Las Vegas'
Dunes
Hotel-Casino

The Mob
The Connections
The Stories

Geno Munari

The Dunes Hotel and Casino: The Mob, The Connections, The Stories
Copyright © 2021 Geno Munari. All Rights Reserved.

Published by:
Trine Day LLC
PO Box 577
Walterville, OR 97489
1-800-556-2012
www.TrineDay.com
trineday@icloud.com

Library of Congress Control Number: 2021949517

Munari, Geno, —1st ed. The Dunes Hotel and Casino
p. cm.

Epub (ISBN-13) 978-1-63424-385-8
TradePaper (ISBN-13) 978-1-63424-384-1
 1. The Dunes Hotel-Casino (Las Vegas, Nev.) -- History. 2. Gamblers -- Nevada -- Las Vegas -- Biography. 3. Executives -- Nevada -- Las Vegas -- Biography. 4. Casinos -- Nevada -- Las Vegas -- History. 5. Organized crime -- Nevada -- Las Vegas -- History -- 20th century. 6. Gambling -- Nevada -- Las Vegas. 7. Entertainers -- Nevada -- Las Vegas -- Anecdotes. 8. John F. Kennedy assassination I. Geno Munari II. Title

FIRST EDITION
10 9 8 7 6 5 4 3 2 1

Distribution to the Trade by:
Independent Publishers Group (IPG)
814 North Franklin Street
Chicago, Illinois 60610
312.337.0747
www.ipgbook.com

For Penny

ACKNOWLEDGMENTS

Special thanks to Doresa Banning for editing and consulting. My appreciation to the following for the help, cooperation, leads, interviews, stories, sources, and encouragement to write this book: Frederic Apcar II, Kimberly Anderson, Autumn Burns, Lem Banker, Rudy Bachman, Tony Braica, Dick Brewer, Earl Brookner, Brian Burton, Christy Burton, Ruben Cabanas, Myron Caplan, Mike Christ, Fran Croysdill, Larry Croysdill, Pat Czajkowski, Deanna DeMatteo, Jimmy Lou Diadone, John Doe(s), Cary Duckworth, Murray Erhenberg, Natacha Faillers, Stuart Feldman, Bruce Fisher, Ray Goldsberry, Danielle Gomes, Oscar Goodman, Jefferson Graham, Morrie Jaeger, Gary Jenkins, Ali Jobe, George Joseph, Dean Harrold, Clarence Hashagen, Paul Herbst, Eda Schivo Herman, Don Hesskamp, Phil Hevener, Leigh Hilt, Gary Jenkins, Harley Kaufman, Joe Kello, Ken Khoury, Gene Kilroy, Duane Krohn, Steve Lake, Michael Landy, Berri Lee, Andrea Lopez, Gary Magnesen, Roger Mennie, John Meier, Denise Miller, Judith Miller, Jack (John) Miller, Bob Miller, Ross Miller, Dan Moldea, Vince Montalto, Tony Montana, Liz Moore, William Ouseley, Nevada Gaming Commission, Nevada Gaming Control Board, Nevada Legislative Counsel Bureau, Nevada State Library, Burt Perelman, Dr. Arthur Quasha, Paul Reyes, John Ritsko, Arolyn Rohac, Rick Ross, Paul Rowe, Artie Selman, Mike Soskin, Lenny Stelly, George Swarts, Dom Taglialatella, Bill & Kay Thompson, Glen Treadwell, Roger Troundy, UNLV Special Collections, Special Collections University of Nevada, Reno, Philip Varricchio, Bob Vigil, Barney Vinson, Blake Whiteside, Glenn E. Wichinsky, Oscar Williams, Christy Whitbeck, Forrest "Woody" Woodward, Dan Wyman, and Dave Wyman.

CONTENTS

INTRODUCTION

The Dunes was more than just a hotel-casino; it was a magical place that held every conceivable amenity a guest could desire. It was also this writer's two-time former employer, which I hold dear to my heart. It was a remarkable place to work, and the stepping stone to my life's journey and that for many other employees. It was a memorable workplace where I earned my "doctorate in real life." I wish I could go back in time and do it again. I am so thankful for the education.

There were eight major management combines that operated the Dunes Hotel during its existence. The operators all were showmen and literally geniuses in their endeavors to please their guests. These hospitality and gaming pioneers deserve to be remembered for their monumental contribution to Las Vegas. They were *real* gamblers, not penny ante pencil pushers. They had good common sense and fine-tuned the operation without the aid of computers and social media tools. They had hearts of gold and never turned away someone who was down on their luck. They created a flagship property coined the "Miracle in the Desert" and the "Miracle Mile." It was THE place to gamble and have a great time. There will never be another hotel as great as the Dunes Hotel & Country Club was when these operators had control of the property.

Charles J. Rich, George Duckworth, Sidney "Sid" Wyman, Howard "Howie" Engel, Dave "Butch" Goldstein, James "Jake" Gottlieb, Major Riddle, Robert "Bob" Rice, Bill Miller, Morris Shenker, and many others, including the numerous fine, hard-working employees, were part of a special brotherhood at this charmed resort.

The intent behind this book is to record the history that would be lost forever if not memorialized. It spans from the Dunes' inception to the final implosion of the fabled gaming mecca. For this project, I researched the subject exhaustively and created a story timeline that took nearly three years to complete. It's a story of good and bad, fierce loyalty and bitter betrayal, underhanded scheming and swindling, and much more.

The Dunes operation was a spectrum of information that is intricate and mysterious at times, protected by a shroud of secrecy and intrigue that is virtually impossible for the outsider to decipher. It featured different operators and characters who, at various times in the history of the hotel, were involved in a multitude of revenue-generating ventures, including gambling, bookmaking, real estate investment, and many other "business" arrangements. Exploring each of these avenues elicits a unique story of interesting characters that interacted in ways that have been described here as thoroughly as possible. Many are impossible to figure out to exacting detail, so I have at times used theories and literary license in explaining them.

A number of incidents described in this book I experienced firsthand, so I wrote them as anecdotes, in the first person point of view. As for other occurrences which are factual, I summarized and wrote in the third person. I have taken this approach so readers may understand this record in the appropriate context intended.

Because I was a Dunes employee and a confidant of the powers that were, I wrestled with whether or not to tell this story for several reasons.

The pros and cons are many concerning whether the true story should be told. Considering the arguments which could be made, one deliberation revolved around whether another writer was working on the true Dunes story. There might be one competitor: Morris "Arthur" Shenker. He once asked me to write a book about his father, Morris Shenker. Had I written that book, I would have told the story truthfully and reported the facts accurately. I believe Arthur would not have accepted my final product. All references in this Dunes book, unless otherwise indicated, refer to Morris Shenker, Sr.

Also, I did not want to run the risk of betraying my mentors in any manner or be viewed by scholars, the curious, co-workers and/or friends as a disloyal whistleblower. I didn't then, and don't now judge my former bosses and co-workers for their actions, which weren't my business. Laissez-faire!

I struggled through many long days and nights with the possibility that my good friends, who had entrusted me with key information, and my confidential sources might think that I'd betrayed them in telling the true story of the Dunes and Las Vegas. Ultimately, I concluded that writing the book was not betraying any secret oath. They had given me the information willingly; I had not obtained it via surveillance, eavesdropping, or any other sneaky or nefarious methods. I simply asked them directly about certain events and topics. They wanted me to know and get the record correct. In the process, I realized that their stories should be told.

Law enforcement agencies and newspaper reporters have long noted that the Dunes had Mob connections. Columnist Jack Anderson, for one, wrote, "Frustrated with Mafia infestation of Las Vegas, the late J. Edgar Hoover schemed to turns the Dunes Hotel over to Howard Hughes in hopes of ridding it of suspected underworld influences."[11]

One individual whom I wrote about in this book intentionally gave me, before his passing, a secret photo of himself taken with the real God-father of Las Vegas and several members of La Cosa Nostra, knowing that someday I would write about him and the image. This gentleman lived and worked as a well-respected casino leader in the city from the early days of the classic casinos and at one time he was President of the Nevada Resort Association. He wanted the record written accurately for historical purposes. I truly believe he wanted the world to know about his dealings with the Vegas operators of the time and the Mobsters.

Was the Dunes Mob controlled? This can't be answered with a simple yes or no, but this question can be: Was the Dunes in an arrangement with organized crime? The answer is a resounding yes. One of the main principals of the Dunes was asked if he would ever write a book about the legendary hotel-casino. He said, "I would, but I'd have to wait until two people were dead." Those "people" were definitely not his direct working associates or employees.

Another problem I faced was limited-to-no access to historical data held by the Nevada Gaming Control Board (GCB) and the Nevada Gaming Commission (GC), and the questionable accuracy of the data that was available for scrutiny. For the most part, the rank and file members of these agencies are above and beyond reproach. They are hardworking, dedicated, and good citizens serving Nevada and keeping casino gambling on the straight and narrow. The following comments are not directed toward these fine people. These comments are directed toward the powers that allow the agencies to continually hide and suppress public information behind several archaic Nevada laws, specifically Nevada Revised Statute (NRS) 463.335(16) and the provisions of NRS Chapter 239.

These laws keep the facts, the historical data, and the truth from the public. The laws make it illegal for the GCB and GC to release anything about a gaming licensee or investigation to practically anyone. This means they won't give you a photo of or information about a past

1   Jack Anderson, Feb. 8, 1974

legendary but now deceased gaming operator or a picture of the interior of an imploded casino, if they even had them. And what about the interesting cases that were investigated 30 or 40 years ago? Everyone in them has passed away, and yet the regulators still won't reveal anything to a person requesting information. A STONE WALL!

Nevada's gaming regulators use these statutes to act, in an unjust manner, as dictators over what should be freely available public information. When they need to inspect, peruse, or examine a fact in a file, they can do so under the pretext that it's legal, yet if a subject of the file needs to defend him or herself, it's practically impossible to get a look at what is in the file pertaining to them.

In the spirit of fair dealing, there must be a reason that the GCB and GC want to keep this information secret. Perhaps a legitimate right to privacy would apply in some cases. Certainly, sensitive personal information that could cause harm to a living subject should not be disclosed. But in the case of deceased gaming licensees and investigations of these persons, keeping this information inaccessible in a vault is beyond reasonable.

The argument that the agencies do it to protect Nevada's gaming industry from innuendo, speculation, and bad press is simply unacceptable in this new age of social media and 24/7 worldwide news outlets.

The information in the hundreds, if not thousands, of files maintained by the state's gaming regulators is critical to Nevada and to the accuracy of Nevada's gaming history. Try to find a picture of Edward "Ed" Torres or Maurice Friedman on the Internet. Good luck!

The Federal Bureau of Investigation (FBI) makes available to the public much of its information via the Freedom of Information Act for a postage stamp. So why then have the GCB and GC not released the same data? Is it because of the fear of litigation? The last time this author checked the law, a dead man cannot file a lawsuit.

Perhaps the high lamas at the GCB and GC do not want this information released and open to research because there are smoking guns buried within it that could implicate past regulators in wrongdoing, unfair dealings, or even flat out criminal activity.

Here is an example of the regulators' response to my simple request for employment verification of Larry Snow (aka Snofsky), a former baccarat gaming executive at Caesars Palace and an applicant who was once turned down for a gaming license at the historic Moulin Rouge in 1951-52:

"Mr. Munari,

"We have looked into your Public Records Request dated November 19, 2017. It is our understanding that you are looking for all documents pertaining to Larry Snofsky's (aka Snow) employment at either the Dunes Hotel or Sands Hotel. The Nevada Gaming Control Board does not maintain employment records from the Dunes Hotel or Sands Hotel. Please contact those companies directly.

"Thank you,

"Nevada Gaming Control Board

Here is another response:

"Mr. Munari,

"The board has no information to confirm whether Larry Snofsky was employed with the Sands Hotel. Please call me if you need further clarification.

"Thank you."

Surely the GCB and GC realize that the Sands and the Dunes are out of business? And to state that they have NO records on a man whom they once denied a gaming license then allowed to work as the baccarat manager at Caesars Palace is beyond ridiculous. It is especially so after I discovered that Snow was in close association with Joe Adonis, and once volunteered information about the suspected Lindbergh baby kidnapper who patronized Snow's garage for a paint job to possibly change the appearance of his automobile.[2]

Adonis was a high ranking member of La Cosa Nostra who operated for 25 years without ever going to prison and did business with Meyer Lansky, Charles "Lucky" Luciano, Benjamin "Bugsy" Siegel, Guarino "Willie" Moretti, and Frank Costello. The Kefauver Committee considered Adonis the dominant influence over Brooklyn's leading politicians. His lavish casino-style craps games in New Jersey earned him more than $1 million per year. Adonis was the executive in charge of Costello's million dollar business.

The University of Nevada, Las Vegas completed an Oral History Program on "Gaming Regulation in Nevada" in which 21 prominent Nevada gaming regulators were recorded on audiotape talking about some very sensitive concerns they had regarding controversial gaming cases and applicants and licensees. The interviewees were Patricia Becker, Paul Bible, William "Bill" Bible, Shannon Bybee, Gerald Cunningham, William "Bill" Curran, Steve DuCharme, Bert Goldwater, Dennis Gomes, Philip "Phil" Hannifin, S. Barton "Bart" Jacka, Bob Lewis, Arthur Marshall,

Wayne Pearson, Harry Reid, Michael Rumbolz, Brian Sandoval, Frank Schreck, Jack Stratton, Roger Trounday, and Sue Wagner. I urge readers of this book to seek out these oral histories for some real inside information.

A researcher may muck out information from the records of the GCB and the GC's hearings but certainly could not write intelligently and accurately about red flags in individual cases based on these sources alone. It is almost an unfair advantage that the oral history participants had over anyone else wishing to discuss or research the topics. There was not a single instance wherein an interviewee refused to answer a question from the moderator based on the confidentiality clause of NRS 463.120 and NRS 463.3407.

Yet, I offer the contentious opinion that the oral history participants crossed the line concerning confidentiality of gaming records pursuant to these statutes. Even though they may have recited information from memory or notes, as the laws are written, any information about investigations is confidential and, thus, cannot be disseminated, whether orally or through printed matter.

Shannon Bybee was appointed to the Gaming Control Board by Governor Donald "Mike" O'Callaghan in 1971. Bybee was asked with respect to Morris Shenker, "Do you recall any specifics of the investigation, such as who headed the investigation and how many agents were assigned to his case?"

He answered, "I don't recall how many agents were assigned; it depended on workload and what else we had to do. I know I got a call from one of our agents in Shenker's office who was going over his things in St. Louis who said that Shenker had a safe in his office that they wanted to get into. Shenker said it had client materials in there that were an attorney-client privilege. I said, 'Put him on the phone.' And I said, 'Morris, you're going to have to decide whether you want to be a casino owner or an attorney.' And he opened the safe and let them in. And that's where they found some old promissory notes where he had loaned money to some of his clients. I think they'd been paid back, but he still had them in his safe. It actually wasn't his clients; I think it was a U.S. attorney that had paid back the money. Shenker had also sold a car at a pretty good deal, when cars were very shorthanded during the war, to an Internal Revenue Service (IRS) agent who 'happened' to be also working on a case involving some of his clients.

"However, when we held the hearing, we had an attorney—I can't remember his name now, but he had been counsel for the Watergate committee—and he said that the ethical standards before Watergate were different than they were after. We also had the IRS agent who said the agent who Shenker sold the car to was not involved in the investigation of Shenker's client. And he also said, 'I was the one who made the determination that there was no criminal case.' And then the IRS agent who got the car said he had no authority to do anything related to that case other than if they prosecuted and recovered the money, then he would apply it against the taxes. That's the kind of thing we ran into on almost every issue with Morris."

As for the Dunes, there are many stories and insider moves that I was not privy to and that could one day yet be discovered. So at the end of a perplexing arrangement wherein I may theorize on exactly what and why a certain action occurred, future writers, researchers, and interested parties may continue where I left off.

In capturing the true story of the Dunes, I had to cross over into the history of some of the other classic Las Vegas hotel-casinos because many of the Dunes operators and associates were connected to these other operations. There is no question that some of these connections, no matter how tenuous, were with the Mob. By "Mob," I mean the Mafia, La Cosa Nostra, the Outfit (Chicago), and the National Syndicate. A common thread links all of these early Las Vegas Strip operations with many of the Dunes operators. What I discovered astonished me, even after being very close to the Dunes situation.

So when I drill down to the particulars and the associates of an individual, it may seem like I am deviating from the Dunes story, which is not the case. As I researched and fleshed out new leads, I discovered a new name associated with Mr. Wyman, for instance. This new person opened up another set of doors to enter, beyond which I found additional stories that heretofore were unknown to me.

A final consideration I had regarding writing this book was that if I were to pass before finishing it, the real story of the Dunes would be lost forever. Hence, I decided to tell it while I'm still able. Doors that I open here, questions that are raised but not fully answered, well, they will be here waiting for the next researcher and writer who care to deep dive down the rabbit hole and explore the labyrinthine world that was Vintage Las Vegas.

CHAPTER 1

THE START OF THE MYSTERY

The movie *Casino* no doubt offered a look at the mysterious affairs of the Mob that was operating in Las Vegas, Nevada, casinos in the 1960s, 1970s, and 1980s. This teased what actually occurred in the early classic hotels such as the Dunes, Stardust, Frontier, Sands, Riviera, Royal Nevada, Sahara, El Rancho, Thunderbird, and Flamingo.

Was there a Mob? J. Edgar Hoover claimed there was no Mafia in the United States, and maybe he was technically correct, but he did recognize the existence of different gangs, such as the Chicago Outfit and the National Syndicate.

Longtime Las Vegas gaming operator Irving "Ash" Resnick, who once ran a sports betting operation for Vincent "Jimmy Blue Eyes" Alo at the Blair House motel on Desert Inn Road, appeared on Ted Koppel's *Nightline* on ABC and said:

> "There hasn't been any Mob in Las Vegas for 15 or 20 years. Most of the hotels are publicly owned hotels. You don't think these public companies have any affiliation with the Mobs? That's just hearsay."[3]

Alo was the New York crime boss and a close associate of Meyer Lansky, who was considered the financial genius behind the Mob's casino operations.

John Scarne, magician and gambling expert, insisted in his book that there was no such thing as the Mafia here.[4] Expanding on his thesis, Scarne purported that attacks on any Italian organized crime figure were nothing more than anti-Italian-American Mafia frame-ups by the federal government, which was determined to deprive the ethnic group of its civil rights. Many viewed Scarne's book, in which he denied the existence of the Mafia, as a mouthpiece for the Mob or Syndicate. However, in one of Scarne's earlier books on gambling, he mentioned the Mob and a New Jersey place called the "Barn," to which he was chauffeured back and forth from New York in a Cadillac limousine.[5] The man who operated

---

3   Reno Gazette-Journal, July 23, 1985
4   The Mafia Conspiracy, John Scarne, 1976
5   Complete Guide to Gambling, John Scarne, 1961

the limo service was Larry Snow (aka Snofsky), who later was the baccarat boss at the Dunes. It was just semantics; Mob, Mafia, Syndicate – they all were in effect the same organization. In his book, Scarne wrote:

"The most successful of all sawdust joints, one which played a prominent part in the Senate crime probe in 1950 and 1951, was located in Bergen County, New Jersey, and was called the Barn. It started in 1937 about eight blocks from my home in Fairview, in the cellar of a local gambler. It housed one money-crap game, and the gambler booking the game was known as the Baron. The game grew in size so fast that the Bergen County racket boys pushed the Baron out and took control. The joint moved from Fairview to Cliffside Park, back to Fairview, to Little Ferry, to Fort Lee and to Lodi, where it was when it folded as a result of the Kefauver probe.

"Lodi is only a few miles from where I live, but when I visited the Barn there in 1945 I first had to go to New York City; local patronage was discouraged. A Cadillac limousine picked me up outside the swank Sherry-Netherland Hotel (a service that extended to all the first-rate New York hotels) and took me to a used-car lot in Little Ferry, N.J., where I met other men with the same destination. Another car took us to the Barn.

"We entered a large rectangular building, formerly a taxi-repair garage, and found ourselves in a small anteroom just about big enough to contain four men. A sliding panel in an inner door moved aside and a pair of eyes gave us the once-over through the small glass window. Then this opened and we passed into another small room, where we were searched for weapons. This was not just a formality; I saw that several pistols and revolvers had already been checked in the "frisk room" by their carriers. It was done to minimize the possibility of the casinos being held up by gunmen.

"Leaving the frisk room, we entered the Barn itself. There were six dice tables, four black-jack tables, and a shimmy [Chemin de Fer] table.

"The Barn's annual gross during its fifteen years of operation was greater than that of any casino in the world. Its monthly gross profits averaged more than the annual gross profit of Monaco's Monte Carlo Casino during its best years. The largest single night's take by the Barn's operators was that of September 1, 1946, when the eleven gaming tables showed a gross profit of $1,250,251.

"It was in this sawdust joint that I saw the biggest dice gambling of my career. Seven of the biggest gamblers and casino owners in the country were present: "Bugsy" Siegel, New York and West

Coast gambler and racketeer; Willie Moretti, then racket boss of Bergen County; his brother, Salvatore Moretti; a wealthy shirt manufacturer; a celebrated New York lawyer; a well- known movie star; and a Chicago department store owner.

"The wagers made that night were all in the thousands of dollars and few bets were made with the bank. The biggest single bet was on the point 4.

"Willie Moretti took $120,000 to $60,000 from the other big-time gamblers. P.S.: Willie missed the 4. At the end of the evening the shirt manufacturer, now long retired, had won $800,000 – in cash, not chips or IOUs.

"Little by little the bootleg mobs began to move in on the casino business and other forms of gambling such as the Numbers Game; former owners like the Barn's original owner, the Baron, were pushed out. By 1934 the mobs had control and the business was organized."

The report to the 81st Congress by the Kefauver Committee, formally the Senate Special Committee to Investigate Organized Crime in Interstate Commerce, which investigated gambling and racketeering activities throughout the U.S., stated in 1951 that there were two major crime syndicates in this country. They were the Accardo-Guzik-Fischetti syndicate (Tony Accardo, Jake Guzik, and Rocco Fischetti), with headquarters in Chicago, and the Costello-Adonis-Lansky syndicate (Frank Costello, Joe Adonis, Meyer Lansky) based in New York.

Evidence of the Costello-Adonis-Lansky operations was found in Las Vegas, Nevada; New York City, N.Y.; Saratoga Springs, N.Y.; Bergen County, N.J.; New Orleans, Louisiana; Miami, Florida; the West Coast; and Havana, Cuba. These syndicates, as well as other criminal gangs throughout the country, entered into profitable relationships with each other, some legal and some not so legal. The top-level Mobsters in different areas of the country had close personal, financial, and social relationships with one another.

The Dunes had relationships with these syndicates and characters. During the life of the Dunes, it crossed paths with people connected to the Chicago Outfit, the St. Louis crime family, the Kansas City crime family, the New York Syndicate as well as the powerful International Brotherhood of Teamsters and its president, James "Jimmy" R. Hoffa. The Dunes' link to the Teamsters in the 1960s spills over to Caesars Palace, the Desert Inn Hotel and Country Club, Stardust, Fremont, and Marina, all of which were in Las Vegas.

CHAPTER 2

THE BEGINNING WITH AL GOTTESMAN

Alfred "Al" Gottesman was a veteran operator of theaters, roadhouses, and nightclubs that had room, food, and beverage amenities which became the standard benchmark in hospitality circles in Reno and Las Vegas. In 1936 he managed the newly remodeled and "ultra-fashionable" Green Gables nightclub in Pennsylvania – on the Hazleton-Wilkes-Barre highway in Butler Valley, Pa. – which opened in 1933 with two big bands, Cato's Vagabonds and Austin Wylie's NBC orchestra. In his new position as manager, he invited the press to taste the food and drink, in hopes they would go back to the city desk and write about the stunning dance hall that had been remodeled to the tune of $50,000, a little over $900,000 in today's dollars.

The media and other select invited guests were given a tour of the new bakery, the gourmet kitchen, a refrigeration plant, and a revolutionary ventilation and air cooling system. Then they were treated to a scrumptious meal prepared by six chefs and entertained with a musical program by Don Carroll and his Golden Gate orchestra as well as a floor show presented by a cast of 25 people. Gottesman was a veteran show producer and knew what the customers wanted. He fed them, entertained them, and no doubt had a crew in the casino parlor that gave them a gamble. Competition was keen, and the weather made the season somewhat short, so the operation could not work financially without the extra casino revenue. The location on the highway was a perfect spot to clean up – or hide – signs of gambling whenever necessary. The building offered a good view of approaching traffic, and the casino games were in an area that could not be seen when entering the business or peering through the windows.

The citizens in Wilkes-Barre were no different than the people in New York state when it came to a love of gambling and drinking. In 1911 Mayor Lewis Kniffen and the police under him were scolded for looking the other way when Harry Moore opened a gaming establishment and then closing it due to complaints from those who frowned on gambling. Even worse, they allowed Moore to retrieve his gambling apparatus from the police evidence room and operate it elsewhere.

Gottesman undoubtedly had some type of connection to Meyer Lansky who operated in New York's Saratoga Springs, which was open to gambling operators, in full action and only a few hundred miles from Wilkes-Barre. Wilkes-Barre, however, was closer to New York City, Gottesman's hometown, which had a greater population density and therefore, a higher concentration of potential gamblers.

Lansky was a partner and involved in a $26 million chain of 50 gambling operations in the country.[6] The Kefauver Committee questioned Lansky about his association with Charles "Lucky" Luciano. They also asked about his involvement in the Arrowhead Inn in Saratoga Springs and the Flamingo hotel-casino in Las Vegas. Committee members discovered tax records that indicated Lansky held a 25 percent interest in the Arrowhead Inn, which offered live gambling and other resort luxuries.

In the early 1920s, Gottesman assumed the lease of Shoemaker's Hall, also known as "Opera," in Shenandoah, Pa. He modernized the playhouse with new chairs and loges and moved the entrance from a side street to the town's main street. He brought in new acts from the Keith circuit, a chain of vaudeville theaters, and special road shows when available. Some of them were: Betty Burke in *La La Lucille* and *Polly and Her Pals* directly from the Casino Theatre in New York City.

Gottesman's forte was producing lavish shows and offering good food, but lacking gambling knowledge, he had to rely on others to run the games. Because of the short season and local opponents of gambling, he sold the Opera in 1937. He went on to affiliate with Danny Shalleck, whose orchestra performed regularly at the Copacabana in New York City, and run various other enterprises in Florida.

Gottesman was briefly the director of the Miami Theater, where he instituted a new policy of bringing foreign motion pictures to the screen. He experimented with Miami audiences by airing three films supplemented by a program of complete news reels.

As the president of the Adrian Corporation, Gottesman announced that a new $50,000 motion picture theater would be built in downtown Miami. His ability to dream and promote was remarkable, along with his sense of quality and professionalism. Perhaps he dreamed beyond his budgetary constraints because he always used other people's money. His style was all about grandeur, and he only wanted the best of everything, no matter the cost. In his trail of fundraising there are some mysterious investment sources despite him being familiar with going to the well. This

6   *Times Record*, Oct. 12, 1950

capital support could very well have been from funders who wanted their name – and involvement – kept out of the limelight. It is likely Gottesman stumbled across the path of the many gamblers in south Florida while searching for and booking talent.

All of the casinos and roadhouses utilized live entertainment to attract gamblers. These early ties paved the way for the grand idea that Gottesman had and for which he was awaiting the right combination of backers and believers. He thought big and played the part as well. He surely might have thought, "It's easy to ask for $5, and it takes the same amount of time to ask for $1,000. If I don't ask, I'll never have a chance to receive."

In 1949, Miami Beach columnist Herb Rau hinted that Gottesman planned to build a hotel in the Virgin Islands but "didn't give any details."[7] Perhaps it was Gottesman's way of stirring up excitement for the idea and engendering talk about his follies.

Somehow, someway, he decided to go westward to Nevada, as did Lansky and his future partners in the Flamingo. He discovered that "The Silver State" was a more amicable place which accommodated legal gambling. He didn't have to worry about paying anyone off or sudden raids and closures in the open state. All he needed was the money to build, he thought. What he did not realize was that he also needed an expert gaming operator who knew how to attract players, not just show patrons. He continued using the press to plant items that helped nurture his grandiose plans.

As of 1951, Isadore Teacher's estate, held by the San Diego Trust and Savings of San Diego, California, owned the land for Gottesman's proposed Dunes. In 1952 L.B. "Tuts" Scherer of Las Vegas purchased the former horse ranch property for $58,000.[8]

The next year, Scherer sold it to Gottesman and Joseph "Joe" A. Sullivan. Sullivan was a former Rhode Island bookmaker and café operator who once sought to purchase the Cal-Neva Lodge in Crystal Bay on the north shore of Lake Tahoe.

Gottesman paid Scherer $58,000 – $20,000 for the initial escrow and $38,000 as down payment for the property. As the full price for the land was $380,000, a balance of $322,000 remained.

Gottesman secured an agreement from a Rhode Island investment group to sublease the hotel in the event it was built. Subsequently, Gottesman invested $600,000, Sullivan invested $400,000, and Charles Fanning, a Providence, R.I. businessman, and Robert "Bob" Rice, a Provi-

---

7   *Miami Beach News*, Nov. 1, 1949
8   FBI file, Nevada Gambling Industry, November 1964

dence costume jeweler, invested $150,000 each, and building hadn't even begun yet. Gottesman paid $16,000, which he was to be refunded, for development of the preliminary architectural plans.

A New York investment firm, Gettinger Associates, put up construction money of $1.5 million and then planned to lease the hotel to Sullivan and his three partners for $250,000 a year, with a six-year option to purchase the property. In the event of an immediate resale of the land, Gottesman was to receive 50 percent of the profits. If a hotel or casino was built on the land, Gottesman was to get 9 percent of any profits from that enterprise, for so long as it was in operation under the lease.

What to name the future hotel there was yet to be decided. "Araby"[9] Hotel was the name used on a January 14, 1954 application to the Nevada Tax Commission. At one time during the planning, the developers wanted to name it Vegas Plaza.

Harvey Bynum opened a club named "The Dunes" in December 1939 on the Boulder Highway, or East Fremont Street. Bynum was one of the first to use the phrase, "Come as You Are" and feature Jimmy Kerr and his Lyric Lads, "the sweetest music this side of heaven."[10] The Dunes advertised that it was the home of the biggest, thickest, and juiciest steaks. Prior to The Dunes, Bynum operated the Santa Anita Inn and Riding Club in California, which catered to the swanky Hollywood crowd. He was arrested on illegal gambling charges in association with this business as a result of having craps and roulette there.

Perhaps Gottesman and the other original owners were influenced by the name of Bynum's previous club, The Dunes, or perhaps they wanted to duplicate the fashionable Palm Springs, California, gambling resort, "The Dunes," operated by Al Wertheimer in the late 1930s.[11]

In June 1954 the Dunes Hotel corporation, comprised of Gottesman et al., announced that the McNeil Construction Company would build the resort at a cost of nearly $4 million. The hotel would have 200 rooms and a theater restaurant that seated 1,200.[12] It was expected to be completed by Christmas, however, construction and other issues delayed the opening.

The principal Dunes stockholders were Sullivan, 32 percent for $576,000; Gottesman, 32 percent for $576,000; Fanning, 11 percent for

---

9   "Araby" is a short story by James Joyce published in his 1914 collection Dubliners. The Araby Bazaar was a marketplace and the beating heart of the community.
10   *Las Vegas Evening Review-Journal,* Dec. 8, 1939
11   *Desert Sun,* Feb. 7, 1936
12   *Oakland Tribune,* June 1954

$170,000; and Rice, 6½ percent for $117,000 – for a total investment of $3.3 million.

The other men who applied to invest a total of $361,000 were Benjamin Lassoff, 9 percent; Jason I. Tarsey, 6½ percent; and Alexander "Bucky" Barad, 3 percent. Barad and Tarsey were approved in May 1955. Lassoff's application was deferred, and there is no record of him being licensed for the hotel subsequently. On July 27, 1955, Kirk Kerkorian was approved for 3 percent. Lassoff, also known as "Little Porky," from Cincinnati, Ohio, was once arrested in Newport, Kentucky, for operating a hand-book clearinghouse, and testified, "I am now out of business because of the federal tax on gambling." Lassoff also applied to the tax commission for 6 percent ($120,000) of the Sands hotel at the same time singer Frank Sinatra applied for 2 percent, in April 1953.[13]

Lassoff was flatly denied a license. What is extremely interesting is that Lassoff later applied in 1967 to the Nevada Gaming Commission, which, with the Nevada Gaming Control Board, took over gambling regulation from the Nevada Tax Commission in 1959 and 1955, respectively, for a 50 percent interest in the Incline Village Casino at Lake Tahoe. He was approved, but only for 10 percent.

The Nevada Tax Commission denied the Dunes' application for live table games and slot machines on March 1, 1955. At their subsequent meeting the following month, they allowed the Dunes to operate provided they removed former Nevada Lieutenant Governor Clifford Jones (1947-1954) from their board of directors. Jones was listed as one of the three owners who controlled voting stock. When the commissioners discovered Jones' association as a voting stockholder and not just as their attorney, Governor Charles Russell, tax commission chairman, said, "Get your house in order and then come back before the commission."[14]

The Dunes' financial plan was that Sullivan and Gottesman would be operating bosses on a 50-50 basis with a five-man board of directors on hand to arbitrate any disputes that may arise between the two of them. In reality, though, the arrangement gave Jones a great amount of power in setting major company policy. The tax commission was worried that if Sullivan and Gottesman got into a dispute, their supporting board members would also disagree. This scenario then would leave Jones with the deciding vote. What appeared strange was that Jones' cash investment was only $250, and his services of general counsel gave him 250 shares of voting stock.

13   *Nevada State Journal*, April 15, 1953
14   *Reno Evening Gazette*, April 2, 1955

Jones withdrew his application and made the point at a related hearing that the tax commissioners, specifically E.F. Loomis, misunderstood the situation. Jones explained that Sullivan, with 1,000 shares of voting stock, would name two directors, and Gottesman, with 500 shares, would name the third. Thus, Jones said, there was no guarantee he would be on the board at all. Jones then noted that he was withdrawing so as not to stand in the way of the other men getting the license.

Attorney Thomas Foley, who represented the group before the commissioners, told them, "The whole situation resulted from a misunderstanding. No deliberate attempt had been made to conceal Jones' interest in the establishment, with his shares listed in a letter furnished to the commission several weeks before the license hearing."

At this same time, Jones was a partner in the Thunderbird, which was built by Marion Hicks. Hicks was the father-by-adoption of John "Johnny" Hicks, who was depicted as Lester Diamond in the movie *Casino*, played by James Woods. Diamond was the boyfriend of Sharon Stone's character.

The Friday before the Dunes hearing, the tax commission suspended the Thunderbird gaming license. Following a lengthy investigation they concluded that Jones and Hicks conspired to protect hidden interests in the Thunderbird.

Prior to his investment with and stint as head of the Dunes, Gottesman resided in Florida, and that was the approximate time that Meyer Lansky, his close friend Vincent "Jimmy Blue Eyes" Alo, and many other gamblers and members of organized crime were there, too. Alo was the Mafia muscle behind Lansky, the Mob's financial genius and gambling director. Alo was the real Las Vegas Godfather.[15]

There is no doubt that Gottesman rubbed elbows with Lansky and Alo in some manner. Gottesman was a political person, endorsing candidates he thought were good for his business affairs. There is no doubt that Lansky, Alo, and the other gamblers were aware of Gottesman's development plans in Palm Beach when he announced a $1.5 million project in 1946.[16] This is strictly conjecture, but there is a good chance that one or several of these gentlemen discussed together the possibility of building in Las Vegas.

Gottesman knew about the competitive show marketing in Las Vegas and story in the press about the Frontier hotel's recent debacle with Mario

---

15   Interview with confidential source, AB
16   *Tampa Tribune*, Feb. 3, 1946

Lanza and having to scramble for a substitute act. Gottesman felt confident in his "don't depend on stars" entertainment policy at his soon-to-be-opened, on May 23, 1955, Dunes hotel-casino. "We're going to offer Broadway musicals and believe the people will agree that the show's the thing," Gottesman said. "There aren't enough name stars in the world to play all the Vegas hotels."[17]

He booked Vera-Ellen for his opening show which was to have a cast of 60. Vera-Ellen seemed excited about this, as did her new husband Victor Rothschild. "I'm not arranging my own act," she said. "The Dunes has arranged Bob Alton and John "Johnny" Brascia with whom I danced in *White Christmas*. We're going to do the dances which received so much applause. I have been married five months so this is really our fifth honeymoon. Victor will try to spend as much time here with me as possible." To star in the Dunes' show, Vera-Ellen had to bow out of the cast of *Tennessee's Partner*, with John Payne and future U.S. president Ronald Reagan.

Vera-Ellen is best remembered for her role as Judy Haynes in the movie *White Christmas* (1954), playing opposite fellow actors Bing Crosby, Danny Kaye, and Rosemary Clooney. Born Vera-Ellen Westmeier Rohe in Norwood, Ohio, she began dancing at the age of 10, and within a few years became one of the youngest Rockettes at Radio City Music Hall in New York City, and a Broadway dancer.

In 1945, she was spotted by film producer Samuel Goldwyn and invited to Hollywood, where she was cast opposite Kaye in *Wonder Man* (1945). There she earned a reputation as a hard worker. She also later danced with Gene Kelly in *On the Town* (1949) and with Fred Astaire in *Three Little Words* (1950). Vera-Ellen also starred in the stage production, *New York-Paris- Paradise*, under the direction of Robert Nesbitt, who collaborated on the special music and lyrics with Carroll Coates and Karen Anthony.

When the Dunes debuted on May 22, 1955, it became the tenth glamorized resort spot to open on the Las Vegas Strip, the stretch of South Las Vegas Boulevard that is known for its concentration of resort hotel-casinos. The two days of festivities included a bathing suit pageant around the swimming pool, in which numerous Hollywood film starlets participated. Among those present at the opening were Jeanne Crain, Cesar Romero, Dan O'Herlihy, Spike Jones, Rita Moreno, Merle Oberon, Reginald Gardiner, Mamie Van Doren, Don DeFore, Virginia Field, Lance Fuller, Claire Trevor, and Ginny Simms.

17   *Tampa Tribune*, April 24, 1955

The Dunes' show, named the "Magic Carpet Revue," featured Brascia, Vera-Ellen's dancing partner; ventriloquist Robert Lamouret and his duck; acrobatic comedians Dick and Dot Remy; Helene Stanton; and Jose Duval. Vera-Ellen was well received and, according to some, "captured the audience" even though there was an obvious lack of costumes.[18] She was paid $15,000 for a four-week contract with an option to renew for another four weeks.

The show was lavish, but the resort just wasn't attracting guests. "The Dunes just didn't have any business," said Morrie Jaeger, one of the original dealers working in the blackjack pit. The Dunes was the only casino on the west side of the Strip that wasn't established to draw the crowds. There was virtually nothing out there except for a small motel just south of the Dunes called the Royal Palms. Howard "Howie" Engel, an original casino boss at the Dunes when it opened but not listed as a licensee, told young Morrie and his brother Ivan, "Someday that little motel will be worth something. You guys should buy it."[19]

They probably would have bought it if they had the money. Land was dirt cheap, as they used to say in Las Vegas, but the average worker just never had the foresight, guts, money, or moxie to even think that land in Las Vegas would amount to anything, especially after seeing an empty Dunes casino.

Being the grandiose thinker he was, Gottesman figured that his big musical shows concept might work in Las Vegas. He built a great property and spent a good deal of the budget on the theater and the opening planned production. He gambled on the drive-in customers from the neighboring states stopping at the Dunes.

But for one, the Dunes' marquee just wasn't attractive to the average family couple arriving in Las Vegas for the weekend. The sign read:

VERA-ELLEN
Starring in Robert Nesbitt's MAGIC CARPET REVUE CAST OF 60
Robert Lamouret – John Brascia – Jose Duval – Helene Stanton Dick & Dot Remy

None of these names were identifiable to the average person, and that was one reason for the lack of business. The show just didn't have drawing power.

There wasn't a mention on the sign of the availability of rooms, casino gambling, or good food at inexpensive prices, the latter which would

18   *Los Angeles Times,* May 23, 1955
19   Interview with Morrie Jaeger, 2019

have enticed live warm bodies to play at the tables. Gottesman was in the gambling business but acted as though he was on Broadway or at some other theatrical venue. He just didn't have the marketing experience to attract players, and evidently, he wouldn't listen to any of his investors' ideas either.

CHAPTER 3

WALLY "MR. PEEPERS" COX
AND MARLON BRANDO

After Vera-Ellen, Al Gottesman made Wally "Mr. Peepers" Cox the star attraction of the Dunes' Arabian Room.

Cox was a comedian who appeared in 20 movies and as a guest on many shows, however, is most readily remembered as the star of his U.S. television series, *Mister Peepers*, which aired from 1952 to 1955. In 1952, Cox was given a Peabody Award which honored a person for distinguished achievement and meritorious public service.

One fan at Cox's show at the Dunes clapped at every line and every joke – Academy Award winner, Marlon Brando. It so happened that Brando and Cox were boyhood friends and remained close for life.

Brando was not as conspicuous at Cox's funeral in 1973 as he was reportedly "ensconced in a back bedroom of Cox's Bel Air home after entering through a back window."[20] Some of the biggest stars in Hollywood were unknowingly within 50 feet of the hidden Brando.

Patricia Cox, Wally's widow, said, "Brando was heartbroken, of course. Everybody was there including celebrities from the *Hollywood Squares* game show, on which Wally was a regular, as well as Tom and Dick Smothers, Vincent Price, Ernest Borgnine, and Twiggy. But Marlon didn't come out."

According to the *Los Angeles Times*:

> Brando made a practice of keeping Cox's remains nearby, sometimes tucking the ashes in a drawer at his home on Mulholland Drive or under the front seat of his car. He did so against the wishes of Cox's widow, who said she considered suing Brando for selfishly keeping the ashes that he accepted under the guise of scattering them in the hills where Cox loved to hike. After Brando died suddenly of lung failure July 1 [2004] at age 80, his family scattered the men's ashes in Death Valley, where the pair had often gone rock hunting. The odyssey of the ashes is one of the more unusual stories to emerge since the death of the eccentric and in-

tensely private actor. Brando had a history of stormy relationships, attributed to a troubled childhood and his upbringing at the hands of a distant father and an alcoholic mother. Much has also been made of his countless liaisons, reputed to be both heterosexual and homosexual, and failed relationships.

Some friends and family of both men insist Brando's relationship with Cox was platonic. Regardless, their bond offers a different perspective on one of the world's most famous, yet little known, men.

Brando, however, was nearly alone in loving Cox's Vegas show, and thus, it was not a success.

To last that many years on a weekly television show meant that Wally Cox did have talent and was funny. However, conveying to a large stage in Las Vegas that same experience that home viewers got on their 9- or 12-inch television set in the intimate setting of their home did not work. People could watch "Mr. Peepers" on television for free but not at the Dunes. There, it cost big bucks. Only the curious or seasoned fans might pay to see Cox as Mr. Peepers live.

The critics were harsh. For instance, Billboard wrote:

> The celebrated, interrupted starring appearance of television's *Mr. Peepers* in the Dunes Arabian Room certainly was a jackpot in publicity, if not in entertainment. After hearing so many show-goers that he had laid an egg at first, Wally Cox himself came to believe it, and, after being barred from the stage for six nights, he returned with new material which drew a lot of laughs, mainly kidding his first unfortunate stint. Consensus along the Vegas Strip: Mr. Peepers should stick to TV.[21]

Gottesman said, "As a result of this lack of an act, Wally Cox did in fact lay the proverbial egg." He added, "In his [Cox's] published statement he implies that we are not qualified to judge his act. I will overlook the fact that I booked talent in my theaters and nightclubs long before Mr. Cox was born. I would like to refer Wally Cox to the reviews of his performance by other 'unqualified' reporters such as the representatives of *Variety* and the *Hollywood Reporter*. Mr. Cox did not only lay an ordinary egg. It was a king-sized omelet that has cost the Dunes untold thousands of dollars."[22]

21   *Billboard*,"= July 30, 1955
22   "Vegas Vagaries," *Las Vegas Review-Journal*, July 25, 1955

Gottesman fired Cox after three performances of a four-week, $44,000 salaried engagement. Gottesman then published a letter in the local press explaining why Cox had been a failure at the Dunes. His letter surely wanted to convey that it was all Mr. Peepers' fault and not that of the Dunes management. Gottesman claimed Cox did not bring or write any new material, lacked orchestrations for his musical numbers, and arrived only a day before his scheduled show.

CHAPTER 4

THE SANDS MARRIES THE DUNES

To save the Dunes, the Nevada Gaming Control Board, in August 1955, approved the leasing of the Dunes by the stockholders of the Sands Corporation, in the first financial combination of its kind in modern gambling history.[23] The transaction called for the Sands stockholders to lease the Dunes for $600,000 a year, to increase to $650,000 after the initial two years of the 10-year lease. The Sands would provide $900,000 as a cash infusion, of which $350,000 was to be used as a gaming bankroll and $600,000 placed in escrow to pay the new hotel-casino operation's financial obligations.

The Sands management announced on August 19, 1955 that they were going to take over the Dunes. An unnamed Dunes spokesman said, "Heavy bettors hit the hotel's casino early and often. Rather than sink another million or so, the Dunes owners preferred to let the prosperous Sands lease the hotel."[24]

The Sands took out an ad in the local newspaper that heralded:

> The SANDS Marries the DUNES. SEPTEMBER FIRST. The same inspired management that has made the Sands Hotel a living legend takes over operation of the Dunes on September first.[25]

Sands executive Jack Entratter inked Frank Sinatra to appear at the Dunes on September 9. A spectacular public relations event preceded Sinatra's opening as well as a bevy of beauties and a caravan, including an elephant.

Sinatra was a hot ticket and a great drawing card for the Sands Copa Room, a far cry from Al Gottesman's offering of Wally Cox, "Mr. Peepers," at the Dunes.

Despite the Sands taking over the Dunes, only four months later, on January 15, 1956, the Arabian Room curtain was lowered for the last time after a performance by legendary French star Maurice Chevalier. In addition, Jake Freedman, president of the Sands Corporation, said regarding

23   *Las Vegas Review-Journal*, Aug. 25, 1955
24   *The Decatur Daily Review*, Aug. 19, 1955

25   *Las Vegas Review-Journal*, Sept. 4, 1955

the Dunes, "We suspended operations at the theater at the close of the graveyard shift this morning." Freedman further stated, "We are keeping the hotel rooms open at this time. We are closing the entertainment room, lounge, and casino because of the tremendous loss incurred during the months of our operation. All personnel, including entertainers, have been paid."[26]

It's conceivable that the Dunes casino was a victim of inside and outside cheating rather than the alleged lucky streak said to have occurred early and often. Interviews with dealers who were employed there said there just was no business in the place, meaning there may have been spotty play, but no continuous play around the clock like at the Sahara and Flamingo. One dealer, whom I will keep unidentified, said, "The boss in the 21 pit was Cleo Simon. I know he was a thief."[27]

26   *Reno Evening Gazette*, Jan. 16, 1956
27   Interview with confidential source, SVR-JM

CHAPTER 5

THE GOTTLIEB-RIDDLE-MILLER ERA

From 1954 through 1957, the property taxes on the Dunes were paid by Al Gottesman and Joe Sullivan, whose mailing address was listed as Jones, Weiner & Jones (Clifford Jones' law firm), 230 South Fifth Street, Las Vegas, Nevada.

In January 1956, Major Riddle, secretary-treasurer of the Dunes under the ownership of Gottesman and Sullivan, went to New York City and finalized a new multi-million dollar sale of the Dunes to a combine headed by James "Jake" Gottlieb.[28]

Gottlieb owned Western Transportation Company in Chicago, was a thoroughbred horse breeder, and a director of Continental Connector Corporation. He had close associations with the Chicago Outfit and was very close to Jimmy Hoffa.

Because Gottlieb was not a gaming operator, he needed someone with experience whom he could rely on to operate and protect the casino. That is where the other members of the group purchasing the Dunes came in.

As identified by Riddle, they were himself along with Bob Rice, the new director, and Bill Miller, the new president of the operating company, M&R Investment Company, the initials of which stood for Miller and Riddle. Those two held 44.1 percent each and Rice owned 11.8 percent. Gottlieb was the major investor in the real estate.

Questions arose as to why Riddle went to New York to finalize the new M&R Investment organization and sale-purchase of the Dunes. Perhaps it was to meet in person with one of his new partners, Miller, who then owned Bill Miller's Riviera in New Jersey. Miller was not a made Mob guy but was associated with many of them. "They were my best customers, and I always got along with them," he said.[29]

On March 2, 1956, an article appeared in the *Las Vegas Review-Journal* with the headline, "New Dunes Operators Prepare for Opening." One section read, "Leasing to the new operators is the Dunes owner, Al Gottesman, who is confident the hotel will enjoy 'the success such an establishment deserves.'" Gottesman then remarked, "We'll have experi-

28 *Reno Evening Gazette,* Jan. 10, 1957
29 Interview with Denise Miller, April 2019

enced management and you can say this time the place will really click!"
The photo with the article depicted the Dunes principals, which included
Gottesman, named as the owner, along with Rice, Miller, and Riddle.

This Gottesman quote about leasing and him being called an owner
directly contradicted the announcement that the Dunes was sold, which
was reported two months earlier, in the January 10, 1956 issue of the
Reno Evening Gazette. It is likely the case that the deal began as a lease and
turned into a sale.

The *Review-Journal* article indicated that Riddle was a newcomer to
the group but Rice was with the Dunes since its inception. This last fact
indicated Rice, a businessman and an acquaintance of Sullivan, who was
friends with Raymond "Ray" Patriarca, surely knew about the hidden
ownership in the Dunes by Patriarca and possibly others. From Providence, Rhode Island, Patriarca was the longtime boss of the Patriarca
crime family that controlled New England for more than three decades.

In a phone conversation with Jimmy Hoffa, which the FBI recorded,
Patriarca acknowledged that he had an original investment of $27,000 in
M&R Investment Company and that he owned a percentage of the cor-
poration that controlled the Dunes real estate.[30] Other captured conversa-
tions between the men were about potential business deals and obtaining
Teamsters pension fund money for them (Hoffa was one of the pension
fund trustees). One FBI report from 1986 indicated that Hoffa sought
Patriarca's permission to kill a man from Massachusetts.

Further proof of Patriarca's hidden ownership is the fact that John
"Johnny B." Baborian was listed on the Dunes property stamp for fiscal
year 1957-1958 as owning 2/3 along with Gottesman, owning the remainder.[31] According to a confidential source, Baborian was the eyes and
ears of Patriarca.

Subsequently, on November 22, 1957, the Dunes was sold at a sheriff's
sale, through litigation, to McNeil Construction Company for $115,018
despite its value of $3.5 million. Gottesman and Sullivan were in Clark
County District Court (Las Vegas is in Clark County) battling with the
creditors and McNeil. Owners Bruce and Lawrence McNeil bought the
title to the Dunes, yet Sullivan and Gottesman were still claiming the
property.

Gottlieb acquired the Dunes building, other assets, and land from Mc-
Neil Construction. He did not apply to be added to the gaming license

---

30   *Hartford Courant*, Dec. 20, 1986
31   The mailing address for Baborian and Gottesman was listed as the Nevada Building,
Third and Fremont Streets, Las Vegas

held by M&R Investment but, instead, remained the lessor of the building and property. His company, Western Realty Company, was listed as paying the property tax on the Dunes for fiscal years 1959 to 1962.

CHAPTER 6

MAJOR RIDDLE, AN INTERESTING MAN

"Despite a house percentage in their favor many big Las Vegas nightclubs have gone broke; my own hotel, the Dunes, has been operating in the red for almost two years because of casino losses."
– Major Riddle in *The Weekend Gambler's Handbook*

Major Arteburn Riddle was born in Louisville, Kentucky, and moved to Indianapolis, Indiana, in 1917 at the age of 11 years old. His father Charles worked in plumbing, insurance, and truck sales before forming the Global Cartage Company of Indianapolis. Charles was considered one of the pioneers in interstate truck hauling and later served as president of the Indiana Motor Truck Association.

The "Maje," pronounced with a long "a," which close friends called him, worked with his father and ventured into some speculative supply and metal fabrication companies, all while getting into Indianapolis gambling circles.[32] Riddle was involved in gaming at the Printers Club and the local Italian clubs with longtime friend, Joseph Jacobson a.k.a. Joey Jacobs and another longtime associate, Dave "Butch" Goldstein. Goldstein later became the executive vice president and co-owner of the Dunes.

When living in Moline, Illinois, Riddle operated the Plantation nightclub with Jacobson/Jacobs. During this time, he courted Virginia Hill, the notorious and legendary girl pal of "Bugsy" Siegel. Riddle moved to Chicago in the 1940s.[33]

During that decade he was in the salvage business with Leo Louis Miroff of Indianapolis, who later became a close contact of the Chicago Outfit. However, Riddle broke ties with Miroff once he learned that Miroff planned to set up a friend of Riddle to be robbed. The friend was James "Jake" Gottlieb, who also was a close friend of Jimmy Hoffa.

In 1953 Riddle employed more than 1,200 people in a surplus business he purchased that was worth $2 million. He also owned a string of 25 oil and gas producing wells in Texas.

---

32   *The Indianapolis Star,* July 10, 1980
33   *Quad-City Times,* Feb. 3, 1957

In February 1954, Indiana's Public Service Commission prohibited Hancock Trucking Company, of Evansville, from using Indiana highways because the company had racked up more than 450 state law violations over a 2½-year period. Riddle, president of the company, testified that his firm never knowingly overloaded its trucks and challenged the right of the Public Service Commission to institute the ban but eventually lost.

Hancock had franchises in cities from Pittsburgh to St. Louis, 17 terminals in seven states, more than 800 employees, 420 trailers, 218 tractors, 106 smaller utility vehicles, real estate in Detroit and Evansville, and a weekly payroll of more than $100,000. The company ran into money problems after the U.S. government filed a tax claim of $465,000 against it for unpaid withholding and highway usage taxes.[34]

A longtime employee of Hancock Trucking since 1949 said the trouble with Hancock began when Riddle took over management after the previous owner Roy L. Friedle retired.

Kenneth Oskins, Hancock's personnel director, said, "Riddle liked to live it up. He went to Las Vegas frequently and the management became slipshod, but when the bankruptcy petition was filed in 1954, there was no reason the business couldn't have been put back on its feet. The company's operating authority was wonderful and we had a 28,000 transportation network."[35]

To resolve the bankruptcy, another company came in and purchased $400,000 in stock. Hancock remained in business but Riddle was out.

In Riddle's own words he explained, "By the time I was 26 I made a million dollars the hard way, in the trucking and surplus business. I lost it the easy way, on the horses."[36] This admission is from the introduction of the Maje's book, *The Weekend Gambler's Handbook*, as told to writer Joe Hyams on methods of wining in the casino, some of the time, if not all of the time.

A risk taker, Riddle once stated, "When I purchased the Dunes, it was the worst gamble I could have made, but I felt lucky and I had enough capital to sit out a fairly long streak of bad luck. I was willing to gamble everything I had on making it a paying proposition. I've always been willing to back my hunches and I had a strong hunch about the Dunes. I was willing to embark on the most foolish gambling venture a man can make, to bet more than I could afford to lose."[37]

---

34   *Indianapolis Star*, Feb. 15, 1971
35   *Indianapolis Star*, Feb. 17, 1971
36   *The Weekend Gambler's Handbook*, Major Riddle, 1963
37   *Ibid*

CHAPTER 7

JOHN GOTTLIEB AND THE TEAMSTERS

"I have known John Gottlieb for 30 years. He was one of the employers who signed one of the first contracts with the Teamsters."

– Jimmy Hoffa[38]

Brothers James "Jake" and John Gottlieb were born into a poor German-Jewish immigrant family that valued the principles of hard work and education. The two boys, their one brother, and two sisters were raised in the toughest of times yet had big dreams and never gave up on them despite enduring the Depression and hard times. Their parents instilled in them that education was power and the means to leave poverty behind for a successful life.

John was admitted to and graduated from West Point military academy and went on to serve in both world wars. He rose to the rank of lieutenant colonel in the U.S. Army and worked in the Washington, D.C. office of the Chief of the Transportation Corps. In 1945 he received the Legion of Merit Award from Secretary of War Robert Patterson and was appointed adjutant general to the president.

He amassed a fortune in various trucking businesses in Chicago and laundries on the West Coast. His road game was business matchmaking, and he excelled in putting the right people together for development of a profitable business venture. For his services, he received a finder's fee in the form of cash or a stake in the resulting company.

One particular deal of the century was in 1977 when John put heiress Joan Irvine Smith in touch with Detroit entrepreneurs A. Alfred Taubman and Henry Ford, II, and California real estate developer Don Bren. This financial group paid $337.4 million in cash to buy the Irvine Company of Orange County, which was one of the biggest real estate transactions in California history.

John also was a founding trustee of the City of Hope hospital and research center and a major contributor to the Music Center of Los Angeles County.

After settling in Los Angeles, John obtained loans from the Teamsters pension fund, officially the Teamsters' Central States, Southeast, and Southwest Areas Pension Fund, to open several businesses, including Abbot Plastic Machine Corporation headquartered in Chicago and with a branch in Los Angeles. John also owned a large amount of stock in the Arizona Savings Bank in Phoenix.

An informant told the FBI the following account, which this writer could not substantiate but thinks is important. The informant was employed by the law firm of Eller and Winton, which represented John and which employed an accountant known by the name of "Printz," as noted in the FBI file. One day Printz came into the office rather flushed and excited and announced that a client [John Gottlieb] had given him $1 million in cash with instructions to buy up motels around the country to help Jimmy Hoffa organize motel employees. The informant said that the accountant was so excited about the situation that he just blurted it out.

Based on this information, the FBI opened a file on John, which grew to 62 pages.[39] They launched an investigation into whether Home Service Company, doing business as Globe Laundry, of which John was the managing partner, received a Teamsters pension fund loan and whether, as a result, John or Home Service paid any cash kickbacks to Hoffa, Teamsters pension fund trustees, Teamsters officials, or others.

A 1961 FBI memo outlined the connections between Hoffa and Jake and John Gottlieb. It revealed that in the agency's investigation, they interviewed John's former private secretary, Eleanore de Terra. She told them she had left Gottlieb's employ in Beverly Hills because she suspected he was involved in illegal activity.

She relayed that John interviewed her for the job at his Beverly Hills residence for three hours, between 10 P.M. and 1 A.M. When he offered her the position, he told her that he would pay her $500 a month to start and if she proved to be a satisfactory employee, she would make more money than she ever dreamed possible.

When she first went to work for Gottlieb, she recalled, she learned that he owned 85 percent of Home Service Company stock. Ben Weingart owned the other 15 percent. She learned that Weingart was one of the wealthiest men in Southern California and owned an abundance of real estate throughout Los Angeles County.

John told de Terra that he had done a favor for a Teamsters official and subsequently received a $1.5 million loan for Globe Laundry. She subse-

---

39   FBI File, Los Angeles, 122-212

quently learned from John's records that the loan was from the Teamsters pension fund, as the documents bore the name James Riddle Hoffa. De Terra noted that she overheard a conversation about John getting the loan prior to an appraisal being done on the involved property.

De Terra recalled that an attorney by the name of Harry Wyatt, whose main office was in Chicago, appeared in person to work on the loan to Home Service Company from the Teamsters pension fund. When Wyatt was in Los Angeles he used the law office of Webster and Abbot, which was located on Wilshire Boulevard, also in Beverly Hills.

Also according to de Terra, John had a Chicago newspaper clipping of a photograph in which he and Hoffa were sitting together in an unknown Chicago nightclub. The caption was something like, *Hoffa and an unknown friend were seen at the nightclub.*

To her knowledge, de Terra added, John's only other business interests were some oil wells somewhere in the vicinity of Borger, Texas, with Ed Pauley, and some oil leases in Denver, Colorado. John also was involved with an unknown man with the Clayton Oil Company in New York.

According to de Terra, John bragged that he was worth about $2.5 million. To her knowledge, his income sources were a monthly salary check from Globe Laundry for a net amount of about $3,000 and dividends from stocks and bonds.

From all appearances, John lived way beyond his means, de Terra said. For instance, during a five-week period in August and September 1961, she wrote checks for him that totaled $55,000. The bulk was for hotel bills, traveling expenses, and other items that did not relate to John's business activities, in her opinion. She could not explain why and how he incurred all of those expenses.

Periodically, she said, John advised her that he deposited money in his bank account in sums up to $25,000 but never explained where the money came from. Home Service Company maintained a bank account at the Union Bank in Los Angeles, and its balance was as high as $400,000. He also had accounts at banks in Chicago and Highland Park, Illinois, whose names she could not recall.

De Terra said that she only heard conversations about two brothers of John. Jake ran a trucking company in Chicago, and Ted lived in Bel Air, California. Once when de Terra talked with John's son, 23 years of age, she recalled, he told her that Uncle Jake, who lived in Highland Park, was a multimillionaire. He said, "If you think my father is a gangster, you should meet my Uncle Jake. He is a real gangster. When Uncle Jake needs a chauffeur, he calls on the chief of police of Highland Park, who drives him around." The son also told de Terra that his Uncle Jake was the man who appoints the mayor of Highland Park.

The person John was most in contact with during the time de Terra worked for him, at least five or six times a week, was a Frank Matula, who she believed was affiliated with the Teamsters union. John also had a significant amount of contact with Weingart, the Los Angeles land developer.

Along with de Terra, FBI agents interviewed a hired agency temporary clerk who worked for John. The clerk told them that John traveled a great deal during August 1961 and that she was required to write a large number of checks on his behalf. This clerk also stated that John did not smoke, drink or chase women, was very devoted to his wife, and was a devout Jew, attending temple every Friday night and Saturday morning.

John also was indirectly linked to U.S. Mobsters.

He filed suit in Reno, Nevada, in 1964 against Dr. U.S. Mitchell, whom John helped obtain financing from Chicago development firm Kirkeby-Natus Corporation. However, Mitchell and his firms failed, as agreed, to transfer the Kietzke-Peckham Lane property rights to Kirkeby-Natus. In his suit John demanded a 75 percent interest in Mitchell's $50 million project at the site for his efforts in helping him obtain the needed capital and for protecting the initiators from future costs and liabilities.[40]

A key figure in Kirkeby-Natus was Arnold S. Kirkeby, who, with his brother Edmund, owned and operated the Hotel Nacional in Havana, Cuba. In the 1950s, Meyer Lansky and Moe Dalitz were behind the casino operation at that very hotel.[41]

Kirkeby-Natus also loaned money to Irvin J. Kahn, who eventually became an owner of the Dunes and a partner to attorney Morris Shenker. Kirkeby was a prominent Realtor-developer who lived in Bel Air in the early 1960s. He held a great amount of real estate in Los Angeles and the surrounding areas and was formerly the key person in his Kirkeby chain of "boutique- exclusive" hotels. As a financier, he made short-term loans to various businesses. (Kirkeby died aboard American Airlines Flight 1 when it crashed shortly after takeoff from New York City in 1962.)

The Kirkeby hotels organization included these properties: Beverly Wilshire Hotel, Beverly Hills, Calif.; The Town House, Los Angeles; Sunset Tower, West Hollywood; The Kenilworth, Miami Beach, Fla.; Belleview-Biltmore Hotel, Clearwater, Fla.; The Blackstone Hotel and

40   *Reno Evening Gazette*, April 21, 1964
41   *The Capital Times*, Lowell Bergman, May 23, 1974

The Drake in Chicago; The Gotham, The Hampshire House, The Sherry-Netherland, The Warwick, and Saranac Inn, all in New York; Hotel Ambassador rebuilt as the Tropicana, Atlantic City, N.J.; Hotel Nacional, Havana, Cuba; and El Panama Hotel, Panama City, Panama.

Kirkeby once borrowed "indirectly" from New Jersey gangster Abner "Longie" Zwillman to acquire the Sherry-Netherland.[42] Julius Endler, a Newark, N.J. restaurant owner who was a front for Zwillman, reported that Zwillman invested $41,000 in bonds of that hotel.[43]

Zwillman was a big political powerhouse in New Jersey and New York and was always ready to write a check to any charity mentioned by any person he was trying to sway. Labor reporter Victor Riesel wrote about Zwillman, "He realized long ago that the labor union can be a thing of beauty to a man with angels and a passionate interest in power politics, without which you can do no favors and get no favors."[44]

Kirkeby also sat on the board of City National Bank of Beverly Hills, which has an interesting background. The bank's first chairman was Ben Maltz, a whiskey broker from Chicago who was a partner in a wholesale liquor business with Alfred Hart. Hart, who became the bank's president in 1955, was, as Mercury Savings & Loan Chairman Leonard Shane told the *Los Angeles Times* in 1985, "a rough, tough cookie" who wound up among the founders of the Los Angeles County Museum of Art and the Music Center.

In his book, *Supermob: How Sidney Korshak and His Criminal Associates Became America's Hidden Power Brokers*, Gus Russo wrote that Hart's past included a stint as a beer driver for Al Capone, eight arrests related to illegal games of chance at a cigar store he ran in downtown Los Angeles, and a stake in the "Bugsy" Siegel partnership that built the Flamingo hotel-casino in Las Vegas.[45]

Hart was a director of Columbia Pictures for 20 years and president of the Del Mar race track in 1953, when MGM boss Louis B. Mayer was its chairman. Hart helped Frank Sinatra resurrect his career by contributing to the capital needed for the film *From Here to Eternity*.

"Another Hart pal was [Sidney] Korshak, a powerful labor lawyer identified in congressional testimony as the liaison between Hollywood and the Chicago Mob. Korshak and Sinatra directed their associates to

42   *Indiana Gazette*, Drew Pearson, April 29, 1961
43   *The Philadelphia Inquirer*, Aug. 17, 1951
44   *Palladium Item*, Victor Riesel, November 12, 1954
45   *Los Angeles Times*, Aug. 5, 2012

the ultra-private new bank, assuring them that their funds would avoid outside scrutiny," Russo wrote.[46]

Bram Goldsmith, who replaced his father-in-law on City National's board in 1964, said he knew of no Hart ties to underworld figures. He recalled Hart as "a very generous human being" for his philanthropy and support of his many friends.[47]

---

46   *Supermob: How Sidney Korshak and His Criminal Associates Became America's Hidden Power Brokers*, Gus Russo, 2006

47   *Ibid*

CHAPTER 8

BILL MILLER

B ill Miller, who was a co-owner of the Dunes and the president of M&R Investment Company, began dancing at 14 years of age. His talent in that regard propelled him to the top, to "Showman Extraordinary" status. As a young man of 16, he won the New Jersey Eastern State ballroom competition and then earned additional trophies, or "cups" as Miller called them, for his terpsichorean talents. Little did he know that he performed in a forerunner to today's *Dancing with the Stars*. His trophies helped him get through the lean years, as he hocked them in shops in Jersey City, New York City, Brooklyn, and Staten Island.

"Just in case some of these cups are still in existence, I'd like it known that I'm ready to buy them back now," Miller once stated.[48]

He developed a dancing act, learned the ins and outs of show business, and at times even performed a curtain act, one in front of the stage curtain without any set or stage design, not even a stagehand.

Young Miller learned what good music should sound like and how it should be presented.

He learned by listening, and his instinctive inner ear told him who was good and who stank.

Miller's first production was *West Point Cadets*, and he even received permission from the West Point military academy to use their uniforms in it. At only 18 years of age, Miller and a partner were cutting up the $1,100 a week they received from the show.

In 1925 and 1926 Miller and dance partner, Nat Peterson, performed in New York's Shubert Theatre. In those early days in New York he met dancer and actor George Raft.

Miller toured with the Alexander Pantages theater circuit for 47 weeks before the 1929 stock market crash, which cost him $180,000. Afterward, Miller quit performing and only produced shows and booked talent.

He then joined Charlie Morrison, the biggest agent in the country, representing names such as Milton Berle, Paul Whiteman, and many more top acts in show business. The experience as a booking agent opened many doors for Miller. Morrison set up an office in Hollywood. Miller started his own business, the William Miller Agency, and specialized in theater, radio, and night club bookings.

Miller booked a tour of the *Streets in Paris* in cooperation with Shubert's RKO Boston Theatre, which earned him $100,000. He parlayed that money and leased the Luna Park Amusement Center in Coney Island, which became a huge money maker. After it burned down in 1944, Miller made more by selling curious spectators a 25-cent ticket to view the burned ruins.

Then on a mission, Miller bought a series of rundown nightclubs on the Eastern seaboard, turned them around, and sold each one for a profit.

Knowing the formula for success in the business, in 1946 he purchased Ben Marden's Riviera in New Jersey.

Marden opened his original Riviera building early in the Depression, but it burned to the ground on Thanksgiving Day four years later. It took eight months for him to reopen his swank new building as an 800-seat nightclub, featuring the top saloon entertainers and fine food. The *New York Times* described the structure:

> "Built on the brink of the Palisades overlooking the Hudson River, the resort features a huge circular room enclosed entirely by glass windows which may be lowered, and is covered by a domed roof which may be drawn back to expose the entire room to the open air."

> "Above all, the Riviera was known for its gambling. The casino's limousines and a succession of cabs shuttled players back and forth across the bridge from a reserved stop on Broadway. Table games were featured on the second floor in the Marine Room. The players' games of choice in that era, in order, were Craps, Roulette, and Chemin-de-Fer. Guards at the bottom of the stairs allowed only known players to walk up, restricting everyone else to the dining and entertainment rooms. The guards specifically turned away the town's local residents to avoid them becoming resentful over gambling losses at the tables. Ben Marden's Riviera was the forerunner of a series of casinos on the New Jersey side of the George Washington Bridge. A key figure in this gambling proliferation was Guarino "Willie" Moretti."[49]

When Miller operated the Riviera, it was the "Showplace of Showtown, U.S.A.," a name that Miller later used at his Royal Nevada in Las Vegas. Miller, however, closed the Riviera in 1953.

---

49   *30 Illegal Years To The Strip: The Untold Stories of the Gangsters Who Built The Early Las Vegas Strip*, Bill Friedman, 2015

Milton Prell and Frank Schivo came to Las Vegas in 1947 and opened Club Bingo, where the Sahara was built after Club Bingo burned to the ground.[50] Prell was the mastermind of the Sahara, Lucky Strike, Mint, and Aladdin hotel-casinos. He was from Butte, Montana, where he owned the 30 Club, which had a small jewelry-gift shop in the front and a small casino in the back.

Prell planned and built the Sahara, which opened in October 1952. It was a fabulous operation with top-notch amenities. Having heard about Miller and his closing the Riviera in 1953, Prell offered Miller a percentage interest in the Sahara as an incentive to get Miller on board. Prell knew that Miller could bring the best acts in the country to the Sahara, which was important in attracting the finest clientele.[51] Miller accepted the offer.

Miller left the Sahara in 1955 and acquired an interest in the new Dunes. There, he assumed the role of entertainment director and booked a show called "Smart Affairs."

"That started all the big production shows you have in Vegas today," said Miller. "From there, they brought in the 'Lido de Paris' and the 'Follies Bergères.'" Miller's former producer in New Jersey, Donn Arden, came to Las Vegas and became one of the city's leading show producers.[52]

Free and clear of the Riviera, Miller could then put his name on the Royal Nevada and applied all of his ideas to the casino-hotel that just could not generate the business needed to keep the doors open. The main investor, Frank Fishman, was overbearing and impossible to deal with. Fishman got sued by the *Las Vegas Sun* newspaper over some advertising bills and appealed when he lost the case. *Sun* publisher Hank Greenspun testified about Fishman:

> "I did ask him about these people who were from St. Louis. I think it was Mr. Moll and Sid Wyman who were going to operate the place and he said, 'It does not make any difference who operates, they are clerks. Frank Fishman is the Royal Nevada, and the Royal Nevada is Frank Fishman. I am the boss over everything there, I am the boss.'"[53]

Eventually, Miller was named the entertainment director at the Flamingo and subsequently, in 1969, brought Barbra Streisand and Elvis Presley to the new International Hotel.

50   *The Montana Standard*, Feb. 16, 1947
51   Interview with Tom Austin, 2019. Note: Austin wrote several books on Bill Miller's Riviera
52   *Las Vegas Review-Journal*, Feb. 7, 1999
53   *Fishman v. Las Vegas Sun*, 341 P.2d 102, 1959

CHAPTER 9

THE DUNES: LICENSING AND OPENING

The Dunes' application for a gaming license was discussed at the May 1956 meeting of the Nevada Tax Commission. Commissioner William Deutsch opposed granting it for five reasons. They were:

- Location.
- Not enough rooms to create its own paying clientele.
- Insufficient bankroll.
- Las Vegas business has increased, but established resorts are sharing in this business and offering competition to the Dunes.
- No inducement for players to go to the Dunes if it does not offer major shows in its big Arabian Room.

Deutsch added, "I can't see how this enterprise has a reasonable opportunity for success at this time."

One important factor that everyone at the commission meeting knew was that the Dunes was closed by two sets of former operators, and Deutsch's key argument, notwithstanding the others, was that the property was located a considerable distance from the other Strip resort hotels. At the time of this meeting, two other hotels located to the south of the Dunes and even further away had gaming license applications pending with the tax commission. These hotels, the Tropicana and the Hacienda, were on the main highway to Las Vegas and near the municipal airport.

Another tax commissioner, William Sinnott, echoed that the financial structure of the Dunes' management team was thoroughly investigated and that the "applications will just have to be decided on their merits."

As for the resort lacking entertainment, Deutsch said, "I can't see where they are going to attract business without major entertainment and a big room." Evidently, Deutsch must not have ever visited the Dunes because there was a big theater that was erected by the former owner, Al Gottesman, which supported casts as large as 60 plus variety acts. It is also dubious that Deutsch looked at the application and personal history of Bill Miller, who was one of the biggest entertainment bookers on the East Coast. Major Riddle and Miller probably projected in their finances a budget for entertainment that was much smaller than what was spent on the former lavish, expensive, and overpriced "Magic Carpet Revue." However, they had a few surprises that they would not reveal until they believed it necessary to do so.

Riddle and Miller chose not to open the extravagant theater right away but offer "back- bar" entertainment and a coffee shop instead. Commissioner Sinnott remarked, "Should the new Dunes policy prove successful, it would break the back of the high priced entertainment in Las Vegas.... It is a Frankenstein that is recognized in Las Vegas."

As far as a bankroll, Miller and Riddle put up $150,000 each, and Bob Rice contributed $40,000, for a total of $340,000. Additionally, the three pledged to add equal amounts to their original investment, if needed, to keep the Dunes in operation.

Deutsch then reiterated that even with $680,000 – about $6.4 million in 2020 dollars – in operating capital, he doubted the Dunes could succeed. He pointed out the Sands management lost $1.2 million in the several months they operated the Dunes. Commissioner Newell Hancock interjected that the actual loss to the Sands was $600,000 and that "even this needn't have occurred."

After all of the discussion, the tax commissioners approved the Dunes license in a 5 to 1 vote, with Deutsch being the lone dissenter.

The new Dunes Hotel and Casino, under the management of Riddle, Miller, and Rice, opened on June 6, 1956.

Miller contracted with Harold Minsky, creator of family-style burlesque shows, whom he knew from New Jersey and Florida, to bring "Minsky's Follies" of 1956 to the Dunes, paving the way for other nude revue shows in Las Vegas. Back in 1948 Ed Sullivan's column leaked a rumor that Miller dropped out of a deal with Minsky to buy the Colonial Inn in Florida, where big stars appeared nightly to attract players to the illegal casino operation owned by Meyer Lansky, "Jimmy Blue Eyes" Alo," and others. "Minsky's Follies," which started in the Dunes' Arabian Room in 1957, featured Lou Costello of Abbott and Costello and a bevy of beautiful women who appeared topless. It was the first topless show in Las Vegas, and Riddle took the credit for it as it quickly became a huge success.

With its many variations and different stars, the Minsky show became and remained a top Vegas attraction for an unprecedented 3½ years. Along with Costello (who died from a heart attack in March 1958), it featured Tony Bennett, Johnnie Ray, Pinky Lee, Lili St. Cyr, and many more, along with bare-breasted chorus girls and dancers.

In response, the local clergy started a campaign against topless stage shows, yet it seemed that they did not object to Nevada having legalized houses of prostitution.

A controversy about nude shows also quickly developed in Las Vegas among hotel owners, with Jack Entratter of the Sands and Ben Goffstein of the Riviera leading the anti-nudity movement. The two believed that nudity and gambling did not mix and that undressed ladies would make the wives of high rolling businessmen limit their gambling to Saturday night poker parties.[54] Beldon Katleman of the El Rancho also was against nudity.

The Dunes and Stardust, on the other hand, were for it. In fact, the Stardust imported Paris' Lido show after seeing the great success of the Minsky show at the Dunes.

Citizen groups took their protest to the Nevada Legislature and the newspapers, but they could not stop the momentum of the Follies show. Miller and Riddle turned a deaf ear to the complaints and sat back and counted the winnings from the casino players whom the featured show attracted. In the first week alone, more than 16,000 people attended the show.

Miller's success came from him always providing top grade, not second rate, entertainment. He was on record as saying, "I will continue to provide entertainment to suit their taste as long as I am able."

The Dunes copied an idea for an overnight casino junket that another hotel was offering, and it was a real bargain. The hotel-casino flooded the Los Angeles market with ads for a free round-trip flight to Las Vegas with the purchase of a $22.95 package that included the "Minsky's Follies" show, the Ink Spots show, cocktails for the lounge and show, a buffet dinner, a bottle of Champagne, limo service, and Champagne in flight. The flights left Burbank and Long Beach in the early evening and returned the following morning between 1 and 4 A.M. These mini-casino junkets were also referred to as "up and backs."

Riddle announced that the Dunes' entertainment budget for 1961 would be $2.5 million for appearances by Jayne Mansfield, Frankie Laine, Zsa Zsa Gabor, Tony Bennett, Johnnie Ray, Frankie Vaughan, "Minsky's Follies," Roberta Sherwood, Lili St. Cyr, Vaughn Monroe, Al Hirt, Billy Eckstine, the Novelettes, the Ink Spots, and Dakota Staton.

Miller resigned from the Dunes in January 1957. Then in March, Riddle bought out Miller's interest, giving Riddle 88.2 percent of the Dunes.[55]

A number of strange occurrences at the Dunes may have triggered these events. A relative of Miller said, "He [Riddle] was caught cheating,

54   *The Record*, James Bacon, Feb. 27, 1959
55   FBI Files 124-90032-10075 and 94-217, April 9, 1959

and Bill didn't want a part of that." This claim could not be substantiated but is consistent with a later November 20, 1961 FBI memo of that stated:

> "Informant learned the owners of the Dunes Hotel had determined that [Major] Riddle has been taking from $40,000 to $50,000 per month from hotel funds without the owner's knowledge and there is definite talk that Riddle will be eliminated for this embezzlement. Since that date informant has repeatedly advised that the owners of the Dunes Hotel are dissatisfied with Riddle and that Riddle will be eliminated in one way or another."[56]

Dorothy Kilgallen, a popular New York columnist who frequented Miller's Riviera in New Jersey when it was open, wrote:

> "Bill Miller is involved in a fascinating tangle with a hotel in Las Vegas. He booked the Minsky show there several years ago, and has been collecting an impressive commission ever since. But the hotel management has decided not to pay him anymore so they've taken the "Minsky" off the advertisements."[57]

In May 1957, the Nevada Gaming Commission approved James C. Adair, a former vice president of the Don Lee broadcasting network, for 7.25 percent of the Dunes. Adair assumed the position of general manager and became an officer and director of the company. However, just four months later, in September, he resigned and sold his stock to Riddle. Adair publicly stated that selling his Dunes stock permits him to devote "an increasing amount of time to other business enterprises."[58] Adair's public statement may have been true, but evidence points to some underlying problems Adair may have discovered. Adair came to the Dunes without any gambling experience and was most likely a square shooter.

According to *The Green Felt Jungle*, written by Ed Reid and Ovid Demaris with former Las Vegas Riviera publicist Ed Becker feeding them tantalizing stories and rumors, the Nevada Gaming Control Board (GCB) mandated a show cause hearing for the Dunes based on allegations of internal cheating and unusual manipulation of large sums of cash.[59] The agency subpoenaed all of the licensed partners for questioning.

At the hearing, Adair testified that the Dunes "was being systematically looted," with the losses always occurring during the graveyard shift (2 A.M. until 10 A.M.). The explanation he was given for the missing money was that

---

56   FBI File, Los Angeles, 92-1010, 1962
57   *The Times Tribune*, Feb. 17, 1959
58   *Las Vegas Review-Journal*, Sept. 6, 1957
59   *The Green Felt Jungle*, Ed Reid and Ovid Demaris, 1963

a "Chinaman" from Boston with a hot hand won the money, he said. Adair reported that some of the dealers on the graveyard shift were mechanics, or card cheats. He also noted that a New York labor leader gambled with "damp and moldy money" and consistently lost to the house. Strange numbers were inked on the bills, the meaning of which Adair said he could not figure out.

Adair also shared that in the fall of the prior year a local figure in the county assessor's office had "put in a fix" with someone in the governor's office, in connection with some business with the Dunes. Adair did not elaborate, for example, on the purpose of this fix. It is probable that all of these incidents are what really were behind him selling his Dunes stock.

Adair also testified that there once was a heated discussion about "cheaters and mechanics" at the boss' table, where Riddle, the major owner, and Jake Gottlieb, the landlord, met every day, and that everyone present was excited. Adair claimed that Gottlieb jumped up and while shaking his fist, shouted, "I'll go to Chicago and get the 'man' to walk up and down the Strip and strike terror in the hearts of these cheating bastards," likely referring to a Mobster from the Chicago Outfit.

This author was employed at the Dunes and was familiar with Gottlieb's demeanor. This statement attributed to him does not sound like it came from his mouth as quoted. It was too dramatic and resembled the patter of a play. Gottlieb would have been more or less rhetorical and would have uttered street lingo.

During the GCB's show cause hearing, Howie Engel, a 5 percent Dunes stakeholder, testified that he went to Miami to get $10,000 to make up for some bad luck the casino experienced. Engel did not reveal the source of that money, and the board members did not question him about it. Why the GCB did not press the issue is not known.

Engel was a class act, well-liked by employees and patrons, a perfect host and an excellent golfer. He was the baccarat manager when the Dunes installed the game in December 1960. He was a bookmaker from the Boston area who moved to Miami in the late 1940s, where he partnered with Samuel "Big Sam" Cohen in operating a fashionable steakhouse called Gray's Inn on Dade Boulevard. On the second floor was a bookie operation.

Cohen was a major principal in the S&G Syndicate, which furnished a wire service and had a co-op of bookmakers. It was virtually impossible for anyone not in with the S&G boys to make book in Miami Beach. Cohen associated with Charlie "The Blade" Tourine, who was a member of the group that had concessions and bookies in every resort hotel. Money flowed, and business was great until the federal government, through the Kefauver Committee, started pressuring them.

CHAPTER 10

SIDNEY WYMAN

J acob Sidney Wyman was a strapping young man who loved sports and gambling. In the 1930s he was a scratch golfer and noted contender in many tournaments in the St. Louis, Missouri, area as well as a top "A" amateur tennis player. He was known as "Sidney" or "Sid" to his close associates and friends. Wyman never forgot his chums from St. Louis and brought many of them to Las Vegas to work in the gambling business. Frank Zemel, a gifted golfer, eventually became Wyman's day shift manager at the Dunes in the 1960s.

In the 1940s gambling was going strong throughout the U.S. and bustled in St. Louis. Wyman made front page news in that city when the police raided the Town Game in the Hamilton Hotel, busting 43 gamblers and operators.[60] Gambling charges were dismissed against all but 13 of the people associated with this "high-stakes dice Town Game." The defendants' lawyer Morris Shenker asked the court to bar all photographers and police witnesses and claimed that the search warrant was not prepared legally.

A newspaper account reported that when the defendants lined up to take the oath, some did so on their knees, with only their hands appearing on the court railing, as the flash bulbs of news photographers popped. Other defendants crouched behind seats, and several, including Wyman and Paul Mayorwitz, wore dark glasses.

On the stand, police captain Charles Wren recalled how he stood underneath the window of the Hamilton Room, which was off of the lobby floor of the hotel, for 25 minutes listening to the activity inside before starting the raid. He heard the rattle of dice in a box and cries of "who is fading me?" he related. As he and his men entered the room, he and a detective sergeant were knocked down in a stampede of startled gamblers, some of whom fled to the ballroom and mingled with dancers at a university hop held in another room. One man ran into a telephone booth to hide whereas a second man tried to jump from a lavatory window but was grabbed.

St. Louis Post-Dispatch, April 30, 1946

Wren testified that in the Hamilton Room were cloth-fitted tables with sideboards, on which there were dice, a money box, a dice box, and a rake. Sergeant John O'Connor told of peering in the gambling room from a ladder raised to the window, which was adorned with Venetian blinds. He identified defendants George Zonnis, David Fixler, Victor Padratzik, Jack Ellis, Phil Grodsky, and Morris Cooper, all of who were sitting around the dice table. Zonnis, one of the livelier participants in the craps game, was heard repeatedly calling for "Little Joe," commonly known as a "hard four," or a 2 on each of the dice.

In the late 1940s, Wyman and his partner Charlie Rich operated a bookmaking company called C.J. Rich & Co.. According to the Kefauver Committee:

> "C.J. Rich & Co., which has also operated under the name of Rich & Wyman, was one of the most unusual bookmaking operations studied by the committee. This enterprise did a gross business of between 4 and 5 million dollars a year and used Western Union telegrams, money orders, and Western Union agents to carry on operations. Most of the business of C.J. Rich & Co. came from more than a hundred miles away from St. Louis through Western Union. Telegrams placing bets would be sent to C.J. Rich & Co. at an address in East St. Louis, Ill. Bets were covered by Western Union money orders. During every operating day the Western Union Telegraph Co. would accumulate the incoming money orders and would issue a single check for all the moneys [sic] bet. The fact that bets could be placed through Western Union with C.J. Rich & Co. was made abundantly clear in the advertising literature which this company distributed. Western Union agents were used as runners and solicitors for bets and were paid a percentage of winnings for their services, or commissions. Cash or presents were also given by the C.J. Rich & Co. to various Western Union representatives. The Western Union company itself profited from the bookmaking business, for C.J. Rich & Co. would receive between 500 to 1,000 telegrams a day. In the month of May 1950, the telegraph bill of C.J. Rich & Co. was $26,700.
>
> "It is quite clear that in the C.J. Rich & Co. operation, the Western Union aided and abetted the violation of the gambling laws of the State, because it was profitable to do so. Only when the

C.J. Rich & Co. was raided on June 26, 1950, did the Western Union do anything to stop its participation in the bookmaking conspiracy. All charge accounts with Western Union of this company were canceled after the raid. One wonders whether the Western Union's obliviousness to its public responsibility not to permit its facilities to be used in violation of State law was in part due to the fact that William Molasky, of St. Louis, a well-known gambler, is one of its outstanding stockholders."[61]

On June 6, 1950, a tip by New Jersey Governor Al Driscoll to the feds set off a raid that wiped out a major nerve center of the national gambling syndicate. State, city, and county police raided the headquarters of C.J. Rich & Co., the multi-million-dollar betting ring from Maine to Texas. They seized two men and a large quantity of horse race and sports betting paraphernalia. Among the items were thousands of telegrams from bettors in various parts of the country. The messages were to place bets on horses at tracks throughout the nation. Also retrieved were invoices from Western Union and acknowledgments from Western Union managers and employees of gifts they received from C.J. Rich & Co. With their gifts, the gambling enterprise was in effect "buying business."

The St. Louis prosecutor described Wyman as the "current kingpin of the gambling fraternity" and said that he was listed in the black book of members taken from notorious Los Angeles gambler and Mobster Mickey Cohen. (Other St. Louis names in Cohen's book were Anthony Giordano, Bennie Greenberg, and Joseph Beckley.)[62]

Wyman and Rich's betting operation introduced them to all of the bookmaking and live game operations and associated Mobsters around the country. These other operators needed a place to lay off bets, and Wyman and Rich took action from all of them, handling $500,000 per day in 1950. They handled bets for horses, baseball, basketball, and football and also specialized in political wagers. They were leaders in setting lines on political races. They were protected by the local sheriff and the old Al Capone crew out of Chicago.

Wyman and Rich did not offer a betting room for watching the board or a loud speaker service wherein a guy in a back room simulated a horse race from reading the ticker tape.

Their brochure, which they sent to Western Union agents, read:

"We pay track odds for $15 across the board and $40-21-10 for the next $85 across. We will accept phone play any time before post time and will pay the charges on all calls."

C.J. Rich & Co. offered Western Union agents 25 percent of the winnings. In April and May of 1950, 12,000 telegrams were sent through Western Union to the bookmaking firm.

61   Kefauver Committee Interim Report No. 3, 1951
62   *St. Louis Post-Dispatch*, Aug. 4, 1950

"It makes the bets that are phoned between New York and New Jersey look like a peanut operation," said Nelson S. Stampler, deputy attorney general of New Jersey.

In 1951, members of the Kefauver Committee subpoenaed Wyman and Rich to appear before them.

Dan Wyman described his Uncle Sid and shared several anecdotes involving him.

"The main thing about Sid for me was not his money or his job; it was his personality," Dan said. "He was charismatic and he oozed charm. He's been gone for 40 years and I remember him so well. There are some actors and musicians who shared some of those larger-than-life traits, who had a great presence. John Wayne and my musical hero B.B. King come to mind. My mother said that Sid was one in a million, and she was right."

Dan relayed how when Sid's sister Belle threw Sid a birthday party, Sid "brought perfume and silk scarves for the women at the party. I was there, and he asked me how old [I thought] he was. I told him he was 60, but he said no, he was 240 because he lived 4 years for everyone else's. That's not too far from the truth, I suspect.

"Uncle Sid always booked show reservations for me, so invariably, I was comped wherever I was in town. I saw Elvis three times. On one of those occasions, when I was 21, I took a blind date to the show. She turned out to be 44 years old. It was not much fun for me," said Dan. "Once, Uncle Sid took my friend and me to a show, when we were teenagers. We saw Sammy Davis. Sid drove us to the show in a T-bird convertible that Ford let him use.

"Sid made reservations for me at another show, at the MGM, which was across the street from the Dunes, before it became Bally's if memory serves me. He told me to go to the invited guest line well before the start of the show, which I did. The person checking the guests in was a security guard. He wasn't very nice to the man in front of me and told him to get into the 'regular' line. I was young and slightly intimidated and when the guard asked me who I was, I made sure to slowly pronounce my last name and tell him that my uncle Sid Wyman sent me over. The man became very solicitous and told me that everything had been taken care of and that I just had to walk in at the start of the show. Sid's name was magic," Dan remarked.

"When I took a girlfriend [who ultimately became my wife] to the Dunes, she wanted to borrow an iron and ironing board before we went to dinner – as you'll remember, you had to get dressed up for dinner and shows in those days. She dialed the Laundry and was told that it was closed, so she asked me to call for her. I called and they promptly sent up an iron and an ironing board, as well as someone to iron her clothes."

Dan continued:

"Sid was incredibly generous. He gave lots of money to charity, including the City of Hope and many others, and he gave many gifts to his family. He gave me my first two cars, including a Plymouth GTX. He gave cars to others in the family, including my brother. Once, he gave a Cadillac to my father, but my father had to return it. He was a salesman and he didn't think it would go over well with his customers if he drove a Cadillac. Plus, the car was too long for our garage! When my father retired in 1970, he bought his company car, a Plymouth. But he soon sold it because Sid gave him a Mercedes that he kept until he died in 1997.

"Sid was very good to my mother, his sister-in-law. He gave her extravagant jewelry and all manner of other gifts, including one of the first microwave ovens. When I got my own apartment, he gave me a microwave as well.

"For Sid's funeral, the Dunes chartered a plane for employees who wanted to attend. During the funeral, a rabbi eulogized Sid and said that Sid had given the temple money to cover the expenses of all the kids who wanted to go to summer camp somewhere in California. The kids wanted to meet the man who had done this for them, so the rabbi arranged for the busload of kids bound for the camp to go to the Dunes. Sid met the kids and gave the rabbi more money so that they could all go to Disneyland."

Dan recalled Morris Shenker arriving at Sid's funeral reception and making the comment to his associate, "Let's get out of here."

Dan continued:

"Sid would give me money when I was old enough to gamble. He'd peel off about $400 from his wad of bills and told me to turn it into something bigger. He said, 'You can't win big unless you bet big.' Now that I think about it, when I was younger, my father would occasionally bring us home money that Sid had given to him for us kids. I don't know if it came from Sid's gambling winnings or from the hotel profits.

"Sid was a great poker player, of course, and is in the Poker Hall of Fame. He told me that he won $250,000 in one hand of poker. That was more than 40 years ago, so you know that was a lot of money."

Wyman believed in the "hit and run" system at the dice table, which was getting to the limit as fast as possible and continuing to play until the dice turned cold.

"Sid always loved gambling. When he was a kid, his father [my grandfather] found money in Sid's pants pockets on one or more occasions. He had won it gambling with someone.

"Not only did my family get to see the shows at Sid's hotels, we got to meet the performers in their rooms or backstage. I remember meeting Red Skelton, The Kingston Trio, Harry Belafonte and others. I was a child and it was very exciting for me. Once, comedian Myron Cohen made a point of introducing my brother and me to his audience."

Dave Wyman, another nephew of Sid, said:

"My memories of Sid Wyman stretch back into the 1950s. My mom and dad and brother Dan would pile into our car to make the trip across the desert to spend a few days visiting Sid, first at the Sands hotel, then the Riviera, and finally the Dunes. Sometimes Uncle Sid would visit us in Los Angeles, too. Those trips were made in the summer before air conditioning came standard on cars, and I remember sweating in the back seat with Dan on those arduously long trips across the Mojave Desert, when the temperature could rise above 100 degrees.

"Our family watched The Red Skelton television show every Sunday night. Red played in the showroom at the Riviera hotel, which Uncle Sid and his partners owned, while our family was staying at the hotel. I was 10 and I loved Red Skelton. When he arrived in front of the hotel in his Rolls Royce, my family and Uncle Sid were there to meet him. We would see several other famous performers during our visits in Las Vegas. I remember seeing Dean Martin, Harry Belafonte, Sammy Davis, and Tony Bennett.

"When Sid visited our home in Los Angeles, sometime in the early 1960s, he asked my dad to bring him a deck of cards and a shoe-box full of poker chips. Then Sid asked my dad to be the dealer in a game of 21. It didn't take long for Sid to show us he had a system for remembering which cards were initially played from that deck, knowing which cards were left, and for winning all the chips.

"One evening my brother and I were with Uncle Sid in his seventh floor suite that wrapped around the north end of the Dunes' 24-story tower building. If my parents were in Las Vegas, too, they must have been out at a supper show. We three were all in Sid's suite to watch the final episode of *The Fugitive*, a very popular TV show. That meant the date was August 29, 1967. I was 19, and Dan was 15. Before *The Fugitive* started, we ordered dinner via room service. I didn't want anything expensive on the menu, as I didn't want to take advantage of Sid's generosity, so I ordered a hamburger. Uncle Sid said emphatically, 'You can't order a hamburger! You're in the Dunes hotel!' I had a fantastic shrimp salad."

Dave recalled further:

"When I was older, I visited Uncle Sid in Las Vegas without my parents, in the company of my brother and our friends. On at least three occasions, when I was in college in Northern California, my uncle paid for me and whoever I was dating at the time to fly to Las Vegas.

"Each time when my girlfriend and I arrived at the Dunes and met Uncle Sid, he'd give us $500. He'd tell us not to leave town with any of that money left unspent. Given that Sid comped everything we did, from our room to our meals to seeing the shows in the Dunes and around town, and given that five C-notes were worth a lot more than they are now, spending all that money was impossible.

"Whenever I visited Sid, whether I was with a date or my brother or a friend, we'd see the 'Casino de Paris' extravaganza in the Dunes showroom. Since we usually spent a couple of days at the Dunes, Uncle Sid would ask us which show we wanted to see on our second night. Whatever that show might be, he'd get us into it. All we had to do, as per Sid's instructions, was announce who we were to whoever was in charge of the VIP line and tip them $20, after which we'd find ourselves somewhere in the center of the showroom, close to the front of the stage.

"Uncle Sid didn't have any kids. He did have four nephews. He gave each of us cars. The first of three for me, when I was 18, was a surprise. The car, a Ford Fairlane, was powder blue and a convertible. And it had an air conditioner. Subsequently, Uncle Sid let me choose the cars I wanted. The first was a muscle car, the formidable Dodge Charger. The second was a far more sedate Volvo.

"In early 2006, I was invited by chance to an annual reunion in Las Vegas of Dunes hotel employees. The Dunes had been imploded some years before, with the Bellagio Hotel erected in its place. Uncle Sid had died about three decades earlier. There were several people at the reunion, though, who worked with Uncle Sid. Everyone who knew him had strong memories of Sid. And everyone, whether they were at the Dunes during Sid's time or not, knew about my uncle. Because I was Sid's nephew, I was treated royally by everyone I met.

"When I told my Aunt Belle – Uncle Sid's sister and a remarkable person in her own right – about my visit to the reunion after the fact, she asked me to take her the following year, which I did. If I was a prince as Sid's nephew at my prior attendance to the reunion, my 93 year-old Aunt Belle was the queen of the ball during her visit."

Dave recounted several stories about Sid's generosity:

"During a strike by employees who were picketing the Dunes, my uncle walked out of the hotel to the picket line, pushing a cart full of sandwiches for the strikers," he said.

"At the conclusion of a private session of Craps for high rollers, none of the gamblers tipped the croupiers. Sid said something to the effect of, 'That's not how we operate here!' He picked up a handful of chips worth hundreds of dollars and gave them to the croupiers.

"One night he walked into the Dunes Sultan's Table, which was completely full. Sid took $3,000 out of his pocket and gave it to the maître 'd and told him to comp all the guests in the room.

"One of the employees couldn't secure a bank loan to purchase a house. He asked Sid if he could make the loan. Sid gave the employee the loan, telling the employee to pay him back as and when he could, without interest.

"An employee told Sid she was taking her parents, who were going to celebrate their wedding anniversary, to dinner at the Dome of the Sea, the swankiest of the restaurants at the Dunes. Sid made the reservation for her and paid for everyone's meal.

"While power failure at the Dunes shut off the air conditioning in the casino, it didn't shut down the action in the casino. Sid's booming voice announced over the loud speaker that all the croupiers could remove their coats and ties.

"By the way, I remember that the loud speakers in the casino as well as out by the swimming pools seemed to have one purpose, to announce that someone, often Sid or one of his partners, had a phone call."

CHAPTER 11

CHARLES J. RICH

Charles "Charlie" J. Rich was sometimes called "Kewpie." In his younger years, he had rosy red cheeks, not much hair, and was a little pudgy, so some neighborhood kids said he looked like a "Kewpie doll," a common carnival prize. The nickname stuck. In adulthood, however, the only ones to call him "Kewpie" were his gambler associates and newspaper journalists who seemed to think it added color to their stories. If they had personally known Rich, they would have realized what a gentleman he was. Even Charlie's longtime business partner, Sid Wyman, never called him Kewpie, and it was never heard in any vernacular in the presence of Dunes employees. Rich's family called him "Cookie," which sounded like "Kewpie." It was easy to tell a young grandson or granddaughter when they heard Kewpie that they really heard Cookie.

Rich's longtime friend Cary Grant probably called him Kewpie, as Grant's daughter, Jennifer Grant, used the name in her book, *Good Stuff: A Reminiscence of My Father, Cary Grant*. She wrote, "Kewpie was maybe five feet tall, bald as they come, with a year-round tan (sometimes orange out of the Coppertone bottle – which Dad heckled him for) and a heart that never stopped giving."

In a 1968 interview, Rich said that he and Grant were intimate friends for 35 years. "I met him in St. Louis when he played at the Municipal Opera there," Rich said. "There's not a greater guy in the world."

Grant was a lover of sports and especially liked baseball and boxing, in which Rich was an expert due to his bookmaking and handicapping experience. This mutual love of sports and the gamble involved cemented their lifelong friendship. Whereas Rich was a real gambler and bookmaker, one step ahead of the law, Grant, who was captivated with his friend's life, only experienced the excitement of it through his movie roles. There is no doubt that Rich invited Grant into his world of sports with box seats to St. Louis Browns games and front row seats at professional boxing matches. Rich tried to buy the Browns, but the timing was unfavorable because he then was being investigated by the Kefauver Committee.

Allegedly a photo exists of Rich, Wyman, and Grant at a championship boxing match. The wide shot captures the referee raising the winner's gloved hand in the air and the three friends in the front row. Wyman and Rich are seated and looking gloomy, seemingly unhappy with the decision of the bout. Grant, though, is on his feet cheering for the winner. Grant likely did not realize that Rich and Wyman had a bundle of money riding on the boxer who wound up losing. Perhaps this book will lead to the discovery of the photo.

Rich loved sports, especially baseball, football, basketball, and boxing. He himself was a champion handball player in St. Louis, winning several titles after graduating from Central High School. His interest in boxing started at the St. Louis Athletic Club from 1922 to 1932 during which time he met many of the champions of the day, including Benny Leonard, Maxie Rosenbloom, Jack Dempsey, and Primo Carnera.

Rich always wanted to own his own boxing gym at which professional and amateur boxers could work out and train. He played a good game of poker and on a wager, won an equal stake in a boxing gym, becoming a 50-50 owner. Rich wanted to put some dice tables upstairs in the facility, but his partner was against the idea. Eventually, Rich bought him out then installed the game tables. Rich also owned as many as four hand-books, which are places that take wagers on sporting events by telephone and telegraph.

A boxing match was scheduled about every two months, and the fighters were required by contract to train for at least two weeks before the match in "Charlie's" gym.

"The best times I ever had were during the Depression. A $2 bet couldn't hurt you," Rich was quoted as saying.

According to Bruce Fisher, grandson of Rich, "Cookie's best friend was Harry Kessler, a boxing referee. Kessler would score a fight, and Cookie would have the exact score for each round. He was really good at this."

Rich followed all major league baseball teams, and many considered him an expert handicapper in professional football and basketball. In a newspaper interview in 1968, Rich said that the interest in horse racing had diminished somewhat.[63]

"You just have to keep up with the horses, you know," he said, adding, "otherwise the fun of handicapping is lost."

Fisher recalled that "Grandma D was attending a Christmas party with her daughter Rowena, and Cookie stops by the party. I don't know why,

---

he's Jewish, but he stopped by this party, and he made a comment: 'Who is that beautiful woman over there?' And I mean, Evelyn was a knockout. She was a stunning redhead, had a beautiful face and a perfect figure. She was just a knockout. Someone told Cookie she's Evelyn McGrath and was a manicurist at a barber shop out on Delmar Boulevard. A few days later, he goes down to get a manicure from her and they start talking and every-thing. She told him about her three kids, one down in Fort Worth and two in St. Louis and trying to get them all back together.

"It was The Great Depression and things were tough. She was living in a one-room apartment with her two girls, Lorayne and Rena. Her son George was with her sister in Texas. Cookie says, yeah, yeah, yeah. And uh, one thing leads to another and of course he leaves a big tip.

"Grandma appreciated his generosity and they became friendly and started dating," Fisher continued. "He came up with a proposal to Evelyn. He said, 'I gamble and play poker sometimes until two, three o'clock in the morning. When I come home, I wake my parents up. They always are complaining about that. What about if we get a two-bedroom apartment and we will bring all, like all your kids together to live in the apartment with us? Let me help you. Cook me breakfast, and you and your children can stay in my two-bedroom apartment. How's that sound?'" said Fisher.[64]

Evelyn was married previously to Harrison Duckworth, with whom she had the three children. He died from complications of pneumonia, leaving her to care for them on her own.

Evelyn accepted Rich's offer, and sent for young George, who by then was almost 8 years old. Charlie and Evelyn married in 1945 in St. Charles, Missouri. Rich loved Evelyn's children as if they were his own.

Once, Rich told Evelyn's daughters to come to the boxing match being held on the weekend to "see me in the ring." They were in disbelief as he was in his late 30s and not in shape. When the two got to the auditorium, they saw him in the ring but dressed in a business suit. He laughed, as his joke had worked. He said to them, "I told you I would be in the ring. I'm the boxing promoter."

Rich's Palm Springs estate was the pride of his life for many years. Grant's daughter, Jennifer, wrote merrily about the great times she had as a young girl at the property belonging to her father's good friend, Las Vegas Dunes owner Charlie "Kewpie" Rich. "Our number-one weekend getaway was to Uncle Charlie's Palm Springs estate. Uncle Charlie was a staple in our life." She went on, "Uncle Charlie lived in a Spanish adobe on

---

64   Bruce Fisher is Charles Rich's grandson and son of Lorayne.

several acres of manicured, palm- tree-lined property. I learned to drive a golf cart and play putt-putt on that lawn. We stayed in the pool house, near the good-for-guppy-hunting pond and gorgeous rose gardens."

The mansion, originally built in 1928, featured 8 bedrooms, 14 bathrooms (not kidding!!!), 13,000 square feet of living space, a four-car garage, a climate-controlled fur storage closet, a swimming pool, a pond, more than 100 palm trees, several 80-year-old Cypress trees, sweeping mountain views, and three standalone guesthouses. The one that Rich built especially for Grant boasted a formal living room, a fireplace, a large bar, a kitchen, two bathrooms, and one large bedroom.

Along with Grant, Rich hosted numerous famous guests at his private estate, including Allen Dorfman, Frank Sinatra, Gene Siskel, and Howard Hughes.

Despite not having any formal education after high school, Rich was extremely smart. He was an astute, intelligent operator with a keen mind for numbers and business. He was a wise, old school gambler with a few superstitions. It was noted but not verified that he did not like yellow pencils to be used in the Dunes gambling pits, the aisles between the rows of gambling tables – craps, blackjack, and roulette. To him, yellow pencils were bad luck. Maybe a yellow pencil had been used to record a sporting bet that resulted in a big loss for Rich during his hand-book days. It was reported he once threw a telephone out a second floor window after losing a baseball game.

Members of the notorious Frank Costello Mob became firmly entrenched in Las Vegas through "Bugsy" Siegel, who constructed and operated the Flamingo, which was, at the time, one of the most elaborate hotel and gambling establishments in America. It debuted in 1946.

Siegel was one of the most notorious gangsters in the country. Before moving to the West Coast, in the East he was involved in numerous illegal activities with Costello, Joe Adonis (who is credited with bringing Siegel to California), Meyer Lansky, Charles Luciano, Longie Zwillman, Moe Sedgwick, Louis Pokrass, and numerous other Mobsters. Also associated with the group in the east was Louis Shomberg, aka Dutch Goldberg, who was one of the most powerful gangsters in America in the early 1930s.

Whereas Rich and Wyman were not known to have a stake in the Flamingo, some unsubstantiated signs suggest otherwise.

At the Kefauver Committee hearing held in Las Vegas (at which time Rich was not a U.S. citizen), the Senators questioned him about the percentage interest in the Flamingo that he had considered buying.[65] Here is an excerpt:

---

65 Investigation of Organized Crime in Interstate Commerce, June 13, 1950

Rich: "I was not negotiating with anyone. There was just the rumor out that the Flamingo was going to be for sale, and I made the comment that I would like to make a small investment in it."

Chairman Estes Kefauver: "Then who did you talk with, who was connected with the Flamingo Hotel, about it?"

Rich: "No one whatsoever."

Kefauver: "That is awfully sort of confused. You wanted to get in on the deal, you heard about it, you got $65,000 out of the bank, and you did not talk with anybody connected with the Flamingo. Who did you hear about it from?"

Rich: "Just general talk in town."

Kefauver: "What made you think it was a good investment?"

Rich: "Well, I just inquired."

Kefauver: "Who did you inquire of?"

Rich: "General conversation around the hotel."

Kefauver: "Mr. Rich, you ought to know who you talked with; after all, it is legal, there isn't anything wrong, legally, with investing in the Flamingo out at Las Vegas. Who told you that it was a good deal?"

Rich: "I do not even know his last name, a party by the name of Jake. I met him out there the first time when I made the trip."

John Burling (Kefauver's assistant): "What was the date of this trip?"

Kefauver: "January 1951. Did you talk with Jake about how much the casino made and how much the hotel made?"

Rich: "Not too much. We just spoke generally and he told me that in his opinion he thought it was a good investment."

Kefauver: "How come you didn't make it?"

Rich: "It was too much for me to handle. I just wanted a small piece, and even with the small piece it amounted to more than I could afford."

Kefauver: "How much did they want for a small piece?"

Rich: "At that time I think it was, for 5 percent I think it was $75,000." Kefauver: "And you got $60,000 or $65,000 out there, didn't you?" Rich: "No, sir."

Kefauver: "What did you do with that cashier's check you got for $60,000 or $65,000? Well, you got either a cashier's check or cash for that much. What did you do with that?"

Rich never answered the question.[66]

It is very probable that the man "Jake" whom Rich referred to was Meyer Lansky's brother.

It is a shame that Chairman Kefauver did not get Rich to give this Jake's last name.

Then there is the mysterious telegram that allegedly was sent to Wyman from Meyer, giving him instructions related to the Flamingo casino immediately after Siegel's murder. This telegram, which is pictured here, has not been verified or authenticated, and thus, could be a forgery. Yet it is a fact that Wyman's partner, Rich, was questioned about a possible investment in the Flamingo.

Analysis of the brief and succinct telegram reveals weak points that make it suspicious, but other information contained in it perhaps tells a secret story.

One big flaw of the telegram is that it is addressed to Wyman at the Flamingo and dated June 21, 1947, when, in an interview with sports writer Jim Murray of the *Los Angeles Times*, Wyman said he'd first gone to Las Vegas 1949, two years later.[67] On the surface, there does not seem to be a reason for Wyman to lie about the date, but perhaps there was. If so, what was his motive, and cui bono – who would benefit?[68]

As for Rich, he testified under oath that the date of his trip to Las Vegas to consider investing in the Flamingo was January 1951. That is even later, four years after the telegram date.

That date coincides with what Rich told the Kefauver Committee when they asked for his last day in business, meaning his last day in partnership with Wyman as C.J. Rich & Co. in St. Louis.

Burling: "When were you last in business?"

Rich: "In June, I think it was."

Burling: "June of 1950?"

Rich: "June of 1950, yes sir."

Burling: "You stopped when you were raided?"

Rich: "Yes, sir."

The line in the telegram, "effective immediately change all locks in the Casino Cage," is suspicious for several reasons. It suggests to anyone who

---

successful.
67   *Los Angeles Times*, Jim Murray, Dec. 12, 1962
68   *Oswald: Assassin or Fall Guy?* Joachim Joesten, 1964. The author maintains that "since Roman jurisprudence, two thousand years ago, a basic maxim of criminal investigation has been cui bono? Who gains? Who stands to benefit from the crime?"

reads it that Lansky was revealing to the public via the telegram, transcribed by a Pacific Telegram employee, that he was giving orders as some sort of director or owner of the Flamingo and, thereby, outing himself as a hidden owner. Also, the instructions given lead the reader to believe that Wyman was staying at the Flamingo and employed in the casino as some type of manager or a hidden representative of Lansky. Were that true then Lansky exposed Wyman, too. Such actions were absolutely out of character for Lansky.

Further, Lansky was an experienced casino operator who more than likely would use correct gambling jargon and not capitalize "casino cage." An instruction like this would have been more appropriate: "Change locks in casino cage and drop boxes. Change combinations on safes."

CHAPTER 12

THE WYMAN AND RICH TAX TRIAL

S id Wyman and Charlie Rich were indicted in New Jersey along with Western Union for conspiracy to engage in bookmaking, but Missouri refused to extradite them to that eastern state.

C.J. Rich & Co. used the Pioneer News Service, which had two Missouri state senators on the payroll, and Rich and Wyman's attorney, Morris Shenker, was quite active in Missouri politics.[69] The two partners were arrested then released on bond in October 1949.[70]

When Wyman was arrested in St. Louis, detectives in Teaneck, N.J., arrested Leo Link a.k.a. J.W. Donaldson. Deputy Attorney General Nelson Stampler described Link as one of the "real big-time bookies" in the east, and called Wyman's organization the "major nerve center" of a national gambling syndicate.[71]

Stampler said that Wyman's gambling operation, C.J. Rich & Co., was based in Wellston, a St. Louis suburb, in a business building using the plating company "Gold Bronze Company" as a front.

"This is no penny ante setup," Wren said. "The book appeared to be doing a nationwide business via telegraph and telephone."

Missouri authorities cleared the way for extradition of Rich, Wyman, Ralph Leon, and Edward Fischer in connection with the Western Union gambling probe in New Jersey. Stampler received assurance from Missouri Lieutenant Governor James T. Blair, Jr. that his office would help clear extradition, however, the four arrested men were nowhere to be found. Newspapers quoted Stampler as saying, "There's something fishy about it."

Later, Wyman, Rich, Fischer, and Leon were indicted in 1953 by a Kansas City federal grand jury on the charge of filing a false annual tax return with the Treasury Department in connection with their nationwide bookmaking operation.

As procedure required, Wyman and Rich's case was submitted to Oscar G. Iden, chief auditor in the post review section of the Internal Rev-

---

69   *Jefferson City Post-Tribune,* Aug. 9, 1951
70   *Mexico City Ledger* (Missouri), Oct. 6, 1949
71   *Courier-Post,* June 6, 1950

enue Service (IRS) in Washington, D.C. Iden supposedly reviewed the case and then abandoned the notion of prosecution. As the chief auditor, Iden exercised broad authority and his recommendations as to whether cases should be prosecuted were usually followed.

Iden revealed to the *St. Louis Post-Dispatch* in April 1950 that Shenker, attorney for Rich and Wyman, obtained a new Oldsmobile for Iden in 1948 when automobiles were in short supply. He said, however, the car was a favor, it had nothing to do with the case against Shenker's clients, and Iden had paid for it.

The Oldsmobile's title was transferred to Iden, but records showed that he did not register it until July 7, 1948, seven days after he retired from the agency at age 60. The transfer of title was notarized by Beatrice Knetzer, who was a secretary at the Park Plaza Hotel in St. Louis, owned by Shenker's father-in-law, Sam Koplar. Shenker lived in the hotel at the time.

When questioned about Iden by the *Post-Dispatch*, Shenker said he had absolutely "no recollection" of buying an automobile for anyone other than his wife or himself. Shenker said he did not know Iden "as far as I can recall."[72]

The Wyman-Rich case was one of Shenker's first tax cases, after which he had unusual success in handling such cases in St. Louis and Washington, D.C.

Shenker arrived in St. Louis in 1922, a 15-year-old Jewish immigrant from Russia who had limited English. His real last name was Greenberg; he later took the name of Shenker. He lived in a small 1½-room apartment with more than eight other immigrants. He worked his way through law school at Washington University and went into practice in 1932.

Shenker once admitted to his love of shooting craps but gave up that pastime in 1944 to avoid public criticism.[73] Shooting craps was illegal in St. Louis and most parts of the country except Nevada then and a violation of his legal oath, which was:

> I do solemnly swear that I will support the Constitution of the United States and the Constitution of the State of Missouri;
> That I will maintain the respect due courts of justice, judicial officers and members of my profession and will at all times conduct myself with dignity becoming of an officer of the court in which I appear;
> That I will never seek to mislead the judge or jury by any artifice or false statement of fact or law;

---

72   *St. Louis Post-Dispatch*, April 20, 1952
73   *St. Louis Post-Dispatch*, April 20, 1952

That I will at all times conduct myself in accordance with the Rules of Professional Conduct; and,

That I will practice law to the best of my knowledge and ability and with consideration for the defenseless and oppressed. So help me God.

Along with Wyman and Rich, another client of Shenker was Lawrence Callanan. Shenker was reportedly the architect of the enormous political fund structure erected in St. Louis by this ex-con who ran Pipefitters Local 562, whose fund the feds closely examined for years, ultimately unsuccessful in finding malfeasance.

In 1953, Callanan was sentenced to 12 years in prison for violating federal racketeering charges in conjunction with Local 562. Shenker pleaded leniency for Callanan, which Judge Rubey Hulen denied. Hulen also was concerned with the use of union funds for the legal defense of Callanan and other officers of the Steamfitters Union when it was discovered that a large percentage of $143,000 distributed in the prior three years covered attorney's fees, bail bonds, and trial transcripts.

Most of the money went to Callanan, and some of it was allocated for political purposes.[74]

Shenker stated in court that every dollar was accounted for and that a recent public audit showed nothing wrong. Hulen interrupted, asking, "Can't you see anything wrong in your client taking union funds to defend himself in this case?"

"These are not union funds," Shenker replied. "The members voluntarily contributed for that purpose. The funds belong to members of the union, not to the union. There has never been 100 per cent contributions to the fund such as there is in paying dues."

"Was it proper for Callanan to seek funds for this purpose?" Hulen asked.

Shenker argued that he did not think it was improper if the membership wished to contribute to Callanan's defense.

"Now that he is convicted, don't you think he ought to put the money back he took for his defense?" asked Hulen.

Shenker said that his client no longer had the money and his only remaining asset was $2,500 of equity in his home.

Shenker stated repeatedly that Callanan came to him before reaching decisions on union matters, which included the time following the return of a federal indictment when Shenker said Callanan wanted to resign as business manager.

---

74   *St. Louis Post-Dispatch,* July 19, 1954

"Why does Callanan always come to you?" Hulen asked. "He was charged with deserting the union. He was charged with betraying the union. If he really did not want to represent the union after these charges, why didn't he just walk into a meeting and say, 'I resign?'"

Shenker sat down at that point.

Prosecutor Tom DeWolfe responded to Shenker's claim that two of the government's witnesses were paid a total of $1,400 by a representative of Callanan to get out of town until the racket case was tried and everything blew over.

Shenker, having complete knowledge of all of the prospective witnesses, had to know that Callanan paid the witnesses to leave town. This certainly could have constituted a violation of his oath as a lawyer.

Shenker did not think a lawyer should refuse to represent a client, regardless of the unpopularity of the circumstances and the case. He was willing to take the risk of representing gamblers and hoodlums even though the public may have thought that he was involved in his clients' crimes. He denied any type of association with his clients other than being their lawyer.

Over the next 20 years, Shenker became a successful defense attorney, a fundraiser for the Democratic Party, an acquaintance of U.S. presidents, and a lawyer for Mobsters. He co-founded the Dismas House in St. Louis, a well-known rehabilitation center for ex-convicts, as well as one of the country's leading fundraisers for Israel, for many years.

He was frequently in the national spotlight representing gambling figures at the Kefauver Committee hearings on organized crime in the early 1950s.

St. Louis hoodlum Richard Westbrook remembered Shenker "standing in front of the St. Louis courthouse pitching to fix traffic tickets for $2 a pop."[75] Westbrook, an associate of many gangsters and gangs in that city, may have hired Shenker himself.

---

75   Interview with Richard Westbrook, 1969

CHAPTER 13

SID WYMAN AND THE SANDS

In February 1952, the Nevada Tax Commission granted Jake Freedman a provisional license to operate the Sands hotel-casino on the conditions that he not sell an interest to or employ anyone who the commissioners considered an undesirable. Freedman was a Texas oilman, a known operator of a gambling house in Dallas, and the owner of a New York stable of racehorses.

Six months later, Freedman applied for a permanent gambling license for the Sands, which then was under construction. During a study of his application, persons claiming they could "influence the state tax commission to approve gambling license applications" drew the ire of individual commissioners, specifically Paul D. McDermott.

McDermott wanted it understood that no individual or attorney or firm of attorneys had influence on the tax commission. He made the point because rumors were floating in Las Vegas that if a gaming applicant hired the "right" attorney, the tax commission automatically issued them a gaming license.

At Freedman's licensing hearing, Harvey Bynum objected to Freedman being granted a gaming license, claiming that as a result of a previous partnership with Dave Anderson and George W. Frisbee, he, Bynum, held a 20 percent interest in a lease on the property upon which the Sands was being built. Accordingly, Bynum should be named on Freedman's gambling license and should receive 20 percent of the Sands' profits, Bynum's attorney, Roy Early, argued. Bynum sued. He lost in Clark County court and then lost an appeal to the Nevada Supreme Court.[76]

The tax commissioners denied Freedman a license because of his relationships with Mack Kufferman and his association with Longie Zwillman and Joseph "Doc" Stacher, who were involved in big time gambling and bookmaking. Kufferman controlled all liquor distribution in New Jersey, and Zwillman ran the state along with Joe Adonis and Stacher. All of them, with second homes in Palm Springs, California, were associated with the Sands.

Reno Evening Gazette, Dec. 19, 1953

The commissioners told Freedman that they would look more favorably at his application if Kufferman was not on it. Kufferman was denied a license in the prior May meeting of the commission and, as a result, had subleased his interests to Freedman. Even though Kufferman had done that, in the eyes of the commissioners he remained in the Sands picture.

The commissioners grilled Freedman about being a front for Kufferman, but Freedman emphatically denied being a front for anyone.

"I have been a star all my life and it's too late to be a stooge," said Freedman, who was dressed in ostentatious Western clothes. Freedman said that he did not need the help of men with money but, rather, men who knew the business and could protect the games, such as Ballard Barron, Edward "Eddie" Levinson, Sid Wyman, and Jack Entratter.

When the Sands leased the Dunes for a short time, Freedman promptly loaned money to its top executives, Chuck Bennett, Charles "Charlie" Turner, and Levinson, as well as celebrity magnet, Entratter, to revive the resort. Turner, a Mob boss and reported associate of Meyer Lansky, lived in a Sands hotel bungalow.

At the time, Wyman and Charlie Rich realized that the heat was on in St. Louis but gaming was going with a green light in Nevada, so the two came out to the Sands at the suggestion of Turner, whom they knew.[77] This meant both Wyman and Rich had to know Lansky and all of the other players involved, like Jimmy "Blue Eyes" Alo.

Of the St. Louis duo, only Wyman bought into the Sands, after being approved by the tax commission on March 4, 1953, for a 6 percent ownership. At the time, Wyman was the night pit boss there, earning $50 a shift, or $480 in today's money.

In December of that year, Wyman sold 2 percent of his 6 percent interest to Carl Cohen, the legendary casino manager who later punched Frank Sinatra in the mouth and chipped his teeth.

Because Wyman and Rich were partners, it is conceivable that Rich also owned a piece of the Sands which Wyman held. No evidence exists that corroborates this, but the Nevada Tax Commission questioned Wyman about Rich's involvement.

Wyman insisted that "despite what you may have heard,"[78] Rich was not in on the deal. Wyman added that he offered Rich a "piece" of his 6 percent interest in the Sands, but Rich declined. He turned Wyman down because he planned on applying for U.S. citizenship, and a St. Louis attor-

---

77   Interview with George Duckworth, 2006
78   *St. Louis Post-Dispatch*, March 29, 1953

ney advised him that holding a gaming interest could negatively affect the outcome of his citizenship application.

In 1951, Estes Kefauver called bluff on that statement, saying that Rich valued his business more than his citizenship given that he lived 40 years in the U.S. as an alien. He added that Rich should become a citizen.[79]

During Wyman's stint at the Sands, a St. Louis grand jury was looking into corruption charges against St. Louis policemen, specifically Detective Captain William Greenspan because his hotel bills were paid by Wyman. Investigators found a note on the hotel receipts that stated, "OK. Greenspan doesn't pay. See me. Sidney Wyman."[80]

The detective stopped at the Sands Hotel en route to and from Los Angeles in January 1955 to transport a prisoner back to St. Louis. He stayed at the hotel for another 12 to 14 days in February when he was on vacation. He stayed at the Sands instead of the Royal Nevada because he was told he could not obtain room accommodations until after the upcoming opening in April.

"I have no idea who took care of the bills," said Greenspan.

Greenspan was one of eight officers questioned by the St. Louis grand jury during their investigation of payoffs to police from brothel owners.

Although Wyman had an interest in the Sands, Greenspan told the *St. Louis Post-Dispatch* he did not think Wyman had enough influence to comp his hotel stay.

"I think Sidney Wyman is over-rated," he said. "He's considered a big gambler here [St. Louis] , but out in Las Vegas he's nothing."

Little did he know. Or maybe he did know, and made the statement to take the heat off of the investigation.

At the Sands, Sherlock Feldman was employed as a pit boss. During his time there, a legendary story about Feldman at the craps table originated that will never be forgotten. A customer who was playing craps leaned over the table to make a bet, and his upper false teeth fell out of his mouth and onto the layout. Feldman pulled out his own upper plate dentures, put them on the table and told the customer, "You're faded!"

Feldman became a legend in the world of gambling and appeared on many television programs such as the shows of Steve Allen, Joe Pyne, Mike Douglas, and others. During Feldman's appearances, he explained the various games in a unique comical fashion. He once even ran for the office of Justice of the Peace in Las Vegas, which was one of the most lu-

---

79   Ibid
80   *St. Louis Post-Dispatch*, Oct. 4, 1955

crative offices in the state because the Justice received an unofficial payment for performing weddings.

Early on, Feldman drove a cab, shot dice in the streets, and then broke into the gambling business when his cronies taught him how to deal roulette, blackjack, and craps. Later, Feldman ran a bookie business behind Sherlock's Tobacco Store at Hamilton and Delmar in St. Louis.

Richard Westbrook recalled an incident when Feldman worked in the Band Box in East St. Louis as a roulette wheel dealer. Westbrook said, "Sherlock had a couple of guys playing on the wheel and lost their entire bankroll. Sherlock felt sorry for them and reached into the change glass and threw them a fifty cent piece. The hots that operated the joint wanted to kill him over that."

Westbrook, originally from Arkansas, knew Feldman and Wyman from East St. Louis. He was a rough character in his early days. He made the front page of the *St. Louis Post-Dispatch* when his car was side-swiped by another, and three shots were fired into his car when he was driving about four miles south of Waterloo, Illinois. Both he and his lady companion were wounded. Naturally, he told police he knew of no reason why anyone would shoot at him. Westbrook's companion, Mary Blakely, was a 25-year-old dice dealer at the Regent Bar in Cairo, Ill., which was operated by Roy Shaw.

Westbrook had a part interest in the drugstore in the Hotel Jefferson in St. Louis, where he had permanent living quarters. The previous Christmas Eve, while in the drugstore, he displayed a German-make sub-machine gun and said he was going "to take care of some people in Cairo." He then sauntered into the crowded hotel lobby, where a police captain saw the butt of the gun sticking out from under Westbrook's topcoat and arrested him.

Westbrook told the police captain he bought the weapon a short time before his arrest from a returned soldier for $30 because he wanted a souvenir. Assistant U.S. District Attorney Herbert H. Freer determined that no warrant would be issued in the case because Westbrook did not have time to register the gun.

Police knew that Westbrook operated slot machines, jukeboxes, and other catch-coin devices and that he was an old-time associate of the notorious Shelton brothers and also a friend to and benefactor of William "Dinty" Colbeck, the former leader of Egan's Rats. Colbeck spent some time in federal prison, and afterward, went into the coin-machine business. Later, he worked at the infamous Hyde Park Club, an East St. Louis gambling casino. Eventually, he met his end and was murdered in gangland fashion.

CHAPTER 14

THE ROYAL NEVADA

In November of 1953, Frank Fishman formally announced that he was going to build a new resort. Work on his Royal Nevada was scheduled to begin on or about December 1, 1953. Fishman operated hotels in Florida, Los Angeles, and San Francisco. His wife, in a divorce suit, claimed Fishman was worth $5 million and had an income of $400,000 a year.[81]

Roughly a year later, the Nevada Tax Commission received an application from Frank Fishman as the principal holder of a new resort called "Nevada Royal." The application proposed the following ownership percentages:

Frank Fishman: 30 percent

Albert B. Moll of University City, Mo.: 10 percent

Roberta Mae Simon of Jennings, Mo.: 10 percent

Herbert "Pitsy" Manheim of Las Vegas: 16½ percent

Samuel "Game Boy" Miller of Las Vegas: 19½ percent

Herman E. Cohen of Miami Beach, Fla.: 7½ percent

Barnett Rosenthal of Miami Beach, Fla.: 4½ percent

Joe Leibman of Miami Beach, Fla. : 2 percent

The commissioners turned down Fishman, Miller, and Manheim, considering them personas non grata. The Nevada gaming regulators told the other partners not to submit another application for a license until Fishman (landlord), Miller, and Manheim were separated from the undertaking.[82]

Miller earned a spot on the Miami Crime Commission's list of "big-time" operators, which included Frank Costello, Joe Adonis, Frank Erickson, Jake Lansky, and Longie Zwillman. Miller was a principal partner in the Island Club Casino in Miami, in which the National Crime Syndicate (NCS) had a hidden interest. The NCS also financed more than $1 mil-

81   *Sedalia Democrat*, March 10, 1955

82   82 *St. Louis Post-Dispatch*, Feb. 4, 1955

lion to complete the Desert Inn Hotel in Las Vegas, which amounted to about a 59 percent interest.

The principal owners of the Royal Nevada then were Harry Moll, his brother Albert Moll, Sidney Wyman, and Simon.[83] Albert Moll invested $150,000 and Simon invested$100,000. Harry Moll pledged $1 million in securities to raise $550,000 cash to buy out the three partners who were considered undesirables by the Nevada Tax Commission.[84]

The Molls were officers of the Paramount Liquor Company located in St. Louis, which was sold to distillery interests in 1949. Charlie Rich once was an investor in Paramount, was associated with Harry Moll in a poultry hatching company, and was an investor in Harry Moll's 905's Liquor store, also in St. Louis. Rich had a different opinion than Albert Moll on how a casino's comping policy should be implemented, so there was some friction between the two.

Morris Shenker, the attorney for Albert Moll, Simon, Wyman, and Rich, tried to secure an interest in the Royal Nevada but was rejected by Alfred Moll because of Moll's relationship with Rich.[85]

At the December 1953 Nevada Tax Commission meeting, the commissioners voted to rescind approval of the gambling license for Fishman after he sold a 35 percent interest in the Royal Nevada to Howie Engel, Herman E. Cohen, Joseph Liebman, and Barnett Rosenthal.

Eventually, however, the agency approved the investors and Fishman after Engel and his associates provided financial statements and evidence that satisfied the commission that racketeers Miller and Manheim, who were in Nevada to work at the Royal Nevada, were no longer involved.

At the same meeting, though, the commissioners discussed another application, this one involving the Riviera.

"We had heard reports that Big Sam and Engel had a share of the gambling concession in the Riviera," Commissioner William Gallagher said, "but after an exhaustive check we could not substantiate these rumors. They may have been part of the original application which has been superseded by one from the present group."[86]

Gallagher directly asked the Riviera's attorney, Harvey Silbert, who represented the applicants that included Harpo and Gummo Marx:

"Are Big Sam Cohen and Howie Engel in this operation?"

"No," replied Silbert.

83	*St. Louis Post-Dispatch*, April 10, 1955
84	*Jefferson City Post-Tribune,* April 11, 1955
85	Interview with Bruce Fisher
86	86 *The Miami News*, March 3, 1955

The Riviera license was granted.[87]

In December of 1954, it was announced: "The Royal Nevada, promoted by hotelman Frank Fishman, formerly of Miami, at $5 million. It boasts a pool of Olympic length and almost as wide."

The year 1955 was a big one in Las Vegas with the opening of three resorts all within a month of each other. The Royal Nevada opened first, on April 15, the Riviera debuted on April 20, and the Dunes premiered on May 23.

The Royal Nevada, was originally primarily owned by Fishman with most of the investors who had invested in the Moulin Rouge, including Joe Louis Barrow, former world heavyweight boxing champion.

Two people who were denied a license for the Moulin Rouge in 1952 were Daniel Tanis, a New York City labor union executive, and Larry Snow of New York and New Jersey. Snow was denied because of his association with undesirable characters. However, later Snow was allowed to work as a baccarat manager at the Dunes and then at Caesars Palace when it opened in 1966.

It is strictly speculation but very probable that Snow was associated with Engel. In the mid-1960s, Engel was the baccarat manager at the Dunes and brought Snow into the position as manager sometime after Engel was licensed as a 5 percent owner of the Dunes in 1964. Bob Rice, an original Dunes investor from the inception, sold Engel the interest for $25,000, a reasonable price at the time and, thus, a terrific opportunity for Engel. The hotel began marketing to high roller gamblers. The Dunes had plenty of rooms and the finest restaurants in Las Vegas. When Howard Hughes wanted to buy the Dunes in the early 1970s, the price was $50 million, making Engel's 5 percent worth $2.5 million.

When the Royal Nevada opened, Sid Wyman was the managing director. Initially, though, Richard Chappell was chosen to be the general manager. Most recently he had been the hotel manager of the Flamingo in Las Vegas and prior to that, the manager of the Park Plaza Hotel in St. Louis.

Sherlock Feldman, close associate of Wyman, was picked to be a gaming supervisor. The two worked together at the Sands when Wyman was a stakeholder.

After the Royal Nevada debut, Wyman had the famous "Dancing Waters" installed and displaying, and booked opera singer, Helen Traubel. The casino lessors took out a $150,000 policy on Traubel with Lloyds of London in case she came down with laryngitis, as tenor Mario Lanza

---

did the week before. Lanza had a $100,000, two-week engagement in the New Frontier's new million dollar Venus showroom, and could not make the curtain call. The press blasted the two-week engagement, conducted by Ray Sinatra, with a headline that read, "Lanza can't sing for his $50,000 a week."[88]

Wyman said, "We anticipate no trouble with Traubel, but we think it is only good business to protect ourselves."[89] Wyman was a smart bookmaker and knew that even a sure bet sometimes lost.

Coincidentally, Traubel also was from St. Louis, and St. Louis was where Rich met his lifelong friend, Cary Grant. Perhaps Grant had some influence on Wyman and Rich's selection of Traubel.

On New Year's Eve, December 31, 1955, a mere 8 and a half months after the Royal Nevada opened, the local musicians scheduled to play at the shows of opera singer Anna Maria Alberghetti voted not to provide their services to the hotel-casino unless their pay was guaranteed. The hotel would not promise pay in advance, so the musicians conceded to playing only two shows. Alberghetti agreed to perform without pay so that the musicians could get paid.

The hotel closed after an employee, who had not received a paycheck since December 15, 1955, began gathering money from the cage and the pit. Then unidentified persons made a "run" on the cage, grabbing handfuls of $25 chips.

The group of St. Louis investors, however, got most of their investment back in mid-summer 1955 through a reorganization in which some Denver businessmen bought most of the stock. Shenker, who was a director of the Royal Nevada, represented the St. Louis group in those proceedings.

"The St. Louis investors, for the most part, got out from under the operation," said Harry Moll. "No one made any money, and there was a loss suffered, but it was not so great."[90]

The Royal Nevada closed on January 4, 1956, because of financial difficulties due to poor crowds and a slack season for Las Vegas that saw more looky-loos than players.

---

88   *The Bulletin*, April 14, 1955
89   *Ibid*
90   *St. Louis Post-Dispatch*, Jan. 5, 1956

CHAPTER 15

THE RIVIERA TAKEOVER

The Nevada Tax Commission approved Sidney Wyman, Charlie Rich, and others on September 26, 1955, to operate the new Riviera hotel-casino in Las Vegas under the direction of Gus Greenbaum. After Greenbaum, Wyman's group invested the highest dollar amount in the enterprise.

Greenbaum, a former bookmaker in Phoenix with long ties to organized criminals, returned to Las Vegas in summer 1955. Greenbaum pledged that he and his partners would lease the Riviera and cover its past due bills. He installed most of his former team from the Flamingo to manage the Riviera and share in its profits. His partners, most of them with Mob associations, included Israel "Ice Pick Willie" Alderman, Wyman, Rich, George Duckworth, David "Davie" Berman, and Ben Goffstein.

Alderman was a Las Vegas casino investor and manager with ties to organized crime. Along with his associates, Meyer Lansky, Siegel, Moe Sedway, Berman and Greenbaum, he not only was involved in the Riviera but, also, in the El Cortez, Flamingo and Las Vegas Club. Prior to living in Las Vegas he was a Mob enforcer in Minneapolis, Minnesota, where he earned his nickname based on his having perfected murder using an ice pick, through an ear specifically. He ran a speakeasy in Minneapolis, in which he claimed to have murdered eleven people in this way. Because his victims slumped over the bar like drunks, Alderman could drag their bodies out of the building unquestioned. He eventually went to prison for tax evasion.

One day at the Dunes, this writer's co-worker Arland Smith was walking into the coffee shop on his break and had to pass the executive booth on his way to the dealers' break area. That day, Wyman was in the booth chatting with a gentleman. He called over Smith and said, "Son, I want you to meet William Alderman." Wyman did not use the names, "Ice Pick Willie" or even just "Willie." Smith shook Alderman's hand and returned to the baccarat area. The baccarat manager, Irwin Gordon, saw Smith with Wyman and Alderman.

When Smith approached, Gordon, with a big grin, asked him, "Do you know who that guy is?"

"William Alderman," Smith answered.

Gordon laughed and said, "You just met 'Ice Pick Willie.'" Smith almost fell over.

Other Riviera investors with Greenbaum were Charles Harrison and Ross Miller (the former Chicago bookmaker and father of future Nevada Governor Bob Miller).

Using his contacts with well-heeled gamblers from his Flamingo days, Greenbaum lured many to the Riviera and turned the business around for its investors, who now included Chicago Mobster Marshall Caifano.

Greenbaum, however, went on to have gambling problems in Las Vegas and became addicted to heroin, which was prescribed for his health problems. By the late 1950s, Caifano accused Greenbaum of taking more than his share of the Riviera's profits. Greenbaum and his pals allegedly were robbing the Mob; Wyman's crew had no part in it. In 1958, during a trip to Phoenix, Greenbaum and his wife were brutally murdered, Gus nearly decapitated. The crime was never solved.

After the Greenbaums were slain and after five years of working at the Riviera, from 1955 to 1960, Wyman and Rich decided it was time to move on to an operation they could control. They, along with fellow gambling licensees, Duckworth and Samuel Gans, sold their interests to Hotel Riviera, Inc. and searched for another hotel-casino to invest in. Ed Levinson, an associate of Meyer Lansky, purchased Wyman et al. and Greenbaum's shares of the Riviera.[91] Levinson listed some of the purchasing group members as Ed Torres and Eddie Barrick of the Fremont; Jack Entratter and Carl Cohen of the Sands; and Bryant Burton of Los Angeles. Wyman was not particularly fond of Torres, who worked with him at the Sands previously. Torres tried to "cut in" to one of Wyman's customers, according to Duckworth, who was also at the Sands when Wyman owned 6 percent of it.

Levinson, Lansky, and Cliff Jones allegedly were secretly involved in some land deals in Alaska.

A couple of stories written by Al Delugach, staff writer for the *Los Angeles Times*, which ran on December 6 and December 26, 1971, were headlined, respectively, *Alaska Mystery – Who Financed Big Land Deals* and *L.A. Man Who Acquired Property Along Pipeline Won't Talk About It*.

Delugach wrote, "Philip J. Matthew of Los Angeles went on an Alaskan land buying spree three years ago. A short time later the route of the Trans-Alaska oil pipeline was announced. The bulk of some 200 parcels

---

91   *Reno Evening Gazette*, May 19, 1959

of land Matthew had bought in central and southern Alaska turned out to be along the pipeline route."[92]

Matthew purchased 500 acres in Valdez, Alaska, for about $300,000. There was an oil boom in the state in 1968, as drillers struck what is believed to be the biggest find in North America. In 1970, Matthew's property there was valued at between $600,000 and $1 million.

The federal government and most Alaskans questioned who he was, but the real question was: Who was associated with him and his Alaskan land deals?

Matthew had a meteoric rise in the world of finance ventures that included savings and loan associations in Los Angeles, Baltimore and, Honolulu. Financing was provided through an obscure but rich Caribbean entity called the Bank of World Commerce, Ltd. in Nassau, Bahamas, which in 1966 had one office and one employee, John Pullman, a native of Russia. Pullman, the entity's president, was known to the FBI as a long-time associate of Meyer Lansky.

The FBI believed that Pullman was a courier for Lansky between Las Vegas and Switzerland and handled investments in Swiss banks for American crime figures.

Along with Jones and Levinson, Matthew's associates included: Meyer "Mike" Singer, an ex-Teamsters official who was widely considered to be Hoffa's West Coast representative. Alvin Malnik, a Miami-based attorney, was the conduit between Matthew and Lansky and a key figure in the 1966 federal grand jury investigation into suspected underworld involvement in the multi-million-dollar stock promotion of Scopitone, a movie-jukebox invention that was featured at the Sands in Las Vegas. People from coast to coast were subpoenaed as witnesses. No indictments were returned.

Other alleged assorted Las Vegas gamblers associated with Matthew were Irving "Niggy" Devine, G.C. Blaine, Charles Turner, Ben Siegelbaum, Jake Gottlieb, and Rich. Their names, however, were not in the public record as being associated with the Alaskan ventures nor is there any public record of who owned the more than 600,000 shares of stock issued by Matthew's firm, Financial Land Investment Corporation, in whose name the Valdez properties were held. Records that Matthew filed in Juneau showed that Financial Land Investment was incorporated in Delaware in February 1969, the month he bought the Valdez properties.

Matthew was listed as the corporation's president and treasurer. The vice president was a retired Los Angeles intelligence agent for the IRS,

---

92   *Los Angeles Times*, Al Delugach, Dec. 6, 1971

Walter E. Schlick. The secretary was Eugene Hettleman, an attorney in Baltimore, which was listed as the corporation's principal place of business. Directors were Matthew, his wife Elayne Matthew, and Hettleman.

One year after Matthew bought the Valdez land, Mel Personett, then Alaska commissioner of public safety, appeared before the state Senate Judiciary Committee. While answering questions about Alaskan law enforcement problems, he voiced concern about associates of organized crime figures entering legitimate business in Alaska. Personett then told of a man operating in the Valdez area who said he had associates who were or were connected to underworld figures. On further questioning, Personett named Matthew as the person about whom he was talking.

CHAPTER 16

George Duckworth

It is a coincidence that when I was just beginning this chapter on George Duckworth I received a telephone call from a relative of his, Bruce Fisher, telling me George had passed on November 16, 2019. It was very sad news, as Mr. Duckworth gave me the opportunity to work at the Dunes. I will never forget him. Reaching 95 years of age, he outlived every major owner of the resort.

Duckworth loved to invite people to lunch and tell them stories about the classic Las Vegas days and characters he knew. He hypnotized his audience, and they begged for more. He could reminiscence for hours without ever repeating a story. A family member called those sessions, "Lunch with Uncle George."

Duckworth once was asked to write a book about the Dunes, and he replied, "I have to wait until two people die." I analyzed that comment intensely. Was he referring to two former employees or two others? I determined that he meant two outside individuals whom no one would easily connect to the Dunes, likely Mobsters. I was certain of this.

A close family source told me of two times that Duckworth had sent his family to Europe for safety but had never explained the reason for doing so. One of those excursions happened on a moment's notice, his family frantically leaving their home for an immediate flight.

I wrote George a letter when I was doing research for this book because I wanted him to tell me the Dunes story that only he knew.[93] No one else was still alive who had direct involvement and extensive knowledge of the Dunes and its secrets. The University of Nevada, Las Vegas' Oral History program did not have any of the key Dunes principals on the record. My letter read:

"Dear George,

"I hope all is going better for you and your family with special prayers and hope that Kim is feeling better and on the road to a recovery.

"I really hate to bother you, but I am driven with compulsion on an issue. Let me explain why, by way of an example:

"A cinematographer can have a million dollars' worth of the finest and latest film cameras; a director can have a stable of actors that get $5 million a picture; a producer can have a studio with a $200 million dollar budget behind him, yet they have no movie without a good story! They have all the ingredients except the most important one, the story.

"You have the story. Your story could be a movie better than *The Godfather* and *Casino* combined.

"The story should be based on YOU and your role in the Dunes Hotel, the Riviera, Sands, and East St. Louis, the used car lot, etc., etc.

"There is no better story than yours! PERIOD! I can't emphasize this fact enough. I know, because I was there to witness it each and every day. This story has fascinated me since I was 19 years old. You were the storyteller and I listened to every word you said.

"I have been researching and studying the Dunes for the last five years and think I have pieced the basic story together accurately, but I need your knowledge and assistance to complete it. I was pulled into the story because I worked side by side with the characters that were part of history. When I say characters I mean good characters that I could never dream up in one thousand years.

"It all began to take shape when I was befriended by Vince Taglialatella. He treated me like a son that he never had, after I helped him interpret a written memo that you had written to the casino staff. Vince called me over as I was going on the stick to call the hands when he said to me, 'Geno, can you make out this small writing, as I was at the eye doctor today and he gave me something to put in my eyes. I can't read it' or something to that effect.

"I very inconspicuously assisted him without any notice to the other dealers or floormen. He was grateful. From that day forward he helped me learn the baccarat game like it was the back of my hand. Vince told me about things that were major points that are remotely connected to the whole story. His connections, his associates, his business of shylocking and betting etc. etc. etc.

"He had a friend, Tommy from New York, who loved to shoot Craps. Tommy was a mystery fellow that was in the middle of the 'action' in the Big Apple. The three of us went to the Horseshoe one night after work and went through $100,000 of Tommy's money betting $5,000 and $5,000 odds. We never picked up a bet! My eyes were as wide open as I could get. To Tommy, it was like a pittance. There was more to the story. Soon I learned who Vince knew, and of course it didn't mean anything to me at the time because I had ZERO knowledge of these people, who never showed up on radar.

"One time Vince said, 'My friend, XXXXX XXXXXXX, would pay $50,000 to walk through the lobby of Caesars Palace.' I just looked at Vince in amazement.

"Jake Gottlieb had a story. Riddle had a story. Your Dad had a story. Sid had a story. Derlachter had a story. Hoffa had a story. Parry Thomas had a story. Howie had a story, and on and on.

"It took me years to unravel this complicated puzzle and all of the players. None of the people are with us anymore. The correct story needs to be relayed in a manner not to hurt or embarrass any living persons. I just hate to see these 'wanna-be' claimers of stories.

"Two years ago, young Arthur Shenker came to me looking for work. He had two front teeth missing and looked like he was living on the streets. He said he wanted to work and needed to get his teeth fixed. I felt sorry for him and gave him $1500 for his teeth. He said his talent was selling cars. I gave him a job selling cars. He told me about his dad and mom and the Dunes and how good they ran the place. I knew better but I listened. I saw his father destroy what you guys put together. Arthur wanted me to write a book about his father and the Dunes. I don't think that will ever happen, and if it did, it would be a bunch of half-truths.

"I think there is an opportunity here for something great. I am not thinking just a book. Everyone and everybody writes books. I am setting my goal high to make this a movie to memorialize the story about the Dunes Hotel and Country Club.

"The lead character will be based on you. The ups and downs, the humorous stories, the sad stories, in the money, out of the money, the flying, the human side and more.

"I am dedicated to doing this project. My motive is NOT money but accomplishment. You write the deal to your satisfaction. I just want to do this with you, not without you. I understand completely there may be trepidation and apprehension about the story, however, sooner or later someone will attempt to write the story without the facts and it will be terrible. I put my hand to GOD and on the Bible to protect you and your family to your satisfaction. I am also protected under the law as a reporter/writer. You can be completely anonymous if you wish. I swear to secrecy.

"I wrote this letter because a phone call to you may last a few minutes, with my words heard once. It is impossible to recall the facts and details of my message in an electronic telephone call. I trust and hope you will pick this printed letter up and read it over and over, so that you may consider my request.

"In addition, I have enclosed a document that I came across in research that is about a former employee, Lenny Shafer. This document indicates he may have been a top informant???????

"Have a very Merry Christmas and may the New Year bring health and happiness for your entire family."

George never answered my letter. Perhaps he was waiting for someone to die. George Duckworth did not have an easy life as a youngster in St. Louis, Missouri, during the Great Depression. His mother Evelyn, a widow with three children, had to send him to live with a relative in Texas to make sure he would be properly cared for because she had to work and feed her two older children.

Evelyn met Charlie Rich, and soon after, he offered his somewhat spacious two-bedroom apartment to her and the children. Evelyn and Rich then married, after which they brought young Duckworth back to St. Louis, where they lived as a family. Rich was a loving stepfather, whom the children enjoyed and loved. Times were indeed tough, but the family always made ends meet and survived.

Young Duckworth was eager to learn all that he could from his stepfather. Rich knew how to handicap and set lines not only for football and baseball, but also for boxing matches, basketball games, and political elections. He could figure out a betting advantage if a match-up had an incorrect betting line or if there was some other abnormality. Duckworth jumped right in, and learned how to take telephone calls and write bets along with the fine art of settling up on winning wagers.

Rich and Sid Wyman invested in a chicken hatchery business with the profits they made and appointed young Duckworth as the manager. This operation was a front for their thriving and profitable hand-book business. In 1944, the two put up $12,000, and a Martin Beldner added $8,000 to acquire the hatchery. In the first year, the enterprise cleared $37,000, but problems arose with a joint bank account. During that time, the hatchery business was shipping nearly 250,000 chicks a week and generating roughly $250,000 a year.

However, in 1949, the gamblers agreed to sell Beldner their interest for $35,000. Beldner paid them $15,000 but could not pay the rest, so Rich and Wyman foreclosed and forced bankruptcy proceedings some months later. Beldner lost his $15,000 down payment and everything else he had invested. Chickens were a speculative commodity but land was an even better speculation for Rich, who had excessive amounts of income. Rich understood the value of buying and selling inventory, but land was one of his better business ventures.

Duckworth was a stickman on a dice game at the illegal Ringside private casino in East St. Louis, Illinois, until he could get a job as a dealer. He went on to work for Rich and Wyman at one of C.J. Rich & Company's hand-books.

One day in 1950 police followed Duckworth, who was driving Rich's automobile, to the hand-book, which was located in the basement of a real estate broker's office. Steve Montefelice, who co-managed the enterprise with Duckworth, was already there, working the phones. The police raided the place and arrested the two. Duckworth gave them the false name of George Werner, but police properly identified him after they traced the ownership of the car that he was driving to Rich.

The police ordered both men to stand with their hands up while the officers "took over" the hand-book and its phones. In a two-hour period, 50 calls came in, in which bets were made that totaled $10,000, or about $100,000 in today's dollars. This was not a $2 bet operation but a high rolling one in which $1,000 wagers across the board were common. The callers placing bets usually used a code and had repartee with the phone answerers.

Suddenly, however, the phones went dead. Perhaps Rich or Wyman had instituted a safety method to immediately cut off service in the event of a police raid.

In January 1951, Duckworth and Montefelice were charged with setting up and operating a gaming house. At the time, Rich was fighting extradition to New Jersey, where a grand jury had indicted him on charges of conspiring with the Western Union Telegraph to have it transmit bets from New Jersey to St. Louis where C.J. Rich & Co. processed them.

George followed his stepfather Rich and Wyman to Las Vegas. There, he worked at the Sands, the Royal Nevada, and the Riviera in various casino positions, and was tutored on the games by the best of the best.

Duckworth was "a young break-in floorman," author J.E. Anderson described, "connected to the Teamster money, who would help straighten out the Riviera problems.[94] "At the Riviera, Chick Berman would always want to be alerted about big cash play," Duckworth recalled.[95] "We had a guy stuck quite a bit of money and I called to inform him. He said to pull the boxes, we are going to count. He came down in his bathrobe at 3:30 in the morning and went to the count room."

94   Ace-Deuce: *The Life and Times of a Gambling Man*, J.E. Anderson, 2011
95   Interview with George Duckworth, 2006

Duckworth's most demanding job was as casino manager, stockholder, president, and board member of the Dunes. It was a tasking role that certainly had pros and cons.

One of the benefits was his meeting Kim Darvos, which led to their marriage and their three beautiful children. A devoted father and family man, Duckworth would do anything to make his family happy and secure. He went to his children's dance recitals and basketball games. He supported them in every way and was a good sport in their growing years and then some.

His England-born wife was cheery and a pleasure to know. She was a stunning beauty who shone on the outside as well as from her heart. She was down to earth yet had the manners of the queen and conducted her household in an English crested manner that Duckworth was never accustomed to in St. Louis. Kim picked out his conservative clothing and taught him to be proper, English style.

Duckworth was so proud of her that he glistened when they walked together in the Dunes to the Sultan's Table for dinner. She was special, and that was evident to all of the employees who could not take their eyes off of her.

Duckworth reciprocated in part to Kim for her kind deeds by introducing her to Cary Grant, his stepfather's best friend for more than 50 years. Kim came to the U.S. as a common British citizen and was only 20 years old when she met the most glamorous English-born movie star of all time. One evening after the three had dinner in the Sultan's Table, Grant put his hand on Duckworth's shoulder and whispered, "Does your wife have a sister?"

Duckworth lost Kim, his wife of many years, in June 2018. It was a tragic loss that he did not overcome.

Not an avid golfer or bowler like many of his counterparts, George, rather, learned to fly an airplane and attained many credentials, first a private pilot's license then a commercial rating and instrument and multi-engine privileges. He loved flying.

"I got my private license last summer, and then decided I'd be twice as safe flying with two engines, especially after my plane had engine trouble over the Rose Bowl," the *Las Vegas Review-Journal* quoted him as saying in 1961. "A fire truck and an ambulance suddenly appeared under me all the way back to Pacific Airmotive (Burbank)." He added, "Now, I'm going to work on my commercial."

Duckworth preferred to fly himself to the West Coast on business rather than wait for commercial airlines' scheduled flights. He was intently interested in aviation and briefly explored a business that developed a fog dispersing machine. As fate would have it, one of the partners in the Thunderbird that his dad and Wyman wanted to operate had an aviation business that manufactured airplanes and other unique specialty parts for the U.S. government.

Duckworth kept his twin-engine Cessna Skyknight with a small fixed-base operator, Vegas Aeromotive, adjacent to runway 19 at Las Vegas' McCarran Field. The operation was small yet had a counter at which pilots could purchase gasoline and other supplies and register for flying lessons. It also had a little place to sit and drink coffee. This was George's favorite hangout. He enjoyed sitting there, sipping coffee and regaling people with flying stories and gambling tales.

This is where I first met him and Kim, when I was 18 years old. I had gone there because it offered flying lessons for $10 an hour wet, meaning gasoline and an instructor were included. I sat and listened in awe to Duckworth as I never heard stories like his. He quickly became my idol. I was just fascinated by this man who was so nice and so interesting.

I offered my help in any way, and occasionally he let me fly with him around the valley. Once we flew to Beverly Hills, landed at the Santa Monica airport, and shopped at a very upscale men's store called Tavelman's. Duckworth wore very classy sunglasses that he knew I admired. He bought me a pair. I was ecstatic.

Duckworth became very friendly with Lewis "Lew" Carlisle, a former Eastern Air Lines pilot, who became the Los Angeles Dodgers' pilot, flying the team's Electra II in 1965 and piloting its 720-B Fanjet in 1971. Carlisle had a ranch up in Idaho, so the Dodgers moved the airplane west, closer to him. They kept it at Vegas Aeromotive, where the climate was dry and the place was safe. Carlisle sat in the airport and told stories along with George. They both had ranches in proximity of one another, which gave them an even stronger bond. Carlisle was a direct descendant of the Pinkertons, which brought more zest to the colorful tales told in the pilots' coffee lounge.

Carlisle once let me and one other pilot take a test flight in Dodger Blue 720-B. What a thrill as he did approaches to a stall over the Daggett-Yermo VOR, or very high frequency omni-directional range. He said, "Listen for the rumble and vibration of the stall come up the aisle on the floor." Wow!

Gene Bowen was a host and pilot for Kirk Kerkorian, who built the International Hotel. Bowen bought and sold airplanes on the side and had just ferried a twin-engine, Douglas B-23 WWII bomber from St. Joseph, Missouri, to Las Vegas. He invited every casino big-shot at the International Hotel to go for a ride over Lake Mead. Duckworth, Bruce Fisher, Alex Shoofey, Jimmy Newman, and even the man himself, Kirk Kerkorian, piled on board. I was asked if I wanted to ride along. "Really? Yes, I would love to go," I said. I was elated. It was October 30, 1966.

Bowen sat as pilot with, I think, Duckworth as co-pilot. I stood behind Bowen. The target was their friend, casino owner and former co-founder of the Sahara, Frank Schivo. They knew he was out at Lake Mead on his fancy Campbell ski boat. When they spotted him, they simulated bombing runs toward his boat. They got pretty close and really had a blast while maneuvering. I look back now and think, what if we lost an engine? That plane was pretty old, and I am sure that the pilot was capable but perhaps in a little over his head so close to the water. He probably did not have a lot of current hands-on experience with an engine-out emergency either. That could have been the end of the line but boy it created great memories.

Duckworth was a stand-up guy and not afraid to help his dear friend, Judge Harry Claiborne. When Duckworth was the president and a minority stockholder of the Dunes, he testified on Claiborne's behalf at his 1984 tax evasion trial, in part about money Wyman gave Claiborne in 1972.

Claiborne's defense attorney, Oscar Goodman, asked Duckworth under oath, "Would you tell the ladies and gentlemen of the jury what then happened?"

Duckworth replied, "Judge Claiborne entered the room and there was a greeting between the judge, Mr. Wyman, Mr. Selman, and myself, and a conversation ensued and after a minute or two, Mr. Wyman said to Judge Claiborne, 'Harry, I have a Christmas present for you,' and took a box from a table which was adjacent to a sofa he was sitting on, and he handed the box to Judge Claiborne and he said, 'This is for you. It's a gift from me to you and I want to wish you a Merry Christmas.'

"Judge Claiborne said, 'Thank you very much. I will take it home and put it under my Christmas tree.'

"Mr. Wyman said, 'Please don't do that. There is $100,000 in that box.'

"So Judge Claiborne said, 'Well, are you serious? Do you mean that?'

"And he said, 'Yes, there is $100,000 in that box, and that's for you. That's a gift from me to you to do with as you see fit, to use it for yourself or your family. Please don't make any investments with it,' or something of that nature."[96]

---

96   *Alabama Journal*, March 30, 1984

"He was a gambler. That was his thing in life," Duckworth said of Wyman. "I've seen him win $400,000 to $600,000 a night. I also have seen him lose that much. He kept as much as $1 million in his safety deposit box in the hotel cashier's cage."

Duckworth also never divulged Wyman's name when asked by the Gaming Control Board about an anonymous note Duckworth received. It instructed him to give Mr. Sanders (really Mobster Nicholas "Nick" Civella) complimentary room, food, credit – anything he wanted. Instead, Duckworth told the investigators that he did not know where the instructions came from. That statement took courage.

Duckworth was an intelligent man with an open mind. He was not afraid to take chances if his calculated risks were manageable. He was receptive to ideas and listened to people. However, the dealers and other supervisory employees knew that it was best to wait until he was in a relaxed mood before approaching him with a request.

An idea came to me while driving to work at the Dunes. About 75 percent of the time I had to wait at the traffic light on the corner of the Las Vegas Strip (Las Vegas Boulevard) and Flamingo Road. While stopped, I noted that a small motel there with 100 rooms, Empey's Desert Villa, was prime for converting into a small casino.

In mid-summer 1973, the Clark County Commission allowed live games to be added to the existing slot arcade that Circus-Circus built next door called Slots-A-Fun. Other small motels were also trying to obtain live gaming as well, such as Little Caesars across from the Dunes.

Empey's Desert Villa met Clark County's minimum room requirement although some rooms would need to be added to house the casino, food services, and entertainment lounge. I thought the Desert Villa would be a perfect spot for small casino-hotel operation, so I waited for a good opportunity to approach and pitch my idea to Duckworth.

In the meantime, I visited the motel, introduced myself to the owner Phil Empey, and inquired if he was in the market to sell it. I was not a real estate broker, and he knew that I was not there to persuade him to list his property.

Despite my limited experience with number crunching and developing a business plan or a pro forma, I had a good feeling about the property and knew that it was ideally located. The area there had plenty of pedestrian traffic, and being on the east side of the Strip, faced oncoming tourists.

Empey told me that he offered to sell the motel to the owners of the adjacent Flamingo every year for the previous 20 years. Empey's would have been the perfect addition to the Flamingo. I thought possibly if we remodeled the Desert Villa and added a casino, in time, the Flamingo would pay a healthy profit to annex it. Empey's asking price was $2 million.

I contacted Duckworth, and he said to arrange a meeting, which I did. I met George at Empey's, and he brought along Arthur "Artie" Selman.[97] The meeting went well, but we did not really examine the physical property. I got the sense that Duckworth was already very familiar with it.

We continued to talk about the deal after we left the meeting. George said, "I want to buy it. We will get a Teamster loan to do the deal. You go back in a day or two and get the final details that Empey is asking for."

My blood was rushing as I knew there would be a way for me to buy a piece of the action or maybe Duckworth would grant me a working equity interest. It was the opportunity I had always dreamed about.

When I saw Empey a couple of days later, I told him my associate wanted to buy the motel. Empey responded that his price was now $2.1 million. I didn't question him. I thought the figure was negotiable and one Empey was using to ultimately get $2 million. I reported back to Duckworth what Empey said.

"Screw him," replied George, and that was the end of the possible deal. Looking back on it, I do not think Empey's minimal price increase was really the deal breaker. Other factors, unknown to me, may have been the true impetus for Duckworth not pursuing the acquisition.

The existing relationship between the Dunes and the Teamsters was one of those factors. Duckworth and his partners were closely associated with Allen Dorfman, who was handpicked by Hoffa to manage the Teamsters pension fund. Dorfman was a guest of Duckworth's stepfather Rich at his Palm Springs mansion on several occasions, and the Dunes employed Dorfman's gal pal as a cocktail waitress.

Perhaps Duckworth did not want to submit a new gaming license application that would guarantee a lot of investigation by the gaming regulators into the 1972 charges of skimming, of which he and other Dunes owners were declared innocent in U.S. federal court. Another theory is that maybe some of the hidden partners in neighboring hotels did not want any competition unless the competitor paid them a street tax, or in other words, cut them in. But that is strictly pulp-fiction conspiracy theory.

Empey's Desert Villa eventually became the Barbary Coast and is now The Cromwell Hotel. When Caesars Entertainment bought it, its value exceeded $800 million.

---

97   Artie Selman is mentioned elsewhere in this book in association with Wyman and Nathan "Nate" Jacobson.

I will always remember George Duckworth as one of the greatest persons I have ever known. He had style and class and knew gaming. I looked up to him and admired everything he did – how he watched the game, how he greeted people with his winning smile. He was someone I wanted to emulate. I respected him so much and will deeply miss him.

CHAPTER 17

THE TERRE HAUTE
BOOKMAKING OPERATION

I n July 1959, seven members of a Terre Haute, Indiana, bookmaking operation were found guilty of a gambling conspiracy, excise tax evasion, and failure to register as a gambling syndicate.[98] They were operating the country's largest nationwide bookmaking ring. Its total betting handle for the 10-week 1957 season was $3.25 million. This would have earned the syndicate roughly $162,500, a little over $1.4 million in today's money, or just over $140,000 a week.

The convicted men were Leo Shaffer, Jules Horwick, Philip Share, James Tamer, Joseph "Joey" Jacobs, Charles "Buck" Sumner, Edgar M. Wyatt, and Irwin Gordon. Gordon was a close associate of Sidney Wyman.

Wyman was one of 169 witnesses subpoenaed to testify in the grand jury investigation that indicted those involved in the Terre Haute operation. Also on the list of witnesses was H.L. Hunt, from Dallas, the owner of Hunt Oil and at the time, one of the richest men in the world.

Bookies Gilbert Beckley, Jerome "Jerry" Zarowitz, and nine others pleaded the Fifth Amendment during their testimony before the 23-member Terre Haute grand jury. Beckley and Zarowitz ran a similar layoff betting ring in Covington, Kentucky. Zarowitz went on to become the No. 1 behind the scenes boss at Caesars Palace in 1966.

During the subsequent trial of the Terre Haute bookmaking operation, testimonies revealed some interesting information. David Gensburg, a Los Angeles businessman and a part owner of the Riviera prior to Wyman and Gus Greenbaum's tenure, claimed he never won a bet placed with the service, and instead, lost $2,500. Gensburg's testimony also linked Gordon to the bookmaking syndicate as Gensburg said that he obtained the book's betting phone number from Gordon at the start of the 1957 season.

Gus Alex and Sam "Momo" Giancana became hidden owners of the Dunes in the early 1960s under the tutelage of Jake Gottlieb and Wyman.

Maurice Dodson, also a bookmaker, became a vice president at the Dunes under Wyman's watch. A close friend of Wyman, Dodson was called to testify in the Terre Haute case as well.

Dan Moldea's book, *Interference*, explained Wyman's relationship with William Kaplan, another of the witnesses:

"Handicapper William Kaplan had created the Kaplan Sports Service during the 1930s. He put out football line information to his subscribers in a scratch sheet called Handicapped. A bachelor, he operated out of Chicago's Croydon Hotel. In the Chicago yellow pages, his business was listed under 'Football Service.'

"Kaplan was also a close associate of Sidney Wyman, a former St. Louis bookmaker and a known frontman for Mob casino operations in Las Vegas. Among other jobs, Wyman had worked at the Flamingo and the Riviera.

"Kaplan paid protection to Ralph Pierce, a former personal adviser to Al Capone. Pierce operated out of Chicago's Fifth Ward, which was represented by Sidney Korshak's brother Marshall, and answered to Chicago Mob boss Sam Giancana.

"In 1957, Pierce – along with two other Chicago Mobsters, Gus Alex, who had taken the Fifth thirty-nine times before the McClellan Committee, and Albert Frabotta leaned on the sixty- year-old Kaplan and allegedly forced him to accept a partner, local Mob soldier Donald Angelini, also known as Don Angel.

"Kaplan was subpoenaed before a federal grand jury in August 1958 in Indianapolis, Indiana, that was investigating a Terre Haute gambling syndicate. Several arrests had already been made of bookmakers Kaplan acknowledged doing business with. 'Sure,' Kaplan told prosecutors, 'I traded information, such as handicapping, with the Terre Haute fellows. I paid them seventy-five dollars for their information, and they paid me seven hundred and twenty dollars during the football season for my service.'"

Kaplan's sports service, "Angel-Kaplan," was one of the two major organizations in the U.S. that set the betting line for sports betting. Kaplan, though, later got arrested for bookmaking and then was banned from Florida horse tracks and the horse racing business.

Kaplan gave Frank "Lefty" Rosenthal his first big break in professional handicapping. Rosenthal, who previously worked at a hamburger stand and met Kaplan as a customer, indeed shared his appetite for sports handicapping and betting. Kaplan hired him as a statistician. Rosenthal's top salary with Kaplan was $150 a week.

In the late 1950s and into the 1960s, Rosenthal played a big part in making line moves, as did Beckley; Dodson out of Birmingham, Alabama; K. Barney Levine in Little Rock, Arkansas; and Sam Mingus in Chicago.[99]

In the 1970s, Rosenthal was forced to submit to suitability and licensing hearings by the Nevada Gaming Control Board on the accusation that he was actually running the Stardust and the Argent Corporation for the Chicago Outfit with Allen Glick as the front man.

The Nevada gaming authorities probably knew that Wyman was involved in the Terre Haute bookmaking operation, either bankrolling it or helping it attract big bettors, but they did not pursue it. No press stories circulated about Wyman being involved, which meant the state would not be embarrassed by it. There was no question that Gordon was a close associate of Wyman and was his personal representative in Terre Haute. Also, Wyman and the Dunes supported the Nevada governor, and the governor ran the Gaming Control Board. Enough said.

99   *The Miami News*, Sept. 10, 1961

CHAPTER 18

FREDERIC APCAR

In 1961, Dunes owner Major Riddle offered Frederic Apcar, Sr. the hotel-casino's main showroom for his maiden musical revue, "Vive Les Girls," which was a hit.

Subsequently, the Dunes management allowed Apcar to debut "Casino de Paris" in December 1963, in a brand new theater designed for the new French spectacular. "Casino de Paris" ran for two decades at the Dunes, headlined by legendary French singer Line Renaud and other guest stars. The marquee read, Casino de Paris – Cast of 100.

"It was announced that on November 29, 1963, the cast of 'Casino de Paris'" would arrive in Vegas from Paris with producer/director Frederic Apcar in charge of the troupe. The production was scheduled to open on December 23,"[100] said Dave Wyman, nephew of Sid Wyman. He added:

> "The Dunes presented the 'Casino de Paris' revue. I fell in love with some of the incredible women who performed in the show. Uncle Sid has his own table in the showroom, where my brother and I (and later our friends, and later still, my girlfriends) would sit, with or without Uncle Sid. It was always an amazing experience when I was a snot-nosed kid to walk up to the 'Invited Guests' line, bypassing everyone else, and give my name to the vaguely menacing men who worked the front of the showroom. Once I or my brother said our name, the demeanor of these gentlemen changed dramatically and we were ushered into the showroom with alacrity."

Many show people felt that Apcar inherited the mantle from the legendary Florenz "Flo" Ziegfeld, an American Broadway impresario who was renowned for his series of theatrical revues, "The Ziegfeld Follies" (1907-1931), which were inspired by the "Folies Bergères" of Paris.

Apcar was born in Tiflis, Russia, known today as Georgia, which was a totalitarian Communist regime. Everyone who lived under the Russian rule became accustomed to hard work and terrible living conditions. The internal desire for self-given rights was a constant goal for young Apcar and his family. They escaped from Russia to Paris and started a new life there. That is where a young Apcar found his love for show business.

At the age of 10, he attended a performance of the French opera, "Le Spectre de la Rose," which translate in English to "The Spirit of the Rose." This short ballet is about a young girl who dreams of dancing with the spirit of a rose that she obtains at her first ball.

Short ballets were typical introductions for individuals, families, and children to the dance form and to the theatre. The performances were usually small, took place in informal settings, were affordably priced and lasted less than 45 minutes. Accessible to all, they offered the public a chance to witness high quality productions.

Hugely successful, "Le Spectre de la Rose" became internationally famous for the spectacular leap the male lead made through a window just before the end of the production. This scene left an indelible impression on Apcar. He was hooked.

Tough times required work for the young man so he tried his hand as a laborer, coal stoker, bookkeeper, printer's devil,[101] waiter, and dock boy. After several of these toilsome jobs, he found work in the theater. Apcar began as an usher in the Rex in Paris, then went on to study classical, modern, and tap dancing.

At age 16 he became a professional dancer, starting as a dancer during the chorus of the "Folies Bergères." However, after showing his talent, Apcar quickly became the show's principal dancer.

Only four years later, he and Florence Waren developed their own act called Florence and Frederic and performed together at the Bal Tabarin in Paris. The duo became one of the most renowned ballroom dance teams in Europe. In 1955, they expanded their adagio act to a 14- member ensemble known as The Florence and Frederic Ballet, which later debuted in the U.S. on "The Ed Sullivan Show."

In 1959, Lou Walters, father of Barbara Walters, brought Apcar and his troupe to the Tropicana to join the U.S. version of "Folies Bergères."[102]

"My father and his cast were in South America at the time, in Argentina, and he got a phone call from Lou," said Frederic Apcar, Jr. "And he said, 'Hey, Frederic, you know, you want to come to Las Vegas for a one-year contract at the Tropicana, right?' Um, and the war was just – the Civil

101   Note: A printer's devil was an apprentice in a printing establishment, responsible for tasks such as mixing tubs of ink and fetching type. A number of famous men served as printer's devils in their youth, including Lyndon Johnson, Mark Twain, Benjamin Franklin, Samuel Fuller, Thomas Jefferson, and Walt Whitman.
102   *The New York Times*, "Florence Waren, Jewish Dancer Who Resisted Nazis, Dies at 95," Denise Grady, Aug. 4, 2012

War was just about to happen in Argentina, and everything was going to hell over there, and he asked his cast if they wanted to come to Las Vegas. And everyone was like, 'Where the fuck is Las Vegas?' It's not like they're taking TWA to get to places. At that time, the majority of people were still taking ships.

"The real thing that catapulted my dad was coming to Vegas, obviously. I mean, the yes to Mr. Walters was probably the best decision he ever made then obviously the opportunity that the Dunes gave him. And that just catapulted to everything else," Apcar, Jr. said.

Apcar, Sr. was so well liked at the Dunes that they let him buy a 5 percent interest in it. Additionally, Apcar loaned Riddle a substantial amount of money when he was building his other gaming property, the Silver Nugget. Apcar became a 10 percent owner of it as well.

Apcar, Sr. remarked to a close friend,[103] "Well, they would, you know, every–every month, they would just have their meetings, and it would just be a bag of cash. Everyone would get a bag of cash, and he would tell me, he was like, 'You know, at the beginning, I would count it to make sure everything was there.' And he goes, 'After the sixth time, or seventh time, I just–I just stopped counting the money.' Charlie Rich told Apcar, 'Frederic, stop counting the money. It's all there. Don't worry about it.'"

Rich, who was compassionate, appreciated Apcar's history of hard work and immigration to the U.S. from a Communist regime, which was similar to his own.

"Charlie Rich really liked my dad a lot, and that's how, you know, obviously my dad got to know George [Duckworth] really well, when George was coming up through the Dunes, um, and, you know, my dad and Charlie went around the world a couple times together. I mean, so, those guys, they had fun," said Apcar's son.

Rich introduced his close friend Cary Grant to Apcar. Grant presented Apcar worthwhile acts that he thought he might enjoy.

Apcar added, "My father socialized with several important Las Vegas high lamas, you know. The crew was Charlie Rich, Wyman, [Kirk] Kerkorian, Moe Dalitz, Riddle, and a few others. There was like six of them that always hung out together. And, you know, it was like, uh, it was like college buddies, just always having fun.

"Those guys [the Dunes owners] were so gracious to my dad, because, you know, they allowed my dad to go work for [Meyer] Lansky in Cuba for like three years. So my dad would like fly back and forth, and those guys were really, really fair with him, and allowed him to grow his entertainment career. They could've said, 'No, Frederic, you got to stay here, and – and this is it, man. If you go anywhere else, we're going to kill you,'" said Apcar's son.. "He went to the Bahamas for Lansky who had two places."

When asked if his father was tight with Lansky, Apcar, Jr. answered, "Yes. One time he had to meet Lansky's guy like at a pier somewhere in Miami. It was just a briefcase, and he gave it to my dad. And my dad like opened up the briefcase, and the guy looked at my dad, and he was like, 'You don't have to count Mr. Lansky's money.' And my dad looked at him, and he thought about it for a second, and just closed the briefcase, and left. It was his payment for his shows."

"Bill Harrah took a liking to my father. They just started a business relationship, and then, he would do things up in Reno and Tahoe, um, you know, every other year, or for six months at a time," said Apcar.

"When [Frank] Sinatra bought the Cal-Neva, Frank wanted him to do a show there, but obviously that didn't pan out for anybody because of the licensing issues that Frank ran into," Jr. added.

Apcar, Sr. went on to conceive, produce, and direct numerous other Las Vegas-based shows, including "Bare Touch of Las Vegas," "Hot Streak," and "Showbiz" along with many more throughout the U.S. He retired in 1993. He was honored in 2006 with a Lifetime Achievement Award from the Nevada Entertainer/Artist Hall of Fame at the University of Nevada, Las Vegas. He died on August 2, 2008 at age 93.[104]

104   *Ibid*

CHAPTER 19

THE THUNDERBIRD:
WYMAN-RICH-DUCKWORTH-FLETCHER

In May 1961, Sid Wyman, Charlie Rich, and George Duckworth set their sights on the Thunderbird. They headed a group that sought to obtain a lease on and operate the Thunderbird with the option to purchase. The lease term would be for 10 years at $50,000 per month for the first five, increasing to $55,000 per month for the rest. The other interested investors were Harry Ulmer, an accountant; Wendell S. Fletcher, an aircraft manufacturer; Elias Lowe, a theater tycoon; and Jerome Steinbaum.

The proposal was that Wyman, Rich, and Duckworth would invest $70,000 for 27 percent of the company whereas Steinbaum and Ulmer would invest $230,000 for 30 percent. Fletcher would contribute the most, at $450,000 (about $3.8 million in today's dollars) for a 43 percent ownership.

Steinbaum and his father Morris Steinbaum were indicted for violating federal liquor laws in 1949 at the Baltimore Hotel in St. Louis. This followed the arrest of Young Steinbaum and bartender William Dover by alcohol and tobacco agents after they discovered evidence of watered down and altered bonded liquor in a upper level room in the hotel. The Steinbaums escaped prosecution by the Department of Justice, though, by offering a compromise. In later years, Jerome became a successful hotel and property developer.

Cash flush, Fletcher was the necessary investor who would give the group enough money to swing the Thunderbird deal. Fletcher's investment and solid background would pave the way so that the gaming regulators would find no areas of concerns. One of the most common problems in casino upstarts was lack of funding, but the proposed Thunderbird operation was properly financed for licensing.

Marion Hicks, the owner-operator of the Thunderbird, wanted to sell it. He was having health problems and was previously deemed unsuitable for a gaming license for protecting hidden interests in the Thunderbird. The *Nevada Tax Commission v. Hicks* explained:

"The ultimate conclusion reached by the tax commission was that respondents Hicks and [Cliff] Jones were unsuitable persons to hold gambling licenses. Five reasons were assigned for this conclusion as to Hicks and three reasons as to Jones. The reasons reflect the commission's standards of suitability, to which we have already referred. By specifying the manner in which Hicks and Jones had failed to measure up, the commission has disclosed its measure to this court.

"We shall consider each of the reasons, together with its factual support. It is apparent from the record, however, that the principal basis for the determination of unsuitability was the concealment from the tax commission of interests which should have been reported. As to Hicks it is stated, 'He conspired with citee, Clifford A. Jones, to violate the laws of the State of Nevada and the rules and regulations of the commission by protecting hidden interests in citee's gambling operation.' Jones is charged with an identical conspiracy with Hicks."[105]

The hidden interest allegedly belonged to Meyer and/or Jake Lansky, the tax commissioners concluded after an investigation. This excerpt from their records noted the relationships:

"From information available to the members of the commission (including the reports of the United States Senate committee upon organized crime, commonly known as the Kefauver Committee) it is apparent that among the figures recognized as prominently active in unlawful gambling beyond the borders of this state and in nationally organized crime are the Lansky brothers, Meyer and Jake (also known as Jack). The former, in particular, is recognized to occupy a position of leadership in organized crime.

"George Sadlo, whose residence for some time prior to the hearing had been at the Thunderbird, is a close personal friend and gambling associate of Jake Lansky. They have operated together in management of gambling enterprises in Florida. Sadlo and Marion Hicks are close personal friends."[106]

In 1947 Hicks borrowed $160,000 from Sadlo. The money was borrowed for use by the hotel corporation in the construction of the Thunderbird and was used for that purpose. At the time of the hearing before the commission, it appeared that Jake Lansky helped Sadlo make this

105   *Nevada Tax Commission v. Hicks*, 310 P.2D 852, 1957
106   *Reno Evening Gazette*, Oct. 27, 1954

loan. Hicks, however, denied any knowledge of Lansky's participation. Hicks repaid the loan to Sadlo in 1954.

Hicks had again borrowed money from Sadlo in 1948, $37,500, for use by the Thunderbird gambling partnership as the "bankroll," the fund that assures a casino has the funds to pay out gambling wins. There is no evidence that Lansky participated in this loan, and Hicks repaid it in 1952. Hicks never reported to the tax commission that either Sadlo or Lansky held any interest in the hotel corporation or in the gambling partnership.

John Hicks, the adopted son of Marion Hicks, confirmed to this writer that his father was a partner with Meyer Lansky in the Thunderbird hotel-casino.[107]

In late August 1961, Marion Hicks said he changed his mind and now wanted to maintain control of the Thunderbird. Thus, the offer from Wyman et al. was canceled, and the group shifted their attention to the Dunes. A confidential insider reported to this writer that when certain documents pertaining to the estates Charles Rich and Sidney Wyman were examined, evidence was found that Wyman quashed the Thunderbird deal as a favor to Meyer Lansky. This confidential source was connected with the transaction and was found to be 100 percent reliable.

Another indicator that Wyman and Lansky were linked was Wyman testifying in 1958 that he was part owner of the Riviera hotel in Havana, Cuba, but refusing to talk about it further.[108] This came out when a federal grand jury was questioning Wyman as a witness in its investigation into the Terre Haute bookmaking operation. Then, Lansky was the primary owner of the Havana Riviera.[109] Also taking the stand at that same grand jury hearing was Dan Peters, who represented himself as the publicist of the Havana Riviera. Further, television and recording star Steve Allen hosted his variety show from Lansky's Havana Riviera in January 1958 and also at the Thunderbird.

An additional revelation from Bruce Fisher: his grandfather Rich, and George Duckworth discovered, in the late 1970s, that Wyman was given a personal finder's fee of $300,000. The fee was likely from Lansky, for Wyman switching his group from pursuing the Thunderbird and then purchasing the Dunes. Wyman never mentioned it to his partners. Fisher said that Rich and Duckworth were quite upset with Wyman after finding out. Fisher also said that Wyman loved to gamble and when he needed cash, Rich would cover the losses and stake him in another venture.

107   Meeting with John Hicks, 1975
108   *Terre Haute Star*, Aug. 20, 1958
109   *St. Louis Post-Dispatch*, March 28, 1982

It is reasonable to suggest that Lansky killed the Thunderbird deal because he and his partners could make more money by selling the property to another group, which eventually happened. In January 1965, gaming regulators approved and licensed the Del Webb Corporation to acquire the Thunderbird for about $10 million. It was worth half of that in 1961 when Wyman et al. pursued buying it.

CHAPTER 20

THE DUNES: GOTTLIEB-RIDDLE-WYMAN-RICH-DUCKWORTH

S id Wyman, Charlie Rich, and George Duckworth looked south on the Las Vegas Strip to the Dunes, where Major Riddle was at the helm and Jake Gottlieb was the landlord. Gottlieb was having a major problem with Major Riddle embezzling from Dunes.[110]

Wyman could smell a thief. He sensed that there were problems at the Dunes and received a lot of information from his invisible hidden network of bookies and gamblers. Plus Wyman knew Jimmy Hoffa through Ross Miller, another Riviera owner, and Hoffa was close to Jake and John Gottlieb. Wyman believed that the Dunes could be saved and that he, Rich, and Duckworth had the experience to do it.

Jake Gottlieb gave Riddle the ultimatum of either selling some of his stock back to the company for Wyman or facing the consequences. Then the deal was struck that gave Wyman the control he needed to make the hotel-casino successful.

Wyman, Rich, and Duckworth filed an application with the Gaming Control Board in September 1961 and along with Wendell Fletcher, received gambling licenses on September 19 for 30 percent of the operating company. The combined investment of the four was $525,000.

It was Todd Derlachter who suggested to Wyman that Wendell Fletcher would be a suitable buyer. Without the cash backers of the likes of Fletcher via Derlachter, the Dunes deal would not have been done. If Wyman was consistent in his generosity with close friends, there is little doubt that he compensated Derlachter in some manner for his part in making it happen.

Derlachter and Wyman – Wyman was five years older – were pals from growing up together in St. Louis, where they both were born. Derlachter's father had a hat-cigar store that Wyman used as a location for his handbook operation, according to Joe Chautin, who was a friend of Wyman and arrested with him during a dice game bust at the Hamilton Hotel in St. Louis in 1946.

Derlachter had the finest education, attending the University of Missouri and the Wharton School of the University of Pennsylvania. He served in the U.S. Army Signal Corps as a major.

Derlachter had a keen business sense and joined Fletcher Aviation Corporation in the mid-1950s, an aircraft manufacturer founded by three brothers, Wendell, Frank, and Maurice Fletcher in Pasadena, California, in 1941. Fletcher Aviation had several patents and developed equipment for use by the armed services.

In 1957 the directors of Fletcher Aviation named Derlachter the treasurer under the chairman of the board, Wendell Fletcher. They also placed Derlachter on the executive committee with Maurice Fletcher, and Leland Launer acting as chairman. In Derlachter's initial treasurer's report, the stockholders were informed that sales for the first quarter equaled sales for the entire prior year of 1956.

In the early 1950s the U.S. Air Force and many American aircraft companies were interested in reviving the Japanese aircraft industry so the troops could be pulled out of Japan. Then the Japanese would have an independent air force. Every American pilot who fought against Japanese aviators had a healthy respect for Japanese aircraft because they were efficient and eminently airworthy.

The activities of the American aircraft companies that wanted to partner with or acquire Japanese aircraft factories and their technology were highly secretive and competitive. Beech Aviation sold the rights to one of their airplanes to Fuji Heavy Industries. Pratt & Whitney negotiated with Mitsubishi for the possible manufacture of jet engine parts, and Bell Aircraft completed a licensing agreement with Kawasaki to manufacture its helicopters. Fletcher Aviation made a similar deal with Toyo Aircraft Company. Fletcher Aviation was playing with the big boys, and Derlachter was right in the middle of the negotiations and planning.

A.J. Industries purchased Fletcher Aviation in 1960, and Derlachter spent 30 years as an executive vice president of A.J. At the time of the acquisition, the company name was changed to Flair Aviation. It produced aircraft fueling equipment, including drop tanks and hose reels for inflight refueling. A shareholder of A.J. Industries was Ben Weingart, a developer in Los Angeles who was from St. Louis and a close associate of John Gottlieb.

When Flair was relocated to El Monte, California, its name was changed back to Fletcher and then, in 1964, Sargent Fletcher before it abandoned aircraft manufacturing in 1966. The rights to the FU-24 went to Pacific Aerospace.

Derlachter became the general manager of Sargent and a board member. An ingenious innovator and a masterful negotiator, he greatly contributed to Sargent's success. He earned a $29,000 bonus for vastly improving its production.

In a strange turn of events, Fletcher was arrested in August 1963 on six counts of illicit acts, including statutory rape, involving two girls ages 12 and 14. On January 22, 1964, he was convicted on two of the counts with the others dismissed. He immediately sold 100,000 shares of A.J. Industries, of which he was a director with Derlachter. The shares sold for about $2.75 apiece. Then in February 1964, the Nevada Gaming Commission permitted Fletcher to sell his 15 percent, or $375,000, interest in the Dunes to Wyman, which took Wyman's holdings to 27 percent. He clearly was the chief operating officer of the resort.

In 1971 Los Angeles police discovered in Derlachter's possession a $100,000 U.S. Treasury bill that belonged to Brown Brothers Harriman, the oldest and one of the largest private banks in the United States. The Los Angeles police investigated Derlachter's possession of the bill, but no charges were filed and nothing was made public of how, where, or from whom he got it.

Wyman and the other new operators went to work at the Dunes and developed it into one of the most successful operations Las Vegas has ever seen. Rich offered Riddle the choice of the title of president or the biggest office, and Riddle chose the former. Titles meant nothing to Rich, who was modest and polite, and Riddle as president really had no power over the majority owners. Rich was happier with the larger office.

Because it was a Meyer Lansky associate who bought the Riviera shares of Wyman, Greenbaum, and others, it is reasonable to think Lansky gave Wyman the $300,000 for leaving the Riviera. The two already had a relationship. For one, when Wyman owned a 6 percent interest in the Sands, Lansky was a hidden owner with "Doc" Stacher, and Anthony "Tony Pro" Provenzano, a New York Mobster and Teamsters leader, carried money off the property for distribution, according to an FBI memo. Two, it is alleged that Wyman backed out of pursuing ownership of the Thunderbird as a favor to Lansky.

Supposedly in May 1962, Gottlieb received a $4 million loan commitment from the Teamsters pension fund though the Los Angeles Times reported that the Teamsters committed back in 1958 to giving Gottlieb the money for the Dunes in 1962, four years in the future.

On January 10, 1962, an informant advised the FBI that he overheard it said that Jimmy Hoffa was ready to loan money to Gottlieb to finance additional construction on the Dunes, but would not make the loan until Riddle was removed from his position there.

Eventually, on August 10, 1962, the Teamsters pension fund loaned Gottlieb $5 million through the Bank of Las Vegas and the Chicago Laundry and Dye Workers Union, to fund construction of a 22-story, 510-room addition to the Dunes.

Behind the $5 million loan to Gottlieb, at someone's request, was the American National Insurance Company (ANICO) and its two chief executives, William L. Vogler and Rollins A. Furbush.

One of the country's largest life insurance firms, ANICO was a major provider of loans in Las Vegas with its investments in the city exceeding $30 million by 1969. Loans in the millions went to Nevada casinos and hotels, and multi-million-dollar loans went to friends of the National Crime Syndicate, or Mafia. Some of the loans were on second mortgages, which were somewhat risky and unusual for a conservative organization like an insurance company. Many politicians were involved with various ANICO loan packages. Several of ANICO's top executives participated in untoward personal enrichment through dummy corporations and complicated clandestine investments.[111]

Vogler and Furbush were officers of American National since 1944. Vogler was made a vice president in 1944 and worked his way up to chairman of the board in 1962. The two were close and ate breakfast together almost daily for 15 years. They had mutual friends in the community, and they attended many social affairs as prominent bankers. Furbush became a company vice president in 1947. He succeeded Vogler as president the year that Vogler became chairman, and later, Furbush became chairman.[112]

According to a *New York Times* article:

> "In 1958, Vogler and Furbush entered into a secret agreement with two St. Louis insurance men, Max Lubin and Jack Molasky, to create a company to manage some of American National's agencies.
>
> "Mr. Lubin and Mr. Molasky organized AMCO, Inc., in St. Louis with $2,500 capital. Each man claimed 50 percent of the company, but it was later shown that Mr. Vogler and Mr. Furbush held a hidden 50 percent of AMCO."

Thomas R. Green was also associated with Molasky and Lubin in the formation of AMCO. This private arrangement meant that AMCO

---

111   *The New York Times*, Martin Waldron, Feb. 6, 1972
112   *Ibid*

would handle the subsidiary offices of ANICO and generate an enormous amount of fees for doing so. This proposition was never put out for a competitive bid and was kept private and undisclosed. It was estimated that in five years' time, the small insider-operated firm made over $300,000 in profit.

The associates connected to Vogler and Furbush in their Las Vegas ventures were Morris Shenker, Wyman, Rich, Duckworth, and Parry Thomas, chairman of the Bank of Las Vegas. Thomas assisted with more than $50 million of loans in Nevada from the Teamsters pension fund.

ANICO then turned around and purchased AMCO for $2.8 million. All of the money was paid to Green, Molasky, and Lubin, with Vogler and Furbush apparently not taking any of the proceeds.[113] It was a legitimate offer and sale even though the purchase agreement stated that $2 million of the purchase price went toward "goodwill, reputation, and the name AMCO."

Shortly after the AMCO sale to ANICO, a partnership named Leonard J. Campbell Enterprises was created. Campbell was Gottlieb's brother-in-law and a minor shareholder. The owners of Leonard J. Campbell Enterprises were the principals of M&R Investment Company (Wyman, Rich, Duckworth, and Fletcher), who held 36 percent; a group of bankers headed by Thomas, who held 12 percent; and Vogler, Furbush, Molasky, Lubin, and Green, who together held 52 percent.

An FBI memo revealed this:

> "An FBI informant advised on February 19, 1962, that he recently overheard a conversation involving Jake Gottlieb at which time Gottlieb mentioned the fact that the Government had subpoenaed all the books and records of the Central States Teamsters Pension Fund which created a real problem for Hoffa. Gottlieb appeared disturbed over this fact but informant does not know why. Informant furnished additional information regarding activities of the associates of Gottlieb."[114]

In January 1963, Hoffa asked Congress to investigate his charge that the Department of Justice used pressure tactics to discourage insurance companies from bonding Teamsters officials.[115]

Hoffa claimed that the Teamsters had been turned down by 260 bonding companies because of pressure brought by both the justice and labor

---

113   *Oakland Tribune*, Sept. 27, 1969
114   FBI File 124-10291-10341, March 27, 1962
115   *Times Advocate*, Jan. 29, 1963

departments. Hoffa pointed out that the Teamsters union was bonded by United Benefit, but the bond was suddenly canceled in 1961.

"This company's license was revoked," he said. "After the company dropped the Teamsters Union, the license was reinstated."

Hoffa then took Teamsters business to the Resolute Insurance Company of Providence, Rhode Island. The company carried the bond for a year and a half and then dropped it without explanation.

"This was the firm that received a visit from representatives of the labor and justice departments," Hoffa said.

An FBI memo dated February 1, 1963, which this writer obtained through a Freedom of Information Act request, captured two phone conversations, in which various Dunes executives discussed a business acquisition that Hoffa wanted to take place.

The FBI had an informant positioned who could listen firsthand to officials of the Dunes regarding management of the operation. The informant may have been a secretary, a casino or hotel executive, or possibly one of the partners. It may have been Sam Landy, who was named as having provided information in another FBI memo. Because the conversations included were described as "verbatim," the FBI could have obtained them via several methods, namely; a room bug, wiretapped telephone lines, and/or someone wearing a wire recorder.

In the first conversation, Gottlieb explained the business arrangement to Riddle:

> **Gottlieb**: "Let me explain the whole thing to you, United Benefit of Omaha is the company. He [Hoffa] talked to Parry Thomas [president of the Bank of Las Vegas] about it and he says it's a very good company. Its price is $1,965,000 and that they have to guarantee to show you that its net cash worth is $1,300,000."

> **Riddle**: "Is this a cash reserve or is it operating cash?"

> **Gottlieb**: "No. This is straight cash, $1,300,000 operating cash. Now he will work it out by putting money in a bank to guarantee it or make me a loan and I will lend it to you or make the loan to you which is no good. I don't want it that way. It will all be worked out so that you will own the company 100%."

> **Riddle**: "Where is he going to get the money to lend me?"

> **Gottlieb**: "He will work it out. He has a bank in Florida. As a matter of fact Parry Thomas will be glad to help him [Hoffa] out on this. In fact, he [Hoffa] has got the La Salle National Bank, too."

Riddle: "Maybe we can put the stock up as collateral."

Gottlieb: "The most you will take a chance on, at the most, is $600,000. The rest is cash in your name."

Riddle: "What you're telling me is that they guarantee the net worth of the company to be $1,300,000 and for the name and goodwill of the company we're paying $600,000."

Gottlieb: "Yeah, but the $1,300,000 has got to be in cash or government bonds. This company can issue bonds up to $60,000 and you'd be O.K.'d to do business in 42 states. Now here's another company. A 100 year old company that a guy by the name of Davis owns who can do business in 47 states and he wants $4,000,000 for it. He's out of Knoxville, Tennessee, and has a bunch of discount stores in the South. But this company hasn't got the O.K. to sell Federal bonds, but they can get it – but it will take 30 days, and I don't think he [Hoffa] can wait. The other company is a better company. They have the choice of either company.

"Let me explain something to you and I won't let you go into it any other way. Number 1. He has got to let you or some insurance agency you elect – a broker like [Harley] Harmon [a large insurance broker in Las Vegas] to write the insurance. You can't write it under Dorfman. I don't want him at all. Number 2, he cannot mess up in this company at any time. You've got to be the boss, the president. You own it and run it like that."

Riddle: "What happens to the stock? Who gets it?"

Gottlieb: "You get it. Who else could get it?"

Riddle: "These guys are going to want some interest in this company."

Gottlieb: "I can't help it. The only guys that can get it is Jimmy [Hoffa], whatever you want to give him. I won't do it with anyone else. If you want to give some to Jimmy, that's up to you. I won't give it to anybody else. I don't want those guys for partners. I never wanted them for partners."

Riddle: "Not openly – hell no."

Gottlieb: "Even closed. Did you hear what I said? You're sacrificing a big thing here, and I'm getting you to do it. As far as right here is concerned, you can go right on. The only thing, you will put in [REDACTED] name. [This is an apparent reference to Riddle's stock in the Dunes.]"

Riddle: "This means right here more to me. After all, consider $180,000 to $200,000 a year in cash and that's better than a million..."

Gottlieb: "You don't have to tell me. Your status will be the same here as ever. But for the books and records you will have to resign."

Riddle: "One big problem, Jake, I know this. Dorfman and those guys are not going to be satisfied to sit back and be cut out of this company. They'll want part of it and they won't push for those bonds. They'll do everything to cut your throat."

Gottlieb: "They can't get the bonds any place else. Listen, under normal conditions you are right, but this is not under normal conditions. The gun is at their head right now. You hear what I say?"

Riddle: "What I will do is go in and give Jimmy [Hoffa] 25% of this secretly, then this guy would throw every bond insurance coverage to this company."

Gottlieb: "You could get all the Teamsters Union insurance business. I'd put out a stock issue after a couple of years and get some real money. You could show $1,000,000 profit or so over three or four years. Issue stock. Keep 51% of it and make some real money."

Riddle: "Yes."

Gottlieb: "Put in a call to him on your private line."

Subsequently, the FBI documented the following regarding the second telephone call, in which Riddle explained the deal to Charlie Rich and Bob Rice. The FBI wrote:

"**FBI Note**: Riddle places a call to Pennypacker 5-0660 in Philadelphia from his private number RE 5-1632. Riddle is told at this number that Hoffa can be reached through his office in Washington, D.C., at WDC number 30525. While awaiting the completion of this call, Riddle tells Gottlieb that the young [Allen] Dorfman is with Hoffa in Washington, D.C."

Gottlieb: (whispers) "These lines are monitored."

"**FBI Note**: Apparently Gottlieb and Riddle write and pass notes to each other for three or four minutes.

"Gottlieb speaks to Hoffa Monday morning, Washington, D.C., 2/4/63. Gottlieb told Riddle that Hoffa told him that he couldn't be any place else other than Washington on Monday because he was waiting for a phone call from across the Hill.

"LV 70-C* [informant] further advised that Major Riddle explained the above business transaction to Charles Rich and Bob Rice, both part owners of the Dunes Hotel. Riddle said that he would have no part of the Dorfmans or [REDACTED] in this insurance business and that Hoffa and his attorneys have already talked over the complete details with Gottlieb. Riddle stated that they almost demanded that Jake take this company because the company is in bad shape and that the policies are being canceled. Riddle told Rich and Rice that after talking to Hoffa on Monday that he would confer with [Nevada] Governor Grant Sawyer and explain the situation to him. Riddle said that if the publicity of him [Sawyer] being connected with Hoffa would be harmful to Sawyer and Sawyer asked him not to make this connection, then Riddle would abide by Sawyer's wishes. Riddle emphasized that he has been closely identified with Sawyer and that he would never do anything to hurt the Governor.

"Rich remarked, 'The Governor will probably say, Major, take it and as soon as I get out of office, I will join you.'

"Riddle also emphasized to Rich that he would promise Sawyer that he would not be tied up with hoodlums or become involved in any illegal activities through this association with Hoffa.

"Riddle stated that Hoffa would make the money available to 'buy this company' and Riddle stated, 'We will still be partners and we can probably make a buck out of this thing.'"

Later in 1963, Leonard J. Campbell Enterprises bought the Dunes buildings, but not the real estate, for $11.25 million, which was much less than the reported value of $15 million. Campbell Enterprises controlled members of the Vogler-Furbush group through a non-operating but legitimate paper corporation with nominal or zero assets. Shenker supposedly established this paper corporation to protect the Campbell partnership from any of Gottlieb's liabilities.

On September 6, 1963, the paper corporation paid Gottlieb $2.8 million in cash and executed a non-interest bearing note to him for $4,598,759. The balance of the announced purchase price was represented by two mortgages the Dunes had on the books: $1,601,241, which was on a joint loan from the Bank of Las Vegas and the Chicago Laundry and Dye Workers Union, and $2.25 million loan from the Teamsters pension fund. Gottlieb, however, agreed to guarantee the two loans even after the paper corporation assumed them. Hoffa, in the Teamsters pension fund notes that accompanied the loans, stipulated that if the Dunes were to be granted additional loans, Gottlieb's name must remain on the notes.

Another FBI memo exposed confidential details of the transaction between Gottlieb and Wyman:

"Informant advised that contacted informant and advised that he had plan worked out where James Gottlieb would deposit $6,000,000 in a bank having numbered accounts and Wyman would then borrow $6,000,000 using Gottlieb's deposit as security. Wyman indicated that he would then use the $6,000,000 to purchase the Dunes Hotel from Gottlieb. As a result of this conversation, informant suspects that Gottlieb has access to $6,000,000 that cannot be shown and is trying to work something out to put this money to work."[116]

On October 24, 1963 Leonard J. Campbell Enterprises paid $2.8 million in cash and took over the deal from the paper corporation.

The FBI received this information from a reliable inside source at the Dunes. Gottlieb, who did not have a gaming license for the Dunes, was calling the shots, as revealed in another FBI memo.[117]

Gottlieb was an extremely close friend of Hoffa and at arm's length of the Chicago Outfit. The Texas group, ANICO, previously helped Gottlieb get $4.15 million in loans from ANICO to be used for other real estate Gottlieb owned: the Albany Hotel in Denver, the Tulsa Hotel in Tulsa, and the Landmark Apartments in Las Vegas, which eventually would become part of the Teamsters pension fund-financed Landmark Tower purchased by Howard Hughes.

In February 1963, United Artists produced a movie titled *Love is a Ball*. They promoted the film by sending 100 top newspaper writers on an all-expense paid trip, which they called the "Love is a Ball Junket," to the Dunes Hotel and Country Club. The hotel wined, dined, and treated them all to shows and gave them true red carpet treatment. The publicity started the ball rolling about the new tower and all of the amenities at the hottest new resort in Las Vegas.

A premier party was hosted at the Dunes' plush Sultan's Table restaurant with legendary Steve Allen filming the action for his television show. Coincidentally, a few years earlier, Allen had filmed his show at the Havana Riviera that was owned by Meyer Lansky. Some say that a potential connection between a Dunes owner and Lansky may have helped facilitate the Allen filming.

In 1964 the Dunes completed and opened an 18-hole championship golf course. They added "Country Club" to the hotel name and called the 7,125-yard, 72 par course the "Emerald Green." The course was designed

---

116   *Ibid*
117   FBI Memo, 124-90032-10075, 1959

by the William F. Bell Company with natural appearing contours that were developed into large, well-trapped greens with five small lakes strategically placed throughout the expanse.

It was not easy to get lakes there due to citywide concerns about groundwater availability. Dunes president Riddle was denied a groundwater well permit, yet his persistence and lobbying to Nevada Governor Grant Sawyer eventually got him the approvals needed in record time.

When the other Dunes owners complained about a situation whose resolution required a $20,000 political contribution be paid to Sawyer, Riddle was overheard by an informant saying, "The guy does whatever we want. Any one of these things he does for us would bring in $20,000." Riddle added, "And besides, the contribution in question was an economy when compared with the $200,000 the Desert Inn had anted up for another influential politician."[118]

In May 1965 the Dunes celebrated its 10-year anniversary and the opening of its 24-story "Diamond of the Dunes" tower of guestrooms. That total investment in the Dunes was more than $20 million, which is a paltry sum today. The month-long celebration was a great reason to invite gamblers to partake in the opening of the Dome of the Sea restaurant, which featured harpist Kippy Lou, who floated magically in a small sea-like water setting and strummed the most congenial sounds that complemented the finest seafood dining.

Also, the Dunes capitalized on the new high-rise by opening the Top of theDunes, featuring Russ Morgan and his orchestra, Art and Dorothy Todd. The cocktail lounge offered unobstructed, panoramic views of the Las Vegas Valley.

Other resort additions were a men's and women's health club, a solaria for nude sunbathing, a Wonderland Nursery, an outdoor Parisian sidewalk café, 12 swanky retail stores in a Garden Arcade environment, a Sea Horse swimming pool, a snack bar, and a cocktail lounge. The Dunes was a city within a city.

On January 1, 1967, M&R Investment bought out the other partners in Leonard J. Campbell Enterprises, which included Vogler and Furbush, for $22.8 million. Later that year, the Campbell partnership was dissolved.

In April 1968, Lee Fisher, Dunes director of advertising and public relations, issued a news release featuring Charles Rich, the resort's executive vice-president, and stating, "It has been estimated that the Dunes' annual gross revenue exceeds $100 million." This statistic came directly from Rich. The Dunes had the best of everything in the way of amenities. The operators believed in offering the finest food, the plushest accommodations, first-class shopping, a championship golf course, and the best gambling.

There were no gimmicks on the tables to lure players, but the casino did offer high betting limits and the best odds. Duckworth and his assistant Artie Selman placed an ad in the local newspaper offering players $5,000 a hand in blackjack or higher if they brought cash. In craps they offered double odds with limits of $5,000 and $10,000. They accepted hard way bets up to $2,000. They offered $500 any way someone could get to a number on the roulette wheel and allowed $5,000 bets on the outside. Topping it all off was the baccarat offering of $60,000 a hand, but if management was given five minutes' advance notice, they would accept $1 million a hand. The message here was if players came with their own cash, they could set their own limit.[119]

In late December 1968, the Dunes began offering, from noon until midnight, daily scenic helicopter flights over the Strip and the City of Las Vegas. To do so, they built a heliport on the grounds adjacent to the Country Club. "The tremendous growth of tourism in Southern Nevada inevitably led to a need for this particular kind of sub-lunar aerial service," Rich said. "After all, a helicopter ride over the Las Vegas Valley, be it by day or night, is one of the most enchanting and exciting experiences a tourist can have." Duckworth was an accomplished fixed wing pilot and progressive in his thinking about aviation and tourism. There is no doubt that he had something to do with the addition of this amenity.

Also, in 1968, Shenker teamed up with three owners of the Parvin-Dohrmann Company to acquire Continental Connector Corporation, a public company. Interestingly, Shenker had gotten one of the lawyers in his firm, James F. Nangle, Jr., appointed as a director of Continental Connector.

However, the Nevada Gaming Commission had two problems with Parvin-Dohrmann Company. One of their directors, Furbush, the president of ANICO, was tied to an owner of another Las Vegas casino and also to the owner of a Bahamian casino.[120] Furbush was linked to the Dunes because he was one of its directors, too.

He also was linked to Meyer Lansky. In 1966, ANICO purchased $1.75 million worth of 6½ percent Series A convertible subordinated notes issued by Resorts International that operated a casino on Paradise Island in

---

119   Dunes advertisement, *Las Vegas Review-Journal*, April 29, 1983
120   Associated Press, May 24, 1969

the Bahamas. The notes were convertible at any time into 350,000 shares of Resorts International stock. This accounted for about 10 percent of the total shares outstanding at the time. Lansky was involved in the gambling operation on Paradise Island. Also, Al Parvin paid Lansky a $200,000 finder's fee for finding a buyer of the Flamingo. Later, in 1971, Lansky was indicted for alleged skimming at the Flamingo.

Another concern of the gaming regulators was that if the Parvin-Continental Connector deal went through, it could lead to a situation in which Furbush held an interest in both a Nevada casino and an ex-Nevada casino, which was prohibited by state law.

In February 1969, the Dunes received Gaming Commission approval to merge with Continental Connector.

Six months later, in August, gaming regulators allowed Continental Connector to buy the Golden Nugget casino located in downtown Las Vegas. During the Gaming Control Board meeting in which the proposed transaction was discussed, board member Dr. Wayne Pearson remarked, "To talk of my previous question, I always try to get these applicants on record about their future plans. You know, you hear so many rumors up and down the street. I just tried to pin Herb Jones [Dunes attorney] down about what Continental Connector was going to do with the Golden Nugget, when they were going to build a 100-story skyscraper."

Jerry Zarowitz held stock in the Golden Nugget, according to a report by the New Jersey Casino Control Commission:

> "Also in the Fall of 1972, it became publicly known that one Jerome Zarowitz had acquired a large amount of Golden Nugget, Inc. stock, in fact 92,000 shares. Philip Hannifin, then Chairman of the GCB, had been aware of Mr. Zarowitz's growing position in GNI since Spring 1972.[121]
>
> "In Hannifin's words, Mr. Zarowitz was a man of 'notorious reputation.' His holdings, in Hannifin's judgment, were not in the best interests of the State of Nevada. Accordingly, Mr. Hannifin, aware also of Mr. [Steve] Wynn's large GNI holdings, and of his wish to gain control of GNI, persuaded Mr. Wynn to attempt to buy Jerome Zarowitz's GNI stock.
>
> "In 1971, other events unfolded that ultimately affected Jerome Zarowitz's sale of his GNI stock. At that time, Mr. Zarowitz's son, Lonnie, then 21 years old, applied for a Nevada license to be able to 'buy into' a business known as a 'slot route.' Nevada's gaming authorities, not satisfied that Lonnie Zarowitz was independent

121   Application of GNAC Corporation, New Jersey casino, License Decided Oct. 13, 1981

of his father, denied his application. The unsuitable reputation of Jerome Zarowitz is not a new revelation to this Commission. We recognized it in the Matter of the Applications of Boardwalk Regency Corporation and the Jemm Company for Casino Licenses, p. 13-18 (Docket No. 80-CL-1).

"His conversations with an attorney for Jerome Zarowitz led Hannifin to conclude that Zarowitz was acquiring GNI stock to embarrass the gaming authorities because of their denial of the license application of his son. In fact, early in 1972, Jerome Zarowitz refused a request of the GCB through GNI, that he submit a license application.

"His attorney, Milton Rudin, questioned the constitutionality of Nevada laws empowering the gaming authorities to require Mr. Zarowitz to submit a license application and threatened litigation. These events, and conversations with Mr. Rudin, led Mr. Hannifin to believe that if Lonnie Zarowitz was licensed, Jerome Zarowitz would sell his GNI stock to Stephen Wynn.

"Lonnie Zarowitz reapplied for a license, which was granted in the Spring of 1973. Mr. Hannifin stated candidly that he voted for Lonnie Zarowitz's new application not because his relationship with his father had changed, but because he believed granting the application would induce Jerome Zarowitz to sell his GNI stock.

"In the Spring of 1973, Stephen Wynn was also granted a license by the Nevada gaming authorities. Thereafter, Mr. Hannifin's expectation was fulfilled. Jerome Zarowitz agreed to sell his GNI stock to a group of investors assembled by Mr. Wynn in May 1973. Mr. Wynn himself purchased 52,000 of Mr. Zarowitz's shares with financing, again, from the Valley Bank.

"Thereafter, through negotiations with GNI Directors, Mr. Wynn was elected a Director and an Executive Vice-President in June 1973. Through further negotiations, during which Mr. Wynn assembled another investor group which made a tender offer to buy 225,000 shares of Golden Nugget, Inc. (GNI) stock, Mr. Wynn became President of GNI and installed a substantially new Board of Directors in August 1973. He had realized his ambition to take control of GNI. The tender offer was completed in September 1973, and Mr. Wynn acquired 25,000 more shares of GNI stock.

"We cannot say that anything now in the record concerning these complicated events reflects negatively upon Mr. Wynn's qualifications. Although Mr. Wynn at one point negotiated personally with Jerome Zarowitz, nothing indicates that their association or the subsequent transaction between them was other than arm's length."

Before Wynn's interest, a connection between Zarowitz on one hand and the Dunes and the Golden Nugget on the other is suggested by some circumstantial facts that link Zarowitz and Larry Snow. Zarowitz without question was the highest authority at Caesars Palace during the construction and after the opening in 1966, and he approved the appointment of Snow to the position of baccarat manager. Snow was previously denied a gaming license at the Moulin Rouge because of his alleged Mob affiliations. A former "eye in the sky" at Caesars Palace when Snow was the baccarat manager reported:

"I was watching the baccarat game one night and a fill slip for $300,000 came, and there were no chips. Then in half an hour later, another fill slip came [$300,000] with no chips. Six hundred thousand in a matter of an hour. That's what they skimmed in an hour. They were stealing a million a month minimum. I reported each incident on my work notes. My boss was a guy that used to be a chief of police. He basically told me to mind my own business."[122]

CHAPTER 21

THE TEAMSTERS
AND BENJAMIN DRANOW

By 1962, the Teamsters pension fund, overseen by eight employer trustees and eight pension fund trustees, including Jimmy Hoffa, had invested more than $45 million in development in the West. On the surface it appeared normal, but a little digging and investigation unearthed interesting characters and curious associations.

It is estimated that 50 percent of the $45 million was loaned for construction of hotel-casinos in Reno and Las Vegas, the latter city receiving about $19 million.[123]

For instance, about $2.75 million in pension funds were invested in Reno's Riverside Hotel where Benjamin Dranow, former financial advisor to Hoffa, stayed from July to September 1962. While there, he cashed worthless checks and exchanged money in a kiting scheme wherein Dranow earned more than $50,000. The purpose of this complicated plot was actually to get a kickback to Dranow so that Raymond Spector could acquire the hotel.[124]

In June 1959, Robert F. Kennedy, chief counsel of the Senate Rackets Committee, investigated Dranow and his association with Hoffa. Dranow, a Minneapolis businessman, obtained a $1 million loan from the Teamsters pension fund for his department store that went bankrupt before the loan was repaid. Then Hoffa had staff order 26,495 Teamsters jackets from Dranow, without accepting competitive bids, enabling Dranow to pocket $6,000 in commissions, equivalent to nearly $55,000 today. Saul Marks and Seymour Svirsky, New York clothing manufacturers, set up a non-union company called Union Local Supply Co. and hired Nat Gordon, a Giovanni "Johnny Dio" Dioguardi[125] henchman, as their only salesman. They paid him $200 a week and sold 30,000 Teamsters emblems for the jackets.

---

123   *Los Angeles Times*, May 16, 1962
124   *Los Angeles Times*, November 30, 1962
125   *The New York Times*, Peter Kihss, Jan. 16, 1979: Note: John Dioguardi was an organized crime leader who specialized in labor racketeering and was an ally of Jimmy Hoffa. In 1954, the Teamsters union forced Dioguardi out after he helped Hoffa create Teamsters locals in New York, which were later exposed by Robert F. Kennedy.

Dranow also was steered to a gain of $56,000 on a stock deal. Hoffa handpicked Dranow to bail out the Sun Valley development, a planned community for retired Teamsters in Florida. Dranow wound up acquiring most of the stock in Sun Valley and promised the developers that he would bail out the troubled project via Teamsters loans he could obtain, if they would help salvage Sun Valley.[126]

George Burris admitted that he was the "dummy" president of a Dranow-controlled corporation, the Union Land and Home Company, which owned 100 percent of the stock in Sun Valley, Inc., the entity that was created to sell home sites to Hoffa's union members. The company sold approximately 1,700 lots with revenue exceeding $200,000, yet one brother Teamster who had purchased a lot had great difficulty finding its exact location.

Burris admitted under oath that the project was hopeless as a development since it was 14 miles from Cocoa, Florida. Burris also admitted that he had borrowed $735,000 from the Teamsters pension fund for a building project in Buffalo and that he and Dranow obtained approval for a loan of $1.4 million for a garden apartment house job in Fullerton, California.

"Dranow is either the world's best salesman or you are its most inept businessman," Kennedy said.

In 1961, Dranow was convicted on 18 of 21 counts of mail, wire, and bankruptcy fraud. Immediately after the trial, he stood in front of the Minneapolis Federal Court building and posed for a picture. Looking at the photo, one would think it was just another day for Dranow, who was dressed in a dapper suit, his shoes shining like a mirror. He looked like he did not have a care in the world. He remarked, "At least they didn't find me guilty on all counts."[127]

In 1963 the Teamsters pension fund became a point of major interest to investigators who attended the conference of Law Enforcement Intelligence Unit that year in Los Angeles.

Senator John L. McClellan, one of the first government officials to delve into the Teamsters pension fund and its loans, praised the *Los Angeles Times* for its stories related to the dubious Teamsters dealings.[128]

The FBI was interested in any information and leads they could investigate regarding Hoffa and the Teamsters pension fund, which they were watching, as indicated in this November 1963 memo:

126   *New Castle News*, June 30, 1959
127   *Star Tribune*, Aug. 20, 1961
128   *Los Angeles Times*, Gene Blake, April 21, 1963

"Informant has furnished extremely valuable information of a general intelligence nature and most of the information pertains to the gambling industry in Las Vegas, Nevada, and the activities and associates of James Riddle Hoffa. Because of the nature or the information furnished by the informant, it has been possible to verify a great deal of the information furnished through independent investigation and/or inquiry. It is believed that if the information furnished by this informant can be developed to the fullest extent, that a great deal of information will be developed on the handling and transfer of funds in and out of Las Vegas."

How these specific FBI sources were recruited is mind boggling. The Supreme Court gave prosecutors the green light to use informants in investigations by exempting informant use from the constraints of the Fourth, Fifth, and Sixth Amendments.

In *Hoffa v. United States*, 385 U.S. 293 (1966), the Supreme Court held that the government could use a criminal informant recruited from a Louisiana jail cell to get incriminating information from Hoffa. Because Hoffa let the informant into his hotel room and spoke freely in front of him, the court decided that Hoffa had no reasonable expectation of privacy regarding that information, and therefore the government could use it without violating the Fourth Amendment's prohibition of unreasonable searches and seizures. The Supreme Court also authorized the use of wired informants to record information electronically.[129]

Also scrutinizing the Teamsters pension fund was the IRS.

A.R. Manzi, assistant director of intelligence for the agency, said, "Unions are an attractive place for racketeers if they can control the tremendous amount of funds. The crux is the union's ability to grant the loans. Through this there are kickbacks and the ability to get control of banks." The comments of the officials who were investigating the Teamsters paralleled those published in *Los Angeles Times* articles about Hoffa and the Teamsters in the years up to 1963. One of the headlines was, "Give Hoffa a $200 Million Piggy Bank to Play with and All Sorts of Strange Things Can Happen." That piggy bank was the Teamsters pension fund, which received approximately $3 million a year in employer contributions.

Millions of dollars of Teamsters pension fund loans were made to known associates of organized crime notables, as late as 1976, to finance hotel-casino operations that were siphoning millions of dollars into underworld coffers. Teamsters trustees and officials tried to give the impression that the fund's suspicious loans stopped in 1967 when Hoffa, who owed a great deal of outstanding favors to racketeers, went to federal prison.

The record shows, however, that the dubious loans continued until passage of the federal pension law, The Employee Retirement Income Security Act of 1974. After it took effect, on January 1, 1975, a Teamsters pension fund loan was made to a man directly linked to Meyer Lansky, according to investigations in Nevada and Florida. The reputed associate of Meyer was on track to receive millions of dollars from the owners of Caesars Palace.

CHAPTER 22

"Big Julie" Weintraub, The New York Junket Master

very other week Julius "Big Julie" Weintraub brought an airplane full of people to Las Vegas from New York City on what is called a junket. Weintraub was named "Big Julie" because of his size; he towered at 6 feet, 4 inches. He visited Las Vegas in 1955 for a friend's wedding and fell in love with the fabulous town. He was a jewelry salesman and had the ability to sell like no other, bar none. He had a knack.

He became friendly with Sid Wyman, Charlie Rich, and George Duckworth at the Riviera and recommended their hotel-casino to his many high-end customers. He received $1,000 a month as an incentive. In May of 1962, after Wyman, Rich, and Duckworth moved to the Dunes, Weintraub proposed an arrangement in which he would bring customers to the Dunes, not in small groups but in a fully loaded airplane.

Rich was not for the idea, but Duckworth saw potential in the opportunity and knew that Weintraub could produce the players. He had some simple rules in those early days for his junketeers: Take cash and gamble, and in return receive complimentary room, food, and beverage. Weintraub changed the rules and format somewhat over the years so that only the best customers received the primo Dunes suites. On a busy New Year's trip, for instance, junketeers were required to have a higher amount of front money to get a ticket to the Dunes and its amenities.

The first junket trip that Weintraub organized to the Dunes was overbooked, to the tune of 140 people versus the planned 125. He wired the Dunes officials saying that they would have to "spring" a few thousand dollars more for the extras, as the Dunes was to pay a flat per-person fee. Weintraub then received this telegram: "TAKE EXTRA PEOPLE OFF YOUR LIST. WE ARE NOT GOING TO PAY FOR ANY COMMERCIAL SEATS."[130]

Weintraub phoned and asserted to an owner that if he did not accept these players, there would be no junket. The owner said the situation felt

"Big Julie of Las Vegas," Edward Linn, 1974

like blackmail. Weintraub said, "Now you got it. Now you're getting the picture. Everybody or nobody. I'd call it a sound business investment, but if you want to call it blackmail, be my guest." The Dunes acceded. Within one hour of that first New York junket arriving at the Dunes, the owners had already won back all of the money they spent on it, which was $25,000 for the cost of the airfare. On Sunday, one of the junketeers lost almost $700,000. Weintraub's junket was a winner.

Weintraub's idea to transport players to the Dunes to gamble worked, and he never looked back as his junket business got better and stronger. He brought customers of every ethnicity. They all considered an invite to his junket prestigious, akin to "keeping up with the Joneses." It became a benchmark status symbol to go to the Dunes for free. It gave customers bragging rights on how well they knew Weintraub. This rolling junket snowball became a multilevel marketing program with customers recommending more customers. Weintraub's junket list reached 6,000 and kept growing.

His players helped fill the Dunes' 1,000 rooms with play that was premium. This action filled the blackjack tables, dice tables, and the exclusive baccarat game. The wives of the players lounged around the pool, visited the health club and solarium, shopped, ate, gambled, and drank – only diet cola. The Dunes was their very own amazing private country club.

Many of Weintraub's Orthodox Jewish customers required a refrigerator for kosher food that they brought with them. At the check-in desk, God forbid, if there was not a refrigerator in Mr. Gold's room, Mr. Gold would flag down Weintraub. Over the rim of his reader glasses, Weintraub would see Mr. Gold approaching.

"Yes, Mr. Gold, I will see to it right now." Weintraub would make a big show and fuss over Mr. Gold while he called to the bellman, "Bobby, make sure that Mr. Gold gets the new refrigerator that we ordered just for him." Weintraub made sure everyone heard him. Mr. Gold was pleased. His "juice at the Dunes," Big Julie, coddled Mr. Gold and accommodated his every whim.

This was how Weintraub worked. Anything that his junketeers wanted was okay unless they did not play. Weintraub told them up front that if they did not gamble, they would not get complimentary rooms, food, or beverages. None of his players wanted to be shunned by Weintraub, so they made sure they followed the rules and played.

Weintraub's junkets were a cash cow and instrumental in making the Dunes extremely successful. The resort recruited junket masters in many other major cities and duplicated the template that Weintraub created, but none of them was as consistent and successful as Big Julie. It is estimated that he brought more than $400 million in casino revenues to the city between 1962 and 1983. Weintraub deservedly became recognized as the most successful junket operator in the U.S.[131]

Weintraub was interviewed by David Hartman for an ABC special on gaming called *Gamblers – Winners and Losers*. The show was an inside look at how gamblers think, act, and play. It presented Big Julie to the nation as the King of the Junkets.

Edward Linn wrote a best-selling book, *Big Julie of Las Vegas*, which tells many hilarious stories about Weintraub's customers and life at the Dunes. In one, Weintraub was preparing to leave the hotel-casino one Sunday afternoon right after many of his big baccarat players beat the game for about $60,000. The players had just enough time to cash in their chips and get on the shuttle for the airport.

The baccarat crew was simulating a real game using shills when Rich walked up, stood about 10 feet from the middle of the baccarat entrance, puffing on his cigar, his hands sort of crossed, and stared at the crew and table. Though his stare was chilling, employees never feared Rich and never considered him a terror. He slowly mumbled, "A bunch of canaries – you got your end," and walked away. "A bunch of canaries" referred to the dealers because when they called winning hands, they sounded like birds singing or chirping. "You got your end" meant that the dealers received a lot of tips after the house had a big loss.

Rich did "sweat the losses" because he was used to winning. During the Great Depression, he handled millions of dollars. On the bets he and his partners booked and on the dice games they operated there was a built-in percentage. Maintaining a winning percentage, called the PC, or percent hold, required constant action. However, with the short-term, one-off play like that by the New York junket members, Rich did not get the chance to win back the $60,000.

Rich loved the employees and never fired anyone at the Dunes. During his time there, no reports were made of him being involved in unfair or questionable business or get-rich-quick schemes. Nobody ever said he treated the dealers or other employees badly. Rich had a heart of gold and helped every charity that asked. He had the tremendous ability to read a person's true character just by listening to them. He listened.

There was a dark moment for Big Julie in early 1969, as he was attacked in New York City by unknown assailants which resulted in both of his legs

---

131   *New Scotland Yard*, Sept. 9, 1983

being broken. Weintraub passed off the incident as a robbery attempt, but it certainly had the look of a Mob shake-down. Yet that did not stop Julie from bringing his junket to the Dunes, albeit on crutches and in obvious pain.

Big Julie was so successful that the Dunes management offered him the chance to buy in to the corporation. In 1964 Weintraub filed a gaming application to purchase 1 percent of the M&R Investment Company d.b.a. the Dunes Hotel and Casino.

The Gaming Control Board (GCB) recommended to the Nevada Gaming Commission (GC) that they deny Weintraub's application on the basis of "questionable antecedents." Yes, the word "antecedents" was spelled incorrectly in the GCB's transcript. In retrospect, it would have been a feather in Weintraub's hat if his lawyer questioned the meaning of "antecedents." What the board was referring to was Weintraub's social background.

At the GC meeting on September 25, 1967, three years later, the commissioners grilled Weintraub. They probed for the specifics of the bankruptcy that he filed. Weintraub told them he paid what debt he could but there was some he could not. No evidence of fraud was apparent.

The commissioners asked Weintraub about his relationship with a Nicholas "Jiggs" Forlano. Weintraub replied, "Well, I know him. He used to be my bookmaker many years ago."

"What was his reputation?" asked Chairman Frank Johnson.

"Not good," replied Weintraub. It appeared to at least one commissioner, Wayne Pearson, that Weintraub was being honest.

The gaming commissioners, who are appointed by the governor, tended to lack knowledge about the workings of casinos, junkets, and gamblers. They, in general, expected licensees to be "lily white" in reputation and as mild as librarians. Gamblers who shot craps, played blackjack and inhabited a casino often did not measure up to the standard expected by these four-year, civil servant employees. If it was left up to this particular appointed commission, the Dunes would not have had any hardcore gamblers, like the New York City craps shooters Weintraub brought there, playing in its casino. It is surprising that Commissioner Johnson did not try to pass a gambling regulation that called for asking customers, before they entered a casino, if they ever lied, cheated, or stole.

Johnson had numerous careers in Nevada, but no experience in gaming. He was a reporter and a newspaper columnist. His method of questioning Weintraub perhaps should have been examined, as it was obvious he tried to belittle him and grandstand. In 1961, when Johnson was a reporter in Carson City, he pulled a stunt that Weintraub's lawyer, Tom Bell, should have called him on. When Weintraub peddled some jewelry out of his pocket, Johnson asked him if he had a business license. Bell should have asked Johnson, "Are you going to have my client arrested, like when Governor Grant Sawyer, Attorney General Roger Foley, and Comptroller Keith Lee were arraigned?"

This question alludes to the formal complaint Johnson made to the Ormsby County Sheriff alleging that Sawyer, Foley, and Lee had violated Nevada's Open Meeting law because Johnson was excluded when Sawyer and members of the state highway board discussed proposed routes for what is now Interstate 80. The case was dismissed a year later.

On June 12, 1962, President John F. Kennedy nominated Foley to the federal United States District Court, District of Nevada (a new federal judicial seat created by Congress). The U.S. Senate confirmed Foley's nomination on June 29, 1962, and he received his judicial commission on July 2, 1962.

As Johnson's questioning of Weintraub continued, it became humorous:

Johnson: "Suppose any of these people – Mr. [Nicholas 'Jiggs'] Forlano, Mr. [Charles 'Ruby'] Stein – any of this group – would you say they would be welcome guests in the Dunes Hotel?"

Weintraub: "Well, Mr. Stein is in jail right now."

Johnson: "He would find it kind of difficult to get there then, wouldn't he?"

Weintraub: "Mr. Forlano...he hasn't been out. He was out that once three or four years ago and never again. I don't think he's welcome in the town."

Commissioner Pearson then praised Weintraub.

Johnson: "Do you have any more questions?"

Pearson: "No, I don't have any questions, but in view of the turn of events that so many things are being made public, I think in fairness to the applicant, it ought to be pointed out that there are several of his acts that have brought him credit, one being that – and I apologize if I'm divulging something here publically [sic] that you wouldn't want divulged, and I would think that you would want yourself presented to the public in as fair a light as possible – that is the fact that he founded a project in Brooklyn to raise funds for a cancer treatment center, specifically, a cobalt treatment center, and through his efforts they have raised over $100,000 to date, all of which has been turned over to that hospital for the establishment of that center. I just mention that because so far everything has been negative, and I thought he deserved something positive."

Johnson continued:

Johnson: "Mr. Weintraub, do you or your counsel have anything you would like to say to the Board before..."

Bell: "I would just like to say this, that the applicant is well aware that he is seeking a privilege and he doesn't have a right to this license. A lot of information, I assume, comes into this board from outside investigators and it is very difficult for an applicant to defend himself against some of these things that are not documented, such as some reference to a credit application. I, for one as his counsel, know nothing about a credit application. I've never been confronted with one. I interrogated Mr. Weintraub and he is not aware of what credit application is being referred to, and in all fairness to him, if there is something that taints his application as the result of some credit application allegedly made, I would think that the best evidence of that would be the application itself, and I think that goes on down the line with any other acts that he's allegedly been involved in.

"We always have this problem of association. I can remember some of my associates in my business I've been involved with that might put me in a bad light, but I think it's a matter of degree in that regard – something in your people's judgment as to whether these associations are sufficient, whether they're simply social, whether they're occasional, whether they're steady, or whether they're business. I think this is something that you people have to decide. I just want to make the point that it's difficult for the applicant to be confronted with something concerning a credit application that he isn't even confronted with, and it may be a statement by some investigator in New York without verification. I don't say they would do something like that but it could happen on occasion, and for that reason I just ask the board to use its own good judgment in passing on this application."

The issue with an alleged credit application was raised because investigators claimed that Weintraub filled out a credit application and listed himself as an owner of the Dunes.

Johnson: "Mr. Weintraub, did you have anything that you wanted to add?"

Weintraub: "I don't know what else I can say. I've been coming to this town for 10 years and I don't know of an enemy I made in this town. I've made a lot of friends, people that I've brought out to Vegas in the last five years. I've brought out 20,000 of them and I've made quite a few friends, and these are the people that helped me build this hospital. I don't know what else I can say."

Johnson: "I guess we are ready for a motion."

Campbell: "I'll make a motion, Mr. Chairman. I'll make a motion that we deny the applicant on the grounds of unsuitable background, without prejudice to his employment in the Dunes Hotel."

Johnson: "A denial without prejudice to his employment?"

Campbell: "In the Dunes Hotel."

Johnson: "Okay. The motion... Do we have a second?"

(No response)

Johnson: "The Chair will step down and second the motion then. Would you like to carry the procedure through, Dr. Pearson?"

Pearson: "Am I in that position?"

Campbell: "I think you can call for it."

Johnson: "Alright, we'll call for the vote then."

"(Whereupon the roll was called by Mr. Johnson and the vote was as follows:

Mr. Campbell: Aye.

Dr. Pearson: No.

Mr. Johnson: Aye)."

How could there be such a strict denial when one commissioner voted in favor of Weintraub? It was a ridiculous decision that did not stop Weintraub from continuing the New York junkets to the Dunes. In fact, he continued running them into the 1980s, then took them to a different hotel.

It is very probable that the presiding governor looked into the situation of Weintraub and quietly let it be known that calling him forward for a suitability hearing regarding him continuing his junkets was not necessary. Kudos to him.

However, Weintraub would again face pressure from gaming authorities. In 1986, New Jersey gaming regulators, in a 4 to 1 vote, found him unsuitable for operating gambling junkets. They cited Weintraub's association with alleged organized crime figures as the primary reason behind their decision.[132]

After a 16-day hearing, Administrative Law Judge Richard Voliva, Jr. recommended that Weintraub be licensed, saying his connections with reputed mobsters and bookmakers were the "inevitable result" of his business.

The Division of Gaming Enforcement, however, disagreed and named several contacts Weintraub had with organized crime figures.

In December 1982, federal law enforcement officials taped a conversation between Weintraub and James Ida, a member of the Genovese crime family, in which Weintraub discussed his personal financial situation. The discussion took place in the office of Matthew "The Horse" Ianniello, a "capo" in the Genovese family. The following year, a New Scotland Yard criminal intelligence report read, "Weintraub has been identified by police and federal agencies as an associate of the Genovese family, being particularly close to Matty "The Horse" Ianniello, James Napoli, and Vincent "The Fish" Cafaro. Ultimately he is said to be controlled by Anthony Salerno."[133]

When Morris Shenker died on August 9, 1989, Ianniello offered his personal assistance to the business operations at the Dunes. Ianniello was very close to Robert "Bob" Amira, a relative of Morris Shenker by marriage. Amira and his wife Pat had several dinners at Ianniello's home in New York.[134]

Amira was brought under the scrutiny of the Nevada Gaming Control Board in 1980 for "unsuitable methods of operation" after his guests were given comps and casino credit. Some of those guests were associated with a New York crime family. Joseph Colombo, Jr., son of the late Mob boss Joseph "Joe" Colombo, was among the alleged Mob associates arrested or detained by Las Vegas police.

In 1981, Amira, Colombo, Jr., and three others were indicted in connection with a scheme that bilked the Dunes out of as much as $2 million.[135] Prosecutors pegged Amira as the group's "inside" man as he authorized airline ticket reimbursements of about $500,000 and approved $1.4 million in casino credit to the New York players, as much as $50,000 at a time.

---

132   *Asbury Park Press*, Feb. 27, 1986
133   New Scotland Yard Criminal Intelligence Report, Sept. 9, 1983
134   Interview with Pat Chzcowski, 2018
135   *St. Louis Post-Dispatch*, Sept. 20, 1981

However, Nevada District Judge Joseph Pavlikowski dismissed the case on technical grounds due to what he deemed an improper communication between the prosecutor and the grand jury foreman.[136]

Junkets organized then in New York, New Jersey, and Chicago for Las Vegas and Atlantic City were permitted only with the consent of organized crime families, and they expected a portion of the proceeds for themselves,[137] U.S. federal sources acknowledged.

As for Weintraub, Steve Wynn and his Golden Nugget agreed to acquire his list of junketeers for $900,000, unaware that the Nevada gaming authorities, on two occasions, disallowed Weintraub to purchase an interest in the Dunes due to certain of his associations. Consequently, the Golden Nugget eventually aborted its relationship with Weintraub because of what it described as its sensitivity to regulatory concerns. However, the Golden Nugget paid Weintraub $585,000 to settle the lawsuit he brought against the casino for failing to pay for his list.[138]

Big Julie went to the "Big Junket in the Sky" on September 21, 1997.

136   *Los Angeles Times*, Oct. 9, 1983
137   New Scotland Yard Criminal Intelligence Report, Sept. 9, 1983
138   State of New Jersey, Sept 19, 1986

CHAPTER 23

PUBLICITY BY
WYMAN-RICH-DUCKWORTH

The Sid Wyman, Charlie Rich, and George Duckworth team welcomed any and all kinds of publicity for the Dunes. They used every approach to getting it for free, including issuing press releases, offering complimentary food offers, providing photo opportunities featuring Tanya the Elephant playing craps and slots, printing pictures of glamorous showgirls, and allowing the casino to be used as a backdrop in movies and television productions.

Publicists Lee Fisher and Jean "Jeannie" McGowan were diligent in thinking up ways to get the Dunes brand into the media. The Dunes had a budget for print ads in the local and certain out-of-town newspapers that, in turn, published the hotel's puffy press releases.[139]

Exposure of the Dunes on the big and small screens included a February 1964 episode of TV's *Arrest and Trial* that was called "A Roll of the Dice." Filmed at the Dunes, the show starred Chuck Connors, Ben Gazzara, Nick Adams, and a cast of seasoned actors.

The episode had the look of a well-produced movie. The camera caught all of the glamour and feel of the real Dunes.[140] The opening sequence depicted the original Dunes' striped front with an iconic Sultan standing on the roof.

The baccarat and blackjack dealing sequences were genuine and not recreated by a Hollywood director. No sets were built for the casino scenes. The director, David Rich, was wise to film the inside of the Dunes in real time, as it was, with the actual crowds and ambient sounds. In doing so, he captured it accurately.

The show provided an inside look at the Dunes management team and some of the employees in their actual work settings. Dunes host Billy Snyder had a speaking part in a scene that took place in the baccarat pit with

139   Note: Las Vegas history aficionado Deanna DeMatteo's website http://www.lvstriphistory.com provides exacting details of many of the Dunes events and milestones. It is highly recommended.

140   Note: A link to this video is posted on the official website for this book: duneshotelvegas.com

actual dealer Ernie LaVerne. The baccarat footage was extraordinary because it depicted the use of real U.S. currency in the game, which Nevada gaming rules then allowed. They later banned it.

Sherlock Feldman, a longtime associate of Wyman, Rich, and Duckworth, was filmed as a roulette dealer. Feldman was a "crackerjack" wheel dealer, and the clip of him handling the game clearly showed his natural ability to deal and supervise the "wheel."

The appearances of Wyman and Rich as acting casino supervisors were rare indeed. It should be noted that Wyman was reluctant to be photographed or interviewed by anyone. At one point in the show, actor Adams asked for casino credit, to which Wyman answered, "Give it to him." This is one of the few clips that portrayed how a real casino manager handled such a situation.

The Dunes was also the location for a March 1963 taping of *The Steve Allen Show*, which was watched by many viewers throughout the U.S. Allen invited Dunes spokesman and gambler Feldman on the show to teach and play the casino games. That exposure was a major help in filling the Dunes' guestrooms.

Allen also filmed shows at the Thunderbird and at the Havana Riviera in Cuba, both connected to Meyer Lansky. It is probable that the connection between Lansky and Wyman paved the way for Allen taping at the Dunes or vice versa.

In 1970 *The Grasshopper* was filmed at the Dunes. Jerry Paris directed it, and Jerry Belson and Garry Marshall wrote the screenplay. It starred Jacqueline Bisset, football legend Jim Brown, Joseph Cotton, and Corbett Monica. Many of the interior and exterior scenes were filmed at the Dunes, including ones of the golf course, the stage areas, and backstage in the "Casino de Paris" dressing rooms. These took viewers behind the scenes of the Dunes' extravagant, 100-person show.

A film reviewer described it:

> "Mise-en-scene: The Las Vegas set pieces are spectacular to witness, filled with color, and akin to something from Hollywood musicals from the 1930s, 1940s or 1950s, but with more revealing costumes than would have appeared in movies from these eras. The settings in the film, in general, are of a high standard, accurately presenting where the main character is at a certain point in time. From the cozy family home in which Christine (Bisset) is first seen, to the Las Vegas theatre rooms, elegant hotel rooms and the tenement she shares with the gigolo, the mise-en-scene in *The Grasshopper* is one of its best aspects."[141]

The movie generated valuable publicity for the Dunes.

In one successful publicity stunt, Rich had a 50-square-foot replica of the Dunes, complete with its eye-catching sign, placed in the lobby of Las Vegas' airport, McCarran Field. The perfectly scaled model, which took nearly three years to complete, got the attention of travelers coming to and leaving Las Vegas.

Some of the Dunes' promotions were the boxing matches and related events that were held on the grounds between 1961 and 1990. They included public viewing of the boxers' workouts and press conferences, beginning with Ash Resnick and others. Some of the matches held at the Dunes were:

- Ossie Ocasio v. Randy Stephens, in which Ocasio, in a unanimous decision, retained the World Boxing Association's (WBA) World Cruiserweight title in 15 rounds on May 20, 1983.

- Greg Page v. Renaldo Snipes, a World Boxing Council (WBC) Heavyweight elimination bout, in which Page won in 12 rounds, by unanimous decision.

- Michael Dokes v. Mike Weaver, a rematch in which Dokes retained his WBA World Heavyweight title in a 15-round draw.

- Larry Holmes v. Tim Witherspoon, in which Holmes kept his WBC World Heavyweight title in 12 rounds, in a split decision.[142]

Gene Kilroy, a close associate of Muhammad Ali, was hired as a host and boxing consultant by Morris Shenker in the 1980s. Kilroy took hotel guests and owners to meet and greet and get their photo taken with the legendary Ali. Everyone knew who Ali was and wanted to meet him. Gracious, he treated every fan like they were the most important person in the room. Such strategies attracted high rollers without the Dunes having to pay the costs of hosting bouts.

The tennis match between Bobby Riggs and Billie Jean King garnered a great amount of publicity for the Dunes before and after, even though it was held in Texas. Riggs was a regular at the hotel-casino in the run-up to the event, and even before that, he was hired as its tennis pro. He was an attraction. He was known to be a decent hustler and admitted to betting on himself when he played at the amateur level. After Riggs lost the match to King, there was speculation that he did it on purpose, that he bet heavily on King to win and then intentionally underperformed to lose.

---

142   Boxrec.com

CHAPTER 24

DUNES: HIDDEN OWNERSHIP

S everal documents indicated that the Dunes had hidden owners during the 1960s. They included men from the organized crime groups in Chicago, New Jersey, New York, Cincinnati, Providence, and Boston.

An FBI informant was told by George Bieber, a Chicago attorney close to the Chicago Outfit, that Jake Gottlieb put together the Dunes hotel deal by providing his parcel of land and then acquiring 28 points in the gambling and hotel operation. Gottlieb allowed Gus Alex to acquire three points and Sam Giancana to obtain points in it. The informant said that Alex and Giancana were the only Chicago Outfit members who had points in the Dunes.[143]

Bieber hosted Alex in Hot Springs, Arkansas, in 1966 and dined with Leslie Kruse and an FBI informant. Kruse was entertaining Michael J. Kennedy, president of Local IBEW 134 in Chicago, who was known to be close to the Outfit and a special contact of Murray "The Camel" Humphreys. The informant relayed to the FBI that Bieber told him that Alex's strength in Chicago's organized crime was superior to that of Felix "Milwaukee Phil" Alderisio and that whenever Alderisio made unreasonable demands on Bieber, he used Alex to "cool down" Alderisio.

The following FBI memo, if factual, lends credence to the other FBI reports of Alex, Giancana, and Peter "Pete" Licavoli being hidden Dunes partners, which may have been just the tip of the iceberg. It is highly probably that Jimmy Hoffa and Allen Dorfman were involved, too.

An FBI file documented the following:

> "In 1962 Frank L. Caracciolo, also known as Frank Carroll, began construction of the Landmark Tower hotel-casino, originally called Landmark Hotel. By the end of 1962 he had expended approximately $2,000,000 in this venture. According to NY T-149 he attempted to obtain a $7,000,000 loan from the Central States Teamsters Pension and Welfare Fund of Chicago in 1963. He made this attempt through Nick Civella, Thomas Lococo, Sam Ancona,

FBI Memo, Oct. 21, 1966

and Roy Lee Williams. Both Civella and Lococo have previously been identified as members of the Kansas City Outfit. Ancona and Williams are officers in the Teamsters locals in Kansas City."

Gottlieb, who was close to Hoffa and bought the adjacent Landmark Apartments, had to know that Civella was involved in the Landmark Tower casino and had influence with Teamsters money.

"In September 1963, Carroll did receive a $5,000,000 loan from the Teamsters Pension Fund so that Carroll could complete the construction of the Landmark Tower. It should be noted that prior to the receipt of this loan from the Teamsters, Radio Corporation of America (RCA) had loaned another $3,500,000 to him in order to complete this project.

"NY T-143 said that the Teamsters loan was obtained for Carroll through the efforts of Roy Williams and Nick Civella.

"In December 1963, Carroll attempted to obtain another loan of $4,000,000 from the Teamsters in order to continue building the Landmark Tower. In September 1966 Carroll received another Teamsters loan in the amount of $5,500,000. NY T-145 said that Morris Klein, Max Jaben, and Nick Civella were instrumental in obtaining this Teamsters loan for Carroll. As a result of this Carroll reportedly granted to the Kansas City individuals a certain number of points in the gambling casino when Landmark Tower opened for business."[144]

If the memo is factual, then it is probable that Jake Gottlieb was more than just a landlord and was involved in the development of the Landmark Tower. At the very least, it was documented that he purchased the Landmark Apartments built near the hotel tower.

The following conversation was the first notation in FBI files that connected Gottlieb and Licavoli. The call was probably bugged.

Licavoli: "I want to get ahold of Joe over at the card room."

The FBI commented that this was possibly Joe Bernstein who was known to frequent the card room at the Stardust. They also postulated that it could have been Joseph "Joe" Pignatello, however, he was not known to hang out at the Stardust. Pignatello, a close associate of Mobster Giancana, operated as a front man at the Villa d'Este restaurant on Convention Center Drive in Las Vegas. Pignatello was one of the finest Italian chefs in Las Vegas.

144   FBI File NY-92-2300

Licavoli: "Is this Mr. Fisher? My son and Bobby Eugel have gone to Lake Tahoe with Sinatra and Towns?"

"Licavoli hung up and resumed a conversation with Jake Gottlieb."

Gottlieb: "He was on business here a couple of weeks ago."

Licavoli: "He was?"

"Then another call interrupted the conversation."

Licavoli checked into the Dunes on July 23, 1962, and Special Agent M.B. Parker observed him there in the lobby.[145]

Even though the one FBI document indicated that Alex and Giancana were the only "Chicago boys" in the operation at the Dunes, it did not rule out the possibility that Mob members from different cities were hidden owners, too. Gottlieb and other principal owners could have distributed points to others. There may have even been such arrangements and I.O.U.s carried over from the first owners of the Dunes.

Further, remember that William Vogler and Rollins Furbush involved American National Insurance Company (ANICO) in several deals with Gottlieb when they owned a piece of the Dunes. Not long after Gottlieb sold the Dunes buildings to Campbell Enterprises, a group started by Jake Gottlieb's brother-in-law Leonard Campbell, for a paper loss to himself, he then sold 86 acres of the Dunes golf course to M&R Investment Company for $3.3 million, which was $1 million more than the actual value. William Vogler and Rollins Furbush arranged for ANICO to lend $2.5 million to M&R Investment to buy the land.

As previously mentioned, Vogler and Furbush helped Gottlieb get another $4.15 million in real estate loans from ANICO.

Another piece of evidence revealing hidden owners of the Dunes was the recording by the FBI of a lengthy discussion in February 1962 between Giancana and Morris "Potsy" Pearl.[146] Pearl was a long-time associate of Chicago hoodlums and was observed at the Fourth of July party of Anthony "Tony" Accardo. Pearl was connected to leaders of the Jewish hoodlum and bookmaking element in Chicago. Here is an excerpt of the transcribed conversation:

> **Pearl:** "Let me ask ya something. When I was out in Vegas I stopped in the Dunes. You know Major Riddle. I hear you went out there. You know I know Sid Wyman. I'm pretty friendly with him. We sat down and were talking and he told me that he's in there since…

---

145   ELSUR 92-703-2-94 93, July 1962
146   FBI File 124-10202-10059, 1962

September. He and his partner, that Charlie Rich, little short fellow originally there from St. Louis. Before that he was in the Sands and before that he was at the Royal Nevada. And the last joint–he was in was the Riviera. Big tall heavy-set fellow, you know him.

"Anyway, Sid and I are pretty friendly and I said to him how the (obscene) did you wind up in this joint. So he said, Potsy, he said if Charlie and I don't get in here, they got me with blowing all this money, you know, that seven or eight million or whatever it was that he had invested in the joint. So I said, how much you got in here, Sid? He says, I got 50 per cent with this group. So like I say, I'm pretty friendly with him. I says, Sid, I says, how's business. Well, he said, Potsy, he said, I'll be honest with ya. Business is much better than it was when we got here... Major Riddle is a real nice guy but he don't belong in a casino. So he says now the setup is Major Riddle ain't got a word to say in the casino. Nothing. He walks around and everything but he's got nothing to do with the casino and the operation of it. He said, I'm here, he said, and Charlie Spretzel.

"So I said, well, is business much better? So he says, Potsy, he says, yes much better. As things go along, he says, if I behave myself and I don't gamble, everything's gonna be all right.

"I said, so how about the under the table stuff? He hesitates a second and he says, you know, I never go into an operation unless I can make money. Anyway, they have 50 per cent of it and there's a few points open, he says. So after all, he knows me and he knows that I know quite a few people you know around Chicago and he figured that if I were to invest in the joint that I might do the place some good and I might do myself some good. So I asked him, I said, how much would it cost to get some points? So he tells me, he says.[147] And then he says, maybe a little bit less. So I says, well, I'll think it over.

"But the main point is this. I said to him I might get a couple of guys that might be interested. So he says, well that's perfectly all right if you're the guy that I have to deal with. So I said, well Sid, I'll think it over and let you know. And if I decide I can always call ya. But when we talked we talked vaguely, you know what I mean? So I didn't pin him down or anything. I just said, Sid, show me what your handle is for the last month. So if he thinks as much of money as I think he does, he'll be more than happy to show it to me. So let me ask you your advice, Mooney. What do you think?"

---

147   It seems the FBI transcript accidentally left out a dollar figure at the end of this sentence

Giancana: "Well, didn't they sell that joint or they're gonna sell it or something? I understand they're just about to complete the sale."

Pearl: "The Dunes?"

Giancana: "That's what I heard."

Pearl: "Now, another thing he told me–so I asked him how much they pay him a month. So he said, they pay me $70,000 a month, you know, for the operation, but he says, they got me to get a commitment from the Bank of Chicago that's already written on paper. The contract is signed and he's getting so much money and they're gonna build 200 or 300 rooms on a high rise, so they'll have around 700 rooms, more or less. Then he says the rent will be $120,000 a month. But you tell me the joint is for sale."

Giancana: "Yeah. I heard that a couple of days ago."

Pearl: "Is that right? Let me ask ya this. If the joint isn't for sale, are you?"

Giancana: "Well, if it isn't for sale then I think it would be a good what ya call it."

Pearl: "Because the way conditions are, Sam, it looks like the only thing left open is Nevada. And with Sid, like I say, one thing about the guy, he's a real high-class fellow."

Giancana: "Maybe you can get that guy, what's that guy's name over at the Tropicana, no, the Stardust, what's his name, that, Ike. He'd be a good man to look out for your interests."

Pearl: "Yeah, he'd be a good man, but this Wyman, he's a high-class fellow. Number one, he's got two factions in that place – he's 50 per cent and then Jake, his end. It's not like Kell Houssels here, the one faction offsets the other in the graveyard counting. The main thing is, about this thing is that Sid has told me that no matter what the operation is, when he gets in there, he says, he takes two or three thousand off per shift. But the reason I say that to ya is you probably hear more about that than I do. Maybe you don't hear nothing, who knows."

Giancana: "I hear very little."

Pearl: "Do you think that it's a good – should I look further into it?"

Giancana: "Yeah, I think it's a good, a good what ya call it because if you build those rooms, your stock will go right up."

Pearl: "So you think I should look into it further?"

Giancana: "Sure. And if I were you, I'd try to cut the ticket."

From a mirror reading of Wyman, a process of putting oneself in the other man's place, one could deduce that Wyman offered the same deal to other "smart money" boys: Tony Giordano, Nick Civella, and Johnny Vitale. Or perhaps those individuals approached Wyman of their own volition.

The following FBI memo described yet another Chicago powerhouse suspected by the bureau to be secretly receiving Dunes dollars:

> "[Gus] Alex continues to reside in apartment IOC 1150 North Lake Shore Drive, Chicago, Illinois. He has been observed in his apartment building on a regular basis through December 8, 1966.
>
> "Alex reportedly visited the Mayo Clinic in Rochester, Minnesota, during October 1966. Alex reportedly continues to receive income from the arcades which are located on South State Street in the Loop area of Chicago.
>
> "Alex allegedly has a hidden financial interest in the Dunes Hotel, Las Vegas, Nevada."

The FBI possessed intelligence connecting Joseph Sullivan, Ben "Little Porky" Lassoff, and Johnny Baborian to Providence, Rhode Island, Mafia boss Raymond Patriarca.[148] An informant reported to the FBI in 1964 information about hidden owners and their points in the Dunes. The FBI documented this:

> "LV T-17 advised on February 19, 1963, that John Baborian had stated that Joe Sullivan, Raymond L.S. Patriarca, and 'Porky' (last name not known to informant) have three points in the Dunes Hotel with him [Baborian]. Baborian was attempting to settle some litigation he had with the owners of the hotel in the amount of $75,000.00.
>
> "LV T-17, on December 3, 1963, stated that Baborian was fronting for Patriarca in the ownership of their investment of the Dunes Hotel, Las Vegas, Nevada. Informant stated the three points actually mentioned above were in the M&R Corporation, which is the operating company for the Dunes Hotel. They also allegedly have a piece of the corporation that holds the real estate of the Dunes Hotel but the informant did not know the exact amount of this.
>
> "Baborian received a check in connection with their interest in the Dunes Hotel in the amount of $25,616.00 which he gave to Joseph Sullivan of Providence, Rhode Island. Patriarca, according to

informant, was to receive $1,000.00 from the above-mentioned check and also another $1,000.00 dollars within 30 days.

"In connection with the Dunes operation, LV T-17 advised that Mickey Redstone of Boston, Massachusetts,[149] had received a payment of $6,000.00 in connection with his interest in the Dunes Hotel.

"[Harry] Doc Jasper Sagansky also is financially interested in the Dunes Hotel. According to LV T-17, Baborian contacted Jake Gottlieb in Chicago, Illinois, concerning the points they allegedly own in the Dunes Hotel but Gottlieb refused to see him, claiming that he did not own any points in the Dunes at this time."

Baborian allegedly invested in the Dunes in 1955 with Sullivan and Patriarca. According to the FBI memo, when the Dunes went out of business shortly after opening due to gambling losses, the management of the Sands agreed to pay all outstanding obligations and operate the Dunes.[150] They were to reimburse the original investors of the Dunes at a later date should the resort become profitable. Baborian, as he was called by the employees at the Dunes when it opened, continued to receive kickbacks for at least a portion of his original investment.[151] He and Patriarca, at the time, were booking horse bets and operated a numbers business.

Later, an FBI informant reported this:

"On 10/7/64 the "informant advised that (Johnny a.k.a. Johnny B.) Baborian intends to meet with 'those guys in New York, Chicago, or Vegas' (apparently in relation) to his alleged ownership of points in the Dunes in Las Vegas.

"Raymond [Patriarca] instructs him to get the points that are owed them. Johnny agrees and said that he would get one point for himself, one point for Patriarca, and Joe Sullivan and 'Porky' can have a half point apiece.

"Patriarca asked Baborian whether Sam Giancana has any connections with the Dunes in Las Vegas. Baborian did not think so but he knew at one time the guys from Chicago were shylocking at the Dunes. Johnny was of the opinion that the guys from St. Louis have it and described them as being three Jews – one being Cutie [sic] Rich, Sid Wyman, and another Jew from St. Louis.

---

149   Note: Mickey Redstone (born Max Rothstein) was a former linoleum peddler, liquor wholesaler and nightclub operator. In 1959, when the business reached down the Eastern seaboard, it was incorporated as National Amusements. His children control Viacom and CBS
150   FBI Memo, Nov. 16, 1964
151   *Ibid*

"Johnny recalled that 'they' [the Chicago Outfit] once tried to get a piece of the Dunes through an attorney.

"The attorney was subsequently beaten up by this mob and Johnny conjectures that they might have obtained a piece of the Dunes at this time. Baborian said he would find out from Patriarca whether or not Giancana has any interest in the Dunes."

Another FBI document also supported the notion that Giancana secretly owned part of the Dunes. It read:

"Special Agent William Roemer, November 21, 1966, reported Giancana was interested in applying for immigrant status in Mexico for permanent residence there. Information obtained indicating possibility Giancana was no longer active leader of organized crime in Chicago area. Information received indicating Giancana has financial interest in Las Vegas casinos, The Dunes, The Tropicana, and The Stardust."[152]

Rich referenced skimming at the Dunes for the hidden Mobster owners in a conversation he had with a seasoned veteran of the gambling industry, who is 100 percent reliable.

Rich was an extremely clever casino executive who made decisions based on facts, previous experience, and occasionally, sought after advice. In those instances, he reached out beyond his tight inner circle of partners and casino executives for opinions from outside businessmen who had similar sensitive methods of operation and secrets that were not for public consumption. Rich never talked on the telephone about anything that could be incriminating, but instead, scheduled one-on-one meetings with several executives who had close associations with the Mob. Rich never met with these people in the Dunes or any other place that could be monitored, but rather in a locals' restaurant-bar.

Once, Rich arranged to meet such a person, a friend, at a Las Vegas bar-restaurant called the Plush Horse, which was about three blocks east of the Sahara. At the meeting Rich told his friend that the Dunes owners needed more cash to supply certain Mob individuals. When I asked the source who those people were, he said that they were probably the Chicago guys, as they often requested more money from him. "If you gave them $5,000, they wanted $5,000 more," he said.[153] Rich did not say the money was for Chicago. There certainly were other candidates, such as St. Louis or Kansas City, and perhaps Detroit.

152   FBI File, CG 92-349, 1966
153   Interview with confidential source, 2020

Rich was an experienced bookmaker who knew every phase of the gambling business, having gained live table game experience and knowledge of credit extension and other casino practices while working at the Royal Nevada, Sands, Riviera, and Dunes. However, Nevada gaming regulations had changed quite a bit since his early days in legal gaming. He wanted advice from an updated casino executive who maintained a squeaky clean operation. Rich also knew that two of his closest confidants at the Dunes ran things the same way that they did when they first got licensed. The advisor to Rich sensed that Rich perhaps did not have the greatest amount of confidence in his confidants' knowledge of gaming regulations, and these meetings suggested that Rich wanted information to stay out of trouble.

Though Rich did not ask about alternative skimming methods, his advisor shared with him that another way to skim money from the operation was via the purchasing department using kickbacks. He told him, "We would use a regular trusted vendor we knew and trusted. The vendor didn't want to lose the hotel's contract so he would do what we asked. If the produce or meat bill was $15,000 a week, we would have him charge us $30,000. We would let the vendor keep a very small portion of the extra $15,000 and give us the cash back. The vendor had no knowledge of who would get the money that he kicked back to us."

The source told me, "Another time Rich met me with an employment problem. One of his Mob associates wanted to put a friend to work at the Dunes. I explained to Rich that I had the same problem on occasion. I explained that a sheriff's card, which was required to work in Clark County, Nevada, would be a valid excuse to use. If the Mob's friend couldn't get a sheriff's card, he couldn't work. I told him who to see that would play ball.

"Sometimes it would work in reverse. There were some guys we wanted to work in the casino who could not obtain a sheriff's card because of a shady background, but if you talked to the sheriff, he was known to help you out, as long as you were straight with him."

CHAPTER 25

AUDIOVISUAL SURVEILLANCE IN VEGAS

A neighbor of this author was a former Central Telephone Company installer whom I'll call "Bruce." We discussed the FBI's wiretaps in Las Vegas and other places. He shocked me when he told me that every hotel where he did work had dedicated lines that were identified with a tag containing some special initials written on them. He said, "When I saw this type of line in the phone room of a casino, I was never to alter or change it. I knew it was some sort of wiretap. It was common knowledge to the installers."

Wiretapping and eavesdropping then were crimes under the laws of Nevada and other states. Under federal law, it was crime for anyone – either private citizens or FBI agents – to "intercept any communication and divulge or publish the existence, contents, substance, purport, effect, or meaning of such intercepted communication to any person."[154] Furthermore, both federal and state courts held that eavesdropping involving a trespass, like secretly installing surveillance equipment in someone's business, is a violation of one's constitutional protections against unreasonable search and seizure.

The FBI was on the trail of bookmakers and gamblers all across the U.S. in the 1960s. They placed phone taps, bugs, and surveillance teams in various Las Vegas locations, which helped them learn about illegal activities and the people behind them. They also planted agents disguised as tourists or bar patrons and even got people hired as employees to work in areas they wanted to surveil. These people, however, were easy to spot by the trained eye.

Sometimes looking at an individual's clothes and shoes revealed a particular detail that was incongruous with the setting. These abnormalities might be referred to as "tells." A tell is exactly what it means – a person subconsciously telegraphs or "tells" what he or she is all about by giving unknowing signals through clothes, actions, words, or presence. Some tells are not readily apparent and others are easy to pick up. It sounds unbelievable, but it's true. For instance, if I notice a player on a 21 game giving me more than a casual glance while I'm the pit boss in charge of the game he or she's playing, there's a reason for it. Perhaps the player is about to make a move against the house by taking unfair advantage with the dealer at the table. In other words, the player is making sure that the coast is clear for him or her to make their move. That's an abnormal condition. If the player was legitimate, he or she would be concentrating on the game, not watching the boss.

The FBI had a secret telephone surveillance program that was operated under the name "Henderson Novelty Company" (HNC) through a Las Vegas post office box. It started in May 1961 under the guise of being a "musical rental service." This was not the case. The real business of the HNC was eavesdropping for the U.S. government. According to news sources,[155] the FBI formed the company to strike a blow against organized crime. Central Telephone leased special phone lines to HNC that HNC used to eavesdrop on casino executives and others. The two entities signed this lease agreement on May 18, 1961. The bills for Central Telephone's service were to be mailed to the Henderson Novelty Company at 301 S. 11th Street – or to Post Office Box 1423.

The bills were to be paid in cash. A Central Telephone executive instructed his subordinates to supply the HNC with "whatever service they needed." These services included installing microphones in hotel-casino conference rooms and executives' offices. The devices were linked to the Central Telephone's landlines. They, in turn, were connected to the FBI's Las Vegas office. The microphone picked up normal conversations taking place around it but in the case of telephone conversations, it only captured the voice of the person speaking near it.

An affidavit of Marvin E. Barr, a special service supervisor for Central Telephone in 1962 and 1963, described the wily ways in which the Central Telephone got the secret equipment installed at the places where the HNC wanted them. "If the intended destination of the new [FBI] leased line was the Fremont Hotel, for example, a Central Telephone employee would then induce trouble on the Fremont Hotel telephone lines down at the central office.

"When the Fremont Hotel called to complain of its disrupted service, a Central Telephone employee would be sent out to make the repairs. Under the pretext of making the repairs, Mallory [a repairman] would install the new, leased line on behalf of the Henderson Novelty Company at its intended destination within the hotel in accord with his directions from

Bob Lee [an FBI agent]. After installation of the line, a service employee would correct the trouble he had induced on the Fremont Hotel lines. The bugs used apparently were supplied and may have been manufactured by the FBI."

For the FBI, these wiretaps were fruitful. In one secret surveillance tape, money wizard Meyer Lansky was heard bragging about the Mob's financial status. "We're bigger than U.S. Steel," said Lansky. The gangsters were in almost everything, foreign and domestic, with holdings ranging from Big Board securities to diaper services.[156]

In another recording, Ben Siegelbaum was caught discussing with Lansky the settling up of the money skimmed from Las Vegas casinos, including the Flamingo, Fremont, and Horseshoe. Siegelbaum suggested that they designate a special number for each person getting a portion of the skim to keep from the courier the recipients' identities and amounts received. Pretty smart. Meyer was given the number 1. Along with Siegelbaum, the list of skim recipients included Jack Cooper, "Jimmy Blue Eyes" Alo," a Teamsters official, Hymie Siegal, and a few others.

In 1962 and 1963, FBI agents monitored conversations originating in the conference room in the Desert Inn's executive office suite. One day, one of owner Moe Dalitz's key managers parked his car in the rear lot of the Desert Inn, got out, and decided to relieve himself in the empty darkness. When he looked around to see if anyone might see him, he saw a man perched on top of the nearby telephone pole along the lot's back border. The manager played it as if he did not see anyone. He got back in his car, immediately drove to valet parking, ran to find Dalitz, and explained what he saw.

Dalitz correctly surmised that the man on the pole was bugging the Desert Inn's telephones. Soon after, Dalitz obtained the services of "Whispering Bill," an electronics expert who could root out listening and other surreptitious electronic surveillance devices.

Once when Dalitz and co-owner Morris Kleinman needed to discuss something confidentially, they did so in the elevator ride from the executive office down to the main lobby, as they suspected their offices were bugged. The topic of that conversation was a particular person and event. Not long after the dialogue, the person the two men discussed was immediately subjected to the obvious scrutiny of the FBI. Dalitz was certain the person's name was only mentioned in the elevator.[157] He and Kleinman

---

156   *LIFE*, Sandy Smith, September 1967
157   Interview with confidential source, MJ, 2016

deduced that there had to be a monitoring device in the elevator. They brought in "Whispering Bill" who, sure enough, located the device.

"Whispering Bill" must have really helped the owners of the Desert Inn group because he was long remembered by a visit to his hospital bed, when he was dying, by a key Desert Inn executive and past Nevada Resort Association head, Alvin "Al" Benedict.[158] Dalitz never revealed Whispering Bill's real name to anyone.

Dalitz was steaming hot when he discovered that J. Edgar Hoover was bugging his offices, especially after friends of Dalitz made sure that the FBI director and his man pal, Clyde Tolson, were treated as first-class high rollers at various horse tracks they controlled, including the Del Mar race track. They made sure that Hoover won at least one bet while relaxing in the Turf Club there. Not far from the Del Mar race track was Mammoth Petroleum Company's office, owned by Dalitz associate, Lansky.

A tap was also hidden in the executive office of Major Riddle at the Dunes. On May 4, 1963, the FBI picked up a conversation in which Dalitz asked Riddle to help obtain a gaming license for Anthony Joseph Zerilli, son of Detroit Mafia boss Joseph Zerilli. The conversation, which follows, provides a vivid account of the quiet maneuvering and close relationships these individuals had with politicians in relation to the gaming business and the Mob:[159]

> **Dalitz**: "You've got to sit down and talk just like we're talking now. These people also have an (unintelligible). They're clean, but the ones these guys sponsor, his name is Zerilli, in Detroit – a terrific kid, a college graduate and he owns a license for the biggest race-track in Michigan. He's successful. Now you know."
>
> **Riddle**: "Well, you know if he holds a license for a racetrack, he can't."
>
> **Dalitz**: "He's going to abandon it. We – you and I – or you have got to see Governor [Grant] Sawyer and tell him it's best for our entire industry. The Frontier [New Frontier Hotel, directly across from Dalitz's Desert Inn], which is the only place left, has to be taken over by responsible people. Also, that we're disturbed over the Frontier's method of operating. That we understand the people that are going to build and put the money - not the operators, we won't tell him [Sawyer] about the operators. We'll only tell him about the builders and the financing people, so we can condition his mind."

158   Interview with Alvin Benedict, 2008
159   *Indianapolis Star*, Dec. 12, 1977

Riddle: "Moe, let me ask you one question. Anyone from Chicago?"

Dalitz: "No."

Riddle: "Well, let me tell you, if so, I won't go for it. Moe, you may have been pressured somewhere along the line and now you have to do something you don't want to."

Dalitz: "No, it's not that at all. It's nothing like that at all."

There was further conversation, including a statement from Riddle that Nevada was a clean state.

Dalitz: "The reason we want to express our feelings with Grant [Governor Sawyer]) is that with the lawyers that come in to him, he will already know that he is not hurting his two friends, Riddle and Rich in Las Vegas. See, there is only the one, Zerilli, and he's clean. That's all."

Riddle then recalled an incident in which Sawyer was offered $50,000 by a gambler with Cosa Nostra connections to get him a gaming license but said Sawyer eventually withdrew from the proposition. Riddle noted that Sawyer "will help us if he can."

Dalitz: "Listen, we were a lot of help to him. We really went the route for him, you know."

Riddle and Dalitz discussed donations for Sawyer's campaign and the fact that Riddle could not get the governor to veto a gambling regulation bill. Riddle then said he did not want to discuss Zerilli with Sawyer over the telephone.

Dalitz: "We can complain bitterly about the operation of the Frontier, and now there is an opportunity to make it a first-class operation. We can show that all of the hotel men see this problem and feel it would be good for the whole industry if the Frontier could be taken over by new people."

Riddle: "Now you know with all these things going on, he'll [Governor Sawyer] probably move down here and maybe we could use him as an attorney for us after he gets out of office."

Dalitz: "Are you kidding? Listen. We'll work strong with you on that. We've got to let Grant know that we are for a new and improved set-up over at the Frontier. There are going to be two lawyers representing the builders and the operator. Woodburn's firm is going to represent the builder and the money people, and Springer is going to represent the operator. You see, we don't want Grant to start off with a no. We want to let Grant know that we are most anxious to see a favorable change be made at the Frontier."

Riddle: "Grant will question the purpose of my visit, knowing that I don't have to come in to him for an okay for any builder."

Dalitz: "That's right, but these people are then going to represent a group of operators for licensing and they want to know beforehand if they will get licensed. They don't want to build and not have operators. So you tell him I don't know who they [the operators] are but I'm sure they're responsible people if law firms like that are representing them.

"You can tell Sawyer that these lawyers are going to come to him and request this and that you want him to know that the gambling industry feels it's good and will be for the benefit of the industry if the Frontier gets new operators.

"You tell him that you want him to listen to their request favorably and ask him to give it his blessings. Now Zerilli has an old man who has a bad reputation – former bookmaker. However, he is now very wealthy.

"The kid, Anthony, is vice-president and operator of the Hazel Park racing track in Michigan. At one time he was even going to buy the Thunderbird."

Riddle: "I'll tell you what I can do. Number one, I'll find out if there are any objections, and if so, tell him to at least keep an open mind on the subject."

Dalitz: But, Major, Ed Olsen [then chairman of the Nevada Gaming Control Board]), he'll fight it because of the FBI. The FBI will tell Olsen that Zerilli is the son of the old bookmaker and he'll say it's a part of the Mob trying to move in."

Riddle then left the room for a moment, and Dalitz told an unidentified person with him, "I won't let the lawyers go in to see him before Major gets his word in with the governor." After Riddle returned to the phone, Dalitz and he discussed whether Riddle should approach Sawyer without mentioning Dalitz's name. After further conversation, Dalitz and the second person left the Desert Inn office.

Then Riddle told Charlie Rich that James Hoffa of the Teamsters called him, and referring to the Zerilli bid, told him, "Maje, I want you to do it as a personal favor for me, and I've discussed it on the phone with Moe today."

Riddle told Rich he was not obligated to Dalitz but was committed to both Dalitz and Hoffa, could not double-cross them and would approach Sawyer casually. Riddle saying that he "was not obligated to Dalitz but was committed to both Dalitz and Hoffa," suggested that Rich and Sidney Wyman held the real power at the Dunes.

In all of the years of my employment at the Dunes, Wyman and Rich ran the show via George Duckworth, even after Morris Shenker bought into Continental Connector Corporation, which owned the Dunes Hotel. It was not until Wyman died that Shenker truly assumed the role as the owner.

On May 6, 1963, Riddle met with Dalitz and Anthony Zerilli, and in the conversation referred to his discussions with Sawyer.

> **Riddle**: "If you're clean yourself, regardless of what happened in the early days that will have no bearing on you. I told him [Sawyer] the whole thing. In fact, I told him I talked to you, Moe, and that Moe had assured me that the Desert Inn had no part in it."
>
> **Dalitz**: "That's right. We're just trying to get rid of an eyesore."
>
> **Riddle**: "That's right. I told him it was an eyesore to you across the street, and he agreed with me. So he's going to make a preliminary check on it. He's going to have some people make a preliminary check. He told me that if he [Anthony Zerilli] is not associated anymore, and I told him that he was going to give up the Hazel Park track, then it looks pretty good."
>
> **Dalitz**: "Major, I think it was fucking big of you to do this. I certainly appreciate it. That's good news for all of us."
>
> **Riddle**: "Now, I've always told you we like you, Moe, and he [Sawyer] told me, 'You have my blessing 100 percent.' Oh, one other thing he told me was that it looked okay if he's [Zerilli] not on the A.G. list (attorney general's list of undesirables). He said there were three things. One, that he's not on the A.G. list, that he himself was not involved with hoodlum operations."
>
> **Dalitz**: "You'll never be embarrassed about this, believe me."
>
> **Riddle**: "I told you, Moe, that when this guy gets out of office we should do something for him."
>
> **Dalitz**: "Oh, sure. In fact, I'm going to give his office some business now."

Later that month, however, Riddle had another meeting with Sawyer, and then had a meeting with Zerilli, with bad news.

According to the FBI:

> "Riddle advised Zerilli he had spent an hour with the governor and the governor had told Riddle that Zerilli could not secure a gambling license in the state of Nevada. Zerilli and several of his associates are on the attorney general's list. And Riddle quoted Governor Sawyer as saying that Zerilli would never be accepted at the present time. He also pointed out to Zerilli that his wife was also reportedly the daughter of someone who is not considered 'desirable.' Riddle stated he was sorry he could not do anything for Zerilli."

In 1972, the nationwide sports conglomerate then known as the Emprise Corporation, now Sport System Corporation, was convicted of violating federal racketeering laws by fronting for Zerilli and others in the licensing of the Frontier in 1966. Also convicted were young Zerilli and five others, including reputed St. Louis Mafia figure Anthony "Tony" Giordano.

The FBI also tapped the telephone lines at the Fremont and bugged owner-operator Ed Levinson's office. For the eavesdropping, the Central Telephone Company installed 25 private phone lines there and a transmitter on the hotel roof.

At the time, Levinson was hooked up with Bobby Baker, who was the Senate's secretary to the majority leader Lyndon Johnson, in the Serv-U Corporation, a vending firm. In addition, Levinson secured a $4 million Teamsters pension fund loan for the Fremont, which led to a fraud conviction of Hoffa in 1965.

From their audio surveillance, the FBI learned that Levinson, with Baker's assistance, was in the process of arranging to have a lucrative architectural contract for the federal building in Carson City, Nevada, awarded to Zick and Sharp, local Las Vegas architects. In exchange, Zick and Sharp only had to buy eight $1,000 tickets to a Democratic fundraiser in Washington, D.C.

FBI agents also overheard Levinson and Fremont Vice-President Edward Torres talk about their association with Lansky and his associates. They captured every word between the two in a special meeting, during which they discussed reducing the skim at the Fremont and Horseshoe and paying a dividend instead. Further, Levinson and Torres prepared a package of money to be sent to Lansky by "Niggy" Devine's wife Ida. She was to take the train from Las Vegas to Miami and pass it off to Levinson's brother-in-law Richard Kornick.

Another time, the FBI captured Levinson and Siegelbaum, an investor in the Fremont, discussing Ben Dranow, who was avoiding federal authorities and was going to be indicted over business dealings he had with Levinson and Hoffa.

Several months later, in April 1963, Levinson decided to redecorate his office. In the course of this beautification project, he asked the telephone company to move his phone. The man assigned to the job was an installer who was friendly with Levinson. Because Levinson comped good workers with free shows and meals, the installer did the work on his day off. In doing so, he uncovered the bug.

News of this discovery spread through the Las Vegas gambling fraternity. In July, two more lines leased to Henderson Novelty and two more bugs were discovered at the Sands, of which Frank Sinatra and Dean Martin owned a piece. Two bugs were found in a bungalow of Carl Cohen, the Sands casino manager.

At that point, all of the wise guys knew they were being targeted but did not know who was behind it and why.

Levinson went to Central Telephone for some answers. After basically being told to hire an attorney, he retained Edward Bennett Williams of Washington, D.C. Williams was politically connected and represented well-known individuals, including Baker and Hoffa.

In February 1964, Williams, on behalf of Levinson, filed a multi-million dollar damage suit against the Central Telephone Company, charging breach of contract, conspiracy, and invasion of privacy. In the months that followed, depositions were obtained from company officials, in which they described, in considerable detail, the FBI's role in the bugging. Levinson was indicted for skimming, entered a plea of "no contest," and was fined by Federal Judge Roger Foley. This effectively dropped his lawsuit against the FBI and Central Telephone.

After discovery of the bug in Levinson's office, the FBI ordered all of the secret lines disconnected and changed the telephone bill responsibility from Henderson Novelty Company to another made-up company called "Clark Associates." Clark Associates' address was the same as that of the Las Vegas FBI office.

The FBI complained about the amount of Central Telephone's bill and never paid it. At this time, in early 1964, when the FBI's investigation into Baker was going full bore, they suddenly realized that there was a big connection between Levinson and Bobby Baker. The FBI was looking into allegations that Baker bribed individuals with money allocated by Congress and arranged sexual favors in exchange for votes and government contracts.[160] Baker later was convicted in 1967 of tax evasion, conspiracy to defraud the government and theft. He went to prison in 1971 and served 15 months.[161]

The FBI was afraid that eavesdropping on Levinson and his related lawsuit might affect the Baker investigation, as Baker was making plenty of noise and crying foul. He told the U.S. Senate Rules Committee in February that the FBI was after him and that "my privacy of communication has been invaded by agents of the government." On the same day Baker said this, Williams supplied the press with pictures of the listening device that was discovered in Levinson's office. In addition, Levinson appeared as a witness in the Baker investigation and testified that the "agents of the executive branch of government and the Central Telephone Company" bugged his telephone in "an unconstitutional invasion of my privacy."[162]

Baker's attorneys served the Las Vegas FBI agents with a $2 million damage suit and possible criminal prosecution. They described the FBI's eavesdropping and wiretapping as "a studied, well-organized, amply-financed criminal conspiracy."[163] This was not the kind of language ordinarily employed to describe the law enforcement activities of the FBI, often called "the most respected, feared, and incorruptible police force in U.S. history."[164] Certain FBI agents were subpoenaed to explain what they knew about the wiretaps and secret phone lines in the Fremont.

The outing of the FBI's wiretapping and the related lawsuits really stirred the pot. They discredited the FBI and the Department of Justice and embarrassed Hoover and the White House. They threatened the success of several government cases, such as the ones against Baker and Fred Black, a Washington business consultant, lobbyist, and neighbor of Lyndon Johnson. Black also was a close friend of Johnny Rosselli and Lansky associate, Jack Cooper. *Washington Post* reporter Richard Harwood wrote that Desert Inn executives Dalitz, John "Johnny" Drew, and Ruby Kolod, then under federal indictment, could perhaps beat the raps they faced.

Ultimately, these public events perhaps weakened the federal government's drive to eradicate organized crime in the U.S. but particularly in Nevada.

---

160   *The New York Times*, Jan. 26, 1964
161   *The New York Times*, Nov. 17, 2017
162   *Miami Herald*, March 3, 1964
163   *Washington Post*, Richard Harwood, June 26, 1966
164   *Washington Post*, Richard Harwood, June 19, 1966

CHAPTER 26

THE DUNES: NICK CIVELLA'S VISIT

While on pretrial bond travel restrictions imposed by the Western District of Missouri, Nicholas "Nick" Civella checked into the Dunes on August 6, 1974, under the name "J.P. Sanders" and gave a fictitious address. Sanders and his female companion, listed as M. Gaustella, were booked to stay for six nights. The Dunes gave the two VIP treatment, comping their suite, food, and beverages, on the order of Sid Wyman. He instructed Artie Selman, casino host, to handle the special arrangement for Sanders.

Selman was previously the captain of the Regency Room restaurant at the Sands when Wyman owned 6 percent of the property. Because Selman made salads and other special food for him, Wyman called him the "salad king." Selman was a likeable guy and showed a keen interest in sports and horse betting.

In 1969, Selman joined Nathan "Nate" Jacobson and Ed Levinson as food and beverage director at the Bonanza in Las Vegas. Levinson and Jacobson purchased the property from one-time Dunes percentage owner, Kirk Kerkorian, who had acquired it previously from Larry Wolf and 20 partners who just could not make it work.

Wolf, however, had foresight when planning and building the Bonanza. The western motif was impeccably executed with a hard-wood-floored casino and a genuine railroad car dining room. The entertainment offerings, which included Lorne Greene of *Bonanza* TV show fame, were good. Wolf planned to buy the adjacent motel and land and erect a 900-room tower there. This certainly may have been the motivation Kerkorian needed to build the MGM Grand Hotel & Casino on this same site.

After the Bonanza, Selman partnered briefly with Jacobson at Kings Castle at North Lake Tahoe. The two visited the Dunes at Wyman's request, and afterward, Wyman hired Selman as a casino host.

After receiving instructions from Wyman regarding Civella, Selman, for one, placed a card on file in the Dunes casino's cashier cage, which contained this note:

"A.S. IS TO MEET MR. SANDERS ONCE ARTIE GIVES
O.K., THIS MAN CAN GET ANYTHING HE WANTS, VERY
IMPORTANT THAT ARTIE IS CALLED BEFORE GIVING
CREDIT.

O.K. FOR WHATEVER HE WANTS.

ANYTHING HE WANTS."

This became a problem for the Dunes. Sanders, really Civella, was the head of the Kansas City Mob. He, along with his brother, Carl "Cork" Civella, was in Nevada gambling regulators' "black book" and had been since its inception in 1960. The state considered those in the book "persons of notorious and unsavory reputation" due to their criminal backgrounds and disallowed them from entering any Nevada casino as long as they remained on the list.

Nick Civella was born to Italian immigrants in Kansas City, Missouri, and began his underworld career committing robberies, bootlegging, and gambling. In the early 1940s he became a Democratic Party precinct worker on the North Side of Kansas City and met Mob Boss Charles Binaggio. Civella became a working soldier in the Binaggio family, which made inroads in controlling the police force in St. Louis and Kansas City.

After the murder of Binaggio, Civella emerged as the successor and head of the Kansas City La Cosa Nostra.

Civella was extremely intelligent, had a keen sense of intuition, and cautiously planned every step he took. Nothing went on in Kansas City and St. Louis that he did not know about. His attendance at the historic Apalachin meeting of Mafia bosses is virtually unknown by most researchers.

Civella was a crafty behind-the-scenes dealmaker and quasi-politician who made it his business to stay close to the Teamsters local in Kansas City. He was friendly with Godfather Carlos Marcello of Louisiana, who was captured on tape by the FBI talking about his influence on the Teamsters leadership.

In the late 1950s, Civella, according to an FBI memo, tried to buy a piece of the Riviera from Sid Wyman and "Ice Pick Willie" Alderman, who were close friends and among the Riviera's owners. Another owner and front for the Chicago Outfit, Ross Miller, reported it to the Nevada Gaming Control Board (GCB).[165]

---

165   Note: According to FBI records: "Miller is alleged to be Hoffa's and Sidney Korshak's man

The FBI's record concerning the event read:

"W.E. "Butch" Leypoldt, Member, Nevada Gaming Control Board, advised the FBI in May 1960 that Ross Miller told the Nevada Gaming Control Board that Nicholas Civella of Kansas City had approached owners of the Riviera Hotel to purchase an interest in the Hotel with a guarantee of a $10,000.00 monthly return. The approach was made on two or three separate occasions to Willie Alderman, former part owner of the Riviera Hotel, to Ben Goffstein, president of the Riviera Hotel in 1960, and Sid Wyman, part owner of the Riviera Hotel in 1960. Alderman, subsequent to the contact by Civella, sold his interest in the Riviera Hotel."[166]

This memo shows that Civella made repeated attempts to obtain a hidden interest in the hotel and was rejected. The actual dates of Civella's requests were probably in late 1958 or early 1959. This proposal to Wyman and other Riviera owners was certainly a major push by Civella.

This rejection and Miller subsequently going to the GCB with information were very unusual. Goffstein was the president, and Wyman's group was the second biggest investor in the Riviera. Were Wyman, Goffstein, and Alderman aware that Miller informed the GCB about Civella? If they were, it might have fractured the relationship between Wyman and Alderman on one side and Ross Miller on the other. Wyman and Alderman would not have supported providing information to the GCB.

The memo also noted that Wyman was a bookmaker out of Kansas City, which was not entirely accurate. He did take layoff action in St. Louis, which meant he certainly may have booked bets out of Kansas City.

The memo stated that Alderman sold his interest in the Riviera after being approached by Civella. Alderman had a criminal history of strong arm arrests, and when this incident occurred in 1960, he was awaiting trial for extortion. He remained friends with Wyman until his death.

Civella at some point may have discovered what Miller did and confronted Alderman, Wyman, and Goffstein about it. A long-time Dunes employee, who later worked at the Stardust under Allen Glick, heard talk in the Dunes pit among the bosses that Wyman was afraid of Civella. Wyman ensured that his personal suite of rooms on the fifth floor of the Dunes high-rise was protected by a special door with a secure locking system.

in the HRI [Hotel Riviera Inc.]. ... LV T-12 advised that Ross Miller in furnishing this type of information to the Nevada Gaming Control Board certainly considered the possibility that he was risking his own life in doing so."

166   FBI File, Nevada Gambling Industry, Nov. 16, 1964

There is no proof that Civella succeeded in obtaining a hidden interest in the Riviera or any other hotel then. But if you asked this writer if it was probable, the answer would be, "Circle the game, don't bet that he didn't."

Once the GCB members learned that Civella was staying at the Dunes, they insisted that the management ask him to leave, which they did on August 9. Next, the GCB charged the Dunes with knowingly and willingly allowing a "black book" listee to stay at their property, and worse, paying for him to do so. In fact, board members claimed, several Dunes personnel knew Sanders' identity before he checked in. They further claimed that the Dunes only asked Civella to leave once gaming agents mandated they do so. Thus, according to the GCB, the Dunes violated Nevada Revised Statutes 463.154, 463.151(3) and Gaming Regulation 28.090.

Casino owners and operators who allowed a "black book" member into their gambling establishment faced losing their gambling license because associations between "undesirables" and gambling licensees were "inimical to the best interests of the State of Nevada and to its gaming industry."[167] However, instead of revoking any licensees, the gaming regulators fined the Dunes $50,000 and required that Wyman, majority owner and operator of the Dunes, apply as a key employee.

Dunes attorney Herbert M. Jones, brother of Cliff Jones, who was the first Dunes attorney, personally appeared before the GC in March 1975 and requested a stay of the execution of its original order. Then Phil Hannifin, on behalf of the GCB, reduced the fine to $10,000. He also rescinded the order that Wyman apply as a key employee, on the basis that it should not have been included in the disciplinary action.

This is certainly a case of some questionable, perhaps politically motivated actions by the GC and GCB.

---

167   Nevada Gaming Commission Regulation 28.090

CHAPTER 27

SHENKER AND CIVELLA

In December 1974, Morris Shenker, then a stockholder of Continental Connector, the parent company of the Dunes, was awaiting his gaming license hearing for complete control of the Dunes. When interviewed by Dennis Baughman of the *Las Vegas Review-Journal*, Shenker said he unequivocally knew nothing about the gaming authorities' case against the Dunes regarding Civella's visit, before an associate brought it to his attention. This vague statement is hard to fathom for several reasons. For one, Shenker was a part owner of the Dunes at the time of the incident.

Also, in their investigation of Shenker for a possible license, Gaming Control Board members discovered he and Civella were connected. In fact, Shenker was indeed deeply involved with Civella.

The FBI had several files on the relationships between Shenker, Civella, and St. Louis crime members, and these files were available to the Gaming Control Board. One of them[168] from 1967 indicated that money was being skimmed at the Dunes and in part going to St. Louis Mobsters. It noted:

> SL T-6 stated that the St. Louis group gets a "flat rate" out of the Dunes Hotel, and as a result they are not bothered with the operations or take at this casino. Their only concern is keeping "their boys" at these casinos out of trouble with the law, which might result in the suspension of their Nevada gambling license.

Further proof of Shenker and Civella's association was captured by FBI agents and reported years later, on October 10, 1978, in a *New York Times* article. It read:

> "Federal agents intercepted a telephone conversation between Mr. Shenker and Nicholas Civella, whom Federal officials identified as chief of organized crime in Kansas City.
>
> "According to an affidavit filed in Federal court here by Shea W. Airey, an F.B.I. agent, Mr. Shenker called Mr. Civella at a Kansas City lawyer's office where Mr. Civella wrongly believed he would avoid surveillance.

"Mr. Civella, who is now dead, advised Mr. Shenker to go to Rancho La Costa, a resort near San Diego financed in large part by teamster pension fund loans, and meet with Roy L. Williams, then the president of the teamsters' union, to discuss Mr. Shenker's financial problems. Two days later, the affidavit said, Mr. Shenker went to Rancho La Costa.

"In the affidavit Mr. Airey described his understanding of the situation in this way: 'Loans of questionable merit, including a loan to the Dunes Hotel-Casino, have been approved through [Allen] Dorfman and Civella influence at the teamster pension fund. Also, informants say Nick Civella has a hidden interest, fronted by Shenker, in the Dunes Hotel.'"[169]

That conversation between Shenker and Civella was orchestrated through a call to the Kansas City firm of Civella's attorney, Quinn & Peebles. On October 10, 1978, Civella's driver and bodyguard, Peter Tamburello, was intercepted placing a call from a Quinn & Peebles telephone to a number for the Dunes in Kansas City.

Carl Caruso answered and was asked by Civella to confirm that he gave something to a person who was supposed to read it. Caruso relayed that he did. Caruso, whose Mob code name was "Singer," was a Kansas City junket organizer for the Dunes and was known to local FBI agents. Civella instructed Caruso to contact the man and tell him "Mr. Quinn" was waiting for him to call back. While Civella waited on one line, Caruso telephoned Shenker and instructed him to call "that party at Mr. Quinn's office." Civella called Caruso back immediately and told him to say only that Mr. Quinn's office would like the person to call them, not that a guy was waiting. Civella stressed that the person they were talking about understood "Mr. Quinn's office" and that Caruso should also.

Shortly thereafter, an incoming call was intercepted over the Quinn & Peebles phone line, in which the caller asked to speak to Mr. Quinn. The switchboard operator first stated Mr. Quinn was not in, but when advised the caller was Shenker, stated that "he" was on another line. Civella then answered and was addressed by Shenker as Mr. Quinn, although the speakers seemed to be well acquainted.

That conversation between Civella and Shenker was this:

Civella: "Well, here, here, tell you what I called you about."

Shenker: "Yeah."

Civella: "Down below there."

Shenker: "Yeah."

Civella: "All them people are down below."

Shenker: "Yeah."

Civella: "Did you know that?"

Shenker: "No."

Civella: "Down there at a, at a, at a, at a, La Costa."

Shenker: "Oh, yeah."

Civella: "Did you know, you know everybody's there?"

Shenker: "Yeah, I knew they were going to be there. They're not there now, are they?"

Civella: "Yeah."

Shenker: "Oh, I didn't know that."

Civella: "Well the fellow from here, local."

Shenker: "Yeah."

Civella: "I think, it, it, he got, if, he's got to be able, he's got to be able to reach for you."

Shenker: "All right."

Civella: "But here, let me make a suggestion to you."

Shenker: "All right."

Civella: "Why don't you reach for him?"

Shenker: "All right."

Civella: "You know who I am talking about?"

Shenker: "Sure, the man, the man a, from your place."

Civella: "Reach for him."

Shenker: "All right."

Civella: "And tell him if you got the time, you'd like to come down there and talk with him."

Shenker: "I can go over there and a …"

Civella: "That's what I want you to do."

Shenker: "I'll go over there."

Civella: "And I think, I think we'll be able to start a legal matter, get it all started and maybe you can draw up all the papers and stuff and have, you have your conversation with him, but I suggest that you have it just you and he."

Shenker: "Oh, let me ask you this. Do you know how long they'll be there?"

Civella: "I think only 'til Thursday. I don't know if they're going to leave Thursday or if they're going to be there Thursday."

Shenker: "Find out, I'll find out."

Civella: "You find out."

Shenker: "And if I can see him, what I could do is go there. Tomorrow night, I could go there."

Civella: "I'll tell you, it would be a good thing if you could."

Shenker: "It would be an excellent idea. I thought they were coming next week. I don't know ..."

Civella: "No, no it's, they're there now and a, I suggested to him that he get ahold of you, but you know how, they get tied up."

Shenker: "Yeah."

Civella: "So if ..."

Shenker: "What I'll do, I'll call over there and find out, and I'll probably go there tomorrow night."

Civella: "Right, and when you do get with him, it's a, just you and he."

Shenker: "Right."

Civella: "And just a, you know, tell him what's on your mind."

Shenker: "Okay."

Civella: "And he, he'll tell you what he can do for you."

Shenker: "All right."

Civella: "And then, then, it is very likely that you may come through here in a few days?"

Shenker: "Well, I was going, planning to go through there within the next two, three days."

Civella: "All right, will you call our office, let us know?"

Shenker: "Sure."

The man that Civella mentioned from his place was believed to be Teamsters official Roy Lee Williams.

Immediately after his conversation with Shenker, Civella unsuccessfully attempted to reach Sam Ancona, another Kansas City Teamsters official who was at Rancho La Costa, using a Quinn & Peebles telephone. On October 12, 1978, Shenker was observed at Rancho La Costa, and the next day, Williams and Ancona were observed arriving in Kansas City on a private jet from the San Diego area.

The purpose of the meeting between Shenker and Williams was to discuss a planned illegal move to give Civella a stronger position in the Tropicana. The plan was for the Teamsters pension fund to transfer $91 million from control of the asset managers to the "B&A account" to pay off the loan that had been given in the so-called M&R Investments transaction involving the Dunes. The FBI called it a "conspiracy to commit offenses involving the fraudulent sale of securities to the investing public."[170] Along with Civella, Shenker would have benefited, too. The transaction was attempted but foiled by the FBI.

Later, a Senate subcommittee unsuccessfully questioned Williams about the meeting at La Costa:

Marty Steinberg (subcommittee chief counsel): "In October 1978, did Nicholas Civella tell you to meet with Morris Shenker at La Costa to attempt to get the Teamsters fund to pay off Mr. Shenker?"

Williams: "I rely on my privilege."

Chairman Sam Nunn: "You are relying on your Fifth Amendment privilege?"

Williams: "Yes, sir, my Fifth Amendment privilege."

Steinberg: "Did you, in fact, meet with Morris Shenker on October 12, 1978, at La Costa?"

Williams: "I rely on my Fifth Amendment privilege."

Steinberg: "Did you discuss with Morris Shenker on October 12, 1978, an arrangement whereby you would attempt to manipulate the Teamsters fund assets to pay off Mr. Shenker?"

Williams: "I rely on my Fifth Amendment privilege."

Steinberg: "Did you use your influence on the present trustees of the Teamsters fund to attempt to get them to increase the benefits and administration account by $91 million to circumvent the independent asset managers?"

Williams: "I rely on my Fifth Amendment privilege."

Steinberg: "Mr. Williams, are you aware of a meeting between Allen Dorfman, Joe Lombardo from Chicago, and Nick Civella at the Crown Hotel in Kansas City on March 25, 1979?"

Williams: "I rely on my privilege of the Fifth Amendment."

Steinberg: "Mr. Williams, after that March 25 meeting, did you personally have a meeting with Nick Civella and Allen Dorfman on April 23, 1979, at the residence of Phil Simone to discuss the manipulation of Teamsters fund assets?"

Williams: "I rely on my Fifth Amendment privilege."

Steinberg: "Did you know Allen Dorfman?"

Williams: "I rely on the privilege of the Fifth Amendment."

Steinberg: "Did you discuss with Nick Civella in April 1979 a meeting he had with the representative of Joe Aiuppa from Chicago concerning the fact that the Chicago mob wanted direct access to your power and influence in the Teamsters fund?"

Williams: "I rely on my privilege under the Fifth."

Steinberg: "Did you at the instruction of Nick Civella insure that John Dwyer resigned as executive director of the Teamsters Central States Pension Fund?"

Williams: "I rely on my privilege under the Fifth Amendment."

Steinberg: "FBI wiretap affidavits reflect that Nick Civella was able to gain a hidden interest in the Tropicana Hotel in 1975 by helping a financially troubled owner with a Central States loan. Did you take any part in the granting of this loan to the Tropicana Hotel in 1975?"

Williams: "I rely on my Fifth Amendment."

Steinberg: "Have you ever participated in filling certain Teamster positions with relatives of Nicholas Civella?"

Williams: "I rely on my Fifth Amendment privilege."

Nunn: "We just have a few more questions, Mr. Williams. We have hundreds of questions we would like to ask you, but I have asked counsel, in keeping with our practice, since you are obviously asserting your constitutional privilege under the Fifth Amendment, to summarize those questions. We, of course, again urge you to testify, but we respect your right under the Fifth Amendment."

Williams: "Thank you."

All this time, Shenker had no idea he was being monitored by the FBI, but he once commented to an associate that agents were probably across the street in a room at Caesars Palace intercepting his calls and watching his movements. Indeed, the rooms at Caesars Palace had a direct unobstructed view of his office and balcony.[171]

---

171   See the notes referring to Morris Shenker as the "Silver Fox" in the addendum.

CHAPTER 28

CIVELLA AND SKIMMING

A t the time that the Dunes visit brouhaha was playing out, in summer 1974, back in Kansas City the four Spero brothers challenged Nick Civella for his home territory. When they tried to get chummy with the Teamsters, Civella and his crew went into action to eliminate the competition. Between 1978 and 1984, all four Spero brothers were murdered, and Civella retained control of the Kansas City Mob. Before Carl Spero was killed, he identified three of Civella's associates as having attempted to assassinate him. The heat was on Civella, but there was no evidence or proof that he was involved in the killings.

Kansas City FBI agents eventually obtained court orders to wiretap Civella and in 1978 put listening devices in the Virginia Tavern, which Civella and his crew frequented. Through that wiretapping, the agents got more than leads to the Spero crime. They uncovered information about Civella's investments and schemes in Las Vegas and learned that he was "behind the scenes," calling the shots at several casinos there. For the FBI, it was like hitting oil. Eureka. They got names and places close to Nick and his brother Carl Civella and their hoodlum friends in Kansas City, as well as information about secret partnerships they had with the Mobs in Chicago, Cleveland, and Milwaukee.

They learned that Nick Civella got control of the Tropicana and did so through Joseph Agosto. Agosto, who was not a U.S. citizen, later told the FBI that he settled in Kansas City with a relative, Sadie Porrello, a made man with two sons, Angelo and Joseph, who were associated with the Kansas City Mafia. Later, Joseph was gunned down by the Mob, and years later, Angelo was jailed for contempt of court for not testifying about the Kansas City Civella Mob having infiltrated the Tropicana.

The process of Civella taking over the Tropicana began in roughly the mid-1970s, when majority owner Deil O. Gustafson, a Minnesota banker, brought Agosto in as vice president of the resort's production company to manage its show, "Les Folies Bergere." Agosto, though, was much more than a show producer; he signed payroll checks for the casino employees.

Agosto previously ingratiated himself with Gustafson by using Civella's influence to block a Teamsters pension fund loan to the group headed by Ed and Fred Doumani, longtime Las Vegas operators,[172] that was trying to take over the hotel.

In late 1974, the Doumani brothers moved into management positions at the Tropicana and infused $1 million into the financially troubled resort. The State of Nevada approved an emergency order for the Doumanis to take it over. Later, the FBI accused Gustafson and Agosto of trying to inflate the stock of the Doumani group, the company that was going to merge with the Tropicana.

Agosto met Nick Civella in 1973 while promoting a legal assistance fund that Teamsters officials could sell to their individual members. Agosto paid $75,000 to Civella for an introduction to the right Teamsters officials. John "Angel" Amaro, associated with Agosto, Joseph in the promotion, was gunned down in his home, and Kansas City police linked Amaro to the Kansas City Mob.

Agosto paved the way for institution of a skimming operation at the Tropicana, in which money was to be moved to the various crime families that were in on the deal.

According to FBI agent William Ouseley, assigned to the Kansas City office: "The intercepted conversations indicate that the Kansas City criminal organization has for years maintained a hidden interest in the Tropicana Hotel Casino in Las Vegas, Nevada, and that the aforementioned Joseph Agosto, who was then entertainment director at that location, was the Kansas City crime group's principal management agent and we developed this fact that our interceptions were made up of a series of regular telephonic contacts between Carl DeLuna, one of the ranking organized crime figures and Joe Agosto. These interceptions or these conversations were normally over pay phones. They are replete with the use of code names, for the principals being discussed, ambiguous and elusive references and the use of Sicilian language. And Agosto would report on and sought direction on a variety of topics through this telephonic link, and as regarded more important management decisions, personal meetings were arranged or messages were sent through the mail, often to places not outwardly connected with our organization, such as lawyers' offices or by means of couriers."

The FBI learned that Civella was and remained very close to Roy Williams, a key Teamster official. Williams met Civella in the early 1950s at a local political event. They eventually became good friends and performed favors for one another. In a deposition, Williams revealed that Civella told him about the Apalachin summit, at which, he said, "Civella had been blessed as boss of Kansas City." Civella also told Williams that he was afforded latitude to have working relationships with Mobs in other cities. Civella slowly drew Williams under his control. Civella's personal Teamsters boss, Williams was willing to do whatever he could for Civella. The two would have a relationship that lasted several decades, from the 1950s through the '60s and '70s to the time of Civella's death.

Williams later testified, in 1985, that Civella first approached him about a Teamsters pension fund loan in 1974.[173]

"[The Teamsters Union Central States Pension Fund] was then giving pensions to our union members. There was money in trust and he [Civella] had asked me if I would go along on a couple of loans," Williams said.

Williams met Hoffa in 1938. "He [Hoffa] called me and asked me to come to Kansas City to help out the strike," Williams said. "The strike lasted 29 days, if I remember right. And after that time, I was asked by Mr. Hoffa to come in and take over Local 41 as a trustee and for me to go to Wichita and get whatever authority I needed from that local union to come to Kansas City and take over as trustee under a man, at that time, by the name of Frank Brown. When this strike was over they asked me to stay in Kansas City and take over this local under Frank Brown."

Williams' relationships with Civella and La Cosa Nostra were addressed in a 1986 President's Report on Organized Crime – Business and Labor Unions:[174]

> "Roy Williams's rise in the Teamsters from 1981 to 1983 was directly linked to his association with organized crime. Williams admitted to the Commission what law enforcement believed for several decades: that Williams had a 'special relationship' with Nick Civella, the boss of the Kansas City family of La Cosa Nostra. Williams and Civella were members of an informal but powerful group of five men. The members of this group, which changed over time, included Civella, Williams, Bill Cerman, Tim Moran, and Sam Gross, the former head of the Carpet Layers, Dyers, and Cleaners Union. The 'group of five' met periodically to settle disputes and to decide which candidates for public office would receive political nominations in the Kansas City area.

173   *The Town Talk*, Nov.1, 1985
174   "The Edge: Organized Crime, Business, and Labor Unions: Report to the President and the Attorney General/President's Commission on Organized Crime," 1986

"The association between Williams and Civella began in the mid-1950s after Williams, knowing Civella's position as the head of the Kansas City LCN [La Costa Nostra], met with Civella to discuss their 'relationship.' The two agreed to assist and promote each other.

"Civella would promote Williams's IBT career with other mob-controlled IBT [International Brotherhood of Teamsters] leaders, especially Hoffa, and reward Williams financially. Williams in turn, would promote Civella's interests, by such means as the placement of people that Civella favored in IBT or industry jobs, and the exertion of influence on the Central States Pension Fund to make loans and arrangements that would benefit organized crime.

"Civella became the man to see to get favors from Williams and the Teamsters. Chicago Outfit territorial boss Joey Lombardo, who was convicted with Williams for attempting to bribe a United States Senator, was overheard by Federal agents importuning Civella: 'Nick, you're the only one who can get to Williams, to have him listen and act. Williams has to be the one to do it, and it has to go through you.'

"Other intercepts reveal that when members of the Chicago LCN approached Civella to obtain favors from Williams, Civella sometimes adopted a protective tone, saying, 'I want to protect Roy. He's a friend of mine.'

"Illustrative of Civella's hold over Williams is a 1979 meeting of Williams, Civella, Allen Dorfman, and Sam Ancona in Kansas City. Dorfman wanted significant new Central States Pension Fund business to be directed to Morris Shenker, Jimmy Hoffa's lawyer-confidant. Williams disagreed. As a result of the disagreement, Williams had to attend a midnight session at the house of an LCN associate at which Dorfman and Williams presented their cases to Civella. Ultimately Civella sided with Williams and tore up Dorfman's contract with Shenker. In this instance, Williams, an IBT president and a fiduciary for the union, had to appeal a union decision to the La Cosa Nostra crime boss of Kansas City.

"Throughout the three decades of their arrangement, Williams and Civella met periodically. When Civella and Williams could not meet or talk on the phone for fear of being observed or overhead, Sam Ancona – an associate of the Kansas City La Cosa Nostra, president of Teamsters Joint Council 56, and IBT International representative – was messenger to both. Ancona and Williams exchanged messages in the union's parking lot outside Williams's office. As a reward, Ancona used Williams's name and gained authority to obtain favors and other assistance from other IBT officers.

"Roy Williams became president of the IBT in large measure because he had the backing of organized crime. When incumbent president Frank Fitzsimmons died, members of La Cosa Nostra set out to choose a new Teamster president. Although there was agreement that someone controlled by La Cosa Nostra should be chosen, the negotiations centered on which faction would have its candidate elected. The key groups were the Kansas City, Chicago, Cleveland, and New York families. One of the participants in these negotiations was Angelo Lonardo, underboss of the Cleveland La Cosa Nostra. Lonardo, now serving a life sentence in federal prison, has provided the FBI with inside information on precisely what transpired."

Morris Shenker's son, Arthur Shenker, invested $1.5 million in the ailing Tropicana on May 7, 1975, which was the same day the Nevada Gaming Control Board (GCB) filed a petition to remove the Doumanis as operators of the hotel. According to the *Las Vegas Review-Journal*:[175]

"Shenker made it clear that he would like to invest in the resort as an owner rather than as a lender. Shenker got the money to make the loan from the Bank of Nevada and placed it into the Tropicana Hotel account in the same bank. Morris Shenker guaranteed the signature, it was confirmed by the Shenkers.

"'If approved by the Nevada Gaming agencies, I intend to be active in the management of the hotel. The Tropicana is one of the finest resorts on the Strip,' said Arthur Shenker."

This writer was asked by Arthur Shenker if I wanted to work in the baccarat at the Tropicana. That did not happen, however, because the GCB ruled that Arthur Shenker's loan to the Tropicana was an illegal loan to a gaming licensee.

About two years later, in September 1977, Jack R. Urich, owner of Urich Oil Company of Southern California, applied to the Nevada Gaming Commission (GC) to invest $6 million in the expanding Tropicana.[176] Urich proposed buying half of the 65 percent Tropicana ownership stock held by chemical heiress, Mitzi Stauffer Briggs. The other owners of the Tropicana stock were Deil Gustafson, 20 percent, with the remaining 15 percent split between Hacienda Hotel owner Paul Lowden, columnist Earl Wilson, Mel Wolzinger, and the estate of Jim Hamil.

---

175   *Las Vegas Review-Journal*, May 8, 1975
176   *Las Vegas Sun*, Sept. 2, 1977

Briggs reportedly agreed to the sale and indicated through a spokesman that Urich's investment would lead to his being nominated to become chairman of the board of the hotel's operating corporation. In the meantime, however, Tony Torcasio, former Tropicana casino manager and friend of Arthur Shenker, was named chairman. As such, Urich would become secretary of the corporation if he was approved as an investor.

The GC denied Urich's request because of his relationship with Agosto.[177]

Eight years later, in 1985, Urich and six other men were charged with fraudulently juggling millions of dollars among commercial accounts in a dozen banks in Nevada, Hawaii, Canada, and Mexico in an elaborate check kiting scheme. The charges followed a 2½-year FBI investigation.

The 52-count indictment alleged that Urich, Richard Fenner, James Whetton, Nicholas Tanno, Donn Smithe, Aref Hanif, and Jaime Zurcher conspired with the late Agosto to carry it out. The indictment indicated that the check kiting practice caused bank account balances to be "artificially and unlawfully inflated by the coordinated exchange of non-sufficient funds checks between bank accounts."[178] This allowed account holders to receive the unauthorized use and benefit of monies belonging to the banks and exposed the banks at which the accounts were located to potential loss. The scheme resulted in the demise of Las Vegas-based Mineral Bank of Nevada and in the loss of more than $1 million to San Francisco-based Crocker National Bank, the indictment charged.

On February 24, Urich was acquitted by a jury on all charges of participating in the check kiting scheme. Four of the other six men charged along with Urich already pleaded guilty in the case, while another defendant, Fenner, a former Mineral Bank officer, was found guilty on 20 counts of the scheme. Zurcher was imprisoned in Mexico.

Several of 1,100 pages of affidavits, containing information gleaned from telephone and microphone surveillance of top Mobsters in Kansas City and Chicago for nine months in 1978 to 1979, confirmed Civella's hidden interest in the Tropicana and the Kansas City Mob's secret control of it. The FBI alleged that the Tropicana's major stockholders, Gustafson and Briggs, knew about and approved the arrangement.

The documents stated that, for one, Agosto was overheard saying that Civella would have the final voice in the granting of the Teamsters pension fund loan to the Tropicana and that Civella would secretly invest money in that hotel resort.

177   *Los Angeles Times*, Al Delugach, Nov. 13, 1985
178   *Ibid*

The affidavits also noted that the FBI overheard Vito DeFilippo of the Joseph "Joe" Bonanno organized crime group say that once that loan to the Tropicana went through, Civella's Kansas City Mob and several other organized crime groups would have hidden ownership in it.

The Tropicana needed that Teamsters pension fund loan, but did not get it. Between 1974 and 1978, it was in the red and hardly able to pay its bills, and that jeopardized its chances of getting it. So to improve the financial picture, Civella put a temporary stop to all skimming at the resort.

An FBI intercepted, day-long meeting between Civella, Agosto, Carl Thomas, and Carl "Tuffy" DeLuna on November 26, 1978, indicated that skimming was taking place at the Tropicana, as they discussed how it was done. DeLuna was a high-ranking member of the Kansas City Mob and in charge of maintaining records of the skims taking place in Las Vegas.[179]

> **Thomas**: "You grab the cashier's keys from the cashier. We take the key, open the box, and snatch the money, just grab the cash like this."
>
> **DeLuna**: "We've been doing it for months, stealing."
>
> **Agosto**: "Like to me, it's like robbing candy on a baby."

Thomas suggested that they open a sports book at the Tropicana. "For one good reason, it would give us another tool to grab some money."

> **Civella**: "Yeah. Each racket's getting tougher and tougher."

Agosto remarked that he had other opportunities to skim utilizing his executive and administration sources. "I told him, I told Carl myself that I'm not a thief on the ground floor. I'm the thief from the fourth floor."[180]

> **Thomas**: "Absolutely brilliant, with the show and the Swiss bank accounts and everything. That would be great, and the money in Switzerland."

A further affidavit[181] indicated that Civella and Shenker hired Carl Thomas as casino manager at the Tropicana to ensure the Teamsters pension fund granted the property a loan.

Civella and Shenker also hired Don Shepard as Thomas' assistant, and Billy Caldwell. During 1976, Shepard frequently stopped in at the Dunes, then run by Morris Shenker, not only to play poker, but also as

---

179   See the Addendum regarding DeLuna's detailed notes
180   FBI Memo, Nov. 26, 1978
181   FBI Affidavit, Aug. 30, 1978

someone visiting a certain Dunes executive, likely Shenker. It is very probable that Thomas also met with Shenker at the Dunes as well.

However, the person who observed Shepard at the Dunes did not know Thomas so could not positively identify him.

Shepard was a frequent visitor to the Dunes. He was observed playing high stakes poker in the card room and also visiting management in their private offices. I knew Shepard from my first job in Las Vegas at the Sahara, where I worked in the dealer's room serving coffee and helping the waiter. I made plenty of tips and learned the basics of gambling from all of the varied personalities and talented dealers, box men, and floor supervisors. Shepard was a nice person and a good casino man. He was extremely friendly to me and also was good natured.

According to another affidavit[182] Civella's Kansas City group had a concealed interest in the Dunes, and Shenker was their front. Further, a Teamsters loan to the Dunes was approved by Allen Dorfman, pension fund trustee, upon Civella's influence. Those two had a strong say when it came to pension fund loans and controlled some of the kickbacks paid for those loans.

Other FBI affidavits revealed that meetings took place between Civella's Kansas City Mob and the Chicago Outfit to discuss the skims at the various Las Vegas casinos.

They stated that on October 22, 1978, Civella and his wife traveled to Chicago for the day to meet with high ranking members of the Chicago Outfit, Joseph "Joey Doves" Aiuppa and Jack "Jacky the Lackey" Cerone. Civella reminded his nephew, Anthony Chiavola, Sr., who at the time was an acting Chicago Police Department lieutenant, to keep the impending meeting absolutely secret from everyone. "*Tu ci dici sente caro mio noialtri non facemo discourse a famigli,*" he told him. This translates to, "You say to him, listen, my dear one, we, we do not discuss the Family."

Civella also instructed Sr. to have his son, Anthony Chiavola, Jr., a Chicago police officer, meet him at the airport and then take Civella's wife to Chiavola's home on Chicago's North Side. Civella was to arrive at the Chiavolas last, according to Mob protocol.

At 12:30 p.m., the FBI observed Aiuppa and Cerone arrive in a car driven by Angelo LaPietra. The meeting lasted until 5:30 p.m. Whatever was discussed is not completely clear nor was it revealed by the FBI, but another meeting was scheduled for January 11, 1979. In another conversation the FBI picked up, between DeLuna and Agosto, it was confirmed that a subsequent meeting would soon be taking place in Kansas City.

182   FBI Affidavit, Sept. 24, 1978

Sure enough, on January 11, 1979, the FBI observed Cerone arrive in Kansas City and then travel to Carl Civella's home. He remained there for several hours before returning to Chicago. Thomas also was likely there, as FBI agents overheard a conversation in which he was told to attend.

The purpose of these meetings was outlined in another FBI affidavit:

> "The Outfit has diverse economic interests which require coordination, negotiation, and consideration of the economic interests of other organized crime groups in other areas of the country. All of this illegal activity requires close coordination between this criminal enterprise and its confederates in Las Vegas, Chicago, and elsewhere."[183]

The competing interests in Las Vegas were casinos, and the primary concern to all was the skim, the money that was being taken from the properties and distributed to various Mob factions.

Typically, the money skimmed in Las Vegas was taken to Chicago. Then LaPietra delivered it to Chiavola, Sr. of Chicago who, in turn, took Kansas City's share to DeLuna and Cleveland's share to Milton Rockman.

DeLuna was the liaison between Las Vegas and Kansas City, and between Chicago and Kansas City.

In February 1979 the FBI discovered and seized DeLuna's records, which were meticulous and thorough. They then had their handwriting expert, Leon Waggoner, confirm that in fact it was DeLuna's handwriting on the documents.

An article about the skim and DeLuna's role in it, by Roy Rowan in *Fortune*, is extremely revealing. Here is an excerpt:

> "FBI agent William N. Ouseley found the books hidden in the basement, attic, and ventilating ducts of DeLuna's house and had no trouble cracking the code that camouflaged the various entries. No. 22, for example, stood for Chicago boss Joe Aiuppa. No. 21 was Aiuppa's enforcer, Jackie Cerone. The nicknames 'Fancypants' or 'Beerman' applied to Frank Balistrieri, the Milwaukee boss. 'ON' (for *onorevole*, meaning honorable in Italian) was Nick Civella, the Kansas City Mafia chief and DeLuna's boss.
>
> "DeLuna was a cautious accountant. If he did not actually see the money change hands, he said so to distance himself from any defalcations. He embarked on an important mission in 1978. His assignment: to force Allen R. Glick ('Genius'), the licensed owner of the Stardust and another casino-hotel, the Fremont, to sell out or

risk the murder of his two children. The mob, which had begun to distrust Glick, thought it could skim more under another owner. In Las Vegas, DeLuna met first with three members of the Mafia's skimming team: Carl Thomas ('CT' in the ledger page below), a gambling boss at the Tropicana; Joe Agosto ('Caesar'), casino manager at the Tropicana; and Frank 'Lefty' Rosenthal ('Craze'), the mob's man at the Stardust. Next he met Glick, who two days later announced his casinos were for sale.

"Four days after DeLuna left for Las Vegas, his wife, Sandy ('San'), followed for the weekend. True to form, DeLuna's accounts show that he paid 'personally for San's fare out and in and also for any personal purchases.' As one of DeLuna's cronies confided to the FBI: 'He kept track of who got what, just so if anybody asked, he could show everything was right, that he hadn't grabbed a dime of that money for himself.'

"The carefully kept records were only partially responsible for the jailing of Chicago's then Mafia leaders, Aiuppa and Cerone. The testimony provided by Glick, who told about the threats the mob used to force him to unload his casinos, also helped.

"So did the mob's avarice. The Chicagoans might never have turned up in DeLuna's ledgers if they had not tried to make the most of their role as conciliators. They tried to mediate between the bosses in Kansas City, Milwaukee, and Cleveland who got to squabbling over the casino spoils in 1975. For their efforts the Chicago mob demanded a 25% fee.

"DeLuna's books depict Mafia benevolence toward both the greedy and the needy. In 1979, $1,500 went to then Kansas City Teamster chief Roy Williams, code-named 'Rancher,' who used his influence to help arrange Teamster loans to the mob-controlled casino-hotels. The skimming money also supported a welfare program. DeLuna once noted that after he, Civella, and the others divided some $30,000, smaller amounts ranging from $1,000 to $3,000 were handed out to elderly Mafiosi and to the families of imprisoned mobsters."

The Dunes appeared in DeLuna's records, including the names of employees who worked in the executive office and two telephone numbers, the main public line and Morris Shenker's private extension. This was more proof of the link between Shenker and Civella. Waylon Manheim, who was a known associate of the Chicago Outfit and who traveled in many social circles in Palm Springs and other California cities, relayed the following about the Windy City Mobsters.

"The Chicago Outfit loved to vacation in Palm Springs," he said. "The weather was just the opposite of Chicago's snow and rain, plus there was 365 days of golfing. Tony Accardo lived there six months at a time and many of his associates were frequent visitors. Accardo's regular hangout was the Marquis hotel that had all the finest amenities and was in close proximity of several great golf courses. Accardo dined at Dominick's, Tommy's steakhouse, Melvyn's and others.[184]

"Melvyn's was a favorite of many celebrities such as Frank Sinatra and many Chicago Outfit associates such as Frank Buccieri. Melvyn Haber, the founder, once asked Buccieri, 'I am waiting for the Outfit to put a street tax on my operation. When are they going to show up?'

"Buccieri told Melvyn, 'Don't worry. No one will bother you here. They want no trouble in Palm Springs. This is their vacation spot.'

"Melvyn had another club in downtown Palm Springs that Tony Accardo and some associates visited and ordered a bottle of wine. The waiter opened the bottle at the bar and then served Accardo. Accardo sent the bottle back and insisted on an unopened bottle. The probable reason is that he didn't want to be poisoned."[185]

Manheim was a regular guest of this small restaurant with a 30-room boutique hotel and of Melvyn's. One evening, Las Vegas and casino gambling was the topic at the bar at Melvyn's, and the name Allen Glick and the Stardust came up. Previously, Manheim ran into Glick at the Sporting House in Las Vegas a few times, and a local restaurateur introduced the two. Since, Glick and Manheim were on a first name basis.

At Melvyn's bar, an Outfit associate, whose name shall remain confidential, talked about the problems Glick encountered at the Stardust and the court trial that resulted in several Chicago Outfit members going to prison. The associate asked Manheim:

"You know, we just want to bury all this old business and just want to talk to Allen. That's all. Just a friendly talk. Do you think you could arrange it?"

"I don't think I want to get involved," Manheim answered. He never went back to Melvyn's. He sensed that behind the 'friendly talk' there was a hidden agenda that would not be too good for Glick.

---

184   Interview with Waylon Manheim, 2020
185   *Ibid*

For U.S. Mobsters, their competing enterprises in Las Vegas were casinos. The Chicago Outfit and the Kansas City Civella Mob had a long-standing disagreement over their mutual interests. They included the casinos owned by the Argent Corporation – the Stardust, Fremont, Hacienda, and Marina. Front Allen Glick purchased them from the Recrion Corporation with two Teamsters pension fund loans, one for $62.75 million, the other for $25 million. Organized crime families in Milwaukee and Cleveland also got in on the Argent skim.

A high level manager at the Stardust maintained that Chicago only wanted money and more money. "They weren't operators, and didn't know anything about operating a casino. Johnny Drew, the first president of the Stardust, was an example of bad management.

"He was always drunk and loved to con anyone out of a buck for the pleasure of it," said the casino official.

In a monitored conversation, DeLuna was heard complaining about the Chicago Outfit.

> "They don't care about nobody, that's their attitude," he told Carl Civella. "They don't give a fuck about nobody. But to me it's showing us a discourtesy for them to treat somebody that we call our acquaintance, our friend – Joe Agosto is our friend."[186]

Further evidence of the dissension between the groups is FBI wiretap documentation of the Kansas City group's plan to carry out a killing.[187]

The skimming eventually culminated, in the 1980s, in numerous indictments, convictions, and sentences. In late 1981 Nick and Carl Civella and 10 other Mob figures were indicted for skimming at the Tropicana. Agosto was the prime government witness against them.

The same year, the Teamsters' Williams was indicted for trying to bribe a U.S. Senator from Nevada. Eventually, he was convicted and became a government witness,[188] the first Teamsters president to do so.

As for skimming at Argent Corporation's casinos, a Kansas City grand jury indicted 15 people in 1983. Most of them went to prison. Nick Civella, however, died before he could be brought to trial.

In October 1985, nine organized crime members were tried on charges of skimming more than $2 million from Las Vegas casinos. Williams testified for the prosecution.

---

186   *St. Louis Post-Dispatch*, Nov. 14, 1979
187   Senate Hearing on Organized Crime and Violence, testimony of FBI Special Agent Ouseley, April 1980
188   *The Kansas City Star*, "Mob Rule," kansascity.com

In 1986, Chicago Outfit bosses Aiuppa and Cerone were convicted of skimming profits from Las Vegas casinos. They told associates that the U.S. government never could have brought their case to trial without DeLuna's records.[189] Subsequently, the Chicago Outfit and the Kansas City Mob severed all ties on an order from Joseph Ferriola, who assumed power in the Windy City after Aiuppa and Cerone went to prison.

---

189 *Chicago Tribune*, July 30, 1987

CHAPTER 29

CIVELLA AND
THE APALACHIN MEETING

N ick Civella and Joseph Filardo were two of nine others who were questioned but not recorded as being at the historic Apalachin summit of the American Mafia, held at the home of Mobster Joseph "Joe the Barber" Barbara, in Apalachin, New York, on November 14, 1957.[190]

An estimated 100 Mafiosi from the U.S., Italy, and Cuba are believed to have attended. Allegedly Vito Genovese, then head of the renamed Genovese family, initially called the meeting as a way to exert his new power as Mafia Chieftain. Others, such as author John Scarne, claimed the meeting was to decide would control Cuba.

The discovery of the Apalachin meeting was pivotal in law enforcement realizing that the Mafia was a large organization that had its own "commission" that dictated policy, settled internal disputes, designated areas for family control and ownership, and coordinated major criminal conspiracies. The confab allowed those present to mingle with other Italian "commissioners" and discuss ways to make money and infiltrate certain businesses.

When state police and federal agents broke up the gathering, several guests hurried off, including Civella and Filardo. However, more than 65 men were rounded up at Barbara's stone mansion that sat on a hilltop 15 miles west of Binghamton. Federal agents were astounded to discover one of the men they apprehended was Genovese, once called the "King of the Rackets" by former New York Governor Thomas Dewey. Genovese's name was just mentioned a few weeks earlier in connection with the Mob killing of Albert Anastasia, the undisputed head of Murder, Inc. Some of the top hoodlums of America's underworld told investigators they were in Apalachin to inquire about the health of Barbara, a friend. Law enforcement called the summit a gangland convention.

As for Civella, once he was back in Kansas City, Missouri, he was questioned at a local police station. Two years later, on October 30, 1959, Major

Halvey, chief of detectives at the Kansas City Police Department, made that interview available to FBI Special Agents Carlton M. Hansen and Leo V. Ewing.

It revealed that during the questioning, Civella stated that he was out of Kansas City and upon returning the previous day, was informed that Halvey desired to talk to him. When asked if he had an attorney with him, Civella responded that he had no reason to have an attorney as he had not committed any crime, in Kansas City or elsewhere.

When questioned about the events that happened in the Apalachin neighborhood on the day of the raid, Civella admitted that he was picked up by New York State troopers near the town of Endicott while in the company of Filardo. They were riding in a taxicab at the time, he said, because they were on business and did not want to bother with a car. Civella stated the troopers took them to a small New York police station, where Civella and Filardo furnished identification, answered a few questions about the raid, and then were released. Civella told New York police that he did not know Barbara or what events the state police were talking about.

When asked if he was in the Apalachin area on the date in question, Civella stated that he accompanied Filardo on a business trip as he does when Filardo's son cannot. Civella stated that he merely went along for the trip and paid no attention to whom Filardo was contacting. He added that he knew nothing about the bakery business and would prefer that Filardo answer any questions regarding their contacts as he did not want to embarrass anyone. When asked how they traveled back to New York, from where they came, Civella stated again that he chose not to answer as it might prove embarrassing to innocent parties.

Civella did not admit to having any acquaintances or connections in the east. When officers read him all of the names of the people they knew were at the Apalachin meeting, Civella denied knowing any of them. He stated that he always lived in Kansas City and did not know anybody in that New York vicinity. He never heard of Barbara and had no reason to go to the home of a stranger, he said.

Civella stated that he had learned about the Apalachin raid by reading about it in the newspapers. He and Filardo happening to be in the vicinity around the time of the raid was merely a coincidence, he said, and while it admittedly looked suspicious, they were in no way connected with the people arrested. Civella further stated that he realized, due to the situation he found himself him, that he would probably have to answer to other investigating agencies, and for this reason, he preferred not to answer any more questions. He stated that he planned to confer with an attorney.

When questioned about his possible connection with the Mafia or any other organized criminal group, Civella stated that all he knew of the Mafia was what he read in the newspapers. He admitted knowing a few people around various cities but stated that, to his knowledge, there was not any close-knit organization among Italian persons other than perhaps ones based on family connections or close friendships.

When Civella was asked about his means of livelihood, he stated that he had a few investments and owned a couple of trucks, which netted him an income. He stated that he did not live grandly and that it did not take much to take care of him and his wife. He admitted that he had gambled with friends on occasion in the past and had good luck doing so but considered himself "retired" from that.

At the completion of the interview, Civella was told that the police department was dissatisfied with his explanation for being in the Apalachin area and that he probably would be called back for additional questioning. He stated that he was available at any time and that he wanted to cooperate with any agency to straighten out the matter. He again commented that due to the seriousness of the matter, he was going to consult with an attorney about his rights when it came to further questioning.[191]

The fact that Civella and Filardo were at the Apalachin meeting confirms the power that these men had. Civella was a very low ranking, but key, member of the commission because he had expertise in gambling. Not everyone there had experience operating a hand-book or a gambling casino. In 1957, many of them did not see the opportunity in Las Vegas gambling or anticipate that it would grow so immensely. Many of the "commissioners" were satisfied to stay in the fields that they knew best, which included extortion, shylocking, transport theft, corruption, vending, food and liquor supply, and various other scams.

Racketeering was cushy where they lived because they controlled their local governments, paid off the politicians, and in exchange, were allowed to operate freely as long as they did not deal drugs to the locals or burglarize residents' homes. Politicians and the police could easily turn a blind eye to bookmaking and back room gambling. Often, they did not see the harm in making a $20 bet on football game or taking a chance on numbers, where 50 cents might bring someone $500. Those taking payoff money were often thankful for the extra cash that they could spend on their family's needs and expenses. As long as the streets were clean and no mayhem was taking place, Mobsters got a green light.

191   FBI File, 124-10214-10333, Nov. 3, 1958

CHAPTER 30

THE ST. LOUIS CRIME FAMILY

The heart of the St. Louis Mob for more than five decades starting in the 1930s were Tony "Tony G." Giordano (born 1915)
and John "Johnny" Joseph Vitale (born 1909), best of friends and
business associates. In contrast to Giordano, who was all business and
had a temper, Vitale was informal, polite, and called by many the "gentleman gangster."

In the 1930s, Vitale was investigated and arrested in connection with
murders, beatings, and bombings and received a felony conviction for possession of a large amount of heroin in St. Louis. Vitale and others smuggled
heroin into St. Louis and Detroit, which were distribution points for cities
across the U.S. In his late 20s at the time, Vitale was brash and in step with
what the New York La Cosa Nostra chiefs were peddling.

Giordano's first arrest was in 1934, when Frank "Three Fingers" Coppola and he were charged in the killing of a St. Louis deputy constable.
(Coppola had established the heroin smuggling ring.)

Giordano and Vitale were closely associated with Al Capone's Mob in
Chicago and later with Anthony "Big Tuna" Accardo.[192] Giordano and Vi-
tale's smuggling shipments were arranged in Europe by Mobster Charles
"Lucky" Luciano.

Vitale and Giordano received a piece of the bookmaking and point shaving business of gamblers Dave Goldberg and Steve Lekometros. James
"Horseshoe Jimmy" Michaels, who was the leader of the Syrian hoodlum
element in St. Louis, was also getting a piece of Goldberg's bookmaking
business.

In September 1963, an informant told of Giordano mentioning that
Goldberg and Steve "The Greek" Athineos were handling the gambling for
his organization in St. Louis. The informant also told of Vitale mentioning
that Goldberg was handling the bookmaking action for him. Vitale added
that he met in Kansas City in August with Nick and Carl Civella and Thomas
"Highway" Simone to compare notes and discuss the "heat" being applied to
them by the federal and local authorities in St. Louis and Kansas City.

---

192   *St. Louis Post-Dispatch*, June 6, 1982

They alleged that Vitale, Giordano, and Nick Civella were receiving skimmed profits from points they held in Las Vegas casinos. Vitale and Giordano controlled Clark Vending Machine Company in Las Vegas.

The FBI had information that Vitale, Giordano, and Ralph Caleca were part of the St. Louis family of La Cosa Nostra. These individuals were associated with various other members throughout the U.S. Vitale and Giordano were involved with all of the gambling activity in St. Louis and were close associates with Sid Wyman, Charlie Rich, Dave Goldberg, and Gilbert "Gil the Brain" Beckley.

When Vitale traveled to Las Vegas, it was with Caleca and in secret. The two took every precaution to not be spotted by the FBI or the local police. They were extremely careful about where they went and who they met. They always returned home immediately by automobile after finishing their business.

Whereas it is not known whom Vitale and Caleca met with while in Las Vegas, it is known that Vitale wanted to buy two more points in the Sands, taking his total to five. This means that Vitale previously had a prior connection to the Sands and three hidden points in it.

One remark in reference to Vitale that was reported to the FBI by an informant who was listed as a businessman and Mob associate, was this: "He and associates had obtained an $8 million dollar loan through the trucking man," subsequently identified as Jake Gottlieb, "[who] was in on the deal in Las Vegas."[193]

When Giordano stayed at the Dunes, the baccarat manager comped it, and the Mobster assumed the name, Mr. Russo. "Tony G.," as we in the baccarat pit called him, was a regular guy and liked sports. He frequently hung around the baccarat pit and chatted with me during a shift.

In 1969, Giordano and Paul Leisure were arrested at the Dunes. Giordano was charged for not registering as an ex-felon. Leisure was charged with vagrancy.[194] Frank Johnson, chairman of the Nevada Gaming Control Board (GCB) said, "Frankly, I think we will simply look into the situation of whether they walked into the hotel and registered or whether they were special guests." Johnson said that they had not heard of the men before their arrests by Clark County Sheriff's deputies.

Sheriff Ralph Lamb described them as "undesirables" and said, "We told the three we didn't want them around."[195]

---

193   FBI Memo, Dec. 17, 1963; Report of SA Robert Bender, SL-92-774, St. Louis office
194   *Reno Evening Gazette,* July 12, 1969
195   *Ibid*

GCB Chairman Johnson said, "It would be difficult to hold the hotel responsible if these men just walked in and registered."

The GCB report described Leisure's duties and subservience to Giordano: "Leisure followed Giordano wherever he went in the Dunes Hotel. He made no comments or no moves of his own in any regard, followed Giordano wherever he went and when Giordano was later observed gambling, stood two feet behind him, constantly observing everything in the immediate area and never left his position."

"When Leisure was arrested he refused to answer any questions until he looked at Giordano and was given a nod or some other movement of permission."[196]

In 1971, Giordano, Vitale, and Anthony Leisure, brother of Paul Leisure, were questioned on suspicion of killing Primo F. Caudera, a Las Vegas junket operator, but the charges were eventually dropped for lack of evidence.

Giordano was the boss of the St. Louis Mob until he went to prison in 1974 for having a hidden interest in the Frontier hotel-casino in Las Vegas. At that time, Vitale came out of retirement and served as acting head until Giordano's release in the late 1970s.

This FBI memo described the key players of the St. Louis crime family:

"In January 1963 SL T-1 advised that a criminal organization consisting of Italian police characters did exist in St. Louis, Missouri. SL T-1 stated that this organization was referred to as a 'family' and that in years gone by this 'family' was active in criminal matters. SL T-1 stated that in recent years there was only limited activity as there had been no new young men trained to take over as the older men passed on and became inactive. As previously reported, SL T-1 advised that other mid-western cities where the 'families' were active such as in Kansas City, Missouri, and Chicago, Illinois, the 'family' had trained young men to take over as the older men became inactive or died. SL T-1 stated that the organization in St. Louis had been in existence for many years and that John Joseph Vitale, one of the members of the St. Louis 'family' had been 'made' in 1934. At the same time, Anthony Giardano [sic][197] and his brother Joe Giardano [sic] were also made. SL T-1 advised that the St. Louis 'family' was closely aligned with the Kansas City 'family' and that Vitale and the Giardanos were close to Kansas City, Missouri, 'family' members such as Thomas 'Highway' Sim-

196   *St. Louis Post-Dispatch*, April 17, 1983
197   The actual spelling of his and his brother Joe's surname was "Giordano."
176

one, [Louis] 'Black Louis' Cangelose, and Joseph Frank Gurera. SL T-1 stated that the 'boss of the Kansas City family' was Nick Civella, brother of 'Corky' Civella.

"On June 14, 1967 SL T-2 advised that there is very definitely a group of Italians living in St. Louis who comprise and make up the core of an Italian criminal organization within the city. The organization is referred to ... as the 'syndicate,' the 'outfit' or the 'Mafia' rather than the La Cosa Nostra (LCN)."[198]

The FBI also described the organization and leadership of the St. Louis crime family:

"SL T-2 stated that the head of the Italian criminal organization in St. Louis and who is referred to as the 'boss' is unquestionably Anthony Giardano. SL T-2 stated that Sam Viviano, who was formerly from St. Louis and who recently died in Battle Creek, Michigan, was the person who groomed Anthony Giardano for his position of prominence in the Mafia. Sam Viviano, Sam Buffa, who are now deceased, and Pete Corrado were all members of the organization and all close friends of Giardano's older brother Joe Giardano. Sam Viviano was born and raised in the vicinity of Seventh and Cole Streets in St. Louis, which was the original location and neighborhood of many of the Italian individuals who grew up and became part of the Italian organization. Anthony Giardano obtained his power and was made head of the 'family' in St. Louis by LCN Commission member Joe Zerrili [sic][199] of Detroit. Zerrili made Giardano the 'boss' of St. Louis when Giardano was released from the penitentiary several years ago. SL T-2 stated that in any major-type decision arising in St. Louis concerning the 'outfit,' Giardano would have to clear it with Zerrili before taking any action. If the matter involved an 'American' and was strictly of a local nature, Giardano could make the decision by himself.

"SL T-2 said that in the old days in St. Louis when Pasquale Miceli was alive and head of the organization the higher-ups in the 'family' in St. Louis met at the council table at the Miceli Funeral Parlor where they decided on matters of policy. Normally these meetings would take place at the mortuary when someone in the 'family' had died and was being buried. This would enable the members of the outfit to have a legitimate reason for getting together at the funeral parlor and it served as an opportunity to discuss problems and decisions to be made within the organization.

198   FBI File 92-6054-2118
199   His surname actually was spelled "Zerilli."

"SL T-2 stated that in those days the policy makers would be such individuals as Pasquale Miceli, Sam Viviano, and others, many of who are now deceased. Other policy makers were Joe Giardano and John Ferrara, both of whom are still residing in St. Louis. After these persons at that time came lesser individuals who were actively engaged in various types of illegal activity such as persons like Anthony Giardano, John Vitale, Ralph 'Shorty' Caleca and Tony Lopiparo (now deceased). SL T-2 stated that all of these persons originally are, or their families, are from the area of Palermo Sicily in Italy. SL T-2 advised that these persons came from different 'dons' and these 'dons' were considered to be the controlling people. Further that the Italians within the organization have something similar to a caste system and that it makes a difference as to their standing within the organization as to where they or their families originated in Italy. An individual coming from the area called Favarotta would be called a Favarottado. The Favarottados are considered by the Italian hoodlums to be the outstanding people from Sicily. The Favarottados are considered to be more important than the Cinisados or Partinicquadoes.

"SL T-2 advised that John Vitale has long been associated with Anthony Giardano and Ralph 'Shorty' Caleca. Vitale has been considered by many persons, because of his reputation of being a top hoodlum in St. Louis, as being the 'boss.'

"SL T-2 stated that Vitale is not the boss but is certainly a highly considered member of the 'outfit' in St. Louis. Vitale is extremely well liked by the Italian hoodlum element of Kansas City, Missouri, and would be close to people like Nick Civella, Thomas 'Highway' Simone, and others but his allegiance would be to Anthony Giardano, the 'boss' of the St. Louis 'family,' who in turn would be answerable to the Detroit organization.

"Joseph Giardano, brother of Tony, is also unquestionably a member of the St. Louis 'family' and derives his power from the same source as his brother, namely Joe Zerrili of Detroit. Joe Giardano is less active but would be considered in all matters of policy and concerning activities taking place in St. Louis.

"Ralph Caleca is also a member of the St. Louis 'family' and close to Giardano and Vitale. Caleca's criminal activities go back to the days of the 'old greenies.' Caleca's opinion would be given more consideration regarding any activities concerning the St. Louis 'family.' Caleca is not as active as he has been in the past but would be completely knowledgeable about all activities concerning the Italian criminal element of St. Louis. Caleca is tied in with the Detroit organization and according to SL T-2 answerable to Detroit. He has recently been training Giardano's nephew James Giammanco in the ways of the 'outfit.' Giammanco has accompanied Caleca to Detroit where he has been introduced and accepted by the controlling element of that city. Ralph Caleca was close to the deceased Alphonse Pazzalo, who was considered in his day to be one of the original Mafioso of St. Louis and a 'hit-man' for them. John Ferrara, known as 'Mr. John,' is also a member of the St. Louis 'family' who would appear to the general public to be a strictly legitimate businessman but who is actually an 'arbitrator.' Ferrara would not be involved in criminal activities as such but would be called upon to give an opinion and arbitrate disputed matters arising within the organization. Ferrara has made a recent trip to Sicily in Italy.

"On May 19, 1967 SL T-5 advised that there is no doubt that James Giammanco is a member of the St. Louis 'family' and appears to be the one who is being groomed by Tony Giardano as the young member of the organization. Giammanco is now used by Giardano for all types of situations and is getting the reputation of being the 'strong-arm' type. SL T-5 stated that Giammanco would not hesitate to kill anyone if told to do so by his uncle, Anthony Giardano."

The FBI discussed that area in which the St. Louis Mob excelled – gambling: "The principal criminal activity of the St. Louis 'family' continues in the field of gambling. Anthony Giardano is a close friend of Dave Goldberg, well-known St. Louis gambling figure. Goldberg in conjunction with his partner Steve Lekometros carried out a large gambling operation prior to being convicted on basketball bribery charges. Giardano, with the approval of Goldberg, moved in on this operation which consisted of bookmaking activity covering horse as well as sports bets. When Goldberg and Lekometros went to the penitentiary after conviction on local charges, this gambling operation was taken over by Giardano's gambling expert, William Spinelli. Spinelli operated with one John Vainikos, who is also controlled by Giardano. William Spinelli was arrested and convicted for his participation in this gambling business. He currently remains free on bond. In the interim, Dave Goldberg and Steve Lekometros have been released from the penitentiary and are currently on parole in St. Louis on the gambling charges for which they were convicted. SL T-10 advised that Dave Goldberg has resumed his gambling activities and is again associated closely with Tony Giardano in this operation. SL T-6 advised in November 1965 that in years gone by the 'outfit' in St. Louis cut themselves in for a percentage of bookmaking action in the St. Louis area. In this respect, the St. Louis 'outfit' had to get the okay from Chicago and New York before they could cut in on the bookies who were operating. When the okay was received, the 'outfit' told all of the bookies that they would take a percentage of their winnings. SL T-5 has advised that the St. Louis 'outfit' continues to move in on local bookmakers who have any amount of business."

As part of its involvement in gambling, the St. Louis Mob fixed boxing matches. In 1960, Vitale was questioned about it at the hearing of the U.S. Senate's Subcommittee on Antitrust and Monopoly that year, but he took the Fifth Amendment on almost every question.

At the start, Senator Robert Kennedy instructed Vitale, "Take the gum out of your mouth, Vitale."

"This is a mint, not gum," Vitale retorted.

Another Kennedy comment that was printed in the press was, "Vitale is probably the leading figure in the St. Louis Mafia."

Here is a verbatim transcript of the questioning of Vitale:

> **Senator Estes Kefauver**: "Mr. Vitale, will you hold up your right hand? Do you solemnly swear the testimony you give will be the whole truth, so help you God? Did you say you do? I did not hear you."
>
> **Vitale**: "I do."
>
> **Kefauver**: "You may question him, Bonomi."
>
> **John Bonomi**: "Will you give your full name and address?"
>
> **Vitale**: "John Joseph Vitale, 3725 Avondale, St. Louis, Mo."
>
> **Bonomi**: "Mr. Vitale, are you presently the president of the Anthony Novelty Co. in St. Louis?"
>
> **Vitale**: "I decline to answer on the grounds I may tend to incriminate myself."
>
> **Kefauver**: "You are directed to answer."
>
> **Vitale**: "I take the Fifth Amendment."
>
> **Kefauver**: "Oh, excuse me. You have a lawyer present with you."
>
> **Lawrence J. Lee**: "I am his lawyer, Senator. My name is Lawrence Lee, in the law office of Morris A. Shenker, 408 Olive Street, St. Louis."
>
> **Kefauver**: "Glad to have you with us. Give Mr. Shenker our regards."
>
> **Lee**: "I certainly will."[200]

---

200   "Professional Boxing : Hearings before the United States Senate Committee on the Judiciary, Subcommittee on Antitrust and Monopoly," Part Two, Frank Carbo, 1960

Vitale was asked about his relationship with Tony Giordano and others. The following excerpt is from later questioning:

> **Bonomi:** "Is it a fact that in 1958 you divided up Sonny Liston with Frank Palermo and Frank Carbo and he is presently managed undercover by you, Frank Palermo, and Frankie Carbo?"
>
> **Vitale:** "I decline to answer on the grounds I may tend to incriminate myself."
>
> **Kefauver:** "You are directed to answer."
>
> **Vitale:** "I stand on the Fifth Amendment."
>
> **Bonomi:** "Is it a fact that you transferred the light-heavyweight fighter Jesse Bowdry to Frankie Carbo's front men, Eddie Yawitz and Bernie Glickman..."
>
> **Vitale:** "I decline to answer."
>
> **Bonomi:** "...during the 1950s?"
>
> **Vitale:** "I decline to answer on the grounds that I may tend to incriminate myself."
>
> **Kefauver:** "You are again directed to answer."
>
> **Vitale:** "I take the Fifth Amendment."
>
> **Bonomi:** "Is it true that at the present time you and Frank Palermo are dividing the manager's share of Liston's purses?"
>
> **Vitale:** "I decline to answer on the grounds that I may tend to incriminate myself."
>
> **Kefauver:** "I direct you to answer the question."
>
> **Vitale:** "I stand on the Fifth Amendment."
>
> **Bonomi:** "Is it true that Palermo is holding his share of the proceeds as the custodian for Frankie Carbo?"
>
> **Vitale:** "I decline to answer on the grounds I may tend to incriminate myself."
>
> **Kefauver:** "You are directed to answer."
>
> **Vitale:** "I stand on the Fifth Amendment."
>
> **Bonomi:** Is it a fact, Mr. Vitale, that you, 'Blinky' Palermo, and Frankie Carbo have Joseph "Pep" Barone as a front man, or on-the-record manager of Sonny Liston?"
>
> **Vitale:** "I decline to answer on the grounds I may tend to incriminate myself."

There is no doubt that the St. Louis Mob had their hands on Liston. It was clear in an anecdote told by John Meier, Howard Hughes' former science advisor. While facilitating the sale of the Desert Inn Hotel and Casino to Howard Hughes, Meier developed a close relationship with the owner-seller, Moe Dalitz. Some say that Meier was a great asset in getting the transaction done, as Hughes was a procrastinator. Hughes personally liked Meier, and Meier had, in Las Vegas jargon, "juice" with Hughes. Meier told a CNN reporter:

> "In reference to your story on the Liston-Ali fights being fixed, they were. I was personal advisor to Howard Hughes and a friend of Moe Dalitz. I sat at a table having dinner with Moe and a few of his friends when Sonny Liston came up to the table. He was either drunk or on drugs. He told Moe that he wanted another $50,000 credit from the casino at the Desert Inn. Moe told him to go to bed. Sonny then made a fist and was about to raise it into Moe's face. Moe told Sonny to not raise his arm and to just look around him. Four men at the tables stood up. They worked for Moe. Sonny then turned and walked away. I asked Moe what was that about. He said that Sonny got big money to lose to Ali twice and should be happy with that. This all took place after the second Ali-Liston fight."

Liston was named the seventh greatest fighter of all time by *The Ring* magazine yet was an enigma to many. He was widely regarded as unbeatable but lost the world heavyweight title in 1964 to Ali. In a 1965 rematch, Ali knocked him out in the first round.

Rumors flew among sports writers and those in the know that the fight might have been fixed.

In 1962 Liston knocked out Floyd Patterson and made boxing history by becoming the first man to win the heavyweight title with a first-round knockout. Liston gave Patterson another match in 1963, knocked him down three times in the first round and was credited with a win with a first-round knockout.

Liston's father Tobe put many scars on the face and body of Sonny growing up. Sonny once remarked, "The only thing my old man ever gave me was a beating." His was a dysfunctional family and his upbringing surely made it easy for young Sonny to turn to crime, which he did, participating in muggings and armed robberies. He was caught in 1950 at the age of 20 and sentenced to five years in the Missouri State Penitentiary.

After his early release in 1952, Liston had a brief amateur boxing career and then signed a professional contract in 1953.

It was rumored that the only boxing managers that Liston could get were underworld figures, who supplemented Liston's income working for them as an enforcer. In 1957, after a scuffle with a policeman, Liston was banned from boxing for the year. He returned in 1958 after getting a new manager, Joe "Pep" Barone, who was a front for hoodlums Frank Carbo and Frank "Blinky" Palermo.

Carbo was nicknamed "Mr. Gray," "The Wolf," "The Uncle," and "The Cousin." Sports writer Jim Murray punched up Carbo's power, saying: "He ruled as boxing's Godfather." Murray wrote, "It was an era in which hoodlums sat at ringside with guns concealed under the newspapers and pointed at the guy who was supposed to lose. It was an era of threats, manipulation, and extortion in which fighters frequently ended up on shoeshine stands or in mental hospitals while the guys in the gray felt hats who owned them wore diamond rings and rode around in bullet-proof cars."

Carbo and associates were the masters of the fight game. Carbo preferred to own both fighters in a match. If he did not own a fighter, the fighter would never have a chance to win a title bout. Carbo did not have to fix every match, but he did get caught doing so with the Jake LaMotta v. "Tiger Jack" Fox bout.

With the sidekicks of Palermo and Vitale, Carbo could easily fix a boxing match. In May 1965, the FBI was concerned that the recent Liston-Cassius Clay fight was fixed. An internal FBI memo stated, "The Liston-Clay fight has received wide publicity by all forms of news media. Included in the publicity have been what appear to be unsubstantiated allegations by sports writers and persons long associated with the fight game that this fight was 'fixed.'"

Despite contacting confidential informants and other sources who were considered experts in the boxing field on a national scale, the FBI failed to develop any positive leads or evidence of bribery or other irregularities connected to the May 25, 1965, fight. They then closed their investigation.

Carbo was no stranger to suspicion in the eyes of the government, especially because of his tentacles in boxing. In May 1958, St. Louis boxing manager Edward "Eddie" Yawitz was ordered to appear before a New York grand jury to answer questions concerning a loan to Carbo. Yawitz's partner Bernard Glickman managed Virgil Akins, a St. Louis contender for the welterweight championship. Glickman extended a $10,000 loan to

Carbo through Yawitz. Subsequently, Yawitz's boxer was victorious over Isaac Logart in the match. Many think the "loan" was really a payoff.

In July 1958, Carbo was indicted on 10 charges of conspiracy and acting as an unlicensed matchmaker and an undercover fight manager. Carbo was the fifth manager indicted by the New York grand jury system concerning fixed fights.

He was not the only secret behind-the-scenes matchmaker in boxing. In 1959, Mafia boss Anthony "Fat Tony" Salerno was an undisclosed financial backer of the Patterson-Johansson fight held in Yankee Stadium. In the 1960s, Salerno controlled the largest numbers racket in New York, grossing up to $50 million per year. Many Mobsters moved out of Harlem and East Harlem when the neighborhoods became predominantly Latino and African-American, but Salerno kept his headquarters at the Palma Boys Social Club in East Harlem and continued working in those regions. Later, the FBI accused him of heading a bookie and loan shark network that grossed $1 million annually. Salerno hired Roy Cohn to represent him. On April 20, 1978, Salerno was sentenced to six months in federal prison for illegal gambling and tax evasion.

Salerno even had his hands in several Las Vegas casinos at which a few key employees helped ensure Salerno and his associates got a piece of the daily drop. One undisclosed shift manager remarked, "My man, Fat Tony, would pay $50,000 to be able to walk through the lobby of the hotel without being spotted." This particular shift manager was a former Sands hotel, "Rat Pack" Era employee with heavy New York connections.

CHAPTER 31

TONY GIORDANO AND ROY WILLIAMS

Tony Giordano, St. Louis Mafia chief, wielded considerable influence on the Teamsters union and controlled its president, Roy Williams, according to the testimony of Los Angeles Mafioso Jimmy "The Weasel" Fratianno in 1981.

Fratianno gave this testimony in a deposition for a lawsuit filed by Teamster pension fund-financed Rancho La Costa against *Penthouse* magazine. *Penthouse* ran a story in which it asserted that La Costa was a haven for organized crime. Fratianno agreed to be a witness for the resort. Ironically, Fratianno was a very important witness of the federal government in prosecuting organized crime.

In the deposition, Fratianno stated, "Underworld leaders in four Midwestern cities shared the influence over Williams before he became Teamsters president, but it was Giordano who had the final authority over matters concerning the Teamsters."

Additionally, he said, "The Detroit underworld exercised its influence in the Teamsters union through James R. Hoffa, the former Teamsters president who disappeared in 1975. The Detroit mob has blood and working relationships with the Giordano crime family."[201]

Fratianno claimed that he introduced Hoffa to Chicago syndicate leaders in Los Angeles in 1952 and noted that it was Hoffa's first exposure to organized crime.

"The St. Louis mob had a secret interest in a Las Vegas hotel and gambling casino," added Fratianno. "Giordano controlled former St. Louis lawyer Morris A. Shenker."

At the time of the deposition, Shenker was and had been the principal owner and officer of the Dunes Hotel and Country Club. According to Fratianno, Shenker negotiated millions of dollars in loans from the Teamsters union's pension fund.

Shenker emphatically denied Fratianno's allegations. "This guy doesn't know what he is talking about. Nobody controls me, especially Tony Giordano," Shenker insisted.

---

201   *St. Louis Post-Dispatch*, Aug. 19, 1981

Technically, Shenker was correct as at the time of the deposition, Giordano was long dead (he passed away on August 29, 1980). However, Fratianno was generally correct, and the FBI had evidence. The bureau had a record on Angelo Marino, a San Francisco Mafioso, who acquired a piece of land in Northern California on which he wanted to build a cemetery and asked an FBI informant to help him arrange a Teamsters loan. The informant told Marino that Giordano knew Shenker, and Giordano would be the key man in getting such a loan through this channel.[202]

Fratianno was asked whether any Cosa Nostra members ran Williams when he was a Teamsters union vice-president. Fratianno replied, "There are three people, four people who go to Roy Williams when they want something." Fratianno identified them as Joey Aiuppa, then head of the Chicago Outfit; Nick Civella, Kansas City Cosa Nostra chief; Frank Balistrieri, Milwaukee chief; and Giordano.

Fratianno relayed that he first met Shenker at Murrieta Hot Springs, a resort near San Diego that Shenker and Irvin J. Kahn developed with a Teamsters pension fund loan. Fratianno also told of conversations with Shenker wherein they discussed common friends, such as Hoffa and Giordano.

During the deposition, Fratianno was asked whether Giordano controlled anybody in the Teamsters. Fratianno replied, "Yes. He controlled Shenker." "Anybody else?" he was asked. Fratianno identified Williams. When asked who controlled Hoffa, Fratianno replied that the Detroit crime family did.

When asked again who controlled Shenker, Fratianno reiterated that Giordano did. Finally, Fratianno was asked if Civella had anything to do with Shenker. He replied,

"Well, they do business together, but Nick gets more or less with Joe [Aiuppa] but with Tony's permission."

CHAPTER 32

ASH RESNICK

I rving "Ash" Resnick was a colorful and well-liked gaming figure who applied for a permit to work in the baccarat game at the Dunes in 1960, according to Clark County Sheriff's Office records. By 1961 Resnick was the director of activities at the Dunes. Those activities were not arts and crafts but related to the gambling and sports crowd.

Prior to his stint at the Dunes, Resnick was involved with "Jimmy Blue Eyes" Alo in a Las Vegas bookmaking operation at the Blair House in the late 1950s. Alo was Meyer Lansky's number one gambling chief and partner and described by a former CEO of the MGM Grand, Al Benedict, as the "Godfather of Las Vegas." Resnick was employed for a short time at the Riviera in July 1955. Other records indicate that he was at the El Rancho in Las Vegas in 1959 when it was rumored that the legendary Joe Adonis was a hidden owner.

The Dunes recently built a new convention hall and planned on hosting Sugar Ray Robinson training sessions in it, which would be open to the public prior to his March 4, 1961, title fight against defending champion, Gene Fullmer, at the Las Vegas Convention Center. The Dunes staff got the dates mixed up and on the wrong day, hung a sign that read, "Sugar Ray Training Here Today – Open to Public." More than 1,000 people showed up trying to get into the training area, the pack jamming itself through the main casino and side door entrances. Dunes President Major Riddle reportedly flipped.

Resnick contacted Robinson's road secretary June Clark, who said that Robinson's gear was packed and scheduled to leave from San Jacinto that morning. The equipment would be set up the following morning. Meanwhile, Robinson was in Bakersfield, California, staging six-round exhibitions with his regular sparring partners, Otis Woodward and Bobby Lee. There was no way Robinson could show at the Dunes to train that day, but he would arrive when he was originally scheduled to.

Fullmer's training sessions for the Las Vegas bout were hosted by the Riviera. However, in the last few days before the fight they closed the sessions to the public, and according to one newspaper account, were under lock and key.[203]

Pre-match advertising was distributed throughout Las Vegas. One piece was a very interesting press photo featuring Barney Perlman, owner of the Hialeah Sports Book, and titled, "Congrats Barney." The caption read, "Barney Perlman is congratulated on his fine betting center, the Hialeah Sports Book in Las Vegas, by three of the top names in the ring today. George Gainford, manager of Sugar Ray Robinson; Perlman; Rocky Marciano; Sugar Ray Robinson; Ash Resnick, sports director at the Dunes Hotel; and three of Robinson's sparring partners." Fullmer was not at all mentioned or represented.

The Dunes recently opened Sultan's Table, where Arturo Romero and his Magic Violins entertained the guests in a fabulously themed, five-star dining room headed by maître d' Joaquin Noriega, who previously was a culinary host at the Sands when Wyman was an owner. Most of the pre-fight talk and rumors buzzed around the lavish tables in Sultan's. Noriega remarked in front of several sports writers, "Sugar Ray is now clawing at the wall." After, two writers ran to the public telephones to call in the information to their editors.

Resnick had a checkered background and a close connection to Lansky and Alo. Resnick was born in Brooklyn, New York, in 1916. He attended Utrecht High School, where he carried a 1937 freshman letter for football and a varsity letter for basketball through 1939. Resnick, however, dropped out for lack of interest and poor scholarship. He made up for what he lacked scholastically, though, with his extraordinary sports skills. Resnick was enrolled for a short time at New York University where he played basketball but did not finish earning a degree.

Resnick played on several "town teams" in New York City that were organized by Davie Banks, who picked up good players and played under the name of the Celtics. Banks was a horse player and small-time bookie who probably was a mentor to Resnick.

The records of the Thoroughbred Racing Protective Bureau reflected the following information pertaining to Resnick, which the FBI obtained in 1962:

> April 20, 1946- subject arrested at Jamaica Race Track.
>
> May 6, 1946: subject ejected from Clubhouse for making book and warned not to return to Belmont Race Track.

July 5, 1946: suspect arrested at Empire Race Track. October 26, 1946: suspect arrested at Jamaica Race Track.

February 28, 1947: Belmont records an undesirable listing and warning not to return.

March 15, 1957: subject ejected from Gulfstream as recognized bookmaker.

Empire, Belmont, and Jamaica were race tracks in the New York City area. Gulfstream was a horse track in the Miami area.

It is most conceivable that Resnick met and associated with some of the most skilled bookmakers in the country and learned his trade by being in the trenches.

Records of the New York Police Department reflected that Resnick was arrested several times for bookmaking in 1946, by the 103rd Street squad assigned to the Jamaica Race Track. The Intelligence Unit of the Internal Revenue Service could not locate any of these records when investigating Resnick.

An FBI informant advised that Resnick was a former New York Celtics professional basketball player, was implicated in a basketball scandal, and was investigated in the alleged fixing of the first Clay-Liston fight in Miami. Also, he allegedly was a friend of Lansky, Alo, and Charlie "The Blade" Tourine.

On April 22, 1956, officers of the Clark County Sheriff's Office arrested Resnick at the El Rancho on the charge of vagrancy. At the time, Resnick was residing and operating his sports bookmaking operation at the Bali Hai apartments in Las Vegas.[204]

At one point, after several unsuccessful attempts to contact Resnick, Alo asked a former bootlegging associate named Meyer "Mike" Benedict to check on Resnick. Benedict was associated with the Old Frontier hotel-casino at the time, which was just across the street from Bali Hai. Benedict took his son Al with him, and they discovered that instead of tending to the bookmaking operation, Resnick was enjoying the pool, the luscious grounds, and the beautiful bikini-clad women there. Alo straightened out the situation, and the bookmaking operation continued. This enterprise accounted for a major amount of revenue for the Mob.

Alo was a major partner of, friend to, and facilitator for Lansky and was the true Godfather of Las Vegas.[205] Alo represented the financial dealings

---

204   Interview with confidential sources, AB and MJ
205   Ibid

of many hidden owners of Las Vegas casinos. When the New York Mob got involved in the new Caesars Palace, so did Resnick.

Going into the Robinson v. Fullmer fight at the Las Vegas Convention Center, both boxers had a win with a draw in their previous three matches. Robinson lost his previous two fights against other boxers. Fullmer was 10 years younger than Robinson.

Practically every casino owner, boss, and bookmaker who lived in Las Vegas attended the capacity crowd match, and many brought guests from around the country. Several of the people in Robinson's corner wore the Dunes logo. The match was to be 15 rounds with no knockouts, scored with a five-point system.

When the opening bell rang, the fighters could not hear it because it was not a proper bell for the type of event. Thus, the start was delayed. The bout restarted, and everyone just dealt with the quiet bell.

Judge David Zenoff gave the match to Fullmer, Judge Jack Tighe to Fullmer, and referee Frankie Carter to Fullmer. Fullmer, a 9/5 favorite, closed at 8/5.

On January 21, 1962, it was reported in the Las Vegas gossip column of Forrest Duke that Sonny Liston and Rocky Marciano accepted Resnick's invitation for the Brown vs. Ortiz light-heavyweight boxing bout to be held in Las Vegas. In the meantime, however, Resnick left the Dunes and re-emerged as the sports director at the Thunderbird. Resnick completed the deal to have Joe Brown train at the Thunderbird and Carlos Ortiz at the Flamingo.

CHAPTER 33

ATTEMPTED MURDER OF RESNICK

After his stints at the Dunes, Ash Resnick was recruited by Stephen "Steve" Wynn to develop the Hawaiian market for his Golden Nugget in Las Vegas, according to the New Jersey Casino Control Commission. Six days after Wynn asked James Powers, vice president of Golden Nugget, Inc., to conduct a background investigation on Resnick, he hired Resnick, on January 27, 1983, at a salary of $200,000 a year. He was also given 10,000 stock appreciation rights, which resulted in his receiving $237,500 in May 1983.

Resnick's hire date was also the date on a memo by Powers about his findings on Resnick, which Powers placed in his own files. Powers apparently discussed his findings with Wynn but did not deliver to him or anyone else in Wynn's company, Golden Nugget Operating Corporation (GNOC), a report in writing. The memo revealed that Resnick was arrested and convicted of bookmaking on two occasions in 1946. Also, it noted that Resnick once received securities as collateral for markers, and instead of holding on to them, he cashed them in. In a third documented offense, Resnick discounted a marker, took the payment in cash, converted it for his own use, and wrote off the marker as uncollectible. Powers described each instance as a "prosecutable case" but wrote that the witnesses did not "hold up."

In his January 27 memo, Powers concluded that the general theme regarding Resnick was that everyone knew he was stealing money, both from marker collection and the baccarat pit, but no one could ever prove it. Finally, Powers noted that Resorts International in Atlantic City considered hiring Resnick but declined to do so because of questions concerning his licensability, a "very adverse investigative report," and "a very real concern as to his basic honesty and integrity based on numerous allegations, although not proven, against Resnick down through the years."[206]

Further, the Jersey gaming commissioners indicated in their records that "we have also been supplied with a handwritten memorandum from the Golden Nugget's file on Resnick, which stated: 'Resnick has a repu-

206   State of New Jersey Casino Control Commission, GNOC Corporation License Renewal, Sept. 19, 1986

tation as a low-class type of guy. Associate of Meyer Lansky and was bag man for Fat Tony Salerno. Was a target on two occasions for bad gambling debts, once they tried to dynamite his automobile, the other, they tried to shoot him.'"[207]

In 1974, bombs were found in Resnick's car in the Caesars Palace parking lot. Nonpayment of gambling debts could have been the motive behind this act as he was a sports bettor and a baccarat player. He was observed playing baccarat at the Dunes, where he knew everyone, and certainly could have been extended credit. It seems unlikely, though, given the way he was treated, that someone there wanted him knocked off.

Maybe the cause was Resnick's theft, perhaps by collecting markers and not taking them to the casino or maybe snatching cash from the count room at either of the places he recently worked, Caesars Palace and the Tropicana.

At Caesars Palace one evening, after the casino drop box count, Dean Shendal went to the men's washroom to wash his hands after handling and counting the cash from the casino take. He then went to relieve himself. Resnick just happened to walk up to the adjacent urinal. Shendal told him, "Pull down your pants. I said, pull down your pants."[208]

Resnick did, and it was evident that he had some cash hidden in a double layer of briefs. What specifically happened after this is not known, but a bad word about Resnick was spread around town to those in the mysterious circle of Las Vegas.

Shendal owned a small piece of Caesars when it opened, having gone there with Jerry Zarowitz, and he worked at the Sands when Sid Wyman owned 6 percent of the casino. Shendal was a tough cookie and a good scrapper, according to his long-time friend, Dave Goldberg, St. Louis gambler and bookmaker.

At the Tropicana, maybe Resnick skimmed the cash from baccarat or extended cash markers to players who walked the money out the door and never repaid them.

What is known is that finances were strained at the Tropicana at this time. When Joe Agosto operated it for the Kansas City Mob, cash was always short.

Once, Paul "Pacy" Perles deposited $200,000 in cash in the Tropicana casino cage, allegedly for safekeeping.[209] The congenial Perles became licensed as a junket representative for the Aladdin in 1977, which paid him

207   Ibid
208   Interview with confidential source, VMTAG, July 2019
209   Conversation with Paul Perles, 1975

192

$2,000 a month. Perles' gaming application was signed by Aladdin President Richard L. Daly, who was a front man for the real boss, James "Jimmy" Tamer. Tamer was a close friend of Wyman and of Irwin Gordon, with whom he worked in the 1950s in the Terre Haute bookmaking operation. Perles ran junkets to other Vegas properties and even took players to the Tropicana when Resnick worked there.

Perles and Resnick were lifelong friends. In fact, the Nevada Gaming Control Board (GCB) recorded Resnick intervening on Perles' behalf one time. Resnick told New York Caesars' junket office manager, Morris Rothenberg, to stop trying to collect a $2,000 marker on a Perles' junketeer-gambler, Frank Mancini.

Perles was known to be a class act by gamblers everywhere. He himself gambled in several casinos around Nevada. At Caesars Palace he had an outstanding gambling marker of $8,500, and at Kings Castle at Lake Tahoe, $15,000. He was a junket representative at Caesars Palace under Resnick before leaving with the unpaid debt. Because he earned $2,000 a month from the Aladdin and had significant markers suggests the $200,000 he put in the Tropicana cage was not his.

The Tropicana casino used the $200,000 as a temporary casino bankroll. There is no question that Perles putting the cash there was an aggressive move by someone, any of the Tropicana's legal or hidden owners, to prevent the Tropicana from closing its doors and to keep the skim alive.

However, a possible second purpose for Perles' infusion was to secretly bolster someone's percentage of hidden ownership. Theoretically, Perles could have put the money up for Nick Civella or even Gordon and Wyman. They could not have been hidden investors outright without having to answer to the other Mobsters with interests in the Tropicana. Perles was the front man, who could fall back on the money safekeeping alibi if need be.

Regarding the failed hit on Resnick, it was theorized, too, that St. Louis mobster Johnny Vitale ordered the hit. In fact, around that time, Vitale was spotted in the Tropicana by Dennis Gomes, GCB agent. Gomes described the sighting in a report:

> "One time I was walking around there with my senior agent, Rich Iannone, and I remember seeing a guy walking away from me, and looked at the back of his head, and I said, 'Rich, I think that's John Joseph Vitale, the mob boss of St. Louis.'[210]
> "He said, 'How could you say that? You're just looking at the back of his head.' I said, 'His ears look familiar to me.' And I was

always good. I had a bad memory with names, but was real good with any kind of facial features. You could wear a disguise, and I'd still know by the eyes or something. And I said, 'I just feel like it.'

"He convinced me I was crazy. So I went back home, and I thought about it all night long. I came back at four o'clock in the morning. I couldn't stand it anymore. I couldn't go to sleep. And I went to the front desk, went behind the front desk and made them show me their records, and I was going through anybody that was staying in-house. And I looked under John Vitale, and there were no Vitales in there. I looked; I couldn't find anybody. So I just started flipping, one by one, through everybody in house, looking at addresses, trying to see if there was anybody from St. Louis. Sure enough, I find this address, and I recognize the address. It was John Joseph Vitale's address. And the guy was staying there under an assumed name. So then I knew he was there. So I started wandering around the place, and I found him in the floormen's lounge, talking to some executives in there. This was a big mob guy. This was one of the biggest. He was the boss from St. Louis. That was a big mob position."

If Resnick was stealing from the Tropicana, it was critical and a serious error on his part because, according to Gomes in his investigative report about the Tropicana,[211] five organized crime families held "hidden points" in it: Kansas City, St. Louis, Chicago, New England-Boston, and the New York (the Gambino) family.

Gomes named an organized crime associate who was a Tropicana employee. That was Joey Cusumano, who was a known associate of Anthony "Tony" Spilotro and the Chicago Outfit. The Doumani brothers were linked to Vitale's St. Louis group. Joseph "Joe The Cat" LaForte was a known associate of the Gambino crime family out of New York. Finally, Joe Agosto was closely tied to Nick Civella and the Kansas City crime family. Gomes considered including Edward "Baldy" Sarkisian as well, but he was no longer running junkets. So Gomes suspected that the Detroit crime family no longer held points in the Tropicana.[212]

Gomes also detailed the surveillance of Vitale in meetings with high level Tropicana casino executives in which Agosto made all of the decisions and called all the shots. (Gomes eventually turned Agosto, the beginning of Agosto becoming a star witness against the Mob.)

---

211   *Hit Me! Fighting the Las Vegas Mob by the Numbers*, Danielle Gomes and Jay Bonansinga, 2013
212   *Ibid*

Gomes suspected Resnick was an associate of the Patriarca crime family out of New England and Boston. Of the many purported reasons for Resnick being the target of an assassination by bombing, the most logical are that he was trying to take control of the Tropicana casino for the hidden group he represented and the cash quantities of the enterprise were falling below minimum operating levels. Perhaps Resnick had sticky fingers and was holding out from Civella's group.

In January 1974, Charles "Chuckie" Berns was arrested and put under house arrest for the attempted bombing of Resnick's automobile. A Nevada court allowed Berns to post a $75,000 bond on the condition that he not leave his home without contacting authorities.

Berns was one of the nicest people anyone would want to know, always pleasant, Jovial, and kind. He fit the stereotype of a friendly Uncle Chuck or a good neighbor Sam.

In 1946 Berns was arrested for gambling in a high stakes "town game" at the Sherlock Pipe Shop in St. Louis, owned by Sherlock Feldman, who worked for Wyman at the Dunes in 1962. Also, Feldman was arrested with Wyman at the Hamilton Hotel prior to this raid.[213]

In 1955, Berns was sentenced to five years in prison for his part in the theft of $20,000 worth of typewriters, razor blades, machine parts, and clothing from an interstate shipping truck. The U.S. prosecutor said he operated the biggest fencing operation in the St. Louis area. Berns' attorney, Morris Shenker, claimed he was a victim. "He was a goat. The thieves that stole the merchandise had taken advantage of him. He formerly operated two liquor stores in downtown St. Louis but went bankrupt after losing heavily at gambling," Shenker said.[214]

Berns and a few other inmates serving their terms at the same federal penitentiary were given special privileges and had special food smuggled into their part of the prison dubbed "King's Row" on account of them being treated like kings, according to sources.[215]

In July 1962, Berns and Oscar Hart were arrested on suspicion of the first degree murder of Realtor John Myszak in St. Louis. Berns was arrested at his car lot without incident. Hart was arrested at his home, where he was found to have a loaded double- barreled shot gun. Paul Spica, originally detectives' primary suspect, who was arrested previously in connection with several burglaries, was reported saying, "Tell my man I am playing it cool," referring to Berns. Eventually, detectives determined

213   *St. Louis Post-Dispatch,* Nov. 18, 1946
214   *St. Louis Post-Dispatch,* March 4, 1955
215   *St. Louis Post-Dispatch,* March 14, 1955

Spica was not the triggerman; he only set up Myszak. Berns, however, was later released for lack of evidence.

As for Berns' alleged involvement in the attempted murder of Resnick, the police were tipped off about it before the bombs were placed. They arrested a James Carl, whose real name was Donald L. Wayton, of Gary, Indiana. Berns contracted to have Resnick killed through another person who was to furnish dynamite to Wayton. However, Wayton rolled over on Berns and worked with the police. They constructed a dummy bomb and then videotaped Wayton as he hooked it up to Resnick's auto on January 5, 1974.

In the interim, Berns fled Las Vegas and could not be located. On January 30, Judge Robert Legakes dismissed charges against Berns after the Clark County District Attorney's Office said they were unable to locate a key witness, Jerry Denonon of San Diego.[216]

Berns' cousin was Dave Goldberg, a higher up in the St. Louis Mob. In 1972, after Goldberg finished parole in St. Louis, Wyman brought him to the Dunes to work as a poker manager along with Al "Henderson Al" Pierro, a seasoned poker player, and Lou Rouso. The trio replaced "Shrimpy" Chautin.

During this time, the Dunes card room was an interesting place, which allowed "short card" games on empty poker tables. Years later the Nevada Gaming Control Board outlawed games that were played "heads-up" between two opponents such as gin, call rummy, and "honeymoon bridge," or turnover. The room was a natural place to sit, meet confederates, plan a scam, book, and do just about anything.

Goldberg obtained a blue box from Jack Molinas, a former associate in a major point shaving scandal that got Goldberg time prior to coming to the Dunes. The blue box erased any trail of telephone numbers that Goldberg called to place or take wagers, which was a federal violation. Goldberg showed it to me, and wanted to know if I wanted one. The Dunes phones or Goldberg's phones were monitored because shortly thereafter, he was indicted and arrested for having the box. I worried that he thought I mentioned it to someone, which I did not do.

Once in Nevada, though, Goldberg immediately ran afoul of Dave Hanson, who worked for Clark County Sheriff Ralph Lamb, who issued mandatory work permits called a "sheriff's card." No card, no work. Lamb was indeed a friend of Wyman, but there is no doubt that Hanson and Goldberg disliked one another. Goldberg was as tough as they come as far

---

216   *St. Louis Post-Dispatch*, Jan. 30, 1974

as being in physical shape, however, he was a perfect gentleman. He did have a temper when pushed.

Hanson was a tough cop. After leaving the Sheriff's Office, he worked at the MGM Grand. He was reported to be a good, loyal employee whom the executives respected.

Hanson stood his ground, and Goldberg would not back down. Their interaction devolved into yelling unpleasant names at each other. Wyman had to intervene, and Goldberg got a work permit. After coming in at the Dunes as a poker manager, he was placed in the baccarat game as a floor-man. Later, he was given managerial authority along with the formal manager, Irwin Gordon.

CHAPTER 34

IRWIN GORDON (QUASHA)

"Cater to a winner. Leave a loser alone. What am I going to tell him, that I'm sorry? He knows I'm not sorry. That's what we're here for. To take his money."

– Irwin Gordon

In all of the years I worked in Las Vegas I was only harassed by one wannabe Mob lackey and only once physically by a legitimate member of organized crime. In 1968 I went to work at the Dunes after a year at the California Club. I thought I hit the jackpot with my job dealing blackjack and sometimes roulette. After six months, I was transferred to the baccarat pit, which was like winning an Academy Award because it was rare for someone my age, 22. There were dealers who worked at the Dunes for years who wanted to, but could not get into, baccarat. It was virtually impossible. At age 22, I was one of the youngest baccarat dealers ever to work at the Dunes. Most of my co-workers were in their mid-30s and older.

That year the United States put a man on the moon. *LIFE* magazine published a pictorial of the gentry watching the historical event, and two of the photos were taken from the Dunes baccarat pit. One of them was of me perched on the table watching the moon walk. In the other photo, the floorman sitting on a ladder chair on the right is Vincent "Vince" Taglialatella. Also notable in the picture is that there is actual currency on the table. We dealt the game with it at the time. The $500 checks (chips) were only used on occasion.

After six years as a baccarat dealer, I was promoted to floorman. This was as good as it got. Floormen received an excellent salary and a full share of the tokes, or tips. Floormen were the gents who made sure the games were dealt correctly.

At the Dunes I made a new set of friends who came from many different parts of the country and even the world. After Cuban casinos were shut down by Fidel Castro, many dealers came to Las Vegas seeking jobs. Several of the Dunes owners had investments in Cuba and knew these dealers and supervisors as good, hard-working employees, which led to many of them finding employment at the Dunes.

A Dunes job was extremely hard to get for several reasons. For one, it was lucrative, and as such, openings were rare and many people applied for each one. Tips were pooled 24/7/365, and the supervisors got an equal share. Because the bosses were cut in on the tokes, sometimes called zooks, they allowed the dealers to be a little more liberal when cultivating players. In other words, we were allowed to hustle, and we did have some "deluxe" hustlers.

Hustling is an action by dealers to encourage casino players to give them tips, or place a bet for the dealers alongside their wager. There is hard hustling, which is strong arming the players by simply saying, "Put a bet up for me so I can win with you," or something like that, and then there is light hustling. Regardless of degree, it's against the rules in every casino.

Two, landing a Dunes job generally required knowing someone there who could vouch for an applicant, ensuring that they were honest, would not steal, and would stay out of trouble. In rare cases, though, applicants got lucky and were hired, say when the casino desperately needed good croupiers.

The baccarat manager Irwin Gordon had just finished a federal prison term for bookmaking. He was very close to Sid Wyman, a Dunes owner. He was a character and an old school gambler.

Gordon liked to rib me because I had longer hair than all of the rest of the employees. Once, he borrowed a comb from someone, got behind us dealers, and combed my hair while remarking, "Look at the beau-tee-ful hair on this young dealer," in his native Brooklynese. He thought it was funny and that because I was the youngest, he could get away with it. I was dating the cocktail waitress who served the pit, and that day, she saw what he did. I snapped. Quietly and calmly, I turned to Gordon and said, so no one else could hear, "You do that again, and I will knock you on your ass."

Oh, my gosh, I thought. What did I say? I am going to be fired right on the spot. No one ever talked to this man like I just had. I panicked.

Nothing untoward happened, though. In fact, he stopped the stupid razzing and treated me like a king thereafter. He even promoted me to floorman after a few years. He became a mentor to me, and I appreciated very much the opportunity to work with him.

Gordon liked employees who knew their job, handled people well, and did not act like a wise guy. If they did not, then good luck. Everyone knew whether he liked them or not. Gordon had the finesse of a bull except when he wanted something. He was one of the smartest bookmakers in the business. He was cunning, street smart, and a great actor when he needed to be. One thing was certain: every employee knew Gordon was Wyman's close friend and advisor.

Gordon, whose real last name was Quasha, was arrested in 1951 for bookmaking in Miami Beach. And then in 1952 he was arrested at the Cavendish Bridge Club in New York with 34 others, including legendary Mobster, Michael "Trigger Mike" Coppola. The Crime Commission of Miami tagged the club as a "hangout for mobsters and smart money boys."[217]

Many of the men who were charged gave assumed names to the police as an inside joke, and at the start of the court proceeding, cheered for each defendant as they arrived. With their bright attire, they resembled a parade of Cadillacs when they departed the police station and they certainly livened up the courtroom. "Why, here comes Hopalong Silverstein," one of them shouted when his friend entered the room. One of the defense attorneys was Ben Cohen, who was the attorney for the S&G Syndicate.

In 1965, Wyman and Gordon became partners in Melodyland in Anaheim, California, a theater for Broadway-style shows and musical acts. Wyman sent Billy and Pete Snyder to run it, and the Dunes advertised heavily in Melodyland playbills and programs.

Sources at the Dunes reported that Gordon was Wyman's front in the Terre Haute nationwide bookie operation of the 1950s. At the related trial, Gordon refused to testify and served time in prison in order to protect Wyman and other associates involved. Gordon was a loyal friend and colleague of Wyman. They were inseparable. Wyman made great efforts to repay Gordon for what he did for him. Gordon could do no wrong in Wyman's eyes, and Gordon had the power to do whatever he wanted in the baccarat pit and around the casino. Not all of the partners of the Dunes liked Gordon, especially Morris Shenker, but there was nothing they could do.

When Gordon was released from the federal prison in Stafford, Arizona, after serving time in the Terre Haute bookmaking case, Wyman sent Dunes co-owner and pilot George Duckworth to pick him up in Duckworth's Cessna 310. Wyman and Gordon wanted to have a laugh at the prison staff's expense, so Duckworth pretended to be Gordon's personal valet. Playing along, Gordon ordered Duckworth, "Get my bags and carry them to my plane."

217   *The Miami News*, Nov. 14, 1952

"Yes, Mr. Gordon," Duckworth replied. Then he picked up Gordon's luggage and followed him off of the prison property. The guards and warden were astonished and taken aback. The Dunes bosses loved to recount this story.

Many evenings on swing shift the FBI was spotted nosing around the Dunes looking for some information on Gordon and Dave Goldberg, who were under constant surveillance. One FBI agent sat in a slot machine chair, acting like he was passionately playing slots when he was really monitoring the baccarat pit.

Usually three supervisors were assigned to a shift in baccarat. They sat in tall ladder chairs, similar to the type used in dice games, which allowed them to look down on the game and the players with an unobstructed view. The floormen stood such that they could monitor the dealers' and the players' actions. If we had to use the telephone for any reason, we covered our mouth with our free hand so that no one could overhear us speaking or read our lips.

Gordon and Goldberg were high bet takers, but they never referred to their gambling business as "taking or booking bets." Rather, they said that "they have action on the Dodgers," etc. so anyone listening could not determine that they were bookmakers. Remember, in Nevada it is not against the law to bet among each other. The only way it becomes illegal is when one of the parties takes a percentage of the bet. This means that if a person wanted to bet a side, he or she would have to lay $11 to win $10. That $1 constitutes the edge that the bookmaker earns.

Duckworth heard many complaints about the baccarat dealers aggressively hustling Dunes customers. The complaints rarely came from the players but from blackjack or dice floor persons who occasionally had to relieve the baccarat crew during lunch or dinner breaks. The complaints also came from other jealous casino employees or bosses. The floor persons and shift bosses in baccarat were cut in on the dealers' tips, so hustling was ignored. No other crew in the Dunes had this unwritten privilege. The two persons who authorized the dealers to hustle were given carte blanche by the highest authority in the Dunes. It was a very unusual situation, but it worked quite well, engendering very few customer complaints about being hustled. It was all one big happy family in the baccarat pit.

One evening a generous "George" of a player was betting $200 and $300 for the dealers. All a dealer had to do was say "koala bear" and the customer bet for the boys. A new young dealer who was intimidated by Gordon was being conservative and hesitated to say the magic words.

Gordon poked him in the back and said, "What are you waiting for? You get your end, don't you?"

"Three hundred dollars for the dealers," shouted the customer.

Once, Sherlock Feldman was observing the baccarat closely and saw the dealer on his side of the table hustle a guy. The dealer was dealing to and hustling the player for about an hour before Feldman came into the pit.

Feldman, a longtime associate of Wyman from St. Louis, was a grave-yard shift manager and relieved the baccarat pit staff on occasion. Feldman was a sharp casino operator and knew all of the tricks. He could spot a hustle a mile away.

Sensing that Feldman would report to the owners what he observed, Gordon yelled at the dealer, "I told you, don't do that." The dealers and the other floormen looked confused because this instruction was the opposite of what Gordon told them 15 minutes earlier. Gordon was not so much worried about Wyman finding out as he was Charlie Rich, who was the stepfather of Duckworth, the casino manager. Duckworth was ambivalent to Gordon; they had a love-hate relationship that could devolve at any moment and cause unnecessary problems.

Gordon was a World War II veteran and not bashful about telling the story of killing 10 German soldiers, or in his words, "those Nazi bastards," with a machine gun that his Army regiment captured. He literally became alive when he described the massacre.

He was politically incorrect and made no bones about it. He was arrested for assault and battery in the late 1950s and "took no shit from anyone." He liked a half-black/half-white cocktail waitress who occasionally worked in the baccarat pit and seemed to respond to Gordon's sexist remarks. Because she was part black, he would not meet up with her in public places where he was known, but it was all right in his mind to meet up with her privately. That way, no one in the casino would know about it.

However, he did tell a few of the baccarat crew about his invitation to the waitress to visit his luxurious Regency Towers apartment, located at the exclusive Las Vegas Country Club. He was ready for her visit, with foods and drinks. Then he suddenly realized that the gate guard and the lobby security officer would see a black woman going to his apartment and surely they might say something to some of his associates, he thought. So Gordon called the girl and told her to stop at the supermarket for a few items he needed and he would give her some extra money for doing so. He asked her to buy a bucket, a mop, some cleaning rags, and a broom. He then called the security guard and said his maid was coming up.

Gordon had a sense of humor that was unique but also had eyes of steel and could size a person up in about a minute of conversation. From his years of street experience, he knew when someone was lying. He was as smart as they come despite having virtually no education other than some high school.

He despised one floorman in the baccarat, Murray Saul, because he ran to Duckworth with anything he thought was improper. Gordon hated "stool pigeons." Saul was also a former small owner of the Riviera before Wyman invested in the place with Gus Greenbaum. Murray's brother Herbie Saul was the blackjack graveyard shift boss. So after a few months of the two working together, Gordon stopped speaking to him. If he wanted Murray to take his lunch break, for example, he told another floorman, "Tell Murray to go on his break." The other floorman then said, "Murray, go on your break." It was crazy.

Gordon also thought that Saul was cheap because he wore the same grey and black striped socks to work every night. In reality, Saul, who was superstitious, wore them all the time because he thought that they brought him luck and would prevent the baccarat from having a losing shift. When Saul was the night shift manager, he said Jewish prayers over the shoe, the container that held the cards to be dealt, in the hopes it would keep players from winning.

The funniest prank that Gordon pulled is one for the record books of all-time best Dunes stories. One evening when Gordon was roaming the casino, he stopped to watch some security guards handle a couple of young ladies who appeared to be prostitutes. Generally speaking, the hotel bellman's desk managed the ladies of the evening, and did so discreetly. They came and went without attention, fanfare, or publicity. If they broke any of the unwritten rules, they were banished from the hotel, and at times, turned over to police. It was suspected that these two ladies were being held for rolling, or robbing, a casino high roller.

Amused at the situation, Gordon joined the conversation and asked the guard for the baggie he had confiscated from one of the women. They gave it to him. Gordon walked into the baccarat pit. Saul and this writer were among the floormen supervising the game that evening. It was a slow night in the casino, and the baccarat had no play whatsoever, except for the game starters, or shills, whose job was to keep the game moving to attract live players.

I saw Gordon take something from his pocket and put it on the pit stand desk, among the supplies needed to operate baccarat. Gordon summoned me over and told me, "Take one of these marijuana sticks and shove it into a Dunes cigar like this. Use a pencil to make a hole and then put the Dunes cigar band around the cigar and bring it back. Go to the second floor where no one will see you."

He had a cheeky smile that only occurred when he was up to something mischievous. I could not believe what I was seeing and hearing.

"Hurry," Gordon said. I briskly gathered up the paraphernalia, including two Dunes cigars, and placed it in my pocket. On my way to the second floor, I thought about what had just occurred. I was flabbergasted. I went onto the balcony to be sure that no one was watching and quickly prepared the cigar. I made sure that the tip of the cigar was packed with the tobacco to hide the rolled joint. I put the band around it and took it back to Gordon. He generally did not smile much, but he was grinning ear to ear.

What is he going to do with that cigar, I thought. In the few minutes that passed, I grew uneasy, sure that something nefarious was about to happen.

Then Gordon said to the floorman, "Hey, Murray, I got a cigar for you." All of the dealers on the table looked at Gordon questioningly, knowing he had not spoken directly to Saul in at least a year. Something was up.

Gordon gave Saul the cigar, even lit it for him. "Thank you," Saul said then got back in his chair and began smoking it. Soon, the faint smell of weed permeated the air. Gordon summoned a few of his associates and brought them in on the ruse. So four men stood opposite of Saul, observing him smoke. "Murray, sit down on the table and shill a little," Gordon told him, and, to a dealer, instructed, "Give him $50,000 to play with." The dealer put up a rim marker and gave Saul the money. Saul started playing $1,000 a hand.

Gordon motioned over a cocktail waitress and told her to take Saul's drink order. He ordered a rum and coke.

It was a sight to see, as Saul had no idea that he was stoned.

CHAPTER 35

THE DUNES:
BOOKING AND WEB OF ASSOCIATES

On November 7, 1975, FBI agents raided the Dunes' cashier cage and unlocked several safety deposit boxes that were in Sidney Wyman's name. They also searched two apartments in the lush Regency Towers, home to the who's who of Las Vegas. Desert Inn Owner Moe Dalitz lived in one of four penthouses. Wyman owned two luxury condominiums there, in one of which Irwin Gordon lived as a gift from his friend.

In all, the agents confiscated more than $700,000 in cash and bookmaking paraphernalia. The cash seized in the probe gave a good indication of the amount of betting action the group was taking. In one weekend, the operation grossed $390,000 and paid out $154,000, for a profit of $236,000.

According to a Dunes baccarat floorman, whose name will remain confidential: "They actually made more money in the bookmaking operation than the Dunes Hotel's baccarat game," referring to those who ran it. "I remember one night when Gordon was the boss and I was his assistant. We had some heavy play and we were in need of a 'fill,' a fill meaning that we needed more cash on the table to operate the game. Several players were having a streak of wins. I walked over to Irwin and started to say that we needed another fill. He had his head down, writing numbers on a piece of paper. I could sense that he was calculating something. Before I could say anything, he looked up at me and said, 'Can't you see I'm busy?' I just ordered the fill and continued watching the game. This was a normal day at the Dunes Hotel."[218]

The fact that the alleged illegal betting operation was lucrative, handling millions of dollars of wagers, may have been the main reason that the Dunes casino did not have a licensed sports book. Morris Shenker was the primary Dunes owner and operator as well as the gaming licensee then. He could have applied, at any time, to get a sports book license added

---

Interview with confidential source, Dunes baccarat floor boss, 2019

to the resort's existing non-restricted gaming license, so why didn't he? Was it because he knew about the bookmaking operation?

It is probable that he did. For one, he had many allies whom he personally placed in the Dunes organization. In addition, it was rumored that Shenker himself was having the telephones in the Dunes monitored.

But who was really calling the shots at the Dunes? The fact that the resort paid for an interior designer to decorate and furnish Wyman's condos suggests that the real boss was not Shenker.

One evening, Shenker stopped this writer in the hotel lobby. He said, "Geno, I am sure you can tell me what Irwin Gordon is doing here at the Dunes."

I was taken aback by the question and certainly wanted to be courteous, but I had no idea what he was talking about.

"I don't know what you mean," I replied.

Shenker did not elaborate and then walked away. I thought this was a strange question coming from the Dunes CEO. I sensed he was looking for information that was unfavorable to Gordon. Why didn't Shenker go directly to Gordon or Wyman and query them? He didn't because he had no control over the situation and already knew the answer.

The incident made me wonder about another statement, one made by a very high ranking Dunes official whose name I will not disclose here. This person, far beyond a regular Dunes employee, was a stakeholder. This person claimed, but never offered me proof of it, that Shenker was an arm's length informant for the government. Because he sought complete control of the Dunes while they allegedly ran an illegal bookmaking operation controlled by Wyman and Gordon, Shenker very well could have cooperated with, or passed information on to, Nevada gaming authorities, who in turn could have given it to the FBI.

The FBI claimed that the Dunes bookmaking operation netted $1.7 million during the 13 days the FBI monitored it via wiretap, from October 25, 1975, to November 7, 1975, according to an article in the *Las Vegas Review-Journal*.[219] The affidavit that the FBI filed with its request to run the wiretap listed Frank "Lefty" Rosenthal as one of the people who told FBI agents about the Dunes' bookie operation. To achieve the cited $1.7 million, the book had to have handled about $2,905,980, which is about $223,540 a day.

At the time of the raid, Dunes cashier Ruben Cabanas was with Wyman at the cage. He recalled:

---

219   *Las Vegas Review-Journal*, David Hill, March 31, 1977

"I remember the federal people came in and they said, 'We have a search warrant,' and they wanted to get into Mr. Wyman's safe deposit box, you know, and he was standing there. I was in there while they drilled it out and, you know, like handed it to them and all that stuff. And, and I was sort of apologizing to Mr. Wyman saying, 'I'm so sorry about this.'"

Wyman replied, "There's no worry, kid. I'll get my money back." "And he did," said Cabanas.

The indictment named seven men. They were Maurice Dodson, a Dunes casino host; Wyman, former majority owner of the Dunes casino operation and now a consultant; Michael Canon and Frank Calahan, both convicted for bookmaking in Birmingham, Alabama; Irwin Gordon, baccarat manager at the Dunes; Joseph R. Berent, a.k.a. "Bobby the Hunchback" and "Hot Horse Bobby"; and Ray Vara, suspected as being the lines maker.

These people corresponded with the names on the 11 strongboxes stuffed with currency, which the FBI agents found in the raid.

Three people, however, were blatantly missing from the indictment. They included Charlie Katz, an associate of Dodson. Katz was one of the best handicappers in the business; he was hands down a genius. His specialty was college basketball. Katz was in the company of Dodson on a daily basis, and there is no question that he was either an arm's length associate or intentionally left out of the indictment because of Katz's past history of beating the U.S. government in the Supreme Court.

When Katz was a bookie in Los Angeles near the legendary Sunset Strip, he suspected that the FBI had bugged his apartment. Most likely the bugging was carried out without permission and a proper search warrant, and a black bag crew did the actual placing of the tape recorder. So Katz began using a public, old-fashioned glass phone booth to make his daily calls. The FBI agents planted a recording device on top of the phone booth and taped his conversations. He was convicted on eight federal gambling charges, but he appealed and eventually took the case to the U.S. Supreme Court. The outcome, decided 7-1 in favor of Katz, added another safeguard to U.S. citizens' right to privacy on one hand, and created one more impediment to law enforcement on the other.

It is very probable that the FBI decided not to pursue an indictment of Katz because if their black bag job with respect to him came out in discovery, it likely would have destroyed the government's case.

Most every weekday morning after the day shift opened at the Dunes, Katz and Dodson stopped and conversed with the baccarat bosses and the crew, especially if there were no active players on the table. The two always talked sports with Vince Taglialatella, a baccarat shift boss, a bookie, and a shylock. Katz had a wonderful personality and sense of humor. He would look and shout a call bet to the dealers on the game, "I want to make a mind bet – $1,000 on the bank side. If I lose, I blow my mind!" After chatting, Dodson and Katz then went to a special room in the Dunes where they conducted the daily bookmaking operation. No records exist today that indicate that the FBI was even aware of this super-secret room.

The other gentlemen who were not indicted were Dave Goldberg and Anthony Daidone. Whereas Goldberg may have been heard on the tapes speaking to Dodson, Gordon, or some of the other members of the operation, the FBI was pursuing another case against him at the time for having a "blue box," an electronic device that allowed him to place calls toll free all over the U.S. The FBI was confident that that case against Goldberg was solid, so it behooved them to leave him out of the Dunes bookmaking trial.

Diadone was well known to FBI agents, who observed him visiting Berent's business, the Tower of Pizza. Daidone was married to Jimmie Lou Stone, the daughter of one of the most respected bookmakers in Dallas, Texas. She was named the director of the Stardust Race and Sportsbook.

Before the trial, a major witness, Gerald Delmann, was murdered in front of his apartment. A sports writer at the Saratoga Club, he was named in court documents as a participant in the Dunes bookmaking scheme. The local police indicated that the killing likely had nothing to do with the trial, and instead cited the motive as robbery. The perpetrators took $30,000 from a briefcase in Delmann's car trunk but failed to take an additional $45,000 from his jacket pocket.

At the jury trial, testimony revealed that Nevada Gaming Control Board Member Jeffrey Silver allowed the FBI into the Dunes casino cage when they showed up for the raid. Wyman and Dodson challenged the government on the legality of the raid, charging that Silver and the bureau had no right to enter the casino cage.

FBI Agent Carl Olsen testified that before entering, agents gave Silver the search warrants, and Silver conferred with another Dunes employee before letting them in. Olsen said he saw that employee hand Silver the key to the cage.

Wyman and Dodson filed motions to have their money returned. Because of his ill health, Wyman was granted a separate trial to be held on November 6, 1976, which his attorney subsequently managed to get postponed indefinitely.

Federal District Judge Roger Foley dismissed three of the nine counts in the indictment because the prosecution could not prove the identity of the people who placed bets on the telephone that the FBI monitored. According to federal law, five or more persons must be linked to the ownership and operation of the bookmaking operation for the first count of an indictment to be valid.

Gordon was jailed in April 1976 for refusing to testify in this case and subsequently released in September. Foley said he did not believe the prosecutors could persuade Gordon and Canon, also jailed, to testify by keeping them in jail. Attorney Gary Logan, who represented Gordon, said of his client, "We would rather die than be branded a stool pigeon." Oscar Goodman, who represented Canon, said the incarceration "certainly is punitive rather than coercive."[220]

The attorneys for the defendants filed a motion to be given the names of the seven informants the FBI admitted to using in the case, however, Foley denied the motion.

FBI Agent James R. Supan admitted that he spoke to two of the seven individuals, and other agents communicated with the other five. He said that the federal prosecutors floated to the informants the idea of immunity in exchange for their testimony but that every informant did not want to be identified and refused to provide any evidence unless they would remain anonymous. This is an interesting statement. If the FBI told the truth about the offer of immunity, it suggests that some or all of the informants were involved with the bookmaking operation, and in doing so, they themselves may have violated the law. On the other hand, they may have been completely innocent of any involvement but merely had knowledge that was crucial to the case.

According to U.S. Prosecutor Kevin O'Malley, Canon was the member of the Dunes bookmaking operation who interacted with the public; he accepted bets via the telephone. Most of the bettors were out of state. During the two days that Canon was not in Las Vegas, Dodson operated the phones in his absence. It also was reported that Canon used a false identity to lease a condominium in the Regency Towers.

O'Malley claimed that Wyman and Gordon were involved in the bookmaking, but their roles were "secretive." The two provided the necessary betting information and were overheard discussing the profits and success of the operation.

The prosecution presented several witnesses. They included the Regency Towers leasing agent, a Realtor, a Nevada Power Company supervisor, a Central Telephone switching supervisor, an attorney for Central Telephone who handled court-appointed wiretaps, and an FBI agent who oversaw the monitoring of wiretapped calls. These witnesses simply explained various procedures.

The other two witnesses were Shenker and Silver. Shenker testified that Dodson was a junketeer. As for Wyman, Shenker said that he "used to be the boss" at the Dunes, from 1969 to 1972, but currently did not own any stock or interest in the resort.[221] He said Wyman currently advised the Dunes on gambling matters and as part of his $60,000 a year consulting fee, was allowed to reside at the Dunes. Shenker said Wyman's knowledge was invaluable to the Dunes in that he knew how, when, and to whom to extend credit. He said that he knew Wyman for 45 years. "He was the one who brought me into the Dunes," he added.

Wyman once had an incident with the owner of a major NFL franchise in California who beat the Dunes baccarat game for about $40,000. The player and his entourage were guests of the Dunes Hotel as well. The gentleman had a $50,000 line of credit at the Dunes and took a few markers of $5,000 each. After winning the money, he paid his markers and left the hotel to play baccarat at the Frontier. After he lost the $40,000 in winnings from the Dunes at the Frontier, he returned to the Dunes to get more credit in the baccarat pit. Wyman canceled his credit. And that was that. Wyman felt that Dunes credit that was extended to customers was for their use at the Dunes. He believed it was bad business to give credit to a player who beats the house and then takes the winnings to a competitor.

One evening Wyman was in the dice pit near the showroom entrance, talking to Major Riddle. When the direct phone line into the casino cage rang, Wyman answered it. It was about a customer wanting to raise his limit another $20,000 and make one bet. Wyman said, "Give it to him." Riddle was worried – he tended to worry about everything – and said to Wyman, "That's an awful lot of money. Suppose he puts it on an even proposition?"

Wyman roared with laughter. "Major," he said, "there's no such thing as an even proposition out there."[222]

Shenker also testified that Dodson, Gordon, and Wyman had telephones at the resort as well as an office. He explained that all Dunes officials had access to the resort's vast telephone system and that their counterparts also used the office available to them.

In May 1977, a jury found four of the original defendants guilty of operating an illegal bookmaking business: Dodson, Gordon, Canon, and Vara.

CHAPTER 36

THE DUNES: BACCARAT PERSONALITIES

Baccarat was the casino's most unique game. It was the most glamorous and prestigious game the Dunes operated. It was specifically designed and placed in a special prominent location within the casino with fancy brass rails to keep the lookie-loos out of the area. The supervisors sat in elevated chairs, sometimes called ladder chairs, so they could observe the entire table, a view which was not possible while standing at the table level due to the heads of the players crowded around the table.

Baccarat was the only game that was dealt with currency, except for the special $500 chips when players were betting the limit of $4,000 and more. The snapping of clean new bills made the game even more interesting and had a history of movie stars, gamblers, Mobsters, and plain old Joes who romanced the game.

It was a sensitive area because of the cash, which needed qualified supervisors who were hand-picked by the Dunes' owners to ensure impeccable service, game protection, and fulfillment of ancillary duties.

It was also very lucrative for the dealers, the game starters (shills), cocktail waitresses, supervisors, and owners. Subsequently, it was the most sought after job in the casino. The people selected to work in the game were honored and privileged. It was understood by all of the other Dunes employees that to work in this area, a person had to have "juice" or a relationship with somebody who was somebody. It could be an owner, a Mob associate, or a relative.

There were some interesting people in this exciting gaming pit, the stories of which would comprise a book in itself. Here are some of them:

> **Larry Snow (Snofsky)** was the baccarat manager at the Dunes prior to opening Caesars Palace in 1966 in the same position. Snow was a familiar face at Joe Adonis' floating craps games in New Jersey. When I first heard of Snow, he was referred to as a "steerer" or "lugger," a person who took customers to a secret or hidden gambling location in safety and comfort, away from the eyes of the police and others.

Harley Kaufman was the baccarat manager of the Dunes in 1969 but started his employment as a busboy and soon after was promoted to room service waiter. Kaufman looked up to Sid Wyman as a father and gambling guru. Kaufman's late father was a dice dealer for Wyman at the Sands in the mid-1950s, which opened the door for Harley to work at the Dunes. Loyalty was big with Wyman, and he loved to take care of his employees.

"Mr. Wyman would order room service and tell me to order something for yourself and come on up and eat," Kaufman recalled.

He addressed the rumor that Wyman, who loved to gamble, went broke a few times and Charlie Rich always bailed him out.

"Only until he got involved with the Dunes," Kaufman said, "because I talked to him about that one day. I said to him—I said, 'Do you go out and play, you know, the way you used to, because I know you used to play high poker and then shoot a lot of craps and loved doing it?'

"Wyman answered, 'Let me tell you something. I don't do it like I used to because the thrill of the gambling is not there. You got to understand something about a player. A player is really hung up on betting far more than he can afford to lose. That is the—the real thrill. And for a player, the moment of truth is when the dice are in the air, not after there's a decision. It's the anticipation of the decision. Now with me, I got more money locked up. Like in the rulers, there's no more thrill in it for me. I've got spendthrift trusts and stocks and bonds and plenty of money, so I don't get the same charge out of it that I used to when I was much younger.'"

Wyman did, however, play high limit poker and gin. "Big Julie" Weintraub, the king of junkets, brought his planeload of gamblers from New York twice a month. Weintraub brought Stu Unger, who was only 19 years old. Unger was raised in a "slosh house" by parents who ran poker and other live illegal gaming in downtown New York City. He could photographically case the deck and play without peers. He was good and was exposed to the best.

Unger played a series of gin rummy games against Wyman and beat him out of $75,000. It was a spectacle. Wyman had a gallery of maybe 15 people watching him play, and Unger had one guy behind him. With every hustler from the Dunes poker pit behind Wyman, it is conceivable that Unger may have had a little help. However, that same afternoon at the craps tables, Unger lost the $75,000 he took from Wyman. Playing craps had become a habit for Unger.

Kaufman continued, "Wyman never left the hotel except for an occasional desire to shoot craps or visit a restaurant. The night before the election, he got Bobby the bellman to drive him up and down the Strip. He went in and out, personally in and out, of every joint on the Strip telling the people in the casino that his choice was Paul Laxalt and it would be good for the Strip. He did it personally." Kaufman added that, "Paul Laxalt thought that Sidney Wyman walked on water."

Brilliant with numbers and a quick learner, Kaufman could have run the entire Dunes resort. He sharpened his observation skills while being elbow to elbow with the bosses at a young age. Kaufman carefully walked the tightrope of casino politics at the Dunes. One could only learn the casino political mind games from being involved, not from lectures or textbooks.

Kaufman worked the cage and the games on his own time. His ability to deal baccarat was as good as any dealer's on the table. Also, he was well-liked by almost everyone. The man with the most power, Wyman, liked Kaufman, and that is what really mattered.

"George [Duckworth] used to watch me. He used to sit at the end of the craps pit with the newspaper, watching me in the baccarat, trying desperately to catch me doing something wrong. He didn't like me. He tried to fire me for 18 years," said Kaufman.

"When I was in the pit, George would never come in there," he went on. "Never ever come into the baccarat pit. No matter what was going on, George would never walk into the pit."

Sources confirmed that the Wyman-Kaufman relationship resulted in jealously and resentment on the part of some of the owners.

"I think George was jealous of my relationship with Sidney. I mean that it's as simple and complicated as that," said Kaufman. "I can remember one time, I'll tell you how much George stayed out of the baccarat pit. Remember Walter Davis? I came in one night, at quarter to nine, I walked into the pit and everybody's walking around whispering, and they're on pins and needles. I said, 'What's going on?' Walter Davis was in and he's stuck $240,000. Now, this was a lot of money. A ton. So, okay, so I'm there about 15 to 20 minutes, I'm watching it and Davis is starting to get out. And the phone rings. 'Harley.' 'Yes, sir.' 'It's Sid.' 'Yes, Mr. Wyman.' He always said 'Sid' and I always said, 'Yes, Mr. Wyman.' He said, 'How's it going?' 'I'll tell you, boss, looks like he is starting to get out.' He said, 'Really?' I said, 'Yes.' He said, 'Game running okay?' I said, 'Certainly.' He said, 'Don't worry about a thing.' I said, 'Yes, sir,' and he hung up."

> **Joseph Chautin** was the baccarat day shift boss and a dear friend of Wyman. Chautin was once arrested along with Wyman at a back-of-the-house St. Louis craps game.

One afternoon, a bookmaker from Minneapolis beat the baccarat game at the Dunes for about $40,000. Chautin was standing between the bankers with cash and the two dealers who paid the players. The third dealer was opposite the other two. The table faced the casino with the money side visible, which was inviting and an incredible curiosity to the public. The dealers counted the money in a crisp, rapid fire method that was unique.

Wyman passed by the pit and asked, "Hey, Joe, how we doing?" Chautin touched the stacks of currency to gauge how much cash was there. He replied, "We're about even." One of the dealers nudged Chautin and said in a low voice, "Joe, we are losing $40,000!"

Joe retorted, "You always tell 'em you are about even."

Kaufman was no dummy about the Chautin situation. He recalled, "I said to Sydney, I said, 'Look, Mr. Wyman, I don't care that Joe Chautin is your friend, and I don't care that you pay him. It's your money. But why don't you pay him to stay home instead of allowing him to be here and have the game exposed?' Sidney looked at me and said, 'Harley, why do you think you're there?' I said, 'Okay.'"

Chautin was a character indeed and never worked a real job in his entire life before the Dunes. He admitted to operating the State Inspector's Association in St. Louis and in Cicero, which published a sham magazine that accepted ads from small business owners that Chautin shook down. His spiel was that "state inspectors" would leave the business alone as long as they placed an ad.

Chautin may not have had enough baccarat knowledge to supervise a game, but he had a lot of grift sense and could smell a fraud in about a second. He had a sharp-witted satiric tongue and acrimony for just about everything.

Baccarat supervisors sat in an elevated chair to have a clear view of the dealers paying and taking bets at the table. A 4-foot-high rail around the pit separated the non- players from the game. Once, a lady walked up to Chautin and said, "Why are you sitting up in that chair?" He replied, "I am waiting for a shoe shine." He never cracked a smile.

Another time, Chautin phoned me on my scheduled day off and asked me to help him do "something." I asked what it was, but he refused to tell me on the line. Chautin was paranoid and maybe rightfully so since the FBI was all over the Dunes watching many of the executives. I went to his apartment, which was less than three blocks from the Dunes, picked him up, and we went to his bank. He told me that he was afraid that the feds were going to raid his safety deposit box. He wanted me to go with him and help carry his cash out of the box and the bank. I will never forget this, the two of us standing in the bank vault courtesy booth, piling bundles of $100 bills into every pocket we had. We left in a hurry. We drove to the Dunes, and Chautin put all of the money into a security box in the cashier's cage.

A few months later, Chautin told me that Morris Shenker needed some money, so he loaned him $100,000. I asked him, "Did he sign a note for the amount?" He replied, "No, I don't need it." To the best of my knowledge, Shenker never repaid Chautin.

> **Vincent "Vince" Taglialatella** was a baccarat supervisor that Chautin relied on to watch his back. If it weren't for him, Chautin would have inadvertently dumped off the entire Dunes baccarat bankroll daily. Taglialatella, "Tag" for short, was a native of Brooklyn, New York, and worked in Harlem paper dice games that were controlled by Anthony "Fat Tony" Salerno and Nick Dicostanzo, a.k.a. "Fat the Butch," "Fat Nicky," and "Nicky Edkins." Dicostanzo was a close associate of William "Lefty Clark" Bischoff, the Detroit Mobster who conceived the Riviera in Las Vegas and was associated with several Cuban casinos. Bischoff was a close friend of Moe Dalitz. Dicostanzo[223] had a piece of the Tropicana Night Club in Havana and was known as a feared enforcer at the Capri Hotel, which was one of the classiest casinos in Havana. Charles "The Blade" Tourine managed the nightclub and Nicholas Dicostanzo ran the casino. Dicostanzo and Tourine were associated with Meyer Lansky and Santo Trafficante.

Larry Snow also worked at the Capri with Tommy Renzoni, who later became the baccarat manager at the Sands in Las Vegas. Snow was friendly with Tourine, Dicostanzo, and Salerno. Snow later brought Vince Taglialatella to the Dunes from the Sands.[224]

When this author was "thrown" into the baccarat pit after just asking to practice on the table without pay, Tag was the only supervisor who offered assistance that was well received. He treated me like a son. I accepted him as my mentor and looked to him for advice and knowledge.

Vince Tag, which he was referred to as, worked at the Sands with Wyman and was one of the most talented paper (currency) dealers in Las Vegas. He learned his special skills in money Craps games where the dealer had bills of $5, $20, and $100 in one hand and rapidly made payoffs by

223   Courtlistener.com/opinion/732555/united-states-v-nicholas-dicostanzo-al-so-known-as-
224   NARA Record, Number 124-90068-10093

retrieving bills from the top, middle, or bottom. It was a sight to see. He taught this writer how to pay all six or seven bets in consecutive order, 1 through 7, and then calculate and place the house vigorish (vig), or commission, backwards. That is 7 to 1. Not a single floorman who was not exposed to this street-style dealing could follow it.

There were times when there were more baccarat players than seats. At times we had 12 seated players and 12 outside players. Tag had a procedure that he taught his crew for handling this unusual betting situation.

He loved sports and accepted wagers and bet on all major sports games; major league baseball, professional and college basketball, pro and college football, boxing, and horse racing. This was before cellular phones and beepers, and thus sports results were essentials to the bookie. Churchill Downs' sports book was across the street from the Dunes, and this writer spent every 20-minute break walking and running to the book to retrieve the latest scores and betting lines for Tag. I was in the best shape of my life from this exercise. God forbid I made a mistake, though. Any mistake could have resulted in a financial loss for Tag. Fortunately, I only made few of them, maybe two in eight years.

Tag taught this writer how to calculate parlay bets, round robins, and every type of bet for baseball and football, without a calculator or computer. He also showed me how to hand notate bets and players' code numbers, which were settled up on Tuesdays.

He recorded his shylocking customers by number and amounts loaned and paid, on a small paper that he folded a special way and placed in the upper corner of a pant pocket in such a manner that if the pocket were patted down or even pulled out, the slip of paper would not be found. He did this in case he was arrested and booked. Fooled everyone.

He also kept a backup copy of his paper files, which were about 6 by 8 inches in size, folded and wrapped in tin foil, and buried in the ground outside his home.

Every Sunday night Tag and his wife Anne invited me to dinner at their home or to an Italian restaurant. In 1969, he introduced me to Joey Cusumano at his restaurant, Joey's New Yorker, next to the Sands. Cusumano was a gentleman, and his authentic Italian restaurant was a favorite of many.

Anne operated a bar and restaurant in New York City before marrying Vincent. She loved to relay stories about Fidel and Raul Castro, who were frequent customers. Anne said that Fidel spoke perfect English.

Vince Tag once said to me, "You know, Geno, I can never be fired from this place. My man would pay $50,000 to walk in the casino here." His man was "Fat Tony" Salerno, who, according to the FBI, was one of the biggest Mob investors in Caesars Palace.

One of Tag's New York associates came in on the junket, and he wanted to take a shot at the Horseshoe downtown. The three of us went to Binion's Horseshoe and played craps, with a first bet of $5,000 and $5,000 odds. It was exhilarating. Tag lost $100,000 but didn't bat an eye.

Tag confided in me that he had been a "button man" in New York prior to coming to Las Vegas. I witnessed him in action one Sunday evening when we went out for our usual Sunday dinner. He had to collect a debt at the Tropicana and asked me to go along. We approached the dice pit, and he called over a pit boss who owed him some money for a bet or a loan. I watched a craps game while Tag handled his business. The man said he did not have the money.

I overheard Tag respond using strong language, which surprised me. "Give me that money or I will bust your head open," he said. As he did so, Tag lowered his right arm and a piece of metal re-bar slid down his jacket arm into his cupped fingers. He got the money in about a minute. Nobody screwed with Taglialatella. He was never "asked" to pay street tax by any other Mob family. He had a free and open license. George Duckworth knew he was a shylock and bookie, as did Wyman, but they did not stand in his way.

I wanted to switch my work shift to swing shift (6 p.m. to 2 a.m.) so I could be home with my newborn son. Tag wanted me to stay on day shift and offered me $15,000 a month to do so. I did not accept and ended up changing my shift. That eventually strained my friendship with him, which hurt, as to me he was like a second father, whom I loved.

> **Freddie Cohen** worked with Taglialatella in New York and was a crackerjack dice dealer. Cohen and 12 other men were indicted in 1966 for operating a Mafia-backed, high- rolling, floating craps game in New York City under the boss Anthony "Tony the Hawk" Arrietta.[225] The group used a fleet of 10 limousines to pick up the players. The game was backed by the Genovese crime family and took 5 percent of the average drop of $100,000 per night.

After he retired in his late 70s, Tag hired him as a game starter, or shill, in baccarat. Shills simulated play so the dealers could be seen calling the hand and paying and taking wagers to entice other people to join the game. Cohen smoked cigarettes and followed that with ingesting Certs

225   *Indianapolis Star*, Oct. 6, 1966

breath mints. He let the ashes build up in the ashtray and then spread them out using the excess paper from the Certs roll. When he went to the restroom or to stretch his legs, he placed the ashtray on top of the shill bankroll. If the baccarat shoe broke, one of the dealers removed the cards left in the shoe and shuffled them with those in use and left in the well.

One afternoon we had some substantial baccarat play just before a New York junket was ready to depart. The shoe broke. Cohen stood, picked up the ashtray, and took only some of the bills under it. He then palmed and crumpled the ones he had left there. Then with his other hand, he dumped the contents of the ashtray into the waste, all the while shielding the money-holding hand as he slid the bills into his pocket. It was a perfect illusion. I estimated he grabbed about $200. I did not do anything. Then about 10 minutes into the new shoe, I got off the chair and approached Tag.

"Vince, " I said, "our boy here just went south with about two bills."

He looked at me and said, "What are you going to do? He's an old man."

An FBI press release identified Cohen as a Dunes employee. However, Las Vegas Undersheriff Lloyd Bell said that Cohen obtained a permit to work as a shill for a different casino years earlier but there was no record of a man by that name employed at the Dunes. It is probable that he was not an official employee on the Dunes payroll but, instead, was paid in cash every time he worked.

> **Atilio "Tut Penny" Pennachio** was a former "roll down" operator in Coney Island, who was gregarious and had the gift of gab like no other I have known in the gaming business. He grew up in New York and rubbed elbows with the "Ma-hoffs" on Mulberry Street, which was his word for members of the Mafia. He had a friendly smile and a calculating brain and was forever on the hustle. He was a "deluxe" hustler, which was the parlance for the finest in the field.

One of the phrases Pennachio used to describe a person's behavior was a classic. He would say, "He is a real cutie-pie" or "He's cute-sy." He said that about a person who he thought was either phony, a liar, or meek. Most often, though, he called someone a "cutie-pie" if they bested him with their wits. According to Pennachio, practically everyone in the baccarat pit was a cutie-pie.

In actuality, Pennachio was the cutie-pie. One evening he was on the job as a floor supervisor in the baccarat, having been promoted to the position less than a few months before. Previously, he worked hand in hand with the dealers who were on the game that night. The dealer calling the cards, or on the "stick" as it was called, had a bad stomachache and was not feeling well yet refused to call in sick, which was a no-no. He could perform his job but could not call the game at the level that Pennachio, aware of the dealer's situation, expected.

Wyman walked up to the rail directly adjacent to Pennachio and asked, "Hi, Tut. What's going on?"

"Listen to that dealer. He just won't call the cards loud enough," replied Pennachio. Wyman immediately yelled at the dealer, "Call the hands right, son," and walked away.

This tattling to Wyman was unnecessary. Pennachio obviously had done it to show Wyman that he, Penny, was doing his job as an observant floorman well.

After the dealer got off the table, he said to Pennachio, "I'm surprised that Mr. Wyman didn't say to you, 'What are you telling me for? You're the floorman.'"

All of the dealers were on to Pennachio. One confided in me that he once gave Penny a pass for scamming the baccarat game.

In the early 1980s, his company, the Tut Penny Gaming Corporation, was allowed to try their new casino game called "crap-ette" in the Dunes casino. In the game, up to 30 players threw two baseball-sized balls into a basket, which then landed on different numbers. The player with the highest sum of those numbers won the game. Also there were over, under, field, and other bets. Pennachio received a patent for this gaming innovation. However, the Nevada Gaming Control Board made him change the name because the negative sounding "crap-ette" could have portrayed Nevada gaming in a bad light. Pennachio's game was later approved as "cice-ette."

Louie Horowitz was a former wrestler and bootleg fighter during the late 1920s and 1930s. At 82 years old, he could break someone's hand with a simple handshake and got a kick out of showing off his wrestling skills.

After getting hired as a baccarat shill, he drove to work in his 1959 Edsel, which was an oddity in itself. Another baccarat shill, Autumn, who never used her last name, hitched a ride to work with Horowitz on a daily basis. Because the shift started at 1 p.m., it was customary for the whole crew to report in at 12:30 P.M. to soap the new bills so they would not stick together.

Somewhat obsessive compulsive, Horowitz was always early. He'd pick Autumn up at 10:30 A.M. and would be circling the Dunes parking lot by

11 A.M. He was the nicest, sweetest man working in the pit, however, everyone knew he was just not quite right. It was suggested that he had received one too many punches in his career, at a time when physical blows, body slams, and wrestling as a whole were the real deal.

One afternoon, the baccarat shoe, which held eight decks of cards, was passed to Horowitz from chair number 12. The dealer who was calling the cards said in a joking manner, "Louie, Smu-ie, here is the shoe-ie."

Horowitz suddenly tensed up and his face turned red. He grabbed the shoe with one hand and made a fist with his other. He looked at the dealer as if he was going to kill him. The dealer continued, "Here is the shoe-ie, Louie." He'd left out "Smu-ie" that time, yet Louie was still enraged. But he did not say anything.

The baccarat card dealing shoe stays with the person dealing as long as the Bank side wins. The Player side won, so Horowitz passed the shoe to the next shill. He abruptly arose from his seat and went directly to the floor supervisor. All of the dealers and other personnel watched. They saw an incensed Horowitz say something to Taglialatella. Tag tried to calm Horowitz and insisted that he take a break and get some coffee.

Horowitz left the pit, glaring at the crew. Tag walked over to the stickman and asked, "What did you call him?"

"I didn't call him anything," the dealer answered. "All I said was 'Louie, Smu-ie, here is the shoe-ie.'"

Tag said, "That word 'smu-ie' that you used, Louie says you called him a woman's vagina."

From that day forward, the dealers tread lightly when interacting with Horowitz. But the story did not end there. Horowitz eventually became friendly with the dealer who used the word that Louie misunderstood. Perhaps Louie realized he made a mistake and now was, in his way, letting the dealer know he was sorry for being angry. Later the dealer got promoted to floor supervisor, and Horowitz appointed himself as his assistant.

Once when the floorman sat in the high chair overlooking the game, Louie sat opposite him, shilling. The floorman brushed something off his forehead a couple of times. Horowitz, jumped up, practically ran over to the floorman, and said, "What did you want?" Horowitz thought the floorman was summoning him.

Another time, in the evening, while working as a supervisor, Murray Saul stood behind the table and smoked a cigar. In doing so, he occasionally touched the top of one of the table chairs. Suddenly, Horowitz leapt out of his seat and knocked Saul down. When one of the dealers went to assist Saul, I corralled Horowitz and guided him out of the pit. He told me he hit Saul because "he was spreading the Hong Kong flu germs on his head." Thank God that Saul was not injured.

Horowitz did not get fired and continued working at the Dunes!

> **Bruce Fisher** is George Duckworth's nephew (Fisher's mother Lorayne was George's sister). Lorayne was a charming, loving, and wonderful woman who treated this writer like a son. Her husband Paul opened an art gallery in the hallway promenade adjacent to the Dunes pool. It was all windows, airy and a perfect location to sell oil paintings of some of the finest artists in the world.

Fisher and I became friends because of our mutual interest in flying, thanks to George. Fisher flew for United Airlines, first as an onboard flight observer, elevated to second officer, then as a flight engineer and retired as a captain. When working, he flew for United about 10 to 12 days a month then returned home to Las Vegas.

He wanted to learn how to deal baccarat and pinch hit for dealers who needed time off, were out sick, etc. Duckworth gave me permission to teach Fisher the game. I did but forgot to tell him something important, the slang word we used for the amount of $1,000.

One afternoon Fisher was dealing baccarat, and Arland Smith was the supervisor on his side of the table. A customer sat down and asked for a "geisel." Fisher did not understand the word, so he naturally thought the customer was talking to a friend who was with him or even to himself. A few hands went by when Smith said, "Mr. B, do you want to play?"

"I asked the dealer for a geisel, but he wouldn't give it to me," the customer said.

"What is a geisel," Fisher asked.

Smith retorted, "Give him $1,000, Bruce."

> **Murray Saul** was the brother of Herbie Saul, another key executive in the blackjack pit. Murray came to the Dunes from the Riviera and became friends with Wyman and Duckworth. He was one of the few employees who knew the sophisticated baccarat and chemin de fer games well.

I was dealing baccarat one afternoon when a male customer sat down opposite me in chair number 1. He asked for $1,000. I put a marker button in his chair number in front of the money rack and counted out ten

$100 bills. Saul said, "Okay," and I gave the player the cash. He played for about five minutes, during which time he came to owe $20 in house commission, or vigorish (vig). This was charged to his account as he won on Bank bets as opposed to Player bets that were not charged a commission. Only Bank bets were charged because they offered a slightly better chance of winning than Player bets. This was how the house made a profit.

The customer suddenly had an attack of some kind, possibly heart. He turned blue and slumped out of his chair onto the floor. Security and First Aid were summoned. While Security tended to the customer, Saul walked up behind me and told me to get the $1,000 from the man's money. I looked at him like he was crazy. He repeated it more authoritatively. I reached into the man's stack of currency, counted out $1,000 and put the remainder back. I said to Saul, "He owes $20 commission." Saul said, "Lock it up."

I thought to myself, "He is giving the man a break, as if the dying man is even aware of it." Only at the Dunes.

But then I remembered Saul often said Jewish prayers, and it made sense. He regularly prayed over the "mixing of the cards" by the dealers before the next shoe in baccarat was dealt.

Many celebrities played and visited the Dunes baccarat pit. Redd Foxx was a regular Dunes keno customer and a frequent baccarat player. One evening several customers spotted him playing baccarat and got Foxx's attention as the dealing shoe was being reshuffled to continue the game. A shoe holds about 80 decisions or hands. As the dealers were shuffling the cards, two African American ladies in their mid-20s, elegantly dressed and adorned with 24 karat jewelry, got Foxx's attention while he pushed his chair back from the table to light a cigarette.

"Oh, Mr. Foxx, Mr. Foxx, hello. We are big fans of yours. We love your shows and TV appearances so much. Can we ask you a question?"

Foxx, in his trademark style and mug said, "Sure, go ahead, ladies."

"Mr. Foxx, do you have any relatives, a brother or sister?"

Foxx did not hesitate and replied, "I am glad you asked. I had a brother one time, but my father left him on a napkin at an Elks picnic."

It was a classic Redd Foxx repartee that sailed over the heads of his fans

CHAPTER 37

HY GOLDBAUM,
BUGSY SIEGEL'S ASSOCIATE

Hy Goldbaum was "the bookies' bookie" on Hollywood's Sunset Strip in California. He and his partners George Capri and Ed Cook operated the largest commission betting house in the US, taking layoff bets from bookies around the country and bets on hot horses that nobody would accept.

The enterprise, operating under the trade name of Golden News Service and conducting all business by telephone, divided the larger bets of other bookmakers into smaller bets and placed them with bookies nationwide. In gambling nomenclature his operation was referred to as a "commission house."

As far as a commission, they only charged one when a bet lost. In those instances, the participating bookmakers paid a commission to Golden News Service of between 2.5 and 5 percent, the amount agreed to when the bet was placed.

Between 1945 and 1949, Golden News Service grossed more than $6 million. In 1949, the trio moved to Las Vegas to operate a commission-style race book at the new, lavish Flamingo hotel founded by Goldbaum's friend, Benjamin "Bugsy" Siegel.

During those years, Goldbaum was one of a group of Los Angeles gamblers that Richard Nixon squeezed for a large campaign donation. Los Angeles Mobster Mickey Cohen, an associate of Goldbaum, told the government during Watergate what happened with Nixon a few decades earlier. Here is Cohen's statement in his own words:

> "I am presently serving a sentence in the federal prison at Alcatraz. At my request I asked for a meeting with a state law enforcement officer and on Oct. 9, 1962, Richard R. Rogan met me in the visitor's room at Alcatraz.[226]
>
> "I informed Mr. Roger [sic] that I wished to discuss with him a question concerning the influence of persons engaged in gambling and bookmaking on the early political career of Richard Nixon.

"I first met Richard Nixon at a luncheon in the Goodfellow's Fisherman's grotto on South Main Street in 1946. The meeting was arranged by Murray Chotiner who asked me to meet Mr. Nixon who was about to start his first campaign as a representative in Congress that year. I was asked by Nixon and Chotiner to raise some money for Nixon's campaign.

"In either 1948 during Nixon's second race for Congress or 1950 in his campaign for the Senate, I was again asked by Murray Chotiner to raise funds for Nixon's campaign. During that time I was running most of the gambling and bookmaking in Los Angeles County. I reserved the banquet room in the Knickerbocker Hotel on Ivar Street in Hollywood for a dinner meeting to which I invited approximately 250 persons who were working with me in the gambling fraternity. Among those who were present, whose names are well known to law enforcement officers, were Joe and Fred Sica, Jack Dragna, and George Capri. Also present was Hy Goldbaum,[227] who is one of the pit bosses at the Stardust hotel in Las Vegas, who also served a term of imprisonment at the federal prison at McNeil Island. Capri was one of the owners of the Flamingo Hotel in Las Vegas.

"Murray Chotiner told me I should have a quota of $25,000 to the campaign. During the course of the evening Nixon spoke for approximately 10 minutes. Chotiner spoke about half an hour. At this meeting my group pledged between $17,000 and $19,000 but this did not meet the quota set by Nixon and Chotiner – and the group was informed they would have to stay until the quota was met."[228]

The sentence, "The group was informed by Nixon and Chotiner that they would have to stay until the quota was met" is especially important. In brief, Nixon and Chotiner demanded the gamblers pay a specific, greater amount. Obviously, the gamblers would expect something in return.

> "I have been asked by several newspaper persons and television employees of NBC during the 1956 presidential campaign to make these facts known," continued Mickey Cohen, "but until now I have refused to do so."

In the early 1950s, Goldbaum, Capri, and Cook were convicted of tax evasion – specifically under-reporting their income on their tax returns during specific years – and conspiracy. The federal grand jury that indict-

---

227   Hy Goldbaum was a bookmaker who once ran the "commission house" inside the Flamingo for Bugsy Siegel and was an associate of Westbrook and Johnny Stone.
228   Drew Pearson and Jack Anderson, *Washington Merry-Go-Round* column

ed them did the same with Los Angeles Mobster Mickey Cohen, also for income tax violations. The three Golden News Service partners served time at McNeil Island Corrections Center.

Along with Siegel, Goldbaum was a friend of underworld figure Anthony "Tony" Brancato, and had a handshake connection with Jimmy Hoffa through another friend, Frank Brewster of Seattle, who was head of the eleven-state Western Conference of Teamsters Pension Trust.

James B. Elkins, in his testimony before Senator Robert F. Kennedy's Senate committee investigating the Teamsters, stated that Goldbaum introduced Brewster to Stanley Terry, a Portland, Oregon, pinball operator who had almost 300 pinball machines on the street. Elkins was Terry's competitor.

Subsequently, Terry reportedly paid Brewster $10,000. Terry's doing so, Elkins said, spoiled his own plan to monopolize Oregon's $250,000 a year pinball industry.

Kennedy surmised that the $10,000 was the cost for Terry getting back in the Teamsters' good graces. Terry needed this because the Teamsters only allowed pinball machines bearing their sticker to be operated in Portland. Businesses using nonunion machines were picketed, and their deliveries of beer, bread, and other supplies were cut off by the organization.

On questioning, Terry denied having told William Capri, part owner of the Flamingo, that he would "take care of Hy Goldbaum" if Goldbaum would arrange with Brewster for Terry to join the Teamsters union.[229] Further, Terry insisted that he "never paid Brewster a cent." He also denied that he paid or promised to pay Goldbaum $7,500 for getting him an appointment with Brewster.

This dialogue and questioning set the stage for the appearance of Goldbaum as an authentic Damon Runyon-type character, one who described himself as a "pit man" in the gaming rooms at Las Vegas' flamboyant Flamingo.

"A 'pit man' is a fellow who stands around to watch that people don't steal," Goldbaum explained. He testified that he "put in a pitch" for Terry with Brewster when he encountered the Teamsters official at the Santa Anita race track in January 1955. However, he denied that Terry paid or promised to pay him $7,500 for doing so.

This conflicted with the contents of an affidavit of Capri. Capri introduced Terry to Goldbaum, he said, and got the impression that Terry would "take care" of Goldbaum. He also said that later he heard Goldbaum complain that Terry "never kept his promise."

229   *St. Louis Post-Dispatch*, March 1957

Goldbaum explained: "What I said was I did him a favor, and he never once even called me to thank me. I pop off a lot. I might have said he bought this favor for $7,500. I could have made this remark." Goldbaum said he might have said that to Lester Beckman, his former cellmate at McNeil Island. He "found out later" that Terry did not keep the appointment with Brewster, he added.

During the late 1960s, Sidney Wyman hired Goldbaum as a casino host at the Dunes, where he worked through the late 1970s. This writer often sat with him on our dinner break, and he relayed some great tales. His cologne, The Baron, was unforgettable. The companion lady's scent was White Shoulders.

Goldbaum introduced me to Russell Douglas "R.D." Matthews, who once was questioned for the Warren Commission's report on the assassination of President John F. Kennedy. His lawyer Harry Claiborne, who represented Wyman et al. in the Dunes bookmaking operation case, went on to become a federal judge, and later was impeached. Matthews would pick up the diminutive Goldbaum like a small doll, and Hy would simulate choking him. Matthews holding up Goldbaum was a sight to see, especially with the black patch Matthews had over one eye.

But this is the best of Goldbaum's stories. Central Telephone Company, the local Las Vegas provider, serviced the Flamingo when Goldbaum and crew operated the commission book there. Las Vegas was a small town so the vendors had a good working relationship with the customers. Central Telephone regularly sent an agent to pick up money from Goldbaum for the monthly phone bill that totaled about $10,000 to $12,000 a month.

Once, the agent asked Goldbaum to consider buying the entire Central Telephone Company for about $50,000 since Goldbaum's monthly bill accounted for almost 20 percent of the total value of the company. Goldbaum told me he was not interested. He must have been making good money if he turned down the opportunity.

CHAPTER 38

THE DUNES:
SKIMMING AND PROJECT JANICE

In December 1971, a federal grand jury returned a three-count indictment against six Dunes officials, alleging that they participated in skimming and concealing money from the dice tables, excluding the revenue from the casino's financial statements, and then falsifying the corporate income tax return. This was the second set of indictments pertaining to skimming in Las Vegas. The first named Meyer Lansky and six others for their alleged skimming at the Flamingo.[230]

The six Dunes indictees were Sydney Wyman, vice-president and chairman of the board of M&R Investment Company and owner of the Dunes; Bob Rice, vice-president and secretary of M&R; George Duckworth, M&R vice-president and assistant secretary; Howard Engel, vice-president; Leonard J. Campbell, a partner in the separate company that held the Dunes' ground lease; and Charles "Charlie" Speck, the Dunes casino credit manager. M&R Investment Co. was the entity that operated the casino and hotel and was wholly owned by Continental Connector Corporation.

In October 1972, the federal government dropped the charges of tax evasion and conspiracy against Speck, the only defendant who was not a co-owner of M&R. Federal Judge Bruce Thompson issued a judgment of acquittal based on the testimony of the government's key witness George Horvath, who did not link Speck to the charges.[231]

The case for the other five defendants went to trial in October 1972. Wyman, Rice, Duckworth, and Engel could not afford to lose the case as they were the gambling licensees for the Dunes. Were they to be convicted, they would have to immediately surrender their gaming licenses and sell their equity in the resort. Also, the likely negative publicity generated as a result would decrease the value of the Dunes. This would undoubt-

---

230   *Santa Cruz Sentinel*, June 27, 1978. Note: Meyer Lansky beat the case thanks to Federal Judge Roger Foley. Foley dismissed the indictment and all of the charges against Lansky because of his alleged poor health.

231   *Albuquerque Journal*, Oct. 24, 1972

edly hinder future attempts to obtain any loans, say for building or other expansions there, or sell the enterprise outright.

As such, the indictments were of great concern to Continental Connector, the directors of which decided to take action to protect their shareholders' interests. In January 1972, Wyman, Rich, Rice, Duckworth, and others announced a proposed sale of about 21 percent of their Dunes' Continental Connector stock, or 500,000 shares, and a majority interest to ATIS, Inc., a Boston-based tour and travel company owned by Meshulam Riklis. Shenker already was negotiating with Riklis in 1970 as Wyman and already-retired Rich wanted to sell their holdings in the Dunes then, prior to the indictments.

The executives compensated Wyman in accordance with his management contract as well. Further, Rice and other minor owners sold their interests in the Dunes to ATIS. Morris Shenker handled the transactions. By making these moves, they demonstrated to the press and Nevada's gaming authorities that they were addressing the issue even though the Dunes executives were innocent until proven guilty.

The proposed sale fell through when, in June 1972, Riklis dropped his planned purchase after "waging an unsuccessful effort to obtain effective control" of the Dunes operation.[232] Jake Gottlieb died in April 1972, and his vast holdings in Continental Connector and the Dunes' land lease were not yet settled in probate. That was probably a major reason why Riklis could not gain total control.

Another factor may have been the alleged hidden ownership of the Dunes, which was acknowledged in FBI reports. Gus Alex, Sam Giancana, Nick Civella, Tony Giordano, Pete Licavoli, and other members of the Mob certainly may have owned a hidden interest in the operation. They certainly may have had something to say about a sale of the Dunes, especially if it would jeopardize their share of the skim, however it was carried out. The skim did not have to be delivered as cash; it could have been concealed in favorable vendor contracts and junket collection arrangements.

The Dunes skimming trial was held in Reno, Nevada, and lasted two weeks. Attorneys for the defense were Shenker in St. Louis and Harry Claiborne in Las Vegas. Claiborne was experienced, knew the Nevada court system well, and was perhaps one of the best defense attorneys who ever lived.

If this writer was in need of a top criminal defense attorney, his first choice would be Claiborne. His disarming style, hidden intellect, and expressive articulation in a courtroom were hard to beat. He graduated from law school in 1941 and quickly passed the bar exam. He went back to Las Vegas where he spent some time as a military policeman while in the service.

Next, Claiborne joined the Las Vegas Metropolitan Police Department and after a year's residency, was admitted to the Nevada Bar. He was promoted to sergeant of detectives and given a special role among the handful of other detectives on the force. He vetted reports by the others and determined whether cases should advance to the district attorney for prosecution. He also prepared and presented evidence to the D.A. Claiborne had a good relationship with District Attorney Gray Gubler.[233]

After being sworn in as a member of the Nevada Bar in December, Claiborne began working for the Clark County District Attorney's Office on January 5, 1947. Claiborne developed one of the most successful law practices in Nevada.

After years of politics and law he was nominated by Senator Howard Cannon for a federal judgeship. President Jimmy Carter used the Omnibus Judgeship Bill to create 152 new federal judgeships throughout the U.S. and nominated Claiborne in 1978 to fill the opening in Nevada. The existing positions were held by Bruce Thompson in Reno and Roger Foley in Las Vegas. Claiborne started his judicial career in Reno and returned to Las Vegas in 1979.

Horvath, the government's key witness in the Dunes skimming trial, testified that Wyman told him about a skimming operation at the hotel. Horvath was a New York businessman with ties to Jimmy Hoffa and Teamsters pension fund loans. Horvath was the prosecution's only witness who saw, heard about, or participated in any skimming at the Dunes.

Jackie Fields, a former professional boxer and then public relations manager at the Tropicana, introduced Horvath to Wyman in 1964 when Horvath was considering purchasing the Dunes. Fields said, "I called Sid and asked if he'd do me a favor. It was a chance for me to make a buck."[234] Fields said he was acting for Horvath, in the hopes that if Horvath did purchase the Dunes, he would receive a finder's fee.

The main evidence that the government proffered was the results of a secret investigation conducted by the IRS penned "Project Janice," during summer 1965. Teams of two and three agents posed as dice players at specific tables at the Dunes and secretly counted the money that was put into the drop box at each of the targeted tables. The drop boxes held all of the cash and foreign casino chips exchanged for valid Dunes chips for play.

233   "Lies Within Lies: The Betrayal of Nevada Judge Harry Claiborne," Michael Vernetti, 2011
234   *Reno Evening-Gazette*, Oct. 26, 1972

Whenever a customer came to play at a game, they handed the dealer cash, and the dealer then converted it into casino chips. Then, using a paddle, the dealer dropped the cash through a small opening into the drop box. This resulted in the terms "the drop" and "the cash drop." When the typically eight hour long dice shift ended, a new drop box was placed on the table, and the old drop box was sent to the cage for counting and game reconciliation. Casino management determined how many shifts to operate based on the amount of game action, or customer business, at the tables. Generally, there were three shifts: day, swing, and graveyard.

The final count, whether a win or a loss, was determined by knowing what the opening bankroll was and adding to it the cash in the drop box and the overflows (credits) sent back to the casino cage and then subtracting the additional chips (fills) brought to the table.

The IRS theorized that taking cash from the drop box would be the easiest way to skim. If they knew exactly how much money went into the sealed box on a dice table for a certain game, they figured they then could compare that to the amounts declared by the casino.

For their investigation, the IRS set up a craps table at the Army Reserve Center in Las Vegas. There they taught 10 undercover agents how to make simple bets and how to count, as part of a three man team assigned to a table, the currency taken in for the game, according to the trial testimony of government witness Robert Smith. Two agents each counted, and the third relieved as necessary. The agents turned in their daily count sheets the following day. The IRS then compared the drop box counts by the agents with the casino's tallies.

From this investigation, the IRS determined that the Dunes skimmed and did not report some $1.5 million from craps table winnings.[235]

The methodology the IRS used in Project Janice, however, raised questions. How could the agents' counts be compared to house records the next day? How was the IRS obtaining the house records? Did they have someone in the cage or a casino boss feeding them the information? Or was the IRS simply holding the tallies to compare them with those on the Dunes' corporate tax return?

Smith admitted on cross-examination that there were problems with the system. For one, the agents' tallies for the same day's worth of drop box income did not always match each other's, and both agents insisted their own count was correct.

Another problem was with the accuracy of the counts because the agents likely did not account for money taken in from the extra craps

---

235   *Ibid*

table that was put on the floor on weekends. They may not have even known about the added table. A former Dunes employee, Jim Sacamono, explained it:

"Throughout the industry the numbers were on the boxes on the games. Now when the IRS was clocking the drop at the Dunes, they were clocking the drop on craps eight because, see, they went one, two, three, four, you know. And that was for start, and then down towards the–to-wards the show, one, two, three, four and then from the show, five, six, seven, eight.

"So eight would be across from one in the middle of the casino. Now they sat, they were clocking the drop on eight all the – all the time. 24/7. The IRS guy standing out there with a – probably a clicker in his pocket and he'd clock the cash being dropped into the box. Now, when they went to court, they produced all this on game number eight.

"Well, on the weekend, on Saturday and Sunday morning, Saturday night, they put in another crap game across from the showroom, down at the end. So now it's one, two, three, four, five, six, seven, eight, nine. So that game turned out to be nine. But they're still clocking it as eight."[236]

One of the defense's tactics at trial was to throw the credibility of the undercover IRS agents into question. Claiborne asked them what a "hop bet" was, and they could not answer. He asked them what a "two way 11" was, and they could not answer. He asked them what a "sleeper bet" was; they could not answer. The defense raised the question that if they were experts to be trusted with the drop box count then why did they not know the fundamentals of the game.

A "hop bet" is casino dealer jargon for a secret bet on the layout in a dice game, similar to In-and-Out Burger's secret menu! A "hop bet" is a one-roll bet wherein a player predicts the number of each separate die. For instance, if a gambler calls "two and three on the hop," it means that one die will show a 2 and the other a 3. Even though the total of the two dice is 5, the gambler is not betting on a total of 5, which could also be rolled 4, 1, for instance. If on the next roll 2, 3 shows, the bet wins. If any-thing else comes up, the bet loses.

The defense argued that all of the charges except conspiracy did not apply as they did not fall within the appropriate statute of limitations. They called the secret cash monitoring during Project Janice an overt act and one that failed to link the defendants to the conspiracy charge. To substantiate that claim, a casino cage cashier, Clifford Erickson, testified that he was never asked to take part in any skimming or improper procedure at the Dunes.

The prosecution, on the other hand, contended that the acts charged in the indictment inferred that a conspiracy existed and that was all they had to prove for a conviction.

Nevada Senator Howard Cannon told the press that "the federal government just didn't have a very good case" and that the trial amounted to "undue harassment by the federal government."[237] He informed U.S. Attorney General Richard Kleindienst that the federal activities in Nevada represented "an undue invasion into our jurisdiction." Kleindienst reportedly responded that the federal strike forces were investigating more in areas like Chicago than in Nevada. That was an interesting comment because there were no legal casinos in Chicago period, only illegal ones run by organized crime. So was the investigation in Nevada about organized crime or skimming? What did Kleindienst mean exactly?

The judge dismissed the Dunes skimming case on October 30, 1972.

However, it still reeks of mystery even as this book is written. No related transcripts, records, or depositions can be found anywhere. A major law firm was hired to search the federal courthouse in Reno for copies of any of the trial documents, but they did not find anything. The court clerk was asked to search for the case records and to search for anything under the name of each individual indicted and tried. Nothing was found. Everything mysteriously vanished.

There are three possible suspects behind the disappearance of these legal records.

1) Harry Houdini, because he owed a gambling marker at the Dunes, broke in to the building, and took the records away without a trace as a favor to the Dunes executives. 2) A federal employee retrieved the records for a federal judge who somehow forgot to have them sent back for storage as a favor in kind to the former Dunes owners, a sort of kindly expungement. 3) The FBI removed the records, perhaps as part of a black operation. Unfortunately, there was no proof that implicated any of them.

It would not have made sense for Claiborne, who later was appointed a federal judge, to have had the documents removed from the archives. He would have preferred to have them available to the public, particularly since he, the other Nevada federal judges, and the federal prosecutors were at odds with the FBI in the Nevada office and with Joseph "Joe" Yablonsky, its strike force chief.

---

237   *Reno Evening Gazette*, Dec. 18, 1972

CHAPTER 39

THE GREEN FELT JUNGLE: WAS IT TRUE?

L as Vegas was both shocked and entertained by *The Green Felt Jungle*, written be Ed Reid and Ovid Demaris and published in January 1963. The authors claimed the book told the truth about Las Vegas, and thus blew the lid off of the entertainment capital of the world. However, much of the material in the book concerning the Dunes was not true or was problematic for one reason or another.

There was a third person behind the book named Edward "Ed " Becker. It was common knowledge that he contributed much of the information contained in it. Becker was an intelligent guy who portrayed a false image to his friends and associates, which was one of being an insider and Mob boss confidant. His employment at and relationship with the Riviera, a major Mob- fronted hotel, did not put him on that level, however.

Becker claimed that Gus Greenbaum was "my friend and boss" and implied he, Becker, was close to the Riviera operation. However, the second biggest investor group in the Riviera was headed by Sidney Wyman, and Becker did not mention Wyman in his book, *All American Mafioso: The Johnny Rosselli Story*.[238] This was odd because plenty of evidence showed that Wyman knew Rosselli and was close to Greenbaum.

Other names that Becker did not mention in the book but should have were Nick Civella and Ross Miller, as they both were heavily involved with the Riviera, too.

Becker was a public relations man at the Riviera when Wyman was a stakeholder. Becker may have worked alongside Wyman but he was never a close enough associate to have been privy to inside information. It seems as though Becker's imagination and drive led him to surmise a great many bits and pieces of information about the owners and operators of the casinos mentioned in *The Green Felt Jungle*, which he then passed along to Reid and Demaris.

Wyman was known to take qualified people with him from hotel to hotel if he liked them and they were capable of doing the job. This writer cannot recall ever seeing Becker in the Dunes or in the company of Wyman or the other executives.

The Green Felt Jungle alluded to the Dunes having had secret owners, according to this passage: "Two well-known pawns, Sidney Wyman and Kewpie Rich, were moved from the Flamingo to the Riviera (Wyman was also at the Sands) and lately to the Dunes, which is having its share of trouble with Chicago."[239]

However, it is clear from the 24/7 FBI surveillance on Sam Giancana that the Dunes owners did not have any conflict with the Chicago Outfit. In 1962, the FBI captured a detailed conversation between Wyman and Morris "Potsy" Pearl in which they discussed a possible investment in the Dunes by Pearl.[240] Giancana also was interested in the Dunes and unless he was lying to Pearl, there was no issue between the resort and the Chicago Mob. This conversation occurred before February 1962, which means that if the group behind The Green Felt Jungle really knew what was going on inside the Dunes, they would have published it. The truth of the matter is that they had no clue as to what the Dunes was all about. They speculated but produced no concrete facts to support their claims.

Further, it is possible that Wyman presented the offer to Pearl of his own accord. Perhaps it was a private arrangement between the two, one that Wyman's partners were not privy to.

The Green Felt Jungle alleged that Wyman and Rich were pawns for someone else. In truth, while the two may have had "investors" who were passive, those investors did not call the shots. These investors were not just anybody, but rather most probably acquaintances from past business associations. One example is Nick Civella, who tried to buy into the Riviera hotel when Wyman was the second biggest investor.[241] Ross Miller vehemently opposed Civella obtaining a secret piece of the Riviera and informed the Nevada gaming authorities that Civella was trying to. Miller was a faction in the Riviera, was a close associate of Jimmy Hoffa and Chicago labor attorney Sidney Korshak who, according to the FBI, represented the Outfit's interests in Las Vegas. Perhaps it was this situation between Miller and Civella that was the conflict to which *The Green Felt Jungle* referred.

Reid, Demaris, and Becker would not have dared called Wyman and Rich pawns to their face. Wyman, who could have been a champion college debater, would have shamed him into being lower than a fly. And their referring to Rich as "Kewpie" was just an insult as there was never a

239   *The Green Felt Jungle*, Ed Reid and Ovid Demaris, 1963
240   FBI File, 124-10202-10059, 1962
241   FBI File, 124-10342-10000, May 1960

classier boss than Charles J. Rich. The remarks hit below the belt. It simply was a rank, sensationalistic tactic to sell books.

The authors claimed that Wyman and Rich moved from the Flamingo to the Riviera, but there is no proof of Rich working at the Flamingo and sketchy evidence that Wyman worked there in any position. It seems the authors inferred from questioning of Rich during the Kefauver Committee hearings that he and Wyman were involved in the Flamingo. During the hearing it came out that the Senate committee had information alleging that Rich was going to purchase an interest in that hotel-casino. Rich, though, denied it. That exchange during the hearing was all public record and available to Reid and Demaris.

The only truth about the Dunes in the book may have been the included quote by Sherlock Feldman, a friend of Wyman: "People in the rest of the world merely go broke and die broke. In Las Vegas you live broke."

Becker, with Reid, was part of a controversy in that he linked New Orleans Mafia boss Carlos Marcello to John F. Kennedy's assassination, a claim that fueled publicity and attention.

The Washington Post, in 1979, described the situation:[242]

"When the House Assassination Committee released its report last month, its most perplexing section concerned alleged organized crime involvement with the killing of John Kennedy. Santos Trafficante and Carlos Marcello were fingered as 'the most likely family bosses' to have participated in any plot, but then the ambivalent report termed the notion 'unlikely.'

"Linking Marcello to JFK's death was an obscure private eye named Edward N. Becker, a shadowy figure who has passed in and out of organized crime circles as a shamus and anonymous researcher of books. Who is Becker?

"He's a 57-year-old, soft-spoken man who today lives in Las Vegas with his second wife. He's currently involved in business with a former assistant attorney general of the U.S., Washington-based attorney Jerris Leonard. And Becker is not delighted his name surfaced in the House report.

"'I expect some kind of retribution,' Becker says today. 'The committee said, We're doing everything in the world to protect you. I didn't believe it. Of course I'm worried.'

"In 1955 Becker signed on as public relations director for the Riviera Hotel in Vegas. His milieu was gambling and men whose occupations were vague, he says, and he eventually helped piece together an NBC White Paper on organized crime in 1966. He also helped gather information for the books, *Green Felt Jungle* and *The Grim Reapers*, both billed as exposés of organized crime.

"Becker says he was in Louisiana in September of 1962 working undercover for a finance company investigating Billie Sol Estes when he struck up a friendship with Carlo Roppolo, a Shreveport oil geologist well-liked by Marcello, according to the House report. The two men visited Marcello at his estate near New Orleans. In the course of a long evening of drinking scotch, Becker remembers Marcello cursing the Kennedy brothers and talking vaguely of trying to kill the president. Marcello denies that.

"That scene (without Becker's name) made its way into Ed Reid's book, *The Grim Reapers*, which led the House committee to Becker, who talked with a committee staffer by phone but refused to testify because he feared the arm of organized crime as well as the wrath of the FBI. The Bureau, according to the House report, worked hard to discredit Becker instead of investigating the validity of his information."

Details were given in *All American Mafioso* about Becker meeting a second time with Marcello. That passage read:

"The same month, Carlos Marcello described a more detailed plan in the privacy of a farmhouse on his sprawling country estate outside New Orleans. Ed Becker, a private investigator and free-lance businessman, was meeting with Marcello and his longtime associates Carlo Roppolo and Jack Liberto when their boss pulled out a bottle and poured a generous round of Scotch. The conversation wandered until Becker made an offhand remark about Bobby Kennedy and Marcello's deportation. The reference struck a nerve, and Carlos jumped to his feet, exclaiming the Sicilian oath, 'Livarsi na pietra di la scarpa! (Take the stone out of my shoe!)'

"Reverting to English, Marcello shouted, 'Don't worry about that Bobby son-of-a-bitch. He's going to be taken care of.' Emboldened by the Scotch, Becker interrupted. 'You can't go after Bobby Kennedy. You'll get into a hell of a lot of trouble.' In answer, Marcello invoked an old Italian proverb: 'If you want to kill a dog, you don't cut off the tail, you cut off the head.' Bobby was the tail, an adjunct, an appendage. If the President were killed then Bobby would lose his bite. Marcello added that he had a plan, to use 'a nut' to take the fall for the murder, 'like they do in Sicily.' Seated again, Marcello abruptly changed the subject, and the Kennedys were not mentioned again."

An interview by this writer of Tony Montana, a Chicago Outfit front man, shed light on the question of whether or not Becker indeed did meet with Marcello in 1962.

In the late 1980s and early 1990s Café Michele on Flamingo Road was a lunch and drink hangout for locals and rounders in Las Vegas. This author frequented the establishment on a daily basis to catch up with friends and share and hear stories about the happenings in the world of gaming, deals, and the Mob. Becker held court at Michele's a few times a week with his business companion and book advisor (working on the Rosselli book), Tony Montana. In fact, Becker introduced Montana to me. Montana was not a lightweight wannabe; he was the real deal. His uncle, John Montana, was a guest at the famed Apalachin Mafia convening in November 1957, and Tony was an employee of the late Chicago boss Tony Spilotro. Tony Montana was an expert food and beverage manager who had the skills to turn profits in bars and restaurants. Because he was loyal, efficient, and a good problem solver, he was highly sought after.

Tony Montana had helped Becker get some interviews with top Mafia bosses, which Becker could not land merely on the claim that he was associated and worked with Gus Greenbaum at the Riviera and Flamingo hotels. My former boss from the Dunes, Wyman, was the second biggest shareholder in the Riviera with Greenbaum. Becker did not hold an inside position in management and therefore was not connected, so to speak.

Becker wanted to interview Marcello in New Orleans but could never connect with Marcello or any of his associates to arrange a meeting. Montana, however, successfully set up an interview, through Joe Pignatello, associate of Sam Giancana and owner of the once famous Villa d'Este Italian restaurant in Las Vegas.

One afternoon this writer interviewed Tony Montana. I was interested in the meeting Tony arranged between Marcello and Becker as described in the book, *All American Mafioso*. Tony told me that he and Becker stayed in a small hotel in the French Quarter and were to be ready the next morning to be picked up by a driver. The pair waited in the outside dining area and soon after breakfast, a car approached. The driver introduced himself as a representative of Marcello. After the pleasantries, Montana got in the front passenger seat and Becker sat in the rear. Becker was demonstrably nervous after the driver said they were going out to the farm in Metairie because he thought that the meeting would take place in a nearby office. The trip to the farm took more than 30 minutes. "Don't worry. If something was going to happen to you, it would have already," the driver told

Becker jokingly with a grin. Montana realized the driver was just being humorous.

Tony continued the story, "We were brought into Marcello's office, and we met Carlos Marcello."

That comment made a light go on for me. In Becker's book he wrote that he and Marcello met in 1962. If that were true then why did the two men have to be re-introduced by Montana at this supposed second meeting? Why would Marcello greet Becker as if he was meeting him for the first time? That did not make sense.

I asked Tony, "Did it appear to you that Ed was meeting Marcello for the first time?" He said, "Absolutely."

The conclusion is that Becker never was at a meeting with Marcello in 1962. It was a fabrication.

One factual story in *All American Mafioso* was about the Dunes and Howard Hughes. Rosselli introduced Robert "Bob" Maheu to Wyman and company, which eventually led to Hughes negotiating to acquire the Dunes.

An alleged incident involving Rosselli and the Dunes was relayed by an FBI informant: "By air-tel dated 4/12/63 in the case entitled 'Dunes Hotel aka Las Vegas Nevada.' The Las Vegas Office advised that LV 70-C* on 3/10/63 advised that Jake Gottlieb (Landlord, Dunes Hotel) and Major Riddle engaged in a discussion involving the giving of markers and they believed that Sid (Wyman-part owner) made a bad mistake in giving credit to an unknown individual. Gottlieb remarked to the effect that Sid had made other mistakes along these lines particularly 'with that fellow Rosselli from Los Angeles.'"[243]

CHAPTER 40

THE DORFMANS AND AL BARON

Paul Dorfman was a former prizefighter who fought under the name of "Red Dorfman." He was managed by Sam Pian, who also managed Barney Ross, a former welterweight and middleweight champion.

In 1955 and 1956, Dorfman was a guest at the Riviera in Las Vegas, then co-owned by Ross Miller, Sid Wyman, and Charles Rich. The hotel's ledger sheets showed that Dorfman was not charged for the rooms he stayed in.

Wyman and Rich had a great love of sports, and Rich once owned a boxing gym in St. Louis. This mutual interest in boxing and sports fueled a long friendship between Dorfman, Wyman, and Rich. It developed over the years and became mutually prosperous. It is conceivable and probable that this friendship led to the start of the Dunes' association with Jake Gottlieb, who was the landlord.

In the late 1950s, the U.S. Senate Select Committee on Improper Activities in Labor and Management investigated questionable activities involving Dorfman and the Teamsters pension fund.

Launched in 1957, the committee operated for more than three years. Because its chairman throughout was John L. McClellan, it often was called the McClellan Committee. Robert Kennedy was its chief counsel. Investigators included Pierre E.G. Salinger, Martin S. Uhlmann, John P. Findlay, James J.P. McShane, and Richard G. Sinclair. During the committee's hearings in 1959, Kennedy stated:

> "Mr. Chairman, over the period of the past day and a half, we have been developing a number of points that we wish to go into further today. There are four major points we have gone into. The first which we have established is that there was collusion in the awarding of the insurance for the Central States Conference of Teamsters, and that is shown through the documents that have been placed in the record here.
>
> "Second, there was collusion in the awarding of the contract of the Michigan Conference of Teamsters, which is shown from

the documents and, for instance, the fact that the bid was submitted to the Michigan Conference of Teamsters the day after the award was made, submitted from Allen Dorfman's company.

"Third, right from the beginning, there were excessive commissions paid for both the Central Conference of Teamsters and for the Michigan Conference of Teamsters.

"Fourth, there is the matter that climaxes all of this, that between 1952 and 1954 the cost to the Michigan Conference of Teamsters and to the Central Conference of Teamsters was increased. The commissions to Allen Dorfman were increased and the benefits to the members of the Central Conference of Teamsters and the Michigan Conference of Teamsters were decreased on three separate occasions.

"All of these matters were handled with the help and assistance and direction of Mr. James Hoffa. When we had our witnesses at the beginning, we developed the fact that this contract for the Central Conference of Teamsters was originally awarded through the efforts and the friendship that existed between Mr. Paul Dorfman and Mr. James R. Hoffa."[244]

Dorfman appeared on the scene and became secretary-treasurer of the union immediately after the founder of the Waste Material Handlers Union, Local 20467, Leon R. Cook, was shot and killed in Chicago on December 8, 1939. Dorfman held this post until the AFL-CIO ousted him in late 1957.

Although never convicted of any crime, he was arrested in 1928 in connection with ballots in the 13th precinct of the old 24th Ward in favor of the Republican State's Attorney Robert E. Crowe, but no disposition related to this charge can be found.

In 1942 he was charged with mayhem in connection with the beating of the executive secretary of the Waste Material Dealers association but subsequently was freed of the charge.

James McShane, who testified at the Senate committee's hearing, revealed some shocking facts in doing so about Paul "Red" Dorfman, his stepson Allen Dorfman, and Hoffa. McShane had more than 21 years' experience in law enforcement with the New York Police Department.

According to McShane, Red Dorfman was a major figure and an associate of most of the leading gangsters in the Chicago area. He was the contact between dishonest union leaders and members of the Chicago underworld.

244   Hearings before the U.S. Senate Select Committee on Improper Activities in Labor and Management, 85th Congress, 1959

Dorfman's many criminal and other associates included Anthony "Tony" Accardo, who was known as the head of the Chicago Mob since the death of Al Capone. Another associate was Abraham Teitelbaum, former attorney for the Capone gang. Teitelbaum often stated, "Alphonse Capone was one of the most honorable men I ever met." Another was Abner Zwillman, one of the top figures in the American underworld, who headed the rackets in New Jersey. Accardo, Zwillman, and Teitelbaum were hidden owners of the Sands when Sidney Wyman was a licensed six-percent owner.

Other Mobsters involved in the Sands were "Jimmy Blue Eyes" Alo, who oversaw construction of its casino for Meyer Lansky and other partners such as "Doc" Stacher, Frank Costello, and Joe Adonis. Lansky, under constant surveillance by the FBI, handpicked Stacher to run the place with Charles "Babe" Baron who looked after the Chicago Outfit's interests there. It is interesting that U.S. President John F. Kennedy stayed at the Mobbed-up Sands in the early 1960s when Frank Sinatra led the "Rat Pack."

Another associate of Dorfman was Harry "Chink" Meltzer, a notorious Michigan hoodlum and finger man who extorted race track bookies, forcing them to pay a street tax for doing business. Meltzer was arrested in Chicago on charges of placing explosives with intent to destroy. After being taken in, he telephoned Dorfman and told him he needed funds. According to the police officers who accompanied Meltzer, "We went to a West Side Chicago bar where he found Dorfman had left $25 for him." Meltzer, reportedly irate at the time, commented to the officers that Dorfman owed him very much more than that.

Dorfman was responsible for securing the charter of Local 102 of the United Automobile Workers Union, AFL, for John "Johnny Dio" Dioguardi, a notorious New York gangster in the garment district who did time in the Sing Sing Correctional Facility with another Teamsters official for extortion.

Dorfman was instrumental in securing a charter for Teamsters Local 805 in New York City, to be headed by Abe Gordon. Gordon was a close associate of Dorfman, Hoffa, and Dioguardi. Gordon's initial organizing activities were in the vending machine industry in New York and New Jersey. A great amount of those machines were controlled by Zwillman.

Dorfman also helped obtain a charter in St. Louis for Harry Karsh, then secretary-treasurer of the Carnival Workers Union, Local 447. Karsh was a partner with Hoffa in the operation of a summer camp in Wisconsin and in the Northwestern Oil Company in North Dakota. Also, Karsh was a partner, with Ted Shulman and Ross Miller, in the management of a heavyweight fighter known as Billy Nolan. Shulman at that time was the executive secretary of the Waste Material Dealers Association, with whom Dorfman negotiated for contracts.

Traced telephone calls indicated that a New Jersey attorney by the name of Harold Krieger called Zwillman at that summer camp. Another associate was Sol Cilento, a former official of the Distillery Workers Union and subordinate of Zwillman. There was a Claude Maddox, a.k.a. "Screwy" Moore, a Chicago racketeer and hoodlum connected with the Hotel Employees and Restaurant Employees Union. The St. Valentine's Day massacre was planned in Maddox's bar in February 1929.

As for Allen Dorfman, Red Dorfman's stepson, he was a partner of Shulman in the Sheridan Lien Company, which purchased property seized due to nonpayment of taxes.

Hoffa developed a unique contract so that Allen Dorfman could handle the insurance for the Teamsters. During the hearing, Kennedy drilled Red Dorfman on the issue, first asking if Allen Dorfman was his son.

> **Red (Paul) Dorfman**: "I respectfully decline to answer because I honestly believe my answer might tend to incriminate me."
>
> **John McClellan**: "You don't mean to imply you have a son that you can't identify and acknowledge without possible self-incrimination? You don't mean to do that, do you?" (The witness conferred with his counsel.)
>
> **Dorfman**: "Yes, I have a son."
>
> **McClellan**: "All right. That is carrying it to the extreme. It is super ridiculous, isn't it? Don't you agree with me on that? I think your silence and giggle is acquiescence with the Chair."
>
> **Robert Kennedy**: "Mr. Allen Dorfman is your son?"
>
> **Dorfman**: "Yes, sir."
>
> **Kennedy**: "The reason for Mr. Hoffa granting this very lucrative contract to this insurance company, to Allen Dorfman, was in order to enable him to get a foothold in Chicago with the Teamsters Union, was it not, Mr. Dorfman?"
>
> **Dorfman**: "I respectfully decline to answer because I honestly believe my answer might tend to incriminate me."
>
> **Kennedy**: "And wasn't that foothold to be obtained through his association with you, and the quid pro quo – for you allowing him

and bringing him into Chicago, the quid pro quo was the granting of this contract on the insurance?"

Dorfman: "I respectfully decline to answer because I honestly believe my answer might tend to incriminate me."

Kennedy: "Isn't it the reason that you had so much power and authority and still do in Chicago, because of your close association with the members of the underworld in that city?"

Dorfman: "I respectfully decline to answer because I honestly believe my answer might tend to incriminate me."

Kennedy: "Isn't it true that prior to 1950 Mr. Hoffa had no following of any kind in Chicago, and that changed after he granted the insurance to Allen Dorfman?"

Dorfman: "I respectfully decline to answer because I honestly believe my answer might tend to incriminate me."

Kennedy: "And wasn't it arranged also that Allen Dorfman would get 50 percent of the profits and the other 50 percent of the profits would go to you, through your wife, Rose Dorfman?"

Dorfman: "I respectfully decline to answer because I honestly believe my answer might tend to incriminate me."

Kennedy: "Wasn't this the arrangement and deal that was made with Mr. Hoffa which ultimately brought about Mr. Hoffa betraying the membership of the Teamsters Union by allowing an increase in commissions to your wife and to Mr. Allen Dorfman at the same time decreasing the benefits to the Teamster Union members?"

Dorfman: "I respectfully decline to answer because I honestly believe my answer might tend to incriminate me."

Kennedy: "In addition to that, Mr. Paul Dorfman, isn't it a fact that on occasion you have paid bills of Mr. James Riddle Hoffa?"

Dorfman: "I respectfully decline to answer because I honestly believe my answer might tend to incriminate me."

Kennedy: Isn't it a fact that during the period of the past 12 months that you have supplied cash on behalf of Mr. James Riddle Hoffa?"

Dorfman: "I respectfully decline to answer because I honestly believe my answer might tend to incriminate me."

Kennedy: "And isn't it a fact also that Mr. Allen Dorfman has supplied cash to pay the bills, some of the bills, of Mr. James Hoffa?"

Dorfman: "I respectfully decline to answer because I honestly believe my answer might tend to incriminate me."

Kennedy: "Wasn't it a double situation: First, that you enabled him to move into Chicago with the control of the Teamsters in that area; and secondly, from the large accumulations of money that you were going to acquire through this Teamster contract, that you would on occasion pay his bills and make investments for him?"

Dorfman: "I respectfully decline to answer because I honestly believe my answer might tend to incriminate me."

The committee did not get the answers they wanted but certainly gathered a lot of attention and scrutiny by the government. The FBI reported that Allen Dorfman allegedly held insurance interests with "Milwaukee Phil" Alderisio, Albert "Obbie" Frabotta, and Santos Trafficante, all prominent racketeers.[245]

More than two decades later in the early 1980s, the FBI, per court order, wiretapped the phones of Allen Dorfman and listened to his conversations for 14 months after receiving tips from informants that he was purchasing hidden interests in Nevada casinos for organized crime in Chicago.[246]

Affidavits filed by the agency indicated that Dorfman inflated casino insurance premiums and split the profit with the Chicago Mob. They also alleged that Dorfman managed the business investments of organized criminals and decided, with input from Accardo and Jackie Cerone via Joey Lombardo, on the loans made to the underworld by the Teamsters pension fund, which at the time had assets in excess of $3.5 billion dollars.

Dorfman's company, Amalgamated Insurance Agency Inc., underwrote more than 90 percent of the insurance for the casinos that had loans with the Teamsters. Many of the Teamsters loan agreements that Dorfman negotiated contained a clause that required that the businesses obtain insurance through his agency. His contract with the Teamsters required that it pay $795,000 monthly to Amalgamated.

Alvin Baron was an attorney and was associated with the Teamsters pension fund, as a trustee and its asset manager. He was a regular around the Dunes in the early 1970s. At the time he owned the Golf Course Motel, which was on the present site of the MGM Grand. He was loud, known for braggadocio, and arrogantly let people know who he was.

245   FBI File, 124-10301-10189, 1962
246   *Chicago Tribune*, April 6, 1982

When he entered the Dunes baccarat gaming area he threw his weight around. He was not a qualified casino man in any sense, but he jumped into the baccarat floorman's "ladder chair" as soon as there was an opening. Baron preferred the chair that faced out into the casino, so he could watch everyone and they could see him. Because he never wore a suit, he looked as though he did not belong in the chair.

After being investigated by a Chicago federal grand jury, he was removed by Teamsters officials. He brought a lot of heat on the union. He then went to work for Allen Glick as a consultant. Subsequently, he was taken to trial and was convicted of receiving a $200,000 kickback on a $1.3 million loan he facilitated for one Foy Bryant in connection to a pet cemetery project.

CHAPTER 41

HOFFA'S BACKGROUND

Jimmy Hoffa was a guest at the Dunes in the late 1960s and a friend indeed to its owners and operators. He had a lot to do with the growth of Las Vegas.

In the late 1950s and early 1960s, Hoffa had a big plan and lots of associates who could help him carry it out. Hoffa's bizarre blueprint for conquest of the American economy stipulated that he would become czar of the nation's vital transportation facilities, as well as boss of millions of policemen, firemen, and government employees across the nation.

He was so powerful that a single order from this brazen brotherhood of Teamsters could halt all trucking, prevent the unloading of ships, prohibit the flow of cargo by air or rail. The Teamsters had direct access to the individuals who ran state and local governments that protected public and private property.

He was politically powerful as well as "thug" powerful, in close alliance with the top Mafia bosses around the country like "Johnny Dio" Dioguardi and Anthony "Tony Ducks" Corallo. When president of the Teamsters, Hoffa used Corallo and Dioguardi in his efforts to capture control of the union in New York City. Dioguardi was an associate who worked under Charles Luciano and was involved in the 1956 acid attack that led to the blinding of newspaper columnist Victor Riesel.

In 1957 Senator John McClellan presented a report to the Senate's Permanent Subcommittee on Investigations entitled "James R. Hoffa and Continued Underworld Control of the New York Teamsters Local 239." During the hearings before this committee it was disclosed that seven local unions of the New York area, five of which were affiliated with the Teamsters, were controlled by the powerful New York Mafia figure and vice president of Local 239, Corallo. The modus operandi in all of these locals was corruption.

In 1958, because of the hearings of the committee and its findings, Corallo resigned as vice president of local 239 but only on paper. He secretly continued pulling the strings. After he resigned, two criminal associates of Corallo, who were complete outsiders to the labor movement, were placed on the local's payroll as union organizers, with salaries exactly equaling that of Corallo at the time of his resignation. Thereafter, a third Corallo associate appeared on the payroll. These three positions were phantom in nature, merely there to provide a means for siphoning off tens of thousands of dollars from the local annually.

Corallo and his fellow officers of Local 239 looted its funds in June 1959, to pay off Sam Goldstein and secure his resignation as president of the local. Goldstein, a major player under Corallo, extorted small businesses to pay up or "else," to keep labor peace. He continued this practice while serving time for an extortion conviction, and all the while collected his $400 a week salary from the local. This situation was an embarrassment to Hoffa.

Goldstein was a regular guest of "Big Julie" Weintraub and his junkets to the Dunes in the late 1960s and early 1970s. Goldstein was no stranger either to many of the casino bosses who were from New York and Miami.

Goldstein was a street hustler and took advantage of every angle at the baccarat game when the game used U.S. currency and not casino chips. He could bet the limit anytime and usually progressed to $2,000 after each successive win on the bank or players. If the Bank side was the winner, say of $2,000, he would say to the dealer, "Reduce the vig and pay me $200 in twenties and $100 in fives." He hoped the dealer would make an error and overpay him, in which case he would not say anything. However, if the dealer underpaid him, he would immediately make a claim, touch the money, and try to confuse the dealer more.

Corallo planned, evidently with Teamsters President Hoffa's acquiescence, to put Goldstein back on the union payroll upon his release from prison in November 1959 and six months later, permit him to resume his role as local president.

Federal investigators, through electronic bugs, obtained recordings that not only implicated Corallo, but also seven other high-ranking Mobsters in other families and provided the first proof that a Mafia commission existed. Corallo and Salvatore Avellino, Jr., who was affiliated with the Lucchese crime family, had long conversations on many topics, captured on tape. Armed with the results of their wiretapping, the government now had the chance to attack the high levels of several La Cosa Nostra families.

The National Crime Syndicate, involved in legitimate labor and business, was graver than was previously revealed. A report prepared in 1958 for New York City Police Commissioner Lee Brown stated:

> "The ramifications of this problem presented the gravest implications for the destiny of our national economy. This close-knit,

clandestine, criminal syndicate has made fortunes in the illegal liquor traffic during prohibition, and later in narcotics, vice, and gambling. These illicit profits help the syndicate with a financial problem, which they solve through investment in legitimate business. These legitimate businesses also provide convenient cover for their continued illegal activities."

The Senate Rackets Committee investigated Hoffa for two years and charged him for specific instances of collusion with employers, conflicts of interest, tie-ups with hoodlums and gangsters, the rigging of union elections, the spending of dues funds "as if they were his own," and suppressing the rights of members through brute force.

The list of crimes the committee members pegged Hoffa for was long and indicated:

- Hoffa "masterminded" the chartering of seven bogus "paper locals" in New York. These locals were gangster controlled, devoid of actual membership, and set up to steal the election of the president of powerful Joint Council 16 for Hoffa's buddy, John O'Rourke.

- Hoffa "obstructed justice" by having secret grand jury testimony in Michigan leaked to him. He then forced a witness, who gave detrimental evidence, to flee to California before testifying.

- Hoffa arranged for $200,000 in Teamsters welfare funds to be loaned to a Minneapolis department store when it was in the midst of a strike against fellow union, the American Federation of Labor, or AFL.

- Hoffa maneuvered $31,953 in union dues to the defense of four Teamsters officials who were tried and found guilty of extorting money from employers.

- Hoffa spent an additional $22,428 in Teamsters funds to defend one of the convicted extortionists, Gerald Connelly of Minneapolis, after he was indicted in connection with the dynamiting of two fellow Teamsters officials.

- Hoffa arranged for Zigmont Snyder to be appointed as the business agent of Detroit Local 299, although he was a "notorious hoodlum" who operated a non-union Detroit car wash, at which he sometimes paid workers less than $1 a day for 12 hours' work.

- Hoffa had $500,000 in Teamsters funds transferred to a Florida Bank to assure a loan of a corresponding amount of money from the bank to a land development scheme in which Hoffa and his chief lieutenant, Owen "Bert" Brennan, held a 45 percent option to purchase.

• Hoffa kept Henry Lower, promoter of the Florida land deal, on the union payroll to the tune of $59,000 in salary and expenses while he set up the real estate scheme.

• Hoffa constantly defended and aided Teamsters officials who "were selling out the interests of Teamster Union members by setting themselves up in highly improper business activities and by entering into collusive agreements with employers."

• Hoffa repeatedly placed hoodlums, ex-convicts and individuals under indictment in high posts in the union. Of the delegates who were selected to the 1957 convention that elected Hoffa president, at least 75 percent, possibly more, were chosen illegally, in violation of the Teamsters union's constitution. These included delegates from Hoffa's own local, 299, and Brennan's local, 337.

• Hoffa and Brennan were aided by Bert "Tito" Beveridge, owner of a trucking firm, in acquiring a truck company for themselves. The two then made special concessions to Beveridge in his labor contract with the Teamsters union, to the detriment of workers.

• The wives of Hoffa and Brennan, using their maiden names, were involved in a series of business arrangements with firms with which the Teamsters were required to negotiate.

• Hoffa formed an alliance with the International Longshoremen's Association (ILA) and attempted to lend it $490,000 from Teamsters coffers after the ILA was ousted from the AFL-CIO because it was bossed by racketeers.

• Hoffa attempted to force 30,000 New York taxicab drivers into a union run by gangster Johnny Dioguardi even though his own union, the Teamsters, was attempting to organize the drivers.

• Hoffa caused the Welfare Fund of the Michigan Conference of Teamsters to lose $600,000 in its first three years of operation because he awarded the Teamsters pension fund's contract to the Union Insurance Agency, run by his pal, Allen Dorfman. Incidentally, Dorfman's lady companion was a cocktail waitress at the Dunes.

• Hoffa forced the Teamsters union to pay between $5,000 and $7,000 to find the runaway wife of his brother, William Hoffa, and made the union pay William's hotel bill and $75 in expenses while William eluded police who wanted him on an armed robbery charge. (It was rumored that Hoffa was related in some manner to Ross Miller of the Riviera in Las Vegas).

The Senate Rackets Committee found that at least 60 executives of the Teamsters union were tried previously for various crimes, from murder on down. In its lengthy 1958 hearing, the rackets panel asked Hoffa why Robert "Barney" Baker, a thug with a police record, was retained in a high union post.

Hoffa answered, "Senator, he is a great organizer, and every one of us has some faults."

Robert Kennedy responded, "I think what [Baker] has done is clear and his associations–and the fact that I read out the names of the people he has been associated with: [John] "Cockeye" Dunn, Meyer Lansky, Joe Adonis, Frank Costello, "Jimmy Blue Eyes", "Bugsy" Siegel, John Vitale, Lou Farrell, and what else do you want? What does it take, Mr. Hoffa?"

Hoffa replied, "I think those names attract you a lot more than they attract me, and I say to you that Baker, being in the capacity of organizing and carrying out his position in organizing, that we would have no way of knowing he was talking to these individuals unless he wanted to tell us, and apparently he didn't. So I cannot be expected to reprimand an individual for something I didn't know at the time it was happening."

Hoffa did not invoke the Fifth Amendment one time throughout this entire Senate hearing.

In mid-December 1966, the Supreme Court affirmed Hoffa's 1964 jury tampering conviction, which carried an eight-year federal sentence. Hoffa also had another five years to serve for 1965 conviction, this one for loan fraud and illegal kickbacks associated with Teamsters pension fund financings. Hoffa's lawyers scrambled for a solution to keep him a free man.

Hoffa attorney Morris Shenker and six in-house Teamsters attorneys filed a petition with the Supreme Court in January 1967 to throw out the jury tampering conviction on the grounds that the prosecution's evidence was obtained illegally through wiretapping.

Missouri Senator Edward Long, an associate of Shenker, "coincidentally" went to Detroit and spoke to the Committee to Preserve American Freedom (CPAF) about the evils of the use of wiretaps by the federal government. The leaders of the CPAF were all close friends of Hoffa and contributed money for his legal defense. At this meeting, Long predicted that the Supreme Court would hand down a major ruling on wiretapping sometime that year.

On February 27, the Supreme Court denied Hoffa's motion. On April 4, Long began public hearings in Washington and called many witnesses who were from the Russell Bufalino lawsuit that was filed in Detroit against the Michigan Bell Telephone Company, an IRS agent, Detroit police officers, and telephone workers, claiming they were a party to the wiretapping against Hoffa.

There was no mistake that Bufalino's lawsuit, the Hoffa appeals, and the Long hearings were connected in a coordinated effort to keep Hoffa free. It was akin to a "concerto" for him.

Allegations were made that Hoffa and Long were more than friends.[247247] An article in *LIFE* magazine accused Long of "misusing" his powers as chairman of a Senate subcommittee investigating wiretapping by federal agencies in an effort to keep Hoffa out of prison, and also sharing legal fees with Shenker.

Long denied the allegation but acknowledged that he received payment of $48,000 in 1963 and 1964 from Shenker. Long claimed that they were referral fees paid by a lawyer to a colleague who steered business his way. Although the American Bar Association does not condone those, they are not illegal.

When questioned by the *LIFE* reporter, William Lambert, about his law practice, Long replied that he "had not been an active attorney since the mid-1950s." As for his relationship with Shenker, he said, "We have been friends for, oh, 30 years."

The *LIFE* reporter than asked, "What services do you perform to justify the money paid to you by Morris Shenker?"

Long did not answer and stared expressionless at the reporter. The reporter broke the silence after 10 seconds and asked, "Senator, we are prepared to document it."

> **Long**: "You had better document it."
>
> **Lambert**: "Is that a denial, Senator?"
>
> **Long**: "You document it."
>
> **Lambert**: "Senator, are you denying it?"
>
> Long paused for a moment and said, "I deny it."
>
> **Lambert**: "Was it for a legal retainer?"
>
> **Long**: "If Morris Shenker paid me any money I feel that you will have to document it… Was this supposed to be before I was in the Senate or afterward?"
>
> **Lambert**: "While you were in the Senate."

---

247   *Detroit Free Press*, May 28, 1967

Long: "I deny it. But even if it were true, I couldn't talk about it because it would be privileged communication between lawyer and client. I make it a practice not to accept government cases since I once represented a man in Missouri… I've never taken any government cases since then. Even if I had, which I deny, I couldn't talk about it."

Lambert: "But Senator, a few minutes ago you told us you hadn't practiced law actively since you were lieutenant governor in the 1950s."

Long: "Oh, a lawyer always has some practice, even if he is not actively in practice."

Lambert: "Senator, you realize, of course, the serious implications of this?"

Long: "I see the implication. It is serious. Don't think I was born yesterday."[248]

Long wanted to know how Lambert found out about the confidential payments from Shenker. He felt that the IRS tipped off Lambert after Long targeted the IRS in his wiretapping investigations. Long claimed it was a strange coincidence that IRS agents recently completed an audit of his tax returns for 1963 and 1964, the years for which Lambert had knowledge of the Shenker payments.

Lambert claimed that he did not get his information from the IRS and would only reveal the source if required by the proper tribunal.

The U.S. Senate Ethics Committee, without questioning, cleared Long in 1968 of any wrongdoing.

"The committee findings were a whitewash," a November 10, 1967 LIFE magazine article declared. The piece also asserted that Long was not exonerated but that the committee discovered serious concerns about his connections and sources of income. Between January 1961 and October 1968, Long missed 546 of 2,055 roll call votes, which is 26.6 percent. This was much worse than the median of 13.6 percent among the lifetime records of senators serving in October 1968.[249]

248   *LIFE*, May 26, 1967
249   Govtrack.us/congress/members/edward_long/406906

CHAPTER 42

THE DISAPPEARANCE OF HOFFA

When James "Jimmy" Hoffa got out of prison in December 1971, he announced that he wanted the Teamsters presidency back, even though he had been warned by Mafia associates to stand down. "I'm not guilty then, nor am I guilty now," Hoffa told union members in the 1970s.

"In 1974, Hoffa starts singing to the government in exchange for a change in his pardon so he could run for union office, and he was murdered. And what was he singing about before he was murdered? The Dunes. He was telling the government how [Frank] Fitzsimmons was skimming money out of the Dunes much as he had done. Hoffa told about Teamsters' loan structure for constructing the property,"[250] a former Department of Labor staff member involved in investigating the Teamsters later recalled in 1976 following the beating of Pete Camarata.

Camarata was a young protégé of Hoffa in Local 299, but no friend of Frank Fitzsimmons. When Fitzsimmons called a "blow off steam" strike for two days in the freight industry in 1976, Camarata led a brief wildcat strike in Local 299 in defiance of the sell-out deal. Also that year, Camarata was the only delegate at the Las Vegas International Brotherhood of Teamsters Convention to vote against Fitzsimmons, who ran for Teamsters general president. Later that day, Camarata was beaten unconscious by Teamsters thugs, but no incident report appeared in the Las Vegas newspapers.

A friend of Camarata and a member of the Providence Local 251, Dave Robbins, said this when he spoke at a memorial event for Teamsters who previously participated in reforming the union:

> "When Fitz's goons beat Pete, they figured they wouldn't see Pete or TDU [Teamsters for a Democratic Union] again. Wrong. Five years later, Pete was again elected a convention delegate and accepted the nomination for Teamster General President. TDU kept building rank and file power, won the Right to Vote in 1989, and we're still here in 2014 and we ain't going away. Pete never stopped fighting the

good fight, and the planet is a better place because of him. Pete, with your inspiration we're keeping the faith. Solidarity forever."[251]

The Mob was concerned that Hoffa might expose the connection between Teamsters loans to Las Vegas casinos and the cash being skimmed from those casinos. Hoffa had to go.

Current Teamsters President Fitzsimmons knew that Hoffa would attempt to use the Teamsters Local 299 as his base to regain power.

Fitzsimmons was a protégé of Hoffa and when Hoffa was sent to prison after being convicted of jury tampering and mail fraud in 1967, Hoffa personally chose Fitzsimmons to direct the operations of the Teamsters. Fitzsimmons was elected president of the Teamsters in 1971 and in December of that year, Hoffa's 13-year sentence was commuted by President Richard Nixon with the restriction that he could not manage, either directly or indirectly, the Teamsters or any other union until 1980. Hoffa filed court motions to have the ban lifted but was unsuccessful.[252]

Another Hoffa loyalist, David Johnson, who was the president of Local 299 and had a great deal of support, decided to oppose Fitzsimmons in the run for Teamsters president and openly promised Hoffa a key staff job if Hoffa succeeded in court.

A series of violent events plagued Local 299 starting in 1970, included the beating of Johnson, a shotgun blast through his office window, and the bombing of his 45-foot-long yacht. George Roxburgh, a Local 299 trustee, lost an eye from an attempted shotgun assassination attempt in 1972. Also that year Eugene Paige, Local 299 organizer, was the victim of a bomb blast outside his home, and then a fire destroyed a barn on the farm of Otto Wendel, who was the secretary-treasurer of Local 299.

International Vice President Richard Holmes mandated a compromise, and in 1975 both Fitzsimmons and Johnson were re-elected to their positions, Teamsters president and Local 299 president, respectively.

Hoffa disappeared on July 30, 1975.

It is highly probable that he did not just disappear, but was murdered.

Hours before he vanished, Hoffa placed a call to Las Vegas. An FBI telex shows that he phoned Morris Shenker at the Dunes, which Shenker previously bought with a Teamsters loan. It is very probable that Shenker bought into the Dunes with Hoffa's help. It is also highly likely that Hoffa was a hidden partner, an arrangement established with Jake Gottlieb and previous owners.[253]

---

251   Teamsters for a Democratic Union (TDU), April 1, 2014
252   *Detroit Free Press*, July 12, 1975
253   Note: See Lombardo-Dorman-Shenker surveillance transcripts

Shenker, Hoffa's attorney for nonunion affairs, said Hoffa told him he was going to Los Angeles to make a speech and might stop off in Las Vegas. He asked Shenker to make hotel reservations for him.

"He sounded cheerful and bouncy as usual," Shenker said. He noted that their conversation was short but "there was no suggestion of anything improper."[254]

According to Eugene Zafft, the personal attorney for the Hoffa family, the relationship between Hoffa and Shenker grew cold after Hoffa's release from prison in December 1971. Hoffa then retained New York attorney Leonard Boudin, who represented Daniel Ellsberg on the charges of espionage and theft when he copied and released the Pentagon Papers to the press. Federal Judge Matthew Byrne dismissed the government case against Ellsberg.

There are several theories about who killed Hoffa and why.

A lead suspect in the disappearance of Hoffa was Anthony "Tony Jack" Giacalone, who was then a senior organized crime figure in Detroit. However, Hoffa and Giacalone were friends since the 1940s. On the day Hoffa dropped from sight, he told his family he was on his way to see Giacalone.

"They [Giacalone and Hoffa] were very close, which is not generally known," author Jack Goldsmith wrote in *In Hoffa's Shadow*. Goldsmith was a Harvard law professor and the stepson of Charles "Chuckie" L. O'Brien, Hoffa's foster son who knew Giacalone since childhood. "And they were both very close to Chuck's mother, Sylvia Pagano, who was a very influential woman in these circles. Chuck's mother was an intermediary between Hoffa and organized crime on a whole set of issues, including pension fund loans and other actions. So Chuckie grew up in both of these worlds. He was Hoffa's closest aide, literally his right-hand man, not his consigliere, but by his side at every moment, starting in '52. He was so close and so trusted by both of them that he served as a go-between between them and between Hoffa and other organized crime figures. He was intimately involved in everything Hoffa did."[255]

O'Brien claimed that "the most explosive rumor of all happened – that in exchange for conditional clemency, [Richard] Nixon demanded and received $1 million in cash from Hoffa – he delivered the bag of money

---

254   Note: Shenker, in his remark, "there was no suggestion of anything improper" meant to convey to the reporter interviewing him that generally everyone felt that Hoffa was a victim of a probable murder. Yet said that after Hoffa disappeared, Shenker talked with Hoffa's son, who said he knew nothing about the incident if there was a murder plot in the works, in Shenker's opinion, Hoffa gave no indication of being aware of it or any possible danger when going to his meeting. It is certain that Hoffa and Shenker spoke about the meeting, and probably, the agenda for it..

255   *In Hoffa's Shadow*, Jack Goldsmith, 2019

from the Teamsters offices on Capitol Hill to a man in a fancy hotel room blocks from the White House."

Goldsmith wrote, "I believe it's true because some of the details [O'Brien] told me I could corroborate."

The author added, "There was circumstantial evidence to think that somebody paid Nixon a lot of money to commute his sentence, but Watergate investigators and Hoffa investigators looked up and down, and they couldn't find any source for the money. They could never corroborate it. And it turned out, according to Chuckie, that it came from Hoffa. It was Hoffa's money. He had these huge stashes of cash, and he paid for himself to get out."

In August 1978, an FBI indictment charged two men, Charles Goldfarb and James Tamer, with secretly managing the Aladdin hotel-casino in Las Vegas for Detroit figure Vito Giacalone. Also named in the indictment as "figuring in" the conspiracy but not charged were Detroiter Raffaele "Jimmy Q" Quasarano and legendary Las Vegas gaming figure Moe Dalitz. According to the indictment, Shenker, owner of the Dunes, across the Las Vegas Strip from the Aladdin, discussed the Aladdin's allegedly shaky financial condition with Goldfarb and Tamer and the possibility of filing fraudulent financial affidavits to get a loan. Shenker, though, was not charged.[256]

Another theory is that Fitzsimmons was behind Hoffa's disappearance or involved somehow. It happened three weeks after the latest series of incidents involving rival factions of the Teamsters union. On July 10, a bomb destroyed the car owned by the son of incumbent Teamsters president, Fitzsimmons. Richard Fitzsimmons was in the middle of a riff between supporters of his father and Hoffa. When questioned, Shenker said he did not believe that there was any connection between Hoffa's disappearance and the bombing of Richard Fitzsimmons' car.

The FBI was investigating whether Frank Fitzsimmons met reputed Mafia figures Quasarano and Peter Vitale at Larco's Inn in Detroit four or five days before Hoffa disappeared. Fitzsimmons and the owners of Larco's all denied that any such meeting occurred. However, one witness, the night auditor at the Fairlane Inn in Dearborn, Michigan, testified that Fitzsimmons checked in to the motel less than four days before Hoffa's disappearance.

Because Louis "Rip" Khoury, an admitted numbers racketeer in Detroit, frequented Larco's, a federal grand jury investigating Hoffa's disappearance called him for questioning. As the "goodwill ambassador" in Detroit Khoury kept all the factions – the Italians, blacks, Lebanese – at peace while at the same time controlled the numbers business. Also, he was a close associate of Giacalone, Giacalone's two brothers, and Hoffa, and an insider.

A few days before his date with the grand jury, Khoury told reporters, "I don't know what the hang I'm here for." After his appearance, Khoury said, "I don't know nothing about this monkey business."[257]

Khoury believed that of all of the theories promulgated about the disappearance of Hoffa, the story about Frank Sheeran, whose account of killing Hoffa was revealed in *I Heard You Paint Houses*, seemed more plausible than any of the others because the description and the facts made more sense than the rest. For one, Sheeran could have gotten close enough to Hoffa to have done it. Khoury's son, Ken Khoury, remembered actually painting Hoffa's house with Hoffa's friend and campaign manager, Mike Bain.

Another theory about Hoffa's murder revolved around a deal to buy 9.3 acres of prime Las Vegas Strip frontage between the Dunes hotel and the Jockey Club condominium units for the purpose of building a casino and hotel there.

The main front man for the operation was Dr. August Juliano, a respected Bergen, New Jersey surgeon who had business relationships with at least two men whom the FBI suspected as being involved in the killing of Hoffa; Thomas "Tommy" Principe and Salvatore "Sally Bugs" Briguglio.

The Mobster behind Juliano was Anthony "Tony" Provenzano, who wanted Hoffa to approve a Teamsters loan for his casino, but Hoffa refused.

Because Hoffa would not finance Provenzano's casino venture in Las Vegas, the two got into a fist fight while they both were in prison, according to newspaper reporter Ed Barnes. Barnes claimed, "I think it's pretty clear. I mean, what we – what we know, particularly once the stuff about Juliano and Briguglio and, and another important hit man for the mob, Tommy Principe, came out, we know, in prison Hoffa and Provenzano came in [to] a fist fight. That was about it. It was not about the presidency. Hoffa didn't mean much to Provenzano, who was on the East Coast and a different, different set of structures and teams or structure. So it was clearly – there was money involved, real money, and Provenzano wanted this, the Central States pension fund, which was out of the

Central States and Midwest, and he wanted Hoffa to make sure he got the money for his casino. Because if you look at the situation at that time, the St. Louis Mob families had a casino, Chicago had a casino. I mean, there's a movie called *Casino*, and that had become basically the Holy Grail for families… That's the motive for the murder."

With a Teamsters loan out of the question, Provenzano turned to the State Bank of Chatham, headquartered in New Jersey and controlled by organized crime. It held major deposits by Teamsters Local 1262, Retail Store Employees, headed by Frank Rando. It also held the account of Teamsters Local 945, which represented the garbage collection industry workers in New Jersey.

The bank was reported to be a "Crown Jewel" belonging to the Genovese crime family of New York and to have approved as much as $10 million in loans for Mafia-controlled businesses, according to a report submitted to Congress' House Committee on Ways and Means by the Professional Drivers Council, a group of Teamsters that tried to reform the Teamsters union.

Two of the loans were given to Juliano and his partner John "Johnny" George in return for the "cardboard box" of cash, which was used as collateral. One loan of $75,000 went to Juliano and another $50,000 loan to George for a "building program in Las Vegas." George was an employee of the Dunes and very friendly with the Chicago Outfit members, especially Jackie Cerone. One evening when Cerone's wife was in the Dunes near the blackjack pit, George immediately recognized her and exchanged pleasantries.[258]

Cerone's mother legally adopted a child who was raised with young Jackie and who was treated by the whole family as if he were a blood brother. His name was Cy. He was a family man and always willing to do a favor for someone. He had a friend whose daughter moved to Las Vegas and was told that she could work at the Dunes as a cocktail waitress. She applied and waited to be called to work. Cy called her a few weeks later, under the assumption that she got the job, wanting to see if everything was all right. She told him she was still waiting to be called by the beverage manager. Cy abruptly ended the conversation and said that he would get right back to her. The following day, Allen Dorfman personally called the young woman with an apology and the message that she could start work the next day.

Previously, George was arrested for suspicion of murder and for bookmaking, which surfaced when he applied in 1968 for a gambling license for a different property, the Valley Inn in Mesquite, a small town in Nevada on its border with Utah. Concerned about his background, the Nevada Gaming Commission turned him down but eventually, after a lengthy battle, granted him a gambling license.

Alexander T. Smith, then president of the State Bank of Chatham, went to Juliano's office and picked up a cardboard box containing $125,000. This cash was the down payment for the purchase of the 9.3 acres on the Las Vegas Strip, which was valued at almost $6 million.[259] Coincidentally (or not), the land was purchased on July 30, 1975, the same day Hoffa vanished.

According to bank records that were uncovered after the State Bank of Chatham failed, none of the "cardboard box cash" was ever credited to any of the accounts of or loans to Juliano, but instead was washed through an attorney's trust account. That attorney, George Franconero, was a former law partner of New Jersey Governor Brendan Byrne and the brother of popular singer Connie Francis.[260] Smith was confident in making the loans because the cash secured by Franconero's trust account was good collateral.

In 1975, the Clark County Assessor's Office (Las Vegas is in Clark County) listed the owner of the property as the George-Juliano-Maltese Limited Partnership. When Anthony Maltese subsequently discovered the Mob links to Juliano, he left the partnership and was repaid his investment. Under these owners, nothing was built at the site and, thus, Provenzano did not get his Vegas casino.

The most plausible theory, based on solid research, of Hoffa's disappearance is that of investigative reporter Dan Moldea, the foremost expert on Hoffa.

"Moldea has been covering Hoffa since before he disappeared and wrote the book *The Hoffa Wars* in 1978, based on dozens of interviews with key figures in the case. He said a new lead brings together the correct cast of characters, the right timeline of events and information from other interviews he has done in his decades of researching the case," the *Detroit Free Press* wrote on December 2, 2019.

Late in that year, Moldea presented new evidence in the case, and further support as of this writing continues to come in. Moldea's key suspect in the murder of Hoffa is Salvatore "Sally Bugs" Briguglio. This, for one, is supported by a passage about the hit in the book, *Tears & Tiers: The Life*

259   *The News*, Paterson, N.J., Ed Barnes and Kathleen Kerr, Nov. 15, 1978
260   Connie Francis was married to Izzy Marion, who was involved with the Aladdin and Frontier hotel-casinos.

and Times of Joseph 'Mad Dog' Sullivan, an autobiography by Gail Sullivan, published in 1978. Sullivan claimed to be a "heavy hitter" for "Fat Tony" Salerno, who was extremely close to Hoffa. Here is the excerpt, which begins in reference to Hoffa:

"Never expected a thing," J.J. [an associate of Sullivan] had gone on, "when he pulled up to the joint and came into the office, leaving Judas [Chuckie] sitting behind the wheel of the car. He was actually relieved getting a chance to bury an old bone. He [Hoffa] had that winning smile in place when he stepped into the office, seeing both Tony Pro and Jack smiling also, but only for the length of a heartbeat before a volley of shots from silenced automatics were fired into his head at close range by the two assassins who lie in wait behind the door. Chuckie O'Brien got out of the car and walked away just as soon as the door had closed behind his father forever. Tony Pro and Jack exited stealthily moments later and went their separate ways. Under the cover of darkness, J.J. and Sally Bugs had no fear of discovery as they worked quickly to dismantle the car, before placing the body in it and moving it into the crusher."

Moldea also deduced that a former New Jersey landfill known as "Brother Moscato's Dump" may be the grave-site of the former, infamous Teamsters boss.

The bottom line is that Hoffa knew too much about the illegal interactions of the Mob and the Teamsters, and he made it known that he was unhappy with the specific Mob influence on the Teamsters with which he did not agree. Certain Mobsters, their hidden rackets, and their scheming that plundered the Teamsters pension fund all were at risk of being exposed by Hoffa if he were re-elected as the Teamsters president. From the Mobsters' viewpoint, that could not happen.

CHAPTER 43

JIMMY GRIPPO,
MAGICIAN AND HYPNOTIST

Jimmy Grippo was the resident magician at Caesars Palace from the beginning, and spent the twilight of his 25 years there performing and hosting customers and friends. Prior to going to Caesars Palace at the request of the Mob, he worked at the Desert Inn, having been hired by Sam Tucker. Not only did he hold the secrets of a magician, he also held the secrets of the Mob.

Jimmy lost his right eye from playing with a firecracker when a small child. Such a disability was difficult for a young man to deal with through his formative years, and it surely garnered remarks that made him feel inadequate. Young Jimmy certainly must have experienced teasing, ribbing, and name calling, yet the prejudice and handicap helped forged the great individual into which Jimmy evolved.

Jimmy lived in Beacon, New York, which was within minutes of the heart of the gambling, drinking, and boxing action in New York City and New Jersey. He hung out at Lindy's in New York City and stayed at the Edison Hotel during overnight trips. Lindy's, which opened in 1921 at 1626 Broadway, was a popular haunt for aspiring Broadway stars, the fight crowd, and Mobsters, and was made famous by the movie *Guys and Dolls*.

U.S. Prohibition began in 1920 and lasted until 1933. Dances, nightclubs, vaudeville, movies, pool halls, illegal casinos, speakeasies, bootleg fights, and boxing events were the entertainment venues of the day. Boxing gyms were a place for young men to go and meet up with their friends. The Great Depression waylaid the country, and survival often meant fighting in one way or another. The Grippo brothers were young, smart, energetic, handsome, tough, unique, and looking for a piece of the action.

Jimmy saw magicians and crafted card mechanics in the area and learned some of their magic tricks. His fascination with this mysterious and secret art became a passion, and he quickly mastered magic and what he became more known for, hypnotism. Jimmy did not get into serious magic, though, until he moved to New York City permanently in the late 1920s.

"I started out back in 1934," Jimmy said. "The way it happened, I always liked fights and there was a bunch of kids in Beacon who fought in bootleg amateur fights [shows] around there. I built a gym for them to work in. It cost me maybe $300, $400. I was in the insurance business at the time."

He went on, "I got [boxer Melio] Bettina accidentally when his mother came to me for help because a school bully was always beating up on her son. When Melio came to me and said he wanted to learn how to fight, I explained I'd hypnotize him so he wouldn't be afraid. He not only knocked out the school bully, but also stopped Tiger Jack Fox in nine rounds for the world title in New York."

Jimmy used the power of auto-suggestion and hypnosis so that his boxer would defeat the foe. People were afraid of Jimmy's power. Boxing opponents avoided his gaze. He received more press than the actual fighters in the ring. It was beyond belief. The boxing commissioner once barred Jimmy from the business because of his methods.

Jimmy went on to be Bettina's boxer-manager. In 1940 Jimmy pursued arranging a fight between Billy Conn and the legendary Joe Louis, who later became a casino host at Caesars Palace.

In 1941, boxing promoter Herman Taylor arranged a match between Bettina and Gus Dorazio, which was fought in Philadelphia.

Dorazio, a fearless but limited contender during the late 1930s and early 1940s, made his name by being pole-axed in two rounds during a championship bid against Louis in 1941. Dorazio is often cited as one of the inspirations behind the character of Rocky Balboa.

Outside of the ring, Dorazio was notorious for his scrapes with the law. On the fringes of the underworld for most of his life, Dorazio even resembled a thug: his craggy face suggested a character Chester Gould (Dick Tracy) might have invented. Dorazio died in 1987, more than 50 years after he first stepped into the Waltz Dream Arena in New Jersey.

The love, money, and excitement of boxing lived with Jimmy from those early days to the years he performed at Caesars Palace and hypnotized Muhammad Ali.

Jimmy was not a boxer himself, but he surely could entertain the guys at the gym and local café. It was a unique method of him overcoming his having only one eye. Due to having to compensate and push his dexterity to the limit, his skills became sharper than the average person with sight in both eyes.

Jimmy's younger brother Mickey Grippo liked boxing and won a match in 1930. Mickey went into the numbers rackets, and his son Ronnie got involved as well. Ronnie later killed a man and died in prison.

Jimmy's brother Jan Grippo parlayed college years at the New York School of Design into an early career as a cartoonist for the New York Herald Tribune Syndicate. He went to Hollywood in 1937, began work as an agent, and then soon began producing movies. What broke the ice at many of Jan's Hollywood movie-star parties was the magic and hypnotism of Jimmy, a popular guest.

Jan produced at least 23 films in the 1940s and 1950s that featured the "Bowery Boys." A band of impish juvenile delinquents, they included tough-talking wise guy Leo Gorcey and his naive patsy, Huntz Hall. Today, these films are featured regularly on the Turner Classic Movies network.

Because Mobster Willie Moretti referred to Frank Costello as the "chief" all the time, Jan inserted the term "chief" in the "Bowery Boys'" scripts repeatedly as an inside joke and homage to Moretti. In the movie *Crazy Over Horses*, Willie was a character named after Moretti, and Duke was a character named after the man who founded Duke's restaurant, Moretti's favorite hangout. Jan included those names for Moretti. This really pleased Moretti, who would boast about being referred to in the "Bowery Boys" movies.

Moretti's love of horses and the racetrack was clearly exposed during the Kefauver Committee hearings, when he stated that he made his living at the racetrack and consistently was a winner. That admission was an amusing highlight of the hearing. When Senator Estes Kefauver asked Moretti about horse racing, he quipped: "Bet 'em to place and show. You've got three ways of winning. Come out to the track some time, and I'll show you."

In another of Jan's movies, *Mr. Hex*, which was about boxing and hypnosis, a story that mirrored the career of his brother Jimmy, Jan included a character named Evil Eye Fagin, based on the boxer, Benjamin "Evil Eye" Finkle. Sach (Huntz Hall) was given a post-hypnotic suggestion that turned him into a championship prizefighter; Jimmy did exactly that to his champion boxer Bettina.

Jan produced some other films, including *Valentino*. He never completed his pet project *Nick the Greek*, which was about the legendary gambler Nicholas Dandolos. The themes of many of Jan's movies were gambling, sports, and wise guys, similar to those in the life of the Grippo clan's associates.

Incidentally, from January to May 1949, Dandolos competed in a two-person "heads up" poker match against poker legend Johnny Moss, former Dunes card room manager, in which the two played virtually every variation of the game that existed at the time. The game, set up by gambler

Lester "Benny" Binion to attract tourists, is widely credited as inspiring the modern day World Series of Poker.

One urban legend holds that Dandolos once had the opportunity to escort Albert Einstein around Las Vegas. Thinking that his gambling friends may not be familiar with him, Dandolos allegedly introduced Einstein as "Little Al from Princeton" and stated that he "controlled a lot of the numbers action around Jersey."

According to Dandolos' own testimony in *Gambling Secrets of Nick the Greek*, just before the end of World War II, he got a call from a friend at the U.S. Department of State, who told him someone was looking to play in a poker game on a weekend in Manhattan. Dandolos reminded his friend that gambling was illegal in New York, but his friend said that he would see to it that no law enforcement would get involved. It was at that game, according to Dandolos, that he introduced Einstein as "Little Al from Jersey."

The Grippo brothers – Jan, Jimmy, and Alex – operated a casino in Beacon in the back of a cigar store. When a fire broke out there in 1940, Jimmy's brother Alex got trapped. While fighting for his life in the hospital, a Beacon city judge donated blood for him. The three brothers must have been respected. Ultimately, though, Alex Grippo died from the burns. His death brought attention to their operation, and an investigation into it began. In December, Mickey Grippo and Frank Romano, former Golden Gloves winner and referee, were arrested.

About the same time, John Roxborough, co-manager of boxer Joe Louis, was convicted along with the ex-mayor of Detroit in connection with a large numbers/policy operation.

Jimmy's talent in magic and hypnosis garnered him a spot in the world of gambling, boxing, the Syndicate, and the Mafia, or La Cosa Nostra. I prefer to call the Mob in New York, La Cosa Nostra, meaning "Our Thing," rather than the Mafia. J. Edgar Hoover refused to believe there was a Mafia, and maybe he was technically correct, but he did recognize the existence of different gangs, such as the Chicago Outfit and the Syndicate. Even Jimmy's lifelong friend, John Scarne, magician and gambling expert and an acquaintance but not close friend of Jimmy's Mob pals as well, insisted in his book, *The Mafia Conspiracy*, published in 1976, that there was no Mafia. In it, Scarne expounded his thesis that attacks on any Italian organized crime figure were nothing more than anti–Italian-American Mafia frame-ups by the federal government, which was determined to deprive the ethnic group of its civil rights.

Many viewed Scarne's book as a mouthpiece for the Mob or Syndicate. His argument that "no Mafia exists" sounded like answers given during the Kefauver hearings by Jimmy's friends and gambler-gangsters, Moretti, an associate of Joe Adonis; Frank Costello; Meyer Lansky; and others.

In 1931, Charles "Lucky" Luciano emerged at the age of 34 as the head of the new National Crime Syndicate. The face he showed to the world in the early 1930s was that of a wealthy businessman. He lived in style at The Waldorf Towers in New York, going out at night to the restaurants and clubs he controlled. Jimmy Durante was a dining companion, and Joe Lewis and George Raft were friends. Raft was a friend of Durante. Luciano invested in Broadway musicals, and to extend the crime empire to Hollywood, played a leading part in establishing Mob control of the stage employees union.

Then in 1936, having been declared New York's Public Enemy No. 1, Luciano was arrested, convicted, and sentenced to a long prison term for running a chain of brothels. Behind bars, however, he long remained, in the words of one scholar, "one of the most brilliant criminal executives of the modern age." Senior Mob associates stayed in constant touch, consulting him regularly on important matters.[261]

He was the covert owner of the Copacabana nightclub in New York, was said to have an interest in the Stork Club in New York City, and eventually, in the Tropicana in Las Vegas.

One of Jimmy's dear friends was Larry Snow, a.k.a. Snofsky, who became the baccarat manager at the Dunes and then went to Caesars Palace when it opened in 1966. The two, about the same age, met in New York.

Larry, or "Labels" as he was known to his friends, operated a garage in the Bronx at East 100 and 82nd streets. At the behest of Mobster Abner Zwillman, he reported to authorities events that occurred at his business in 1932. On April 7 and 9, Bruno Hauptmann, the kidnapper of Charles Lindbergh's baby, went to Snow's garage to have the fenders of his car painted black and its trunk rack straightened.[262] Snow told authorities he forgot about that happening until he reviewed some prior work orders.

The timing of Snow coming forward was interesting. Around then, Zwillman, a Jewish-American gangster whose career in organized crime dated back to the early Prohibition days, offered a $30,000 reward for the capture of the Lindbergh kidnapper. Zwillman hoped the reward and the added testimony from Snow might foster a better feeling among the public and law enforcement about the Mob's gambling and bookmaking operations.

261   *Sinatra: The Life*, Anthony Summers, May 30, 2006
262   *Miami Daily News-Record*, (Oklahoma), Jan. 11, 1935

Zwillman was a founding member of the "Big Seven" Ruling Commission, a member of the National Crime Syndicate, and an associate of Murder, Inc. Zwillman later became a hidden owner in the Sands with Gerardo "Jerry" Catena and others.

Jimmy Grippo knew many of the owners of the Dunes, but he was extremely friendly with Jake and John Gottlieb, who were extremely close to Jimmy Hoffa. Hoffa was a big fan and friend of Grippo. Once when I was coming on shift at the Dunes baccarat pit, my fellow workers, who knew that I had a love of magic, told me, "You just missed Jimmy Grippo. He was sitting on the table and did some great card tricks." This occurred a few times, so I decided to meet Grippo. He became a great friend and confidant.

Jimmy talked about Duke's restaurant all the time. Duke's address was 783 Palisade Avenue, Cliffside Park, N.J., and it was, in the 1940s and 1950s, the meeting place of and safe sanctuary for the leaders of the National Crime Syndicate. Moretti was there every day. Presiding over Duke's, which sat directly across the street from the Palisades Amusement Park, was Joe Adonis, one of the leading Mafiosi not only in New York and New Jersey, but also in all of the country. I heard about Duke's from Jimmy, not in a book and long before the Internet. I could not imagine what he was conveying to me. I wish I'd asked more questions. All of the people in the Grippo part of this story were frequent guests at Duke's.

It was easy to connect the dots between Jimmy Grippo and Adonis, Moretti, Lansky, Costello, Hoffa, "Fat Tony" Salerno, and others. Some of these characters were dubbed Mob or Syndicate members, La Cosa Nostra members, or members of the "mythical" Mafia by name, yet they really did not have a secret ceremony for initiation. In fact, of all of the real players who were connected, or in the so-called Mafia, I never ever heard the secret initiation ritual even brought up as a mythical story. My mentor at the Dunes, who was a "button man" in Brooklyn, never mentioned this mythical initiation rite, yet he taught me all the rest.

There are direct links between Duke's, from the past up until the 1980s, to a legitimate casino operation in Nevada. This association was, in Jimmy's words: "Joe Adonis, the Mobster, a long story."

There were frequent card games at Duke's, and this was not a very big place but intimate and cozy. Adonis was considered to be an "expert" gin rummy player.

Jimmy said, "In this one game with Joe Adonis and some other Mob guys playing, Adonis asked me to beat two Mob guys out of about $60,000 and then return it, just to prove a point."

This certainly put Jimmy in a good position with Adonis, the real god-father of the times.

Gambling was Adonis' specialty, and he especially loved Grippo's card handling. Jimmy made his own "juice" and was a lifelong friend of Adonis. It was discovered that Adonis had secret compartments built in his traveling luggage or trunks to hide his personal belongings and valuables.

The senators conducting the Kefauver hearings tried to portray Adonis as a bad guy. Although indicted on charges of kidnapping, extortion, and assault, which were later dismissed, he was actually a soft-spoken, conservatively dressed family man who lived in a respectable neighborhood and only had an occasional drink. His family and children worshiped him. According to Adonis, his idea of a big evening was "gin rummy with friends." He built up a lucrative haul-away business that he ran efficiently. Adonis, however, was an ex-bootlegger (who wasn't?), a big time gambler, a notorious underworld figure, and according to the Kefauver Committee, one of the most important figures in the U.S. crime network. He also had enormous behind-the-scenes political power.

Over the years Adonis engaged in many legitimate businesses. He said that he "does not object to profits just because they are legitimate." But along with those enterprises, according to an indictment pending against him in New Jersey, he ran a "carpet joint" as opposed to a less opulent and less swanky "sawdust joint." In doing so, he was developing the "flagship" model casino that later was replicated in Las Vegas.

He did not mind the indictments, being called a big gambler, or even being hauled before the Kefauver Committee, which could have resulted in his going to prison for the first time. (He went to prison in May 1951.) He did, however, bitterly resent the fact that as a result of the Kefauver grandstanding fiasco he lost his car hauling business and a big contract with Ford Motor Company. The committee sent a letter to Ford, suggesting that they cease doing business with Adonis. Adonis called it persecution. He was 100 percent correct, and I believe local law enforcement felt the same. Talk about the McCarthy hearings and justice – Kefauver intentionally ruined a legitimate business.

The godfather of Las Vegas-style gambling, Adonis operated a floating craps game at 8th Avenue and 15th Street in New York City, which was frequented by everyone until Mayor Fiorello La Guardia turned on the heat.

In 1937 three Italian hoods thought they could rob Joey A's floating craps game. The trio came in, grabbed all of the money on the layout, and emptied the customers' pockets of cash and jewelry. They got away with it for the time being, but within two months all three were found murdered.

In a 15-minute interview by the police, Adonis said that he could not imagine who had done in the three boys. He was a reputable businessman, and such bloody incidents were completely foreign to him. He was "truly sorry he couldn't help and didn't understand why the police thought he could." The lesson to the hoods on the streets was this: "You don't cross the Mob!" You can bet this didn't happen again.

Frank Costello made a solid connect with the legendary Mills Novelty Company of Chicago, the largest manufacturer of slot machines in the country. He and Phil Kastel placed over 5,100 machines in New York City and the surrounding communities. They grossed about $100,000 per day in the mid-1930s. In today's dollars that would be about $1.8 million a day. They probably netted anywhere between $500,000 and $700,000 after paying the winners and splitting the profits with the local operators.

Adonis and Moretti could not have machines in the "floating" craps games because they were not mobile and could not be easily hidden or moved when there was a bust. But you can bet that the two had a piece of the action.

In the mid-1930s La Guardia literally busted up many of the machines in the New York City area. So Adonis and Moretti looked for other places to operate, like New Jersey, Florida, and Cuba.

Jimmy wrote in his notes to me: "Floating crap games in Lodi, New Jersey, with Moretti and Adonis." Lodi, N.J. was home of the fabulous "Barn," which became a Las Vegas style casino at night. What was an ordinary garage during daytime hours was transformed into a big craps game at night.

The garage owner and operator, John Garrantano, was arrested and brought before a grand jury along with seven employees of the gambling operation. Seven others, who were described by the attorney general as "stick" or "dice" men in Lodi, were slated to appear at the hearing. One of the "inside men" who talked with jurors was James Grippo, allegedly a nephew of Willie Moretti. But like a magic trick where doubles are used, this particular James Grippo was not Jimmy Grippo, which is what I have ascertained through my research.

What is even stranger, though, is that not a word of this "coincidence" was ever mentioned by Jimmy Grippo, nor was it picked up in any of the stories that appeared in newspapers across the country. Jimmy previously received many write-ups and garnered lots of publicity by the nation's top sports writers, yet there was *not one* mention of this incident.

Was this a cover-up? There is *no* question that the real Jimmy Grippo, magician, was aware of this incident, as were Moretti and the rest of the crew in and around Duke's restaurant.

In another note from Jimmy to me, he wrote, "The police arrested the bookmakers at Duke's restaurant, [James] 'Piggy' Lynch saved me from the rap." This statement said a lot, as Jimmy was involved with the New Jersey and New York Mobs in bookmaking and gambling. Jimmy had to keep his name clean and to appear above reproach in the boxing world, so undoubtedly he had to be very careful in his daily activities.

The incident to which Jimmy referred is this. The rampant gambling and over-the- top political corruption in Saratoga County, N.Y., which virtually allowed the Mob to operate there carte blanche, came to a crashing halt with the arrest of Meyer Lansky. In the 21-count indictment against him, Lansky was charged with forgery in the third degree, being a common gambler, and participating in a conspiracy to gamble. Lynch was one of the other people named with Lansky. Jimmy was very close to being indicted and arrested as well.

The indictment mentioned how Lansky, Lynch, and the other defendants conspired by using a restaurant as a front for the gambling operation. It explained the M.O.: "Mix an excellent restaurant that loses money, add a good local 'front' and have a passageway to the casino."

Sounds like Las Vegas!!! Lansky et al. had the perfect business model way before the Flamingo.

The grand jurors explained: "The restaurant should be operated on a lavish extravagant scale and provide food of choice quality and of greatest delicacy, and should entertain its guests with performances by stage and screen celebrities of national reputation and with widely popular dance orchestras." The indictment alleged that the lavish casino at the Arrowhead Inn in Saratoga Springs, N.Y. gave Carmen Miranda a check for $10,000 for a week's engagement in 1947. In today's dollars that would be over $110,000.

The "restaurant" front, the indictment explained, should lose money "and incur a deficit that would be met from casino proceeds." (How would these old-time operators feel about Las Vegas casinos now charging for local parking?)

The grand jurors added that the operators' aim was "to attract the maximum number of patrons of appropriate economic position who should be induced to proceed from the restaurant to the casino and [once] there, to engage in games of chance."

Lansky and Lynch testified that they knew one another, but they refused to answer questions about their mutual business dealings. Lynch admitted that he did not have a legitimate business, but the Senate Committee introduced evidence of $5 million in checks that were endorsed by Lynch and deposited into a New York City account over a five- month period in 1947 and 1948.

Jimmy said to me, "Write this down: Mobster Willie Moretti, the real 'Godfather,' a great story." Guarino "Willie" Moretti, a.k.a. Willie Moore, was a notorious underboss of the Genovese crime family and a cousin of the family boss Frank Costello. Costello was the best man at Moretti's wedding.

Moretti was born in 1894 in Bari, Puglia, Italy on February 24, 1894, four years before Jimmy. His family immigrated to the U.S. in the early 1990s. They settled in New Jersey, where Moretti met brothers Frank and Eddie Costello, and eventually the three formed a street gang.

Moretti was a bootleg fighter in New York's Longacre, which was at the heart of a neighborhood broadly known as the Tenderloin or Satan's Circus. In 1901, the area from 37th to 47th streets and from 5th to 8th Avenues was home to 132 brothels and at least as many saloons. Moretti boxed in the same venues where Mickey Grippo competed in the flyweight class.

On January 12, 1913, at the age of 19, Moretti was arrested for the first time, convicted of robbery in New York City, and sentenced to a year in state prison. He was released after a few months due to his young age and relatively minor crime for the time period. After his release, Moretti continued working with the Costello brothers, committing crimes such as robbery, extortion, theft, and burglary. It was known early on that Frank Costello was the brains, Moretti was the muscle, and the two worked well together.

By the late 1920s and into the early 1930s Moretti, who had continued his life of crime, became a very powerful man in New Jersey working for the Genovese crime family of New York. He ran a successful gambling racket throughout New Jersey and upstate New York and had other Mafia notables such as Adonis and Zwillman working alongside him. His gang eventually consisted of at least 60 men.

Duke's was a daily hangout for Moretti and the boys in Cliffside Park, N.J. When asked by Senate investigators about the place, Moretti said, "Well, I would class [sic] Duke's restaurant like Lindy's on Broadway; there is no difference."[263]

---

263   Investigation of Organized Crime in Interstate Commerce: New York-New Jersey, Dec. 12, 1950

When Moretti was asked who the actual customers were, it was discovered that Adonis, Zwillman, Catena, Lynch, and many others were patrons.

According to the 1951 Kefauver Senate Report about domestic gambling and racketeering, two major crime syndicates operated in the U.S.: the Accardo-Guzik- Fischetti (Tony Accardo, Jake Guzik, and Rocco Fischetti) syndicate headquartered in Chicago, and the Costello-Adonis-Lansky group based in New York. Jimmy Grippo was allied and associated with the latter.

During one of the hearings, the following exchange took place between Rudolph Halley, chief counsel to the Kefauver Committee, and Moretti, a political fixer and front man operator for Adonis et al.

> **Halley:** "You are not a member of either the Mafia or the Unione Siciliano?"
>
> **Moretti:** "What do you mean by a member, carry a card with Mafia on it?"
>
> **Halley:** "No. I am not being humorous now."
>
> **Moretti:** "I mean, to be a member you've got to carry a card. You got to be initiated."
>
> **Halley:** "It is a secret organization. You have read that, haven't you?"
>
> **Moretti:** "That's all just in newspapers."
>
> **Halley:** "And I ask you if you belong to such a secret organization."
>
> **Moretti:** "No, sir, I don't."
>
> **Halley:** "Have you ever?"
>
> **Moretti:** "No, sir."
>
> **Halley:** "And do you know anybody or have you ever known anybody who did?"
>
> **Moretti:** "How could I know if it don't exist?"
>
> **Halley:** "You know nothing about it?"
>
> **Moretti:** "For my knowledge it don't exist."

A 1951 Bureau of Narcotics document concerning the Mafia stated flatly that Frank Sinatra was "discovered by Moretti after pressure from Costello and Luciano." An FBI document quoted an informant as saying that Sinatra "was originally 'brought up' by Frank Costello of New York." And a 1944 report on crime in New Jersey noted that Moretti "had a financial interest in Frank Sinatra."

Later, engaged in conversation by agents on a pretext, Moretti "admitted his association" with Sinatra. The son of the senior policeman who wrote the 1944 report, himself a former New Jersey investigator, recalled his father discussing the Sinatra-Moretti matter. As Matthew Donohue, Jr. remembered it, "Willie Moretti and big guys like Joe Adonis used to go into the Rustic Cabin. People like that were often there. And Willie took a liking to Sinatra."[264]

Sinatra maintained, in testimony to the Nevada Gaming Control Board in the 1980s, that Moretti "had absolutely nothing to do with my career at any time." However, in a much earlier closed session with U.S. Senate investigators, Sinatra made a crucial admission, according to the transcript.

Attorney: "I will ask you specifically. Have you ever, at any time, been associated in business with Moretti?"

Sinatra: "Well, Moretti made some band dates for me when I first got started."[265]

In 1950 Moretti and other Mob associates were called to testify before the Kefauver Committee. Most of them refused, invoking the Fifth Amendment. Moretti, however, talked rather openly. Miss Mary Gilbert, Intelligence Unit, Miami Police Department, made available on April 6, 1959, a recorded conversation that took place during the Kefauver hearings between George White, U.S. Treasury Department, and Willie Moretti. Here is a portion of it:

White: "Willie, why do you keep insisting that there is no such thing as the Mafia? You look silly saying that with what we know today."

Moretti: "Of course there's a MAFIA. And I'm just what you claim I am. I'm the head man in my territory [New Jersey]. But what's so bad about that? We don't bother anybody outside our own people. We just don't run to the cops when someone gets out of line. We settle things among ourselves."

This statement by Willie probably helped get him murdered. Vito Genovese felt that Moretti was losing his mind because of the syphilis he contracted and used this slip as a reason to have him bumped off. According to Jimmy, Johnny Roberts killed Moretti, and later, Roberts was killed in Brooklyn.

Genovese had this done, against the wishes of Costello, Adonis and, I will stick my neck out and say, even Albert Anastasia, all of whom liked

264   Ibid
265   Ibid

Moretti. Genovese did not think the same way as the others and had an underlying motive for removing Moretti. It is possible but not certain that Genovese and Santos Trafficante, Jr., who wanted to take over the gambling in Cuba as early as the 1950s, killed Moretti for two reasons: as a warning to others to not become loose lipped and to remove Moretti from the gambling enterprises that he adeptly controlled in Cuba and New Jersey. A master, Moretti held all of the employees together and ran a smooth, fine-tuned operation.

An FBI informant reported that by early 1957, Anastasia, in connection with his control of the waterfront in New York, developed a powerful organization known generally among hoodlums as the Anastasia Syndicate. Although Anastasia was a member of the Mafia, the very size of his organization posed a threat to the Mafia itself, and the Mafia foresaw an eventual bitter struggle for power if Anastasia decided to "break out of the waterfront area," which was assigned to him.

According to the FBI, in summer 1957, the Mafia, through Trafficante, offered then Cuban president Fulgencio Batista a large sum of money for the gambling casino concession in the Havana Hilton. Subsequently, Trafficante learned that Anastasia was interested in turning over the waterfront to Anastasia's brother, Salvatore, and moving into Cuban gambling, and that in fact representatives of Anastasia already proffered a higher dollar figure to Batista than the Mafia had through Trafficante. Trafficante suspected that Batista would accept the highest bid no matter whom it came from and that the only solution was to try to convince Anastasia to back off.

Trafficante took the problem to New York, where he conferred with several high ranking leaders of the Mafia. They agreed to pressure Anastasia to stay out of Cuba.

Trafficante and others had numerous conversations with Anastasia, without results. Anastasia insisted that he was tired of the waterfront, that Cuba should be open to anybody, and that he wanted to move in. The final sign that he was serious came in October 1957, when he turned over the New York waterfront to his brother, Salvatore. The Mafia tried one last time to reason with him, in a conference held in the latter part of the month, again to no avail. Anastasia was murdered on October 25, 1957.

Immediately after the Apalachin Meeting of Mafia heads on November 14, 1957, Salvatore Anastasia let it be known that he was going to get the people responsible for Albert's death, including Trafficante. In February 1958, someone shot at Trafficante while he was driving his car in Havana, but he survived. According to author Scarne, "The Apalachin meeting was about who would run the gambling in Cuba, not about setting the rules for the Mafia."

In a story published just a few days after Moretti's murder, the Kefauver Committee, after hearing testimony, named Meyer Lansky, "Doc" Stacher, and "Piggy" Lynch the heads of the New York ring. Under the name of L&L Trading Company, they operated the Arrowhead Inn and held interests in Florida, in The Club Boheme, The Colonial Inn, and the Greenacres Club. The committee members named Lynch, Adonis, Catena, Anthony "Tony Greeno" Guarini, Salvatore Moretti, and James Rutkin the heads of the New Jersey ring. This group operated under the auspices of the G&R Trading Company in Lodi, N.J. and the L&P Trading Company, the B&T Trading Company, and the Pal Trading Company in Palisades, N.J.

The heat was on in both states, and boxing was not the same for Jimmy, so he booked more performance venues and entertained around the country. Miami was the forerunner of Las Vegas and full of action, so Jimmy worked there in various clubs and venues.

In the *Miami News*, columnist Herb Rau reported that Jimmy's friend, Snow, of the Havana Hilton hotel, was in Miami Beach. This was not a coincidence. Snow was there for the grand opening of Grippo's 21 Club in the Sea Gull Hotel on Friday, November 20, 1959. This was the same year that Castro closed all of the casino operations in Cuba.

The ad for Grippo's grand opening did not contain anything like "featuring Jimmy's act," or even give the time of his appearance. It only noted, "entertainment nightly." This suggested that gambling was the main draw, and that Jimmy was the front man for that operation there. The words in the ad, "Jimmy Grippo and 21 Room" said it all. "Jimmy is your host for playing blackjack!"

Jimmy's 21 Room at the Sea Gull Hotel featured dancing, music, food and, in fact, gambling in a casino; this writer confirmed that there was a casino in the 21 Room.

At his 90th birthday gala at Caesars Palace in Las Vegas, Jimmy introduced me to Gerald Christopher. Later, I found a letter written by Christopher that mentioned special cards to be used for cheating.

Christopher's friend, Larry McTiernan, worked for Jimmy at the 21 Room and elsewhere in New York. Jimmy discovered a few months later that McTiernan was a bust out dealer when Jimmy saw him make a move. After it, Jimmy inquired, "Who hired him?" That suggested that, one, Grippo did not hire McTiernan and, two, that Grippo had a partner in the gambling there who was one of the Mob's key operators. If that was the case, who was it? Was he a partner of Grippo? Perhaps a silent partner? Did this partner have connections in Las Vegas? Did this partner have Grippo move to Las Vegas?

The gambling at the Sea Gull Hotel operated full bore as if gambling were legal. Clearly, the operation had plenty of protection from the Mob and from the police. The Sea Gull Hotel was a favorite meeting place and spot among the top Ma-hoffs.

Trafficante frequented it, according to numerous FBI documents.

```
        On November 4, 1963, Departmental Attorney KENNEY
advised that his source had not learned where NOUEL was
residing in Miami; however, NOUEL had met SANTO TRAFFICANTE
on the night of November 3, 1963, by chance, at the 21 Club.
KENNEY advised that the trip was apparently only for pleasure
but he understood that TRAFFICANTE had obtained two Latin
girls for NOUEL, however, NOUEL did not like the girls.
```

I believe Trafficante was a competitor of Grippo's group, which consisted of Genovese family-connected individuals, including "Fat Tony" Salerno, Sam Di Carlo, and many, many others. The FBI secretly obtained guest registration cards from the Sea Gull for handwriting analysis to determine if any of guests were Mobsters who were on their watch list. One such guest who registered under the name Sal Mann was suspected of being Kelly Mannarino, who was the Pittsburgh crime boss, attended the Apalachin meeting, and worked in Cuba, protecting the interests there of his Mob family.

```
        On December 11, 1959, JEfferson 1-7000 was called
by SA JOHN P. LENIHAN. This is the telephone number for
JIMMY GRIPPO's 21 Room at the Sea Gull Hotel, where RABIN,
ROTHMAN, MANNARINO, COTRONI and ROBERT have stayed in the past,
so for that reason no attempt was made to interview the LOWENTHALs :
this matter.
```

Hoffa regularly visited Grippo's 21 Room, as did Salerno. There is a mention in a Miami 1962 newspaper of one of Hoffa's visits on page 276.:

Years later in Las Vegas, Jimmy Grippo confided in me that Hoffa frequently visited Caesars Palace and spent a great deal of time with him. Hoffa, who really liked Grippo, had him pick him up from or drop him off at the airport on his Las Vegas trips. The last time Hoffa visited Las Vegas before his murder, Grippo saw him off, he told me.

Grippo said that Hoffa wanted to build a small boutique hotel, maybe 150 rooms with an intimate showroom, just for Jimmy's magic. The hotel would have the finest restaurant to be found anywhere. It would be

RENICK   HOFFA   KENNEDY

FOUR YEARS LATER, September, 1962, this is how things shaped up here: New York columnist reported that "saleswomen in some of Florida's best stores have been told in no uncertain terms that they must speak Spanish fluently or lose their jobs" . . . U-M freshman coed was given aptitude test to determine what she was best suited for. Turned out she was best suited for high school . . . Quote from this column, Sept. 10, 1962: Jimmy Hoffa, three nights out of four last week, caught Jimmy Grippo's magic act at the Seagull. (Maybe he's trying to pick up some pointers on how to make Bobby kennedy disappear?)" . . . Prominent circuit Court judge explained why he never appointed a woman attorney to fill an opening as a Special Master: "How could I explain to my wife that I have a Special Mistress?"

the best of the best. Unfortunately, Hoffa's death precluded fruition of the concept. But I will bet my last dollar that Hoffa would have been Grippo's partner in that operation as he perhaps was in Jimmy's 21 Room in the Sea Gull Hotel.

The owner of the Sea Gull was Jerry Zarowitz, who was probably a partner of Grippo. It surely is logical that Hoffa and Zarowitz became very friendly. There's no doubt that later, when Caesars obtained financing from the Teamsters pension fund, Zarowitz's friendship with Hoffa clinched the deal, with a little help from Grippo not romancing, but polishing, the stone. Incidentally, Zarowitz was the New England bookie and gambler who was convicted for fixing the 1946 New York Giants-Chicago Bears National Football League championship game.

The Mob was interested in developing gambling operations in the Caribbean Islands. Prior to Grippo opening his club in the Sea Gull Hotel in 1959, he composed a letter to Sir Stafford Sands, finance minister of the Bahamas, requesting authorization to operate a casino there.

This letter was a major move on the part of Jimmy. There was absolutely no way that he acted solo in this formal request to Sir Stafford Sands. It would have been extremely harmful for him to write such a letter without approval from his associates.

The paragraph in it, "It is commendable that your Island has been free from what we call in the U.S. the syndicate. I have no such affiliation," is significant. Jimmy carefully worded the letter, as he did with everything he wrote, never using the word "Mafia," "La Cosa Nostra," or "Mob." Instead, he used the gentler term, "syndicate." By definition, "syndicate" means organization, group, or consortium, which are perfectly legal as-

---

Miami Beach, Fla., July 2, 1958

Honorable Sir Stafford Sands,
Nassau, Bahamas,
British West Indies.

Dear Sir Stafford Sands:

Although I have not had the pleasure of meeting you personally, I have been fortunate in visiting your Island and performed on numerous occasions at the Emerald Beach and British Colonial Hotels. During these shows and my visits, I have met many fine people and developed a keen interest in your way of life. As a result, my aspiration at the moment is to work and live there.

I understand that the gambling Casino at the Bahamas Club is for sale due to the ill health of the present chap who heads the establishment. If this is so, I would be most appreciative to be able to avail myself of the opportunity to enter a bid for the concession.

Principally, I am known as an entertainer who performs hypnotism, mind reading and sleight of hand magic. However, I understand all phases of gambling, having made a study of it for many years and was consultant for many casinos in the United States.

It is commendable that your Island has been free from what we call in the U. S. the syndicate. I have no such affiliation.

If the Bahamas Club is not available, perhaps there is a possibility of a second club. I believe that I would be a credit to such an organization as I am very well known and have a large following.

Thanking you in advance for any information you can give me on the above, I remain,

Respectfully yours,

JG/TG

sociations. Jimmy suggesting to Sands, without the Mob's approval, that there was a syndicate would have been disastrous for him. One can bet that the Mob was behind him and using him as a front man, which was their modus operandi.

An FBI memo detailed the various characters who were associated with Jimmy, the Bahamas operation and Las Vegas. The familiar names and connections are evident. George Sadlo was Meyer Lansky's No. 1 man in the gambling business that caused problems for Marion Hicks of the Thunderbird with the Nevada Gaming Control Board.

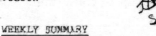

TO: DIRECTOR, FBI (62-9-29)

FROM: SAC, MIAMI (92-515) (P)

RE: CRIMINAL INTELLIGENCE PROGRAM
          MIAMI DIVISION

WEEKLY SUMMARY

KM ████ C-TE reported that ROBERT "MUSCLES" MARTIN, who was one of the dispatchers in a big dice game which took place in Dade County, Florida, the past winter season and who was formerly connected with the Plaza Hotel gambling casino in Havana, Cuba, has been designated the individual who will process and screen individuals to be employed in the Lucayan Beach gambling casino at Freeport, Grand Bahama Islands. He was also told GEORGE SADLOW, a former gambling casino employee in Havana, Cuba, and Las Vegas, Nevada, has gone to Freeport, where he will become the casino manager. FRANK "RED" REED is scheduled to be the credit manager of this operation. He further learned that DAVE GEIGER (NM 165-250) formerly of New York City and also a former casino employee in Havana, Cuba, who has been a gambler and bookmaker in the Miami area the past several years, will be connected with the casino.

GEIGER recently returned to the United States from London, England, where he allegedly had been instructing prospective employees in the art of casino gambling. Reportedly GEIGER, with his partners, JERRY ZAROWITZ (NM 165-256) and ANTHONY SALERNO (NM 92-406), will have five to ten points in the casino. GEORGE SADLOW, with his partner, WILLIAM O. BISCHOFF (NM 92-89) will also have some points in the casino, possibly a like number.

When the law cracked down on Miami Beach, Mobsters sent Jimmy to Las Vegas. Caesars Palace was just starting to become an idea, and the Mob was making a deal to buy into the brilliant concept of Jay. J. Sarno.

There was a meeting in Palm Springs that the FBI monitored very closely. The attendees were all old-time acquaintances of Jimmy. The FBI learned that the Genovese family boss, Salerno, was buying a controlling interest in the operation and planning to install his trusted operator, Zarowitz, there to run it.

Bernard "Bernie" Einstoss promoted the Caesars Palace concept, circa 1963 and 1964. He was associated with Mobster Johnny Rosselli, who was hired with Sam Giancana and Trafficante to kill Fidel Castro, by Howard Hughes' employee and former CIA-FBI operative Bob Maheu. Einstoss went to Reno, Nevada, from Los Angeles in 1947, and when the Mapes hotel opened that same year there, he, Leo Kind, Frank Grannis, and Louis "Lou" Wertheimer, whose brother Myrton "Mert" Wertheimer ran a casino for Lansky in Florida, leased the casino from owner Charles Mapes.

When Einstoss suddenly passed away in 1966, Zarowitz assumed the role of finding additional investors who were willing to buy points. One individual purchased 3 percent during the formulation stage of Caesars but later backed out because he did not like Zarowitz.

Rosselli, aware of Zarowitz's checkered background, knew that he would have difficulty obtaining a Nevada gaming license for Caesars Palace, if at all. A master of the shakedown, Rosselli figured he could make a few bucks by offering to help Zarowitz obtain a gaming license. I wonder who Rosselli's co-conspirator was in this scheme.

The FBI was surveilling Rosselli electronically, and here is their official document about his scam:

```
OF CEASAR'S PALACE AS ONLY ZAROWITZ HAD PUT MONEY INTO

OPERATION AND NONE INVESTED BY JAY SARNO OR NATE JACOBSON,
                      A
OWNERS OF RECORD.  ZROWITZ CONTACTED ALO AND ANTHONY "FAT

TONY" SALERNO WHO CAME TO PALM SPRINGS AND ACCORDING TO

LOUGHRAN PUT IN "MILLIONS OF DOLLARS." EXACT AMOUNT

INVESTED OR POINTS RECEIVED NOT KNOWN BY LOUGHRAN.

    ACCORDING TO LOUGHRAN, GAMBLING AT PALM SPRINGS WAS

  INCIDENTAL.  THIS STORY NEVER PREVIOUSLY TOLD SOURCE BY LOUGHR

    AUSA, LOS ANGELES ADVISED MAY THREE INSTANT THAT FGJ

  INSTANT MATTER CONTINUED TO MARCH NEXT SO RUBY LAZARUS

CAN REMAIN IN CUSTODY UNTIL THAT TIME.

    LAS VEGAS ADVISED AIR MAIL.
```

Rosselli may have gotten the money from Zarowitz, as $200,000 was petty cash to this operator to pay for help in getting a gaming license, according to a 1959 FBI note.

Zarowitz was tighter with the New York Mob than Rosselli ever could be. The evidence showed that Zarowitz was wise to Rosselli, and because of this scam, kept the Chicago element out of Caesars Palace. On December 29, 1966, Rosselli was arrested by Ralph Lamb in Las Vegas after being in the Desert Inn. He once tried to shake down the owner, Moe Dalitz. As a matter of record, Dalitz was very close to Hoffa and the Teamsters, and was since his Detroit laundry days. So who fingered Rosselli? It is more than probable that Dalitz fingered him to Lamb.

In February 1970, a guest of Caesars Palace sent Jimmy Grippo a note, gushing about his recent trip to Las Vegas and his experience in the Bacchanal Room where Grippo performed. At the end of the letter, the guest wrote, "Please give my regards to Jerry Zarowitz." Indeed, there was more than just an employee-employer relationship between Grippo and Zarowitz.

Zarowitz was the real boss at Caesars Palace, even though Sarno and Nathan "Nate" Jacobson fought with each other over who should be the president. Zarowitz once told Sarno in a rather heated tone, "You see that carpet? Don't ever cross this line and enter the casino."[266] Sarno didn't.

The unpleasant side of Zarowitz came out in an incident involving Sinatra. In Anthony Summers' book, *Sinatra: The Life*, he wrote, "Some prominent critics suggested, when the hardcover edition of our book appeared, that we had been unfair to the man and his artistry. We say they are wrong, and we stand by every line."

Summers got some of the story correct about a confrontation Sinatra had with a Caesars Palace executive, but Summers never found out or simply did not reveal who the executive was. He wrote, "The mob had again failed to back him up. Giancana, who mostly lived abroad following a spell in prison, was a spent force. Angelo DeCarlo and Jimmy Alo were in jail. Joe Fischetti soon would be." The executive was Zarowitz.

Here is what actually happened, which was told to me by Morrie Jaeger, whom I have known for 35-plus years and who witnessed the incident.

"One early evening Zarowitz came by the casino and said, 'Come on, we are going up to Sinatra's room. He doesn't want to go on. The showroom is full and they just had dinner. Our customers won't like this. Let's go see what the problem is.' We went to his suite and Zarowitz told Sinatra that the showroom is full and the customers just finished dinner and were waiting for him to perform. He asked Sinatra why he wasn't going on. Sinatra replied, 'Because I don't feel like it!'

---

266   Interview with anonymous source, MJ, 2016

"Zarowitz got red and lost his temper. He looked at me and said, 'Open the sliding glass door.' Frank's longtime friend Jilly Rizzo jumped up and Zarowitz yelled at him, 'Sit down or you're dead!'

"Zarowitz pointed his finger at Frank and said, 'You're going on and you're going to do two encores or I am going to throw you off the balcony!' Sinatra got up and went downstairs and did the show. We waited in the other side of the wings and saw him do the encores. I was as nervous as hell as a witness to this incident. This story has never been told anywhere."

My associate also wanted it known that Zarowitz was a kind, thoughtful, and stand-up individual who always was on the side of the "little guy" or average working man. He spent as much or more time talking with a bus boy as he did a hotel president. He really cared about what people had to say. If he liked someone, there was nothing he would not do for them.

Jaeger was also present when the FBI raided random boxes in the casino cage at Caesars looking for skim money and bookmaking records with which Zarowitz was associated. One of the senior FBI agents said as they were confiscating money, "We finally got those Jews."

Jimmy Grippo wanted me to help him write a book about his life based on his short notes, which included: "The dinner party with gourmet cook Joe Adonis and Meyer Lansky" and "I hypnotized Walter Winchell every Sunday night for his famous broadcasts, 'Mr. and Mrs. America' and all the ships at sea. His stomach would swell up from nerves, and hypnosis kept him calm and reassured. Winchell would meet me every night at midnight to make the rounds at all the New York late night hangouts to gather information for his daily newspaper column."

In Jimmy's anecdotes, there was a mystery, the real identity of someone he repeatedly referred to as "Fat Tony Baloney." There was no Mobster with that name.

In reality, that person was Jimmy's friend, "Fat Tony" Salerno, one of the hidden owners with the biggest interests of Caesars Palace. Grippo never referred to Salerno by his real name to protect him because Salerno was still conducting business as usual at the time. Jimmy never tipped his hat. What a story.

CHAPTER 44

THE ALADDIN AND IZZY MARION

I never saw it coming. Whack! Bang! Thud! I was knocked out in a fraction of a second, and I never saw the car T-bone me. I was driving North on Eastern Avenue in Las Vegas at about 45 m.p.h. in a 1972 Mercedes 500SL coupe. The car that collided with mine ran through a posted stop sign and halted my cruising. I was spun around, knocked out, cut my forehead, and landed in the front yard of the residence of Izzy Marion. My telling of this story is solely based on the accounts of eyewitnesses.

Marion, in his kitchen, heard the collision and immediately went outside to discover his new uninvited guest. I was stone cold out. Marion opened my car door, and I fell out as far as my seat belt allowed. Thank God I was wearing it.

"What are you doing here?" I asked, now in a groggy, semi-conscious state. "What are you doing here?" Izzy replied.

I felt relieved that I saw an old friend. It was consoling just to see his face, yet I could tell he was concerned about my condition. He asked repeatedly if I was okay. I felt all right, got out of the car, sat down on a cement step, and tried to make sense of what just happened.

I first met Marion in about 1963 while I was visiting family in Las Vegas. I was considering moving to Las Vegas as soon as I graduated from high school. Marion was having a Sunday backyard party to which my son Matthew and I were invited. I can clearly remember all of the male compares playing a popular Italian card game called Briscola. Briscola is a Mediterranean trick-taking card game for two to six players with a standard Italian 40-card deck. A standard Anglo-American deck can be used by stripping out the 8s, 9s and 10s. The objective of the game is to win tricks with valuable cards in them.[267]

After Briscola they played Morra. In its ancient form, Morra is a hand game played for points by two people.[268] Both players show either one or

---

267   A trick-taking game, either card or tile based, is one in which play of a hand centers on a series of finite rounds or units of play, called tricks, each of which is evaluated to determine the winner, or taker.

268   *Introduction to the Theory of Games*, J.C.C. McKinsey, 1952

two fingers, and simultaneously call, out loud, in Italian, the number of fingers they think the other player will show. A correct call wins the number of points showing as fingers (2, 3, or 4); if both players call correctly, there is no winner. This would be a great place for a referee as there are more fouls and arguments in this simple game than in hockey.

A winner was determined, and the "Boss" elected an "Underboss" and they continued in their Cosa Nostra-style game of reward and revenge. One of the women brought out a tray of small miniature beer cans and put them in front of the Boss. The women were forbidden from playing a game like this. The Boss conferred openly with his Underboss. Marion was a master at this clever game in which he could say how bad a certain member was, how he could never be counted on for help in times of trouble, or that he was never loyal. He then asked his Underboss what he thought of the member. The Underboss either defended him or also knocked him. The Boss then could flag that member by not giving him any drinks that round, because he was "not-ta nice-a." This was the Boss' show of retaliation.

The next compare was then judged and may have been approved by the Boss to have a drink, and then the Underboss might have suggested that he have two drinks, and then the Boss may have said he needed three drinks. Before long, this compare was drunk, but the first member was dry. It was an interesting type of fun. Those whom the Boss liked drank. Those whom the Boss was unhappy with were prohibited from drinking. It was a hoot. Some of the Boss' true feelings were often shown to the other compares to set an example. It was so simple, yet so effective. It almost paralleled the real inner workings of the Mafia bosses. They kept everything nice and simple – and private.

I still had no grasp of what all of these guys did for a living, but I wanted to be just like them. They dressed to a T, looked sharp, and expressed themselves like I never witnessed in my life. I really wondered about Marion. He was good looking and could have been an actor on the big screen, not just an actor but a leading man playing opposite any woman he told the studio head to cast. Little did I know that I would really get to know this mysterious, yet outgoing, individual.

He was a macho man and his character appealed to the Italian blood within me. His ways were what most, if not all, young Italian men were taught. It was cool to be like Izzy. At 15, I thought he was really a trip.

I learned how to deal cards and went to work in my cousin's casino, The California Club, to "break in," learn the business and all of the games that the little casino on the corner of First and Fremont Streets, now swallowed up by the Golden Nugget, had to offer.

The California Club had a small show stage right in the middle of the casino. Some great acts appeared there at one time or another, such as Fats Domino, Little Richard, and many others, including the regular house act, Robert "Sunny" Spencer. One evening I went to work, and there he was in living color, the star of the show. Izzy Marion entered the building. He was a terrific act, as he appeared to me, especially since I met him a few years earlier. I had no idea that he was a friend of my cousin, Frank Schivo.

But Marion was everyone's friend. I realized that he was a real politician and moved as swiftly as a halfback in the NFL. He was impressive as an entertainer, in my young opinion, and he could even carry a tune. He did the job well, and the people really liked him. He was there probably to showcase his act, break it in, and get it smoothed out for better venues. After all, right outside the entrance on First Street there was a city sign that read, "No spitting on the sidewalk."

At the same time, Marion was working a deal with his friends at the Frontier. A full-page ad that appeared in the *Las Vegas Review-Journal* showed Marion and Jack Shapiro standing in front of the Frontier. The caption read something like this: "We welcome Izzy Marion to the Frontier Hotel and wish him a huge success in his new beauty salon in the hotel. Also, we wish Izzy great success in his new advertising agency."

I could never figure out this ad, other than it indicated that Marion was more than just the Izzy Marion I knew. He was doing other surreptitious things for undisclosed people. I did a little investigating. I wholeheartedly believe, and will bet my last dollar, that Izzy Marion, the singer, hair-stylist, and entrepreneur, convinced Anthony "Tony" Zerilli, one of his closest friends, to let him help watch Zerilli's interest in the Frontier hotel-casino.

In February 1972, during the trial of Shapiro and others, the government presented evidence that ex-Teamsters boss Jimmy Hoffa agreed in 1964 to lend $6 million to the hotel in which Zerilli and Michael Polizzi each would have a hidden interest. Federal prosecutor Thomas Kotoske claimed that Frontier developer Maury Friedman first contacted Shapiro in 1964 to attract investors for the then proposed International Hotel Casino. It is a real coincidence that years later, Kirk Kerkorian developed the other super-sized hotel in Las Vegas, aptly named the International Hotel.

Friedman was a key government witness, testifying for two days under a grant of immunity from prosecution. He provided plenty of information about Zerilli, Polizzi, and "Tony G" Giordano having secret ownership of the Frontier. When there was concern about some construction costs at the Frontier, Friedman quoted Shapiro as saying, "Don't worry. You know that Mike [Polizzi] and Tony [Giordano] are behind this thing. You'll get your money."

Friedman told of many meetings during 1966 and 1967, in Las Vegas, Los Angeles, Anaheim, Detroit, Toledo, and New York, about how control of the hotel passed to the Detroit group. He revealed that they were giving orders as early as May 1966.

Friedman, Johnny Rosselli, Zerilli, and Polizzi met in Palm Springs, California, in March of 1964. Friedman was trying to get investors for his new hotel-casino venture, the Frontier. Polizzi and Zerilli both wanted in on the deal provided they could remain silent partners, even unknown to all other investors. A week later in Buffalo, Zerilli, Polizzi, and Friedman met with Lou Jacobs of the Emprise Corporation, now Sport System Corporation. They discussed the proposed resort and wanted Jacobs to invest in concessions at the property.

Then in April, they had the big meeting. Zerilli, Polizzi, Friedman, and Rosselli met with Hoffa in Chicago to arrange a $6 million loan for the hotel-casino. They had a basic deal put together, but it fell apart in a few weeks. It could have been because Hoffa was about to go on trial in Chicago for allegedly defrauding the Teamsters pension fund in connection with other loans with which Hoffa was involved.

According to Ed Becker and Charles Rappleye,[269] Rosselli was also instrumental in arranging financing for construction of new hotels and expansion of existing ones, often through the offices of the Teamsters Central States Pension Fund, which was controlled by Chicago Mob figure Paul Dorfman and his son, Allen.[270]

Fred Black graphically explained in an interview, "If John Rosselli told Allen Dorfman to go shit on the courthouse steps in Carson City, he would shit on the courthouse steps."[271] Black was a lobbyist who gained national notoriety as an accomplice to Capitol Hill dealmaker Bobby Baker, and he was a close friend of Rosselli.

At the trial, Kotoske also said he would prove, through another witness and partner in the Frontier, Sam Diamond, that Shapiro suggested a similar deal in 1965 for a different property. Zerilli and Polizzi tried to secretly

---

269   *All American Mafioso*, Ed Becker and Charles Rappleye, 1991
270   Note: Hoffa did not loan the Frontier money, which suggests that he did not like the operators and/or that Moe Dalitz, who owned a competitive property, influenced Hoffa in that regard.
271   *Ibid*

invest $400,000 to $500,000 in the Silver Slipper casino located adjacent to the Frontier and across the street from the Desert Inn. The government had documentation that confirmed that Shapiro not only was the front, but also had about a 10 percent stake in the Frontier, as a "handmaiden and mouthpiece" for Zerilli and Polizzi.[272]

When questioned during the trial, Zerilli denied having an ownership in the Frontier, as reported by the *Reno Evening Gazette*:

> "A defendant in the Frontier Hotel trial, angered over questions about his reputation stemming from ties to organized crime, has told the court his reputation is as good 'as anyone else's in this courtroom.' The outburst came from Anthony Zerilli Thursday during questioning by Assistant U.S. Attorney Thomas Kotoske.
>
> "Zerilli, 43, five other men and the Emprise Corp. of Buffalo, N.Y., are accused of conspiring to conceal true ownership in the Las Vegas, Nev., hotel. Kotoske triggered the outburst when he asked Zerilli, 'Isn't it a fact your reputation would have prevented you from becoming licensed in this venture?' Nevada gambling laws prohibit the licensing of persons involved in organized crime. 'I take exception to that, have as fine a reputation as you have,' Zerilli answered. During cross-examination Zerilli said he approached former Teamsters Union president James Hoffa in 1964 for a loan to invest in the International Hotel in Las Vegas. Zerilli said the deal, which involved the Emprise Corp., never developed. Zerilli denied that he ever had a hidden interest in the Frontier or gave any orders in its operation. 'I take an oath before my maker that I never had a financial interest in the Frontier Hotel at any time,' he said."[273]

Friedman and Louis Feil, another witness who testified to the illegal involvement of some defendants, offered no evidence that implicated Giordano. None of the four government witnesses knew of any involvement by Giordano in the conspiracy or directly implicated him.[274]

Giordano had a financial interest in some valuable real estate in downtown St. Louis. The property was once the location of a B-girl bar operation. The property was sold to the St. Louis Civic Center Redevelopment Corporation that subsequently built the St. Louis baseball stadium. Giordano received a substantial sum of money from the transaction and then started looking at deals in Las Vegas in which to invest his money.[275]

272   See picture of Jack Shapiro in *Las Vegas Review-Journal* advertisement with Izzy Marion
273   *Reno Evening Gazette*, March 24, 1972
274   *United States v. Polizzi*, 500 F. 2d 856, July 18, 1974, openjurist.org/500/f2d/856/united-states-v- polizzi#fn92_ref
275   *Riverfront Times*, June 11, 1997

The stadium developer and concessions contractor was Emprise, which helped shield Giordano and the Detroit Mafia's joint hidden interest in the Frontier.

A local restaurant operator, Frank Cusumano, made three unsecured loans to Giordano totaling $50,000 between 1964 and 1968 for the purpose of Giordano's drive to invest in the Frontier.

A St. Louis real estate tycoon named Anthony Sansone, Jr. was also brought into the Frontier opportunity by Giordano. Sansone is the son-in-law of the late James Michaels, then the Syrian crime boss of St. Louis and a close ally of Giordano. Sansone was a business partner of former St. Louis mayor Alfonso J. Cervantes. Sansone and Giordano both traveled to Las Vegas together to make the original investment.

As for Giordano and Zerilli, they were close friends. Giordano lived in St. Louis, Zerilli in Detroit. There were telephone calls between the homes and offices of both of them, as well as other calls charged to Zerilli's credit card and placed to Giordano's numbers, at various key times in the course of events between June and November 1967. Giordano knew the Cusumanos and the Sansones in St. Louis, but the Sansones did not know Zerilli.

The need for additional money, which resulted in the issuance of the Class C debentures that Sansone later bought, developed in early June. There were calls between telephones listed to Giordano and Zerilli at that time. Zerilli went to St. Louis for two days on June 8.

The Sansones began gathering money for their VFI (Vegas Frontier Hotel) investment after Zerilli visited St. Louis, but before the Class C debentures were officially issued. They could have learned about the investment opportunity only from a person with knowledge of the inner operations of VFI.

In early August, Giordano repaid an overdue loan to the Cusumano family trust. Less than three weeks later, Sansone took out a loan from the same trust. This loan was part of the money Sansone planned to invest in VFI, and it was the only business transaction ever consummated between Sansone and the Cusumano family. It was unsecured. Although the VFI debentures in which Sansone invested yielded 4 percent interest, the loan from Cusumano was at 7 percent, an anomaly for which Sansone had no convincing explanation.

Giordano made five trips to Las Vegas between July and November 1967. The Giordanos had no business interests or relatives in Las Vegas, and Giordano was not a gambler. Each of these trips was closely preceded or followed, or both, by telephone contact between Giordano telephones and Zerilli telephones or phone calls charged to Zerilli. Each trip coincided with an important event in the unlawful scheme. For example, trips in September and November coincided with the beginning and end of the $150,000 investment.

On September 12 a series of phone calls took place between Zerilli's home and Giordano's home and business. The next day, Sansone marshaled the entire $150,000. On that same day there was a call from a Zerilli phone number to Giordano's phone number. On September 14 Sansone flew to Las Vegas with the money to make the investment. He checked into the Frontier, and 16 minutes later, Giordano checked into the Dunes. Four days later, Sansone deposited the $150,000 in VFI's account, received the debentures, and left Las Vegas. Giordano departed the following day.

In November, a telephone call to Giordano was charged to Zerilli on the same day that the Nevada Gaming Commission sent a letter to Sansone. Giordano went to Las Vegas on November 9; Zerilli arrived and checked into the Frontier Hotel under an assumed name on November 10.

Sansone arrived on November 11, less than 60 days after making his $150,000 investment, to withdraw it.[276] He did so after Nevada gaming regulators told him that he would have to apply for a gaming license, disclose the source of the invested funds, and provide fingerprints. Sansone testified that he backed out only because "I never anticipated that I would have to be classified as a gambler when I bought the debenture." But from the outset the Sansones admittedly knew they were investing in a gambling casino.

Former local FBI Special Agent in Charge Jim Nelson, deemed by the Supreme Court as an expert on the Mafia, agreed that St. Louis was a second-tier Mob city. "Historically, they had access to the [ruling] commission through Detroit. And the Syrian mob was stronger here than the Italians," he said.[277]

Both James "Horseshoe Jimmy" Michaels and Giordano, along with John Vitale, were considered among the last of the big-time, alleged crime-boss figures, not that the so-called Mob here was any great shakes, said retired policemen.

One of them noted, "We never had mainliners; here they came under the jurisdiction of Chicago. Even Kansas City had more of a Mob, and more muscle, than St. Louis."[278]

276   Ibid
277   St. Louis Post-Dispatch, John M. McGuire, March 19, 1997
278   Source wished to be unidentified.

By the 1960s, Giordano emerged as St. Louis Mafia boss, continuing what would be three decades of harmonious coexistence with the South Side gang run by Michaels, whose underworld pedigree dated to 1929.

Emprise was convicted with the Mafia members of hidden interests in the Frontier, which was not a coincidence because three of Giordano's sisters married Detroit Mafia members.

During Prohibition, Peter and Thomas "Yonnie" Licavoli, Joseph "Joe" Bommarito, and other St. Louis gangsters migrated to Detroit to act as gunmen for the Purple Gang, a group of notorious Jewish bootleggers. Later, Peter Licavoli moved to Tucson in 1944 at the request of Mobsters "Bugsy" Siegel and Moe Dalitz. Peter Licavoli shared power in Arizona with Joe Bonanno, the exiled boss of one of New York's ruling Mafia families.

Aaron Herman, a Dunes key employee and personal friend of Charlie Rich and Sid Wyman, also was very close to Bonanno and Licavoli. Herman had this writer teach Bommarito how to deal blackjack, Las Vegas style. Bommarito's sister was married to Peter Licavoli.

In July 1972, Zerilli and Polizzi were sentenced to four years and a fine of $40,000 each. Giordano was sentenced to four years and fined $10,000. All three appealed the conviction and were denied. The three began serving their sentences in 1975. In 1976 they were denied parole.[279]

---

279   FBI Report MM 92-517

CHAPTER 45

THE ALADDIN:
WEBBE, TAMER, SHENKER

Three partners purchased the Aladdin hotel-casino in Las Vegas from the Recrion Corporation for $5.25 million in 1972: Peter Webbe and Richard L. Daly, both St. Louis attorneys, and Sam Diamond, a Las Vegan formerly from Detroit.

In an interview with the *St. Louis Post-Dispatch*, Morris Shenker revealed that a total of $500,000 to $600,000 was invested by the trio.[280] It was confirmed that Daly and Webbe invested $125,000 each, and Diamond invested the balance. Diamond was the front for James Tamer and Charles Goldfarb, who were the fronts for other Detroit underworld characters. Webbe and Daly were fronting for the St. Louis Mob, headed by Tony Giordano and Johnny Vitale. When negotiations for the sale were conducted, Giordano was present in a private room at the Aladdin, calling the shots.

On the sale, Shenker received a $500,000 finder's fee that he shared with Sorkis Webbe, St. Louis attorney and Peter Webbe's brother. According to the Nevada Gaming Control Board (GCB), three other persons shared the fee: Jack Catain, Jr., J. Fihn, and Samuel "Sam" Ray Calabrese, a Los Angeles crime figure. Giordano was livid that Calabrese claimed part of the finder's fee, as Calabrese once disrespected Giordano on the telephone.

The original Detroit investors whom Shenker arranged for the deal were denied gaming licenses because of their underworld associations. Diamond, who was approved in the second group assembled by Shenker, had to assume their obligations. This group consisted of Charles Goldfarb; his brother, Irwin Goldfarb; and George George. Gaming authorities discovered that the three were associated with well-known Detroit syndicate members. One such associate was Jack Shapiro, who operated the Frontier in Las Vegas. The Frontier had three hidden owners – Tony Zerilli, Chuck Polizzi, and Giordano – all of whom were convicted and served prison time.

Sorkis Webbe, the de facto boss of the Aladdin since 1971, was a regular visitor to the Dunes. He dined three or four times a week at the Sultan's

Table or one of the other restaurants. He had several friends in the baccarat pit and often stopped by the game on the way to the Sultan's Table. According to eyewitnesses, Webbe did not sit at a baccarat table. Instead, he stood by the game and called bets.

"Two thousand dollars on the Bank side," shouted Webbe in his clear, strong, radio voice. If he lost the bet, he made another but never more than one or two. If Webbe lost both bets, the dealer put up the game marker buttons on the table between the seat numbers. Webbe said he would be back. He never signed a paper I.O.U., but played on what is called RIM markers, or I.O.U.s. Whatever happened as far as collecting his losses is a mystery. He was a personal friend of Shenker, who indeed had many of his cronies around the casino and was undoubtedly fully aware of the situation. The game was surveilled through video cameras and easily monitored physically from every angle.

Webbe was amiable, unarrogant, friendly to everyone, and well-liked by the dealers and staff. He was approachable, and his winning smile made it seem like he was everyone's long lost friend.

Sorkis Webbe was the general counsel for the Aladdin hotel-casino, and many suspected he was a front man for the Kansas City and St. Louis Mobs. In July 1973, the Nevada Gaming Commission (GC) demanded that Webbe apply for a gaming license because, according to one commissioner, he was acting as a "key" employee of the casino. GCB Member Shannon Bybee said Webbe, through an attorney, indicated he was unwilling to seek a license because he was undergoing an IRS probe and did not want to submit financial statements to Nevada gaming authorities.

GCB Agent Dennis Gomes worked up a 44-page report on the Aladdin and its cast of characters. The report detailed every aspect of the Aladdin sale that started with Shenker and included every Mobster who was comped at the Aladdin and all of the gangsters who were employed there. It was thorough, and could have been used to strip the Aladdin of its gaming license. Gomes gave the report to GCB Chairman Phil Hannifin, who presented it to the GC.[281]

The GC did not want to do anything about the Aladdin, which shocked Hannifin and Gomes. According to the GC, they did not want to tarnish Las Vegas' image. Neither Hannifin nor Gomes could find any logic in the GC's rationale or decision to let it be.

Hannifin's hands were tied, though. He was legally obliged to follow the commission's final ruling in all gaming matters. However, he suggest-

---

281   *Hit Me! Fighting the Las Vegas Mob by the Numbers,* Danielle Gomes and Jay Bonansinga, 2013

ed to Gomes, "Hand your Aladdin investigation over to the feds, and then leak it to your guy in the press."[282]

Bybee said Webbe's attorney was aware that the state wanted Sorkis licensed and that the GCB got the GC to demand that Webbe apply within 10 days or face a possible GCB complaint. Webbe was from St. Louis and not part of the original group that was licensed to operate the Aladdin.

In August, Aladdin President Sam Diamond wrote a letter in which he discharged Webbe of his duties as general counsel. In it, Diamond wrote, there was "no alternative but to discharge you."[283]

This was an interesting move on the part of the Aladdin management and necessary because the GCB had evidence that Webbe was making management decisions at the hotel, decisions that were not in the best interests of the Detroit group that was running the operation.

As one author noted: "He was afflicted with other investor representatives, none of which seemed to understand that casinos have a finite earning capacity. Aladdin management spent $1,500,000 on 'The Theater for Performing Arts,' which was only capable of drawing rock-band audiences – who didn't gamble. The Aladdin failed."[284]

In February 1979, federal prosecutors claimed that Shenker, a close associate of Webbe, arranged to get a loan from Valley Bank of Nevada, via his association with the banker there, Parry Thomas, for two underworld characters who were secretly managing the Aladdin. The attorneys maintained that Detroit businessman Goldfarb and convicted felon Tamer were the real operators of the Aladdin and had the final word on any deal or issue.

Tamer was convicted of bookmaking in the Terre Haute bookmaking ring in which Dunes owner Sidney Wyman held a secret interest. Tamer and Wyman's close friend Irwin Gordon took the rap. After Gordon's release from prison in the late 1960s, he was employed as the Dunes baccarat manager.

Federal prosecutors had a wiretapped tape recording of Goldfarb, Tamer, and Shenker from 1977. In this three-way conversation, Tamer and Goldfarb sought Shenker's advice on how they could raise cash to save the failing Aladdin. The company had excessive cost overruns from two construction projects. Goldfarb did not think any bank would loan $2 million based on his contingent liabilities of $20 million, stemming from his bail bond business.[285]285 Shenker suggested that the trio see the

282   Ibid
283   Reno Evening Gazette, Aug. 25, 1973
284   Ace-Deuce: The Life and Times of a Gambling Man, J.E. Anderson, 2011
285   Reno Evening Gazette, Feb. 3, 1979

banker [Parry Thomas]. The day after this conversation took place, Las Vegas- based Valley Bank loaned $2 million to Sorkis Webbe. He then funneled most of the funds, about $1.7 million, to his brother, Peter Webbe, an Aladdin stockholder.

When reporters contacted Shenker and asked about the recorded conversation, he denied that he referred to Thomas specifically and denied that a meeting with Thomas discussing the loan ever took place.

"I didn't get them a $2 million loan," Shenker said. "To my knowledge, the loan they were asking about was never presented to any bank. They abandoned the idea."[286]286

A reporter then asked whether Shenker was aware of the U.S. prosecuting attorney's records that showed that Valley Bank loaned $2 million to the Aladdin the next day.

"I don't know about that. Maybe that loan was from a previous application," he said.

According to the Associated Press, Shenker was listening on January 1977 when Goldfarb mentioned the possibility of submitting a loan application to a lending institution and omitting from it his $20 million contingent liabilities. Federal prosecutors on the case said the participants in the conversation never went through with that idea after agreeing to seek the money from Valley Bank. Here is a snippet of that conversation:

> **Goldfarb**: "Here is my situation, Morris, in a nutshell. I can show assets of about $3 million."
>
> **Shenker**: "Yeah."
>
> **Goldfarb**: "And absolute liabilities of maybe $200,000."
>
> **Shenker**: "Pretty clean statement."
>
> **Goldfarb**: "Yeah, but I've got contingent liabilities of $20 million."
>
> **Shenker**: "You mean on bonds, on bail bonds?"
>
> **Goldfarb**: "Right."
>
> **Shenker**: "That don't mean nothing."
>
> **Goldfarb**: "Yeah, but at the bank it does."
>
> **Shenker**: "At the bank it means a whole lot, yes."
>
> **Goldfarb**: "Yes, but I can – I would – I'd – if I gave you that statement that way I wouldn't mind, you know without the $20 million."

Goldfarb then said that the Detroit bankers knew him for the liabilities.

286 *Ibid*

Shenker: "Oh, sure."

Goldfarb: "But in St. Louis, or California, or something, I'll put it in without that. But locally they know."

Shenker: "Well, let's do the following. Let's talk to the banker today at 12:30."

Reporters tried to reach Thomas for comment, but he was unavailable. At the time, Thomas also was the vice president of Continental Connector Corporation, the holding company of the Dunes.

Gaming regulators denied Tamer and Goldfarb gaming licenses because of their ties to the underworld.

The federal investigation into the Aladdin constituted a major campaign against organized crime, however, many of the informants stopped leaking information to the prosecutors because they feared retaliation from the Detroit Mob.

Associated Press reporters uncovered the fact that Tamer was visiting Las Vegas every other week. Before they learned this, a Michigan judge surreptitiously expunged the 1939 bank robbery conviction from Tamer's record. Informants reported to the FBI that Tamer was in effect the No. 1 boss at the Aladdin, answering to his Mafia associates in Detroit.

Architect Lee Linton, who worked on the Aladdin remodeling, was charged in a kickback scheme. Before the trial he was contacted by an anonymous person who wanted to build a commercial building in Las Vegas. Linton met two men at the supposed location of the raw land in Southwest Las Vegas. They were gentlemen during the introductions, standing in the open air on the property, until one of the men pulled out a picture of the automobile of Linton's daughter. Linton immediately recognized it and turned white.

"Lee, you know whose car this is?" asked one of the men.

"Yes," Linton replied.

"You better do the right thing."

Linton refused immunity from prosecution and accepted jail time. He served his time at the federal prison in Lompoc, California, and became friendly with the warden after the warden discovered that he was an amateur cabinetmaker. Linton designed and built office shelves for him.

In July 1975, a federal grand jury in St. Louis accused two top backers of the Aladdin hotel- casino, Sorkis Webbe, Daly, and Calabrese of conspiring to defraud the U.S. The indictment alleged that the three tried to impede an IRS investigation of Webbe. The charge centered on business deals involving Colorvision Studios, Inc., a defunct Hollywood firm formerly headed by Calabrese. Coincidentally, a federal indictment against Calabrese was dismissed in Kentucky in the wake of two mistrials for 1970 criminal charges of misapplying $2.25 million of bank funds. Calabrese was known to law enforcement agencies as a business associate of organized crime figures.

Sorkis Webbe was charged in a separate count of the indictment of filing a false income tax return for 1968. The charge was based on a loss claimed on a nonexistent sale of a 25 percent stock interest in Colorvision, according to the indictment. Webbe was the agent for a St. Louis group that lent $230,000 to Colorvision that year. The group included Shenker, who then was recently licensed by Nevada gaming authorities as the controlling shareholder of the Dunes near the Aladdin on the Las Vegas Strip.

The *Los Angeles Times* revealed in 1975 that the previous December, in 1974, under Webbe's control, the Aladdin gave free rooms, meals, and liquor to at least 20 reputed organized crime figures and associates from St. Louis and Detroit.[287]

Sorkis Webbe, a lawyer and public administrator in St. Louis, once was going to run for lieutenant governor, and had many of the unions, the Teamsters and the Steamfitters, behind his war chest.

He was indicted in September 1979 and went to trial in Las Vegas on charges that he masterminded a $1 million fraud and kickback scheme involving $34.2 million in three pension fund loans to the Aladdin in 1974 and 1975. The federal indictment charged that Webbe and five other individuals and two corporations, including the Aladdin, participated in the fraud. The indictment specified that an important part of the conspiracy was Webbe's negotiation of the pension fund loans. Certain Aladdin owners were convicted in federal court in Detroit in 1979 of allowing hidden control by the Detroit Mob beginning in 1973.

Sorkis Webbe was also allegedly involved in trying to get the Tropicana a Teamsters pension fund loan in 1975. A source who wished to remain unnamed told the *St. Louis Post-Dispatch* in July 1981 that Webbe helped the Tropicana with negotiations to borrow $49 million from the Teamsters pension fund. The loan was never issued. The source said that just after Webbe was indicted on an income tax charge in 1975, he met in Las Vegas with Jimmy Hoffa and Shenker at the Dunes. Webbe, however, denied meeting with them.

---

287   Los Angeles Times, June 5, 1975

The source also claimed that Webbe and Tropicana officials went to Chicago in January 1975 and met with the Teamsters fund trustees and pitched them for a loan. It transpired just after Webbe negotiated a $22.9 million loan from the Teamsters for construction of the Aladdin. Joe Agosto, entertainment director at the Tropicana and named by the FBI as a front man for Kansas City Boss Nick Civella, also was at the meeting. Webbe denied being there.

Webbe's relationships with the Teamsters and those who controlled the fund were very close. One of the trustees, Alvin Baron, was very familiar with the Tropicana, especially since he owned the Golf Course Motel, which was on the grounds of the Tropicana golf course directly across the street from the Tropicana hotel-casino. Baron was a regular guest at the Dunes and a close associate of Shenker, who had a great success rate in obtaining Teamster loans.

The same *St. Louis Post-Dispatch* source claimed that the Tropicana then was controlled by the Kansas City Mob.[288] Unsealed FBI wiretap affidavits showed that Civella and associates took control of the Tropicana in 1974, just before it requested a $49 million Teamsters loan. The affidavit claimed that Civella had a very strong influence on Teamster loans and that he "controls a portion of the kickbacks paid in connection with approval of loans."[289]

The affidavit additionally said that Civella's control was through Teamsters president Roy Williams, who was indicted and convicted on charges of conspiring to bribe a U.S. senator in connection with trucking deregulation.

While testifying at his trial in 1987, Williams said, "I think that organized crime was filtered into the Teamsters union a long time before I came there, and it'll be there a long time after I'm gone."[290]

New York prosecutor Mark Hellerer asked Williams if other members of the top executive board of the Teamsters knew about his Mafia connection.

"Yes," Williams answered, "because I made no bones about it. Nick Civella – I was controlled by Nick.

"And when he threatened me, why, that's when I became his boy," Williams added, recalling that two of Civella's men visited him in 1967 and told him he better cooperate.

"They named my two children, my wife," he went on, "and they said, 'You'll be last.' That's the threat I got."

288   *St. Louis Post-Dispatch*, Ronald Lawrence, July 14, 1981
289   *Ibid*
290   *The New York Times*, Arnold H. Lubasch, June 2, 1987

The prosecutor then asked, "When they said that you would be last, what did you understand them to mean?"

"Well, they were going to kill the others first and then me," Williams replied.

After the threat, he said, he cooperated when Civella requested a Teamsters pension fund loan for casino hotels in Las Vegas. He added that Civella then sent him cash payoffs of $1,500 a month from 1974 to 1981 for his help in getting him the Stardust loan.

Williams said Hoffa told him not to get involved in the union's activities in New York and New Jersey.

"Hoffa told me to stay away from them because they all had their own method of operating," Williams said. "And it didn't make any difference what kind of contract we negotiated. They lived under their own rules."

According to sworn testimony by Williams in 1974 or 1975, Jackie Presser, then a trustee of the Central States Pension Fund, offered a bribe to Williams, who then was a Teamsters vice president and pension fund trustee. Presser sought Williams' active support and vote for a loan to the Tropicana. The meeting between Williams and Presser probably took place in Chicago.

Although Presser and Williams were alone when the bribe was offered, pension fund records indicate that in 1975 the Tropicana submitted a one-page loan application seeking $49 million for Hotel Conquistador, Inc., doing business as the Tropicana Hotel and Country Club of Las Vegas.[291]

The bribe, however, was not carried out, and the Tropicana loan was never made because a new federal law, the Employee Retirement Income Security Act of 1974, or ERISA, prohibited it. The law, which required that the Teamsters fund diversify its loans, went into effect just before the Teamsters received the Tropicana's loan application.

That same year, 1975, Sorkis Webbe was acquitted of the income tax charge. Hoffa disappeared in July and was never found.

291   President's Commission on Organized Crime, 1986

CHAPTER 46

THE STARDUST-RECRION DEAL

In addition to the Aladdin, the Dunes was also linked to the acquisition of Recrion Corporation, which owned the Stardust and Fremont hotel-casinos in Las Vegas.

In 1974, Allen Glick's Argent Corporation bought Recrion Corporation, formerly the Parvin-Dohrmann Company, using a loan from the Teamsters pension fund and a $500,000 loan from Tamara Rand, a San Diego, California real estate broker and investor. Glick was introduced to Recrion owner Delbert Coleman by Todd Derlachter, for which Glick paid Derlachter a $1.26 million finder's fee.

"Coleman sold it out from under me," said Morris Shenker, referring to Recrion. "I haven't got the slightest idea how Glick got the financing."[292]

Shenker claimed his financing deal with the pension fund to acquire Recrion was all but finalized when he learned, to his surprise, an arrangement was sealed with Glick.

"I'm not in a position to say if the Teamsters dealt privately with Glick or what they told him," said Shenker.

He said that he learned sometime later that Glick and Derlachter went directly to Coleman and offered him $5 million more for Recrion than Shenker offered.

Shenker met with Coleman on Saturday of the weekend and was told Coleman accepted a higher offer. Shenker asked Coleman if he could have more time to think about raising his bid, but found out the following Monday that Coleman closed the deal with Glick.

"They threatened Coleman and told him if he went through with the deal to me, they would go over his head to the stockholders," Shenker said.

If Shenker's statement was true, he did not know that Allen Dorfman shut him out of the transaction. Dorfman, who was rock solid with the Chicago Outfit, basically handed the deal over to Glick on a platter. Shenker caused Dorfman to build resentment against him by not coming through with stock for Dorfman and Jimmy Hoffa in several developments that were built with Teamsters pension fund loans. If Shenker did owe this stock to Hoffa, Dorfman, and un-named others, Dorfman would have prevented Shenker from receiving a finder's fee related to the Recrion acquisition.

It is highly probable that Sid Wyman was the impetus behind excluding Shenker from the Recrion deal by having his longtime friend Derlachter facilitate the purchase by Glick, who represented the Chicago and Kansas City Mobs that Wyman aligned with many years before.

After Derlachter became the executive vice president of the Dunes, he was seen regularly on the property, but many employees did not know who he was, what position he held, or what responsibility he had. Derlachter was mostly seen in the company of Wyman. Occasionally, Derlachter stopped by the baccarat pit and chatted with Sam Bernstein, an acquaintance. Wyman placed Bernstein, who was considered an inexperienced baccarat supervisor by most of the dealers and other supervisors, in the cushy baccarat floorman position. One person said Bernstein could not spot an "elephant" pass by the game. Inexperience in high-stakes baccarat cost the Dunes lots of revenue.

When Wyman was at the Sands, Derlachter met Pennie Levy, the widow of Leon Levy, a Sands owner. Eventually, Derlachter and Levy married.

Regarding the Recrion purchase, an FBI investigation underway in February 1974 was one of several reasons why Glick was handpicked over Shenker as the buyer. Federal agents were looking into more than $100 million of questionable Teamsters loans that were made to entities in various cities. One was to Shenker and Irvin Kahn for more than $180 million for their Penasquitos land development near San Diego.

Kansas City Mob Boss Nick Civella, who controlled Teamsters loans through Roy Williams, did not want Shenker to take over the Stardust or the Fremont for several reasons. Shenker was somewhat controversial and loyal to Hoffa; he defended the Dunes owners in their skimming trial; he was being investigated by the Nevada Gaming Control Board for the Dunes purchase; and many other allegations were thrown against him.[293]

Civella orchestrated the takeover of Recrion, which was documented in Glick's testimony. Glick claimed that Civella threatened him in March 1975 when the two met in a Kansas City hotel room.

---

293   "President's Report on Organized Crime – Business and Labor Unions." Ultimately Nick Civella sided with Roy Williams, and tore up Allen Dorfman's contract with Shenker. In this instance, Williams, a Teamsters union president and a fiduciary for the union's pension fund, had to appeal a union decision with La Cosa Nostra crime boss of Kansas City.

Glick quoted Civella as telling him, "I have partners in this casino business and owe them $1.2 million for arranging the loan. If I had my choice, you would never leave this room alive, but if you listen, you may."[294]

Recrion had hidden Chicago Mob owners who did not trust, and previously, did not do business with Shenker. These individuals also had a stake in the Dunes through Wyman and Jake Gottlieb, as shown in FBI documents.

In an October 20, 1962 newspaper article about the groundbreaking of the Dunes 24-story high-rise, all of the main principals were photographed: Jake Gottlieb, Wyman, Duckworth, Charlie Rich, Parry Thomas, Major Riddle, and other Dunes executives and associates. Shenker was not among them. Further, he was never listed as a director or officer of Continental Connector Corporation, which purchased the Dunes.

There were two main powers at the Dunes in 1962: Gottlieb and Wyman, the latter including Rich and Duckworth. Wyman's group had the controlling interest in the casino. He ran the show, period. Even in February 1975, after Shenker was approved by the Nevada Gaming Control Board and the Gaming Commission for a license, he did not control the Dunes casino. Wyman's group was the undisputed high lama at the Dunes, which operated as if Shenker was not even licensed.

A former casino cashier remarked, "Shenker had just taken it over, if I recall correctly. And, uh, Sid Wyman was still, you know, around the place a lot. And I think he was actually the person that was, you know, in fact in charge."[295]

In his book, *The Teamsters*, Steven Brill wrote about the Derlachter-Recrion- Shenker situation. Brill quoted "a lawyer involved directly in the deal," who gave this version of what happened in the Recrion acquisition:

"Shenker had to get out because Dorfman and the others at the fund wanted him out. They were afraid of all the bad publicity because of all the other loans he had at the time for the Dunes [and other properties] and because of his past reputation. Also, he had been Hoffa's lawyer, and with Hoffa trying to come back they were worried about Shenker's loyalty. I heard Dorfman say this.

"So Bill Presser [another powerful figure in pension fund activities] remembered Glick and said how clean he was and everything. 'Let's give it to that nice kid, what's-his-name,' he probably said."

The same source informed Brill, "We told Shenker we couldn't give it to him, but that he could deliver it to Glick and take something out for himself and his people. So Shenker had Derlachter contact Glick. I think Derlachter's payment [the finder's fee] went to Shenker and to the mob guys Shenker was involved with. That way Shenker didn't feel so bad."[296]

Brill noted that the alleged finder's fee payment to Derlachter "is made more plausible" by the fact that Derlachter was known to be an associate of Shenker. This does not make sense for two reasons. One is that it is more than likely that Derlachter did not answer to Shenker or do his bidding. In actuality, Derlachter was Wyman's soldier. The other reason is that Shenker would not have said that they "pulled the rug" from under him if he in fact was in on the Recrion deal.

Shenker reported to the *Las Vegas Review-Journal* that he was never contacted or interviewed by Brill.

"If this fellow had called me, I would have told him the story right," said Shenker. Shenker recounted that Derlachter was kept on the Dunes payroll to honor what he understood was "a moral commitment" between Derlachter and Meshulam Riklis. He said that Derlachter must have "overheard" a telephone conversation about the Recrion deal, which was kept confidential, and somehow conveyed the information to Glick, or perhaps got the information from "a close friend," the late Dunes executive, Wyman.[297] It is not clear if Shenker actually mentioned Wyman by name in this quote or if the reporter added it.

With this remark, though, Shenker was not protecting Wyman, but, rather, informing on him. Perhaps he figured since Wyman was dead, it did not matter.

In addition, in what seemed like almost a slip of the tongue, Shenker indicted Derlachter by saying, "I'm not involved in the Mob, never was." This implied that Derlachter was, specifically with the Chicago Outfit, and that Dorfman and the Outfit were involved in the deal. How else could it be interpreted? And how did the Mob get into the conversation? The two parties of the Recrion deal were Glick, who was basically a square shooter, meaning he was not in the Mob, and Coleman, who owned a public company and was not a Mob member either.

Shenker also said, "Derlachter never gave me a quarter, and to this day he can't be paged in this hotel [the Dunes]."

This statement suggested that Shenker ordered the hotel operators never to page Derlachter. It also implied that Derlachter was not associated with Shenker and was unwelcome at the Dunes. This was yet another

---

296   *The Teamsters*, Steven Brill, 1978
297   *Las Vegas Review-Journal*, Sept. 17, 1978

factor that separated the Wyman camp and the Shenker camp. Wyman, Duckworth, Howie Engel, Irwin Gordon, and Dave Goldberg just did not like Shenker.

When Shenker was asked what he thought about the circumstances presented in Brill's book, he said that its only accurate claim was that "I felt bad about losing the deal." Shenker pointed out that he was not merely an associate of Derlachter, but was his employer at the Dunes. He said Derlachter was hired as a consultant by Riklis, who was the principal shareholder of the Riviera and who controlled the Dunes before Shenker took over.

That, however, was not entirely correct. In reality, Riklis bought the Dunes in January 1972 through his public company, ATIS, Inc., when the Dunes owners were under indictment for skimming and awaiting trial. Riklis then rescinded the offer in June 1972, intending to sell the Dunes, after the owners were found not guilty, to a group that included Thomas, Shenker, and Kahn. Kahn and Shenker were stockholders of Continental Connector, which was the holding company of the Dunes at the time. Continental Connector did not suspend or fire those on trial for skimming, but had them temporarily sell their stock holdings. The powers that be felt that the move would appease the stockholders. At the trial, Shenker was a member of the legal team that got Wyman and his co-defendants acquitted.

Again, this series of events highlighted the fact that Wyman, not Shenker, had the power at and control of the Dunes during the 1970s. It is also clear that Shenker did not have the ability or crew to operate a casino properly. He had no casino personnel on his team who could make crucial game decisions.

Another twist to the Glick-Derlachter finder's fee was discovered in August 1982 at the tax evasion trial of Richard "Ritchie" Gordon, the owner of a car leasing company. Gordon was a frequent guest at the Dunes. At the trial, Glick testified under immunity that he agreed to pay a $420,000 finder's fee to Derlachter. Derlachter agreed to split the fee with Gordon because Gordon introduced Derlachter to Glick and sat in on a few of their meetings.[298] Derlachter was also given immunity for testifying about bringing together Glick and Coleman. The question, though, is: "How did Ritchie Gordon meet Derlachter?" The answer is, probably through Wyman. Wyman was extremely friendly with Gordon and was seen with Gordon many times in and around the Dunes. It is also probable that Wyman wanted a liaison between himself and Derlachter and that Gordon was perfect for it.

---

298   *Las Vegas Review-Journal*, Jane Ann Morrison, April 30, 1982

THE STARDUST-RECRION DEAL

The Dunes' telephones were under constant monitoring by the government, and there were FBI agents in the hotel 24/7. The agency may have intercepted a phone call in which Wyman and Gordon discussed some of these issues, which in turn fueled the FBI's investigation of Glick, Wyman, and Gordon.

In his 1982 tax evasion trial, Gordon was convicted and ordered to serve four months in prison, pay a $37,500 fine, and remain on probation for five years. Additionally, he had to pay the IRS more than $100,000 in back taxes and penalties for the years 1974 and 1975.

After the conviction in Judge Harry Claiborne's federal court, Gordon appealed in 1993, hoping to reverse the tax penalties in his favor. He submitted the following records in the appeal:[299]

"In December 1969, petitioner incorporated Luxury Rental and Leasing, Inc., a Nevada corporation (Luxury), for the principal purpose of leasing so-called exotic cars. Luxury also leased trucks, boats, and conventional automobiles. From 1969 through the years in question, petitioner was a full-time employee of Luxury, a member of its board of directors, and its president. Luxury's federal income tax returns for the years 1970 through and including 1972 each state that petitioner owned 76 percent of Luxury's stock. The record of this case does not reveal the identity of the person or persons who owned the remaining 24 percent of Luxury's stock during those years.

"Luxury's federal income tax returns for the years 1973, 1974, and 1975 each state that petitioner owned 100 percent of the stock of the corporation. The parties have also stipulated that during 1974 and 1975 petitioner was the sole shareholder of Luxury. Nevertheless, petitioner's personal financial statement dated September 30, 1974, under the category of other assets, lists '85 percent stock' of Luxury. The record does not explain this discrepancy.

"In 1972, Mr. Allen Glick or a corporation controlled by him, Saratoga Development Corp., acquired the Hacienda Hotel and Casino in Las Vegas. Petitioner became acquainted with Mr. Glick at that time due to the fact that Luxury was then leasing an automobile to the Hacienda. The two men developed both a business and a personal relationship with each other.

"In early 1974, petitioner and Mr. Glick considered buying an automobile leasing company in southern California, Ralph Williams Leasing (Williams Leasing). The leasing company was then undergoing reorganization under the bankruptcy laws. Because of his experience in the automobile leasing business, petitioner undertook to investigate the proposed acquisition. In that connection, he visited Williams Leasing and its creditors in southern California, and he examined the company's records. The acquisition was never consummated.

"Also in early 1974, Mr. Glick informed petitioner of his interest in acquiring other casino properties. Petitioner told his long-time friend Mr. Todd Derlachter about Mr. Glick's interest, and in late February or early March 1974, petitioner introduced Mr. Derlachter to Mr. Glick. After discussions with Mr. Glick, Mr. Derlachter arranged a meeting in New York City between Mr. Glick and Mr. Delbert Coleman, the controlling shareholder of Recrion Corp. (Recrion), a corporation which owned the Stardust and Fremont Hotel-Casinos in Las Vegas.

"As a result of that meeting, in the summer of 1974, Mr. Glick, acting through a corporation which he had formed for the purpose, Argent Corp., made a successful tender offer for Recrion's stock. The tender offer was followed by the merger of Recrion into Argent Corp. which thereupon succeeded to the business and assets of Recrion, including ownership of the Stardust and the Fremont. Petitioner played no role in the Recrion deal beyond introducing Mr. Glick to Mr. Derlachter and attending several meetings between them.

"Before the deal closed, Mr. Derlachter and petitioner had orally agreed that they would share equally any finder's fee earned through their efforts. No mention was made of Luxury. Shortly thereafter, Mr. Derlachter informed Mr. Glick of his agreement to share any finder's fee with petitioner.

"After the Recrion transaction was completed, Mr. Glick agreed to pay a finder's fee of approximately $421,000 to Mr. Derlachter. On August 31, 1974, Mr. Glick filed a Form 10-K with the Securities and Exchange Commission (SEC) explaining the details of the Recrion transaction. The filing mentioned the roles of Mr. Derlachter and petitioner in the deal and the fee paid to Mr. Derlachter, but it did not allude to any part that Luxury might have played. The Form 10-K states as follows:

"'Registrant [Argent Corporation] agreed to pay a finder's fee to Mr. Todd Derlachter in the amount of $421,844 in connection with Registrant's acquisition of certain outstanding shares of Recrion stock. Although Mr. Derlachter originally indicated that he was the sole finder, Registrant was informed subsequently that Mr. Derlachter had agreed to pay part of his fee to Mr. Richard Gordon. Neither Registrant nor its parent, Allen R. Glick, has at any time had any contractual arrangement with, or obligation to, Mr. Gordon in respect to any finder's services or related activities. Registrant paid $321,844 to Mr. Derlachter on August 29, 1974. The balance of $100,000 is payable to him on or about the first anniversary of this initial payment.'

"At Mr. Glick's request, petitioner signed a letter dated September 1, 1974, acknowledging receipt of $210,922 from Mr. Derlachter and stating that he had been paid in full by Mr. Derlachter for his role in the Recrion transaction. The letter states as follows:

"Argent Corporation, Las Vegas Hacienda 3950 Las Vegas Blvd., South Las Vegas, Nevada 89119 Mr. Todd Derlachter 35283 Beach Road San Clemente, California 92624

"Dear Sirs:

"Receipt is hereby acknowledged of the sum of $210,922.00 from Todd Derlachter in full payment for all services rendered by the undersigned in assisting Mr. Derlachter in bringing together Delbert W. Coleman and members of his family and Allen R. Glick as agent for Argent Corporation, resulting in the execution of an Agreement of Purchase and Sale dated April 8, 1974 with respect to shares of Common Stock of Recrion Corporation. "The undersigned represents that the payment acknowledged hereby was neither promised by nor the result of any agreement, arrangement or understanding between Argent Corporation, its officers, directors or agents and the undersigned and was made pursuant to an arrangement between Mr. Derlachter and the undersigned. In connection with such payment, the undersigned agrees to indemnify Argent Corporation, its officers, directors, agents and sole shareholder against any and all costs, liabilities or expenses, including attorneys' fees, which may result, or in any manner be connected with, any claim by any person that the payment hereby acknowledged is improper or was caused by, made with the knowledge of, or was the result of any agreement, arrangement or understanding between Argent Corporation and the undersigned.
"Very truly yours, Richard Gordon"

Gordon lost the appeal.

Two years later, he tried again to get his conviction overturned, this time on constitutional grounds. In May 1985, he filed a petition charging that Judge Claiborne violated U.S. federal law and judicial ethics by not recusing himself from presiding over Gordon's tax trial. Gordon cited a federal law that mandates that a judge must recuse himself from a trial if the defendant is being represented by an attorney who also is representing the judge in a criminal action.[300] Gordon claimed that at the same time that his attorney Oscar Goodman represented him in his tax evasion trial, Goodman also represented Claiborne in Claiborne's tax evasion trial.

Gordon's petition claimed that Goodman became Claiborne's attorney around the time that Goodman received a telephone call from Nevada brothel owner, Joseph "Joe" Conforte, who told him he would testify against Claiborne. In the conversation, Goodman allegedly told Conforte that he would talk to Claiborne.

It is likely that Claiborne did not like Gordon because he felt that there was more to the story. Even if he did not like Gordon, he still would have been 100 percent fair. Had Claiborne's friend Wyman been alive at the time, Claiborne may have asked him, "What is the story behind Gordon?" Wyman would not have been happy with Gordon for making such a charge against Claiborne. Wyman died in 1978.

In June 1980, the U.S. Securities and Exchange Commission (SEC) filed an amendment to their 1978 complaint against Glick. In the new version, they wrote that Glick concealed certain financial arrangements in his 1974 acquisition of the Recrion Corporation. The SEC charged that Glick made "false statements" about a finder's fee he paid to Derlachter.

Additionally, the complaint indicated that Glick failed to disclose a deal with Tamara Rand, who was murdered in 1975 in what police described as a gangland killing. San Diego Chief of Police Bill Kolender said that Rand's murder was similar to that of Chicago Outfit member, Sam Giancana. In the movie *Casino*, Anthony "Tony the Ant" Spilotro was the alleged killer of Rand, but there is no proof that he committed this act in real life.

Rand allegedly was murdered because she threatened to expose the Recrion deal to authorities. This was because Glick allegedly reneged on his promise to give her 5 percent of Argent in exchange for her $500,000 loan to him so he could purchase Recrion. Rand visited Glick in Las Vegas but cut short her visit because, she told her friends, her life was threatened.

Rand and Glick should have disclosed to Nevada gaming authorities her loan to him, and because she made the loan, she should have applied for a gaming license, as required by Nevada law, but she did not do that either. As such, an investigation regarding Rand's involvement in the Recrion transaction could have nixed Glick's chances of getting a license. As future hidden owners expecting a skim from the Stardust and Fremont, the Chicago Outfit and Kansas City Mob needed Glick to get that license.

If it came down to Glick being refused a license, Lefty Rosenthal, who was a front man for the Mafia in those two cities, would have been replaced or killed himself for allowing the situation to get out of hand.

Although Glick denied that the agreement that Rand claimed existed, investigating authorities had "reasonably good evidence" that it did. Rand sued Glick, and afterward someone amended that very agreement, changing Rand's description in it from "investor" to "long term consultant to Glick."[301]

If Rand was a long term consultant, she would not have had to apply for a Nevada gaming license unless the Gaming Control Board requested her do so. More than likely she was promised some equity in the Stardust but Glick and Rand never discussed applying for a license. This implied that he was hiding her involvement.

Glick refused to cooperate with the authorities regarding Rand's murder. Though he may or may not have threatened Rand, it is more likely that an associate did it, in Glick's presence. If Glick did cooperate with police, he, too, undoubtedly would have been killed.

301   *Los Angeles Times*, Dec. 20, 1975

CHAPTER 47

THE DUNES:
SHENKER AND LICENSING

T he Nevada Gaming Control Board's (GCB's) "six-month investigation of nationally known attorney Morris Shenker revealed a pattern of improper relations with public officials, questionable business ethics and questionable business and personal associations."[302]

Shenker applied for a gambling license for the Dunes in 1975, for which the GCB held a hearing and recommended approval. Then the Nevada Gaming Commission (GC) held several meetings and approved Shenker as a licensee on February 27, 1975.

At the proceedings, Shenker presented a slew of character witnesses who extolled his upstanding morals and honesty and portrayed him as a having a good character. Shenker cast doubt on every area of concern that the gaming regulators raised.

Shenker's defense approach in general was clever. He relied more on highlighting the prosecution's failure to make a case or faults with the prosecution's case than on presenting a defense.

He openly admitted that he never would ask a client whether he was guilty or not guilty, but would ask, "What did the police say to you? What did you tell the police?"

He also paid special attention to jury selection and told the jurors that they had a great responsibility. Shenker's theory, based on research, was that jurors tended toward leniency; a man was innocent until proven guilty; the burden of proof was on the state; and where there was reasonable doubt, the defendant should be favored. Shenker relied on this when he represented himself before the Nevada gaming authorities.

Shenker frequently avoided contesting facts, but tried to fit a reasonable theory of innocence into the stated facts. One of his "pet devices," according to courtroom observers, was to confuse the witnesses. Shenker explained this by saying he tried to make it easier for certain witnesses to testify the way he wanted them to. His method was to rephrase witnesses' answers repeatedly, adding a bit of his own idea, until the witnesses found themselves acquiescing. His tack in state court, however, was different than his approach in federal court, wherein he pulled no shenanigans.[303]

Shenker admitted that he was not concerned with a person's morals, only their legal rights. For instance, when he defended Pioneer News Service, he fought for their right to have telephones, even though the business of Pioneer was deemed illegal by the Missouri Public Service Commission.

Only Nevada Gaming Commissioner Walter Cox seemed to be on to Shenker. Cox was born in Virginia City, Nevada, in 1900 and moved to Yerington in 1906, where his father worked for the *Yerington Times*. His father purchased the *Mason Valley News* in 1919 and the *Yerington Times* in 1932. Walter Cox eventually became the owner, publisher, editor, and columnist of the *Mason Valley News*. His homespun manner, political views, and examination of the government were published in his weekly "Cox's Column." He had outstanding literary skills and journalistic flair. He was an honest man and could not be fooled easily.

During the questioning at the hearing, Cox injected a bit of humor in his truth. He said, "Well, Mr. Shenker, we damn near pumped the well dry, and you have been on the hot seat long enough. I will tell you something, and I think the boys are familiar with it. Attorneys are not my favorite subject, to start with."

Shenker retorted, "At least I got a lot of company."

Cox said, "You know, I'm going ass backward on this because I wanted to get Jones [Clifford's brother Herb].[304] There are some things I don't like. This term he used, of a 'write-over.' I think in English, I think, we would call it 'failure to disclose.' I don't know whether Mr. Jones would take it that way or not, but if a title company fails to disclose, a couple other guys have a piece of the action.

"However, I understand that you guarantee it, but I think it would be more simple if you would use English like 'failure to disclose' instead of 'write-over.' It confuses us lay people."

Shenker and his attorneys hoped the "write-overs," or the "failure to disclose" liens against a property would slide by the commissioners, which it

---

303   *St. Louis Post-Dispatch*, Ralph Coghlan, June 23, 1950
304   "Jones" refers to Herb Jones, Shenker's attorney at the meeting. Jones made a statement about a procedure called "write-overs" that were, in effect, debts or liens that were not revealed on a title policy that Shenker used for business transactions

did except for Cox. He did not miss a trick. The GCB recommended that the GC approve Shenker for a license for the Dunes, which it did.

However, when the GCB members investigated Shenker beforehand, they certainly did not dig deeply enough into his past. For example, the board did not mention or ask Shenker about the details of the tax case in which he represented Sid Wyman and Charlie Rich, specifically the testimony about Shenker buying a car for Oscar Iden, the IRS auditor involved.

Also, the GCB questioned Shenker's role in a suspicious transaction involving Pipefitters Local 562 pension funds but later dropped it. In 1970, those monies were used to buy $500,000 worth of fictitious Swiss Enterprise, Inc. bonds from a stockbroker Edward A. White, who was a business associate of Shenker. On May 17, the Pipefitters pension fund demanded an explanation from White for why the interest on the bonds was not paid. On that same day, Shenker and Irvin Kahn applied for a $6 million loan for their company, B.A.I., from the Pipefitters Union. On May 18, the following day, B.A.I. bought back the phony bonds from the union for $540,000, the same amount the union paid for them.

When the GCB questioned Shenker about it, he said he was unaware of the whole transaction and unaware that the bonds were worthless when B.A.I. bought them. He said that the union asked Kahn to buy the bonds, and that Kahn handled the purchase for B.A.I.

"He was the boss. He signed the checks. It was done. What could I do?" he said.[305] Shenker's response was typical Shenker, begging for mercy, "What could I do?" Shenker could have done a lot being a lawyer and an officer of the court. Was he saying in reality he did not know right from wrong? Shenker obviously knew that a dead person could not answer so he put the blame on his deceased partner, Kahn. Shenker believed in Ovid's *Heroides*, which says that "*exitus ācta probat*" ("the outcome justifies the deeds").

GCB Chairman Phil Hannifin said that the events appeared somewhat suspicious but the board did not investigate further, which is ludicrous. Hannifin seemed above reproach and a highly skilled administrator, but something stopped him from taking the issue further. Hannifin gave Shenker a pass, for whatever reason. It is very probable that Governor Mike O'Callaghan had a say in Shenker's licensing.

The GCB members also failed to examine Shenker's moral character with respect to the advice he gave his clients. In Shenker's own words,

---

305   *St. Louis Post-Dispatch*, Jan. 29, 1975

his client Lawrence Callanan, who ran the Pipefitters Local 562, came to him about everything, so certainly Shenker and Callanan discussed paying $1,400 to the two government witnesses to leave town and not testify in the case against Callanan.

Rubey Hulen, the judge at the Callanan trial, mentioned that he was impressed with some of the witnesses, especially one who feared for his life. That man testified that he set up a dummy company at Callanan's request to conceal payoffs. His testimony was "devastating" to Callanan's defense.

Shenker's repeated argument that he never went into business with his clients and that his involvement was only professional, on an attorney-client basis, was not true and misleading. He may not have been in business with them or cared about their moral fiber, but it is beyond doubt that he gave them advice that was unethical and amoral.

Also, there was mention at the Dunes that Shenker somehow betrayed Sid Wyman. Christy Whitbeck, who was a former employee there, recalled:

> "All I remember, I overheard Jo Melland, my aunt, in a conversation that 'Morris Shenker betrayed Sid Wyman.' I've been trying to think back what else was said. I can't remember, but do we know of any transaction where Sid Wyman would have given his percentage of ownership to Shenker, maybe Shenker was representing him?"[306]

A Massachusetts agency that reviewed the Shenker gaming licensing case a decade later issued a report on the investigation's shortcomings. It read:

> "Shenker's case raised several major issues related to the licensing process, among them:
> (1) the fairness of the hearing procedure, (2) the manner of assessing an applicant's reputation and the weight to be given such assessment, (3) the proper method of making a financial investigation, (4) the applicant's past relations with public officials, (5) the applicant's past business history, (6) the reputation of the business and social contacts of the applicant, (7) whether such relationships suggest the presence of undisclosed interests in the casino, and (8) the predictability of future conduct of the applicant as a licensee. Despite the adverse public notoriety that Shenker was given in the press and the reluctance of the Nevada Gaming Control Board to see Shenker licensed, the Gaming Commission, concerned about constitutional guarantees of procedural due process, granted the license."[307]

306   Interview with Christy Whitbeck, niece of Jo Melland, 2010
307   "The Commonwealth of Massachusetts Legislative Research Bureau Report Relative to

Shenker's dubious ethics brought to mind a mandatory gaming employee meeting at the Dunes after he received his gaming license. He told the employees about his new management team and policies and then fielded questions. A floorman stood and asked, "Why won't we have health insurance as we did before?"

Shenker replied, "You won't need it because you won't be working here."[308]

Another time, Shenker asked all Dunes employees to consider not taking a paycheck during one of the slow periods just before Christmas. He made this request through a memo, in which he explained the reason was to help the Dunes through its then financial hardship.

One employee did a little research and found that the Dunes made record profits just prior to that time and that Shenker was given a raise or bonus.[309] Further, Shenker's law firm got more than two-thirds of almost $2 million in legal and other fees paid by the Dunes for defending casino executives against federal skimming charges and for the investigative fees charged by the State of Nevada to investigate Shenker for his gaming license.

The employee noted it to a local newspaper, which immediately sent a reporter to interview Shenker. Shenker then rescinded the request that employees refuse a paycheck, probably because he feared being publicly exposed.

In all of the history of the Dunes, under the various other owners and managers, there never was even a suggestion that employees forfeit their paycheck to benefit the resort.

Shenker had a reputation of being money hungry.

"Shenker would sell his mother if he could get five bucks!" Charlie Rich once said, according to his grandson, Bruce Fisher.[310]

Fisher qualified, "Cookie – we never called him Kewpie – never knocked or bad rapped anyone that I can remember. But one day he was visibly upset and made this remark.

Casino Gambling," April 1983
308   Interview with Barney Vinson, 2019
309   Interview with confidential source, EB, 2019
310   Interview with Bruce Fisher, 2020

CHAPTER 48

THE DUNES:
SHENKER AND ENSUING PROBLEMS

In 1975, Morris Shenker and Major Riddle were in trouble with the Nevada Gaming Control Board (GCB) because a top Chicago Outfit member, Anthony "Tony the Ant" Spilotro, appeared to have made the Dunes his second home and was operating his own illegal business from the casino poker room.

Riddle stated that Spilotro registered at the Dunes under an assumed name and while they had information that he was an undesirable, the picture of him was 20 years old, so hotel personnel did not recognize him. "It was about as innocent as anything that ever happened," Riddle said. "Mr. Shenker didn't know he was here, and of course, with me, I never met this man in my life, don't even know him. I didn't even know there was such a name." Riddle added, "I've never met this man in my life, but Shenker knew him."[311]

However, the GCB authorities had intelligence that contradicted Riddle's statements. They contended that Spilotro was well known to the Dunes management and spent long hours in the poker room there. Riddle was even observed playing poker with Spilotro. Also, Spilotro was allowed to return to the Dunes after the GCB warned management about him.

The GCB and the Nevada Gaming Commission (GC) were 100 percent correct about Spilotro being a regular at the Dunes. Irwin Ross, a former New York pen manufacturer and distributor of novelty items who later became a Dunes casino host to players, was friendly with Spilotro. He told this writer that Spilotro left him an envelope with $2,200 as a toke from the winnings he accumulated in the Dunes poker room. Spilotro had a lot of things going for him at the Dunes. He was making some money by shaking down bookmakers, shylocking, and bankrolling other players. He had a unique scam going in high-stakes poker games.

This writer observed Spilotro hanging around the poker room with a few of his associates, several of whom Spilotro bankrolled in poker. Spilotro had cold eyes and his chilling presence was palpably nefarious. His body language sent the message to those who knew about his past that he had permission to be there and nobody could do anything about it.

Eventually, though, Spilotro was banned from the Dunes on the order of the GCB to Shenker, the gaming licensee.

The next year, another problem arose for Shenker and the Dunes. In May, the GC allowed Shenker to accept a $40 million loan from the Teamsters pension fund for a $75 million expansion of the Dunes, the groundbreaking for which was scheduled for July.

Shenker made an interesting comment to the GC, that he doubted that any other large Teamsters pension fund loans would be made in Nevada in the near future. Based on what happened next, the gaming authorities should have asked Shenker why he thought that, before they unanimously voted to approve the loan. They also should have looked into a January 1975 federal grand jury subpoena for Shenker and Irvin Kahn's records concerning their land business in an investigation of possible fraud and misuse of Pipefitters Union funds.

The Teamsters backed out of the $40 million commitment.

In June 1976, the Dunes sued the Teamsters, asking that the union be forced to comply with the terms of the loan agreement. In the suit, Shenker claimed that damages to the Dunes would be $100 million if the loan was not carried out.

Shenker noted that the pension fund could not make the loan due to a perceived conflict of interest that violated a new law, the Employee Retirement Income Security Act of 1974, or ERISA. The U.S. Department of Labor informed the pension fund that M&R Investment's parent company, Continental Connector Corporation, owned a trucking company in Chicago, Western Transportation Company, and that Teamsters who worked for that business contributed to the pension fund. Federal law prohibited pension fund loans to entities wherein employees contributed to the fund. The loan also may have violated the "diversity of assets" provision of ERISA. Shenker reported, however, that Continental Connector sold Western Transportation to eradicate any conflict.[312]

Previously, that same year, when Shenker was pursuing the $40 million loan from the Teamsters pension fund, the Department of Labor filed motions against him after investigating the fund for 18 months or more. They reported that Shenker became a millionaire as a result of his dealings with the Teamsters pension fund.[313]

312   *St. Louis Post-Dispatch*, June 25, 1976
313   *The Washington Post*, George Lardner, March 6, 1983

Two related complaints were filed in the U.S. District Court for the District of Nevada, one by I.J.K. Nevada, Inc., the initials in which stood for Irvin J. Kahn, which was reported to own about 35 percent of the common stock of Dunes Hotels and Casinos, Inc., and the other by Shenker, reported to be the 100 percent owner of I.J.K.

The complaints sought damages of $30 million and $50 million, respectively, as contractual compensation. The case continued for several years. Finally, in September 1979, the trustees and the Dunes-Shenker proposed a settlement by the pension fund, making an additional $85 million loan plus $6 million to restructure the old loan. The settlement was conditioned on approval by the court and the fund's counsel.

The Department of Labor and the U.S. District Court both objected to the loan, deeming it would be an inappropriate transaction. The court also denied Shenker's claim for damages.

An FBI informant advised that Roy Williams and Shenker met at the Rancho La Costa country club in October 1978 concerning the civil suit that Shenker filed against the Teamsters pension fund. Williams wanted Shenker to withdraw the suit and agree to a settlement, of which Williams and Nick Civella would get a piece.[314]

Williams testified in a Kansas City federal court in late October 1985 that he was pressured in 1979 to help Shenker in his dealings with the Teamsters pension fund. He told a jury that Civella asked him to settle the suit filed by Shenker for the full $80 million asked. He offered this testimony during the trial of nine men accused of skimming money from Las Vegas casinos financed by the Teamsters.[315]

Williams also testified that Allen Dorfman, a protégé of Jimmy Hoffa and main facilitator of Teamsters loans, wanted more business to be sent to Shenker's firm. Williams said that both efforts on Shenker's behalf were decided at a meeting in April 1979 between Civella, Dorfman, and Williams, at the home of a Kansas City trucking company executive. Dorfman was assassinated in Chicago on January 23, 1983. That same year, Civella died of cancer.

Williams also revealed that Shenker was known to the Teamsters and Civella's associates as "The Old Gray Fox."

In May 1981, Williams was appointed interim president of the Teamsters, succeeding Frank Fitzsimmons who died that same month. The Senate Permanent Subcommittee on Investigations issued a report on

314   FBI Field Surveillance Records, WT-79-4-3
315   *St. Louis Post-Dispatch,* Nov. 1, 1985

Williams' past activities, which cited his indictments for embezzlement of union funds, of which he was acquitted, and his involvement in the attempt to persuade the new pension fund trustees to manipulate a fund account known as the B&A account to complete a loan to Shenker that was blocked in federal district court.[316]

The Senate subcommittee report also provided evidence that Williams was controlled by Kansas City Mob Boss Civella. The report was authenticated by the Organized Crime and Racketeering Section in the Department of Justice's criminal division.

The Teamsters pension fund backing out of the $40 million loan to Shenker should have piqued the curiosity of the GCB, but Chairman Phil Hannifin said that the major responsibility of gaming officials in overseeing loan deals was to determine the credibility of the lending source. He said that "if a casino owner shuttles the loan money into another business, the state can do little unless it can be proven that the transaction worked to the detriment of the financial stability of the casino itself."[317]

That statement does not make sense because the licensee who seeks approval of a loan from a third party uses loan proceeds to pay the GCB for their investigation. Any deviation from a plan should have been a reason for gaming authorities to investigate. Some of the funds could be diverted and a portion of the funds might be given as kickbacks for obtaining the loans. The use of funds should have been scrutinized thoroughly. Ironically, Hannifin said that the GCB's ultimate responsibility was to find the evidence to bring a complaint before the GC.

Hannifin, who later became a vice-president of Howard Hughes' Summa Corporation, said that only a handful of Teamsters loans were made to Nevada gaming operations while he headed the GCB from 1971 until mid-1977. He did not know what government attorneys were referring to when they alleged that those loans were "questionable" and said that the gaming authorities deferred license applications so that further investigation could be done and more information could be collected.

If Hannifin's board did not know why the loans were questionable, they should have dug more deeply and contacted the Department of Labor and the FBI to find out why.

GCB Member Jeffrey Silver said, "Teamster loans always have been considered legitimate money from legitimate people."

I guess he was not aware of the February 1974 indictment against Dorfman for fraud involving $1.4 million in loans made by the Teamsters pension fund to a plastics manufacturing company in Deming, New Mexico. Indicted along with Dorfman were Joseph Lombardo, Tony Spilotro, Irwin Weiner, and several others.

Daniel Seifert was the key witness who was going to testify for the government regarding a conspiracy to defraud the Teamsters pension fund. He was murdered in front of his son on September 27, 1974. Dorfman was the main person behind approving the loan in which Seifert was involved.

More problems concerning loans made to Shenker arose, but these were financings by a different union. In March 1977 the Department of Labor accused Al Bramlet, president of the Las Vegas Culinary Union, and other trustees of that union pension fund of making illegal loans of more than $30 million to Shenker and four of his controlled companies.[318] The government filed suit in federal court to stop future loans, to remove the trustees, and to repay the money lost to the fund through the investments made by Shenker.

The loans violated ERISA, a law that required trustees to act prudently and solely in the interest of pension plan participants and to diversify their loans to avoid risks that could lead to large losses.

Among the defendants were seven persons who were active or former trustees of the Culinary Union pension fund and four Shenker-controlled companies, which included I.J.K. Nevada Inc., Sierra Charter Corporation, Murrieta Hot Springs Corporation, and S&F Corporation.

For some reason, Bramlet was adamant that he would not turn over his union's pension fund to the International, as later indicated in a report on labor and management racketeering by the President's Commission on Organized Crime. It recounted:

> "As boss of the HEREIU Local 226 in Las Vegas, Elmer 'Al' Bramlet adamantly refused to let the International take over his local's health and welfare fund. LCN [La Cosa Nostra] Associate Joseph Hauser, a mob expert on insurance swindles, testified before the Senate PSI [Permanent Subcommittee on Investigations] that he was present when he, LCN associate Sidney Korshak, and a Los Angeles HEREIU official who later became International secretary-treasurer, Herman 'Blackie' Leavitt, tried to persuade Bramlet. Hauser testified Leavitt warned Bramlet that the Chicago LCN had ordered [Edward] Hanley to merge Bramlet's fund with the International's. "Korshak, according to Hauser, told Bramlet ominously,

---

318   *The New York Times*, March 31, 1977

'You know something, Mr. Bramlet, I would listen to Mr. Leavitt, he makes a lot of sense.' Bramlet became very upset, ripped off his tie, and asserted the funds would go to the International only over his 'dead body.' Leavitt responded, 'You'll be six feet under the desert if this is not done.'"

Department of Justice prosecutors purported that Sidney Wyman and a Mob associate bribed Bramlet to obtain loans from the Culinary Union pension fund for the Dunes. They also believed that Wyman was involved in payoffs to Bramlet for those loans.

Bramlet called Wyman at the Dunes on February 24, 1977 and asked for $10,000. Wyman delivered the money to one of their mutual friends. About three weeks later and prior to the government accusations, Bramlet's body was found buried in the desert, he having been murdered.[319] Wyman was one of the last people to talk to Bramlet before he died.

Another memo from the Department of Labor's enforcement chief dated March 4, 1977 stated:

> "Why should the Dunes Hotel executive [Sidney Wyman] want to pay $10,000 to Al Bramlet? This gives some credence to a theory that Bramlet was possibly involved in a kickback arrangement with the Dunes Hotel, since it is owned by Shenker, and Shenker received loans from the fund, which is dominated by Bramlet."

Wyman became acquainted with Bramlet at the Riviera, where Bramlet was a daily guest at the executives' lunch table. Wyman introduced Shenker to Bramlet, whom Shenker considered responsible for having made the loans to his companies, Murrieta and Sierra Charter.

Wyman, protected under the veil of the title of "consultant" to the Dunes, was the conduit between Bramlet and the St. Louis and Kansas City underworld. He also was a friend to the New York Mob and the Chicago Outfit.

A 1977 audit of the Las Vegas Culinary Union pension fund, occasioned by the murder of the boss, Bramlet, revealed that about 60 percent of the fund's $43 million was lent to Shenker.

Of those loans, $750,000 received by Sierra Charter from the pension fund was given to Wyman and used to buy U.S. Treasury bills, which were secured in Wyman's safety deposit box in the Dunes casino cage. Wyman kept no secrets about the money in the box and exposed it to the adjacent baccarat crew that was just steps away from the cashier's cage. The crew

---

319   *St. Louis Post-Dispatch*, March 28, 1982

watched on one occasion wherein Wyman emptied the box into the open arms of his poker playing friend Sam Angel, on the pretext of looking for a very large diamond ring he buried in the box with the cash. Another $20,000 loan to Wyman was never repaid.

Subsequently, the Department of Labor filed suit in U.S. District Court against Shenker, accusing him of obtaining Culinary Union pension fund loans by fraud and diverting them for his personal use.

Thomas Kane, a labor department official, wrote a subsequent report for Edward F. Daly, the director of enforcement for the labor department, which noted:

> "The Department of Justice has become deeply involved, since they received an allegation of a $100,000 kickback to a person associated with the culinary fund."

Another memo to Daly in January 1978 revealed that the FBI was conducting another investigation of the Culinary Union pension fund. The agency specifically was looking into reports of a $200,000 kickback to a union official for $2.7 million in loans.

CHAPTER 49

THE DUNES:
SHENKER AND MONEY WOES

Morris Shenker plodded on at the Dunes. In 1979 he had the South Tower added, expanding the hotel to 1,300 rooms. However, the hotel-casino still had difficulty attracting high rollers, except for Adnan Khashoggi and bought business. The property just could not compete with the newer and bigger hotels, such as the MGM Grand and Caesars Palace, both across the street, which boasted many more new luxurious rooms and unequaled entertainment. The MGM Grand, then the biggest, brightest, and finest hotel in Las Vegas, drew customers from Caesars and the Dunes at an alarming rate. The competition caused a severe decline in the Dunes' casino drop.

Shenker was visibly upset about this, according to another confidential source, as well as the looming repayment of $5 million that was loaned to him by Dadi Darma, who was the director of Far East junket operations for the Dunes.

Darma was a gambler at the hotel for many years before Shenker became the licensee, and a problem gambler at the baccarat table when the game was dealt in currency. Because Darma bet the house game limit of $2,000 on every hand, Baccarat Manager Harley Kaufman had the crew prepare bundles of $2,000 comprised of $100 bills with a regulation $2,000 printed bank wrapper. This special preparation allowed more hands to be dealt per hour, which meant more betting action.

After each decision, Darma placed the bundles in his pocket but secreted away a bill or two from each one before making his next bets. Once, one of the dealers counted the bundles after one of Darma's losing bets and discovered the discrepancy. In response, Kaufman, one of the brightest and gifted up-and-coming casino executives, stapled together a $2,000 packet, making it impossible for Darma to extract any bills from it. Darma never complained and kept on playing.

Shenker struggled to keep the Dunes open due to cash shortages. Occasionally on weekends he called and borrowed cash from the MGM

Grand, using the excuse that the Dunes had some losses and they could not get to the bank in time to replenish its monetary inventory. When Shenker did this, he played the Jewish card with the MGM executive, saying in Yiddish, "Vas makhstu, Macie? "(How are you, Macie?)"

Even though such borrowing was illegal under Nevada gaming regulations unless the transactions were reported to the Gaming Control Board (GCB), many operators discreetly borrowed from one another.

The same MGM official had a very good customer of his resort request a favor of him. The customer was having a bad year with reduced cash flow but previously purchased a lot at Shenker's Murrieta Hot Springs. This customer wanted help canceling the deal and getting a refund from Shenker. The customer tried on his own but could not even sell back the land to the corporation.

The MGM official told the customer that he would see what he could do. Because he knew Shenker on a personal basis, although the two were not social friends, he figured that Shenker would return the simple favor. When the MGM official asked Shenker, he said, "Sure, Macie, I will take care of it myself." However, Shenker did not do anything, so the customer did not get what he wanted. After that, the MGM official never spoke to Shenker again.

After Shenker borrowed money from the MGM a few times, their management decided that that was it, they would not allow it anymore.

A confidential source and friend of James Tamer revealed that Shenker also borrowed cash for the Dunes' cage bankroll on occasion.[320]

On November 21, 1980, a fire devastated the MGM Grand and took 85 lives. This unfortunate incident indeed troubled owner Kirk Kerkorian and his staff, which included Al Benedict, Bernie Rothkopf, and Morrie Jaeger.

The Clark County Fire Department investigated the fire and determined the cause was an electrical ground fault in a pie display case along with some scraping and chafing metals due to improper installation of a refrigeration compressor.

However, key management, including Benedict, the president, speculated that it was an arson attack,[321] carried out by unsavory characters who used bombs and fire as everyday tools. The local Culinary Union's president was involved in some local restaurant fire and bombing incidents. Benedict retained a lawyer to investigate, but no evidence was found to prove the fire was arson.

---

320   Interview with confidential source, KQ
321   Interview with confidential MGM employee, 2018

The Dunes continued having cash problems, and they tried every marketing method to increase revenue. Shenker placed his niece's husband Robert "Bob" Amira as his key man in the casino. This led to many problems and a major clash between Amira on one side and Sid Wyman, George Duckworth and their loyal, trusted casino team on the other.

A cage employee recalled, "Duckworth came over to me one day when Bob Amira was screaming at him. Amira then came over to the cage and told me to do something about a customer. He said, 'This guy's good, don't worry about it.' Amira was being real loud and showing off. Amira walked away. Then Duckworth came over, and he asked me to pull somebody's credit card, and he just holds it in his hand and doesn't even look at it. He kind of used the card to shield the purpose of his next remark. He says, 'Listen to me carefully.' He says, 'Don't make any mistake about it. You work for me. Do not do what that fellow just told you.' And he walked away."

The cashier continued, "One day Shenker called down and he says, 'You know, I have a really good friend that's coming over from the Aladdin, Sorkis Webbe. I want you to give him $10,000.' But at the time the Dunes controller, my boss Duane Krohn, said, 'Nobody gets a cent, unless I say so.' So Webbe shows up, and I tried to call Duane. I couldn't find him, and I can't give this guy any money. I'm under orders not to give anybody money unless Duane approves it. So the guy left upset. And I went to lunch and somebody came to the dining room and said, 'You can't come back to the cage.' I asked why. 'Shenker fired you, and you can't come back.' I said, 'Okay.' So I went back to the cage and Duane was there. He says, 'No, no, you're – you're in. You're okay.'

"Later on I was talking to Shenker directly, he asked me to do something. He says, 'Now, are you going to do what I tell you to do?' And I said, 'Sir, I've always done what you told me to do except when I was instructed to do differently by my supervisor.' And he kind of stopped for a second, and he goes, 'Yeah, that's what I understand.' But even after that he was always a little bit cold when talking to me."

In 1981 Amira, Joseph Colombo, Jr., and three others were indicted in connection with a scheme that bilked the Dunes out of as much as $2 million.[322] Prosecutors pegged Amira as the group's "inside man," authorizing airline ticket reimbursements of about $500,000. Additionally, he personally approved $1.4 million in casino credit to the New York players, as much as $50,000 at a time.

322   *St. Louis Post-Dispatch*, Sept. 20, 1981

Nevada District Judge Joseph Pavlikowski, however, dismissed the case on technical grounds. This was because of a communication between the prosecutor and the grand jury foreman that the judge ruled as improper.[323]

Several Dunes casino cage cashiers were called in for questioning by the GCB about one member of this group, Alphonse "Fat Allie" Merola. He was called the whale not because he was a high roller, a term that was never used in the 1970s, but because he was quite overweight. The GCB had information that Merola and others were setting up dummy credit card lines at the Dunes and bringing other Mobsters into the hotel-casino. The case went to trial.

About those involved, a former cashier said, "We identified everybody. And then what happened? During that trial we found out, you know, they had befriended one of the girls in the cage and that she was the one that was falsifying how we were supposed to get ID. And I think at the time we were taking a picture of the license or something. Anyway, she was setting up all these guys' accounts, um, falsifying them to look legitimate. And so when I found that out, I didn't know it until the trial. And of course it was disappointing and they asked if I knew anything about those guys. And now the only thing I remember is that Johnny Pradella was running the junkets by then. Andy Pradella [father of John] was the guy that originally ran them. Andy is the one that actually set it up and then Johnny assumed it. He was working with a couple of guys that were called the Scibelli brothers.[324]

"I remember the two of them, but there was this one they called 'Sky-balls,' the little one. They were both short. That one was just as nasty as can be. He would always come to the cage and say, 'I want you to do this, that, and the other.' And I would fight him, you know, and say, 'No, you're not going to do that, it's against the rules,' you know. And the guy would curse me out and I would curse him back, then we'd have like this big feud. I just thought he was a nasty old cranky guy. And then one day Johnny Pradella told me, 'You should be more careful with this guy because he's actually an enforcer. This guy actually goes out when people don't pay. He gets the money,'" the cashier continued.

"Johnny always told me, 'Just don't do what he wants to do 'cause it's against the rules.' But he says, 'Be more careful how you address him because he can be really nasty.'" Then the cashier told me a story about a time

Johnny Pradella, Francesco/Frank "Skyballs" Scibelli and someone else had dinner at the Dunes' Sultan's Table. "The casino host, Artie Selman, came into the room, and Skyballs called him over. Selman was starting to put pressure on the junket, and Selman said, 'You guys aren't producing' or something to that effect. There was some disagreement. Artie didn't feel that they were doing the job.

And of course they thought they were doing theirs. Then Skyballs says, 'I want to talk to you.'

"And remember, Artie was I think six feet tall and he said, 'What?' And Skyballs says, 'Well, lean down here. I don't want to shout to you.' And so Artie leans down to get next to Skyballs. Skyballs grabbed him by the tie and put a fork to his eye and said, 'I hear you want to get rid of us. Is that true?'

"Johnny tried to shield the violence from people around them. He called the musicians over and they started playing."

"And then towards the end of my relationship with Johnny he came to me and he said, "Whatever you do, pretend that you and I don't know each other,' he says, 'because I got some problems with the feds. There's some people that are following me, and you need to stay out of the way.' He wanted to protect me."

The cashier went on, "Several of the players on the junket were stereotype Italians with many gold chains on their necks and open shirts. It turned out that these players were FBI agents."

"Skyballs" Scibelli got into a "beef," or argument, with a Dunes dice dealer that was not pleasant. The dealer said something to Scibelli that just hit him the wrong way, and he threatened the dealer. Casino Host Irwin Ross had to calm Scibelli down.

Ross said, "I had to have Duckworth give the dealer a day off until Skyballs went back on the junket. He wanted to kill the dealer."

Scibelli and eight associates, alleged members of the Genovese crime family, were arrested after a Springfield, Massachusetts, grand jury indicted them on racketeering charges as part of the Department of Justice's national crackdown on organized crime.[325] The FBI obtained evidence that Scibelli and his associates engaged in bookmaking and sponsored gambling trips to the Dunes in Las Vegas and to Atlantic City, New Jersey. The FBI claimed that the group used threats to establish bookmaking operations in upstate New York as well.

Two of the men indicted with Scibelli were Mario Fiore and John Pradella, who brought junkets from upstate New York and Boston to

---

325   *The Boston Globe*, Oct.31, 1985

the Dunes. Fiore was a perfect gentleman while visiting the Dunes and well-liked by the casino bosses as well as the employees.

The FBI used an electronic bug to gather the evidence against the Scibelli group to obtain the indictment, which went back to 1978 and Scibelli's interaction with the Genovese crime family. Anthony "Fat Tony" Salerno, the alleged head of the Genovese family, was described in the indictment as an unindicted co-conspirator. In a conversation recorded by the FBI between Scibelli and Salerno at the latter's Palma Boys Social Club at 416 East 115th Street, Salerno was described as the "chieftain" in New York.[326]

At this meeting Scibelli said to Salerno, "We're doing a good job up there, you know, running the *Thing* [La Cosa Nostra] there. You got me, I'm being a good capo."

Many of the casino bosses saw the paranoia that Shenker had about casino players, especially the high rollers who occasionally won. A seasoned casino operator he was not. He could not bluff his way through running the Dunes, and it showed. He would have the winning dice taken off of a game in the middle of a hot hand and get rebuked by the players, but he did not care. He once told a blackjack floorman that he should not let a high player parlay his bet more than twice. Shenker's casino methods were disastrous and quickly alienated the best customers. He slowly dug himself into a hole; his other businesses were draining him of cash, and he was constantly seeking more money.

One evening in 1979, a high rolling customer gambled and won $60,000 at the blackjack table. A casino host tried to get the customer to put the money on deposit in the Dunes cage to get him to play later at the Dunes, during which the casino could get the money back. The customer refused and left. However, the host found out that the customer was staying at the Jockey Club next door, which did not have live gaming. The next day, the host visited the Jockey Club and learned, with some light bribery of the talkative front desk clerk, which room in which the customer was staying.

When the casino host and casino boss called upon him, the customer looked different. He was clean shaven and bald, yet the day before he had a mustache and a full head of hair. It was evident that he used a disguise at the Dunes.

The customer immediately recognized the casino host. Before the host could say anything, the player said, "Okay, I don't want any trouble, just take the money." There was no doubt the customer was an experienced card counter and perhaps had some help from the dealer. He never expected to see the Dunes host and when he did, he thought he was caught. The customer thought he might get hurt because he believed the casino boss who accompanied the host was a "heavy." The customer immediately gave back the $60k, which was returned to Casino Manager George Duckworth to put in the Dunes cage. Shenker found out about what occurred and asked the casino host, "Why didn't you bring me the money?"[327]

Shenker settled certain markers privately, such as those of Adnan Khashoggi, an international arms dealer and an extremely good player at the Dunes. During these private settlements, anything could have happened with the markers and how they were paid, if they were. The records of the play were carefully guarded and practically untraceable. Shenker did not follow Nevada gaming regulations while settling them, so an exact paper trail of Khashoggi's action did not exist. This irregular internal control procedure between Shenker and a casino guest certainly could have been a cover-up for a skim.

The Dunes catered to Khashoggi like he was an almighty ruler, which he was by way of the saying, "Whoever has the gold makes the rules." They built a rooftop pool adjacent to his suite for him, they stopped games to allow him to eat, and they even afforded him a private gaming pit in which to play and lose $250,000 and upwards each evening.

Though he catered to Khashoggi, Shenker treated the Dunes employees much less generously.

Dana Petrarca, a former Dunes pit clerk, recalled with pride at a Dunes employee reunion how fun it was to work with people "who weren't under the corporate microscope." Those days were gone with the Shenker team. "We were like a family," Petrarca said. "We really were."[328]

Shenker required polygraph tests be done on dealers and other workers, which was a far cry from the days of Wyman and Rich. This duo knew when someone was not telling the truth and did not need to use a lie detector machine.

Glen Treadwell, a Dunes casino host and nephew of Clifford "Cliff" Perlman, Caesars Palace' president and CEO, had a child who was born with spina bifida. The Dunes allowed Treadwell's spina bifida support group to meet in one of the hotel's small meeting rooms free of charge. The group sometimes had a pot luck dinner with members providing

327   Interview with Gene Kilroy, 2019
328   *Las Vegas Review-Journal*, John Smith, Feb. 9, 2011

homemade dishes for the evening meeting. In those instances, Shenker's wife, Lillian Shenker, went into the group's meeting room and personally inspected the food to ensure it did not come from the Dunes' kitchens. Treadwell said this happened on many occasions.

The Dunes' financial position continued to slowly erode, and the gross gaming drop continued to decline. Cash, coming in one door and out another, continued becoming scarcer. In December 1982 the IRS was about to close the Dunes because of $3 million of unpaid and overdue federal taxes and penalties. Additionally, the Dunes owed $2.5 million to employee welfare funds and another $5 million to other lenders, which were due by January. Further, the Dunes was in arrears with numerous vendors.

A Dunes affidavit to the GCB in support of obtaining a loan from Clifford and Stuart Perlman, former principal owners of Caesars Palace, revealed the Dunes lost $2.8 million dollars in the previous month (November) and was expected to lose more than $1 million in the present month of December. The GCB did not have time to audit the Dunes in December to determine where the losses occurred.

The affidavit claimed that a major factor in the Dunes' declining revenue was the instability of Mexico and the $46 million in Mexican players' gaming markers, or I.O.U.s, $20 million of which were uncollectible. This claim alone should have been a red flare to the GCB. Mexico was not the problem. Neither was it the target of Shenker's standard claim: "My partner was in charge then. Ask him." Shenker had no one to blame but himself and his inadequacy in operating a hotel-casino business.

In a related emergency meeting of the Gaming Commission in December 1982, they approved the Dunes to receive a $10 million loan from the Perlmans. The Perlmans signed a $185 million agreement with Shenker to buy the Dunes. The Perlman brothers previously were denied a gaming license in New Jersey because of their association with underworld figures, including Mob financier Meyer Lansky.

Bill Bennett of Circus-Circus was also interested in the Dunes and sent several executives to delve into the property's complex maze of debt and mystery and determine the facts. Former GCB Chairman Richard Bunker was the corporate treasurer of Circus-Circus but left the company in 1985 to become the president of the Dunes. Subsequently, he was appointed its bankruptcy trustee.

Bunker was an extremely good negotiator and administrator whose presence at the Dunes enhanced its image, which by that time was one of a sinking ship. His gaming control knowledge could have kept the Dunes

327

out of trouble with Nevada regulators, and he knew enough influential Las Vegans to keep some of the financial pressure workable. What the Dunes needed the most at the time, however, was revenue, and Bunker could not generate that. He did not have a player list or the ability to garner casino play. He did not have a set of players who followed him to the Dunes, and frankly, he lacked the experience needed to walk into a pit and know if a major conspiracy was in operation. He just did not have that actual hands-on casino experience. In time he would have been fine, but time was ticking on against him.

It is interesting that when four suspected Mafia members, including Colombo, Jr., were indicted on charges of obtaining money under false pretenses in an airline ticket reimbursement scam at the Dunes as guests via Amira, Bunker said the hotel complementaries did not violate any Nevada law or gaming regulation. Then, as chairman of the GCB, he took no action.

In the next year, 1983, Shenker opened The Oasis Casino at the Dunes, a satellite gaming enterprise, on the corner of Flamingo Road and Las Vegas Boulevard. The building was beautiful and unique. However, it was considered to be a design mistake in terms of people flow. Pedestrians walked in and gambled, never knowing there was a larger, main casino with high-stakes gambling along with quality entertainment, shops, gourmet restaurants, buffets, dancing, and more at the Dunes proper. So guests likely would not visit again. A people mover from the street to the main casino and hotel entrance would have been more profitable.

Attrition through percentages brought some of the guests into the main casino area, but two casinos required double the personnel and security. At best, the Oasis was a break-even proposition, depending on who did the bookkeeping.

An anonymous source close to the Dunes controller said, "When Morris Shenker, Sr. was building the new high-rise and the Oasis, they were supposedly buying the best or [sic] ever was, but the fact was they were buying something that was either normal or, you know, it wasn't the best. So what was happening is they're pocketing the difference."[329]

The Dunes marketing team did its best, through slot tournaments, golf tournaments, Elvis impersonators, the Comedy Club, and cheap airline junkets in which $5 and $10 bettors qualified for the trips, to bring in customers to gamble. On some days the Dunes made more money through the junket operators than directly through the casino itself. Former owners Wyman and Rich would not have operated the casino in this manner.

329   Interview with confidential source, 2019

Jeannie Magowan, who was the Dunes publicity director for 20-plus years, described the hotel-casino as being "like a glamorous lady who has fun and survives good times and bad with a sense of adventure and expectation.

"The Dunes always had a personality of its own. No matter what happened, even during the culinary strike that almost closed the town in the 1970s, its people did what they had to do but they always were loyal and usually managed to keep a sense of humor. I hope that spirit is not gone. I believe it survives today," she said.

But in reality, Magowan was dreaming, as was Norma Desmond in Billy Wilder's movie, *Sunset Boulevard*, about the Dunes making a triumphant return to stardom. The sad part was that the Dunes was sinking, and sinking fast, as it approached the point of no return.

There were always outside cheaters and thieves looking to capitalize on a hotel- casino that was in trouble and make a quick buck. They could smell the openings via the back door of the butcher shop or liquor storage area, or even from a property in storage to which certain security chiefs had unlimited access without any checks and balances. An unnamed former GCB employee who later worked for Shenker removed Dunes property for himself. This person cannot be named herein for fear of retribution.

Even the Dunes reservation office in Los Angeles was affected. Abby Cooperman, who was the manager, said that the Dunes office was billed for middle-of-the-night calls to a pornographic telephone recording and to soothsayer Jeane Dixon.[330]

Junket masters were slowly weaning off of the Dunes for other markets. The GCB was cracking down on them and calling them in to determine their suitability. Sigmund "Captain John" Kassap from Baltimore resigned when the GCB told him to file an application. Fellows like Kassap needed to acquire good junket players. He knew the players through personal relationships with some of the biggest bookies in his area.

Ash Resnick returned to the Dunes to help bring more high play to the resort. While employed there he sued the GCB, asking that they be required to let him see the investigative reports they compiled on him. His case was denied in local district court, and he lost an appeal to the Nevada Supreme Court.

A clever marketing guy, Resnick used connections like writer Percy Ross and his nationally syndicated column, "Thanks a Million" to give some of his readers a complimentary dinner for two at the Sultan's Table.

It is probable that the down-on-their-luck beneficiary did not have the money to get to Las Vegas, but the names Resnick and the Dunes were certainly seen by many people and likely sparked the thought that the Dunes was a great place to visit and contact the charming host.

All of this led to Shenker filing a bankruptcy petition on January 3, 1984. It listed 49 creditors' claims totaling about $184 million.[331] It was a record high in bankruptcy court in St. Louis and more than four times the total of the previous record holder. The last straw for Shenker was a $34 million court verdict against him for money he borrowed from the Culinary Workers and Bartenders union pension fund for resorts in Southern California and other projects.

Shenker failed to list all of his creditors in his bankruptcy petition. For one, he owed Dunes baccarat supervisor Joseph Chautin $100,000, which he borrowed in 1976.[332] Chautin, originally from St. Louis and a close associate of Wyman, said that Shenker needed the money badly at the time. Many of the newspaper stories about Shenker ramping up to take over the Dunes referred to him as a millionaire. It is incongruous that he borrowed money, $100,000 no less, from a 75-year-old employee of the Dunes who was on the edge of dementia.

Chautin also knew Shenker's wife Lillian back in St. Louis, when she was younger. Chautin said that Lillian's father, Sam Koplar, who founded the Chase Park Plaza and Forest Park hotels in St. Louis, paid Chautin and other young Jewish men to keep her company at dances and school parties.

Shenker had plenty of assets that he could liquidate, including $1.2 million in Dunes stock, 1,500 acres of land in Roseville, California, and 260 acres of land in San Diego County.

Shenker's lack of experience in operating a casino and bad business decisions contributed to his having to declare bankruptcy. Shenker could not survive with the big boys. Greed also played a key role in his destruction of the Dunes.

Also during 1984, lawsuits against Shenker regarding some of the loans made to his companies were resolved, compounding his money problems.

The Department of Labor filed a civil ERISA, or Employee Retirement Income Security Act of 1974, lawsuit against present and past trustees of the Culinary Workers and Bartenders pension trust fund along with Shenker and the Shenker-controlled corporations of I.J.K. Nevada, Mur-

---

331   Annual Report of the U.S. Secretary of Labor
332   Interview with Joe Chautin, 1976

rieta Hot Springs, S&F, and Sierra Charter.[333] The government agency claimed that the defendant trustees breached their fiduciary responsibility, failed to diversify fund assets, and made illegal loans to parties related to employers contributing to the trust parties of interest.

Shenker-Sierra Charter filed counterclaims, asking for damages resulting from the labor department's allegedly negligent investigation, unwarranted institution of litigation, failure to discuss settlement, fiduciary breaches, and pursuit of a "vendetta" against Shenker.

The court ruled on May 15, 1984, ordering Shenker to pay $33.9 million in restitution to the trust. Also, it awarded interest on that figure through May 15, 1984, along with costs and attorney fees, and allowed the trust to retain the collateral properties. In addition, the court ordered that the amount of post-transfer property expenses be assessed to Shenker.

T.L. Karsten, Associates, the Teamsters pension fund's asset manager, sued Shenker, Sierra Charter, and I.J.K. Nevada, charging them with fraud and seeking restitution to the trust. Shenker-Sierra Charter filed counterclaims against Karsten, and the former asset manager, Upper Avenue Bank, now Lakeshore Bank of Chicago, for failure to preserve the value of the collateral properties.

In November 1983, a jury found Shenker liable for the loans. The court ordered him to pay the trust $33.9 million and allowed the trust to retain the collateral properties.

Although the Department of Labor had indications of loan irregularities and problems involving the Culinary Workers and Bartenders union trust in 1975, they did not begin to investigate them until 1977. In 1975 investigators obtained information about two loans to Shenker companies, Murrieta and Sierra Charter, amounting to $7 million in illegal loans under ERISA.[334] The labor department knew then that Shenker received $57 million in illegal and imprudent loans from two other pension funds. They also had evidence that Shenker had connections with organized crime members.

Key sources at the Department of Labor believed that they should have launched an investigation when they learned about any one of these loans to Shenker.

The Pipefitters Local 562 pension and welfare funds granted five loans totaling $24 million to Murietta, Mission Hills Enterprises, and B.A.I., all represented and negotiated by Shenker and Irvin Kahn. The FBI in-

---

333   "Handling of The Abuses of the Southern Nevada Culinary Workers and Bartenders Pension Trust Fund," U.S. Department of Labor, September 1983
334   The Employee Retirement Income Security Act (ERISA)

vestigated Shenker and these loans in early 1975. Shenker made most of the presentations about the loans and was always the only person who discussed the handling of the loans, the collateral and security in favor of the pension fund.[335]

The FBI reported that during these presentations and discussions, the pension and welfare trustees made it very clear to Shenker and Kahn that the loans had to be secured by a first deed of trust. This meant that if any of the loans was not repaid, the pension fund would be in the first position of taking the property that was put up as collateral. The trustees were emphatic about this stipulation because, as they stated, they held a position of fiduciary responsibility to the members of the Pipefitters Union. All of the transcribed meeting minutes verified that these were stipulations of the loans.

In 1974, Shenker tried to substitute a piece of property for one that had collateralized a loan. A trustee had some doubts about the value of the substitute property and decided to physically examine it. Along with another trustee and the fund's attorney, they traveled to Northern California to inspect the property.

The trustee said, "After viewing this property, I was convinced that Shenker was trying to do a big con job on them, as the value of the property did not come anywhere near the amount of the loan." Shortly thereafter, the trustees decided to reject this proposed substitution. They also stated that payments on all of the loans they made to Shenker were always delinquent. Further, they said that after several restructurings of the loans, they discovered that they did not hold a first trust deed on the properties.

A title officer at Title Insurance and Trust Company in Riverside, California, who was a redacted FBI source, revealed what happened regarding two Pipefitters pension fund loans.

One was a $5.5 million loan for Mission Hills Country Club that was jointly controlled by Kahn and Shenker. For this loan, certain parcels of real estate in Palm Springs, including Mission Hills, were pledged as collateral to the Pipefitters pension fund.

Shenker's office handled the escrow. A title policy was issued to the Pipefitters, which referred to a recorded lien on the property. The lien was originally in the amount of $2.9 million, however, it was reduced to $500,000 at the time that the Pipefitters made the loan.

The title officer called this non-documented or reported lien a "write over." He further stated that Kahn and Shenker were personally present at the closing of the Mission Hills loan and both played an equal role in

<hr>

[335]   FBI File, 156-20-309, February 1975

representing it. The officer said, "There is no way at all that Shenker could not have known about the write-over of the Mercantile lien."[336]

The title officer revealed that another loan, a $5 million loan to Murrieta, had write- overs associated with it. Supposedly the write-overs were necessitated because Shenker and Murrieta wanted to negotiate a discounted payoff on the prior liens on the property before making the final payment. The title company issued a title policy in favor of the Pipefitters, deleting any references to the existing liens, which made it appear as though they were paid off.

This title officer stated that he was never involved in write-overs prior to getting involved with Shenker and Kahn. Also, his firm did not have a policy concerning write- overs but used them when competing for title business in Southern California, as other title companies did. If a loss resulted in a transaction wherein a write-over was used, the title company made up the amount.

The FBI learned that Shenker had a pattern of defaulting on payments he owed on properties he purchased. The source for much of the information provided to the agency was a shareholder of Sierra Charter.

One property owner who sold his land to Shenker described that transaction to the FBI. Prior to October 1971, that landowner received a letter from an individual representing Shenker that indicated Shenker wanted to purchase the owner's specific, 33-acre parcel of land, the owner stated. The owner noted that the letter sounded more like a threat because the writer stated that they were going to research the property and thereafter buy the surrounding pieces of land owned by other persons, which would leave this owner's property divided and inaccessible.

The owner decided to hold out but eventually sold his parcel to Shenker for about $130,000, which was comprised of a cash down payment of $32,000 and annual installments of $28,545. Shenker was delinquent on the first and subsequent payments, causing the seller to file multiple notices of default, beginning just two months after the sale.

One parcel acquired by Shenker's company, B.A.I., only had a balance of $15,330 with a monthly payment of $125, yet the record of payment was always "extremely" bad.

Shenker and Kahn's actions related to their land transactions and their representations to the Pipefitters Union were scandalous.

It may seem unfair to compare Shenker to the other Dunes management teams, but they did not have the problems that Shenker had while

336   FBI File, SL-156-20, 1975

running the hotel-casino. The others never hurt the working man or took money from them in any way that was improper.

In mid-December 1985, Valley Bank of Nevada and the Culinary Union pension fund acquired half of Shenker's interest in the Dunes as he could not come up with the funds agreed to in their settlement.

CHAPTER 50

THE DUNES:
THE TEAMSTERS AND SHENKER

T he reason for the disappearance of Jimmy Hoffa involved the Dunes, University of Nevada, Las Vegas, professor Dr. William N. Thompson purported in his book, *Gambling in America*.[337] About the Teamsters leader and pension fund trustee, Thompson wrote:

> "The Dunes just may have provided the motivation for the murder of Jimmy Hoffa. It was money from the International Brotherhood of Teamsters that went to finance the Dunes – and Teamsters' money was spread around Las Vegas – but the Dunes was the main place. The Teamsters' loans had all sorts of crooked things around them. There were invitations to skim, and Hoffa got kickbacks on the loans. Hoffa's successor Frank Fitzsimmons kept the loans going after Hoffa was in prison and then he kept them going after Hoffa was pardoned, but Hoffa could not run for union office.
>
> "Hoffa wanted to ingratiate himself with the Nixon administration. The federal government passed a new law in 1974 called the Employee Retirement Income Security Act, giving the Department of Labor and the Federal Bureau of Investigation special powers to investigate and prosecute union pension funds that were being misused. I worked for the new pension administration in 1976 and 1977, and the story was still in the rumor mill. In 1974, Hoffa starts singing to the government in exchange for a change in his pardon so he could run for union office, and he was murdered. And what was he singing about before he was murdered? The Dunes. He was telling the government how Fitzsimmons was skimming money out of the Dunes much as he had done. Hoffa told about the Teamsters' loan structure for constructing the property."

This quote was from the first edition of Thompson's book, however, the account, in its entirety, was omitted from the second edition. I find

337   *Gambling In America: An Encyclopedia of History, Issues, and Society*, William N. Thompson, 2015

the exclusion strange, and the reason for it is unknown. Maybe it was left out because it was inaccurate. Perhaps Thompson's publisher or the University of Nevada or former Dunes associates who were unhappy with it pressured Thompson to delete it.

What is certain and factual is that, as evidenced in an FBI surveillance tape, a May 22, 1979 meeting took place between Allen Dorfman, the protégé of Hoffa and the main facilitator of Teamsters loans; Joey "The Clown" Lombardo, high lama of the Chicago Outfit; and Morris Shenker, the owner of the Dunes and an attorney of Hoffa. There was no mistake that Dorfman and the Chicago Outfit did not like Morris Shenker.

Before Shenker arrived at the meeting, Dorfman and Lombardo protested that Shenker was holding back money that Dorfman had coming to him as kickbacks in return for facilitating Teamsters pension fund loans. Dorfman claimed that Teamsters loans went to a company called I.J.K. Nevada, to other companies that Irvin Kahn and Shenker controlled and to the Dunes. Dorfman was adamant that the day Shenker and Kahn appeared for their first loan in 1966, Hoffa and Dorfman were entitled to 25 percent of everything. Yet Kahn died a few years later, and for the last 12 years, Dorfman said, "We have received absolutely nothing."

Shenker denied ever having met Lombardo and said he did not recall the meeting."[338]

In another meeting, this one between Dorfman, Lombardo, and Tony Spilotro, held at Dorfman's insurance company in Chicago, Dorfman was captured by the FBI talking about an agreement he and Hoffa had with Shenker. Dorfman explained:

> "According to the agreement that we have had, Hoffa and myself, we had 25 percent of Kahn and Shenker's holdings, which was Penasquitas [sic], Mission Hills, Apto Seascape, and then they acquired the Dunes Hotel. It was acquired through I.J.K. Nevada, which was the holding company over all it. The money to buy the Dunes Hotel came out of the loans that I gave him. That's all the money that was transferred from Penasquitas in I.J.K. Nevada to buy the Dunes."[339]

I.J.K. Nevada also held controlling shares of stock in Continental Connector Corporation and the Continental subsidiary that owned and operated the Dunes Hotel and Country Club, M&R Investment Company.

---

338   *The New York Times*, March 1, 1983
339   FBI transcript of conversations overhead via microphone in William Webbe's office, May
1, 1979

Shenker did not agree with Dorfman and Lombardo's allegations, insisting that Dorfman "never had an interest in I.J.K. Nevada, never."

Shenker may have been correct in that his deal may not have been with Dorfman per se but, rather, with Hoffa. Because Hoffa vanished, no one knows what transpired between the two. The original Teamsters solidification with Hoffa began when the Dunes underwent a reorganization in 1961-1962, in which Jake Gottlieb was a major player, attending planning meetings and having a say. By 1979, Gottlieb was deceased.

Dorfman and Hoffa did not have a problem with Sidney Wyman and Charles Rich. There is evidence that Hoffa was a guest of Rich on two occasions in Palm Springs prior to this meeting. Also, Hoffa was occasionally seen at the Dunes.

"We [employees] always knew Jimmy Hoffa was around, but somehow never discussed it. Why, I don't know. It was an 'Open Secret,' said Christy Whitbeck, a former employee.

Whitbeck relayed an incident involving Hoffa and her aunt, Jo Melland, who was the secretary of Major Riddle.

> "One afternoon Major Riddle instructed Jo Melland to go to the front desk and pick up some room keys and bring them back to the office. As Jo walked back to the office, Jimmy Hoffa stepped out from the side of a slot machine and said 'Jo, those keys are for me.'[340]
>
> "She handed the keys to Jimmy Hoffa. When she returned to the office, she told Mr. Riddle Mr. Hoffa had said the keys were for him and had given them to Hoffa. Mr. Riddle was very angry with Jo. He said, 'Jo, do you understand if you are asked by the feds, 'have you seen Jimmy Hoffa,' you will have to answer truthfully.'"

Whitbeck added, "This is just an amusing little story that I wanted to mention. When there would be heavy rains, we would always have buckets behind the front desk catching the drips from the rain. Where it came from we didn't know. But one time [during rain] we looked up in the overhead panel light, and it looked like a clump of something was at the edge of the panel. One of the assistant managers said, 'Wanna bet, it's Jimmy Hoffa.' He had disappeared (obviously) by that time."

Later in Dorfman's conversation with Spilotro and Lombardo, he told the two about another arrangement he tried to make with Shenker.

"Now, when I met with Shenker, he's gonna build this other 1,000 rooms, whether the financing is here, or he has a commitment out of a German financing house," said Dorfman. "So I said to him, I says, 'You know, I expect to get some stores in that place [Dunes], Morris. You make sure they get allocated to me now.'"

Spilotro told Dorfman that many of the stores in the Dunes were operated by Shenker's relatives.

"What do you wanna do?" Dorfman asked. "I've been hanging on this for how long now? It's over a year."

Lombardo said, "I know what I would like." Lombardo then claimed that he discussed the situation with "The Old Man," a nickname for Lombardo's superior, Joseph "Joe" Aiuppa, the boss of the Chicago Outfit. "The old man said he will handle it."

The conversation then shifted to the money that Shenker owed Dorfman, Spilotro, and Lombardo, although the reason that he owed them was not mentioned.

Lombardo said, "Shenker is the only guy who knows his hole card, knows his trump card, knows how it originates, knows how he got his money. This ain't no fucking thousand dollars. This is fucking millions."

Dorfman replied, "Every fucking thing that comes out of it, you know, he gets legal fees. I just looked at the [Dunes'] statement. A million dollars a year his firm gets in legal fees out of the Dunes Hotel."

Lombardo then remarked, "Well, do you know what I hear from this guy all these years? This guy is the dirtiest fucking person, fucking rattlesnake."

Lombardo continued, "We gotta take a ride up there, you [Dorfman] and I. We gotta estimate it [the amount owed] and just go and get it. Don't you see, he's used up his usefulness?"

Dorfman replied, "Listen, it's our money." "Let's do it then," Lombardo said.

"I just lost the insurance on the Dunes Hotel to some friends of his [Shenker] in St. Louis," Dorfman said. "I just saw the letter on the casualty insurance."

Dorfman then told Lombardo about a previous meeting he had with Civella in Kansas City. "I say, 'Hey, Nick, I got some rather large lines of commitments coming from Shenker and so far all I get is nothing but conversation.'"

Shenker insisted that he still did not owe Dorfman anything for the Dunes, and Lombardo suggested that Dorfman document his claim. Dorfman said he could, but there was no evidence presented in the court hearings that Shenker ever did have to make any of the talked about payments.

Shenker was mute to Dorfman's claim concerning the Dunes, but he certainly did not have any issues with Dorfman's girlfriend, Maja Doherty, a cocktail waitress working at the Dunes.

According to government witness James "The Weasel" Fratianno, who once was an acting Mafia boss on the West Coast, Shenker "belonged to [the late] Tony Giordano," the crime boss in St. Louis.

"If Shenker had any problems," Fratianno testified at a hearing, "he would go to Tony Giordano, and Tony Giordano would take care of them."

"What if Shenker got a threat against his life?" Fratianno was asked.

"I don't think anybody'd threaten him – if they knew what I knew." When asked if Shenker did get a threat, Fratianno said, "Shenker would go to his man."

Johnny Rosselli and Fratianno talked about Shenker in *The Last Mafioso*.[341]

Fratianno said, "I introduced him to Bomp and Louie Dragna," referring to Los Angeles Mobsters Frank Bompensiero and Louis Tom Dragna. "You can't make any fucking money with that guy."

Dorfman told Lombardo about a recent get-together that Dorfman had in Kansas City with Roy Williams and Kansas City Mafia boss Civella. Dorfman said he learned that Shenker did not belong to Civella, as Dorfman thought.

"That's true," Lombardo agreed. "He don't belong to Nick. But the guy that's got him never got a penny from him either." Lombardo indicated that he talked to Giordano about Shenker in blunt terms, and told Giordano to "either shit or get off the pot." For talking to Giordano, Lombardo said, he was lectured by Aiuppa, who warned him such talk could touch off Mob warfare.[342] Aiuppa was referring to the St. Louis and Detroit Mobs with which Shenker was associated.

"'The Old Man' says, 'What is this with you? 'Shit or get off the pot?' You can't talk to those guys like that.' He says, 'They're the same people like we are. You can't start – you'd have a fucking war going through this country.'"

Lombardo continued, "You know where you belong, and he [Dorfman] knows where he belongs and the other guy knows where he belongs – we all belong to certain people you account to. It's a big world."

Lombardo then told Shenker: "You know, you're a lawyer, you've been around St. Louis a long time."

Shenker: "Yeah, a long time."

Lombardo: "You got a place to go for help, you know what I mean?"

Shenker: "Well, I don't think I – I need any help."

---

341   *The Last Mafioso*, Ovid Demaris, 1984
342   *The Washington Post*, George Lardner, March 6, 1983

Lombardo: "Listen, if you don't owe nothing, you got nothing to worry about."

Shenker: "I owe everybody. I owe everybody."

Lombardo: "You will reach 73 then, you've no problems."

Shenker told *The New York Times* that he never met Lombardo and that he did not recall that meeting."[343]

When Aiuppa warned Lombardo about starting a war in the country, he was not kidding. It seems that when Shenker was running the Dunes after getting licensed in February 1975, he had all bases covered with various Mafia connections plus the Chicago Outfit that were closely tied to the Dunes. It was a fact that he knew Giordano. Giordano was more than just a past client of Shenker and close to him; he also was a guest of the Dunes in 1976, unbeknownst to the Nevada Gaming Control Board.

Giordano was nominated in 1975 for entry into Nevada's List of Excluded Persons from casinos, called on the street the "black book," but his name was withdrawn in 1976.

As the boss of the St. Louis Mafia, Giordano was closely allied with the Detroit factions and in the middle of the action with the Aladdin group of owners. Giordano was a close friend of Irwin Gordon and Dave Goldberg, who were bookies and who operated the baccarat game at the Dunes for Wyman in the late 1960s and early 1970s. Goldberg was especially close to Giordano.

Gordon was written up in *LIFE* magazine[344] many years ago when he was arrested for bookmaking in Terre Haute, Indiana.[345] James Tamer of Miami, who became the Detroit's Mob chief operator at the Aladdin in the 1970s, also was arrested. The same went for Leo Shaffer and Jules Horwick, both of Chicago; Philip Share, Minneapolis; Joseph Jacobson and Charles L. Sumner, both of Indianapolis; and E.M. Wyatt, Terre Haute. All of the arrestees were charged with evading taxes on gross wagering receipts of $3,263,150.

They all were classic bookmakers who took betting action from all over the country. Some of the more illustrious gamblers who bet with the Shaffer book were oilman-gambler Ray Ryan, once a partner with actor William Holden; Zeppo Marx, actor and comedian; and H.L. Hunt, Dallas oilman.

343   *The New York Times*, March 1, 1983
344   *LIFE*, Sept. 1, 1958
345   *The New York Times*, August 1958

It is conceivable that Giordano had a piece of the secret bookmaking operation that Goldberg and Gordon were operating out of a hotel guest room at the Dunes, considering this FBI note:

> "John Vitale and Anthony Giardano [sic], in St. Louis, Missouri, have allegedly 'moved in' on Dave Goldberg and Steve Lekometros and are now taking a piece of their gambling operation."

It is also possible that Giordano had a hidden piece of the Dunes casino action, just like he did with the Frontier, for which he was convicted.

CHAPTER 51

THE DUNES: THE INFORMANTS

T he Dunes, like every other Las Vegas hotel-casino, had its share of internal informants. John Winn, who was a slot manager in the early days at the Dunes, looks to have been one, according to this FBI file:

> "On February 25, 1959, John Winn, operator of slot machines at the Dunes Hotel, Las Vegas, said that [Eugene] Warner is a 'runner' for Joseph 'Doc' Stacher, who has an undisclosed interest in the Sands Hotel. Winn said Warner relays information to Stacher, who spends much of his time in Los Angeles, California. Stacher was described as a notorious gambler and underworld figure from New Jersey and California. Winn was unable to furnish any details on Stacher's interest in the Sands. Warner is not known to have any interest in the Sands or any other hotel in Las Vegas and is not known to be employed by any of them."[346]

Winn continued working at the Dunes after Sid Wyman and Charlie Rich obtained controlling interest of the hotel. Wyman, Rich, and George Duckworth certainly would not have been pleased to know that Winn cooperated with the FBI.

Another FBI document suggested that Sam Landy was an FBI informant, too.

> "In March 1957 Major Riddle bought out Bill Miller's interest giving Riddle 33.2% of the Dunes. Although his name does not appear on the license as a percentage owner, Al Gottlieb, owner of a large trucking concern in Chicago, Illinois, appears to have a financial interest in the Dunes, as he is very frequently in residence at the Dunes, sits in on meetings, and is consulted on policy matters, according to information furnished by Sam Landy, Public Relations, Dunes Hotel."[347]

First, the name "Al Gottlieb" was an error; in fact the person of reference was Jake Gottlieb. Landy knew Gottlieb's name so either Landy was not

346   FBI File, 124-90088-10046, April 16, 1959
347   NARA 124-90032-10075

the source or the FBI misheard the name or it was transcribed incorrectly. Additionally, it is hard to believe that a public relations representative would ever make such a comment.

There is the possibility that Landy, who was from Illinois, may have been familiar with Bill Miller's Riviera in New Jersey, and it very well may have been Miller who hired Landy at the Dunes. A newspaper profile of Landy stated that Landy had close friends in Tampa, Florida, was a runner for a bookie, and worked in a casino in the Bahamas. It also said he came up with the junket concept and welcomed them at the casinos he ran.

In the profile, Landy mentioned an "up and back." The Dunes operated "up and back" junkets in 1957, which were successful. So this marketing tool of buying business via junkets put Landy, as a public relations person, in the middle as a facilitator of the daily flights to the Dunes from Los Angeles, Burbank, and Long Beach.

When and how Landy left the Dunes to go to the Thunderbird is not clear. In August of 1963, Landy was mentioned as an executive there,[348] which means he could have been working at the Dunes when the FBI memo of February 5, 1963 was written.

Landy billed himself as the "Professor of Chance," which he said was "known throughout the nation"[349] because he gave lectures on how to gamble. He was very active socially in the community and was in the charitable group known as the "Saints & Sinners." He rubbed elbows with the Who's Who of Las Vegas at parties and events for the elite.

He left the Dunes in 1966 to be the administrative assistant to Oscar Agron, casino manager at Milton Prell's Aladdin. A *Las Vegas Sun* article about Landy said that he worked at the Dunes in 1955 and left in 1961 to join Revlon as assistant to the senior vice president. The same article said he came back to Las Vegas as assistant secretary at Electronics Capital Corporation, a position he held since 1963.

Curiously, Morris Shenker, Irvin Kahn, Wyman, and Rich all were involved with the Electronics Capital Building. However, there is no documentation to show that this property was in any way related to the company with which Landy was associated.[350]

348   *Valley Times Today*, Aug. 8, 1963
349   *Tampa Tribune*, April 19, 1985
350   *Morris A. Shenker and Lillian K. Shenker v. Commissioner of Internal Revenue*, 804 F.2d 109 (8th Cir. 1986) Note: Regarding the Electronic Capital Building, "On April 4, 1967, Mr. Shenker, Kahn, and Penasquitos executed a new agreement providing that Mr. Shenker and Kahn terminated Penasquitos's agent status, agreed to hold Penasquitos harmless from all claims connected to its operation of the Electronic Capital Building (ECB), and assumed all liabilities and obligations incurred by Penasquitos in operating ECB. That same day, Sidney Wyman and Charles Rich entered an agreement with Kahn under which each acquired a 25 percent interest in ECB from Kahn in exchange for

Landy resurfaced at the Dunes again in 1976 in the position of baccarat manager, placed there by Shenker to be his eyes and ears. Landy bragged to the dealers that he had a meeting with Shenker and after the meeting, he wrote and sent a memo to Shenker about the topics discussed. His boasting to the regular baccarat employees about the private memo was inconsistent with the actions of a genuine loyal employee. He wanted those around him, especially the ones who he believed were inferior to him, to feel that he was something special and more talented than most of the casino bosses in the Dunes. It became obvious that the owners, excluding Shenker, were not happy with Landy.

One evening in 1976, Landy was sitting in one of the two baccarat ladder chairs that were on opposite sides of the table. Landy always sat in the chair that faced the entire casino floor. Holding court in that chair, in his mind, showed all of the other people in the casino, from the bosses and dealers to the players and guests, that he was an important person.

Once when Landy was in the chair, Duckworth and Howie Engel, two major owners of the Dunes, approached the baccarat entrance and talked to one another. Then Duckworth, the acting casino manager, yelled across the pit, in front of the crew, "Landy, let me tell you something. You do that again and you will be sorry!" Duckworth was so mad that the veins in his neck appeared about to burst. He was enraged like the crew had never seen before. Whatever Landy did, it was disrespectful to Duckworth and was likely meant to undermine him in some way. Chances were that what Landy did was point out to Shenker, in a manner meant to belittle Duckworth, a casino decision or policy rendered by Duckworth. That was a no-no.

By his admonition, Duckworth told Landy that under no uncertain terms would he tolerate his behavior, no matter how much influence he had with Shenker. When Duckworth finished his tirade, he turned to Engel and said, "Come on, Howie!" then grabbed Engel's arm and led him away. Inadvertently angry, Duckworth nearly pulled Engel's arm off of his body. Duckworth, who stood at 6 feet, 2 inches and was in great shape, towered over Engel's diminutive 5-feet, 7-inch frame.

The entire baccarat crew rarely ever saw anything like this. It embarrassed Landy. Though he did not explain what made Duckworth irate, the staff knew that it had to have been a serious indiscretion. Landy's embar-

$200,000 previously advanced to Kahn. This agreement also authorized another entity controlled by Kahn, the Kahn Organization, to act as Wyman's and Rich's agent in operating and managing ECB, in return for a fee of 50 percent of ECB's net income. After April 1967, Wyman and Rich paid this fee to the Kahn Organization, but it appears that Penasquitos continued to play some role in ECB's operation."

rassment showed that he was not an ally of Duckworth. Because Shenker hired Landy, this was just another reason why Duckworth was not happy with Shenker. The employees clearly saw the rift developing and had to be careful not to get caught in the middle.

Based on information from a confidential informant, the FBI circulated the following memo that implicated Gottlieb's brother, John, in being involved with the Teamsters and Jimmy Hoffa when in reality, Jake Gottlieb was the one with those ties.

> On November 20, 1962, informant furnished the following information in the case entitled, "JAMES RIDDLE HOFFA, Home Service Corporation, Colonel JOHN O. GOTTLIEB, Miscellaneous - Information Concerning (Accounting and Fraud Section)," OO: Los Angeles, Bureau file 63-7179, and Los Angeles file 62-5136. Informant advised that GOTTLIEB has resided in Beverly Hills, California, for approximately two years and that GOTTLIEB owns the Globe Laundry in Los Angeles. Informant stated GOTTLIEB is very close to HOFFA and that during the last two years approximately $2,000,000 in cash has gone to HOFFA through GOTTLIEB. Informant described GOTTLIEB as a powerful man in the trucking industry and as a man who can fix a Teamster strike practically anywhere in the United States.
>
> GOTTLIEB is a close friend of FRANK MATULA, Los Angeles Teamster official and that GOTTLIEB and MATULA are partners in a number of business ventures in this area.

As mentioned previously, Jake Gottlieb purchased the real and personal property of the Dunes and vested it in Western Realty Company, which he wholly owned. He then leased out the casino.

Many years after leaving the Dunes, this author was interviewed by a prominent gaming writer, whose identity will be kept private, who specialized in gambling and Las Vegas. After the interview, while we were talking off the record, he asked me, "You worked the Dunes Hotel a while back?"

"Yes, I did."

"Did you know Sam Landy?"

"Yes," I answered, my facial expression changing upon the mention of his name.

"Sam Landy tried to get me to assist him in helping FBI agent, Joe Yablonsky, set a guy up."

"I am not surprised. He was a real creep and probably got someone to help him on the setup. I am proud of you not getting involved with that sleazy plan," I replied.

It is not a coincidence that Landy somehow was made the baccarat manager at the Dunes after Irwin Gordon was indicted and arrested for bookmaking. Also, it is no coincidence that Landy and Yablonsky lived in the same building, Regency Towers, at which the Dunes' alleged bookie operation control center was located. Gordon lived there as well.

There is no doubt that Landy fed every bit of information he could obtain about Gordon and Wyman to Shenker directly, or through Shenker's relative by marriage, Bob Amira. It is probable that Landy passed on to Yablonsky every single detail of any connection between the Dunes and Harry Claiborne. There is no doubt that Landy informed Shenker that Wyman employed one of Claiborne's daughters as a pit clerk for many years and then placed another daughter in the baccarat pit as a "break-in" dealer, both at the Dunes.

Wyman's baccarat manager Gordon personally asked this writer to teach Claiborne's daughter, in the back meeting rooms opposite the Sultan's Table, how to deal the game.

Gordon said, "Wyman would like you to teach Shirley how to deal the game."

"I will," this writer said.

She was immediately put on the game, and the crew carefully led her through the intricacies of the baccarat. She was a quick learner and soon could handle every situation. She was the first female baccarat dealer employed at the Dunes, and the crew realized it was a big advantage to have her on the staff. She was attractive, and the male customers loved her. The dealers were happy as their tokes (tips) increased.

If Shenker knew that Landy was a close associate of Yablonsky, there are two possibilities for Shenker's position on it. Shenker wanted that relationship to continue as it could be beneficial to him down the road. For instance, Shenker could perhaps leak certain information to Landy that put heat on Wyman, Gordon, and Dave Goldberg. Maybe Landy told Shenker that he could keep him out of trouble with the FBI in exchange for Landy helping Yablonsky get Claiborne. If that were the case, then Shenker would favor keeping Landy around.

The second possibility is that because he was previously linked to Rich and Wyman, Shenker wanted to get rid of Landy because he was informing the FBI.

One unlikely confidential FBI source was Leonard "Lenny" Shafer, who was the director of convention sales for the Dunes. An FBI report claimed that he "often utilizes the telephone in the coffee shop of the Dunes Hotel for business calls. He has, for the past approximately six years, been a symbol informant of the Las Vegas Office."[351] A symbol informant was one to whom the FBI attaches a code for identification so that their name is kept secret.

---

351   FBI File, DOCID-32140935, March 30, 1964

Another FBI memo references a confidential informant, who may or may not have been Shafer:

"LV 25-C advised SA M.B. Parker on 9/26/62 that the Plan-It Travel Agency, 6931 West North Avenue, Oak Park, Illinois, which is owned by Anthony R. Accardo, son of well-known hoodlum Anthony J. Accardo, and Robert Nitti, son of the old-time hoodlum Frank Nitti, have booked a short convention into the Dunes Hotel, Las Vegas, for an organization known as the Oak Park Fellowship Club. CI advised that this is composed of only those individuals of Italian extraction.

"CI advised that the group is scheduled to arrive sometime on 10/3/62 by chartered aircraft. They will be in Las Vegas for approximately two days.

"CI advised he had received a call from Nitti that in addition to the usual room reservation, he desired a deluxe suite reserved for a 'VIP.' CI stated that he is not sure but he believes that Nitti stated the name of the VIP was Sam Mooney [Giancana].

"On the morning of 9/26/62, in the presence of SA Parker, LV 25-C telephonically contacted Nitti to confirm that the deluxe suite had been reserved, and CI asked Nitti what name should be used in making the reservation. Nitti replied to reserve the deluxe suite in his name. CI replied, 'We can do that but do I know the individual who will be using it?' Nitti replied, 'You might know him. You'll see him when he gets there,' and would make no other statement.

"CI is departing Las Vegas on 9/29/62 to Chicago and points East on convention business and he made a definite appointment to see Nitti in Chicago on the morning of 9/30/62, and at that time will obtain a definite arrival time for the group to reach Las Vegas on the basis that the Dunes Hotel has to provide transportation from the airport to the hotel. Upon ascertaining the arrival time of the chartered aircraft in Las Vegas, CI will telephonically contact SA Parker from Chicago, at which time he will furnish same and the identity of the individual to use the deluxe suite if he can determine the same.

"Las Vegas, upon receipt of the information of the arrival of the aircraft, will take appropriate steps to attempt to identify all of those individuals arriving. If possible, photographic surveillance will be instituted and copies will subsequently be furnished to Chicago. Chicago, if any information developed as to identity of any individual planning to make the above-described trip, should advise Las Vegas since same will be of benefit in attempting to identify those individuals."[352]

There is no positive identification of this informant but it is highly probable that it was Shafer because of the personal service and communication that were given to a Chicago hoodlum's son, Robert Nitti. It is also possible that a second person in the Dunes convention sales office was an informant. It is also very probable that the convention reservation was referred to the Dunes convention sales office by a Dunes owner who was familiar with the principal, Giancana. A lower level employee in the sales office would not have been given this assignment.

Shafer was approved for a 1 percent interest in the Dunes by the Nevada Gaming Control Board in August 1964. What was interesting, though, were the comments made by its chairman, Edward Olsen:

> "Item 64-88, Leonard Shafer seeks a 1% interest in the M&R Investment Company doing business as the Dunes Hotel. Whose phrase was the 'elastic tongue?' Was that yours, Andy? Well, Mr. Shafer otherwise seems to be satisfactory, however."
>
> **Charles LaFrance**: "You mean you have not met Mr. Shafer, Mr. Chairman?"
>
> **Olsen**: "Oh, yes, I've met Mr. Shafer. You have heard the motion and its second, all in favor say 'Aye.'"
>
> **Ned** Turner: "Aye."
>
> **W.E. "Butch" Leypoldt**: "Aye."
>
> **Olsen**: "Aye. No opposing vote, the motion is carried."

What were the commissioners referring to by suggesting that Shafer had an elastic tongue?

What did they mean by that? Did he do a lot of talking? Maybe. To whom? The FBI.

CHAPTER 52

THE DUNES:
PAUL LAXALT AND HOWARD HUGHES

In the late 1960s Sidney Wyman walked into the Dunes blackjack pit, stopped at every table, and had a short chat with each dealer. The Dunes dealers had a secret signaling system that was started by the Cuban dealers in the pit. If a dealer said the word, "paco" or "pacone," it meant to watch out and be on your best behavior. In this case the code words were "pacone grande," meaning the big boss was coming around.

Wyman stopped at this writer's table and said, "Geno. Do me a favor, and vote for Paul Laxalt."

In November 1968, Nevada Governor Paul Laxalt said, "Corporate ownership would be the salvation of Nevada gaming. It would minimize the so-called underworld taint and provide financing for the industry." Laxalt also predicted that Nevada would become the tourism center of the world in the next 10 years. He was right on both counts.

Laxalt was the recipient of many political contributions from figures with links to organized crime, according to an article in the *Wall Street Journal*.[353] The newspaper could not find any illegal conduct on Laxalt's part in an extensive investigation of his life. Rather, the article noted: "What it does provide is evidence of his long and continuing associations with men alleged to have unsavory ties. And it raises serious questions about the judgment of a man who advises the president."

The article named some of Laxalt's associates. Moe Dalitz, then 83, was a Las Vegas developer and casino landlord identified in a 1978 California Organized Crime Control Commission report as a major underworld figure. Laxalt simply called Dalitz a longtime political supporter. Other political supporters named in the article included Charles Baron, a Las Vegas casino employee described by state and federal authorities as an associate of underworld figures; Sydney Wyman, who died in 1978 while awaiting trial on bookmaking charges; and Allan D. Sachs and Herbert Tobman, casino owners described by the FBI as fronts for the Chicago crime syndicate.

A *Sacramento Bee* story by seasoned investigative reporter Denny Walsh started a hailstorm of controversy for Laxalt. The opening statement in the article hurled a claim that made headlines, turned heads, and probably stimulated attorneys' fees in the thousands of dollars. The sentence read:

> "Substantial sums of money were illegally skimmed from the proceeds of Carson City's Ormsby House Hotel Casino during the time it was owned by Paul Laxalt, now the powerful senior U.S. senator from Nevada and head of President [Ronald] Reagan's re-election campaign, according to federal tax agents who gathered the evidence 10 years ago."[354]

This writer interviewed a local gentleman by the name of Bernie Sindler, who was a former owner of the Frontier and the Silver Slipper, both in Vegas.

"What happened at the Frontier with Paul Laxalt?" this writer asked. Sindler replied, "Very simple. We were applying for a license and one day I was asked by Maury [Friedman] to go to the Tropicana Hotel and give a large manila envelope to Paul Laxalt. Maury said there was $25,000 inside. I looked into the envelope, and there certainly was more than $20,000 inside. I did not count it, and Maury did not seal it, other than the metal clasp that held the lid [flap] together. Maury told me we were having trouble getting our gaming license for the Frontier, and we had to take care of Paul Laxalt to straighten things out. I went to room number 519, knocked, and said, 'Hi, I'm Bernie Sindler. I think you were expecting me.' I gave him the envelope, he said, 'Thanks' and I left. Soon we received our gaming license after being postponed several months on the Gaming Control Board agenda."

There is no proof to substantiate that what Sindler said was fact or fiction, however, this writer has a video recording of him making the statement. Sindler initially contacted me to write a book about his association with Meyer Lansky and used a "carrot" to entice me to do the work by saying that he had information about Mobster Johnny Rosselli that never was revealed. Sindler claimed that he, Sindler, fronted the money for a financial interest in the Silver Slipper casino for Rosselli. I researched this and deduced from all of the facts and information that I uncovered that there was a big ring of falsehood to it. I confronted Sindler about it. He finally admitted that it was not true and that he told me the lie to enhance his book sales.

---

354   *The Sacramento Bee*, Denny Walsh, Nov. 1, 1983

In another interview Sindler claimed that he and another MGM Grand employee embezzled as much as $1 million in airline ticket reimbursements. Based on the previous false information he gave about Rosselli, this new statement might also have been false, however, he openly furnished that name of his accomplice, who was alive at the time of my interview with Sindler, unlike Rosselli, who was murdered.

Sindler also gave permission for the FBI to release to me information about him through a Freedom of Information Act (FOIA) request. This document alleged that he was approached and cooperated with the FBI in the Frontier hidden ownership prosecution and was being groomed to be an informant.

In July 1970, Sindler was called to the grand jury as a witness in an investigation into hidden interests in the Frontier.[355] According to a *Los Angeles Times* article, "… Bernie Sindler, a former stockholder in the Frontier Hotel-Casino on the Las Vegas Strip, apparently testified at length, emerging from the jury room frequently to confer with his attorney. A fifth witness, alleged underworld figure Johnny Rosselli who is appealing convictions for card cheating at the Beverly Hills Friars Club and for violating alien registration laws, was excused from appearing."

Sindler told this writer,

> "I sat in the waiting room outside the Grand Jury room and recognized Tony Accardo and Paul ("The Waiter") Ricca; however, neither of us acknowledged the other. I'd met each separately years before via Johnny Rosselli. Any recognition would have been more problems for all of us.[356]
>
> "They wanted the names of the people who had met with Maury [Friedman] and Mal [Clark], and who had put the money up for the Frontier hotel. All I could tell them was that I was told that they were from Detroit. [Attorney] Adrian [Marshall] and I conferred several times, and he was finally called in to meet with the agents by himself. They told him that if I testified for the investor group, they would severely restrict my freedom to do anything outside Leavenworth. They didn't know they were doing me a great favor. That meant I couldn't testify for anybody. I couldn't testify for them or against them."

Another part of the FOIA document revealed that Sindler was approached to get information on Martin "Tiny" Levine, a very colorful employee at the MGM Grand who was very close to the top upper management.

355   *Los Angeles Times*, July 17, 1970
356   *The Hand You're Dealt*, Bernie Sindler, collaborated by Geno Munari, 2013

Sindler also stated that if the FBI came in and requested information on a casino customer, he retrieved the customer's credit file without a search warrant and allowed the agents to view it. I asked him, "How many times did you do this?" He replied, "Maybe 200 or 300 times."

My only regret is not informing my dear friend Al Benedict, MGM Grand executive, about these incidents before he died.

Another confidential source, who learned of Sindler's assisting the FBI, told this writer in an interview that if Benedict learned about Sindler's actions, "Sindler would have a lot to worry about, if you know what I mean! Not a promising future."

Another big backer of Laxalt was Ruby Kolod, who contributed more than $200,000 to have him re-elected after Kolod was put in Nevada's "black book" for threatening to kill Robert Sunshine over an oil venture. Wyman's former partner, "Ice Pick Willie" Alderman, and "Milwaukee Phil" Alderisio also were convicted. Kolod had so much influence on Nevada gaming that his and Alderman's names were subsequently removed from the "black book." This never before occurred in the State of Nevada, being included and then removed, except when an excluded person died.

Another big figure in Nevada's gambling industry, with ties to the Dunes, was Howard Hughes. In Jack Anderson's February 8, 1974 column titled, "Hoover Wanted Mafia out of Vegas," he wrote that he learned that J. Edgar Hoover wanted to turn the Dunes over to Hughes, hoping that would rid it of its underworld influences. While the column centered on the Dunes, nowhere did it specify which Mafia group to which Hoover was referring.

Hughes decided that he wanted to live in Southern Nevada and got his sights set on the Dunes.

In 1966, Hughes' Nevada executive, Bob Maheu, came to Las Vegas to arrange for a place for Hughes to reside, one that pleased the eccentric millionaire. Maheu was referred to the Dunes through his relationship with Johnny Rosselli, who was a friend of Wyman from the Sands. Through Maheu, the CIA recruited Rosselli and Sam Giancana to assassinate Fidel Castro.

George Duckworth, the Dunes casino manager and a points holder, showed Maheu around the newly remodeled casino, pointing out the improvements in the wall coverings and chandeliers that adorned the expanse in colossal style. It was obvious that Duckworth was selling, and Maheu was the patient prospective customer listening to the sales pitch. Duckworth was excellent in his presentation.

Rumors quickly spread throughout the casino and the hierarchy that Howard Hughes' No. 1 man in Las Vegas was spotted with Duckworth. The bosses in baccarat only knew that it was Maheu because Duckworth spread the word he was showing around a Hughes executive, not because they identified him from past association.

The potential reasons Hughes decided to move to the Dunes were varied. An obvious one was the impressive presence of the magnificent highrise; there was nothing in Nevada quite like it. It stood above the desert floor in beauty and magnitude. In fact, the McCarran airport control tower operators often used the Dunes as a reference point for large and small aircraft that were landing. "Report downwind over the Dunes Hotel" was a familiar Federal Aviation Administration order to pilots who were landing on runway 19. Perhaps Hughes made a mental note about the Dunes when he landed at the Las Vegas field.

He did land at the McCarran airport on many occasions and even kept a car in a hangar owned by fixed base operator George Crockett's Alamo Airways. Hughes also stayed at Crockett's home, which was just south of McCarran. Katie Crockett, daughter of George, recalled Hughes keeping food in the family refrigerator. A historical display of Alamo Airways with an airplane hanging from the ceiling is in the lobby area of McCarran airport in a fitting tribute to Las Vegas aviation.

Before Maheu came to Vegas, the Hughes advance team rented one of the top floors of the Dunes' 24-level high-rise. These best suites in the main tower, in which special telephones were installed at the request of Hughes, sat unoccupied but paid for, awaiting Hughes' arrival. It was widely talked about in the casino pit that the Dunes owners were unhappy with empty rooms, from which they were losing a great deal of play. Those accommodations could have been filled with regular gamblers, such as those that arrived with the New York junket twice a month.

The owners decided to curtail Hughes from continuing to rent the suites, and terminated their agreement. Hughes did not purchase the Dunes then, but why not? Perhaps his terms at that point were unacceptable to the behind-the-scenes Dunes powers that were. They were not going to take petty cash for an operation that brought the Dunes partnership millions in revenue.

If the Dunes did not end Hughes renting of the suites and he eventually moved in, he probably would have acquired the resort at an acceptable price.

Once the suites were again available to guests, they soon were filled with potential players.

Subsequently, Hughes moved into the Desert Inn and eventually purchased it. He also bought the Frontier, Landmark Tower, Silver Slipper, and Sands, all in Las Vegas.

Later, according to an FBI memo, Rosselli met with Dalitz at The Brown Derby restaurant in Los Angeles. Rosselli took an unidentified person, a heavy, with him, and Dalitz took Yale Cohen. Rosselli told Dalitz that he wanted the rest of the money that he said was owed to him for bringing the parties together in the sale of Dalitz's Desert Inn to Hughes. An informant who was in frequent contact with Rosselli told the FBI everything that Rosselli talked about. Rosselli had no idea that the person was an informant, and many sensitive subjects were leaked to the government from their conversations.

Regarding the legendary Frank Sinatra incident at the Sands, the FBI report told of Sinatra's wife, Mia Farrow, losing $20,000 in the casino. Sinatra was furious and lost another $30,000 trying to recoup her losses. He managed to get another $20,000 and lost all of it in a drinking, screaming, cursing episode with the employees that lasted 45 minutes. When Hughes heard of this, he immediately canceled Sinatra's casino credit, further fueling the crooner's anger. Sinatra went to his hotel room and destroyed it. He returned to the casino and tried to get more chips to play but was refused.

He grabbed one of the Sands' golf carts and drove it into the walls of the restaurant. Casino manager and part owner, Carl Cohen, tried to calm Sinatra, but Sinatra threw chips into Cohen's face and said some choice, disrespectful words to him. Cohen punched Sinatra in the mouth, causing him to lose two teeth. An FBI informant indicated that their impression was that the Sinatra incident was planned so that Sinatra could get out of his Sands contract and work at the new Caesars Palace.[357]

Hughes still wanted to purchase the Dunes, but by then, he reached the limit before he would violate anti-trust laws, and President Richard Nixon's justice department was scrutinizing Hughes' Nevada casino-hotel investments. Hughes sent employee Richard Danner, a former FBI agent, to Washington, D.C.

Danner was fired from his position as Miami's city manager in 1949 after the city council accused him of "playing both sides against the middle" in a gangland dispute over control of the police department. When Danner was Congressman George Smathers' campaign manager, Smathers introduced him to then freshman congressman Nixon. In the mid-1960s

---

357   FBI File, 92-6045-2141, September 1967

Danner went to work for Hughes as his liaison to Nixon. Danner introduced Nixon to Charles "Bebe" Rebozo, who became a pivotal character in the Watergate scandal.

"Everyone had a price," Hughes told a longtime employee, Noah Dietrich, who recalled that the billionaire "contributed up to $400,000 each year to councilmen, county supervisors, tax assessors, sheriffs, state senators and assemblymen, district attorneys, governors, congressmen and senators, judges, yes, and vice-presidents and presidents, too."[358] Nixon was one of the many beneficiaries of Hughes' largesse.

Danner scheduled a meeting with Attorney General John Mitchell and laid out Hughes' proposal to buy the Dunes. Danner had two private meetings with Mitchell, who eventually justified approving the Hughes purchase because then Governor Laxalt "was deeply concerned about the hoodlum infiltration of the hotel's casino – infiltration that the current owners couldn't control."[359] This last part of the quote is shocking and, perhaps intentionally, ambiguous, since Laxalt was very close to the Dunes major owners. The current owners were Continental Connector Corporation. About two weeks after receiving the green light, Danner delivered a second $50,000 to Rebozo for Nixon. Despite getting the okay to acquire the Dunes, Hughes did not go through with the deal.

Investigators for the Watergate Committee then believed that the Dunes issue and related "quid pro quo" was the motive behind the 1972 burglary of Democratic headquarters. Senate investigators contended that Mitchell tampered with the Dunes case. The theory is that the burglars broke in to open the safe of Democratic Chairman Lawrence O'Brien, photograph his papers, and tap his telephone line. This unsuccessful break-in subsequently led to the Watergate scandal and Nixon's downfall.

---

358   *Rolling Stone*, "Strange Bedfellows," Howard Kohn, May 20, 1978
359   *The Wall Street Journal*, May 6, 1974

CHAPTER 53

WYMAN AND
THE NEW YORK JUNKET CUSTOMER

Hustling – prodding a customer into giving the dealers tokes – was prohibited at the Dunes unless it was done discreetly and politely. If it was done in conjunction with providing good service, it was acceptable. Blatantly asking players for money, strong-arming them into paying, and making them feel uncomfortable were prohibited and grounds for termination.

One day, the baccarat table was full, and the customers were all betting on the Bank side and winning. I was dealing on the left side, Ron "Ronnie" Steinman was on my right, and both of us were dealing to six players with two outside players standing and making call bets.

Steinman was hustling a Jewish man, trying to get him to bet for the dealers. Steinman said to him in Yiddish something like, "A bissel gelt for the kindle-la," meaning "a little bet for the kids," or dealers. He repeated this a few times.

Suddenly, the player slammed a fist on the table, got up, marched out toward the dice pit to the junket master, "Big Julie" Weintraub, and spoke to him. The player was at the Dunes on one of Weintraub's junkets. Weintraub looked at us, over his reading glasses. I dropped my head, and Steinman remarked, "Oh, shit, we are in big trouble now."

Just then Sid Wyman, who overheard the conversation, approached Weintraub and the customer. At the top of his lungs, he yelled, "They did what?"

I told Steinman, "We are going to get fired over this one."

Steinman and I were busy, and sweat was pouring out of me. When I looked up, I saw the parade heading toward the baccarat pit. Wyman and Weintraub were fuming, and the customer was smirking. When they got to the baccarat pit, Wyman yelled at us, "Who do you think you people are? You will never hustle anyone in the Dunes again. You will never work in the State of Nevada," etc., etc., etc.

I was petrified. I looked up. Wyman continued his tirade for about five minutes. After, he started to walk away but turned back and said, "And another thing. I warned all of you before. This is it."

We thought that really was it. Our immediate floormen wanted nothing to do with us because they knew they were in trouble as well. When the shift ended, we went to the time clock office where employees punched out, expecting pink slips. There were not any, so we thought they just did not have enough time to prepare them. The next day, I went to work, again anticipating a termination slip, but, surprisingly, I was not given one when I clocked in for the day.

The floormen were icy; they would not speak to us. On my first break of the day, I headed for the dealer's lounge, taking the hallway that passed the main elevator of the Dunes high-rise.

As I was about to pass the elevator, a door opened and out walked Wyman. Wearing a bright reddish-colored baccarat blazer, I felt and looked like a target on a gun range. I could not avoid Wyman as he approached me. I put my head down but knew I had to acknowledge him when he got closer. Before I could say anything, he blurted loudly, "Morning, son," and walked right past me.

I never heard another word about the incident. But I learned my lesson.

CHAPTER 54

ELIAS ATOL AND
THE DOGNAPPING CAPER

This incredible story has to be told by keeping the now-deceased protagonist anonymous to protect their relatives. Herein, he will be referred to as "Joe Doe." Do not let the indifferent name dim your interest. This is a doozy.

Joe Doe was working as a break-in dealer in "Glitter Gulch," also called "Downtown," where all the so-called "sawdust joints" were erected on the road that led to the Union Pacific train station. Some of Las Vegas' original gaming casinos were built on both sides of this active gaming area. There were not many fancy hotel rooms and gourmet restaurants in these small, smoky casinos that dealt 10-cent chips to gamblers.

Many of the players were unsophisticated but knew every angle of cheating and stealing from casinos. They were a band of scammers, swindlers, and cheats. They were sometimes banned from play for past posting, taking one-time shots on a roulette wheel claim, or claiming that a slot machine did not pay out when it should have. They were not welcome in every casino, only at the California Club. They could drink, gamble on the square, and hang out as long as they did not cross the line. They used the place to dream up their next scheme.

Break-in dealer jobs paid minimum wages and sometimes tips. If the tips amounted to $5 during a shift, it was considered a banner day. A person could hardly make a living and meet his bills, which mandated that workers share apartments, use the limited bus routes, and carpool. Money was short and times were tough, but the goal of getting a lucrative job on the famed Las Vegas Strip made it worth it.

Doe was a likeable, former New York policeman who moved to Las Vegas. He could talk the talk, walk the walk, and was extremely amiable, however, he struggled like everyone else. His wife worked as well and helped keep the family, a couple of children and a dog, together. Doe loved his family's dog.

One day, Doe spotted a man walking a dog. Doe immediately saw that something was different about the man. After all, Doe was a former cop whose street sense and wits kept him alive in New York City, where survival was a way of daily life.

An associate of Doe told him that that the dog walker was Elias Atol, one of the owners of the Riviera.

Atol was a seasoned Las Vegas hotel operator, first as an executive with the Eldorado Club in 1947 and then as co-owner of the Flamingo. After he sold his interest in the Flamingo in 1954, he purchased a portion of the Riviera in July 1955. He was president, secretary-treasurer, and chairman of the board for the Riviera until he sold his stake in 1965. Afterward, he joined the staff at the Aladdin under the leadership of Milton Prell in 1966.

Atol was a partner of Sidney Wyman, Charlie Rich, Gus Greenbaum, "Ice Pick Willie" Alderman, Dave Berman, Ed Miller, Ross Miller, and Bernard "Bernie" Nemerov. They all were fronts for hidden interests in the Riviera. Atol was the front for the Chicago Outfit.

Bingo! Doe realized how he could land a lucrative Strip job. He snatched Atol's dog, the center of Atol and his wife's world. Their dog was like a child that they nurtured, fed, loved, and adored. There was nothing more important in their world. Money, fancy cars, vacations, and many other luxuries that a millionaire could buy meant nothing to them. The dog was their life.

The full details of the caper could lead to Doe's identity, so here is what can be revealed. After the dog-napping, Doe waited for a notice about the missing dog to be posted or printed in the newspaper. In the meantime, he kept the dog well fed and cared for. Sure enough, the following day, a "dog lost" want ad appeared in the newspaper. Doe waited a day then answered the ad. This resulted in an almost instant meeting between the two parties, at which Doe returned Atol's dog, which was in good shape, to him.

Atol asked Doe many questions about finding the dog, which Doe answered cautiously. Thrilled that he got his dog back, Atol insisted on buying Doe a meal. "I would love to have lunch with you, but I will be late for my blackjack audition," Doe told him. "I am trying to get a job."

"You need a job?" Atol asked. "I have one for you at the Riviera if you can deal blackjack.

Meet me at the hotel tomorrow."

"Okay, thanks, Mr. Atol. I will be there," Doe said.

When Doe showed up at the Riviera, he was introduced to the day shift manager and given an apron and a shift schedule. He began work there as a dealer the following day.

After a few days, Atol checked on the dealing ability of his new hire and seemed pleased with the reports that Doe was a good clerk. Atol did not want any ill feedback from his Riviera partners.

Atol had a daily routine of eating lunch in the executive booth in the Riviera's coffee shop. The other bosses congregated there and swapped stories about the hotel-casino, discussed business, and entertained pals. This exclusive off-bounds table was equipped with a private telephone and was persona non grata to anyone unless they were invited.

One day, Atol phoned the blackjack pit and requested that Doe be sent to his booth. The shift manager obliged, and Doe became Atol's guest for lunch. Atol was so pleased that Doe returned his dog, he felt he could not do enough for this seemingly innocent young man. Atol bent over backwards for Doe. This surprised the bosses at the Riviera because Atol was not someone who warmed up to just anyone. They thought his doing so with Doe was unusual.

Soon, Atol promoted Doe to a floorman position and summoned him to his lunch table every day. Because Doe was now a regular at the executive table, he began meeting and getting to know the Riviera's other owners and bosses. Doe mixed well with these different casino personalities and held his own in conversations. He was accepted into the group.

One such regular visitor to the group was Al Bramlet, who was the chief of the Las Vegas Culinary Union. Bramlet knew who the boss was at the Riviera, to whom to buddy up – Atol, the president. As the chief administrator, Atol signed all of the Riveria's contracts.

Bramlet discussed and made deals with Atol and proposed investments that were potentially enticing to Atol and his associates, particularly since he controlled the Culinary Union's million-dollar pension fund. Bramlet had to be careful, however, with any deal he made involving union funds that they could not be traced back to him. This was because such deals included kickbacks and simple fee interests in construction projects and land acquisitions.

Bramlet told Atol about a certain shopping center opportunity and said he could not be a part of it due to a conflict of interest with the Culinary Union, which would provide the funds upon his approval. Bramlet needed a front man.

"I got the guy for you," Atol said. "Joe Doe."

Bramlet knew Doe from the daily lunches and agreed he would be the perfect "front man." Soon, the deal was codified by an agreement, and Doe had a small piece of the action as the front for the investment in which the hidden participant, Bramlet, would benefit.

Afterward, another deal came to Bramlet, and the same arrangement was made. Ultimately, many successful investments, as many as 12, were carried out in this way. All of them turned out to be choice real estate projects with substantial revenue.

Then the unthinkable happened. Bramlet was killed. In the contracts for the deals, Doe was listed as the only investor. He remarked, "I wonder who my new hidden partner will be."

However, a new hidden partner never showed up. This indicated that Bramlet did not share any of the opportunities with the Mob or any of his many wives. Consequently, Doe and his family became very wealthy through this portfolio of investments that were financed by the Culinary Union and facilitated by Bramlet.

Doe went to work at the Dunes in the mid-1960s after Wyman took over control of its casino.

CHAPTER 55

SAM ANGEL AND SID WYMAN

Sam Angel was a poker player and jewelry peddler whom Sid Wyman befriended. Wyman allowed him to display and sell his merchandise at the Dunes casino cage window which was in the hallway that led to the Sultan's Table. Because the Sultan's Table was the finest gourmet room in Las Vegas, customers were like a who's who of the world.

During the evening hours, Angel opened his jewelry cases to show rings, watches, gold bracelets, and trinkets, which caught the eye of gamblers, customers, and employees. Angel also offered staff members a good deal, and his prices were half of those in a legitimate retail store. He had no overhead or employees and unlimited inventory.

Angel pulled various stunts that entertained the dealers in the baccarat. One was producing a ridiculous looking, giant, oversized pocket watch that was a sight gag and saying, "It is time to make a bet."

Then he extracted from his coat pocket a $100 bill that was ten times the actual size, placed it on the baccarat layout, said, "Money plays," and waited for the crew to laugh.

He was known as a high-stakes poker player who occasionally played baccarat. Once, he came over from the adjacent cashier cage to the baccarat railing that separated the game from the crowd. He looked the game over and called out a bet (a call bet is the terminology).

"Five hundred on the Bank," he shouted. Angel lost the bet, sat down at the table, and called another bet to get even. He lost that bet as well. Angel said that he had $48,000 on deposit in the cage, and on checking, the money was there. He drew markers against the 48 grand, and lost everything except one $500 chip. He also owed $500 in vig, or commission.

Angel looked to the floorman, held up his last chip, and looked at the commission marker he owed. It seemed he expected a favor of locking up, meaning removing the commission, and betting the last chip. The floorman obliged, which was proper in this instance because Angel just lost $47,500. The floorman would have been justified either way. Angel made his bet, and he managed to win back every bit of his money. Although the floorman was technically correct and acted on precedence, he never heard the end of it from the casino executives who heard about the incident.

One evening, Wyman was at the cage conducting some business, and Angel was nearby. "Sam, let me show you the diamond ring I bought for Loretta," said Wyman in a jovial and rather loud voice. Certainly he was putting on for the baccarat crew, showing off.

Wyman pulled his lock-box key out of his pocket and gave it to the cashier. The box was brought over to the window under the cage bars. The lid of the box nearly opened itself from the pressure of cash that was stuffed into it.

"Sam, look here, the ring is here somewhere," shouted Wyman. "Put your arms out and hold the money until I find it."

Angel held out his arms, and Wyman started piling the cash onto them. Angel had to use his chest and chin to keep the money from falling on the floor.

"It is here somewhere. It is a 22-karat stone," Wyman said with an obvious grin.

Angel held at least $1 million, in numerous $10,000 bundles, while Wyman repeated over and over that the big diamond was in the box somewhere and emphasized the huge amount of money in Angel's arms. Then Wyman found the ring. Angel's eyes popped open when he saw it. Wyman put the ring on his pinky finger, held it to his own eye, and said jokingly, "Something in my eye, Sam?"

Wyman was not bashful about showing off the cash that was stored in a lock-box, for which he had the only key. Lots of people were watching – the cage employees, the baccarat crew, customers, and the FBI agents, some incognito and others not, who were in the hotel constantly, farming their informants and acquaintances.

CHAPTER 56

SPRINGFIELD SAM MANARITE

While I was a dealer at the Dunes, my friend Dominic Manarite wanted to get into the baccarat pit. I realized that he started working in the casino there long before I did, and I helped him in every way I could. His dad hung around the place and was associated with the Boston junkets. His name was Sam Manarite, and he was also called "Springfield Sam."

Sam was a Mobster with felony convictions dating back to the 1940s, including "assault with a deadly weapon, money laundering, conspiracy, transporting obscene materials, and suborning perjury. In 1970, he was convicted of extortion in New York, where the judge called him 'the ultimate manifestation of success for criminals.'"[360]

Sam was playing 21 at the Dunes one afternoon, and Dominic was dealing on the table next to him. Dominic got into a beef with an unruly player, a wise guy, and words were exchanged between them. Sam overheard their interaction and jumped right into the argument. Before one could blink, the dispute got physical. The player was about to really hurt Sam, so Dominic set down the card deck and rounded the table to help him. A cocktail waitress was at the table serving drinks. Dominic grabbed a coffee pot off of her tray and hit the player in the head with it.

Eventually, the fight was broken up, and Dominic went back to work like nothing happened. Can you imagine if something like that happened today?

Later that year I was walking into the coffee shop for a 20-minute break during my shift. Sam came up, walked with me a bit, and said, "You better get Dom into the baccarat or you won't be too happy." He grabbed me by the collar, shoved me up against the wall, and repeated the remark. I pushed him off, and he casually walked away. Someone saw the incident and reported it to Irwin Gordon, who asked me what happened. I told him.

After that, I never had another problem with Sam, and in fact never saw him around the Dunes again. And Dominic never got a chance to work the baccarat pit.

Only at the Dunes.

Much later, in 2002, after going in and out of prison, 84-year-old Sam allegedly opened fire at Astro Auto Sales in Las Vegas, where his son reportedly bought a car. The owner got hit in the wrist.[361] Consequently, Sam faced attempted murder charges.

361   *Ibid*

CHAPTER 57

DAVEY WEINSTEIN'S GIFT

D ave "Davey" Weinstein was a nephew of two legendary Las Vegas gambling experts, brothers Murray and Herbie Saul. These guys were old-time classics who learned their trade from working for top-notch racket bosses their entire career. One of the original owners of the Riviera in Las Vegas, Murray was weaned working at Ben Marden's Riviera in New Jersey and dealing roulette in Cuba. His brother Herbie was right behind him. Murray also was one of the founding points holders of the Moulin Rouge, the stylish Vegas hotel casino that was built amid the black community in Vegas' Westside.

Realizing the Saul brothers were honest, conscientious workers, Charlie Rich, Sid Wyman, and George Duckworth brought the Saul family to the Dunes.

In 1964, the brothers Saul got their nephew Davey Weinstein a job at the Dunes, but his manner and reputation were the opposite of classy Murray and Herbie.

Working as a blackjack floorman, Weinstein complained every day about his boss, Aaron Herman, but he was relatively nice to him face to face. Weinstein also was jealous and resentful that the dealers got tips and floormen did not. Dealers made an average of about $90 a day whereas floormen made about $70. Every morning each dealer received a small envelope with their name on it, inside of which were their zukes (vernacular for tips) from the previous day in crisp new bills. Weinstein could not wait to find out each day how much was in the dealers' envelopes.

He did not befriend any of the staff, only pretty cocktail waitresses and customers, but even those attempts of his were shallow. He often presented attractive cocktail waitresses with a dollar bill he folded origami style to resemble a winged goddess, believing that gesture alone would garner their friendship or get him laid. He never came to the defense of any of these so-called friends when he had the chance to. One dealer thought Weinstein had his tie color preference and shirt size on the back of his Dunes business cards. The dealers saw through Weinstein.

He really he was an internal terrorist. Weinstein's remarks, wisecracks, and bull definitely drew a line in the sand in the Dunes gambling pit. He was so annoying that all of the dealers and other bosses really disliked him.

One day, after listening to Weinstein belly up to a customer who sold color television sets, hoping the player might gift him one, the dealers decided it was "coup de Dave" time. It was time to shut him up.

Earl Brookner, a seasoned blackjack dealer, went to the local TV appliance store and found an RCA color television box in the trash bin. He and some of the other dealers found a rock that fit in the box and weighed about the same as a TV. They wrapped the box and even strapped it so that it looked as though it came right from the factory. They topped it with a red bow.

They delivered it to the Dunes bell desk and gave the bellman $20 to deliver it to "Mr. Dave Weinstein."

Later that morning the bellman approached the extremely busy pit and proclaimed to Weinstein, within earshot of the dealers and customers, that a giant, brand new TV was at the front desk for him.

During that whole shift, from 10 AM until 6 PM, Weinstein bragged about how a customer gave him a TV. He even asked a few of the dealers to help him load it into his car.

The next day, though, Weinstein was silent. No one heard anything about his new "TV." Only at the Dunes!

CHAPTER 58

WILLIE CUTLER AND TONY TEGANO

The classic 1960s Las Vegas casinos were not complete without interesting pit bosses and floormen. The bosses working in the Dunes in 1968 were for the most part all unique, had wonderful personalities, and could create their own special fun which some may describe as mayhem. I could not wait to get to work to see what crazy stunt or practical joke would happen on my shift.

The bosses' ability to manage the dealers and the customers was second to none. Their occasional frivolity might have given outsiders the impression that they were not capable, but any such notion was erroneous. They were sharper than a needle's point. They could immediately recognize hand muckers, past posters, daubers, and card counters.

The stories they relayed were sometimes better than Dashiell Hammett's detective novels or O. Henry's amusing surprise-ending tales in New York City.

On my first day at work, I met Willie Cutler, who grew up in Brooklyn playing stickball. He volunteered to show me where the dealers went on their breaks for coffee or food. I could figure this out myself, but he insisted.

Off we went to the coffee shop. He stopped at two open counter seats where employees were permitted to sit.

Cutler turned to me and asked, "You want coffee?"

"Yes, please," I replied.

The waitress, Betty, approached us to take our order. She was not the type of waitress I expected, especially when she popped off with, "I am not a mind reader, Willie. Take your time but hurry with your order."

My eyes opened wide. I had never heard this style of humor before. Cutler quickly barked back with, "Yeah, yeah, yeah, Betty. Turn your hearing aid up and bring us two cups of coffee."

I added some sugar to my coffee as it cooled. I picked up the cup, about to sip some, when Cutler placed a hand on the wrist of my arm holding the cup, and asked me a question. To answer, I had to set down the coffee, which I did. While I answered, he consumed some of his coffee.

When I again tried to take a drink, he asked me another question, this one about my experience dealing. So I again set down the cup and responded. While I talked, Cutler took some gulps.

This question and answer, coffee cup up and down bit went on a few more times. Then he said, "Great coffee. Come on, we got to get back to the pit. Our 20 minutes is up!"

I did not get even one sip of coffee.

Cutler put down a buck and told me, "Hurry, we'll be late."

Because I was the new kid on the job, I never realized that that routine in the coffee shop was a prank on Cutler's part. I was young and believed everyone at the Dunes.

Cutler was one of the great bosses, as was Tony Tegano, who was in the blackjack pit waiting to place me on a game. "How was your coffee?" he asked, the hint of a knowing grin just visible on his otherwise serious face.

CHAPTER 59

THE COWBOY WITH
DIAMOND-TOED BOOTS

For certain special events and holidays, the Dunes management wanted two baccarat games operating instead of the standard one table in a sunken pit near the casino cage. Increased room occupancy, more walk-in business, and capacity-filled junkets all meant more gamblers.

A real gambler, who knows the business and has qualified staff observing and dealing the game, can operate anywhere. Elaborate furnishings and décor are not necessary to create a game atmosphere. A hard core player just wants a place to play and the best possible odds.

So the owners decided to use a portion of the poker room, which was moved once before from its original position near the coffee shop entrance, for the extra baccarat setups. The space was equipped with two baccarat tables, a pit stand to handle the paperwork, and four high ladder chairs.

Cheaters who worked in tandem with one or more dealers preferred high volume times for executing their nefarious acts. A scam perpetrated by the outside, meaning a person or persons working solo without any help from the dealers (the inside), or a combination of the outside and the inside, would prefer a great deal of betting action and cash on the table game to hide their stealing.

In the 1970s the Dunes baccarat game usually opened with a cash bankroll of about $31,000; $1 chips and $500 chips were on the table as well. The $1 chips, called checks in gambling terminology, were used for change and never used for betting. The $500 checks were used when the betting amounts were $2,000 and higher. The checks were not as glamorous as snapping currency but allowed the game to operate faster, allowing more hands to be dealt per hour.

Plenty of action helped cover the swindling by the cheaters because they were not the only players that the supervisors had to watch. Often, smaller amounts of theft would not be noticed with a high volume of action on the busy game.

A big long weekend came around, and we had the temporary baccarat pit operating to handle the increased play. Business boomed, and the two games were constantly full. This writer was a floorman on the evening, or swing shift, and during that time, we were jammed with action. All 12 seats were used, and on occasion, there were outside bettors, too.

Just prior to the weekend, Casino Manager George Duckworth used his influence to grant the request of a casino host to have a Dunes dice dealer, R.J., transferred to the baccarat to learn the game. This transfer was a political one and happened without the seal of approval of Irwin Gordon, who controlled the baccarat. The host was an old friend of Duckworth, Sid Wyman, and Charlie Rich from their days working together at the Sands. Perhaps to justify the transfer, Duckworth used the pretense that baccarat needed another set of eyes on it.

In the mid-1970s, Nevada's gaming authorities banned the use of currency in baccarat to pay winning wagers. Instead, casino chips, called checks by the casinos, were used. So rather than there being $30,000 plus of cash on the table for an opening bankroll, there were long tubes of chips on the layout, like with blackjack.

During one particularly busy game, I was off of the chair standing close to the long end of the table, monitoring the action. A high roller whom I will call Mr. L was in seat number 8. He wore a cowboy hat and cowboy boots that had diamond studs on the toe tips. He made sure everyone saw the studs, as he was proud of them. When I met him, my "fraud intuition" was piqued. He was a little too friendly, and I sensed that he was a thief. Sometimes you can just smell a scam in the making. I purposely turned away from the game for a second or two and then, unexpected by the suspect, turned back. He was looking at me and then quickly looked away. Why was he watching me? This was definitely a "tell" with a capital T.

R.J., the new dealer, knew the player from craps, so I watched both of them covertly.

After a decision of paying and taking bets on the Bank side or the Player side, I glanced at the chip tray then started to get into the ladder chair. On looking again, I noticed that a group of about 40 or 50 black chips ($4,000 to $5,000 worth) in one tube was separated from and about two inches higher than the others. The dealer quietly and nonchalantly put the chips back into their correct position to form one interrupted row. That allowed me to calculate the number of chips in the tube.

Instinctively, I knew that the dealer was going to hand off those chips to a player, so I thought I would set a trap in advance. However, I turned away as I got into the ladder chair, and when I quickly turned back, I saw that the tube was missing chips and that they were not on the table. I looked at everyone. The dealer calling the hands (stickman or caller) was making sure everyone had their bets down, and the other dealers were making change and getting ready for the next decision. Mr. L was stuffing something into his right coat pocket.

A full game played out, and when the action started to settle, Mr. L quietly stood and walked into the main casino area. I pondered how I should handle the situation. Were the other dealers in on it, too? Were other players in on it, and should I try to find that out? Also, R.J. just went on his 20-minute break. Gordon was not present that evening, Duckworth was not available, and I did not want to tip off any of the cheaters. I did not have any hard proof, just what I saw.

And I was busy, with the paperwork after the play, and another good honest customer wanting a reservation. Twenty minutes went by rapidly. R.J. came back into the pit and prepared to call the game.

I was furious that he made the move at my observation station. I wanted to punch the jerk. I called him over, and he looked like he was going to panic. I said, "Nice move. Why did you do that in front of me?"

He sort of stammered and acted like he did not know what I was talking about. He went back on the game. I planned to let Duckworth know the next day what happened.

The following day, I went in and found out that R.J. had himself transferred from the baccarat.

CHAPTER 60

THE GUN INCIDENT

The Dunes had a men's washroom that was a classic operation. The attendant, Lonnie, was an interesting black man. A born hustler, he knew exactly how to hustle a toke from every customer. When you washed your hands, you saw a small money tray behind the sink, for bills, coins, and chips. As you were about to get a paper towel to dry your hands, he handed you a linen cloth, and you could not refuse it. You were practically forced to leave a tip, merely by the prospect of being embarrassed by not giving one, and especially after drying your hands with his fancy towel.

If you told Lonnie that you did not have any change, he countered, "I have change right here." He could break any bill with the pre-counted change in each of his four trouser pockets, one for each denomination – $100, $20, $10 and $5. The small counter trays had coins in them to give the idea that no amount was too small.

In the restroom, Lonnie had every brand of cologne, mints, mouthwash, razor, and whatever else a man needed to spruce himself up. There were ice cubes in the urinals, and even a first-class shoe shine stand that generated a ton of cash. He walked down the avenue of stalls reminding customers to please flush the toilets, as if he was trying to put a guilt trip on them.

One day I walked into the mini-corporate bathroom for a shine. The attendant took my suit jacket and hung it on a solid wooden hanger. I got into the chair. He cleaned my shoes, applied polish, and began to spit shine with his cloth. Aaron Herman, the 21 shift manager, who was the best friend of Pete Licavoli, Detroit's No. 1 Mafia kingpin, stepped up to the sink to wash his face and hands. He talked to me by looking in the mirror that stretched across the wall and made the room look twice as big. He said, "Hi, kid."

Herman was a sharp ex-bookie who ran several gambling operations in Detroit. There was not much about the gambling business that he did not know, and he was well respected.

His wife, Eda Schivo, is this writer's cousin, and the couple had two children, Andrea and Jeffery. Young Jeffery drowned at a boarding school in Arizona. That was a horribly sad day for everyone who knew the family. This writer was in the pit when the news arrived. Terrible day. Things never returned to normal for Herman or his family.

Herman could smell a thief in the room. He either liked someone or did not, meaning either he talked to them or didn't.

Then into the restroom walked Murray Lang, who was recently brought in to the Dunes by Howie Engel from Miami Beach, as a favor to some wise guy, and placed in the role of casino host. Lang was not Mr. Warmth to any men, only women. Herman did not particularly like Lang, and the two had several run-ins before. They made eye contact via the mirror.

Herman said, "What are you looking at?" It got worse from that point on. Words led to a shove, and soon after, Lang produced a small pistol and hit Herman on the head with it. There was a scuffle, and someone yelled, "Gun!" Everyone ran out of the bathroom, including the shoe shine attendant, who left the cloth and polish on my unfinished shoes.

I was stuck in the chair that was no more than four feet away. I tried to duck out of the line of any fire. Eventually Casino Manager George Duckworth and security came in, and Lang was fired.

Herman was angry at me for more than a year because I did not take away the gun when it appeared.

Only at the Dunes.

CHAPTER 61

LILLIAN SHENKER AND
THE BLACKJACK SKIM

The person who is trustworthy in very small matters is also trustworthy in great ones; and the person who is dishonest in very small matters is also dishonest in great ones. If, therefore, you are not trustworthy with dishonest wealth, who will trust you with true wealth?

– Gospel of Luke 16:1-13

After a string of bizarre events, I was fired from my job as a baccarat floorman at the Dunes, under Morris Shenker's control, in 1975. Until that day, I thought that I would retire from that very job.

While working at the Dunes, I became acquainted with Frank Kish, who practically lived in their poker room. Kish bet 20 dimes (one dime is $1,000) per game without blinking an eye. As well as a gambler, he was a good bookmaker, who learned his trade in South Bend, Indiana, near Notre Dame. He had unwritten privilege to make and accept sports bets at the Dunes, and was a frequent high-stakes poker player.

Kish remained under the radar of law enforcement and did not break any laws other than sports betting without a license. Bettor-players like him were commonplace in Las Vegas. In those days there were no big sports books in hotels. The betting action was on the street as it had been for years. It was all on the up and up, with relatively few problems.

There was plenty of business, and the Nevada Gaming Commission had no comprehension of its scope or of the amount of money being wagered day to day. Tuesday mornings, following the Monday night NFL game, was the time to settle up, for which bookie to bookie, bookie to player, and others involved in the intricate system of sports betting usually met at the Castaways Hotel, now the Mirage.

In 1964, Kish and several partners built the Skyline Casino on the Boulder Highway. Kish chose the name because he previously made a fortune in the stock market, cleaning up with a company by the name of Skyline Homes. John Ligouri and Joe Antonio were the casino gaming licensees whereas Kish and the others were the landlords. Skyline originally had about 54 slots, a couple of blackjack games, a bar, and a decent restaurant.

The operation, though, just could not make it, so the co-owners closed it and boarded up the building. In early 1975, the partners decided to sell the Skyline Casino, so they spruced up the outside, cleaned the inside, and opened the doors. Kish told everyone at the Dunes about the Skyline, hoping that the dealers and cocktail waitresses would visit and possibly have an after-shift cocktail and/or grab a bite to eat and maybe gamble there.

One night I went to see it because it always was my dream to own a gambling operation. I walked around looking for Kish and learned that he was out but would be back within the hour. To kill some time, I sat down, broke a $100 bill on the blackjack game, and played $10 to $15 a hand. In less than 25 minutes I was betting the limit of $50 a hand and won over $800. Then in walked Kish. I was somewhat embarrassed at the money that I won because I was not even trying; cards in my favor just kept coming. My $800 win put a dent in the night's gaming win at this little "joint."

I was interested in buying the Skyline – it was perfect – but the money I had would only cover 30 percent of the cost. Eventually, co-owner Ligouri promised me 30 percent if I went to work there in the pit, managing a shift.

My boss at the Dunes, Irwin Gordon, gave me permission to take a leave of absence to work at the Skyline and get a feel for the operation. Sid Wyman and George Duckworth agreed that I could give it a go as they considered buying it themselves. In the past, I told Duckworth about another property for sale, Empey's Desert Villa motel, perfect for converting into a casino. He intended to acquire it, but the deal did not go through.

The Skyline Casino deal did not work out either, so after about six months away, I returned to work at the Dunes, in January 1976. My previous job was not available, so I worked in the blackjack pit. One day, I was assigned to watch four tables, and the floorman next to me, Jimmy Thacker, watched four tables. Thacker was an experienced gaming boss and came from a family of experienced casino workers. He motioned me to look at one of his tables then walked over and quietly told me to watch the play at it, which I did.

The dealer, Fred Perlove, broke the hand and paid the players. However, instead of paying them even money, he paid two of the players even money and topped off their bets with an extra stack each. The payoff to each was double what it should have been. I moved in to take action, but Thacker mentioned that the dealer was getting off in just a minute and

Thacker would handle the situation then. He did not take back the extra payoff right away because the recipients were Lillian Shenker, an attorney and former city judge, and her friend. Thacker knew who Lillian was, that she was the wife of the Dunes owner, Morris Shenker, and did not want to embarrass her in front of her guest.

Soon after, though, Thacker reprimanded Perlove and ordered him to never do that again. Perlove said he overpaid to help Lillian and her friend because Lillian was not winning and he felt sorry for her. Thacker was furious.

The main shift manager, Aaron Herman, saw Thacker and me huddled with Perlove, came over and asked what happened. Herman, who did not tolerate acts like what Perlove did, fired Perlove on the spot. Perlove walked away and said with a grin, "You can't fire me. I will be back."

A week went by, and I was transferred back to the baccarat pit. My work life seemed back to normal.

About a month later, however, the new baccarat manager announced that Perlove was being placed in the baccarat pit as a floorman. I could not believe it. Perlove, who was seen stealing and got fired for it, now was not only back at the Dunes, but also promoted to one of the most prestigious and most profitable positions in the casino. This was a great job for a floor supervisor because he received a floorman standard wage and a full share of the baccarat dealers' tips.

It was tough for me, having to work alongside Perlove, but I maintained my dignity and kept my cool. I think that it really must have irked the other dealers at the Dunes that Perlove was rehired. It sent the message that the Dunes owner rewards those who steal for his wife's benefit. It was a bad, immoral precedent to set.

About a month later, I was on duty in baccarat when Nevada Gaming Control Board Agent Ernie Rivas approached me, flashed a badge, and asked, "Are you Geno Munari?" He handed me a subpoena, on which were the words: "In the matter of Fred Perlove."

After the theft, the Dunes' cadre of lawyers acted as lobbyists for Lillian. One of them was Jim Zimelman, who worked in the firm of Morris Shenker and was his attorney. He approached each of the supervisors who directly witnessed the incident and told them Lillian would never intentionally accept money that was not justifiably hers. The attorneys gave excuses for why she did so, from her not knowing she was given the money illegally to her not being able to see well out of one eye.

The poor eyesight alibi was similar to the one she used when charged with a traffic violation, which ended up in court. There, State Trooper J.B.

Upton testified that a bus, heading westbound, stopped at about 3:30 p.m. to let off some children. Lillian, heading eastbound in her automobile, drove past the bus.

The trooper said that "the bus' blinker lights were working, and the stop arm was extended," but Lillian, represented by Morris, testified that she did not see either of them. On cross-examination, Morris brought out that Upton did not inspect the bus equipment at the time of the offense to see if it was working properly. Lillian was found not guilty.

Regarding the blackjack incident, Shenker's lawyers continued lobbying the case in defense of Lillian. Their actions certainly could have been considered witness tampering and in violation of Nevada law. According to Nevada Revised Statute 199.230, "preventing or dissuading a person from testifying or producing evidence" has two central elements. The first is that the defendant act with an intent to obstruct the course of justice. The second is that the defendant use persuasion, force, threat, intimidation, or deception either to: prevent (or attempt to prevent) another person from appearing before any court (or person authorized to subpoena witnesses) as a witness in any action, investigation, or other official proceeding; or cause or induce another person to be absent from a legal proceeding or evade the process which requires the person to appear as a witness to testify or produce a record, document, or other object.

In other words, it was unlawful to bully or deceive a potential witness into not providing evidence or testifying in a case. It was irrelevant whether the defendant's actions ended up having no effect on the outcome. Simply, the action of intimidating or deceiving a witness was criminal in Nevada.

Each one of us who was involved with the incident was called to testify and answer questions posed by the GCB. I did not lie, magnify, bear false witness, or confer with the other witnesses beforehand, and answered honestly as to what I witnessed. I could not refuse to go to the meeting, and even though I had a constitutional right not to testify, it would not have been a good move.

A month later George Duckworth called me into his office and asked me to resign or be fired. I was not given any reason for this or any information at all. I offered to take a polygraph test and answer any questions that they might want to ask. I had nothing to hide. I refused to resign, and Duckworth told me to go back to work. One day, after another week in the baccarat, I was told that it was my last at the Dunes.

Frank Fertitta, Sr., who later founded Station Casinos, was given my position in baccarat. When one of the baccarat dealers asked him why he was working at the Dunes, Fertitta replied, "I'm just passing through."

I applied with the Nevada gaming regulators for a non-restricted gaming license, which allows a casino to have more than 15 live table games with dealers and slot machines. GCB agent Mac Belmont instructed me to never mention the Dunes blackjack incident involving Lillian to any of the state's gaming authorities, but I was not given a logical reason why I should not.

When GCB agents started looking into my background in connection with my application, I learned that I was being secretly followed and my comings, goings, and other activities were being recorded by agents disguised as everyday citizens, all as part of a separate investigation, about which I knew nothing. They may have tapped my home telephone line and done who knows what else, I don't know.

It was scary, especially because, unlike the U.S., Nevada has no Freedom of Information Act through which one can obtain copies of the gaming authorities' records on them. Nevada law allows the Gaming Commission (GC) and the GCB to keep all files, investigations, reports, remarks, rumors, and any other materials they have on gaming employees and gaming license applicants completely sealed. Someone in the gaming industry can be accused of something and never be told any of the facts surrounding the allegation. In my case, I had and still have no rights under Nevada law to know the who, what, why, where, when, and how of the GCB's tracking and investigating me.

Later, the GCB agent working on my gaming license application asked me to bring by a document that was needed to finalize my request. I arrived at the GCB offices a little early, and the receptionist waved me over to my investigator's work area. As I rounded the corner to get there, I saw Sam Landy sitting there, talking to the investigator. I thought, What is he doing here? Shenker had recently hired Landy to replace Irwin Gordon as baccarat manager. When Landy saw me, he jumped up like a jackrabbit and said, stuttering and mumbling, "I, I, I was just passing by and just happened to stop by. Ah, ah, ah, see you later." Landy had to be involved somehow in my being terminated.

My application finally came up for a vote at a hearing of the GC, whose chairman was Harry Reid, from 1977 to 1981. He was thought to be the man behind the name, "Mr. Clean-face or Mr. Clean," which the FBI picked up in a conversation about "fixing" things with the state gaming authorities. Reid denied the allegations, and a five-month investigation cleared him.

Reid asked me why I was fired from the Dunes. Before I could answer, Commissioner George Swarts, in my defense, said that I was used as a "smokescreen" at the casino. I remember him using that specific word, but it was not in the official transcript of the meeting. Nothing more was asked or said, and the commission voted unanimously to grant me a license.

Little did I know that Reid and the gaming commissioners were well aware of Shenker's previous efforts to ruin my chances of getting a license. Reportedly, Shenker paid $4,000 to a fugitive, who had stolen more than $250,000 through securities fraud, to falsely accuse and falsely testify about me to Shenker and to the GCB. This mystery man claimed that I propositioned him to "take off" the baccarat game. I never exactly learned what was in or saw the statement of what this mystery witness said about me. I never was given a positive identification of the accuser. The GCB agent asked if I knew a Mr. Lewis.[362] I said that I did not know the man. But I did recall a Dunes customer and an incident involving lunch that was indeed a mystery to me.

There was a baccarat customer, about 33 years of age, whom this writer knew as Jim Reed. It was the duty of the floor supervisors to "cut in" to new players and offer them assistance with making dinner or show reservations, and obtaining other hotel services to help develop the gambler into a loyal Dunes customer. Reed and I seemed to get along well, as we had mutual interests in sports, snow skiing, and aviation. He had a very attractive, sandy colored and short-haired gal pal with him who Reed said was an airline attendant. When the baccarat dealing shoe was spent, there were a few minutes in which I could talk to customers, yet still observe the dealers shuffling the cards. During that time, Reed boasted about having a Learjet and flying it to Las Vegas often. He offered to take me for a spin on his next trip to Vegas. That certainly roused my attention. The date to expect him, which I noted on my calendar, was exactly two weeks from the day we spoke. He said he would call when he arrived.

However, that day came and went without a call. That should have been a clue to me, but the chance to fly in a Learjet was the dangling poison that kept me from suspecting that Reed was a fraud. I just figured something serious must have prevented him from coming or at least calling me. He told me his line of business was the trendy bar and restaurant chain, Bobby McGee's.

---

362   Lewis is a pseudonym due to this writer's lack of memory.

Two weeks later Reed called and invited me to lunch. He said that I should pick the place and that he would meet me there. I suggested Nishon's owned by Nish Kerkorian, today Chateau Vegas. At lunch, Reed told me of a mechanical problem he had with his airplane on the day we were supposed to fly and apologized for not notifying me. We made small talk about our mutual interests until he asked me, "Could you get me credit at the Dunes Hotel?"

This was the first time he or I ever talked about the Dunes. The question sent double red flags into my brain.

"I wish I could help you but only the owners of the hotel can approve casino credit after you apply formally at the casino cage," I said firmly, yet politely.

He seemed disappointed and that was about the end of the conversation on the topic. We shortly left and I never saw or spoke to the man again.

Despite knowing his history, the GC refused to censure or penalize Shenker for framing me, for his handling of the blackjack theft incident at the Dunes, or for trying to influence the witnesses.

The GCB has all of the inside details and the identity of the accuser but will not allow me, by Nevada statute, to learn what exactly occurred.

Despite the injustice concerning this incident, I survived. Surprisingly, many years later, I was given the highest compliment by Duckworth, who was right in the middle of the situation. He and his close friend Irwin Ross, a former Dunes host, on two occasions wanted to invest in my business. The two of them showed me that they respected what I did and trusted me. That meant more to me than any amount of money on this planet.

CHAPTER 62

THE DUNES: CURLY, RAZZ, KEM CARDS, & MOBSTERS

After Morris Shenker relieved me of my duties at the Dunes sometime in 1976, Jimmy Newman, a former Sahara stakeholder, arranged a job for me at the Flamingo. He was a friend of George Duckworth, who was the casino manager at the Dunes. I knew Newman from the Sahara. My cousin Frank Schivo, who was Milton Prell's protégé, gave Newman a big break in the gambling business.

In those days, as today, if there was a problem with an employee, the word got around and a "jacket" was put on that person. A "jacket" was basically a "bad rap" or "NG," meaning "No Good," which indicated the employee was not a good risk for a casino. Word spread quickly in the industry about someone's reputation and if a person had a no-hire attached to their name, it was near impossible for them get another casino job.

While I was working at the Flamingo, an opportunity arose to buy into a small business in Henderson, Nevada, named the Drug Store Tavern. I later bought out my partner, applied for a non-restricted Nevada gaming license, and opened with two blackjack games, one poker, slots, four pool tables, and a 66-foot-long bar. In 1979 I renamed the place Cowboy Gene's Casino. It was a grind.

I purposefully relaxed all of the rules for blackjack players, which drew the interest of the local card counters. They played right into my slack rules. Buzz traveled around that Cowboy Gene's was an easy target. Comments about how "easy" the game was were even published in a local "mailman's" blackjack newsletter. If they only knew the truth, that this was what I had hoped would happen. This strategy worked for me, and if I was going to open another casino, I would do the same thing but more of it.

One Saturday I arrived early to do some paperwork, do the hard count, and make sure everything was in order for the day and evening shifts. In walked Curly, who worked in the Dunes high stakes poker games and who still gambled, drank, and chased all night after work. Curly would get busted (lose his money gambling) and stop off at my place for a nightcap or to borrow a "Cecil" or two. A Cecil is gambling slang for a $100 bill. Curly needed some cash and he knew he could always get a bill from me any time he asked. It was good business. This gesture is unheard of in to-day's casinos; owners will not give you the time of day if you need a quick bill or two. Instead of reaching in their pocket, they will give the lame ex-cuse that the state's gaming regulations do not allow the loaning of money to a player without the proper paperwork being filed. That is if you can even find an owner in a casino.

So on a subsequent Saturday morning, when Curly came in to repay me, he threw a deck of Kem playing cards on the bar top and said, "See if you can see the marks on these cards!"

Curly knew I liked the subject of marked cards and all the other gaffs that existed. He looked at me like he was thinking, "That dumb mother-fucker will never figure out this scam."

He was right. I picked up the cards and intensely scanned the back of each one. I flipped the deck like a cartoon flip book, looking for the marks to animate. I saw nothing. I was stumped.

He then asked, "What are you doing looking on the backs?"

I did not understand what the heck he meant. I looked on the faces but saw nothing on them either. Then Curly pointed out small scratch lines cut into the hair and face on all of the court cards – the Jacks, Queens, and Kings. The color and design of the hair on each side of the faces easily disguised the marks that were meticulously placed, typically with a razor.

Curly explained that those very cards were used at the Dunes. Curly told me that at the Dunes he took off many high rollers, even Major Rid-dle and many other Dunes owners, for Chicago Outfit enforcer, Tony Spi-lotro, and others.

The method, which went undetected for years in many card rooms, was extremely effective in the game of seven card stud low, or "razz," as the 12 altered cards hugely advantaged the cheater. When placing cards to the players, the person dealing could feel with their index finger the special markings on the face cards. The slightest groove enabled the dealer to dis-tinguish whether the card was a high or a low one. The dealer could then signal the value of the player's hole card, the one dealt face down.

CHAPTER 63

THE BIG BACCARAT SCAM

O ne evening in 1981, the graveyard baccarat shift was quiet at the Dunes until some players sat down to play. They were very chatty, talking with everyone else at the nearly full table, and we were conversing with them. At first the play was normal.

In baccarat, players make their bets, and two separate hands are dealt, one for the Player side and one for the Bank side. Initially, the two cards are alternately given to each hand. The dealer who is conducting the game adds the values of cards and subtracts all 10s from it. For instance, a total of 13 would be 3, and a hand of two face cards would be 0. The hand that is closest to 9 is the winner. Depending on the total of each hand, specific baccarat rules call for a third card for either hand. There also is a tie bet proposition that pays 9 for 1. Then the losers' money is taken, and the winners are paid.

The Bank side has a slight advantage of winning. To compensate for that edge, the house charges a 5 percent commission on all winning Bank side bets.

Players must place all bets before the cards are dealt, but as a courtesy, a player may switch his bet once before any cards are exposed, for whatever reason. No player should be allowed to switch their bet repeatedly.

In this game that night, suddenly one or two of the players changed their bets more than once, sometimes after the first card was dealt, sometimes after all four cards were dealt. In the initial deal, two cards are dealt for the Player side and two cards for the Banker side, then according to the rules, which depend on the totals of the hand dealt to each, the Player side (place to wager on like red or black in roulette) and/or the Banker side may get another card for a maximum of three cards each.

In this game that night, the dealer who was responsible for their bets previously was told by a higher up that dealers were not allowed to stop players from changing their bets.

"Can they switch?" the dealer asked the floorman.

"Yeah, they can, they can switch. You know the rules," the shift manager said then went on a break, disappearing for hours. He left two floormen (supervisors) or possibly one floorman watching the game.

"I'm not sure if he was there much of the time at all. He was trying to just duck everything," said Ray Goldsberry, a baccarat dealer on the game that evening.

Goldsberry added, "Shenker said do not stop the players from doing anything, these Asian players, because they are honorable people and they won't be cheating you. And that's when Dadi Darma was also telling Shenker how to treat the Oriental players. He's the one that allowed the man from Hong Kong that lost $1 million in about seven hours to get another $1 million credit. Then he didn't even make a bet. He just pulled the first card out of the shoe and looked at it very innocently and he says, 'Oh, I forgot to bet.' He pulled out a nine. So he put about a $1,000 bet on the players, and they said, 'It's all right. It's all right.' The floorman said, 'It's all right. It's all right. Dadi Darma okayed it.'

"Well, it took him about four hours to lose that second $1 million. And they [the baccarat boss] held over the graveyard shift. They wouldn't let us go home. He [the player] wanted the same dealers, so they wouldn't let us go home. The day shift dealers sat down in the break room, doing nothing all day and getting paid for four hours, until this guy lost the second $1 million. That's how all this came about," said Goldsberry.

"So now it was just a few weeks later that this man and a group of people came in and started playing and they seemed very, very, uh, uh, normal players for a while. Then they started the bet switching after a little while."

That very night, September 6, 1982, the Dunes baccarat was beaten out of more than $250,000 by the suspect group that changed their bets, however an exact amount could not be confirmed. After the Dunes reviewed the videotapes of the play, Shenker fired three baccarat floormen and four dealers. The Dunes also confiscated more than $465,000 of the suspected players' cash and chips that were in a deposit box in the cashier's cage.

The Nevada Gaming Control Board (GCB) investigated the incident and found no evidence of cheating. They took the confiscated money and chips. The GCB did notice irregularities in how the baccarat games were conducted, namely letting players switch their bets, which resulted from illegal policies set by the Dunes management. The rule change allowing the Asians to do whatever they wished was based on the greedy belief that the Dunes would win more money by having more Asians play.

A dealer who wanted to remain anonymous reported that Shenker and Darma allowed and encouraged the dealers to permit players to add or change bets after the first card was played but not after the first card was turned face up.

This was not the first time Darma or Shenker allowed irregularities at the Dunes gaming tables, as previously noted in this book.

The three accused baccarat players hired Attorney Hank Gordon to help get their money back and clear their names. He filed a civil suit on their behalf, asking that the cash and chips be returned to them. The Dunes countersued.

Both parties, however, reached a settlement, in which the Dunes was to return to the players $200,000 in cash. In exchange, the players were to return $130,000 in Dunes baccarat chips that the GCB took during their investigation. They also agreed to return $90,000 in Dunes chips that they had taken back to Hong Kong. Both sides agreed to drop their lawsuits, and they were formally dismissed by District Judge Charles Thompson, with each side paying their own legal fees.[363] Shenker publicly stated that that agreement was unfavorable to the casino.

Goldsberry, one of the dealers who was fired over the incident, also filed a lawsuit, contending that he was wrongfully terminated. He also claimed that it was the job of Baccarat Manager Paul Weintraub and Floormen Arland Smith, Dean Harrold, and Robert Gross to "watch, secure, and protect the game" and, thereby, keep Goldsberry from being fired.[364] Goldsberry did not sue Weintraub or the floormen, however. He only sued Shenker, Darma, and miscellaneous John Does.

Weintraub denied any involvement. He said that he was in bed sleeping in his Dunes room when the game was played, and thus, he should not be held responsible. Goldsberry's attorney Eli Leslie "Les" Combs, Jr. said that he did not mean to imply that Weintraub actually was supervising the game, only that he was the baccarat manager in charge and therefore responsible in absentia.

One of the fired dealers, Tom Dewey, was rehired because he tried to prevent the changing of the bets during the game.

This writer was called by Dunes Surveillance Manager George Joseph and asked to come over to look at the tapes. I was familiar with Joseph. My former baccarat boss Irwin Gordon was a dear friend of Joseph's uncle, James Tamer. Gordon and Tamer were convicted of illegal bookmaking in Terre Haute, Indiana. Joseph also was a friend of noted magician Jimmy Grippo. Grippo casually introduced me to Joseph at a convention for magicians.

Joseph learned that I recently detected a baccarat scam at the Imperial Palace, where I was working, which was similar to the one at the Dunes.

---

363   *Las Vegas Review-Journal*, Jan. 14, 1983
364   *Las Vegas Review-Journal*, Dec. 10, 1982

The Imperial Palace management decided that they wanted to open a baccarat game, and my job was to assist the general and casino managers with setting it up. During a few meetings, I advised them on the different ways that the game could be operated. I furnished rules and procedures that would safeguard the game against cheaters, both on the inside and on the outside.

Management asked if I would like to work in the baccarat game, and I accepted. I was told that I would be phoned to start soon. I waited and waited for the call, but it did not come. I called the casino manager, Joseph "Smokey" Claycomb, to follow up, and he told me that he did not have a position for me. I sensed that something was wrong. Immediately, I arranged a meeting with the two managers to see if I could possibly figure out why my services were suddenly no longer needed.

I soon learned that I was the only outsider who was considered for a baccarat position there. The rest of the crew was handpicked by the newly appointed baccarat manager, who lacked any direct baccarat experience in Las Vegas. He never was a floorman or even a dealer. I thought, *Does this person have the experience necessary for a high rolling baccarat game?*

Finally, I was hired at the Imperial Palace as a floorman. I had more experience in the game than anyone in the entire pit. I sensed though that I was an outsider. I was not treated as a part of the crew and felt unwelcome. From the moment I started the job, the baccarat manager gave me nothing but a hard time.

On opening night we had quite a bit of business for a new baccarat game, especially since the Imperial did not advertise its debut.

An interesting lady, adorned with expensive jewelry and donning the finest of garments, sat down to play. Even her name, Madame Yu, was intriguing. She was Asian looking and charming. She deposited $10,000 in the cashier's cage with which to play. Yu gave one the impression that she was a big player with a lot of money. The crew was happy to have landed a good, high rolling baccarat player.

Yu did have a lot of money, and she did play heavily, but something was off about her. Her purse was inexpensive and did not match her attire. Though she appeared Asian, the more I observed her, the more I was convinced that she was not, that she was trying to make us think she was.

Her play was hot and cold as far as where she placed her bets, meaning she played the Bank side and then suddenly switched her wager to the Player side or vice versa. Sometimes she switched in the middle of a hand, after the cards were already dealt. According to traditional baccarat rules, switching is not permitted after a card has been dealt from the baccarat shoe. Occasionally, a courtesy switch is permitted before any cards are exposed but never continuous switching.

Yu was tipping the dealers heavily, which is a common misdirect by cheaters. Money tended to blind the dealers and the floormen to anything out of the ordinary.

I felt that Yu was violating the rules, but the shift manager told me to let her play the way that she wanted. This went against the grain for me and was very dangerous for the house.

Finally, I noticed that every time that Yu sat down to play, two other gentlemen also joined and always in the same seats. One man was Asian, the other a redhead, both about 50 years of age. I grew suspicious and made every attempt to talk to all three of them to get the slightest clue as to what their scam was.

The redhead told me that he was a wall coverings designer. He even went over to the walls in the baccarat pit and talked as if he knew exactly the brand and manufacturer of the paper. He was a master of deceit. The Asian man would not converse at all. He just smiled or stared at me.

Again I took my suspicions to my supervisors and was told that I was paranoid. I returned my full attention to the developing problem. That evening, Yu began to lose, which made my theory look baseless. At the close of the evening, however, she won a little and gave the dealers thousands in gratuities.

The following morning Yu returned to the game bearing a gift for the shift manager and me. I was honored with a solid sterling silver Gucci pen, which I still have as a reminder of the Imperial Palace swindle. I became even more cautious.

Eventually, I saw one of the gentlemen flash his cards, after they were dealt, to the player sitting opposite him. That player decided whether or not to have the bet changed based on the numerical total of the Bank side's cards. That player secretly signaled Yu, who was at the other end of the table. She acted like she was not even watching the game, but following a signal, she asked to switch her bet from the Bank to the Player side or to put down a bet after the cards were already out. She was a master!

When the players determined the value of the Player hand, they knew which hand would probably win. It simply was a matter of switching bets to make it happen.

This was one of the cleverest schemes I ever saw. No marked cards. No extra cards. No gaffs of any kind. Because the floorman allowed the changing of the bets, he technically allowed the scam to happen.

The trio won quite a bit of money before I raised a big enough stink so that the play was stopped.

The next week, the three returned and were arrested at the baccarat table. One of them confessed, vindicating me and my theory. I still have questions about it, though. Was anyone other than the three involved in the operation? How did they know that the baccarat game even was open in the casino?

The card flashing at the Imperial Palace was done by the dealer with the shoe, who dealt the cards methodically and accurately: one for the Player side and one for the Banker, one for the Player and one for the Banker. The cards for the Banker were supposed to be dealt under the corner of the shoe, however, this player dealt them about an inch away from its edge then slipped them under. This is when the player made the cheating move.

As he slid the cards under the shoe, he raised one corner of them slightly. He positioned them at just the right angle for his accomplice to see them. The trio worked out their strategy prior via a computer simulation, and it beat the game.

When I reviewed the tapes of the baccarat cheat at the Dunes, I saw the flashing of the cards when they were dealt, but it differed slightly from the way it was done at the Imperial Palace. Yet there was no doubt that the bet switching aided the players.

The common factor between the two scamming incidents was that the casino did not adhere to the true rules and, thus, compromised the integrity of the game. The cheating could have been prevented.

If Sidney Wyman was alive to witness this mess at the Dunes, he would have laughed at how little Shenker knew about gambling

CHAPTER 64

JOHNNY HICKS AND *CASINO*

Martin Scorsese's movie, *Casino*, which came out in 1995, delivered a better than average portrayal of Las Vegas in the late 1960s and 1970s. Many parts of the film were based on actual events and people. One of the characters in the movie, played by James Woods, was Lester Diamond, the boyfriend of Sharon Stone's character. In real life, Diamond was my longtime friend, John "Johnny" Hicks, son of gaming pioneer Marion Hicks.

I first met John when I was "breaking in" to the gambling business while working at the California Club. Built on First Street and Fremont, it was a small casino with four blackjack tables, two craps, one wheel, about 140 slot machines, keno, a snack bar, and a comfortable, 50-stool bar next to the pit. Every rounder, thief, and booster called the bar home. The bartender, Big Bob, was a weightlifter-bodybuilder around 65 years of age (in 1966) who tightly shook people's hand until they smiled.

What a place to work. It had an eye in the sky and one on the floor that we called the eye in the rug. One employee was an old time cheat from Montana, Mike Sarkis. He was an expert cold deck operator who worked with many teams. The California Club owners hired him on the belief that "it takes a thief" to catch a thief. They were right, as long as the thief can be controlled.

Sarkis sat at the bar watching blackjack and counted down the deck by tracking the most important cards for the dealer. If a player was beating the house, we shuffled or continued dealing down to the bottom of the deck and then reshuffled when cards were still in play on the table.

Usually, we shuffled after dealing one or two hands. The idea was to keep the most important cards for the dealer in play and the most important cards for the player out of play.

The most important cards for the dealer are the five, the six, and the four, in that order. If a player sat down to play and in the first round, the fives and sixes came out but no aces, Sarkis signaled me to shuffle. If the cards were not shuffled, the chances of the dealer busting and a player getting a blackjack increased.

Johnny also was breaking in, but across the street at Binion's Horseshoe. The Horseshoe was a popular place to gamble, had great food, and offered guests the chance to take a photo in front of an actual $1 million. After posing for a free picture, they had to wait around for the print. It was a great way of inducing tourists to gamble.

It was well known on the streets that getting caught cheating the house at the Horseshoe was to be avoided. Otherwise, it could get a person roughed up. A former Horseshoe casino manager told me that once a dealer was handcuffed to a water pipe for several days for stealing. When the owner found out that the dealer stole from a customer not the house, she let him go.

John was a friend of the Binions, and they allowed him to learn the games at the Horseshoe. Bucky Howard was the shift boss at the California Club and his dad, Buck Howard, Sr., was a floorman at the Horseshoe. Sr.'s relative was Ma Beachie from Phenix City, Alabama. They were hard core gamblers. Hicks dropped in at the California Club occasionally, and I was introduced to him by Bucky Howard.

Las Vegas was still a small town, and we all socialized after work. Many of us frequented Dirty Sally's, which was on the corner of the Las Vegas Strip and Spring Mountain Road, now the site of The Venetian. Dirty Sally's had live music and a single, $10 limit blackjack game that was great for suckers. A few of the dealers were bust-out artists, so it was not a game for betting serious money.

Johnny, age 24, and I, age 21, became great friends. He had a Cadillac Eldorado convertible and was the man about town. Once he had to leave town for a few days and asked me to take his car in for servicing. Wow, what a chance! I could drive his convertible around town and meet some chicks.

Or so I thought. That morning I took his car to the Cadillac dealer and waited in the service line. Once when the line moved, I went to do the same. However, because I was not real familiar with the pedals, I pushed on the gas instead of the brake, rear-ending the car in front of me. A little person jumped out of the car, and in a heavy accent and with a speech impediment, he loudly berated me. I was horrified. I caused about $500 of damage to his car and about $1,000 worth to Hicks. I paid off every penny.

John forever ribbed me about the incident. He thought it was hilarious. It was not so hilarious to me.

Hicksie, as his friends called him, was a real rounder. He loved women, golf, gambling, drinking, and telling stories about his dad and Meyer Lansky. One morning at about 3 a.m., someone knocked on my door. It was Hicks, who had been out and was in the neighborhood. He stopped by to show me his dad's personal pistol, a small .25-caliber handgun, which he carried all of his waking hours. Hicks wanted me to see it shoot, but we could not do it outside because it would wake all of the neighbors. So we decided to shoot at a target in my fireplace. We were pretty stupid 20-somethings.

Johnny's father Marion Hicks built the Thunderbird and, later, the Algiers next door. The Algiers did not have gambling because by that time, the state gaming authorities deemed Hicks unsuitable for a gaming license.

The general manager of the Algiers for many years was Jack Walsh, who worked directly for Hicks. He also was a member of the Nevada Gaming Commission (GC) from 1973 to 1985. Here are excerpts from an obituary of Walsh that ran in the *Las Vegas Sun*:

> "In 1961, Walsh took a job he would relish for the rest of his life: general manager of the Algiers. The small hotel was built on the north end of the Strip to handle overflow guests of the Thunderbird, which later became the Silverbird, the new El Rancho, and now is closed.
>
> "Walsh served as the Thunderbird's general manager in the late 1950s.
>
> "For the past 35 years, Walsh, wearing his ever-present white tam o'shanter and smoking his ever-lit pipe belching honey Cavendish, was as much a fixture at the Algiers as the chandeliers and tiffany lamps that adorn the ceilings and walls of the old hotel.
>
> "'He and his wife both lived on the property since the very beginning so he was just the lifeblood of the Algiers,' said Marianne Kifer, the owner of the Algiers and the daughter of Marion and Lillian Hicks, who built the Thunderbird and the Algiers. 'He knew everything and knew an awful lot of people in town.'
>
> "Walsh's reputation for finding simple, workable solutions to complex problems was reflected in the way he managed the Algiers.
>
> "When a reporter asked Walsh in 1995 why he kept a turn-of-the century look at the Algiers through the years, he replied: 'I like it. A lot of people like it ... There haven't been any big changes. Just pictures and paint.'"

It is interestingly ironic that Walsh's boss at the Algiers was unsuitable for gaming, yet Walsh was a member of the GC. That is how Las Vegas ran.

Johnny gave me a very special photo that was given to him by his father and Meyer Lansky's partner, George Sadlo. Sadlo et al. owned a fully functional casino in Mexico, with table games and a sports and race book.

Sadlo had a panoramic picture taken of the operation, which is priceless. Looking closely at the boards in the sports book, one can see the price for the Willard-Johnson heavyweight boxing match in 1916. It was held in Havana, where Lansky and Sadlo eventually operated casinos. I still have this picture hanging in my office.

After I got a job at the Dunes, Johnny would visit me there and tell me what was going on in his world. Occasionally, I stopped by his house in the Las Vegas Country Club. He lived near "Lefty" Rosenthal and his wife Geri McGee, who were depicted in *Casino* as Sam "Ace" Rothstein by Robert DeNiro and Ginger McKenna by Sharon Stone. (Execute a Google search for "Geri Rosenthal" and there will be photos of "Lefty," Geri, Tony Spilotro, Siegfried and Roy, and others.)

John told me that he was seeing Rosenthal's wife Geri and that the two of them took the contents of "Lefty's" safety deposit box and went on a spending spree with it.

One evening in 1972, John invited me to his place, where we hung out with Pete Griffith, a craps dealer whom I knew from the Sahara, and two or three cute girls.

A few days later, John was murdered while leaving or arriving at his home. He was shot behind the ear with a .22 pistol.

I tried to contact Griffith, but was told by a mutual friend that he was "scared shitless" and left without a trace, perhaps because he saw who killed John. I have not seen, spoken to, or heard from Griffith since.

I did not attend John's funeral out of fear. I thought that perhaps Griffith was killed, too. I thought that maybe John was being followed before the shooting, and the people involved might want to find Griffith, me, and the others who were at John's house that night. I regret that I did not have the guts to pay last respects to my friend.

In *Casino*, John's character was beaten up and tossed into his Eldorado, the infamous Cadillac Eldorado. The movie avoided his murder altogether.

After I conducted some research into who shot my good friend, a reporter wrote me this:

> "Geno,
>
> "Nice to hear from you. Most of my information on Johnny's final days comes through his running mate at the time.
>
>   "I think everything you stated about Hicks is right on the money. I think Tony [Spilotro] killed him, or perhaps he had Joey Han-

sen or one of his other friends do it. [Frank] Cullotta was never suspected of it, to my knowledge.

"It's interesting. My knowledge of Cullotta is pretty fair, and I don't think he was often used as a hitter. He is called a hitman, of course, and I don't doubt he participated in several murders. He also admitted shooting Jerry Lisner in Las Vegas. But other people in Spilotro's crew have told me Cullotta wasn't trusted like some of the other guys. He worked hard to get involved with Tony and worked his way next to him. That irked a lot of Tony's loyal friends.

"But as to the Hicks murder, it certainly would have been Tony depending on how much heat was on him at the moment. He was quite clever, switching cars, wearing disguises, etc.

"As to specifically who pulled the trigger, I will ask Cullotta when he's available again. "It's funny. Spilotro, the Italian-American, was the mob guy. But what does that make all the casino executives who catered to him or turned a blind eye to his activity?

"In this town, the ability to dummy up has been raised to an art form.

"Your friend,

XXXXXXXXXX"

Years later, in 1994, a dealer friend of mine from the Dunes, Gene Strolien, called me and said that he was taking a guy around town who was making a motion picture about Las Vegas. Strolien was familiar with my card dexterity and wanted to have the "guy" watch me do some moves.

I was in my first store at the MGM Grand when the two stopped in unannounced. Strolien introduced me to the moviemaker, but I did not register who he was. I was busy with customers that day, but I did some of my false shuffles and second deals, and we briefly talked.

Afterward, Strolien told me that I was too clean cut for a part in what was going to be the movie *Casino*. Strolien did not know that I knew John Hicks, and I did not know that John would be a character in the movie. Otherwise, the three of us might have talked for hours.

Little did I realize that the "guy" was Scorsese and that he'd auditioned me for *Casino*

CHAPTER 65

THE LAST DAYS UNDER SHENKER

In February 1984, Cliff Perlman bowed out of the Dunes and sold his rights to John Anderson, a California tomato grower, for $25 million, which was about a $10 million loss. The sale diluted Morris Shenker's holding to about 18 percent. In May 1984, Anderson was unanimously approved by the Nevada Gaming Commission (GC) to acquire 41 percent of the Dunes for $25 million. Anderson was already licensed as the owner of two Nevada properties, the Maxim Hotel and Casino in Las Vegas and the Station House in Tonopah.

Perlman backed out of the Dunes purchase because he could not completely control the Dunes and the different land parcels and indebtedness on the property.[365]

Anderson increased his investment in the Dunes to 51 percent by buying the stock held by the estate of Major Riddle. Shenker and his family retained 2.2 million shares of the outstanding 8.5 million Dunes shares. The majority of Shenker's Dunes stock was controlled by the U.S. Bankruptcy Court in St. Louis, which also handled the reorganization of his personal debts.

In June 1984 federal prosecutors charged that Shenker paid $600,000 to the Milwaukee crime family of Frank Balistrieri as kickbacks for receiving millions of dollars in loans from the Teamsters union pension fund.[366] The government documents filed in court claimed that Shenker switched allegiance to Balistrieri from the Kansas City crime family of the late Nick Civella. The government also filed transcripts of conversations that were monitored under court order that backed up their claims. Also included were copies of relevant documents seized by FBI agents who executed search warrants in Kansas City.

Among the documents seized by the FBI from the bedroom of Balistrieri was a handwritten list of payments, from the 1970s, totaling $600,000. The list was in code and said the payments were from "Fox" to "Berman." The FBI identified "Fox" as Shenker and "Berman" as Balistrieri. The FBI

365   Interview with Glen Treadwell
366   *St. Louis Post-Dispatch*, June 26, 1984

specialist, Fredrick Thorne, said that the list was written by Carl "Tuffy" DeLuna, second in command of the Civella crime family.

There was also a transcript of a monitored conversation on November 7, 1979, in a Milwaukee restaurant between Balistrieri and his son Joseph, an attorney. The elder Balistrieri talked about Shenker and how Balistrieri's Mob owned the Teamsters pension fund.

In the transcript Balistrieri said, "The thing is, then, let Frank work on Shenker and let's nail Shenker down, cause Central belongs to us. I got – I can follow it up. Kansas City is out. I'm handling it."

In an interview Shenker said, "I have no idea what Balistrieri was talking about. I never belonged to anyone."

Shenker categorically denied all claims that the federal government made about him, all of which were recorded in the transcripts of the FBI's electronic monitoring of him.

Shenker believed the press and public would believe his denials, which certainly may have been phobic. Fear of being chastised as a criminal would have threatened his credentials as a lawyer and his gaming license.

In one document that DeLuna prepared about various meetings was information discussed at a meeting involving Carl Civella and Shenker on February 16, 1978, at the Kansas City airport.

In August 1985, the Dunes sold its Atlantic City, New Jersey, property that was dormant for several years to Anderson. The Dunes then bought the Rancho Murieta Country Club near Sacramento for $42.2 million. The following month Anderson placed his Carson Valley Land Company into Chapter 11 bankruptcy. His other Nevada properties, the Dunes, the Maxim, and the Station House were not affected by the filing, however, he faced lawsuits on defaulted loans totaling $76 million.

In October, federal marshals stormed the Dunes and seized cash from the casino cage to pay a $2.7 million judgment obtained by the Culinary Union. They accepted a $200,000 check and left the cash in the cage. The Dunes did not pay the health, welfare, and pension benefits for about 1,510 culinary workers for six months, from August 1984 through February 1985.

On November 1, the marshals returned to collect the remaining $2.7 million judgment but they were stopped by a last minute restraining order. On November 6, 1985, the Dunes' operating company M&R Investment filed for reorganization under Chapter 11. This filing circumvented local District Judge Robert "Clive" Jones' order and the threat of having a receiver being appointed to run the company. Shenker kept the hotel open, and the stockholders retained control over the management.

Shenker hired Sam Dash, famed special counsel in the Watergate break-in, to assist with his personal bankruptcy filing and with I.J.K. Nevada. As part of the settlement with secured creditors, Shenker sold his remaining stock in the Dunes, but was retained as a consultant. This came to an end when the Dunes filed for a Chapter 11 reorganization.

As of November 1985, Anderson became a majority owner of the hotel with 51 percent of the operation, with Shenker and his son Arthur retaining consulting contracts worth nearly $500,000. Bankruptcy Judge Jones ordered Anderson's attorneys, not Shenker's, to pay the 2,300 hotel and casino workers.[367]

In December 1985, the Dunes defaulted on a major bank loan of $68.6 million. Local Valley Bank moved ahead with the necessary legalities for a foreclosure sale scheduled for December 23. Valley Bank requested an appointment of a trustee to protect its interest in the Dunes from the influence of Anderson and Shenker.

Shenker rejected an unsolicited offer of $115 million cash from Steve Wynn and his Golden Nugget, Inc. but stated he was willing to negotiate. Shenker said that the Golden Nugget and the main creditors of M&R Investment were colluding to force a distress sale. The Dunes wanted to sell for a minimum of $143 million.

On December 10, 1985, Shenker's California land was sold at public auction. "I'm 79 years old and I'm tired of fighting," said Shenker. "I wanted this to come to an end. I think that if I did choose to litigate this all the way to the end that I would have won. But I was tired of those people chasing me for years. I'm glad to get rid of them."

For the year ending 1985, the Dunes reported a loss of $15.6 million, which compared to the net loss of $2.6 million in 1984.

In January 1986, long-time gaming figure Burton Cohen was named president of the Dunes. He refused to step foot in the hotel-casino until Shenker was completely out so that Cohen could operate autonomously, without influence from Shenker and his associates.

Nine months later, in September, Cohen announced that a mystery buyer, approved by Anderson and Shenker, was in place. Cohen refused to name the buyer and claimed disclosure would "kill the deal."

Simultaneously, there was a second offer on the table by Jack Blumfield, which called for selling "junk bonds" to raise the capital to fund the sale. Cohen's mystery buyer agreed to assume all union contracts while Blumfield was noncommittal on the point.

The next month, the New York-based brokerage firm of E.F. Hutton revealed itself as the secret partner in the Dunes sale and presented an offer of $144.5 million for it. This experienced brokerage felt that $144.5 million was below the fair market value of the property and that they could easily flip it and make a huge profit through a syndication. Cohen participated in the offer as a general partner. For this sale to go through, it had to be approved by the bankruptcy court.

On November 25, 1986, Jones approved the purchase of the Dunes by a limited partnership headed by E.F. Hutton. Cohen would be president and the group would have to sell 30,000 limited partnership interests of $5,000 a unit, for a total of $150 million. The deal was scheduled to close on March 31, 1987.

The Hutton firm, however, withdrew from the Dunes deal in February 1987 and refused to comment to the press why.

Then Southmark Corporation, the parent company of 7-Eleven, came to the rescue in May 1987, acquiring the first and second mortgages of the Dunes.

On July 22, 1987, Hilton Hotels Corporation put its hat in the ring to purchase the Dunes for $122.5 million. John Giovenco, who was the president of the company, announced that they would spend an additional $110 million on the property, adding a 1,000-room tower and completely refurbishing the existing 1,156 rooms and casino. Hilton's offer was an all-cash deal and was to close within a month.

A second offer came in from a Japanese company, Minami Shoji. Cohen signed a letter of intent to sell the Dunes to Minami's owner, Masao Nangaku, for at least $135 million. The Hilton and Minami offers were to be considered at a hearing held by the gaming authorities, scheduled for August 3, 1987.

Then over the weekend of August 2, 1987, Henry Lewin, former president and long-time associate of Hilton Hotels and recent president of the Las Vegas Hilton, also made an offer on the Dunes in partnership with Sheldon Adelson and his company, The Interface Group.

Subsequently, Honolulu attorney, Jon Miho, representing an unidentified Indonesian group, offered $135 million for the Dunes as well.

Kirk Kerkorian also was negotiating to buy the Dunes, with Al Benedict handling the offer. As of August 1, 1987, Benedict was ready to make the final offer, which would have closed the deal. In a letter to Cohen and Jones, the president of MGM Grand, Inc., Fred Benninger, called Kerkorian's offer "significantly superior." It noted that the Kerkorian offer "provides for a substantially greater cash purchase price than the Hilton offer." It also noted that the Japanese offer was "contingent upon a receipt of a gaming license for a group of previously unlicensed investors." Kerkorian filed an application with the Nevada Gaming Control Board (GCB) in anticipation of acquiring the Dunes. Kerkorian was ready, willing, and able to buy the hotel until a 1 A.M. telephone call to Benedict ordered him to back off, which he did. No explanation was ever given to Benedict or Benninger for Kerkorian's sudden pullout.

It is interesting to note that Kerkorian purchased the Desert Inn and the Sands in September 1987, and appointed Cohen to operate the former. According to an undisclosed source who worked at the Desert Inn baccarat game, Cohen received an X envelope[368] from the baccarat game. This X envelope was an equal share of the dealers' tips each week. According to the same source, Cohen received an X envelope from the main showroom maître d's tips. Cohen did not explain this "mystery" to anyone. Under Sid Wyman, Charlie Rich, and George Duckworth's management of the Dunes, they never took an X share of tips as that was beneath them. If Wyman was alive and aware of Cohen's actions, he may have sarcastically remarked, "He could get away with it because he was a lawyer."

On August 3, 1987, Judge Jones and the Dunes stakeholders accepted the offer of billionaire Nangaku. His final bid for the Dunes was $155 million. Nangaku outbid four others, including three top names in the Nevada gaming industry. Nangaku's attorney and spokesperson, Wallace Fijiyama, urged Jones at the hearing to approve his client.

"This man has come to Las Vegas and wants to be part of your community," he said. "You will have an outstanding businessman, others will follow. He is very community minded."

Ironically, just after the Dunes sale was approved, Shenker was hospitalized at the Jewish Hospital in St. Louis, suffering from a heart ailment.

The chances of Nangaku getting a gaming license were almost 100 percent as Nevada Governor Richard H. Bryan encouraged Japanese business investment in the state, which was on an uptick.

"When you think of Nevada's future, you have to think about foreign investors," said Michael Rumbolz, chairman of the GCB under Bryan. "Governor Bryan has continually sought this new money."[369]

---

368   Note: An X envelope is one without a specific name on it. It contained tips that were divided by the dealers. Regular envelopes have a last name on them so they can be distributed to the dealer or floorman who was entitled to the share of tips. The X made sure no one had a record of the recipient.
369   *Chicago Tribune*, Sept. 8, 1987

Part of Bryan's economic program was to open up an office in Tokyo to garner new business that was independent of the state's primary industry of gaming.

Rumbolz said, "The strong yen played a major role in Nangaku outbidding the Hilton corporation for the Dunes."

Rumbolz said that it would take several months for the GCB to complete its background investigation of Nangaku. This task included an investigation in Japan involving a detailed look at and compilation of the records of Nangaku's companies and interviews with Nangaku's friends, relatives, and business associates.

Cohen announced that the Dunes had $10 million in cash versus the $1 million at the time of the bankruptcy filing in November 1986. The sale to Nangaku closed on December 15, 1987.

After, Cohen appointed Forrest Woodward as the executive vice-president of the Dunes. Woodward, who was an extremely competent casino accountant and internal auditor with plenty of casino experience, came on board in February 1987. He implemented free bingo sessions in the casino theater showroom as a way of thanking the residents of Las Vegas for their support over the years.

"Through good and bad times, the people of this town have supported our efforts," said Woodward. "We felt this would be a great way to show our appreciation. Everyone likes to play Bingo, especially when there is no obligation. We want everyone to enjoy themselves while they are playing, so we will be giving away free coffee, wine, or whatever during each evening session."[370]

Woodward's offer was certainly inviting and a tool of the old-time Las Vegas operators. It was a start to getting local and tourist foot traffic into the casino. Woodward's real talent was watching the numbers, finding the leaks, and stopping them. He initiated the first numerical sequential marker system and the controls in the State of Nevada. He discovered that anyone could go to the local office supply store and buy counter checks that were exactly like those used in many hotels, which was an open door to marker fraud. Woodward's counter checks were independent and printed in a different marker format, including a version that was legal in Mexico.

Woodward knew Dennis Gomes from a group that had formed, which was called the Hotel Association. Accountants, controllers, and assistant controllers were members. Gomes, who was on the GCB at the time, heard about the system and called Woodward to obtain a copy of his marker procedures. Gomes directed the rewriting of Nevada's Gaming Regulation 6 to include Woodward's procedure. Regulation 6, which set the controls for money and markers, was the bible of gaming then. After Woodward obtained a copy of the rewritten regulation, he called Gomes:[371]

"Hey, you didn't change anything. I looked at my procedures that I sent out, and they're exactly what the new regs are," said Woodward.

"Well, they were written good enough to where that's all we need to do," replied Gomes.

Woodward was a perfect fit for Cohen to clean up the Dunes and its maze of irregular gaming procedures of nepotism, slimy hangers-on, and associates. Every agreement, every employee, every casino program, and sales and marketing program had to be examined thoroughly. Woodward was uneasy and had areas of concerns about every key employee. It was a dirty mess.

Phil Hannifin, then running Howard Hughes' Las Vegas properties, wanted Woodward to run the Frontier. Hannifin went to Cohen with the idea, and Cohen told him, "No. I think that he could do better for me here rather than him going over there and running the Frontier."

Woodward replied, "Hannifin had already talked to me about the Frontier and I told him I spoke to Burton about coming over to the Dunes. Then Dennis Gomes went over to the Frontier."

In April 1988, Gomes was approved to manage and operate the Dunes pending the licensing of Nangaku. Gomes negotiated to operate the hotel and casino under a lease agreement that called for up to an $850,000 monthly payment.

Previously, Gomes was the chief operating office of the Aladdin, which was owned by another Japanese businessman, Ginji Yasuda. Gomes, who had a great deal of integrity and justice, defied the order of Yasuda to fire an Aladdin dealer whom an Arab sheik wanted terminated. Gomes looked into the matter and determined that the dealer had done nothing wrong and should not be fired. Gomes simply moved the dealer to another area and kept him out of the sight of the sheik. The sheik was alerted that the dealer was still working there and complained to Yasuda. Yasuda insisted that the employee be fired, but Gomes would not do it. Yasuda threatened Gomes' job, and subsequently Gomes quit. Of note is that when Gomes later took over at the Dunes, he hired the dealer to work there.

Nangaku's attorney Barry Gould said that his client wanted Gomes in at the Dunes and the current operator, Cohen, out because he thought Gomes "will be of greater benefit to the hotel."

371   Interview with confidential source, FW, 2019

Rumbolz also thought highly of Gomes as Gomes detected a major skimming operation at the Stardust when he was a GCB agent. Gomes' experience and knowledge of the gaming laws certainly should have kept the Dunes and Nangaku out of trouble.

Nangaku personally got to know Gomes and his likeable and trustworthy personality. His winning smile and warm personal manner gave Nangaku confidence in his selecting Gomes to operate the Dunes Hotel and Country Club.

Gomes' Clark Management group took over the Dunes on July 1, 1988. Gomes technically terminated the existing Dunes employees and required that they re-apply for their jobs. It was all legal and advantageous to Gomes. He did not waste any time going after high rollers and stepping up the sales and marketing programs for the tour and travel business. His operating "nut" was a maximum of $850,000 monthly. He could easily fulfill his budget goals and make a healthy profit if there were qualified players and hotel guests occupying the rooms all year.

Based on the GCB's 1990 abstract of gaming revenues for hotels and casinos on the Las Vegas Strip with revenues between $36 million and $72 million, which is on the conservative side, the Dunes should have generated a healthy profit. The abstract used average revenues for each department, but with Gomes' management team in place, the Dunes' numbers were expected to be better than average.

The average revenues were as follows:

Average pit revenue per day	$71.86
Average slot revenue per day	$118.24
Average food revenue per day	$35.86
Average beverage revenue per day	$18.23
Average room rate per day	$42.39
Average room occupancy per year	
	89.26%
Average cost of sales	6.7%
Average departmental expenses	52.4%
Average G&A expenses	31.0%
Average net income	12.3%

Based on these numbers, the Dunes' projection was:
Total rooms = 1,156
Rooms at 89.2% occupancy = 1,031.84
X $286.58 per room revenue = $295,706 daily revenue X 365 days = $107,932,803 yearly revenue
Divided by 12 = $8,994,440 monthly revenue$8,994,440 monthly revenue minus
$8,103,954 total monthly expenses
$890,486 total average monthly profit

The $890,486 number was low because the numbers were based on a lower revenue tier to be conservative. When the Dunes was in its heyday in 1968, Lee Fisher, who was the director of advertising and public relations, issued a news release featuring Charlie Rich, the executive vice-president, that noted, "It has been estimated that the Dunes' annual gross revenue exceeds $100 million."

According to a rumor that circulated among pit supervisors who were not owners, each point in the Dunes was worth $9,000 a month. If one divided $890,486 by 100 points, it equals $8,904, just under $9,000. Maybe those rumors were true? And that was in 1968 not 1988. Funny how numbers work!

In November 1988, the Dunes and Morris Shenker received publicity in the press regarding past associations with infamous high rollers. Former Sun Savings and Loan Association President Daniel W. Dierdorff, who was no stranger to Dunes employees, pleaded guilty to two felony charges. In a pre-sentencing report he recalled Shenker telling Dunes casino cage manager Ruben Cabanas, "Take good care of Dierdorff. He's a good friend and he's got lots of money."[372] Cabanas testified that Dierdorff received more favorable treatment than the typical $250,000 Dunes Hotel gambler."

The Sun Savings and Loan Association, which was seized by federal regulators in July 1986, lost $200,000 from an "imprudent" $500,000 personal loan that Dierdorff negotiated for Shenker, according to the pre-sentencing report. Shenker arranged for Dierdorff's use of the Dunes' private jet, complimentary rooms, a credit line, and other perks "to discreetly divert money to Dierdorff to obtain favorable treatment" for the loans that were seriously in default, according to the report.

The investigation of Nangaku for a gaming license, which involved GCB agents going to Japan, took about 11 months and cost a record $730,000.

The licensing hearing was scheduled for December 7. However, the GCB members felt that the date, the anniversary of the Japanese bombing of Pearl Harbor, was inappropriate because Nangaku was a former member of Japan's Navy during World War II. So the hearing was moved to Dec. 8.

On that day, the GCB recommended that the GC approve Nangaku for a limited, two-year gaming license for the Dunes with 15 restrictions. Rumbolz publicly expressed doubt that Nangaku understood Nevada business ways. GCB agents also had concerns about the conduct of some of Nangaku's employees. Further, the GCB's recommendation allowed for Gomes to continue his lease of the Dunes, and thus, Nangaku would have to deal directly with Gomes, without any intermediaries, about the casino operations. The GC followed the GCB's recommendation and granted Nangaku a limited license.

Consequently, Nangaku raised the specter of discrimination against the Japanese being behind it. Rumbolz, however, responded that he personally abhorred racial discrimination and noted that the GC awarded more than 30 similar conditional licenses in Nevada in the last four years.

This writer's opinion is that the gaming authorities had no business limiting Nangaku's license due to lack of gaming experience and lack of Nevada operating know-how. Plenty of capable management teams were available and willing to offer their services. Severe limitations only stifled and hindered an operator and could lead to failure.

Nangaku's acquisition of the Dunes' 1,200-room hotel, casino, and other amenities, which sat on 163 acres of real estate, for $157.7 million closed. Subsequently, he hired Gomes as a Dunes manager, and gaming veteran Ash Resnick was terminated.

The Dunes had 200 employees, who were members of five different labor unions, who worked without contract agreements for a year. As such, Gomes' Clark Management group was accused in June of trying to force unions out of the hotel-casino. He responded by saying that the Dunes would follow the lead of other Strip resorts in negotiations with the unions.

Veteran casino operator Jack Speelman became Nangaku's chief operating officer. With plenty of competition from all of the surrounding hotel-casinos, management decided to spruce up the Dunes with new carpet and paint, having the work done during the slow time just prior to Christmas. In September 1989, Speelman announced that the Dunes would spend $9 million on a facelift. The bulk of the renovation was scheduled for the second floor of the satellite casino, The Oasis, including a new lounge, a nightclub, a 240-seat bingo hall, and a two-level race and sports book. The Dunes Hotel was to have most of its 1,200 guestrooms remodeled.

Speelman made it clear that Nangaku wanted to erect a new Dunes guestroom high-rise but would not do so until he received a permanent, unrestricted gaming license.

Cost cutting measures were on the agenda as well. One of the first items to get the axe was the Dunes' Top of the Strip restaurant in the sky, which offered a truly fabulous view of the Las Vegas Valley. There was no nicer dining, dancing, and drinking facility anywhere in the town. Top of the Strip was scheduled to be closed after Bob Anderson performed the New Year's show.

In December, the Dunes announced a buyback of outstanding shares of Dunes Hotels and Casinos, Inc., or DHC, stock. The Dunes ended up in bankruptcy within two years of Nangaku's ownership, and Nangaku's management agreement with Gomes ended in a dispute over control.

On February 17, 1989, Lillian Shenker died of infirmities in St. Louis. She was an active civic leader, lawyer, judge, and wife of Morris Shenker.

Less than two weeks after her death, her husband was indicted for conspiring to defraud the IRS and the U.S. Bankruptcy Court by funneling hundreds of thousands of dollars to his children to avoid paying back taxes and bankruptcy creditors. In an elaborate scheme, Shenker supposedly diverted money from a California partnership that his children owned to individuals in Canada and then back to Shenker's secretary in Las Vegas. The indictment also charged him with diverting to his children the proceeds from the sale of a St. Louis-based commuter airline, Resort Air.[373] Shenker faced up to 10 years in prison.

It was a sad situation for Shenker, losing his wife of many years, being very sick himself, and getting indicted by the government. Shenker felt hopeless at this point. This writer hopes that the government did not purposefully indict Shenker within a week of his wife's death to break his spirit. If they did, that was unfair, immoral, and bad karma.

Enduring all of the related stress did not help Shenker's heart condition. He succumbed on August 8, 1989, at his daughter's home in Santa Monica, California.

Shenker has his name front and center on the largest preschool in Las Vegas, Shenker Academy. Shenker Academy's website says they "are committed to excellence, nurturing, and creative individual learning." The preschool has been well received and seems to be doing an outstanding job,

---

373   *Reno Gazette-Journal*, Feb. 19, 1989

but on the "About Us" web page there is not a word or mention of the sponsor, Morris Shenker. There is not a "History" page that gives background of the school's beginning and leads one to wonder why Shenker's name is not mentioned.

In March, Nangaku broke ground on a $90 million office building, to be called Minami Tower, and said that "it would send a signal around the world that Las Vegas is a good place to do business." He also planned to add a $35 million non-gaming hotel to the site at a later date. This sent the message to Nevada gaming authorities that he was willing and had the money and the opportunity to invest in the state but would not expand the Dunes proper without the gaming license he wanted.

Two years after the GC granted Nangaku an initial gaming license, the commissioners gave him a permanent, non-restricted one.

During 1990 and 1991 many hotels laid off workers due to a slowdown in business that began in 1989. Caesars Palace, across the street from the Dunes, cut 370 employees due to the economic downturn caused by a recession and the Persian Gulf War,[374] according to Debbi Munch, the spokesperson. The Dunes laid off about 150 employees in May 1991.

Reports began surfacing in June that Nangaku was looking for a buyer or a joint venture partner for the Dunes, which was in financial trouble. He was actively looking for a partner that could operate the gaming because, as he reported to the GCB, the hotel was losing about $500,000 a month. The Hilton Nevada Corporations showed interest but nothing developed.

Nangaku also stopped the work on Minami Tower and tried to give the land underneath it back to the City of Las Vegas. Nevada Senator Harry Reid then got the federal government interested in the property, and it eventually became the Lloyd D. George U.S. Courthouse.

Ted Gottlieb reported that the Dunes started to use the "Win Cards" that he invented. Win Cards must have been well received because sales reached 1,000 units weekly. This is ironic because the Dunes was on its last legs, and Gottlieb's Win Cards, which helped blackjack players, likely hurt the Dunes blackjack win.

In August, a five-member delegation of the Chinese Ministry of Construction and a Chinese investment group toured the Dunes. They were interested in acquiring the property, tearing down the existing structures, and replacing them with a new hotel and theme park that would resemble the Forbidden City palace complex in Beijing.

---

374   *Reno Gazette-Journal*, March 7, 1991

GCB member Steve DuCharme queried, "How do you license a government?" The theme park idea, however, slowly fizzled.

In October, Steve Wynn's Mirage Resorts, Inc. purchased the Dunes. The price was kept confidential, but insiders speculated that it was probably less than half of what Nangaku paid for the resort.

In late October, Richard Goeglein, head of the transition group that ran the Dunes during its final months, said that Nangaku ordered the closure of the hotel-casino within 60 to 90 days as required by federal law.

CHAPTER 66

HARRY CLAIBORNE, ATTORNEY AND JUDGE

A long with Sid Wyman and Charlie Rich, Harry Claiborne defended some big names in the Las Vegas gaming industry, including "Bugsy" Siegel, "Lefty" Rosenthal, and "Benny" Binion. Binion previously oversaw an illegal gambling empire in Dallas, and was involved in numerous shootings, beatings, and other criminal activities and police corruption. Binion acknowledged that he committed two murders in his past and surrounded himself with similarly tough associates. When he left Dallas for Las Vegas, he brought with him two suitcases stuffed with $3 million in cash.

According to author Michael Vernetti:

> "Claiborne described the day in 1948 when he bumped into Binion and another acquaintance on the street, the first time they laid eyes on each other since Claiborne had sent Binion's bodyguard Cliff Helms away for life the year before. The third party asked Claiborne about his recently announced decision to leave the DA's office and enter private practice. Hearing the exchange, Binion told Claiborne, 'I want to hire you.'
>
> "Since Binion was none too pleased to have his good friend Helms imprisoned – and had made known his displeasure – Claiborne was taken aback. 'Well, Mr. Binion, from all I hear, you don't like me very well,' he said.
>
> "Binion looked him in the eye and responded, 'I didn't know there was a goddamn law that said you have to fall in love with your lawyer.'
>
> "Claiborne laughed, shook Binion's hand, and 'represented him a lifetime.'"

In 1979, after Claiborne become a federal judge, there existed in Las Vegas "an atmosphere of animosity and hostility" between the state's federal judges and certain attorneys in the justice department's strike force.[375] The latter made their sentiments known through offensive caricatures of

---

Claiborne, his defense attorney Oscar Goodman, and others displayed in their offices in 1980.

The document containing the Nevada Supreme Court's opinion on *State Bar of Nevada v. Claiborne* explained:

"Chief Judge [Roger] Foley learned that insulting materials and caricatures were prominently displayed on a bulletin board in the offices of the strike force. Oscar Goodman claimed the derisive items on the bulletin board were in full view of, and had an intimidating and prejudicial effect upon, members of the grand jury, as well as potential grand jury witnesses.

"These materials consisted of a mock man-on-the-street interview with numerous individuals including former Clark County Sheriff John McCarthy, Judge Claiborne, Judge Foley, defense counsel Goodman, and other individuals, some of whom were reputedly connected with organized crime in Nevada. Sardonic responses to the question, 'Does organized crime really run the casinos and the State of Nevada?' appeared beneath the photographs of those depicted. In the space reserved for Judge Claiborne's photograph appeared the notation, 'no pictures please.' Judge Foley, on the other hand, was depicted as a clown dressed in circus regalia.

"We do not deem it appropriate to set forth the statements attributed to those ridiculed in the item in question. We observe, however, that although the unknown author of this sarcasm ostensibly compiled it in jest, the fact that it was displayed within the confines of the United States Department of Justice, and apparently within the purview of members and witnesses of the grand jury, demonstrated an appalling arrogance, contemptuousness, and lack of decorum. On April 4, 1980, Judge Foley ordered United States Marshals to remove these items. Thereafter, the problems between the strike force attorneys and the federal district judges became so acute as to attract the attention of Nevada's congressional delegation, the highest officials in the Justice Department, and the Clark County Bar Association."[376]

Consequently, Foley decided to no longer preside over cases involving the strike force. Claiborne, as chief judge for the district of Nevada, took over Foley's administrative duties in May 1980.

"Respondent [Claiborne] claims that these facts, in addition to the fact that he had ruled adversely to the government's position and had criticized strike force tactics in several cases which had come

---

376   *Ibid.*

before him, eventually motivated some within the strike force and the FBI to view him as an obstacle in their path, and to seek his removal from office.[377]

In April 1980, Claiborne became a target of the strike force and the FBI. At their request, a grand jury investigated allegations that Claiborne, prior to his judgeship, hired Las Vegas detective Eddie LaRue to illegally surveil someone as part of a defense investigation. According to the case summary:

"Upon learning of the grand jury activity, on April 10, 1980, Judge Claiborne publicly stated that he had been cleared of these same charges prior to his appointment to office. Additionally, he publicly denounced the strike force, called for disbandment of the grand jury, and suggested that the grand jury had been tainted by the improper tactics of some strike force agents and attorneys. Specifically, the *Las Vegas Sun*, in an article entitled, 'Judge Says Strike Force Must Go', quoted Claiborne as follows: Charging they were a 'bunch of crooks,' U.S. District Judge Harry E. Claiborne said Wednesday Las Vegas Strike Force attorneys should be thrown out of Nevada and their Special Federal Grand Jury disbanded. 'I think they have outlived their usefulness, and they should be removed from this community,'" Claiborne said. 'The grand jury has become tainted and should be disbanded.'

"Claiborne said the strike force, which he believes is responsible for 25-30 illegal wiretaps, also conducts illegal arrests and other such far-reaching illegal activity. 'They're a bunch of crooks, and they know I know it,' Claiborne angrily said. 'I'm not going to let them ride roughshod over this community. I'm going to stop them.'

"We note, however, that in May of 1980, Judge Claiborne voluntarily removed himself from presiding over any further strike force cases."

Subsequently, federal law enforcement officials conducted four grand jury investigations of Claiborne, first in Las Vegas, then Portland and then Reno.

"In the course of its investigation into the allegations that respondent and [Ed] LaRue conducted illegal electronic surveillance, the Las Vegas federal grand jury subpoenaed Charles Lee in April of 1980. Lee was then employed by the Las Vegas Metropolitan Police Department as a homicide investigator and polygraph operator. His testimony before the grand jury concerned a polygraph examination he had administered to respondent in 1977. Lee told the grand jury that, in his expert opinion, respondent had truthfully denied any participation in activities involving the illegal electronic surveillance into which the grand jury was inquiring.

"In an affidavit submitted to the federal court, Lee averred that following his appearance before the grand jury, he was summoned to the office of his superior, Sheriff John McCarthy. McCarthy informed Lee that he 'had been visited by two Federal Strike Force agents sent by [FBI Special Agent In Charge] Joseph Yablonsky. According to Lee, McCarthy further stated that as a result of Lee's exculpatory grand jury testimony, Yablonsky considered Lee to be an 'uncooperative witness' and that Yablonsky was going to 'come down on [Lee] like a ton of bricks.'

"Lee's attorney, Michael Stuhff, also has attested to the fact that information subsequently released to Lee pursuant to requests under the Freedom of Information Act and the Privacy Act 'confirms that Lee was targeted [for investigation] by Yablonsky because of Lee's refusal to join in or cooperate with Yablonsky's vendetta against Judge Harry E. Claiborne.' Lee and his attorney maintain that, as a result of Lee's testimony before the grand jury, and at the direction of Yablonsky, Lee was demoted and reassigned to a desk job answering telephones, and was further subjected to an intensive three-year investigation. The investigation into Lee's activities involved extensive covert and electronic surveillance of Lee by the FBI. Ultimately, however, the investigation was terminated having disclosed no wrongdoing upon which criminal charges could be based. It can thus be inferred from the record that Lee may have suffered extensive harassment and intimidation solely because he provided exculpatory testimony to the grand jury investigating respondent.

"Similarly, the grand jury investigation into the allegations that LaRue conducted illegal electronic surveillance at respondent's direction failed to result in any indictment against respondent. LaRue, however, was formally charged with six counts of installing illegal listening devices. These charges were unrelated to the previous allegations involving respondent. In an affidavit, LaRue has attested that after his indictment, an FBI agent advised him to 'give up' Judge Claiborne. Further, LaRue has attested: 'The agent advised me that if I would do that, all federal charges [the indictment against me] would be dropped. I told him to 'give up' Judge Claiborne would be false since I didn't know a single thing illegal or unlawful that Judge Claiborne had ever done. The message was clear to me, I could rid myself of all the expense, embarrassment, intimidation, and sorrow that I had suffered and was about to suffer simply by lying against Judge Claiborne. This I pointedly refused to do and went to trial.'

"'I went through the anguish of defending myself against these false charges in Reno Federal Court. The Government removed the trial to Reno, Nevada, 500 miles from my home, which added additional financial burden in travel expenses for myself, my attorney, and witnesses. After a week-long trial I was acquitted.'

"'This trial cost me $35,000 in attorney fees alone, to say nothing of the expense of taking my witnesses all across the state to the trial.'

"'I was wrongfully indicted for the sole purpose of giving the FBI leverage to make a deal with me. The sole purpose and object of my indictment was to 'get' Judge Claiborne. He was their target, not me.'

"Thus, the record reveals some factual basis for concluding that despite a lack of significant evidence of any wrongdoing, LaRue suffered harsh and retributive treatment as a result of his inability to provide inculpatory evidence against respondent.

"Respondent [Claiborne] contends that additional questions concerning the propriety of his pre-indictment investigation are raised by a curious event that took place on March 19, 1981. On that date, respondent opened his monthly American Express bill and found that an American Express statement addressed to Nevada State District Judge Thomas O'Donnell was included along with respondent's. On April 9, 1981, respondent wrote to the American Express Company requesting an explanation and observed:

"'In the envelope containing my last billing was also the bill for Judge Thomas J. O'Donnell. It would not be surprising that someone's bill was also included with mine but our curiosity is more than aroused in view of the fact that Judge O'Donnell is my closest and best friend. For his bill to be included with mine is a very unusual circumstance.'

"'If I were of a suspicious nature, I might suspect that someone is monitoring our accounts and replaced both of them in the same envelope by mistake. If this is true, then both Judge O'Donnell and I desire to pursue it further.'

"'Thereafter, the American Express Company replied that it could not explain the mix-up.'"

As for Yablonsky, FBI Director William Webster censured and placed him on probation in 1983 for "improper inquiries Yablonsky had made to the United States Air Force about the personnel records of a candidate for state office in Nevada, Brian McKay. At the time of Yablonsky's inquiries, McKay was running against Yablonsky's friend, Mahlon Brown, in a hotly contested race for the office of Nevada State Attorney General."[378]

"Reportedly, Yablonsky first denied that he had made any such inquiries, then later admitted that he had done so but denied that he was fishing for disparaging information about

McKay that would benefit his friend's campaign. Although Director Webster characterized Yablonsky as a 'highly competent and experienced field manager,' Webster was also quoted as stating that Yablonsky's actions 'were inappropriate and made at a time and under circumstances likely to bring into question the integrity of the FBI's inquiries.' Director Webster also characterized Yablonsky's actions as involving 'extremely bad judgment in utilizing the files of another agency to inquire about Mr. McKay for a reason I did not consider adequate or sufficient.'

"Additionally, after his retirement, Yablonsky was investigated by the FBI and a federal grand jury concerning his failure to inform bank officials that his bank account had been mistakenly credited with $40,000 as a result of a computer error. The mistaken credit apparently went undiscovered for three years until it was ultimately revealed by a bank audit. The grand jury, under the direction of the Justice Department's Public Integrity Section, declined to return a criminal indictment against Yablonsky."[379]

Jack Miller, a former special agent of the U.S. Air Force (USAF) Office of Special Investigations (OSI) and a Nevada State Gaming Control Board member, relayed to this writer the following about Yablonsky and Jerry Young's inquiries about McKay:

"Brian McKay wanted to be the Nevada Attorney General in 1982. He had served as enlisted airman USAF for a four year hitch but only served three years. Richard Wright, Major, USAF, was assigned to Nellis Air Force Base (AFB) as detachment commander [Air Force Office of Special Investigations] in the late '70s or early '80s. Young was a graduate of the Air Force Academy. I served with him in Korea in 1968-69. I don't think Wright was aware of the political scene or that Brian McKay was running for office.

"'YOBO' [Joe Yablonsky] called Wright and asked why McKay had not served a full four years. YOBO probably felt there would be some derogatory information in the USAF files. Wright was asked to contact the Military Personnel Records Center to determine why

378   *Ibid*
379   *State Bar of Nevada v. Claiborne,* 104 Nev. 115, 145-46 (Nev. 1988)

McKay had received an 'early out.' Wright felt the request was for official purposes.

"Wright did not make the connection between the name and the politics or he was too new to the area to know McKay was running for political office. Wright checked the records and I believe the reason was a normal 'reduction in force.' In any event there was nothing derogatory.

"The information was passed to YOBO.

"Later, OSI Command learned of the incident. I believe Wright probably learned that the request from YOBO was for political purposes and notified OSI Command himself.

"USAF personnel have to be apolitical, and I'm certain headquarters felt Wright did not use good judgment in the matter. Wright was transferred to Minot AFB, North Dakota, and probably received a letter of reprimand, which would be a career killer. I doubt if YOBO had any action taken against him.'"[380]

Miller also described the roles of FBI Special Agent Howard Sharpe as a "black bag" agent and anti-skyjacker.

"I met Sharpe when I was working as an investigator for the District Attorney's office. We had a common interest as he knew I had been a special agent with the OSI and worked in the counter-espionage area as a mother to a double agent spy and he had received special training by the bureau in the area of 'illegalities.' In these areas, 'illegal' is defined as a sick bird (Ill Eagle). Anything to get the job done.

"During our association a trust was developed and he told me he had been assigned as a 'black bag' agent and received training in surreptitious entry using lock picks and in the area of 'flaps and seals' used when intercepted mail and packages are received, secretly opened, contents examined then the mail resealed and allowed to proceed. (Sometimes this action is authorized by warrant but very seldom.)

"He also said that he had been one of the FBI supervisors at Ruby Ridge and was an anti-skyjack team member. His job was to dress as a pilot or navigator and carry a map case onto a plane which had landed for fuel with the passenger still on board. In the map case he would have a concealed weapon, and at first chance, to shoot and kill the skyjacker.

"One other thing I happened to think of was one time he took myself and another retired OSI agent to the third floor restaurant at the Mint Hotel and Casino. I saw well-known Las Vegas judges, lawyers, businessmen and politicians in the restaurant drinking and eating. This was exclusive and required membership. I was told that there was no cash handled in the restaurant. Members signed for everything and once a month received a statement. A great way to pay off others for favors."[381]

In his manuscript, *Conforte: Portrait of America's Biggest Little Criminal,* Oscar Dey Williams told the story of Claiborne, Yablonsky, and Joe Conforte, former brothel owner.[382] The author wrote:

"Harry Claiborne had been a Las Vegas police officer, a Clark County assistant district attorney, a city attorney for North Las Vegas and Henderson, a state assemblyman, and Nevada's first Director of Probations. He helped create the Las Vegas Police Protective Association and pushed for civil service status for cops and firemen. He topped Nevada's list in private practice for trial lawyers willing to represent the poor, the indigent, and policemen pro bono.

"Harry Claiborne also had a stellar history of defending mobsters – and the Confortes. "Harry Claiborne donned the black robe of justice in 1978, vowing to protect the common man from abuses of federal government, which he had seen firsthand as a criminal defense attorney.

"Judge Claiborne was true to his word and often clashed with prosecutors from the bench, at times ruling against them. He once threatened IRS agents with jail for disobeying his order to return cash to a gambler.

"'Those bastards are out to destroy Nevada and I'm not going to let them do it,' Claiborne said, referring to the Las Vegas-based federal strike force targeting mob activities."

JOSEPH YABLONSKY.

"FBI Special Agent Joseph Yablonsky was known as the King of Sting for his undercover work infiltrating the mafia. Yablonsky was assigned to lead the Las Vegas office because Nevada, he said, acted like 'a foreign protectorate.... We've had to plant the American flag in the desert.'

"Nowhere was his statement more apropos than in Storey County. But rather than build the case against Joe Conforte that his predecessors had been working on for years, Yablonsky sought a bigger target: Judge Harry Claiborne.

---

381   *Ibid.*
382   Oscardeywilliams.com

"Judge Claiborne criticized the FBI and prosecutors to the local news. He obstructed the Justice Department's efforts to clean up Nevada and at one point even refused to hear any strike force cases. Claiborne appeared to Yablonsky to be in the mob's pocket.

"'I'd rather have ten Confortes walking the street than one corrupt federal judge,' Yablonsky said of Claiborne.

"Joseph Yablonsky had one of his agents enlist Joe's attorney, Stan Brown, Sr., to orchestrate a bribe from Joe to Claiborne. Yablonsky offered no deals for Joe. The important thing was that Joe not know of the FBI's surveillance or of Stan's complicity.

OUT OF THE FRYING PAN

"Harry Claiborne had been an employee and friend of the Confortes as well as a customer with a lifetime pass to the feminine pulchritude in their stable – until he became a judge and distanced himself. He told Joe, a convict-in-waiting, to never call him again. Still, he threw Joe and Sally a bone when he stalled the subpoenas of the two Mustang Ranch girls who were to testify on voting fraud.

"Joe once made a pledge to himself to never accuse someone unless he had proof. He lived by a code: Don't talk to cops, don't screw over your friends, trust and loyalty matter, show fidelity to your patron. Joseph Conforte was a man of principal, yet he would rather chew off his foot to escape the shackle than be caged for the next five years.

"U.S. Attorney Geoffrey Anderson, chief of the Las Vegas-based strike force, had received his share of rebuke from Judge Harry Claiborne: 'Geoff Anderson has no respect for decency, and he has no respect for people's civil liberties.'

"Joe telephoned Anderson and offered to provide damaging information on Judge Claiborne in exchange for a deal to avoid prison. He didn't give any specifics, said he would call back in a week, then changed his mind.

"Joe was to appear before Judge Ed Reed on December 23, 1980, for a final hearing on his tax evasion case. The day meant the end of his freedom: he had lost, and the Feds had won. Joe skipped court, drove south into Tijuana and on to Mexico City, flew to Acapulco for a short respite, and then flew to Rio de Janeiro, Brazil where he stayed for the next three years.

"With that, Yablonsky's hope of knocking Claiborne off the bench went out with the tide.

But then ... the tide came back in.

THE STING

"Joseph Conforte worked on his tan on his penthouse deck near the beach while formulating a strategy to beat the rap and return to the U.S.A. A little over six months after jumping bail, Joe contacted the FBI about bribes he allegedly gave to Claiborne years before. He was very convincing on the telephone. Meetings with IRS and FBI agents and officials from the Department of Justice – Public Integrity Section followed: twice in Rio, once in San Juan, Costa Rica, and once in Acapulco.

"Conforte was a treasure trove of knowledge during these meetings, with details of corruption of city officials on up to governors, U.S. senators, and one federal judge. Using methods he had learned in Army counter-intelligence training in the late 1940s, Joe gave them a mix of truth, half-truths, and omissions to gain their trust.

"And, he lent a helping hand in a sting of two of three Lyon County commissioners: "Back in 1979, two Lyon County commissioners had tried to extort money out of Conforte for a brothel license. Joe refused to pay and didn't get the license. He then attempted to bribe the district attorney to harass or close his competitors, and offered to work together to catch the commissioners being crooked. '…not only will you do some justice to me,' Joe said to the DA, 'but you'll also stop this goddamn corruption that there is in Lyon County.'

"Jump to 1981: the two commissioners who had screwed over Conforte were caught red- handed by the FBI, trying to extort money out of another brothel license applicant. The third county commissioner's insight into the situation was, 'I firmly believe [Conforte] is behind the whole thing.'

"It was sweet revenge, with a touch of irony that Conforte played a role in cleaning up Lyon County.

"The more Joe talked, the more the Feds believed him. U.S. Assistant Attorney General D. Lowell Jensen wrote to the FBI Director about Joe: 'There are few, if any other individuals who would be in a better position to know about corruption in the State of Nevada.' By the time Joe finished dropping his bait, they had bought his Claiborne bribe stories hook, line, and sinker. A plea agreement was ironed out, granting Joe immunity and a reduced sentence in exchange for his testimony before a federal grand jury.

"On December 4, 1983, the Feds got their man when Joe flew from Rio de Janeiro to Miami and into their cold embrace. He next flew to Washington D.C., where a judge lowered his five-year sentence to fifteen months. Joe then flew to Reno.

"Joe testified before the Reno federal grand jury on December 7th about giving two cash bribes to Claiborne: $30,000 to stall the voter fraud probe, and $55,000 to influence Joe's tax evasion conviction or sentence. Joe was shipped to federal prison in San Diego from there.

"Judge Claiborne was subsequently charged with bribery, filing false income tax returns, and making false statements to the Judicial Ethics Committee based on Conforte's assertions and other evidence in a seven-count indictment.

"'I have never taken an illegal penny on the judicial bench,' Claiborne said.

"At Harry Claiborne's trial, in March 1984, Conforte again testified, but unlike a grand jury, which is merely the prosecution's side, here Claiborne was able to defend himself. Claiborne swore his innocence during his testimony. He successfully refuted the date and location of the first bribe Conforte alleged to have made. He denied most of Conforte's details of the second alleged bribe. At the end of the day, both bribe claims were Joe's word against Harry's, and Joe was a tax-evading pimp behind bars who had a lot to gain from implicating the federal judge. The trial of the Honorable Harry Eugene Claiborne ended in a mistrial.

"Joseph Yablonsky and others in the Justice Department at some point had to accept that Joe had lied and lied big. When asked why the Feds didn't enforce Joe's plea bargain agreement to answer truthfully, Yablonsky replied, "We felt [Conforte] would get in trouble again on something more serious and we'd get him." The statement seemed to be a deflection of what the editor of the Las Vegas Sun newspaper had characterized as a Justice Department 'vendetta' against Claiborne, and the fact that Conforte conned a lot of smart people, including the King of Sting himself.

"The taxes that Joe and Sally owed the IRS amounted to $25 million. In what some people felt was a major coup, though more likely the result of extensive litigation and reassessments, the IRS shaved nearly $17 million off that – a sixty-eight percent reduction.

"Joseph Conforte was released from federal prison on December 10, 1984, having served twelve months of his fifteen-month sentence of what was originally a twenty-year sentence. It was his birthday. He was fifty-nine."

After being convicted of tax evasion in 1984, Claiborne began his two-year prison sentence on March 16, 1986. He did so with the intention of returning to the bench in two years' time. He did not resign his judiciary post, and continued to receive his salary of $78,700 a year.

This placed the U.S. Congress is a difficult position. Clearly, Claiborne was no longer fit for office in their opinion, and yet the Constitution allowed only one method for removing a federal judge – impeachment.

Members of Congress did not discuss at length whether Claiborne's alleged tax fraud constituted "high crimes and misdemeanors" or whether a convicted felon could be permitted to remain on the federal bench. After only a few hours of debate, the House Judiciary Committee unanimously passed four articles of impeachment on July 22, 1986. The Senate received those articles on August 6, 1986.

Rather than convening The High Court of Impeachment, the Senate agreed that evidence in the Claiborne impeachment trial would be first heard by a 12-member panel created for that purpose. Acting upon a Senate rule adopted in 1935, but never before used, the Senate Impeachment Trial Committee examined evidence and heard testimony before reporting its findings to the full Senate on October 7, 1986. Sitting as a court of impeachment, the Senate heard closing arguments, including the argument by the defense that the use of a trial committee was unconstitutional.

The following excerpt from Goodman's cross-examination of Claiborne in his impeachment trial reveals the government prosecutors' dislike for Claiborne. (The entire cross-examination of Claiborne by Goodman is available here: https://www.c-span.org/video/?150519-1/claiborne-impeachment-hearing-cross-examination.)

Goodman: "As of April 11, 1980, did you have any other suspicions that you were being followed, or being investigated by the government?"

Claiborne: "I knew that I was under surveillance. I knew I was being followed, as events of the last few days have established. I knew that my friends were being questioned concerning me, and my lifestyle, and my history, and every conceivable thing. And of course I had known for a long time, and, frankly, misjudged that the head of the Las Vegas office of the Federal Bureau of Investigation, somehow, took a personal dislike to me, I think, even though he was a very ambitious man, and he came into Las Vegas with an idea of, as he said, "planting the American flag in the Nevada desert." And I think that his idea of doing that was to get rid of a lot of people, and, unfortunately, for me, I was, I believe, foremost in his ambitious path. And I think somewhere along the way, he recognized that he was going to have to deal with me in order to be able to accomplish the things he wanted. But he didn't know me very well. So I think he, he misjudged situations with me.

"I think when he came here that he – that he heard that I was a, a criminal lawyer, and that I was. And that immediately, to them, I was a threat. But I have said this to everybody who would listen. If they will find two prosecutors in the federal system, outside of the strike force, that will say that I ever was unfair to the government, or that I was on the side of a defendant, then I'd resign tomorrow and they won't have to have these proceedings.

"But it wasn't what was presently there that bothered them. It was what I think would be down the road in the future, from the number of public officials in – that they later began to try. And those cases were in the mill in some minor ABSCAM-type sting operations."

Claiborne's claim that Yablonsky had a vendetta against him was valid. The facts showed that the FBI used everything in their arsenal with which to attack Claiborne. In the early 1970s Claiborne defended a group of the Dunes owners on the government's charge of skimming. There is no question that Claiborne met with many of these defendants and had many telephone conversations that very well could have been recorded. The Dunes was indeed a location of wiretaps and monitoring. This unlawful wiretapping pointed to other issues and associations the government could have used in building evidence against Claiborne and others.

Senators then voted on October 9, 1986, on all four articles of impeachment. The vote on the third article held particular significance in the history of impeachment trials. It essentially stated that Claiborne's conviction by a jury trial in the district court proved that he was guilty of "misbehavior" and "high crimes." With a vote of 46 to 17 (35 voted "present"), Article 3 was the only article not to achieve the required two-thirds majority for conviction. Senators expressed concern that adoption might set a troublesome precedent: by declaring that a court conviction was automatic grounds for conviction in an impeachment trial, the reverse situation – an acquittal in a court trial – therefore might require an automatic acquittal in an impeachment trial.

With the conviction, Claiborne was removed from office and his judicial salary was terminated. It the first time the Senate impeached an official who already had a criminal conviction.[383]

383   "United States Senate: The Impeachment Trial of Harry E. Claiborne U.S. District Judge, Nevada," 1986

CHAPTER 67

LINKS TO THE KENNEDY ASSASSINATIONS

I didn't want to write this chapter for many reasons, however, I would be negligent if I did not touch on this sensitive issue. Years ago I helped a local Las Vegas gaming executive write a book about his alleged connections to Meyer Lansky. After 18 months of research and writing, I found a major flaw in his story and decided that I did not want to work on his book any longer. The time I spent was not wasted even though I was not paid a penny for my work. What I gained, which I consider worth more than money as remuneration, was valuable knowledge and research about the Kennedy assassinations. Additionally, a few years later I assisted John Barbour, a former Hollywood producer and writer, in creating a documentary about John F. Kennedy's murder. To top it off, I met John Meier, a former employee of Howard Hughes.

Suddenly, like a bright red light that went on in my head, I saw connections between the Kennedy assassinations and the Dunes and other Mob associates whom I knew or knew about in Las Vegas. These people were Robert Maheu, R.D. Matthews, Jimmy Hoffa, Nick Civella, Moe Dalitz, Carlos Marcello, John Meier, Tony Montana, Joe Segretto, and John "Johnny" Stone.

Several casino bosses whom I worked with, such as Joe Slayton, Irwin Gordon, and Dave Goldberg, knew Jack Ruby. John Stone's daughter lived in the same apartment building as Ruby. Of course, the legendary Matthews was questioned by the House Select Committee on Assassinations, accompanied by his attorney, Harry Claiborne. The committee investigators showed a keen interest in the relationship between Ruby and ex-convict Matthews, a former Dallas resident with numerous arrests. Matthews was questioned because when Ruby gunned down accused assassin Lee Harvey Oswald, he had Matthews' telephone number with him.

Matthews was asked many questions about Ruby:[384]

> **Question:** "Did anybody hire Jack Ruby to kill Lee Harvey Oswald?"
>
> **Matthews:** "I don't know."

Question: "Did anybody hire Lee Harvey Oswald to kill President Kennedy?"

Matthews: "I have no idea."

Question: "Is there any general information you could tell us about Jack Ruby that would be helpful to the Committee in investigating the assassination of President Kennedy?"

Matthews: "I don't know anything I could tell you, sir. I don't know. He was a very slight acquaintance of mine, just a passing acquaintance."

The committee looked into any contacts Matthews may have had with Ruby in Cuba in 1959 when Matthews worked in the casino of the Hotel Deauville in Havana. Recently declassified federal documents indicated Ruby was actively trying to free organized crime figure Santos Trafficante from a Havana prison that year. The Warren Commission, which investigated the assassination of President Kennedy, made no mention of Matthews' phone number being on Ruby or in any of his notebooks.

The Committee investigators also uncovered phone records that revealed a 13-minute long distance call from Ruby's Carousel Club in Dallas to Matthews' ex-wife in Shreveport, Louisiana, on October 3, 1963. The call to Elizabeth Ann Matthews was made on the night of the day that Oswald arrived in Dallas after a 10-day trip to Mexico City. In Mexico City, Oswald tried unsuccessfully to get a visa to travel to Cuba. After the assassination, Elizabeth Ann said that she "could not recall having received a long distance telephone call from Dallas on or about October 3, 1963," according to an FBI report. However, R.D. himself might have received the call. R.D. said he was only a "passing acquaintance" of Ruby for about 12 years. However, Charles Duarte, a longtime friend of Ruby, told the FBI several days later in December 1963 that Matthews was "well acquainted with Ruby."

Warren Commission Assistant Staff Counsel Burt W. Griffin placed several long distance calls inquiring about a Ruby-Matthews link just two days before the commission submitted its final report to President Lyndon Johnson. Griffin called Ruby's sister Eva Grant, his roommate George Senator, business partner Ralph Paul, and Carousel Club bartender Andy Armstrong. None said that they knew of any connection between Ruby and R.D. or Elizabeth Ann.

Walt Brown, a former FBI agent said, "I also visited the weapons dealer in Oklahoma where R.D. had the tools of his trade specially made."[385]

---

385   Walt Brown e-mail, Nov. 25, 2013

This statement suggested that R.D. kept a good supply of guns that were tailor-made to his specifications, yet I still could not put a smoking gun in his hand.

After learning that the American public believed that the assassination of John F. Kennedy was not just the work of a "loan nut" and that other theories about a conspiracy surfaced, I read Mark Lane's book, *Rush to Judgment* in 1968. This book opened my eyes to the possibility that more than one person conspired to kill JFK. In 1966, half of those polled believed that more than one person was involved, and only 36 percent believed that it was a single shooter. In 2003 only 19 percent of Americans believed that it was a single shooter.

I was privy to several sources of rumors, hearsay, and casino chatter, the latter being a valuable conduit of underground information. Casino dealers, floor-persons, pit bosses, cocktail waitresses, porters, valet car parkers, front-desk clerks, and many other employees all had sources of information. Some of the information was true and 100 percent accurate, and some was fallacious. In many cases, a story might have gotten its start from a dealer who overheard a casino boss talk about an incident or from an employees' dining room worker who had a relative in the police department. The information moved around in an amazing manner. I was in the middle of this underground super rumor mill for years and had many sources. Sometimes there is truth to the adage, "Where there's smoke, there's fire."

The most firsthand information that I uncovered in my research of the John F. Kennedy assassination is probably the most interesting, and it involves Jimmy Hoffa, who was associated with the Dunes during its prosperous years. Hoffa's association with Mobsters was something that could not be avoided. His philosophy was to let the Mob do their thing while he did his own thing. It was a capricious co-existence. Hoffa met Moe Dalitz in Detroit in the early days. It was speculated that they were introduced in the workplace of Hoffa's mother, a laundress.

Joseph "Doc" Stacher, a hidden owner of the Sands in the early 1950s, said, "We knew Jimmy Hoffa right from the early days because of Moe Dalitz – Jimmy Hoffa met Moe when he was just a young man in a group of Jewish boys who worked for Norman Purple in the Purple Gang [Detroit]. There was a war among Detroit gangs, and when Dalitz's boys got the worst of it, Moe left the Purple Gang and set up his own in Ohio."[386]

---

386   *When Hollywood Had a King: The Reign of Lew Wasserman, Who Leveraged Talent into Power and Influence*, Connie Bruck, 2003

Dalitz and Meyer Lansky were close associates and business partners in the 1920s when they set up a bootlegging network.

Several sources asserted that Hoffa had something to do with the assassination of JFK. Frank Ragano of Tampa, Florida, who represented Hoffa for 15 years, told the *New York Post* the former Teamsters boss asked him to carry a message to Florida Mob Boss Santos Trafficante and New Orleans Mob Head Carlos Marcello in January or February 1963, nine months before Kennedy was slain.

"Jimmy told me to tell Marcello and Trafficante they had to kill the president," Ragano said. "Hoffa said to me, 'This has to be done.'"[387]

A year later, on May 15, 1964, *LIFE* magazine ran an article titled, "Scheme to Kill Bobby Kennedy." In this story, Edward "Ed" G. Partin, who turned state's evidence against his once close associate Hoffa in his jury tampering trial, detailed a chilling story about Hoffa wanting to kill Robert F. Kennedy. *LIFE* checked every detail of the story and submitted Partin to a grueling lie detector examination, which he passed without any deception. It was conducted by the most foremost expert in the field, Leonard H. Harrelson.

Although Hoffa's plot to have Robert Kennedy assassinated never occurred, just the plot, idea, and suggestion by Hoffa to Partin suggests that Hoffa was capable of coordinating the assassination of JFK.

Talented researcher and writer Dan Moldea published *The Hoffa Wars*, the first book to theorize that Hoffa recruited Mobsters Marcello and Trafficante to arrange President Kennedy's assassination.[388]

A September 1967 *LIFE* article alleged that Louisiana Governor John J. McKeithen looked the other way while Marcello offered a $1 million bribe to Teamsters official Partin to recant his testimony. The magazine said the "bribe" meeting was held in the home of Aubrey Young, a key assistant of McKeithen.[389] The article also asserted that McKeithen and New Orleans District Attorney Jim Garrison allowed Marcello and his rackets to operate "with a remarkable degree of official tolerance."

During the 1940s, Marcello became associated with New York Mafia leader, Frank Costello, in the operation of a slot machine network. Their association in various Louisiana gambling activities came about following a reported agreement between Costello and Senator Huey Long that allowed for the introduction of slot machines into New Orleans. Costello and Marcello were involved in various gambling operations. Marcello,

387   Associated Press, Jan. 14, 1992
388   Associated Press, Nov. 22, 1993
389   Associated Press, Nov. 22, 1993

Phil Kastel, and other associates gained control of the two best known casinos in the New Orleans area, The Beverly and New Southport Club; The Beverly brought Marcello into partnership with Syndicate financier Lansky. Marcello was a hidden owner of the $50 million Tropicana, Johnny Rosselli's first major deal in Las Vegas, according to the *Las Vegas Sun*.[390]

Marcello did not attend the national Mafia conference in Apalachin, New York in 1957. Instead, he sent his brother Joseph Marcello, the family's underboss, to represent him.

Costello himself was the target of an assassin's gunshot that nearly killed him, in May 1957. This was after authorities found a note in his pocket that read, "Gross Casino Win as of 4-26-57, $651,284. Casino win, less markers – $434,695. Slot wins $62,844 – markers $153,745. Mike $150 a week, totaling $600; Jake $100 a week, $400, L. $30,000, H. $9,000." Investigators soon determined that those numbers exactly matched the gaming revenue at the Tropicana. Furthermore, the note was written by Michael J. Tanico, a former Tropicana cashier who was previously employed by Kastel at The Beverly in Louisiana.

Then came the bombshell, from someone in a position to know some extremely obscure details that were relevant to the JFK assassination.

A veteran casino boss who worked at the Desert Inn in the 1950s until it was closed, serendipitously ran into me at a local coffee shop. He saw me writing in my notebook and said, "What are you writing, Geno?"

I explained that I was writing a book with a fellow who was around Lansky and his dealings in Florida and Las Vegas. At that point in my notes, I was reviewing some of the characters who were coincidentally linked to the John Kennedy assassination in some way. He then said, "I could tell you a story you may find interesting."

He began by telling me about the special mission he was part of as a scout sniper in the Marine Corps and how he came to meet and work for Moe Dalitz.

> **Anonymous:** "Okay. So in 1946 they pulled out 50 Marine scout snipers–now, scout sniper–there's a shooter and a spotter so you're always in two man teams–and they sent us–what they wanted to do–what [President Harry] Truman wanted to do was make sure that the Nazis and the fascists didn't come back into power. So he sent us out to kill all the top ones all over the country, all over the world."
>
> **Munari:** "And where were you when you say all over the world?"

Anonymous: "I went to Germany, I went to France, I went to Argentina, because there's a big concentration of Germans that went down there, and I just went all over."

"Go out there and kill all–they'd give us the names of the people and we'd have pictures of them. So, we'd go and sometimes it'd take us a day to do it, sometimes it'd take us a week, week and a half. But we always–we stayed away from everybody that was in the Marines, or Army or anything else, because we were on our special mission and we–they didn't want anything slipping up about Truman."

Munari: "You didn't want them, the public, to know it was our forces killing these guys?"

Anonymous: "Right."

Munari: "So were you in uniforms?"

Anonymous: "No, no. We dressed like bums sometimes, and we'd dress like businessmen other times. It's just according to where we were going. So we went and did all that. Then when I got out of the Marine Corps in '49, I did a little moonshining. Got in trouble in North Carolina for that, and I went down to the guy that I hauled moonshine for. Knew the guy that ran the gamut in Phenix City, Alabama."

Munari: "Do you remember his name?"

Anonymous: "The one in Phenix City? Patterson, or something Patterson. I don't know. Yeah, well they were all down there. And they taught me the wheel and 21 and craps. But I was never a good crap dealer for one reason. I don't have a strong voice and–you're a crap dealer, right? You got to have a strong voice if you're on the crap table because all the yelling and all. Well, the dealers couldn't hear what I was saying, neither could the box man. So they put me on the base and I never went on the stick again, but just all in the base. But my main thing was the wheel. I could deal that wheel. I loved that wheel.

"But Moe Dalitz called my boss and he said, 'I'm looking for a wheel dealer that can deal a gaffed wheel.' So he said, 'Well, I got the perfect guy for you.' And he said, 'He's got another bonus for you, too.' So I don't know what he said, you know, but – "

Munari: "That means he's saying that you could do something else with another tool."

Anonymous: "Yeah."

Munari: "What was that?"

Anonymous: "A rifle."

Munari: "Oh, okay."

Anonymous: "So he sent me out–he called me into the office, and he was saying, 'A friend of mine out in Vegas needs a wheel dealer.' And he said – "

Munari: "Do you remember the year of this?"

Anonymous: "'53. Yeah, 1953."

Munari: "Wow. [The Desert Inn] just opened."

Anonymous: "Yeah, well, they'd opened two years before, '51 they opened. So I said, 'All right, I'll go.' Hell, I'm only about 20 years old at that time. And I come out–so I reported to Dalitz, and we talked about the wheel and everything. And he says, 'Well, I wanna see what you can do.' So I said, 'All right.' So I went down and the guy that was in charge of the roulettes and Everything – so I went down and everything and they had some play down there. But I kept hitting the numbers that nobody was on.

"And a boss walked up to me and says, 'I don't know what the hell you are doing, but it isn't right.' I looked at him and I says, 'You ever dealt a wheel?' And he never had, he never dealt a wheel. I said, 'Well, then you wouldn't understand it.' So I got off and the boss told Dalitz, he called Dalitz in because Dalitz told him he wanted to try me out. And he told him, he says, 'I would stay away from this guy, there's something wrong with him, he's crooked or something.' And so Dalitz called me over there, and he says, 'Well, you're all right, you're gonna work and everything.' And he said – . By the way, Patterson's first name, I forget his first name."

"But anyway, he said, 'You're pretty good with a rifle.' I said, 'Yes, sir, I was a scout sniper in the Marine Corps.' He said, 'Well, I wanna see that.' So three or four days later, I'm working on the table and I get a call. And so I go up, and Dalitz says, 'I'd like to take you out and see what you do with a rifle and target practice.' So we went out and he had a quarter. He said, 'I wanna see if you can hit this.' And he goes way out there, I guess it must have been a quarter of a mile.

"So he put that quarter up on–he has a thing like this, it was like a little log-like thing, stood about this high and it had a little slit in it and you stuck the quarter in there. And he come back and he said, 'Let me see you shoot that.' Well, I shot it, and I said, 'Actually, you can take it further than that.' So I said, 'If you want to, go out there and change the quarter to a dime.' And I said, 'I'll hit it.' So he did that, and I hit it. And he said, 'Yeah' – he said, 'That's gonna be a bonus in the years to come.' So I said, 'All right' because I had no qualms of shooting somebody if they deserved – I thought they deserved it."

Munari: "If you thought, though. You were told that they deserved it?"

Anonymous: "Yeah."

Munari: "That was just a job?"

Anonymous: "Yeah. I had two rules, though. Never a kid and never a woman. I've never hurt a woman or a kid in my life, and I wouldn't do it. Even when we were in the Marine Corps and all, I wouldn't shoot a woman, and there were some women they wanted taken care of. But I wouldn't shoot a woman."

Munari: "What if you had to protect yourself?"

Anonymous: "Well, that's a different story. But just to go out and assassinate them, I wouldn't do that."

Munari: "So you guys were assassins? Was that a special division? Was it called anything?"

Anonymous: "If it was, I never knew it."

Munari: "Do you remember your commanding officer?"

Anonymous: "Chesty Puller."

Munari: "Was he a lieutenant?"

Anonymous: "No, he was a general."

Munari: "He was a general? Chesty Puller. Okay."

Anonymous: "He wasn't a politician. He was strictly a Marine. I mean he loved the Marine Corps. But he told us one thing, no prisoners. We don't take prisoners. One shot, one kill, no prisoners. That's not our job."

Munari: "And if you wounded them, you had to kill them?"

Anonymous: "Well, we didn't wound them. That one shot had to kill them."

Munari: "What kind of gun were you using?"

Anonymous: "It was a Marine Corps sniper, I forget what the hell – a Springfield, I think. But it was modified. It had – the bullets, instead of being this long, were about this long. It was modified with extra powder and everything. It would reach out there – "

Munari: "Was it a magazine loader or was it a bolt action?"

Anonymous: "Bolt action. It held eight shots or eight bullets. I don't know of ever having to shoot twice. I've seen the time where the subject was with a kid or something, well then I'd pace until later on and go back at them."

Munari: "So the ones that you had to do, were they Nazis?"

Anonymous: "They were Nazis and fascists."

Munari: "Did you know who the people were? As far as name-wise, recognition?"

Anonymous: "No. All we got was a picture and approximate where they were at. And we'd go into that area and stake them out. And we had good scopes back then, you know."

Munari: "Just to back up a second, what layer of prominence were these guys that you were doing? Were they high ranking officers?"

Anonymous: "They were ex-high ranking officers and high ranking government officials and Nazis."

Munari: "In the cities?"

Anonymous: "Yeah. And there were traitors that went on to the German side and collaborated with the Germans and had all these people killing all - and with the justice system the way it was, they couldn't kill them, so we went in and killed them."

Munari: "So have you killed a lot of people?"

Anonymous: "Oh, yeah."

Munari: "You did?"

Anonymous: "Yeah."

Munari: "How many, do you think?"

Anonymous: "I would say in the – 260, 270, about."

Munari: "You, yourself, or your team?"

Anonymous: "Myself. Oh, no, we killed a few – take all 50 guys, we probably killed 3,000."

Munari: "And how many – would you go out together? Just one of you or together?"

Anonymous: "No, two, two guys to a team. Say like they send one team into Germany, take care of a certain amount, and then we'd pull out. While we were in Germany, there'd be another team in France or Belgium or someplace else. And then, what they didn't take care of, when we pulled out of Germany, we'd go in and clean it up. And what we didn't take care of, the others come in. Now seven guys on my team were killed. Seven guys."

Munari: "Did your own forces ever kill our guys?"

Anonymous: "No."

Munari: "What was it called, this particular assignment? Was there a code name for it?"

Anonymous: "No."

Munari: "Really?"

Anonymous: "Just – there had to be one, but we just thought –. Well, yeah, if there was – I'm sure Chesty Puller and Truman had a code word for what they were."

Munari: "Oh, yeah."

Anonymous: "Our transportation would be a military cargo plane going into Germany and all. But we always stayed away from the soldiers or Marines or whatever. And you know, we'd get snide remarks and everything, but we never said anything. And once in a while we'd go onto a base and meet with Chesty Puller. We'd meet usually in a hangar that they're not using or something. We'd meet them in the hangar and we'd talk over everything and all. And he'd have papers with him and everything, and then before he left he'd burn the papers. But we never associated with any of the Marines or Army or anything else. Had a colonel one time that – he was gonna find out who the hell we were, boy. He didn't like us being around at all. Of course, we never talked to anybody."

Munari: "You were not supposed to."

Anonymous: "No. So he went after us like a hound dog."

Munari: "And where were you based?"

Anonymous: "North Carolina."

Munari: "Do you remember the base?"

Anonymous: "Yeah. Camp Lejeune."

Munari: "Camp Lejeune. Camp Lejeune."

Anonymous: "Yeah."

Munari: "That's a famous place."

Anonymous: "Yeah, it is."

Munari: "Yeah. And when did you leave that service, approximately?"

Anonymous: "1949. I think it was November 27th, 1949."

Munari: "Do you remember a country you went to? Do you remember a particular country?"

Anonymous: "Germany. I don't know all of the countries we went to."

Munari: "Did you go to South America at all?"

Anonymous: "Yeah. Argentina. They had a big concentration – "

Munari: "You went into Argentina?"

Anonymous: "Yeah, we been into Argentina. I killed probably 80 to 90 people in Argentina alone."

Munari: "Nazis."

Anonymous: "Because there were so many of them in there. And I don't know how many of the other teams went in there."

Munari: "So this was finishing the war up, wasn't it?"

Anonymous: "Yeah. It was cleaning it up, yeah."

Munari: "So this is stuff that people don't know about."

Anonymous: "No."

Munari: "No. You know, you hear a little bit about it."

Anonymous: "Yeah."

Munari: "But they put it over to the CIA and then they – but people don't understand this is necessary."

Anonymous: "The CIA, no. Even CIA and them didn't know about us. For the simple reason, I later learned that Truman didn't want a blemish on his record. And this would be a blemish. In fact, when we came out–now this is something that surprised the hell out of me, was when we came out of it, all of us out of 50 guys, three guys survived. Everyone else was killed, 47 was killed."

Munari: "You said a minute ago that a few were killed on your team."

Anonymous: "Seven."

Munari: "Seven on your team, but out of the whole thing, only– how many survived?"

Anonymous: "Three."

Munari: "So they all were killed?"

Anonymous: "Yeah, except me and three other guys."

Munari: "How many total guys were there?"

Anonymous: "50, 47 gone."

Munari: "Wow."

Anonymous: "But I didn't have a scratch. Chesty Puller says, 'You know, you're the luckiest son of a bitch in the world.' He said, 'Seven guys on your team been killed and you ain't got a scratch.'"

Munari: "So there's two of you, okay, on a team."

Anonymous: "Right. You got a shooter and you got a spotter. I was always the shooter. I never was the spotter."

Munari: "And tell me what the spotter would do."

Anonymous: "He would look through the scope or glasses and he'd tell you what the range was and you'd adjust your sights to that range, and you click. You'd always find something to find out where the wind - which way the wind's blowing."

Munari: "You could see a leaf or something."

Anonymous: "Yeah, anything. But that comes from being a kid."

Munari: "Experience. So if you saw the wind blowing, you would compensate your–?"

Anonymous: "Yeah, the scope."

Munari: "The scope. Not the aim, the scope."

Anonymous: "Well, the scope would make you compensate the aim."

Munari: "So this was a pretty sophisticated gun, wasn't it?"

Anonymous: "Yeah, it was. It was really – but I looked at what they got now, and hell, that's like a bow and arrow."

Munari: "Yeah. So how did you practice? Or did you practice?"

Anonymous: "We didn't practice on – we practiced by killing the people."

Munari: "So you couldn't shoot a shot to see where you were?"

Anonymous: "No. No."

Munari: "Because you had no silencer, did you?"

Anonymous: "Nope."

Munari: "Yeah."

Anonymous: "They didn't have them back then."

Munari: "Did you ever have any close calls?"

Anonymous: "Yeah, I was sitting with a guy, like here, and I hear something go by my ear–and his brains blew out. So that was a close call, in my book."

Munari: "And you guys would hit the ground?"

Anonymous: "Yeah, I just flipped over like I was shot and then I started searching for where he was and I found him and I killed him. But we had – everybody had a body bag, two body bags per team, because if you got killed, you can't leave your buddy there. So we would take him and put him in the body bag. And this is horrible to say, but we had to drain the blood out. So we'd let the blood drain out because the body bag – you don't wanna be walking with the body bag and it dripping blood. Back then, though, I was in great shape. Man, I could lift a ton. So we would take the body bag, and we would take them and put them at the command center. And we'd walk away."

Munari: "So it's clear, why would you never leave the body there? For family?"

Anonymous: "No. Marines never leave a body."

Munari: "Oh, that's the Marine Corps…"

Anonymous: "Motto."

Munari: "…rule."

Anonymous: "We never leave a body on the battlefield."

Munari: "I see. No matter what?"

Anonymous: "Out of respect for him and his family and the Marine Corps."

Munari: "That's interesting."

Anonymous: "But everyone was carrying a flag. So when they died, we would put them in the body bag and then when we got to headquarters, you would wait and wait until you could put them somewhere where they'd find them. We would drape the flag over him. We always did that. That's why when I see someone burning our flag, I go crazy. It just drives me crazy.

"Dalitz – back in those days, they wouldn't kill anybody in Vegas. When people talked about, oh, Lake Mead was the burying ground, that's not where we buried people. There's mine shafts out in Searchlight and Pioche, out in Potosi. That's where we dumped them. We dumped them in mine shafts. Just boom."

Munari: "Now you say we dumped *them*, you're implying that you killed a lot of people?"

Anonymous: "A few, yeah."

Munari: "From Las Vegas?"

Anonymous: "Yeah."

Munari: "Who were doing what?"

Anonymous: "Doing something – whether they were threatening Dalitz or somebody else, they were doing something that would endanger them."

Munari: "It wasn't a regular citizen, it was usually a Mob guy, wasn't it?"

Anonymous: "Yeah, it was like if somebody was doing something that would threaten their gaming license, they get rid of them. Somebody that was threatening them or their family, they get rid of them. It's like [Louis] 'Russian Louie' [Strauss]. You know 'Russian Louie?' Well, Jimmy Fratianno killed 'Russian Louie.' He took him out of the Desert Inn and the night he took 'Russian Louie' out of the Desert Inn, he was over there, I was having a drink with him and everything and he said, 'Do you wanna go to California with us? We're gonna do a little trip down there.' And I knew what he meant by a trip."

Munari: "Who's speaking to you?"

Anonymous: "Jimmy Fratianno, 'The Weasel.'"

Munari: "So you knew him?"

Anonymous: "Oh, yeah. He was a little bitty guy, but strong as a - fierce and tough. He had no conscience at all. But the reason they got rid of 'Russian Louie'] was because 'Russian Louie' was putting the squeeze on Benny Binion. So Benny said he couldn't have anything to do with the killing so he paid us, arranged it with Jimmy Fratianno."

Munari: "What was 'Russian Louie' trying to do to Benny Binion?"

Anonymous: "Extort money out of him."

Munari: "Because he wanted street tax?"

Anonymous: "Yeah, 'Russian Louie' was a big, mean son of a bitch. He was big and mean."

Munari: "Did he have anybody behind him?"

Anonymous: "No. They all hated him."

Munari: "So he was just a guy out on his own trying to get whatever he could get?"

Anonymous: "Yeah."

Munari: "A wild card."

Anonymous: "But he was mean enough and strong enough and all, that people knew that he could do what he said and all. That he was threatening his–actually he was threatening Jack. He was gonna take Jack [Benny's son] out if Benny didn't give him money and all."

Munari: "About what year was this? Was this before he sold the [Horseshoe] to Joe Brown?"

Anonymous: "Yeah, yeah."

Munari: "The first time he had it, right?"

Anonymous: "Right."

Munari: "Okay. Jack was a younger kid then."

Anonymous: "Yeah. But this guy didn't care. You know, he – "

Munari: "So Benny told Moe about it?"

Anonymous: "Yeah. Benny and Moe knew each other very well."

Munari: "Okay, so you're working in the pit, and you're doing all this. Did you always stay at that position?"

Anonymous: "No. I got up to floorman. After Dalitz and them sold the Desert Inn, Hughes came in and [Robert] Maheu, and they bought it. Dalitz left and everything. But Maheu brought him back, brought Dalitz back. And the Hughes people, scared to death of them. So they made Maheu fire Dalitz and everything. But Dalitz told Maheu, he said, 'Listen to this kid, to what he's got to say and everything.' So I went from dealer, floorman, up to assistant general manager."

Munari: "On the hotel side?"

Anonymous: "I was assistant general manager."

The interview turned to Mobster involvement in the Desert Inn.

Munari: "So who did Dalitz have to answer to?"

Anonymous: "Dalitz didn't really answer to anybody."

Munari: "Well–no, they had Mob guys involved, right?"

Anonymous: "Yeah."

Munari: "So which Mob guys were involved?"

Anonymous: "Giancana. Nick Civella out of Kansas [City]."

Munari: "A Cleveland bunch was there too, right?"

Anonymous: "Yeah."

Munari: "The Cleveland Mafia was pretty tough."

Anonymous: "Yeah, they were."

Munari: "They were Detroit, Cleveland basically."

Anonymous: "That's where Dalitz came from, Detroit and Cleveland."

Munari: "Yeah, and do you think Hoffa had something to do with it?"

Anonymous: "Hoffa was – yeah, but he – you know who Allen Dorfman was?"

Munari: "Yeah."

Anonymous: "Well, Allen Dorfman was in there all the time."

Munari: "He was?"

Anonymous: "Yeah, and there was another guy. But Allen Dorfman, a week before he was shot, he was in the Desert Inn. In fact, Dalitz told me, he said, 'He's a walking dead man.'"

Munari: "Why'd they kill him?"

Anonymous: "Because he was gonna turn state's evidence against the Mob and all to stay out of prison for all the loans and stuff. But here's the thing about those loans, every hotel that borrowed money from the Teamsters, paid it back with interest. There was nothing–they didn't welch or they didn't nothing. But when the money welchers started and everything was when [Morris] Shenker came in to the Dunes. There was another guy there before Shenker, and they started the scamming stuff. But before then, every hotel that borrowed money from the Teamsters paid it back with interest."

Munari: "Do you think [Meyer] Lansky had anything to do with the Desert Inn? He had a little bit, didn't he?"

Anonymous: "Yeah, yeah. But his big interest was the Flamingo, Lansky."

Munari: "Yeah. So, what about Rosselli? Did you see him around there very much?"

Anonymous: "Yeah, he was there."

Munari: "Did you have any dealings with him?"

Anonymous: "But he was the force. I'd say hello to him, and he'd say hello to me. But, we weren't, you know."

Munari: "Did you know Bob Maheu? Maheu used to work for the FBI."

Anonymous: "Right."

Munari: "He retired and he opened up his own agency with the hopes and probably the approval of the CIA because he knew people who were in both. And they used him to do special things for them because now he's a private citizen. But he can do things that they couldn't do and he could be the front, the beard. So Maheu is involved with the CIA and [Richard] Bissell and a few other guys and he's asked to–they wanna kill Castro, so somebody suggests some of the Mob guys, that they used the Mob before in New York City.

"So Maheu hires Rosselli and they met him–first of all, Maheu wants to go to Las Vegas. And so this guy says, 'If you need to meet anybody, you should meet Johnny Rosselli.' So Johnny Rosselli meets them at the El Rancho. It just so happens, when they're in the El Rancho, here comes Beldon Katleman. Beldon Katleman sits down. And Maheu had a subpoena for Beldon Katleman. That was the first time he met Johnny Rosselli and that was the reason he wanted to come to Vegas and he couldn't pull the subpoena out now because his friend introduced him. So that's how he knew who

Rosselli was. So then when they went back, they hired Rosselli to kill Castro. And then Rosselli got Giancana involved. So, now, you got a situation that's very interesting. And there's a lot of people that say Rosselli had something to do with [John F.] Kennedy dying. He may have known who did it, but I don't think he would kill Kennedy.

"Let me just get to the point here. So because he was with the CIA and Giancana was killed in his basement, a lot of people say it was the CIA that killed Rosselli. They think that maybe that's why he was killed, because he knew too much. I say no. I asked around a little bit and Rosselli met a girl, Al Rothman's wife. Al Rothman was a dealer at the Desert Inn. You knew him, right?"

Anonymous: "Right."

Munari: "So he was a dealer – "

Anonymous: "I knew that his wife was cheating on him, yeah."

Munari: "She was a cocktail waitress. And Rosselli took her away from him. And a friend of mine contends–now I'm gonna tell you this. He passed away, but I'm gonna tell you this in confidence, okay? XXXXX seemed to believe that could've been the problem, and so did XXXX. Now, XXXXX was involved with Dalitz because of the Stardust. His father was a Mob guy, XXXXX. So he knew those guys pretty well. And that's what he told me. So, I tend to believe him. So, then XXXXX confirmed it even more, because he kinda–the kid bragged about it a little bit. And now, the way they found Rosselli, Rosselli was cut up, put in a drum and they took his penis off and stuck it in his mouth. Now, you don't do that if the guy's a stool pigeon; you just shoot the guy in the mouth."

Anonymous: "Right."

Munari: "You don't take the time for that. So he wanted to make a point when he did that. And he's dead now, but his father was Chinky Rothman, another guy that was a hoodlum and he was around Philadelphia or somewhere, or Baltimore and he was a bad guy, too. He did some bad stuff for the Mob guys. And he worked for the Stardust. So that's where the story's coming from. Did you hear anything about any of that?"

Anonymous: "Well, there was rumors and everything, you know, but I didn't – "

Munari: "What kind of rumors did you hear?"

Anonymous: "I heard that the kid killed him."

Munari: "You did hear that?"

Anonymous: "Yeah. Because of screwing around with his wife."

Munari: "You did hear that, though?"

Anonymous: "Yeah, but the thing is, when you're involved in stuff like that, you just–once somebody tells you something, you just, you never say it again, you know, it is – "

Munari: "Yeah, it is just out of your head because it didn't really make any difference to you."

Anonymous: "Right."

Munari: "Because Rosselli was not a well-liked guy in some ways. So, you know, I've got an FBI memo, in black and white, which details how Rosselli meets Dalitz, and Yale Cohen. Rosselli has a third unidentified person with him and they go into the Brown Derby restaurant in Los Angeles or Hollywood. Rosselli wants the rest of the money that he says is owed to him for the sale of the Desert Inn that he set up to Hughes. And I would have to say that he's probably right about that. He did have a lot to do with getting that pushed to Hughes because of Maheu."

Anonymous: "Maheu, yeah. Also, you know his son was at the DI [Desert Inn] and everything. His son was an epileptic and he swallowed his tongue so – "

Munari: "Peter?"

Anonymous: "Yeah, Peter. He had a seizure in the pit, and I took a ballpoint pen and pulled his tongue out and held it down and all until the medics got there."

Munari: "Really?"

Anonymous: "Yeah. So he had it really bad."

Munari: "You saved his life. Well, you know, Bob bought my cousin's house on Cochise, you know. And a friend of mine was with my cousin that day. When he sold it to Bob, and they were good friends, he says Bob took him over to the Silver Slipper and paid him cash out of the cage for his house."

Anonymous: "Yeah. They use that stuff for–Baker, Bobby Baker, he was Johnson's–well, he was the money man for Johnson. He'd come out and he'd just be– Another person that was a bag man was–do you remember the clothing store in the airport? Steve–I think it – "

Munari: "Steve Gordon."

Anonymous: "Gordon."

Munari: "Yes, I do remember that."

Anonymous: "His mother, she always – she would go into the DI, she would go in the Flamingo, different places, get the money and all and she would ride the train. She never flew, she never did. Always a train. But she was a big bag woman."

Munari: "In this particular conversation at the Brown Derby, Dalitz tells–first of all, they–Rosselli's presenting the story as, 'I gotta have my money, I'm getting some pressure.' And he points to this third party that – we don't know who this is. The FBI would not reveal in this memo who that person was because that was the informant. So Rosselli didn't know the guy that he was with was an informant for the FBI. Okay, so he was probably wired. So this memo was pretty accurate. I found it – I could go through here and find it for you and show it to you."

Anonymous: "That's all right."

Munari: "So, Dalitz says – and this is in Dalitz's writing, this is black and white, this is not a rumor, this is black and white – Dalitz says something like this to Rosselli, he says, 'Well, I'm not gonna get shaken down, blah, blah, blah, blah, blah. I thought you had… if you need money, we can get you some money. Blah, blah, blah, blah, blah, blah, blah.' And he says, 'I'm gonna have to speak to Lansky and Bobby Gordon over this.'

"So, let's talk about skimming a little bit. So, everyone has a conception of how skimming works, okay? I have a conception, you have a conception, but is there anything unusual about the way the Desert Inn did it? Do you have any knowledge of how they did it?"

Anonymous: "Yeah. The DI and the Stardust was almost the same thing. Back in the old days, you didn't have these machines that count money and all.

"So here's the thing about the Desert Inn, the count room had a hidden door. You couldn't tell, it just looked like a wall. But you opened that door and there's a stairway right up to Moe Dalitz's office. And you know how they found it? When Howard Hughes bought it, they moved the cage. So they tore it all down, and moved the cage over here and all of a sudden they found the door. They could go in there and open up the safe.

"They wheeled the money in and – let me see, now, the scales were on the coins, it wasn't on the cash. They'd move the money in and everything – and the thing is, they knew the tables that had really strong – but at the Desert Inn, you know how they are – the dropboxes are about like this and about like this, about like this. Well there were times that you'd take that paddle, and the paddle's sticking up this high. There's so much hundred dollar bills in it, you can't put the paddle down.

"So they would come and they'd open those boxes, take out whatever they wanted, or whatever they thought there was and they'd divide it up, Cincinnati, Chicago, all these places and then they would take them up to Dalitz's office. But underneath the Desert Inn was a catacomb. You could come in and go down under the Desert Inn and it'd go right out by the pool. The pool was like this. It was like this and then it had a hill like this. Well, there was a place there that you could walk into and everybody thought it was pool equipment stuff, but it wasn't. That's where they took the money out of there and took it down next to the golf course. It'd come right there, right in front of the golf course. And he just took it right out.

"He took the money up to his office and then they'd take it out. I don't know if they divided the money in the count room or in Moe Dalitz's office. But they'd take it to Moe Dalitz's office and that's when they'd go down into the catacomb."

Munari: "There's no telling how much money they would take in a day, huh?"

Anonymous: "No. I tell you, that Desert Inn, not just one table, but you'd see 10, 15 tables where the paddle's up about – you know how those paddles are – and they're sticking up like this. You can't get in anymore, and the floorman's shaking the thing. It's just so full of money. It was surprising to me when they sold it, sold the Desert Inn, because they only sold it for about 13 million, something like that."

Munari: "So, it was worth more than that?"

Anonymous: "Oh, yeah, yeah. I mean the skim, they probably skimmed two or three times that much a year out of that place. It was really strong."

"Going back to me, though. From when I first went to work there, I never got a paycheck, it was always an envelope. Always an envelope. I was never on their payroll. And I never figured why and didn't give a damn, really."

Munari: "What'd you care, right?"

Anonymous: "Yeah, I get my money."m"And I'm making more than any dealer in there."

Munari: "He took care of you, didn't he?"

Anonymous: "Yeah, yeah. When Hughes and them come in and all, I had to get a sheriff's card."

Munari: "You didn't have a sheriff's card?"

Anonymous: "No, I didn't have nothing. They knew when the–if the Gaming Control Board came in, they'd let me know."

Then the former sniper and Desert Inn casino boss relayed a stunning story related to the murder of John Kennedy.

Munari: "This morning you said something about you had a take on the [John F.] Kennedy assassination. Let's hear it."

Anonymous: "Carlos Marcello hated the Kennedys. They were after him, they dropped him off down to South America, no passport and everything else."

Munari: "Guatemala, they left him there."

Anonymous: "Yeah, and when he come back in and everything, there was a meeting at the Desert Inn. Now, when Lansky and Civella and all these people come into the Desert Inn, you know where they met? The Country Club. Up above the Country Club was a convention thing. And they liked to sit up there and look at the golf course and talk and everything. And they knew it wasn't bugged because they –"

Munari: "Desert Inn was bugged pretty heavily."

Anonymous: "Yeah, but not there because they swept it pretty good. The one really bugged was the Fremont.

"I had done something for Dalitz and he wanted to – when I got through and everything, he wanted to talk to me about it and all. So, it was about 10, 11 o'clock at night when I finished. And I searched it for him. So I knew that the Country Club closed down, the only time anybody was in the Country Club was when he was having a meeting with someone. So I went down to the Country Club and I was going up to the thing, there was two big guys sitting at the bottom of the stairs and they wouldn't let me in. And I said, 'I need to talk to Dalitz.' So they went up and everything, and then they came back down and let me back up there. Well sitting at this table was Dalitz, Nick Civella, Sam Giancana, Johnson, Lyndon Johnson and, who else? There was two other guys there, I think –"

Munari: "Lyndon Johnson?"

Anonymous: "Yeah, Lyndon Johnson."

Munari: "The vice president of the United States?"

Anonymous: "Vice president of the United States."

Munari: "Are you sure about that?"

Anonymous: "I knew Johnson. No way would I mistake Johnson. So I went up to [Dalitz] and told him how the deal went. And he looked at Nick Civella and he said, 'This is the Marine I was telling you about.' And Civella, he's a – you ever meet him?"

Munari: "He came in the Dunes. I never knew him though."

Anonymous: "God, he looked like he's frozen. He looked at you like he could freeze you with ice. He had dead eyes, what you call dead eyes. Then he said, 'Thank you. And I was surprised he brought me up with all those guys. And about two days later, Dalitz said, 'How'd you like to apply your special talents to get rid of a politician?' I said, 'No. I don't mess with politicians. It just causes too much trouble. Unless it's another country and it's against our country, but I won't go against a politician.' And nothing was ever –"

Munari: "That's pretty strong."

Anonymous: Nothing was ever said –"

Munari: "So you weren't introduced to Johnson, though?"

Anonymous: "No."

Munari: "Who was he with?"

Anonymous: "Bobby Baker was in the hotel, but he wasn't at that meeting."

Munari: "What year was this? '60? '61?"

Anonymous: "It was three weeks before President Kennedy got shot. Three weeks. And Carlos Marcello was there. Who in the fuck was those other two guys? But as soon as I heard that Kennedy was killed, I knew why. In my mind, I flashed back to that meeting. And knowing how Marcello hated him. So they can say what they want to about who killed him – "

Munari: "Yeah, but why would Dalitz expose that? Three weeks before wasn't enough time to –"

Anonymous: "Dalitz actually trusted me. He knew I wouldn't say nothing."

Munari: "That's pretty risky. Why would the vice president be there and talking about something like that?"

Anonymous: "You've got me."

Munari: "You sure it was him?"

Anonymous: "As sure as you're sitting there, son."

Munari: "Did he say something to you?"

Anonymous: "Never said a word, just looked at me."

Munari: "Were they all sitting at a table together?"

Anonymous: "Yeah, they were all at a table. But here's the thing. How did the shooters know their route? Because they changed it just before Kennedy was killed."

Munari: "Well, there's reasons about that."

Anonymous: "Yeah. But I figured –"

Munari: "But this is a new one. So what would Johnson be doing in Las Vegas at that time? That's interesting."

Anonymous: "Because nobody knew Johnson was there. Nobody."

Munari: "Well, he had to have had some protection."

Anonymous: "If they were, I never saw them."

Munari: "Were those guys Secret Service that were downstairs?"

Anonymous: "No, they were Mob guys."

Munari: "Wow, that's an interesting story. Did Dalitz ever say anything more to you about it? What about after Kennedy was killed?"

Anonymous: "The only thing he said was, 'Forget that meeting.' I said, 'I don't even know what meeting you're talking about.'"

Munari: "So you're talking about serious business. You know that, right?"

Anonymous: "Yeah."

Munari: "That's an interesting story."

Anonymous: "But Dalitz knew that I wouldn't say nothing. I'd killed some people for him. Why would I go blabbing about –"

Munari: "No, I understand that. But the only thing I'm thinking of is how Johnson would let himself be exposed with all those people there."

Anonymous: "I don't know."

Munari: "Of course, he doesn't know what Dalitz said to you either. You just walked in a room, and there's the guys. That was not discussed in front of Johnson. It was discussed in front of you."

Anonymous: "Right. The only thing I told Dalitz is that the job's been completed."

Munari: "When did he ask you about that? The next day?"

Anonymous: "Yeah. The next day he called me into his office and asked me if I'd be willing to get rid of a politician. He didn't mention no names. He didn't say nothing like that. He just said a politician."

Munari: "That's pretty strong. That's a strong one. That's a very interesting one. That corroborates things that were said before, you see? Wow!"

Anonymous: "But that wasn't the first time that Dalitz had had meetings up in the Country Club. When all those Mobsters – Sam Giancana was there also. But when all those Mobsters come into town though, and they had a meeting, it was always up there. And sometimes they'd have meals served to them. But when they got down to talking the business, there was nobody around."

Munari: "Well then, I gotta take the other side of the coin here for a second. The day that Kennedy was killed this guy by the name of [Rolando] Cubela was in Paris near an embassy with a CIA officer and he was asking for a gun to kill Castro. Cubela was a double agent. But he was a guy that we thought was on our side, and they were still trying to kill Castro. So now, there's a very good possibility they're talking about Castro, because Giancana was involved with Rosselli to kill Castro. And Rosselli wasn't at that meeting?"

Anonymous: "No. No."

Munari: "But you're saying Giancana was there, though?"

Anonymous: "Yeah."

Munari: "He had a piece of that joint, I think."

Anonymous: "Of what?"

Munari: "DI."

Anonymous: "Yeah, he did."

Munari: "No question about it."

Anonymous: "Phyllis McGuire was his girlfriend."

Munari: "Right, right."

Anonymous: "She was dangerous. She'd come up to you, and she'd be on the table, talking to the people, and she'd [make obvious sexual innuendos] while you're standing there dealing, and he's over there talking to Moe Dalitz and everything. She didn't care. She was a strange girl, boy. But she could get you killed."

Munari: "That could get you killed."

Anonymous: "Yes, it could. I was surprised that the Smothers Brothers, that guy, one of the Smothers Brothers was –"

Munari: "You mean Dan Rowan of 'Laugh-In?'"

Anonymous: "Yeah, I'm surprised he didn't get killed."

Munari: "They roughed him up."

Anonymous: "Well, I tell you, everybody that I knew in the Mob hated Bobby Kennedy with a passion. And they didn't like JFK –"

Munari: "Well you see, this is where the incongruent thing is here. That's not the way you get rid of Bobby Kennedy. You get rid of Bobby Kennedy by killing Bobby Kennedy."

Anonymous: "Yeah."

Munari: "You don't kill the president to get rid of Bobby Kennedy. That's where I have a problem with that. See, if it was me thinking –"

Anonymous: "But it was John F. Kennedy that gave the okay to deport Carlos. That was the thing with Carlos. When he was going to get his visa and everything updated and all, that's when they nailed him. And he hated both of them."

Munari: "Well, how come then none of those guys did any time? None of those guys got in any trouble. None of them were even arrested for this. All the rumors that you hear about them, how come nothing happened to them?"

After my interviews with the former Desert Inn casino boss, I asked an FBI agent, Gary M., for his thoughts on what I was told. Here is his response:

"November 5, 2019 "Geno,

"I read the information with interest. At first I thought no way, but as I read more I now lean towards the truth of what he said. I fully believe that the mob was in a conspiracy with the CIA regarding the Kennedy assassination and he confirms that.

"I believe that Giancana's man, Jack Ruby, was responsible for enlisting officer [J.D.] Tippit to kill potential witness, Oswald, but he turned the table by killing Tippit.

"The rule of the mob is that if your guy fails to carry out a hit then you are responsible and must make it right. That is why Ruby had to take care of Oswald. Additionally, VP Johnson established the farce of an investigative commission led by Earl Warren who was to protect Johnson at all costs.

"When Ruby told Warren that he had the answer to the Kennedy killing, but he wanted to be protected in Washington D.C., Warren said he couldn't move Ruby from Texas to Washington, D.C. and basically dismissed him. Are you kidding me? The Chief Justice of the Supreme Court and head of the so called truth commission couldn't move Ruby as a vital witness? As unbelievable as it seems, I think Johnson was at the D.I. when your source saw him there.

"I need to read what you sent me again. It is full of interesting stuff. "Thanks,

"Gary"

This writer's feeling is that the confidential source told the truth in our interviews together.

He did not waiver on any facts and was consistent throughout the questioning.

The only problematic piece of information to me was the date on which the source said that Johnson, Dalitz, Civella, Marcello and Giancana met, which was three weeks before the JFK assassination. Perhaps the source remembered incorrectly. I then did some research at the LBJ Presidential Library and discovered that Johnson did visit the Desert Inn and stayed in Room #340 on January 15, 1963. Johnson also went to shows at the Stardust, which had hidden Mob interests, and to the show at the Tropicana, of which Marcello was a hidden owner.

There is proof that Dalitz and Hoffa spoke to one another on a regular basis. Robert Kennedy staff member Walter Sheridan revealed in 1969 that the FBI, without notifying anybody, bugged Dalitz's office and recorded his side of a phone conversation with Hoffa. Also, they monitored several Hoffa conversations that took place in Teamsters cars.[391]

Arthur M. Schlesinger, Jr. wrote in his book, *Robert Kennedy and His Times*:

"The pursuit of Hoffa was an aspect of the war against organized crime. The relations between the Teamsters and the syndicates continued to grow. An FBI electronic microphone, planted from 1961 to 1964 in the office of Anthony Giacalone, a Detroit hood, revealed Hoffa's deep if wary involvement with the local mob. For national purposes a meeting place was the Rancho La Costa Country Club near San Clemente, California, built with $27 million in loans from the Teamsters' pension fund; its proprietor, Morris B. Dalitz, had emerged from the Detroit underworld to become a Las Vegas and Havana gambling figure. Here the Teamsters and the mob golfed and drank together. Here they no doubt reflected that, as long as John Kennedy was President, Robert Kennedy would be unassailable. (And here Richard Nixon in October 1975 made one of his first sallies from his San Clemente fastness to play golf in the company of Frank Fitzsimmons, Hoffa's successor as head of the Teamsters, Anthony Provenzano, a leading suspect in Hoffa's murder, and the ex-convict Allen Dorfman.)"

I started looking at the associates of Dalitz and Hoffa for any possible links to the Kennedy assassinations. There were many – coincidences or not?

391   *Robert Kennedy and His Times*, Arthur M. Schlesinger, 1978

One connection involved Texas oil billionaire H.L. Hunt, who was a big gambler and who was probed in the Terre Haute bookmaking investigation. Researchers linked Hunt to the assassination of President John F. Kennedy.[392] For one, on November 21, 1963, Eugene Hale Brading (also known as Jim Braden) visited Hunt's office, and it is believed that Ruby was there at the same time. Brading was a regular at the Rancho La Costa resort, Moe Dalitz's exclusive country club and Teamsters hangout.

Earlier in the day, Brading arrived in Dallas with a man named Morgan Brown. They stayed in Suite 301 of the Cabaña Motor Hotel of Dallas.

Brading developed a long criminal record while living in California. Arrested 35 times, he had convictions for burglary, illegal bookmaking, and embezzlement.

After the assassination of John Kennedy, Brading was arrested, on November 22, 1963, and taken in for interrogation because he had been "acting suspiciously" in the Dal-Tex Building that overlooked Dealey Plaza. Brading told the police that he was in Dallas on oil business and had gone into the building to make a phone call. In the affidavit that the police had him prepare, he wrote:

> "I am here on [oil] business and was walking down Elm Street trying to get a cab and there wasn't any. I heard people talking saying, 'My God, the President has been shot.'
>
> "Police cars were passing me coming down toward the triple underpass and I walked up among many other people all watching them. I moved on up to the building across the street from the building that was surrounded and I ask [sic] one of the girls if there was a telephone that I could use and she said, 'Yes, there is one on the third floor of the building where I work.'
>
> "I walked through a passage to the [freight] elevator they were all getting on and I got off on the third floor with all the other people and there was a lady using the pay telephone and I ask [sic] her if I could use it when she hung up and she said it was out of order and I tried to use it but with no success. I ask [sic] her how I can get out of this building and she said that there is an exit right there and then she said wait a minute here is the elevator now.
>
> "I got on the elevator and returned to the ground floor and the colored man who ran the elevator said, 'You are a stranger in this building, and I am was [sic] not suppose [sic] to let you up.' And he ran outside to an officer and said to the officer that he had just

taken me up and down in the elevator. And the officer said for me to identify myself and I presented him with a credit card. And he said, 'Well, we have to check out everything,' and took me to his superior and said for me to wait and we will check it out. I was then taken to the Sheriff's office and interrogated."

Brading was released without charge and returned to his room at the Cabaña. It was later established that around midnight Ruby visited the Cabaña, one of the many enterprises financed by Hoffa's Teamsters union pension fund.[393]

It may be a strange coincidence, but Brading also was in Los Angeles the night that Robert Kennedy was murdered.

Starting in 1959, years before the John Kennedy assassination, the CIA began conspiring with certain Mafia bosses about invading Cuba and killing Fidel Castro. At least eight organized crime figures had ties to American intelligence, military and civilian, to anti-Castro Cuban agents and, directly or indirectly to Ruby. Two of them were Russell Bufalino and James "Jimmy" Plumeri. Bufalino was the Mafia boss of all of industrialized northeastern Pennsylvania and credited with arranging the 1957 Mafia summit in Apalachin.

After the initial attempts to kill Castro failed, the CIA turned to other assets, to Bob Maheu, and through Maheu, to Rosselli, Giancana, Richard Cain, Charles Nicoletti, Trafficante, and Salvatore Granello.

Maheu, who purchased his home from one of my relatives, lived five doors down from me. One of his sons was my paper boy. Maheu was one of the most fascinating people anyone would want to meet. He led a life that most people dream of living. Once an FBI agent, Maheu left to pursue a career as a private detective at the behest of someone at the CIA. In a special arrangement, he was to work for them, shrouded by a layer of secret protection so that the CIA could never be accused of being involved, which was the standard CIA modus operandi. Creating layers and giving orders or commands through a series of different people made it difficult to discover the actual true source. Maheu's small business was the front for his doing the bidding of the CIA. He was paid a small monthly retainer, and it was the start of a long career.

He worked on projects for Aristotle Onassis and Howard Hughes and eventually became the head of Nevada operations for Hughes. He rented suites at the Dunes long before Hughes settled in at the Desert Inn, however, was asked to leave because the Dunes owners needed the rooms for their high-rolling gamblers.

393   *Legacy of Doubt: Did the Mafia Kill JFK?* Peter Noyes, 2010

In August 1960, CIA agent Richard M. Bissell approached Colonel Sheffield Edwards to determine if the U.S. Office of Security had assets that could assist in a sensitive mission requiring gangster-type action. The mission target was Fidel Castro.

On September 24, 1960, an initial meeting was held between CIA Operations Support Chief Jim O'Connell, Rosselli, and Maheu at the Plaza Hotel in New York to plan the assassination of Castro. Rosselli then asked Giancana to participate. Giancana agreed and approached Trafficante, who agreed to recruit an "asset" to carry out the murder.

A follow-up meeting of Rosselli, Giancana, Trafficante, Maheu, and O'Connell took place in early October 1960 at the Fontainebleau Hotel in Florida. When Maheu explained the plan to Rosselli and Giancana, his client Hughes contacted him and asked him what he was doing in Miami. Maheu told Hughes about the CIA plan to kill Castro.

By 1977, six of the eight known Syndicate figures used by the CIA in the plot to kill Castro were murdered, and all of their murders were unsolved. Only Trafficante of the second group and Bufalino of the first were still alive on December of that year. Trafficante appeared before the House Select Committee on Assassinations in March 1977 but refused to answer any questions about the murder of John F. Kennedy.

Maheu, Giancana, and Rosselli were also linked in an eavesdropping scandal in which CIA resources were used for a personal romantic matter.

Giancana, a jealous man, was hot and heavy for singer Phyllis McGuire. He discovered that Dan Rowan, a Laugh-In comedian, was courting her. Giancana, or more likely his good friend Rosselli, hatched the idea of eavesdropping on Rowan. Rosselli went to Maheu with the request, then Maheu had an associate, Arthur Balletti, perform the "black bag" operation.

Balletti was arrested on October 31, 1960, for listening to the phone calls that Rowan made and received in his room at the Riviera. The Clark County Sheriff's Office learned about it after a hotel manager stumbled upon suspicious looking equipment in Balletti's hotel room, also at the Riviera. The hotel manager being in the room was unusual; it likely was a ruse by management to find out what was going on inside. It is probable that management thought the eavesdropping they discovered was the work of the FBI. A subsequent search of Balletti's room yielded dates, times and notes about Rowan's phone conversations and a suitcase full of electronic devices, including transmitters, receivers, wall plugs, a Minifon wire recorder, and a set of 17 professional lock picks.

This incident was in 1960 just after Sid Wyman left the Riviera. It was a regular hangout for Rosselli, and this is where Wyman and he crossed paths many times.

After being transported to the county jail, Balletti admitted that he was hired by Investigations Incorporated of Miami, Florida, which was owned by former FBI agent Edward DuBois, and that the company had a client who wanted information on Rowan's private life. According to Balletti, investigator Fred T. Harris entered and installed the listening device in Rowan's room. He admitted eavesdropping on Rowan's conversations for about five days, since October 25.

Rowan was told what happened, but, on November 1, he agreed to drop all charges against Balletti. Rowan did so, after and as a result of getting threatened and roughed up by an unidentified individual, a source told this writer. The beating likely also was a warning to stay away from McGuire.

Robert Kennedy was furious when he found out that Maheu approved and directed this black bag job for Giancana. Kennedy, who had to square it all, hated Giancana to start with, and then on top of that, they used the CIA to bug Rowan's room for Giancana.

This led me to wonder how many other taps were placed on unsuspecting people in Las Vegas and elsewhere when someone wanted information. If Giancana and Rosselli could get CIA operatives to bug Rowan's telephone, it is a very good bet that they might have bugged the Desert Inn's offices as well. By doing so, Giancana and the Chicago Outfit could have gleaned valuable information. How many conversations about the casino skim did they overhear? They could know the answers to questions before asking.

The methods involved in the Rowan bugging were even more interesting. For one, a full crew of operatives was involved, much like with the break-in of the Democratic National Headquarters in the Watergate building. Also, Maheu instructed T.W. Richardson, a manager at the New Frontier, to pay a gentleman $1,000 for a password, which really was a retainer for Balletti's eavesdropping services. What is strange is how Maheu involved an uninvolved casino employee in the scheme and made it mysterious by saying the money was for a password. Wouldn't that have made Richardson suspicious? All Maheu had to do was tell Richardson, "I want you to give a guy whose name is Mr. Brown (or whatever the name) $1,000 for me. I will reimburse you when I see you." But he didn't. I will always wonder why. Maybe this was common practice for Maheu and Richardson. Covert ops were old hat for Maheu.

Many years later, Maheu talked about another incident involving surreptitious surveillance of another unsuspecting person. He said, "Mr. Hughes was interested in rumors that were abounding to the fact that Ava Gardner, in whom he was very much interested at the time, was at Lake Tahoe and seeing Frank Sinatra, and wanted surveillance placed on Ava Gardner. I hired a private eye, a former FBI agent in Reno, and gave him the assignment."[394]

In an interview for public radio, Maheu explained Hughes' zeal for communication and his "need to know." Perhaps Hughes was the impetus behind all of the latest listening mechanisms employed by the National Security Agency, the CIA and every other intelligence gathering source in the U.S.

Maheu said,

> "I mean, in the case of Hughes, people seem to want to forget about the accomplishments. And I'm talking about the accomplishments in communications. Everyone thinks of Hughes as a movie mogul, a woman chaser. They don't realize that when he flew around the world, when he set a record flying around the world, he was as proud of the fact that throughout that whole trip he was in constant communication. He was a communications buff. I mean, who soft landed the first vehicle on the moon? It was Hughes Aircraft. Imagine that many years ago we soft-landed a vehicle on the moon that sent messages back to Earth upon command from Earth, not once but twice. We marvel about our communications today in the world of space. Who set the first space vehicle synchronized to Earth? The Early Bird, which was a Hughes Aircraft manufactured vehicle, we did that in the middle '60s when four-fifths of the world had been incapable of receiving instantaneous communications. You understand that better than I do at that time. But we don't talk about these accomplishments. We don't talk about the things, the helicopters, and the other accomplishments of this man. And I think it's time that we do. And as long as I live, I'll do my share in that world, I'll tell you."

Maheu's own words confirm in my mind that Hughes was a full-fledged partner of the CIA and Maheu likely was the go-between.

Maheu came from the old school of law enforcement and was a strong anti-Communist. He was a loyal patriot who acted on the belief that one had to do what they had to do for the benefit of the U.S. This is evident in a journal entry of Meier, which captures the sentiments of Maheu and Richard Nixon's brother, Don Nixon, immediately following Robert Kennedy's assassination.

"June 5, 1968. Wednesday

"I got up at 4 A.M., went to shower and shave and put on the morning news about the primary. The newscaster was talking about the sadness of the shooting of Kennedy and I assumed he was talking about the JFK assassination in relation to the Robert Kennedy primary results. He then said that Robert Kennedy was shot at 12:15 a.m. I was so totally shocked at this news that I cut myself deeply while shaving. I began frantically trying to reach either Paul Schrade or Harry Evans on the telephone when the newscaster reported that Evans and Schrade had also been shot. He listed some others as well.[395]

"2:30 p.m. I reached Harry Evans at the Kaiser Hospital in Hollywood (213/667-4011) where Paul Schrade was taken after the shooting at the Ambassador Hotel. Evans said that he was trailing a bit behind Schrade and was entering the doorway into the Ambassador's serving pantry when gunfire broke out. Because of the crush of people, he was unable to get much closer. He knew that the Senator, Schrade, and several others had been shot. Evans said that an enormous number of shots were fired and that Schrade took a bullet in the head. Evans said that Frank Mankiewicz, RFK's press secretary, had called and said that although the Senator is still alive, it does not look promising for him. Evans said that Elizabeth Evans, who was hit by a ricocheting bullet, was no relation to him.

"5:00 p.m. Don Nixon called from the Vegas airport, demanding to know where I was and why nobody was there to pick him up. When I explained the reason, he became even more agitated and said words to the effect of, who cares, what about my hotel room? His concern over Kennedy was nonexistent and placed well behind who was going to pay for the taxi and the room.

"He checked into the Frontier Hotel and made several calls to me, which I did not return. I went to bed totally exhausted, shocked, and sick about the events of the day."

"June 6, 1968, Thursday

"5 a.m. Bob Maheu called to ask about the Don Nixon meeting and suggested 8:30 for breakfast at the Desert Inn Country Club. I went to the club. Maheu was all smiles and Don Nixon walks in all

395   *Age of Secrets: The Conspiracy that Toppled Richard Nixon and the Hidden Death of Howard Hughes*, Gerald Bellett, 2015

smiles. What followed next had to be seen to be believed. They embraced each other and Don Nixon said, 'Well, that prick is dead,' and Maheu said, 'Well, it looks like your brother is in now.' At the time I did not even know what they were talking about.

"Maheu joked that they should now be calling Don Nixon 'Mr. Vice President.' I still did not realize that Robert Kennedy had died and when they saw that I was unaware, Maheu told me, 'John, you are out of it. Why don't you go home and Don and I will carry on without you?' The last thing I recall was Don worrying about who was going to take him to the airport to catch the Western 1:05 flight to L.A. Maheu said he would take him personally as they had much to talk about."

CHAPTER 68

THE END

The Dunes closed for good on January 26, 1993. On that Tuesday, 1,400 people became unemployed.

"We raised each other's children," said Denise Watson, who was a casino cashier there for 14 years. "We've buried each other's parents. We've lived each other's lives. That's what we'll miss, the unity part."

Pit boss Earl Brookner said, "It was the jewel of the Strip." Brookner, then 56 and now deceased, spent half of his life working at the Dunes. "Celebrities of the highest magnitude were patrons here. You were rubbing elbows with the elite of the entertainment and sports world."

Steve Wynn described the Dunes property as "the site of the next extraordinary leap in resort design in the history of this remarkable city." He planned to demolish the Dunes, and in its place, build a 3,000-room resort around a 14-acre lake. He planned to market the finale of the historic property in conjunction with the opening of his newly built hotel-casino, Treasure Island.

In advance of the Dunes implosion, planned for late October, Wynn and company were trying to sell the film rights of it to a movie studio. Mirage officials were willing to delay the implosion until November to get national network TV coverage. Wynn purchased an hour of prime-time air on NBC to broadcast the event.

The implosion was budgeted at a cost of $1.6 million plus liability insurance of $315 million.

A Mirage spokesman, Alan Feldman, sarcastically remarked, "We'll make sure we miss Caesars Palace."

One of the issues with the planned implosion of the Dunes was not mortar or debris damage, but rather the deadly asbestos that was identified in the Dunes structure. Hal Newman, a Clark County plan check supervisor, remarked, "If they do blow it down, it will be one hell of a dust cloud."

Caesars Palace, located directly north of the Dunes but separated by Flamingo Road, was concerned. Spokesman Phil Cooper said, "Caesars wants to make sure that the implosions don't hurt casino guests or property. We're talking about possibly an enormous dust problem. Everything that brings air into Caesars is on that side."

Nobody seemed concerned about the employees or hotel guests.

In March, Wynn hired a liquidator to dispose of all of the furniture, fixtures, and equipment in a giant, maximum 60-day sale. The Dunes was completely vacated.

On October 27, 1993, Wynn threw the switch that started the initial fireball display that led into the explosion of 600 pounds of dynamite placed throughout the Dunes structure. Simultaneously, a cannon shot off at the new 3,000-room Treasure Island.

Wynn described the event as "a wonderful bittersweet moment for Las Vegas." He went on, "The Dunes, in its best moments, was a wonderful, exciting place. There came a time when that was not true anymore. We're taking the first step in making it wonderful and exciting again. This is not an execution; this is a phoenix rising."

More than 200,000 people watched the Dunes fall, from various protected areas along the Las Vegas Strip.

"It was like a bomb hit the place," said Kathy Markowski, a gambler.

Many of the past Dunes employees looked on in shock and wept as if they were at the funeral of a close family member. Among them was a palpable animosity toward Wynn, a person whom they did not even know. They objected to the final hour of the legendary Dunes.

"How could this end like this?" remarked a former cocktail waitress. Her thoughts were echoed by many standing in the chilled air as the crowd witnessed the hanging dust of death.

Nothing lasts forever.

The stray animals that made the Dunes their home now wandered onto the grounds, aware that something was wrong. For years they received complimentary lodging, food, and beverage there from the employees, several of whom now scrambled to look after the frightened critters.

In the minds of the employees, the Dunes was a mother ship. It raised families, paid mortgages, bought cars, paid for vacations, and in some ways, contributed to vices as well.

There would be no more of that. There would be no more stealing, hustling, skimming, or gambling. There would be no more legends hanging around the gaming pits. There would be no more cups of coffee or cocktails in the Royal Box lounge. There would be no more cutting the tokes and trips across the street to shoot craps. There would be no more after-shift drinks. This was the end of the last shift.

The Dunes was done, gone, no more, with one exception: the memories. They remained. Only the memories could not be taken from the employees, guests, and owners. Yes, thanks for the memories.

The end.

Addendum

EXHIBITS

Former FBI agent William Ouseley was kind enough to furnish these exhibits.

ITEM # 1: Two excerpts from Affidavits in support of requests for court authorized electronic surveillance.

Telephone call from Morris Shenker to Nick Civella. It is appears the conversation was concern over the M&R suit filed by Shenker. This telephone call was never entered as evidence in the court hearing and is the only public record of it.

The person Civella is telling Shenker to meet with at La Costa is believed to be Roy Williams, Teamster Vice President and Director of the Central Conference. Williams is totally under the control of Nick Civella.

The Sam Ancona mentioned in the excerpt is a Teamster Official, a Kansas City resident, and part of the Civella organization. Ancona acts as the go-between for Civella and Williams.

ITEM # 2: Testimony of Joe Agosto. Agosto testifies concerning using Shenker to infuse much needed funds into the financially troubled Tropicana. Agosto was beholden to the Civella organization, and had wormed his way into a position at the Tropicana, without being licensed as a key employee, calling the shots and reporting to on a regular basis by phone to Carl Deluna, Civella's street boss.

ITEM# 3: Records seized by FBI agents, pursuant to a search warrant on March 5, 1980, at Milwaukee, from Frank Balistrieri, Milwaukee Mob Boss.

"Fox" is the code name used by the mob for Shenker

A - This record was determined to be in the handwriting of Carl Deluna of Kansas City. It shows money being paid by Shenker to Balistrieri, whose code name was "Berman," and divided into 3 shares. It is connected to the following notations.

B - This record of the "Fox Account" indicates the three-way split was: "FM" is Balistrieri; "Ch" is Chicago crime family; "Ni" is Nick Civella in Kansas City.

C - E - Further breakdowns of the Shenker payments.

ITEM # 4 - Records seized by FBI agents pursuant to a search warrant on February 14, 1979, at Kansas City, from Carl Deluna, ranking Kansas City mob member.

F - Note showing monies received from what Deluna calls the "Berman Acct." Note that the 33,333 matches that figure for "Ni" on note "B" seized from Balistrieri.

G - Two notes dated 10/9/77 re getting $40,000 from Shenker. "Cp" is the code for Charles Moretina, Kansas City mob member. It is not clear how they got the money as I don't believe they were in Las Vegas, but Deluna has his own codes for such things. This appears to be a separate Shenker debt than the "Berman acct."

The "On" mentioned was Nick Civella, The last little line "gave the 40 to Lgs" is a reference to Pete Tamburello another of the Kansas crime family.

H - Deluna note of his visit to Las Vegas 4/24 to 4/30/78. The first line refers to his visits with "Cease" – short for "Caesar" – code name for Joe Agosto. "Craz" is Frank Rosenthal. "CT" is Carl Thomas.

"Fox" is Shenker. "San" is his wife. Of interest, it was on this trip that Deluna, chosen by the Chicago and Kansas City Bosses, visited Allen Glick to order him to sell out his Argent Corp. interest, or else.

I - Note of meeting with Shenker at Kansas City airport along with "MM" – Carl Civella, acting Kansas City Boss. Mr. Ozark part is not pertinent. Lawsuit with "monkeys" (Teamsters) is a reference to the M&R matter. The last part of monies delivered = the figure 27-1/2 matches the figure in the note labeled "G".

J - L - These Deluna notes show that Shenker is "Fox." All these items except for "H" are public record.

WT 79-4-3

174. The following conversations were intercepted over telephone number 816-471-3100, located at 1104 Oak, Kansas City, Missouri.

174A. On September 25, 1978, at approximately 2:29 pm, an outgoing call was placed by a female, at a time when Nick Civella was on the premises of Quinn and Peebles law office, to 816-924-1650, identified as subscribed to by Teamster Joint Council 56. When the call was answered this female asked for Sam Ancona. At this point, the interception was terminated.

175. On October 10, 1978, at approximately 2:13 pm, Morris Shenker placed an incoming call to Nicholas Civella. Civella told Shenker that "all them people are" at "La Costa," including "the fellow from here local." Civella told Shenker to "reach for him" and "tell him if you've got the time, you'd like to come down there and talk with him," adding, "that's what I want you to do." Civella further instructed Shenker as follows:

176. "And I think, I think we'll be able to maybe to start that legal matter, get it all started and maybe you can draw up some papers and stuff and have, you have your conversation with him, but I suggest that you have it just you and he."

177. Civella told Shenker to, "tell him what's on your mind," and "he'll tell you what he can do for you." Shenker told Civella that he would meet with Civella "there" within the "next two, three days."

178. At approximately 3:17 pm, Civella called telephone number 1-714-438-9111, identified as "LaCosta" by the person answering, and attempted to unsuccessfully to reach "Mr. Sam Ancona," who Civella stated was "with the teamsters."

179. Special Agents of the San Diego Office of the FBI advised your affiant on October 12, 1978, that an IBT meeting was held at LaCosta Country Club and Spa, Carlsbad, California, on October 10-12, 1978. On October 12, 1978, Frank Fitzsimmons and Morris Shenker were observed at LaCosta, and on October 13, 1978, Roy Williams and Sam Ancona were observed boarding an IBT jet in Carlsbad and departing for Kansas City.

WT- 79-4-3

in the interim "Yarborough" will run things until "we find out where we're going."

Williams continued that he set out the alternatives for the trustees, that they will either trust "the guy that goes up there", they will find someone the trustees do trust, or they will change the trustees, but they will stay away from the "fund".

19. As set forth at paragraphs 175-177 of Exhibit D, on October 10, 1978, a court-ordered electronic surveillance of telephone number 816-471-3100, located at 1104 Oak Street, Kansas City, Missouri, revealed a conversation between Morris Shenker and Nicholas Civella. Civella told Shenker that "the fellow from here local" was as "La Costa". Civella directed Shenker to contact "him", to 30 to La Costa, and meet with "him". Civella suggested that "just you and he" meet together, and that "he'll tell you what he can do for you." Shenker responded that he would also meet with Civella "there" within the next "two, three days".

As set forth more fully in paragraphs 175 through 180 of Exhibit D, a confidential informant, whose qualifications appear in paragraph 113 of Exhibit D, advised that Morris Shenker and Roy Williams met at La Costa Country Club in October, 1978, concerning a civil suit Shenker had filed against the CSPF. Williams wanted Shenker to withdraw the suit and agree on a settlement, and the informant concluded that Williams and Nick Civella will get a "piece" of the settlement figure.

FBI surveillance confirmed that Williams, Ancona and Shenker were observed at La Costa on October 12 and 13, 1978.

20. This same informant advised during the week ending September 21, 1979, that the matter involving a suit by Morris Shenker against the CSPF regarding a loan that had been agreed to but not completed for the Dunes Hotel and Country Club, Las Vegas, Nevada, is still pending. The source advised that a proposed settlement of this case would result in monies being funneled to organized crime figures in Chicago and Kansas City through Roy Williams and Allen Dorfman, and that Williams, therefore, favors a settlement being reached. The M & R case resulted in CSPF Administrator Dwyer having to step down, in that

Q   And did you do anything with them in terms of recommending people for hire?

A   Yes, I did recommend them to hire Mr. Carl Thomas as previously agreed to follow-up Mr. Nick Civella's instruction.

Q   And had you discussed the hiring of Carl Thomas by the Tropicana with anyone else prior to making this recommendation to the Doumanis?

A   I discussed this with Mr. Civella in the light booth.

Q   I'm sorry?

A   I discussed this with Mr. Civella at the meeting I had in the light booth. He recommended that I hire Carl Thomas.

        THE COURT: Mr. Agosto, it would be better, when you are referring to one of the Civellas, to be specific as to which one you are referring, so that we would appreciate it if you would refer either to Mr. Nick Civella or Mr. Carl Civella, or whoever. But rather than just Mr. Civella, because it is difficult sometimes to know which one you are talking about.

        THE WITNESS: Yes, sir.

        THE COURT: In this instance, which one are you talking about?

        THE WITNESS: I am talking about Mr. Nick Civella with whom I had the meeting in the light booth.

        THE COURT: All right.

Q   (By Mr. Helfrey) Did you discuss the employment potential

1   of Carl Thomas with anyone else from Kansas City?

2 A   I discussed it, yes, with Mr. DeLuna.

3 Q   And in what format did you discuss it with Mr. DeLuna, in

4   person or over the telephone?

5 A   Over the telephone.

6 Q   Was, in fact, Mr. Carl Thomas hired by the Tropicana Hotel?

7 A   He was hired by the Doumanis.

8   MR. RUSSELL: I would like to narrow down as to

9   the time frame we are talking about.

10   THE COURT: I think you are entitled to that.

11   Get him to be specific as to the time frame.

12 Q   (By Mr. Helfrey) Do you remember the time frame Mr. Thomas

13   worked in the Tropicana Casino?

14 A   In the spring of 1975.

15 Q   And do you remember what position he occupied?

16 A   He was hired as a casino manager, to the best of my

17   recollection.

18 Q   And do you recall how long Mr. Thomas remained an employee

19   of the Tropicana Hotel Casino?

20 A   A very short period of time, approximately two months.

21   MR. RUSSELL: I am willing to stipulate he worked

22   there from early April to early May of 1975.

23   THE COURT: That is agreeable, Mr. Helfrey?

24   MR. HELFREY: Mr. Russell, will you stipulate he

25   commenced work on April 7, 1975 at the starting rate

of $60,000 per year, and the last day he worked as

May 11, 1975 as casino manager?

MR. RUSSELL: That is right, 30 days.

THE COURT: All right, ladies and gentlemen, it

has been stipulated by the lawyers that Mr. Thomas's

period of employment as a casino manager at the

Tropicana was from April 7, '75 to May 11, 1975 at the

rate of $60,000 a year.

MR. HELFREY: And I believe, Your Honor, that

Plaintiff's Exhibit 434 has been received in evidence.

If not, I would offer it at this time.

MR. RUSSELL: It hasn't.

MR. HELFREY: I will then offer Plaintiff's

Exhibit 434, which was authenticated by the custodian

of records of the Tropicana Hotel Casino.

MR. RUSSELL: In light of the stipulation, I don't

think it is necessary. I am stipulating that he worked

there 30 days.

THE COURT: Is there any other purpose in 434,

Mr. Helfrey?

MR. HELFREY: No, I can't think of any at the

moment.

THE COURT: Then let's be satisfied with the

stipulation.

MR. HELFREY: Okay.

1   Q   (By Mr. Helfrey) Now, why did you seek a position for

2   Carl Thomas at the Tropicana Hotel as casino manager?

3   MR. GOODMAN: Objection. I believe that assumes

4   facts not in evidence. I don't believe that is the

5   witness's testimony thus far. I thought he said the

6   Doumanis recommended Carl Thomas.

7   THE COURT: On his recommendation.

8   MR. GOODMAN: I did not hear that.

9   Q   (By Mr. Helfrey) Do you recall the question?

10   A   Would you say the question again.

11   Q   Why did you seek a position on behalf of Carl Thomas as

12   casino manager at the Tropicana Hotel Casino?

13   A   Mr. Civella and I discussed -- Mr. Nick Civella and I

14   discussed Mr. Carl Thomas, and Mr. Civella told me he was

15   the man capable to take charge of the Tropicana Casino, be

16   in charge of the stealing.

17   Q   During this time period, did you have any discussions with

18   Carl Thomas?

19   A   I had discussion with Carl Thomas as my intent to recommend

20   to Doumani to be hired as casino manager.

21   Q   And did you discuss with Carl Thomas the nature of your

22   discussions with Mr. DeLuna and Mr. Nick Civella concerning

23   the stealing from the Tropicana Hotel?

24   A   At that time I did not.

25   Q   Did you discuss at any time with Carl Thomas the ultimate

55

1   goal at the Tropicana Hotel of stealing?

2 A   A little bit later, yes, I did discuss in detail.

3 Q   How much later?

4 A   In 1978.

5 Q   And did Carl Thomas indicate to you whether or not he was

6   in contact with Nick Civella or anybody else from Kansas

7   City?

8 A   Yes, Carl Thomas indicated to me that he was in contact

9   with Mr. Nick Civella in Kansas City at all times.

10 Q   Did you discuss with Mr. Carl Thomas the hiring of any

11   other individuals at the casino?

12 A   Mr. Carl Thomas requested full authority as the casino

13   manager in order that he may hire his crew, as he classified

14   them, meaning assistants and others, clerical workers.

15 Q   And did he indicate why he wanted to have that autonomy, that

16   authority?

17   MR. GOODMAN: Could we have a time for this?

18   THE COURT: Yes, you are entitled to that.

19 Q   (By Mr. Helfrey)   Are we still confining ourselves to the

20   spring of 1975, Mr. Agosto?

21 A   Yes. He did not indicate why he had to have such authority.

22 Q   Did you discuss Carl Thomas with the Doumani brothers?

23 A   Yes, I did.

24 Q   And after he was hired, did you have further discussions

25   with the Doumani brothers concerning Carl Thomas?

5

1	A	The Doumani brothers had hesitancy on hiring him.
2	Q	Did you have any discussions with them approximately in
3		May, or around May 11, 1975, concerning his continued
4		employment at the Tropicana Hotel?
5	A	Yes, I told the Doumanis, if they would keep Carl Thomas,
6		they might have an opportunity to obtain the teamster loan.
7	Q	And did you have any discussions with anyone in Kansas City
8		concerning the retention of the position for Mr. Carl Thomas
9		at the hotel, the Tropicana Hotel?
10	A	I conveyed to Mr. Nick Civella and Mr. DeLuna that the
11		Doumanis were not too happy with Mr. Carl Thomas.
12	Q	And did that precipitate other meetings or other contact
13		with Mr. Nick Civella or Mr. Carl Civella?
14	A	Yes, I flew to Kansas City and had a meeting which was
15		attended by Carl Civella, Nick Civella, and DeLuna.
16		I discussed it, that possibly I was not going to
17		be able to maintain Carl Thomas in a position of manager of
18		the casino due to the pressure I was getting from the
19		Doumanis.
20	Q	Did the four of you discuss what should be done about that
21		situation?
22	A	We decided that we should keep Carl Thomas at all cost.
23	Q	Did the four of you agree to that plan, to implement that
24		decision to keep Carl Thomas at the Tropicana Hotel?
25	A	I was told to go see --

Q   By whom?

A   By Nick Civella -- to go see Mr. Morris Shenker, the owner
    of the Dunes Hotel, which nickname was the Fox, and to
    seek with him the possibility of him putting enough money
    in the Tropicana in order that we may retain control and be
    able to save Carl Thomas's position.

Q   Did you, in fact, visit with Mr. Shenker?

A   Yes, I visited with Mr. Shenker.

Q   And what discussions after this meeting with the two
    Civella brothers and Mr. Carl DeLuna in Kansas City, what
    conversations, if any, did you have with the Doumani brothers
    concerning Carl Thomas?

A   I was stalling for time with them, not to terminate Carl
    Thomas's position.

Q   And did you offer them any inducement not to terminate Carl
    Thomas?

A   Yes, I told them I would be able to provide more money, and
    I told them that by retaining Carl Thomas, possibly the
    teamster loan, which had been denied from month-to-month,
    might be allowed to them.

Q   To your knowledge, did Mr. Shenker cause any money to be
    invested in the Tropicana Casino Hotel in the spring of
    1975?

A   Mr. Morris Shenker, in the spring of '75, caused money to be
    invested, number one, to an associate of the Tropicana in a

1   small amount through his son, Arthur Shenker. And after

2   my visit to him, during the so-called Carl Thomas crisis,

3   Mr. Morris Shenker did invest a million and a half into the

4   Tropicana Hotel.

5 Q   And prior to Mr. Shenker investing a million and a half

6   dollars in the Tropicana Hotel, did you have any relationship

7   with Mr. Morris Shenker, yourself?

8 A   Yes, yes, a very good relationship with him, with Mr.

9   Shenker, very good.

10 Q Were you able, then, on your own to secure a million-and-a-

11   half-dollar investment from Mr. Shenker for the Tropicana

12   Hotel?

13 A   Yes, I was able to talk to a bank in Nevada for which I was

14   a customer of it, and induce them to make a loan to Mr.

15   Shenker for a million and a half, which they did.

16 Q What role if any, did Mr. Carl Civella, Mr. Nick Civella,

17   and Mr. Carl DeLuna play in this million-and-a-half-dollar

18   investment by Mr. Shenker?

19 A   None.

20 Q Who originated the idea, then, for this investment to save

21   the position of Carl Thomas?

22 A   The idea was conceived and decided in my meeting in Kansas

23   City with Mr. Nick Civella, Carl Civella, DeLuna. After

24   the implementation was made by me by contacting Mr. Shenker,

25   assure his cooperation, and by me talking to the banker to

allow the funds to belong to Mr. Shenker, which used his

personal financial statement to do so.

Q   And this was a disclosed investment subject to the gaming

rules?

A   Yes, it was disclosed subject to the approval of the Gaming

Board.

Q   And did this investment preserve Carl Thomas's position at

the Tropicana Hotel?

A   Only temporarily.

Q   Would the investment by Mr. Shenker give him any ownership

interest in the Tropicana Hotel?

A   Yes, if he would have been approved by the Gaming Board, yes.

Q   Was he approved by the Gaming Board to make this investment

in the Tropicana Hotel?

A   No, it was not approved.

Q   And how long after that, or what time period in relationship

to this proposed investment by Mr. Morris Shenker did Carl

Thomas leave the Tropicana Hotel?

A   Well, once the Gaming Board denied the approval of

Mr. Shenker to have permission for the infusion of this

million and a half capital, the board gave to the Doumanis,

I think, 30 days for them to repay Mr. Shenker the money

which there were already some spent during this period of

time. The Doumanis sought new investors, because they were

violently opposed to Mr. Shenker investing, violently opposed

1   to retaining Mr. Carl Thomas, and they sought new investors

2   which was in the name of Mike Davis in a period of 30 days,

3   repay Shenker and terminate Carl Thomas. The Doumanis

4   terminated Carl Thomas the same day they repaid Shenker.

5 Q   Did Mike Davis then come to exercise an ownership interest

6   in the Tropicana?

7 A   Yes, he did.

8 Q   And for how long a period of time, to your knowledge?

9 A   Mike Davis also came as a so-called emergency investor to

10   relieve the Doumanis out of a situation which was intolerab

11   according to them, which existed at the time when Mr. Shenk

12   tried to interject his capital.

13 Q   To your knowledge, what was the financial condition of the

14   Tropicana Hotel Casino at that point in time; that is, the

15   spring of 1979, early summer?

16 A   It was living day-by-day. Had a financial crisis every day

17 Q   Was the investment interest of Mike Davis ever repaid, to

18   your knowledge?

19 A   Yes.

20 Q   By whom?

21 A   In the summer of the year 1975, after Mike Davis came into

22   the Tropicana, Mrs. Mitzi Stauffer Briggs came as a stock-

23   holder, a majority stockholder, to the Tropicana, with an

24   infusion of six million two capital, which repaid Mike Davi

25   the investment which was used to repay Mr. Shenker.

A

ITEM 3

CLERK U.S. DISTRICT COURT
Exhibits:
P 610 b   D

Case No. 83-00124-CR-W-8

Fox to Berman
Lists Fox 7/4 — 75 - 75 —
3/7 — 50 - 125 - 15
4/8 — 50 - 125 - 15
8/8 50 — 50 - 125 - 15
Approx 9/10 (4 mos) 50 — 275 - 15
9/8 (SD) — 325 -
Cont Fox to 50 = 375 —
9/29 50 = 425 —
50 = 475 —
50 = 525 —
50 = 575 —
600
450

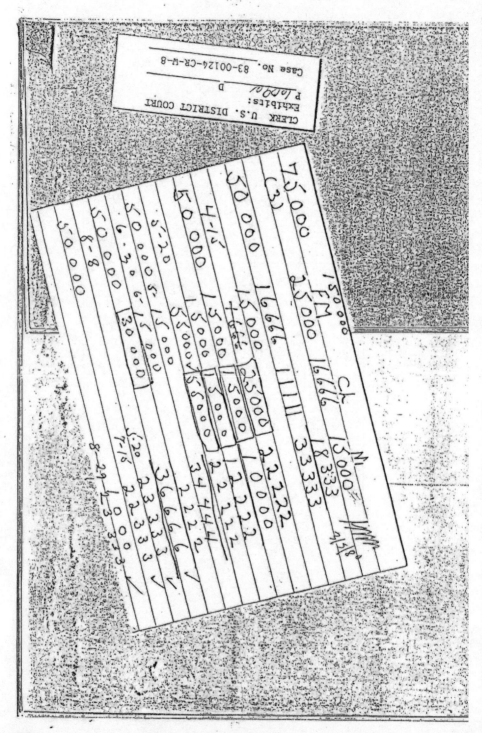

"C"

Fox

3- 75,000
4-15 50,000
  2,000
5-20 50,000
  5,000
6-30 2,25,000
  17,000
8-8 50,000
  2,75,000
  3,25,000

3/5/80

FRONT

4b

6093

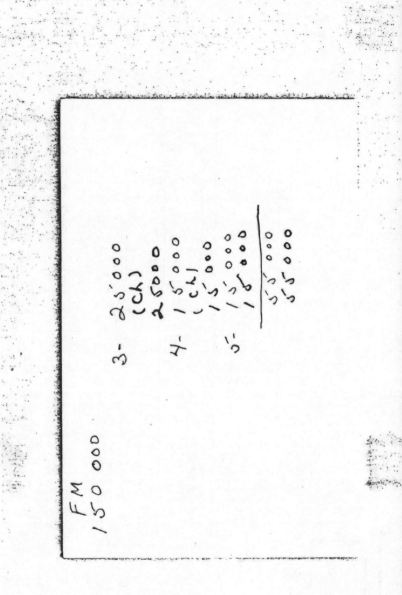

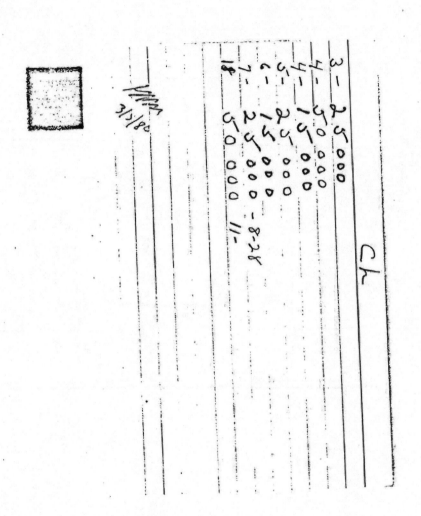

FRONT

$$383 \quad 4\text{-}15 \quad 558$$

$$
\begin{array}{ccc}
183 & 150 & 333 \\
25 & 12 & 25 \\
11 & 5 & 11 \\
11 & 6 & 11 \\
1 & \underline{1} & 1 \\
\overline{231} & 174 & \overline{381} \\
 & 4\text{-}15 &
\end{array}
$$

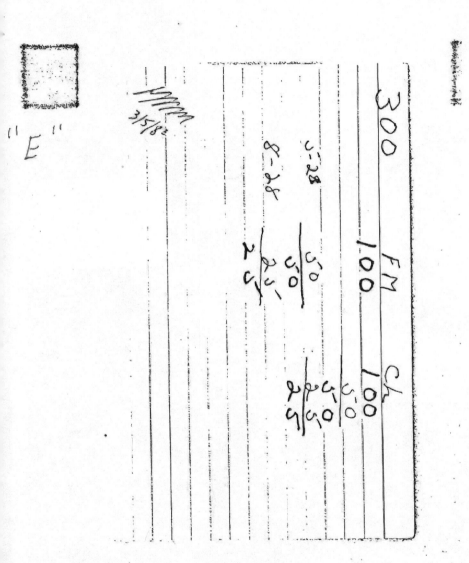

"E"

4f

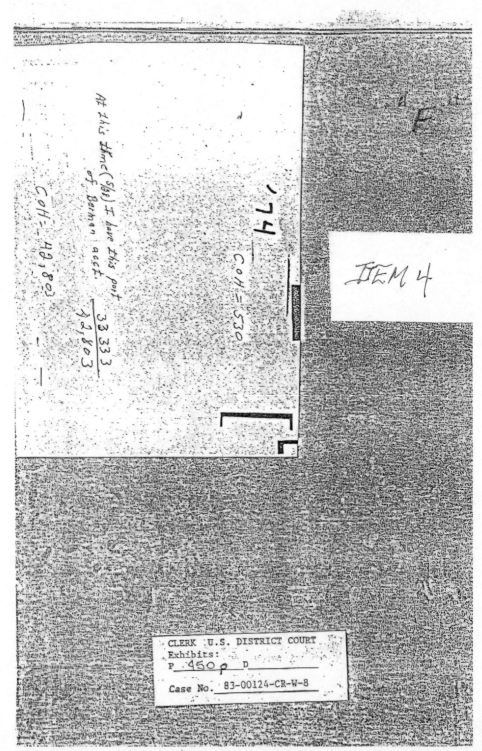

"G"

10-9 Sun '1977
4000 fr Sly today at his
office at home. Promised the balance
of 2750 by end of month. Cp gave
the 4000 to /gs.

1977   Memo.
10-9, Sun. Cp & I took a ride
to see Fox - Saw him at his
office at home. We picked up, from
Fox, 40. That leaves a balance of
27½ which he said he would give
by end of the month. This 67½
(when paid) is the balance (he paid 7½ to on
quite a while back) of an agreement with
on for 75. (The agreement in reality was to
          only for 50) Gave the 40 to gs

.28

479

"H"

4/24 to 4/30/78
Saw Cease, Craze, CT, Fok & est,
San came Fri 4/28

San (in & out)   365
Clothes for Carlo, RK & me - about 1235
"6" ——————   about 10,400
                                    12,000

brought personal - 5000
   borrowed   11,500
San brought 920+337 1257
                         17,757
Ret. w/ about   5,757
                         12,000

Exhibit 14a
81-00107-CR

CLERK U.S. DISTRICT COURT
Exhibits:
P 451 L   D

Case No.   83-00124-CR-W-8

2-16-78

MM & I met Fox
at KCI.

Subject matter: UV
54
Mr. Ozark ref to ON
transfer ref to Cunya
he claimed recent
no contact
by mutual freinds in
regards to merger or
anything else
Small talk ref to lawsuit
with monkeys. claimed moves
by monkeys are detrimental
to his cause (suit)
Gave us 16 towards his
bal of 27½. His bal is now 11½
Gave the 16 to lgs. lgs now has 56

THE DUNES HOTEL AND CASINO: THE MOB, THE CONNECTIONS, THE STORIES

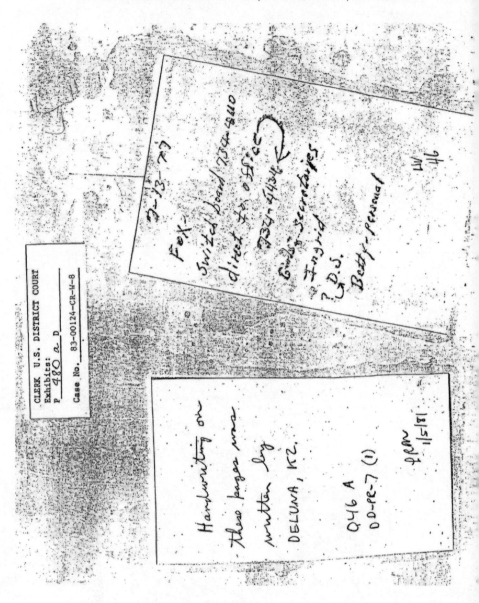

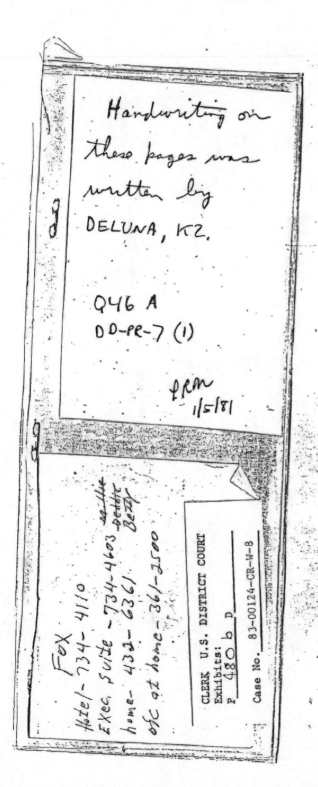

"K"

483

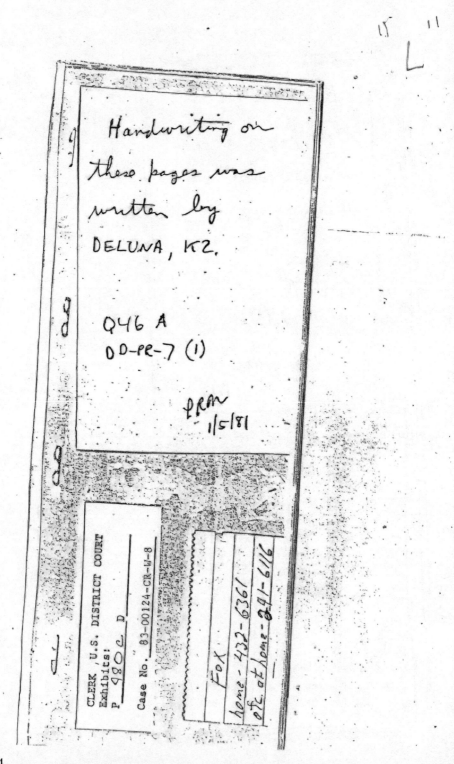

George Duckworth & Artie Selman in the dice pit.

Ground-breaking ceremony of 24-story, 250-room hotel tower, known as Diamond of the Dunes. Front row: fourth from left, Governor Grant Sawyer, Jake Gottlieb, Mrs. Lois Gottlieb, Major Riddle, Parry Thomas. Back row from left, unidentified, unidentified, George Duckworth, unidentified, Sidney Wyman, Robert Rice, Clifford Jones, Charles Gustin, unidentified, unidentified.

485

Joaquin Noriega, unidentified, unidentified, unidentified, unidentified, Governor Grant Sawyer, Jake Gottlieb, Robert Rice, Sidney Wyman, George Duckworth, unidentified, unidentified, Charles Gustin.

George Duckworth, Robert "Bob" Rice, Sidney Wyman.

Big Julie "Weintraub, New York Junket Master.   Charles "Kewpie" Rich, Robert Rice

Irwin Kahn   Morris Shenker

Irwin Gordon   Charles Rich

Cary Grant, Kim Duckworth, George Duckworth

Jimmy Grippo, Walter Mondale, President Jimmy Carter

Frank Sinatra with Dunes showgirls.

Shenker and Hoffa.

Wyman and Feldman.

Tanya, the Siamese elephant who performs at the Dunes Hotel and Casino in Las Vegas, 1966

Al Gottesman and Dunes cocktail server.

Preliminary rendering and artwork of Dunes Hotel circa 1951-52

Dunes circa 1965

First Dunes Arab style marque

Frankie D., Mike Broadhead, Arland Smith standing. Sam Bernstein in chair.

At The Sands: Ron Steinman (leaning) Vince Taglialatella opposite dealing, Tommy Renzoni, John Scarne, Carl Cohen (hand on Scarne) Murry Kraden dealing.

Left to right. Paul Rowe, Shirley Lorato, Norm Luoni, Dick Brewer, Geno Munari.

Dealers from left to right. John Ritsko, Dick Brewer, Lenny Stelly. In back, Geno Munari, Dave Goldberg, Irwin Ross.

Index

Gottlieb, John 31, 32, 98, 99, 266
Gottlieb, Ted 406
Gould, Barry 401
Gould, Chester 262, 401
Grant, Cary 53, 71, 81, 92
Grant, Eva 422
Grant, Jennifer 53
Grasshopper, The 127
Greenbaum, Gus 72, 73, 87, 100, 203, 233, 237, 359
Greenberg, Bennie 47, 61
Greene, Lorne 148
Green Felt Jungle, The 43, 233, 234, 236
Greenspan, William 66
Green, Thomas R. 101
Griffin, Burt W. 422
Griffith, Pete 393
Grim Reapers, The 236
Grippo, Alex 264
Grippo, Jan 263
Grippo, Jimmy 261-264, 266-271, 274-277, 280, 281, 386
Grippo, Mickey 262, 264, 270
Grippo, Ronnie 262
Grodsky, Phil 46
Gross, Robert 386
Guarini, Anthony "Tony Greeno" 274
Gubler, Gray 229
Gustafson, Deil O. 158, 159, 162, 163
Guys and Dolls 261
Guzik, Jake 11, 271

H

Haber, Melvyn 168
Halley, Rudolph 271
Hall, Huntz 263
Halvey, Major 172
Hamil, Jim 162
Hammett, Dashiell 368
Hancock, Newell 41
Hancock Trucking Company 30
Hanif, Aref 163
Hanley, Edward 317
Hannifin, Philip 110, 111, 151, 291, 310, 316, 401
Hansen, Carlton M. 172, 393

Hanson, Dave 196, 197
Harmon, Harley 104
Harrah, Bill 93
Harrelson, Leonard H. 424
Harris, Fred T. 450
Harrison, Charles 55, 73
Harrold, Dean 386
Hart, Alfred 35, 36, 195
Hartman, David 119
Harwood, Richard 139, 147
Hauptmann, Bruno 265
Hauser, Joseph 317
Hellerer, Mark 296
Helms, Cliff 408
Henderson Novelty Company (HNC) 139, 146
Herman, Aaron 68, 69, 262, 289, 317, 366, 373, 374, 377
Hettleman, Eugene 75
Hicks, John "Johnny" 390
Hicks, Marion 17, 94-96, 278, 390, 392
Hill, Virginia 29
Hirt, Al 42
Hoffa, James "Jimmy" R. 11, 26, 27, 29, 31-33, 74, 78, 85, 98, 100, 102-107, 113-116, 129, 130, 143-146, 149, 160, 161, 185, 186, 225, 229, 234, 240-243, 246-260, 266, 275, 276, 280, 284-286, 295, 297-300, 315, 335-337, 345, 421, 423, 424, 435, 446, 448
Hoffa Wars, The 259, 424
Hoffa, William 249
Holden, William 340
Hollywood Squares 21
Holmes, Larry 128
Holmes, Richard 254
Home Service Company 32, 33
Hoover, J. Edgar 9, 141, 147, 264, 352
Horowitz, Louie 219,-221
Horvath, George 227, 229
Horwick, Jules 87, 340
Houssels, Kell 133
Howard, Buck Sr. 391
Howard, Bucky 391
Hughes, Howard 56, 70, 107, 182, 238,